50 YEARS OF THE EUROPEAN TREATIES

The essays which appear in this work are based on the papers presented at a two-day conference held in Liverpool in July 2007 to celebrate the 50th anniversary of the signing of the Treaty of Rome establishing the EEC. The collection reflects critically upon some of the EU's historic characteristics and speculates imaginatively on some of the diverse challenges facing the Union in the future. Contributions from both established and emerging scholars of EU law and policy are united by two main themes: the paradox of the resilient yet unstable basis of the Union's constitutional fundamentals, and the ever-contested balance between the EU's core economic mission and its broader social values and aspirations. For any student, scholar or practitioner interested in the dynamic nature of the constitutional relationship between the Union and its Member States, and in the complex tensions underpinning the EU's substantive policies, these essays will be essential reading.

50 Years of the European Treaties

Looking Back and Thinking Forward

Edited by

Michael Dougan and Samantha Currie

·HART·
PUBLISHING

OXFORD AND PORTLAND, OREGON
2009

Published in North America (US and Canada) by
Hart Publishing
c/o International Specialized Book Services
920 NE 58th Avenue, Suite 300
Portland, OR 97213–3786
USA
Tel: +1 503 287 3093 or toll-free: (1) 800 944 6190
Fax: +1 503 280 8832
E-mail: orders@isbs.com
Website: www.isbs.com

Hart Publishing Ltd, 16c Worcester Place, Oxford, OX1 2JW
Telephone: +44 (0)1865 517530 Fax: +44 (0)1865 510710
E-mail: mail@hartpub.co.uk
Website: http://www.hartpub.co.uk

British Library Cataloguing in Publication Data

Data Available

ISBN: 978–1-84113–832–9

Typeset by Columns Design Ltd, Reading
Printed and bound in Great Britain by
TJ International Ltd, Padstow, Cornwall

Contents

List of Contributors

ARIANNA ANDREANGELI is a Lecturer in Law at the Liverpool Law School, University of Liverpool.

CATHERINE BARNARD is a Fellow of Trinity College and Professor at the Faculty of Law, University of Cambridge. She also holds the Jean Monnet Chair in EU Law.

FIONA BEVERIDGE is Professor of Law and Dean of the Liverpool Law School, University of Liverpool.

PETER CAMERON is Professor of International Energy Law and Policy at the Centre for Energy, Petroleum and Mineral Law and Policy at the University of Dundee.

VLAD CONSTANTINESCO is a Professor at the Law Faculty of the Robert-Schuman University of Strasbourg.

PER CRAMÉR is Professor at the Department of Law, School of Business, Economics and Law, University of Gothenburg.

SAMANTHA CURRIE is a Lecturer in Law at the Liverpool Law School, University of Liverpool.

ALAN DASHWOOD is a Fellow of Sidney Sussex College and Professor of European Law at the Faculty of Law, University of Cambridge.

MICHAEL DOUGAN is Professor of European Law, and Jean Monnet Chair in EU Law, at the Liverpool Law School, University of Liverpool.

JEFF KENNER is Professor of European Law at the School of Law, University of Nottingham.

PANOS KOUTRAKOS is Professor of European Union Law at the School of Law, University of Bristol.

DOMINIC MCGOLDRICK is Professor of International Law at the Liverpool Law School, University of Liverpool.

LEE MILES is Professor of Politics, Jean Monnet Chair in EU Government and Politics, and Co-Director of the Europe in the World Centre at the University of Liverpool.

ROBERT SCHÜTZE is a Lecturer at the Durham Law School, Durham University.

ELEANOR SHARPSTON is Advocate General at the Court of Justice of the European Communities.

ELEANOR SPAVENTA is a Reader in Law and Director of the Durham European Law Institute at the Durham Law School, Durham University.

SAMANTHA VELLUTI is a Lecturer in Law at the Lincoln Law School, University of Lincoln.

DERRICK WYATT is a Fellow of St Edmund's Hall and Professor of Law at the University of Oxford. He is also a Queen's Counsel.

Table of Cases

European Court of Justice

Opinions

Court of First Instance

Commission Decisions

European Court of Human Rights

International Court of Justice

Germany

United Kingdom

Table of Legislation

Regulations

Directives

Decisions

South Africa

United Kingdom

Editors' Introduction

MICHAEL DOUGAN AND SAMANTHA CURRIE

2007 marked the 50th anniversary of the signing of the Treaty of Rome establishing the European Economic Community. By happy coincidence, 2007 was also the 800th anniversary of the granting to Liverpool of its Royal Charter by King John. It therefore seemed a particularly apt year during which to organise at the University of Liverpool a conference intended (according to the publicity bumph) 'to reflect critically upon some of the EU's core characteristics and achievements ... and to think imaginatively about the diverse challenges facing the EU for the future'. The conference, *50 Years of the European Treaties: Looking Forward and Thinking Back*, was held at the Liverpool Law School on 5 to 6 July 2007. We are very grateful to all of our speakers and chairs for their contributions to the event: Louise Ackers, Catherine Barnard, Fiona Beveridge, Peter Cameron, Vlad Constantinesco, Per Cramér, Alan Dashwood, Tamara Hervey, Jeffrey Kenner, Panos Koutrakos, Dominic McGoldrick, Lee Miles, Jim Rollo, Robert Schütze, Jo Shaw, Eleanor Sharpston, Eleanor Spaventa and Derrick Wyatt. We are indebted to our funders—the Liverpool Law School, the Vice-Chancellor of the University of Liverpool and the Jean Monnet Programme of the European Commission—for making the event possible in the first place. Kayte Kelly at the Liverpool Law School was unfailing in her excellent administrative support and good humoured tolerance of our academic whims. Bleddyn Davies and Ruth Lamont provided much appreciated practical assistance over the two days of the conference. The Mersey Partnership also provided valuable assistance with the organisation and hospitality.

This edited collection is principally based on the conference proceedings, although with some alterations: other commitments meant that a few speakers were unable to write up their papers for publication; conversely, the collection seemed to present a good opportunity to showcase the diverse work of some of the EU scholars working at the Liverpool Law School itself. The resulting collection is not intended to explore a single coherent theme in EU law. Rather, the essays cover a broad range of topics and approach them from a wide variety of perspectives: some emphasising the historical aspects of the subject, others tending to stress more the future prospects of their chosen field; some providing a general discursive overview of the topic, others focusing in greater detail on a few particularly troublesome aspects of their specialism. Nor is this collection meant to provide a comprehensive analysis of the main challenges facing the modern European Union. Some major issues included in the original conference programme—such as the difficulties posed by economic and monetary union, and the problems arising from recent and potential future enlargements—are not specifically addressed in this publication (although other authors do touch upon them in their contributions). Other important developments—not least the continuing failure of efforts to secure a deal on constitutional reform of the European Union capable of being ratified by all 27 Member States, as illustrated by the negative result in Ireland's referendum held in June 2008—occurred well after the deadline for submission of final drafts by contributors.

Nevertheless, we hope that the collection emerges as more than just a sample of interesting essays on various aspects of European integration. In fact, certain themes are recurrent across several chapters, and indeed seem to permeate much of our scholarly thinking about European integration, of which two seem particularly striking.

First, there is the desire to understand what constitutional principles and processes contribute to keep the Union ticking after 50 years of success and growth mixed with setback and upheaval. Those principles and processes concern the regulation of relations both between the Union institutions and between the Union and its Member States. Chapters 1 to 3 each offer their own reflections on this profoundly important yet profoundly complex and difficult question. Alan Dashwood focuses on two aspects of the Union's institutional structure that reveal its inherent genius for responsiveness and flexibility: its ability to find solutions for overcoming Member State reticence about integration and indeed to harness the Member States' political will more effectively to the fulfilment of the Union's objectives; and the progressive introduction of an acceptable level of democratic accountability into the Union's decision-making processes (especially through the role of the European Parliament, but, increasingly, also the contribution of the national parliaments). Lee Miles complements Dashwood's legal analysis with one derived from a political science perspective. He argues that a useful macro-model for understanding the Union as a system of governance—especially its stability, but also its sub-optimality—lies in 'fusion theory', ie the merging of resources by Member State and EU-based actors into joint institutions and complex procedures. That theory stresses the importance to the Union's constitutional structure of the consent of national political elites, based on the Union's ability to deliver on domestic policy goals; such consent cannot be taken for granted and is as capable of producing a more differentiated and loosely bound Union as a more integrated and cohesive one. Per Cramér also draws upon the insights of political science—this time involving theories of mutual trust as a precondition for effective governance and economic growth—to explain the Union's constitutional cohesion: for example, mutual trust between

Member States in fields such as fundamental rights monitoring; between the national and Union legal orders when it comes to securing (conditional) respect for the principle of supremacy; in the guise of mutual recognition in the operation of the Treaty free movement provisions and the need for Community level harmonisation; and as regards the constitutionally contested functioning of the European Arrest Warrant.

Chapters 4 to 9 carry this constitutional debate further along two (inter-related) axes. The contributions by Robert Schütze, Derrick Wyatt and Samantha Velluti focus on the constitutional problems associated with the complex division of competences between the Community and its Member States within the First Pillar. Schütze highlights the importance of the distinction and inter-relationship between competences, instruments and procedures in understanding the legal nature of Community power, before examining in detail the evolution of highly differentiated categories of competence to explain how such Community power interacts with the existence and exercise of Member State competences. Wyatt then offers a searing critique of how such carefully negotiated limits to Community power may actually be less effective and more malleable than the theoretical framework alone might suggest: through a detailed analysis of the case law before and since the famous ruling in the *Tobacco Advertising Directive* dispute, he argues that it is difficult to escape the conclusion that the European Court of Justice (ECJ) has interpreted the Treaty provisions so generously as to confer upon the Community institutions a general competence to regulate the internal market. If Wyatt expresses concerns about the effective limits of the Community's 'hard' competences within the core of economic integration according to the classical Community regulatory method, Velluti demonstrates that reservations also abound in respect of the Community's 'soft' powers for the pursuit of social policy goals in areas typically associated with innovatory governance techniques. Through her examination of the open method of coordination in the field of employment policy, Velluti highlights difficult problems, such as shortcomings in the levels of participatory and even representative democracy, in the functioning of the European Employment Strategy.

Subsequent chapters broaden the discussion by exploring aspects of the Union's institutional framework under the Second and Third Pillars. The contributions by Dashwood and Miles had both already highlighted the specificities of Union external action, especially under the Common Foreign and Security Policy (CFSP), as an essential part of the constitutional package for securing the participation of Member States in an extremely sensitive policy field. Those specificities are further examined in the contributions by Panos Koutrakos and Dominic McGoldrick. Koutrakos notes that the development of the CFSP has been marked by its incremental, *sui generis* and obsessively procedural nature, before considering three current and future trends in the operation of the Second Pillar:

the quest for greater coherence in EU external action; the emergence of the European Security and Defence Policy; and (in an observation which tallies with Miles' speculation about the possible trajectory of integration in this field) the accommodation of greater flexibility and differentiation among the heterogeneous Member States. McGoldrick is also concerned with the search for a mutually acceptable constitutional framework for the pursuit of the EU's external objectives, this time as regards the conferral of legal personality upon the EC and the EU, culminating in the suppression of the EC as a distinct legal entity and the express recognition of the EU's international legal personality pursuant to the Treaty of Lisbon—a reform which McGoldrick considers to be not merely a legal technicality, but of symbolic and political importance, not least for the Union's international identity and its ability to promote European values effectively on the global stage. Specificities of a different sort are highlighted by Eleanor Sharpston in her contribution concerning the Area of Freedom, Security and Justice. Focusing on the jurisdiction of the ECJ in both Title IV, Part Three EC and Title VI TEU, Sharpston reminds us that the complex constitutional settlements underpinning the functioning of the Union also extend to debates about the proper scope of the judicial contribution to the inter-institutional balance and the interaction between the Union and the national legal systems, particularly in contested fields such as immigration and asylum or cross-border criminal cooperation.

The second pervasive theme in this collection is the contribution of Community law in the creation of an effective framework for greater prosperity through economic integration and enhanced competition within the Single Market, inextricably linked to the perennial problem of how (and how far) to balance those economic goals against the protection and promotion of non-economic rights and values in spheres such as employ-ment policy, the environment and fundamental rights. Of course, those dilemmas and tensions have a strong constitutional dimension, as the chapter by Samantha Velluti will have already shown, and later contribu-tions (especially those by Peter Cameron, Jeff Kenner and Eleanor Spaventa) will further emphasise. Nevertheless, the discussions in Chapters 10 to 16 focus more squarely on the substantive aspects of the Communi-ty's interlinked economic and social policies.

Arianna Andreangeli deals with competition law, one of the Communi-ty's oldest economic policies, yet one which has undergone a radical process of modernisation in recent years. She focuses on the transforma-tion in the role of the individual in Community competition policy: their involvement was once almost entirely focused on participation in the administrative proceedings undertaken before the European Commission, but has increasingly been reconceived in terms of the private enforcement of competition rules through legal actions initiated before the national courts, particularly in the light of rulings such as *Courage v Crehan* and

Manfredi, but also under the influence of the Commission 2005 Green Paper and 2008 White Paper. Peter Cameron's contribution concerns another of the Community's long-standing yet less well understood policies: energy. He demonstrates that, ever since the founding ECSC, Euratom and EEC Treaties, the Community institutions have struggled to work within the framework of their available competences so as to manage the amicable co-existence of the three corners of a triangulated policy: economic efficiency in the energy sector within the context of the Single Market; security of energy supply and price; and compatibility with the Community's environmental goals and international commitments. Those challenges have moved steadily up the Union's political agenda in recent years, as affirmed in the 2007 *Energy Policy for Europe*, and their legal framework would be recast by the introduction of a dedicated Energy Chapter by the Treaty of Lisbon.

Jeff Kenner examines another Community policy in the throes of adjusting to the complexities and uncertainties of the modern Union in its changing global context and with its evolving global roles: labour law. The idea of 'flexicurity' set out by the Commission in its Green Paper on Modernising Labour Law is intended to balance more flexible employment laws and working practices so as to facilitate and stimulate economic growth, with the promise that workers are actively supported in the challenge of adapting to the changing workplace and labour market (for example) through retraining and appropriate social support. Kenner critically interrogates the relationship between that emergent 'flexicurity' model and the personal scope of existing EU employment protection legislation, particularly in the case of vulnerable categories of individuals such as agency workers. Catherine Barnard is also interested in how Community law manages the tension between the forces of economic competition and the safeguarding of employment rights, but this time, as regards the interaction between free movement, social dumping, regulatory competition and Community harmonisation. She argues that, in the absence of clear and compelling empirical evidence, the spectre of social dumping is by turns invoked or derided, by employees, employers, Member States and Community institutions alike, so as to lobby for or legitimise particular legislative choices at the EU level. Ultimately, despite the enhanced prominence given to various aspects of social policy in the modern European Union, Barnard is unconvinced that a genuine balance between economic and social considerations will be struck anytime soon.

Two of the main cases considered by Barnard—*Viking Line* and *Laval un Partneri*—provide the basis for Eleanor Spaventa's critique of how the ECJ has chosen to structure the balance between economic freedoms (on the one hand) and fundamental rights (on the other hand) in its case law under the primary Treaty provisions. Spaventa argues that the ECJ in such rulings has elevated free movement to the status of a fundamental right, so that it competes on equal terms with more traditional freedoms such as those embodied in the European Convention on Human Rights and national constitutions, and as a consequence, the applicable standards of fundamental rights protection have become centralised in the hands of the ECJ rather than determined (where they should be) within each national legal system. Judicial creativity also forms the basis of Samantha Currie's chapter, which concerns the rapid evolution of Union citizenship in the hands of the ECJ since the groundbreaking rulings in *Sala*, *Grzelczyk* and *Baumbast*. Union citizenship might seem like a field where Community law has made a determined effort to overcome the accusation of bias towards economic integration, in favour of a more equitable sharing of the social benefits of European integration. However, Currie (like Spaventa) is sceptical about how far the rights associated with Union citizenship can truly be considered fundamental—not least given the continuing need to demonstrate a cross-border dimension, however artificial and arbitrary, before being able to trigger the application of the Treaty provisions— although she concludes with the intriguing observation that the strengthening of democratic and participatory rights as promised under the Treaty of Lisbon could provide an alternative means of enriching and empowering (static) Union citizens.

In the penultimate chapter of the collection (Chapter 16), Fiona Beveridge addresses another key area of EU social policy. Whereas some of the contributions (particularly those by Kenner and Barnard) are concerned with the extent to which the EU is able to balance the promotion of both economic and non-economic objectives, Beveridge is interested in the relationship between the process of EU enlargement and the implementation of gender law and policy. The chapter not only considers the manner in which gender law is experienced by the states that accede to the Union, but also explores the impact that enlargement itself might have in turn upon the development of EU gender policy. Drawing on the 2004 enlargement, Beveridge considers the impact of both the formal equal opportunities *acquis* and the broader commitment to gender mainstreaming in the national polities of the accession states. Whilst she is critical of the failure to incorporate a formal role for mainstreaming into the pre-accession process, she argues that EU membership can allow actors at the national level, such as non-governmental organisations keen to promote the rights of women, to achieve a more empowered status.

Thanks in large part to the pressures (real and perceived) generated by the 2004 and 2007 enlargements, much of the recent history of European integration has, of course, been dominated by the struggle to forge a new constitutional settlement for the next stage in the Union's development. Many of the contributions in this collection incorporate that struggle into their analyses, especially in their reference to the relevant proposals contained in the Treaty of Lisbon 2007. Vlad Constantinesco closes this volume with some overall reflections on the post-Laeken constitutional reform process (Chapter 17). Those reflections need now, of course, to be read in the light of the Irish 'no' to Lisbon delivered in June 2008—and the resulting uncertainty about whether and in what form the Treaty of Lisbon, or some of its proposals, will ever enter into legal force. However, even if events may appear to have overtaken some of Constantinesco's optimism about the survival of the Constitutional Treaty through its substantial reincarnation as the Treaty of Lisbon, the underlying spirit of his contribution remains very pertinent: can we really claim that Lisbon provided answers to the burning questions about how to place the relationship between the Union and its peoples on a more secure footing of legitimacy? Did Lisbon merely postpone for another day the task of establishing a clear link between the enormous policy challenges the Union must tackle, and popular acceptance of the institutional and constitutional framework required to discharge those responsibilities effectively? If anything, the Irish 'no' to Lisbon could be interpreted as a vindication of Constantinesco's closing reflections.

Last, but not least, the editors would like to express their sincere gratitude to Richard Hart and his sterling team at Hart Publishing for their unflagging patience and assistance.

1

The Institutional Framework and the Institutional Balance

ALAN DASHWOOD

... Resolved to substitute for age-old rivalries the merging of their essential interests; to create, by establishing an economic community, the basis for a broader and deeper community among peoples long divided by bloody conflicts; and to lay the foundations for institutions which will give direction to a destiny henceforward shared ...

I. INTRODUCTION

THE MOVING WORDS of the final recital of the preamble to the Treaty establishing the European Coal and Steel Community (hereinafter, 'ECSC Treaty' or 'ECSC') encapsulate the project that was launched in the 1950s to provide a solution to the 'age-old rivalries' that had made Europe the cock-pit of the world, arguably since the seventeenth century, but most catastrophically in the twentieth. The aim, eloquently proclaimed by the Schuman Declaration of May 1950,[1] was to bind together the nations of Europe politically and economically in such a way as to make it inconceivable that they would ever fight each other again. This was to be achieved step by step, by first establishing an economic community and then going on to broaden and deepen the relationship, a development that would be channelled by a carefully designed set of institutions.

An essential feature of the institutional design that may loosely be identified as the 'Community model' has always been the interaction between institutions composed of representatives of the Member States and 'supranational' institutions with a duty to act independently of national governments: the role of the former being to involve national political

---

[1] For the French text of the Schuman Declaration, see *Documents on International Affairs* (1949–50) 315–17. There is an English translation in 22 *Department of State Bulletin* 936–7.

leaders directly in the enterprise of shaping a common European future; that of the latter, to consolidate the gains made (the *acquis communautaire*) and, if practicable, to carry the integration process forward. Finding and maintaining an appropriate balance between the two groups of institutions has been an essential requirement of the sometimes faltering progress of the EC/EU during the half century since the signing of the Treaty of Rome.

Under the system of the ECSC Treaty, the heavyweight institution was the supranational High Authority. It headed the list of institutions in Article 7 ECSC, with the Special Council of Ministers coming only third, after the Common Assembly and before the Court of Justice. It was the High Authority that was charged explicitly with responsibility for attaining the objectives of the Treaty; and, with a few exceptions, it was also the decision-making body of the Community, empowered to adopt the formal instruments defined by Article 14 ECSC.[2] The High Authority was authorised, among other things, to: procure funds[3]; fix maximum and minimum prices for certain products[4]; ensure compliance by the Member States with their obligations under the Treaty[5]; and fine undertakings guilty of infringing the ECSC's rules on competition.[6] The role of the Council was more particularly to harmonise the action of the High Authority with that of the governments of the Member States, acknowledged as being 'responsible for the general economic policies of their countries'.[7] The characteristic involvement of the Council in decision-making was by way of a requirement for it to be consulted, or for its assent (*avis conforme*) to be obtained,[8] on actions the High Authority was proposing to take.

In broad terms, therefore, it can be said that the institutional balance of the ECSC was tilted towards the supranational side. Doubtless this can be explained in part by the political context in which the ECSC was created: with World War II still a vivid memory, and the perceived threat posed by the military strength of the Soviet Union and its sponsorship of Communist-led coups in several central and eastern European countries, there was a receptiveness in West European political circles to the grand design set forth in the Schuman Declaration of laying 'the first concrete

---

[2] The binding ECSC instruments were decisions and recommendations, the latter corresponding to EC directives. Decisions could be individual, in which case they became binding when notified to the party concerned, or general, in which case they took effect by the fact of publication: Art 15 ECSC.

[3] Art 49 ECSC.

[4] Art 61 ECSC.

[5] Art 88 ECSC.

[6] Arts 65 and 66 ECSC.

[7] Art 26, first para ECSC.

[8] Assent was sometimes to be given by a special qualified majority, as defined by Art 28, second paragraph ECSC, and sometimes by unanimity.

foundation for a European Federation'. At the same time, reassurance was provided by the gradualist strategy encapsulated in the recital to the ECSC Treaty recognising 'that Europe can be built only through practical achievements which will first of all create real solidarity, and through the creation of common bases for economic development'. The scope of the ECSC was limited to the organisation of a common market for coal and steel, the mechanics of which were laid down in considerable detail by the treaty itself.[9] The High Authority's very considerable powers were, therefore, executive in character, the parameters for their exercise having been clearly and firmly set by the primary law of the Community.

The European Economic Community (EEC) was endowed with a similar institutional framework to the ECSC (as also was the European Atomic Energy Community (EURATOM)). There was a council consisting of representatives of the Member States, to which each government was required to delegate one of its members, and a supranational body—the Commission—corresponding to the High Authority. The initially separate Councils and Commissions of the EEC and EURATOM, together with the ECSC's Special Council of Ministers and High Authority, would be replaced, as from 1 July 1968, by a single Council of the European Communities and a single Commission of the European Communities, acting for the purposes of the different treaties in accordance with the respective powers and procedures laid down therein.[10] However, pursuant to a Convention signed at the same time as the Treaties of Rome, the three communities that would exist from 1958 were to be served by a single Assembly and a single Court of Justice.[11] The Assembly, soon to re-name itself 'the European Parliament',[12] was still composed of national parliamentarians, and its powers remained limited. It was not yet a branch of the budgetary authority, and its involvement in the legislative process did not go beyond the right to be consulted on certain Commission proposals.

As compared with the ECSC system, that of the EEC showed a marked adjustment of the institutional balance in favour of the Council, as the main decision-making organ of the Community. The familiar tag, 'the Commission proposes, the Council disposes', accurately expresses the interaction between the two institutions that characterised the legislative process originally established by the Rome Treaty: the Commission had a

---

[9] See Title Three ECSC comprising 'Economic and social provisions', in particular the detailed provisions on investment and financial aid (Arts 54–6), production (Arts 57–9), prices (Arts 60–4), agreements and concentrations (Arts 65–6), interference with competition (Art 68) and wages and movement of workers (Arts 68 and 69).

[10] Treaty establishing a Single Council and a Single Commission of the European Communities, signed in Brussels on 8 April 1965.

[11] Convention on Certain Institutions Common to the European Communities, signed in Rome on 25 March 1957.

[12] The change of name was formally acknowledged only in 1986 by the SEA.

near monopoly of the initiative, the Council a near monopoly of the power of final decision, and it was also the sole budgetary authority. The Council's role as the organ that must positively approve any development of the body of primary rules contained in the Treaty was highlighted in the reference in Article 145, second indent EEC (now Article 202, second indent EC) to its having 'power to take decisions'; the Commission was stated to have 'its own power of decision', but this was confined in practice to areas, such as the completion of the customs union, where legislative discretion was circumscribed by detailed Treaty provisions.[13]

The shift in the institutional balance may have been influenced by the failure of the over-ambitious projects for a European Defence Community and a European Political Community, which foundered when the French National Assembly voted against the ratification of the former.[14] However, it reflects very real differences between the two Communities. The substantive scope even of the primordial EEC was vastly greater than that of the ECSC—the establishment of a general common market, covering all economic sectors other than those within the purview of the ECSC or EURATOM Treaties, and of a potentially interventionist agricultural policy and a transport policy,[15] complemented by a variety of flanking mechanisms, policies and principles.[16] Moreover, the Community was much less fully realised by the Treaty itself: in the jargon, the EEC Treaty was a *traité cadre*, while the ECSC was a *traité loi*. The bare bones of the Treaty provisions would have to be covered with flesh, through the legislative activity of the institutions.

Many changes have taken place in the institutional framework of the EC/EU over the ensuing 50 years. Practical considerations mean that only the most significant can be noted here, and their selection is necessarily, to some extent, a matter of individual judgment. Leaving aside the immense contribution of the Court of Justice, which is a subject for another paper, I venture to suggest that the main institutional developments have been broadly of two kinds: those designed to overcome reticence on the part of the Member States, and to harness their political will more effectively to the objectives of the EC/EU; and those seeking to introduce an acceptable

---

[13]   Art 155, third indent EEC (now Art 211, third indent EC).

[14]   See A Arnull, A Dashwood, M Dougan, M Ross, E Spaventa and D Wyatt, *Wyatt and Dashwood's European Union Law*, 5th edn (London, Sweet & Maxwell, 2006) (hereinafter, *Wyatt and Dashwood*) paras 1–004–6, and the references there cited.

[15]   Designated 'Foundations of the Community' and the subject of Part Two of the EEC Treaty.

[16]   To mention only some of them: rules on competition (Arts 85–94 EEC), tax provisions (Arts 95–9 EEC), the approximation of laws (Arts 100–102 EEC), coordination of aspects of general economic policy (Arts 103–9 EEC), a common commercial (external trade) policy (Arts 110–16 EEC) and social policy, including the principle of equal pay for equal work and the establishment of a European Social Fund (Arts 117–28 EEC). The substantive scope of the EC has since been greatly enlarged by the series of amending treaties that began with the SEA.

level of democratic accountability in the legislative process of the Union. I shall indicate, quite briefly, the key changes in each of those categories, as they appear to me, and then attempt, in my conclusion, to assess what effect they may have produced on the institutional balance.

II. OVERCOMING MEMBER STATES' RETICENCE AND HARNESSING THEIR POLITICAL WILL

It became apparent very early on that adjustments to the Community's institutional arrangements for this purpose would be necessary, when the Community experienced its worst ever political crisis—that of France's 'empty chair' strategy—which began in the summer of 1965 and culminated in the so-called 'Luxemburg Compromise' at the end of January 1966.[17] The crisis was precipitated by an activist EEC Commission, under its founding President, Walter Hallstein. The Commission had put forward a proposal in the form of a 'package deal', linking the introduction of a system of 'own resources' to fund the Community's budget, with arrangements for the financing of the common agricultural policy (CAP), in which the French Government had a particularly strong interest. Part of the context was that the EEC Treaty provided for the introduction of qualified majority voting in place of unanimity for Council decision-making in a number of policy areas, including the CAP, with effect from 1 January 1966, the end of the second stage of the Community's transitional period. After that date, it would theoretically be possible for France's position on CAP financing to be overridden by a Council majority.

Everyone is familiar with the outcome. As part of the Luxembourg Compromise, it was agreed that, on a matter capable of being decided by qualified majority voting (QMV), when 'very important interests of a Member State are at stake', the Council must attempt, within a reasonable time, to reach a solution acceptable to all of its Members; the view of the French delegation, that discussion must continue until unanimity was reached, was noted but not accepted by the other delegations. Other elements of the compromise were designed to constrain the behaviour of the Commission in putting forward proposals, especially its tactic of seeking to balance elements liable to be seen as more or less palatable by different Member States, within artificially constructed package deals.

Even though, as we shall see, the Luxembourg Compromise has been formally invoked on very few occasions, the crisis of 1965/66 cast a long shadow. To borrow form Robert Browning, it would never be a 'glad,

---

[17] See the account in *Wyatt & Dashwood*, para 3–010. The full text of the Luxembourg Compromise was published in *Bulletin of the EC*, March 1966, 8–10.

confident morning again' for the Community.[18] Nevertheless, the intransigence of De Gaulle's France may be seen in a positive light, as a salutary reality check. The lesson was learned that Member States could not be compelled to accept constitutional changes through subtle manipulation of the institutional framework; if their 'very important interests' were perceived to be at risk, the framework itself was liable to buckle. The survival and further development of the new European constitutional order would depend upon finding ways of ensuring that its component entities—states in the full sense of public international law, and the main focus of their citizens' collective loyalty—could be comfortably accommodated within it.

Three such expedients were: the establishment and expanding role of the European Council; Council practice on QMV; and the 'pillar structure' of the European Union created by the Maastricht Treaty. I shall deal with these in turn.

A. The European Council

The habit of holding regular summit meetings of the European Community's political leaders developed at the end of the 1960s. The meetings, bringing together the heads of state or government of the Member States and the President of the Commission within a 'European Council', were set up on an established, although still informal, basis by a decision taken at the Paris Summit in December 1974. The first European Council convened under that designation took place in Dublin in March 1975. There was no such body envisaged in the original EEC Treaty and the earliest mention of the European Council by a treaty was in the rather meagre Article 2 of the Single European Act (SEA), which said nothing about its function. The treaty basis of the European Council is presently Article 4 of the Treaty of European Union (TEU). This states in its first paragraph that '[t[he European Council shall provide the Union with the necessary impetus for its development and shall define the general political guidelines thereof'; and it goes on to regulate the composition of the European Council, the rhythm of its meetings (at least twice a year) and its chairmanship (the head of state or government of the Member State holding the Council Presidency during a given semester). If it ever comes into force, the Treaty of Lisbon (TL) will give the European Council the formal status of a Union institution, with power to take legally binding decisions, including for

---

[18] The quotation is from 'The Lost Leader', Browning's attack on Wordsworth for abandoning his earlier radicalism.

some purposes by QMV; and it will have a full-time president for a period of two-and-a-half years, renewable once, instead of the present six-monthly rotation.[19]

In broad terms, the European Council has two main functions: as the 'demiurge' or 'moving mind' that guides the Union's strategic development on matters such as the reform of the institutional structure, the accretion of competences to the Union and the accession of new Member States; and as a kind of 'cabinet' determining political priorities. These are functions that could not be effectively or properly performed by the institutions formally established under the foundational treaties. No single formation of the Council can speak with the collective authority of the governments of the Member States; and the Commission lacks both the power and the legitimacy to set an agenda that is not supported by a consensus among the democratically responsible governments whose coercive and administrative resources will be needed for its implementation. This was first seen at the time of the 'empty chair' debacle; and it has become increasingly apparent as the Union has become involved in the 'high politics' of foreign affairs, security and defence. The European Council should, therefore, be regarded, not as an interloper or a usurper of functions that belong elsewhere, but as filling a gap in the institutional framework created by the primordial treaties.

A well-functioning European Council need not mean that the Commission is relegated to a subordinate, essentially administrative role. The Commission President is a full member of the European Council and, therefore, part of any consensus that has to be reached. The extent of the Commission's influence at the fundamental level of constitution- or policy-making will depend on how well its president plays his or her hand. Jacques Delors was perhaps the most influential president after Hallstein. He got most of what he wanted on the single market and on economic and monetary union, including the arrangements under the Maastricht Treaty that led to the introduction of the single currency. On political union, however, the Commission went off on an extravagant frolic, which lost it all influence in that part of the Maastricht Treaty negotiations.

B. Council Practice on Qualified Majority Voting

As noted above, the possibility of acting by QMV, which became available to the Council in January 1966 for many purposes connected with the establishment and functioning of the common market, was one of the

---

[19] See Arts 13 and 15 TEU (as amended) and Art 235 of the Treaty on the Functioning of the European Union (TFEU), the re-named EC Treaty. For consolidated versions of the Treaties as revised by the Treaty of Lisbon: [2008] OJ C115/1.

factors that precipitated the crisis of 1965/66, eventually resolved through the adoption of the Luxembourg Compromise. In fact, the famous invocation of 'very important interests of a Member State' has been formally made only very rarely—perhaps about a dozen times. However, the Council's practice was profoundly affected by the crisis and, until the early 1980s, decisions were normally taken by consensus, except on the budget and staff matters.[20] When I first arrived in the Council's Legal Service in 1987, we still used to count the occasions on which a vote was taken, because there was a group of Members of the European Parliament who regularly asked questions about this[21]; whereas by the time I left in December 1994, majority voting had become normal Council practice and ceased to attract political attention. What made the difference was the internal market programme, launched by the Delors Commission in 1985, which the Member States wished to see enacted by the deadline of 31 December 1992, while being aware that it would be unachievable if consensus had to be found on every proposal; and this had a spill-over effect in other policy areas.

Nevertheless, as I have repeatedly insisted,[22] a disciplined practice of seeking the greatest possible measure of consensus still prevails within the Council—'disciplined' because delegations are aware that, if they are intransigent, a vote can be taken and they risk finding themselves in the minority. Presidencies set out to build a qualified majority around a compromise solution, which is also acceptable to the Commission (so that the latter will 'make the compromise its own', by amending its proposal)[23]; but every effort is made to cater for the genuine problems of all the Member States. The Council has become an effective decision-making organ, but one where Member States in the minority on a given issue are able to feel confident that intelligent and persistent negotiation will prevent their 'very important interests' from being ridden over roughshod.

The legal bases enabling the Council to act by QMV would be further extended by the TL, mainly as a result of the generalisation of the co-decision procedure (a point to which I return below). However, it appears there is an irreducible minimum of issues that some, at least, of the Member States regard as touching their sovereignty so nearly as to require

---

[20] See JL Dewost in F Capotorti *et al* (eds), *Du droit international au droit communautaire; Liber amicorum Pierre Pescatore* (Baden-Baden, Nomos, 1988) 167 *ff*; and A Dashwood in J Schwartze (ed), *Legislation for Europe* (Baden-Baden, Nomos, 1989) 79 *ff*.

[21] See, eg answers to WQ No 1121/86 (Elles) [1986] OJ C306/42; WQ No 2126/86 (Fontaine) [1987] OJ C82/43.

[22] A Dashwood, 'The Role of the Council of the European Union' in D Curtin and T Heukels, *Institutional Dynamics of European Integration*, Vol II (Dordrecht, Martinus Nijhoff 1994) 117; and 'States in the European Union' (1998) 23 *EL Rev* 201.

[23] Because of Art 250(1) EC, which provides that the Council can only amend a Commission proposal by unanimity.

retention of the unanimity rule. That is certainly the position of the United Kingdom (and other Member States that shelter behind its back) with respect to tax harmonisation.[24]

C. Pillarisation and the Foreign Policy Infrastructure

I have written elsewhere about the technique of 'differentiation', which has been developed within the constitutional order of the Union to allow the organisation, within the single institutional framework referred to in Article 3 TEU, of activities in respect of which some or all of the Member States are unwilling, at least for the time being, to accept the thorough-going application of the Community model.[25] I argued then, and remain convinced, that the technique should be celebrated rather than regretted, because it makes possible the extension of Union competence into important new fields and avoids the risk of certain Member States' taking forward the integration process outside the Treaties by unsatisfactory arrangements like Schengen. It is a prime example of the capacity of the constitutional order to respond sensibly and realistically to the exigency of having states as its component entities.

For reasons of space, I am focusing here on what I have described as 'structural differentiation', namely the establishment by Titles V and VI TEU of the special institutional and procedural arrangements of the Second and Third Pillars. This was due to the unwillingness of some Member States to agree to the conferral of competence on the newly created Union in the fields of the common foreign and security policy (CFSP) and of justice and home affairs, if the Community model were to apply there. The establishment of the 'pillared structure', the progressive assimilation of the Third Pillar to the First (Community) Pillar, and the preservation of the particularity of the Second Pillar, even under the regime envisaged by the TL, vividly illustrate the way in which differentiation works and why it is needed.

The constitutional arrangements that were established in 1993 by Titles V and VI TEU deliberately altered the institutional balance, by giving the Council a predominance it does not enjoy under the First Pillar. In the original Maastricht version of the Treaty, the Council invariably acted by unanimity, the Commission was denied its usual monopoly of the initiative, the European Parliament had no direct involvement in the adoption of

---

[24] See Arts 113, 114 (2) and 115 TFEU, which preserve the unanimity rule for the harmonisation of both indirect and direct taxation.

[25] See A Dashwood, 'The Relationship between the Member States and the Community' (2004) 41 *CML Rev* 355.

specific measures and the jurisdiction of the Court of Justice was completely excluded. Nevertheless, I have always taken the view that it was misleading to describe the systems of the Second and Third Pillars as 'inter-governmental'. That is because powers were conferred on the Union as an entity distinct from the Member States; and in exercising those powers the institutions of the Union function as themselves, under their usual rules of procedure and serviced by their own officials.

The Treaty of Amsterdam started the process of integrating the Third Pillar into the First Pillar. Those aspects of the original Title VI that had to do with the crossing of external borders and the treatment of third-country nationals, as well as with judicial cooperation in civil matters, were transferred to Title IV of Part Three of the EC Treaty, reducing the scope of Title VI TEU to police and judicial cooperation in criminal matters (PJC). At the same time, a new set of Third Pillar instruments was introduced,[26] including 'framework decisions', which resemble EC directives in all respects, except that they are said not to entail direct effect[27]; and the Council was required to consult the European Parliament before adopting such measures.[28] Last but not least, the Court of Justice was given an admittedly rather truncated jurisdiction with respect to certain instruments adopted under Third Pillar powers.[29]

The assimilation process would be completed by the TL, with the transfer of the whole of PJC to the Title of the TFEU on the Area of Freedom Security and Justice.[30] This would bring PJC fully within the legal order that has been developed under the First Pillar, mainly through the creative jurisprudence of the Court of Justice. The resulting enhancement of the legal protection afforded by EU law to individuals, in an area where fundamental freedoms are liable to be directly affected,[31] would be a major constitutional gain. However, the progressive dismantling of the Third Pillar has been achieved only through recourse to less drastic forms of differentiation. The Protocol that allows the United Kingdom and Ireland to hold aloof from measures adopted under the present Title IV of Part Three of the EC Treaty, unless they opt into them, was an expedient to secure the initial transfer of Third Pillar competences at Amsterdam; under the regime of the TL, the Protocol would be extended to PJC measures and strengthened in some respects. There would also be a new 'emergency brake' mechanism, allowing for the referral to the European Council of a draft harmonisation measure in the field of criminal law, which was

---

[26]   Art 34(2) TEU.
[27]   *Ibid*, point (b).
[28]   As well as before it adopts Third Pillar decisions or establishes Third Pillar conventions: see Art 39(1) TEU.
[29]   Art 35 TEU.
[30]   Title V of Part Three of the TFEU.
[31]   As, for instance, through being the subject of a European Arrest Warrant.

regarded by any Member State as liable to affect fundamental aspects of its criminal justice system; such referral would effectively block the proposal, since consensus within the European Council would be needed for it to be remitted to the Council.[32]

In the case of the Second (CFSP) Pillar, the development has tended to be in the opposite direction, towards strengthening its particularity. This is especially noticeable in the executive role assumed by the Council, as the body that not only takes decisions on matters of foreign and security policy, but also that is primarily responsible for the preparation and implementation of such decisions.[33] To enable it to function effectively for this purpose, the Council has been equipped with an increasingly complex infrastructure. This now includes:

(i) a presidency more specifically tasked than in other fields of Union activity[34];
(ii) the Secretary General/High Representative, whose job is to contribute to 'the formulation, preparation and implementation of policy decisions' and to conduct political dialogue with third countries[35];
(iii) the Political and Security Committee, which, besides monitoring the international situation and contributing to policy formation, exercises political control and strategic direction of crisis management operations, and may be authorised by the Council to take any necessary decisions for this purpose[36]; and
(iv) in order to assist with planning and with the running of operations, the Military Committee and Military Staff of the EU.[37]

The intention of the TL to preserve the specificity of the CFSP seems evident from the fact that the relevant provisions are retained within the TEU,[38] instead of being placed with the other substantive provisions on External Action by the Union in the new Part Five of the TFEU. Whether this intention can be reconciled with the establishment of a common list of objectives for the whole range of the Union's external action,[39] and with

---

[32] See Art 83(3) TFEU. If a proposal were blocked in this way, a group of at least nine Member States would automatically be authorised to take it forward by way of enhanced cooperation.

[33] For a fuller exploration of the particularity of the CFSP under the regime of the Treaty of Nice, see A Dashwood, 'Issues of Decision-making in the European Union after Nice' in A Arnull and D Wincott (eds), *Accountability and Legitimacy in the European Union* (Oxford, Oxford University Press, 2002) 13.

[34] Art 18 TEU.

[35] Art 26 TEU.

[36] Art 25 TEU.

[37] These were established by, respectively, Council Decision 2001/79/CFSP [2001] OJ L27/4 and Council Decision 2001/80/CFSP [2001] OJ L27/7.

[38] In Chapter 2 of Title V TEU (as amended).

[39] Art 21(2) TEU (as amended).

the new-style High Representative, wearing his double headgear as an officer of the Council and Commission Vice-President,[40] remains to be seen. At all events, it is my clear view that continuing Council control of the CFSP is an indispensable condition of the policy's further successful growth. This is for the brutally simple reason that the assets of foreign and security policy—diplomatic influence, historical and cultural ties, troops and military hardware—belong exclusively to the Member States, and indeed to rather few of them. Therefore, political realism argues in favour of the maintenance, for the foreseeable future, at least of a two-pillar structure.

III. DEMOCRATIC ACCOUNTABILITY IN THE LEGISLATIVE PROCESS OF THE EUROPEAN UNION

The other main theme of the constitutional development of the European Union has been the perceived need for greater democratic accountability in a legislative process that seemed to be growing ever wider in scope. How could a satisfactory level of accountability be achieved in a *sui generis* order like that of the Union, composed of highly self-conscious political entities, each providing a forum in which the democratic game is vigorously played under local rules?

Inspiration could not be drawn from national models, because the familiar division of powers between the legislature and the executive is not reflected in the relationship between the European Parliament, the Council and the Commission. The solution that has won acceptance, although not without difficulty, is that legitimacy has to be sought in two parallel ways: *directly*, through the full participation of a European Parliament, elected by universal suffrage, in the enactment of Union legislation; and *indirectly*, through links with the parliamentary systems of the Member States. Links of the latter kind are provided, in part, by the participation of national leaders in the European Council, and of Ministers in the Council, all of them politically responsible to parliaments and electorates at home; and, in part, by the fact that national parliaments themselves 'contribute actively to the good functioning of the Union', as the TL puts it.[41] Indeed, it is interesting to find the principle of dual accountability expressly espoused by the TL, something that would surely have been unthinkable in earlier reforming treaties.[42]

---

[40]   Art 18 TEU (as amended).
[41]   Art 12 TEU (as amended).
[42]   Art 10(2) TEU (as amended) provides: 'Citizens are directly represented at Union level in the European Parliament. Member States are represented in the European Council by their

A. The European Parliament in the Union's Legislative Process

In my opinion, the enhanced role of the European Parliament in the legislative process of the Union is the constitutional change that dwarfs all others in importance, with the possible exception of the evolution of the European Council as the body responsible for the Union's strategic direction.

As I have recalled, in the system of the primordial EEC Treaty, the limit of the European Parliament's involvement in law-making was its right to be consulted by the Council before certain measures could be formally adopted. In practice, this amounted to very little. The Council was only entitled to act definitively once it was seised of the opinion of the Parliament[43]; and, if it intended substantially to amend the original text on which consultation had taken place, there had to be a re-consultation.[44] However, so long as those procedural requirements were respected, the Council could completely ignore the substance of the opinion rendered by the Parliament, and usually did. The only practical way for the Parliament to influence the legislative outcome would be if it could persuade the Commission to amend its proposal, which would mean that the Council had to act unanimously to override the amendment.[45] That situation continued even after the European Parliament was transformed into a body directly elected by universal suffrage in June 1979. Although it has been superseded in many policy areas, the 'consultation procedure' is still prescribed by some legal bases, for example, by Article 37 EC for the purposes of the CAP.

The first big advance came in July 1987, with the entry into force of the Single European Act, which established a new 'cooperation procedure', available mainly for the enactment of legislation connected with the implementation of the internal market programme.[46] The procedure (which still survives in the field of economic and monetary policy)[47] involves two readings of draft measures. The principal innovation was that, if the European Parliament rejected the common position adopted at first reading by the Council, its veto could only be overridden by a unanimous Council decision, even if QMV was the voting rule prescribed

---

Heads of State or Government and in the Council by their governments, themselves democratically accountable either to their national Parliaments or to their citizens'.

[43] Case 138/79, *Roquette Freres v Council* [1980] ECR 3333.

[44] Case 41/69, *ACF Chemiefarma v Commission* [1970] ECR 661; Case 1253/79, *Battaglia v Commission* [1982] ECR 297; and Case C-65/90, *European Parliament v Council* [1992] ECR I-4593.

[45] Art 250(1) EC.

[46] It is now set out in Art 252 EC.

[47] See Arts 102(2), 103(2) and 106(2) EC.

by the relevant legal basis. Otherwise, the Parliament remained dependent on the Commission to take its proposed amendments on board.

The co-decision procedure was introduced by the TEU and further refined by the Amsterdam Treaty. In its developed form, the procedure places the European Parliament on an equal footing with the Council, as co-legislator. The Commission's proposal is submitted to both institutions at the same time. If, after two readings at arm's length, there are still amendments on which the Parliament and the Council remain divided, their representatives meet face to face in a Conciliation Committee, to attempt to reach agreement on a joint text. In order to become law, a proposal has to receive the positive approval of both institutions. Once adopted, the instrument is authenticated by the signatures of their two presidents.

When it was introduced, co-decision replaced cooperation as the legislative procedure on internal market matters and in some other policy areas, and its scope has been progressively extended by later amending Treaties. The further step that remains would be the 'generalisation' of co-decision, by according it formal recognition as the ordinary procedure to be used for the adoption of all legislative acts, other than those for which the Treaties lay down a special legislative procedure. This will be finally achieved by the TL, assuming it comes into force.[48]

On paper, therefore, pretty much everything that needed to be done would have been done, under the regime of the TL, to enable the European Parliament to fulfil its role in the legitimisation of the Union's law-making process. However, at the level of harsh political reality, it remains a question whether the Parliament is capable of living up to that role. There is as yet no sign of the development of a political process at the level of the Union, under which Members of the European Parliament can expect to be rewarded or punished at the ballot box for anything they, or the political grouping to which they belong, may achieve or fail to achieve in Brussels and Strasbourg. Until such a democratic link has been forged, while the Parliament may do an efficient job as a revising chamber, its contribution to solving the accountability conundrum will remain largely aspirational.

B. National Parliaments in the Union's Legislative Process

Heads of state or government may be called to account by their national parliaments and/or by public opinion for the decisions they agree to in the European Council, and the same is true of ministers when they take part in meetings of the Council at which legislation is adopted, whether by co-decision or some other procedure. How effective such control is

---

[48]   Art 289 TFEU.

depends upon various factors, in particular the flow of information from the political organs of the Union to the national level, and the arrangements established within national parliaments to monitor the progress of proposals through the decision-making process of the Council. In this regard, amendments envisaged by the TL to strengthen the Protocol on the role of national parliaments in the European Union, notably the requirement that the Commission forward its legislative proposals directly to national parliaments at the same time as they are submitted to the European Parliament and the Council,[49] would clearly be helpful.

A real innovation of the TL would be the new subsidiarity mechanism that would be created by amending the Protocol on the application of the principles of subsidiarity and proportionality. This would give national parliaments a formal role, independent of governments, in helping to ensure compliance with the principle. They would be able to intervene directly in the legislative process of the Union, by adopting a reasoned opinion explaining why they considered that a draft measure was not in conformity with it. For this purpose, every national parliament would be assigned two votes, one of them to be exercised by each chamber in a bicameral system.

Under the so-called 'yellow card' procedure, if reasoned opinions on non-compliance with the principle of subsidiarity represented at least one-third of the available votes, the originator of the draft measure (normally the Commission) would be required to review it. The outcome of the review might be a decision to maintain the draft or to amend or withdraw it, and reasons would have to be given.

The 'orange card' procedure would apply only to Commission proposals under the ordinary legislative procedure (co-decision). If reasoned opinions on non-compliance with the principle represented at least a simple majority of the available votes, a review would have to be undertaken, with legally prescribed consequences in the event of a decision by the Commission to maintain its proposal. The Commission would be required to adopt a reasoned opinion; and this, together with the opinions of the national parliaments, would have to be submitted to the Union's legislator, ie the European Parliament and the Council. During the first reading of the proposal in both branches of the legislator, there would have to be a formal moment when consideration was specifically given to the issue of its compliance with the principle of subsidiarity, particular account being taken of the reasons expressed and shared by the majority of national parliaments, as well as of the Commission's reasoned opinion. If, by a majority of 55 per cent of the members of the Council or a majority of the

---

[49] Art 2 of the Protocol.

votes cast in the Parliament, the legislator was of the opinion that the proposal was not compatible with the principle, no further consideration must be given to it.

I am an enthusiast for the new mechanism. Because of its heavy policy load, the principle of subsidiarity is much more effective as a guide to action by the legislator than as a basis for ex post review of a measure's legality. National parliaments are exactly the right bodies to apply the principle, because it is they who will lose out if it is abused. If the mechanism is introduced (and this could be done without the TL, by way of an inter-institutional agreement), they would have a real opportunity to influence the course of the Union's legislative process, although a considerable investment of time and effort would be needed. I am not one of those who considers the mechanism toothless, because the author of the draft measure in question would have the option of leaving it intact; within the Council, it would be a bold minister indeed who would join a qualified majority, in the teeth of a negative opinion from one or both of the chambers of the national Parliament. Indeed, it would not be necessary for the yellow or orange card procedures to be formally triggered; any significant number of negative opinions would alter the political dynamic of decision-making.

In my view, therefore, useful steps are in prospect to strengthen the national limb of dual democratic accountability in the legislative process of the Union.

IV. CONCLUSION

Have those developments, and others there has not been space to consider in detail, brought about a shift in the Union's institutional balance? On that question, I would offer these thoughts.

First, the idea that was once in the minds of some of us—myself included—that the old Marxist fantasy would come true for the Community and the Member States would simply whither away, has not happened. Nor will it. If anything, they are more confident and assertive now than they were in the 1960s. The institutional framework has been changed to accommodate that ineluctable fact, notably through the establishment of the European Council and the extension of its remit over the whole range of the Union's high politics, as well as in the particularity of the arrangements under which the CFSP is carried on.

Secondly, and in spite of that fact, I believe that the Council/Commission relationship, shorn of the unrealistic hope that the Commission could single-handedly force the pace of European integration, remains substantially unimpaired. Frank acknowledgement of the character of the Union as a constitutional order of states merely reinforces the need for an independent Commission, strongly led and technically competent, in order to counter the centrifugal pressures inherent in such an order.

Thirdly, there has been a substantial shift towards the European Parliament in the legislative process of the Union. I welcome that development, as one limb of the system of dual democratic accountability, although I do not believe it yet to be sufficiently articulated politically. The other (national) limb is beginning to show signs of promising muscularity.

Finally, a point which I hope shines out from this brief analysis is the wonderful adaptability of the Communities/Union. Willingness to entertain unorthodox solutions (like the pillar structure), until either they constitute a new orthodoxy (like the Second Pillar) or a return to a modified version of the former orthodoxy (as with the Third Pillar), is surely the mark of a constitutional order well equipped for Darwinian survival.

2

A Fusing Europe? Insights for EU Governance

LEE MILES

I. INTRODUCTION

O NE OF THE central themes of this volume is to reflect upon past achievements as well as to think more clearly about the future evolution of the European Union. This author has argued that, at least in terms of policy analysis, EU external relations policy[1] represents an area where the interface between past achievements and propensities for further EU development is obvious.[2] This chapter has three tasks. First, it provides a thematic survey of the EU today and argues that scholars of European integration (in both political science and law) should, once again, begin 'to think bigger'. Secondly, this chapter proposes that fusion approaches and the concept of a fusing Europe provide a useful, and somewhat familiar, starting ground to 'think bigger', since fusion approaches offer useful insights and conceptual tools to explain current EU development, especially in relation to the Treaty of Lisbon 2007,[3] and also to EU external relations. Finally, this chapter offers tentative conclusions regarding the future of the EU in the context of fusion approaches.

---

[1] In this chapter, the term 'EU external relations policy' encompasses the full breadth of EU instruments with third countries across more than one pillar of the existing EU. It includes trade policy mechanisms of the first (EC) pillar as well as foreign and security policy instruments pertaining to the second pillar, such as the Common Foreign and Security Policy (CFSP) and the European Security and Defence Policy (ESDP). It also adopts a fundamentally political science-orientated perspective.

[2] L Miles, 'Editorial: A Fusing Europe in a Confusing World?' in L Miles (ed), *The European Union: Annual Review 2004/2005* (Blackwell, Oxford, 2005); and L Miles, 'Still a Fusing Europe in a Confusing World?' in A Haglund Morrissey and D Silander (eds), *The European Union and the Outside World: Global Themes in a European Setting* (Växjö University Press, Växjö, 2007).

[3] [2007] OJ C306. For consolidated versions of the revised Treaties, see [2008] OJ C115.

II. THE EU TODAY: UPGRADED EU AMBITION; DOWNSIZED
SCHOLARLY ENDEAVOUR

With some simplification, the challenges confronting the European Union today broadly fall in to four main categories. First, there are the *ongoing debates on the future configuration of the EU that have culminated in the signing of the EU Reform Treaty in Lisbon in December 2007*. The Union has made progress in moving forward, especially in the development of EU external relations portfolios, institutions and instruments. Secondly, there are the *discussions on further EU enlargement*: the Union is digesting the impacts of the 2004 and 2007 accessions, as well as handling pressures emanating from a list of formal applicants (Croatia and Turkey being the most notable). Enlargement signifies that the Union is regarded by third countries as a successful operation, for some worthy of joining and accepting the *acquis*, with its mix of intergovernmental and supranational features. Thirdly, there are the *challenges surrounding an ever-expanding and ambitious external relations policy*. The development of, for example, the European Neighbourhood Policy (ENP) that is designed to handle the demands of the Union's closest neighbours—including those where EU membership is a longer-term prospect or not even on offer—ensures that external relations questions will require constant EU attention. In addition, the Union is strengthening its crisis management and military capabilities (under CFSP/ESDP auspices) and coordinating reactions to the 'war on terror' that also ensure that relations with third countries will feature prominently on EU agendas. Finally, there are the *external implications of existing integrative policies, such as Economic and Monetary Union (EMU)*, where EU relationships with third countries are affected by the deepening of existing portfolios. These integrative forces enhance, directly and indirectly, the role of the Union's trade and external relations as a force for global change.

As this volume signifies, such a broad agenda warrants greater attention, given that 2007 represented the 50th anniversary of the signing of the Rome Treaties, and provides a rationale for the EU to reflect on past successes. As Swedish Foreign Minister, Carl Bildt, remarked in a major speech given at Chatham House on 15 March 2007, the EU is successful because:

... it is easy to see that old divisions between domestic and foreign policies don't really apply any longer ... National policies are increasingly for national consumption—it is the common European policies that are there to handle the global challenges that increasingly are affecting our citizens.[4]

This can be taken as testimony that 50 years of European integration have been characterised by a form of fusion of national and EU competencies—a theme that this chapter will return to later. Furthermore, 2007 represents another phase in EU development since EU leaders found agreement on the principles of a new Reform Treaty (in June) and then signed the final Treaty of Lisbon (in December). There is, once again, a rather fuzzy blueprint for further European integration, that will, most likely, remain even if the new Treaty is not ratified.

In contrast to upgraded EU policy ambitions, scholarship on European integration and the EU as a system of governance is moving in the opposite direction. EU scholars have, over the last decade, been moving away from the search for any single 'meta-theory' that can explain large aspects of the Union as a system of governance.[5] Many are content to apply 'middle-range' approaches that focus on *some* of the dynamics associated with the Union. This selective concentration of effort among EU scholars has advantages and disadvantages for those contemplating EU external relations. The impact of international politics on the EU is panoramic, not confined to one or even a small number of specific EU policy domains and can, more accurately, be described as a *phenomenon*. Theoretical considerations also apply not only to the Union, but also, albeit to a lesser extent, to the applicant and/or candidate countries. When searching for conceptual and theoretical pointers, it is necessary to continually widen the traditional horizons of European integration theory.[6]

There is, of course, a limited amount of scholarly effort in this regard. Important contemporary contributions discuss EU international identity,[7] and conceptualising the impact of the EU as a 'force for good' and as a 'normative power',[8] as well as notions of flexibility in determining EU capabilities.[9] As Warleigh-Lack illustrates, most works focus on what constitutes EU external relations and the exporting of EU ideas to other

---

[4] 'Europe 1957–2007–2057', Speech by HE Carl Bildt, Minister for Foreign Affairs, Royal Institute of International Affairs (Chatham House, London, 15 March 2007).

[5] There are some notable exceptions, such as S Bartolini, *Restructuring Europe: Centre Formation, System Building, and Political Structuring Between the Nation State and the European Union* (Oxford, Oxford University Press, 2005).

[6] L Miles, 'Theoretical Considerations' in N Nugent (ed), *European Union Enlargement* (Palgrave, Houndmills, 2004).

[7] I Manners and R Whitman, 'The "Difference Engine": Constructing and Representing the International Identity of the European Union' (2003) 10 *Journal of European Public Policy* 380.

[8] I Manners, 'Normative Power Europe: A Contradiction in Terms?' (2002) 40 *Journal of Common Market Studies* 235.

[9] A Warleigh, *Flexible Integration: Which Model for the European Union?* (Continuum, 2002).

regions. Consequently, he calls for further linkages between disciplines (including law) and for research on 'new regionalism'.[10] Nevertheless, at least in political science, existing scholarship explains only a small part of EU external relations. Above all, the specific relationship between the supranational trajectories of European integration and the evolution of the EU external relations policy remains largely under-developed.

III. UNDERSTANDING EUROPEAN INTEGRATION: THE FIVE 'S'S'

If scholars are to 'think bigger', they must address five specific research themes that underpin discussions on the evolution of the EU as a system of governance—labelled here as the five 'S's'. The primary focus of the first two research themes concentrates on what we are trying to explain in terms of 'thinking bigger' on the EU. First, *stability*: it is necessary to explain *not just change, but the fundamental stability that underpins contemporary EU evolution as a system of governance over time.* The primary research question is: *how can the fundamental stability of the EU as a system of governance be explained?* Secondly, *sub-optimality*: there is the requirement to explain *the continuing sub-optimal sustainability of the European Union as a system of governance.* Put as a research question: *how can we explain sub-optimal innovation in the EU as a system of governance, especially when such developments may not produce optimal solutions to the economic and political challenges that the EU faces?*

When reflecting on these two primary research themes, it is necessary to outline what should be examined when 'thinking bigger' and thus, two secondary research themes should be considered. First, *systemic linkages*: a need to recognise the *systemic* nature of European integration. As a research question: *why and how does the EU as a system of governance contain a potent mix of supranational and intergovernmental features that span not just internal EU competencies, but also external relations portfolios?* In other words, understanding the EU as a *supranational system of governance primed to deliver internal and external outcomes that are intrinsically related to the transformation of the European nation state itself.* Secondly, *synergy*: it is essential to understand the *synergy* of the European Union as a system of governance. As a research question: *how does the EU accommodate synergy as a system of governance?* At this point, several forms of synergy can be identified. First, there is an 'internal EU' synergy that centres on the relationship between European integration

---

[10] A Warleigh-Lack, 'Toward a Conceptual Framework for Regionalisation: Bridging New Regionalism and Integration Theory' (2006) 13 *Review of International Political Economy* 750; and A Warleigh, 'In Defence of "Intra-disciplinarity": European Studies, the "New Regionalism" and the Issue of Democratisation' (2004) 17 *Cambridge Review of International Affairs* 301.

(supranational EU evolution) and Europeanisation (adaptation of national and sub-national actors and institutions to EU evolution). This internal synergy highlights not just the implications arising from the 'legal', but also the 'living', organic capabilities of the EU; and, since there will be differentiated impacts *on the Member States*, ensures that concrete classifications among the supranational, national and sub-national are difficult. In addition, there is an 'external EU' synergy that recognises EU evolution impacts on national and sub-national actors in third countries, and prompts national and sub-national adaptation in differentiated forms for the former as well. Ultimately, there are new synergies developed between EU and Member States' actors and those in third countries as they jointly react to the pressures of European integration. Robust understandings of the EU as a system of governance must accommodate notions of differentiation in terms of scope and depth of integration.

This formulation of this '2+2' should then enable scholars to focus on a fifth research theme, reflecting on how such stability, sub-optimality, systemic linkages and synergies enable us to 'think bigger' about the future of the EU, and thus consider *scenarios*: EU scholarship must show greater ambition in producing future *scenarios* for the EU as a system of governance. As a research question, can the acknowledgement of *stability, sub-optimality, systemic nature* and *synergies* produce future scenarios for the EU?

IV. A FUSING EUROPE AND THE FIVE 'S'S'

If existing EU scholarship equated with 'thinking bigger' is surveyed, then one body of work that may offer food for further thought is that of fusion; an approach (or perhaps more accurately a set of approaches) that offers numerous conceptual tools to understand both the trajectory of European integration and the perspectives and adaptation of participating political elites. Collectively, these approaches produce an understanding of the EU as a system of governance as a 'fusing Europe' that may not only accurately identify the state of play of the Union today, but also provide conceptual tools to explain future EU evolution.

According to the intellectual architect of the macro-fusion thesis (MFT), Wolfgang Wessels,[11] fusion represents a dynamic macro-political thesis explaining the development of the Union, whereby Member States and EU-based actors increasingly merge resources in joint institutions and complex procedures. The MFT argues that European integration is 'the logical product of fundamental choices by member governments' in which

---

[11] W Wessels, 'Nice Results: The Millennium IGC in the EU's Evolution' (2001) 39 *Journal of Common Market Studies* 197, 199.

constituent steps are taken primarily through package deals that make Member States agree to invest competencies and resources in the EU.[12] The fusion thesis addresses directly one of the research themes outlined in this chapter—namely how to explain the *fundamental stability and stable evolution of the European Union as a system of governance over time.*

A. A Stable Evolution

The MFT offers numerous insights, since it recognises that the *stable* supranational development of the European Union is intrinsically linked to, and facilitated by, the ongoing transformation of the nation state that has been largely affected by growing interdependence among countries that makes utilisation of domestic instruments to deliver the welfare needs of citizens increasingly difficult.[13] Political elites accept the supranational obligations of EU membership, the pooling of sovereignty and the logics of supranational institutions in order to harness solutions that fulfil the welfare needs of citizens that are otherwise no longer achievable using exclusively national mechanisms and policies. According to the MFT, the EU develops as a stable international platform precisely because 'the national state is alive, but not well'[14] and that national and sub-national elites favour stable, closer European integration (and thus EU membership) because of fundamental alterations in the style and emphasis of governance that are occurring within the Member States. By accepting these supranational obligations, political elites participate in European integration that spurs on a blurring of sub-national, national and supranational competencies that accompanies, and also accelerates, transformation within the Member States. Put another way, and as Bartolini argues, in a format largely compatible with the MFT, European integration represents the sixth developmental phase in European history since the sixteenth century in which 'European integration can therefore be interpreted as a response by national elites to the weakening of the European state system'.[15]

According to the MFT, EU joint problem-solving is perceived as meeting needs emanating both from domestic politics and the imperatives set by

[12] W Wessels, 'An Ever Closer Fusion? A Dynamic Macropolitical View of the Integration Process' (1997) 35 *Journal of Common Market Studies* 267, 274.
[13] *Ibid*, 273.
[14] W Wessels, 'Comitology: Fusion in Action. Politico-administrative Trends in the EU System' (1998) 5 *Journal of European Public Policy* 209, 217.
[15] S Bartolini, above n 5, 366. Bartolini provides an instance of scholars 'thinking bigger'. This is readily conceded since the work of Bartolini is highly compatible with that of fusion. It is not fusion or Bartolini; rather it is more accurately a case of fusion *and* Bartolini. This warrants further investigation in future works.

international interdependence.[16] Yet, fusion also explains why elite support is somewhat conditional.[17] Even though elites largely accept that EU participation also leads to further changes in the statehood of Western Europe, and that 'for the sake of its own stability, the state has to promote a process which leads to its very erosion',[18] fusion also explains why European integration may go through fits and starts. If the benefits are not discernible or not delivered, elites (and citizens) question the advantages of further integration. European integration, unlike that outlined by neo-functionalism, is neither linear nor automatic. The MFT accommodates the fact that the EU faces real and potential rejection, as with the Constitutional Treaty in 2005 and the Reform Treaty in 2008, yet still evolves.

B. Sub-Optimality

There is a second strength of fusion—in explaining the *sub-optimality* of the EU as a system of governance and future EU trajectories. The MFT proposes that European integration is an elite-driven, open-ended process without a clearly defined *finalité politique*, in which political elites are building a system of governance that, in political terms, goes well beyond intergovernmental cooperation. Nevertheless, fusion approaches recognise the sub-optimality as a normal part of the EU's *modus operandi* and, consequently, a fusing Europe falls short of establishing a fully fledged constitutional settlement akin to a federal Europe. Such a federal future would require agreement on constitutional arrangements that are beyond the present scope of policy-makers given its high degree of political symbolism and the requirement of having extensive consensus on specific constitutional arrangements.

According to the MFT, European integration is establishing a blurred, rather messy system of governance in which sub-national, national and supranational competencies are fusing together, with citizens finding lines of political accountability difficult to trace.[19] In fusion approaches, this blurred, sub-optimal, political space is actually something that national and sub-national political elites rather like. Such a fused political space is the result of what Bartolini may call[20] a process of 'centre formation', in which elites seek to turn natural international arenas, where there may be resource asymmetries, into governmental political arenas, where such

[16] W Wessels, above n 12.

[17] A Johnson, 'The Diffusion Thesis? EU Governance in the Social Policy Field', Paper at European Union Studies Association (EUSA) Biennial Conference (Madison, Wisconsin; 31 May–2 June 2001).

[18] W Wessels, above n 12, 286.

[19] W Wessels, above n 12, 274.

[20] S Bartolini, above n 5, 27–8.

solutions can be accessed through cooperation and conformity with others. The result, as Bartolini contends, is elite consolidation resulting in an alliance and integration between national rulers (national governments and parliamentary elites) and supranational techno-bureaucratic centre builders (the EU institutions):

> ... based on cooperation towards shared goals, but also on institutional competition and mutual controls that take the form of persistent fused powers, unclear competence distributions, and weak legitimacy sources. Any attempt to separate the powers, distribute the competencies, and strengthen more direct forms of legitimacy more clearly, would probably upset the inter-elite form of control on which this consolidation rests to date.[21]

C. Systemic Linkages

A further strength of fusion approaches is that they offer specific insights into the *systemic nature of the EU and how such systemic trends affect future EU trajectories*. In the MFT, Wessels identifies indicators to detect fusion trends in the EU system.[22] Among them, fusion can be detected through *the growth of EU binding decisions that impact on national and sub-national actors and institutions*.[23] Fusion assumes that there is an explicit, systemic link between decisions taken by the EU and adaptation, and thus between European integration trajectories and Europeanisation, whereby national and sub-national actors respond to growing EU legislation. In addition, fusion assumes that the EU has developed a *mixed system of competencies* that have only limited, sectoral impacts on Member States. The MFT acknowledges that the impacts of European integration are differentiated and 'sectoral constrained' across national and sub-national governmental and policy remits.[24] For Bartolini, such differentiation amounts to weak 'system-building', with a very thin level of identification and loyalty to common EU purposes or visions outside the elite level.[25] Furthermore, fusion approaches expect a *growth and differentiation of EU institutions and procedures* that offer new opportunities for actors to develop systemic relationships directly with the supranational EU institutions, sometimes independent of national government structures.[26] Actors are neither excluded nor crowded out, leading to intensive, differentiated

---

[21]   *Ibid*, at p 176.

[22]   W Wessels, above n 12, 275–84.

[23]   M Lindh, L Miles, C Räftegård and H Lödén, *Understanding Regional Action and the European Union: A Fusion Approach* (Karlstad University Studies, Karlstad, 2007).

[24]   W Wessels, A Maurer and J Mittag (eds), *Fifteen into One? The European Union and its Member States* (Manchester University Press, Manchester, 2003); and L Miles, *Fusing with Europe? Sweden in the European Union* (Ashgate, Aldershot, 2005).

[25]   S Bartolini, above n 5, 244.

[26]   M Lindh, L Miles, C Räftegård and H Lödén, above n 23.

incorporation of national and sub-national actors into the EU system. Finally, the MFT envisages *systemic widening and deepening of channels of access and influence for intermediary groups*, evidenced by national and sub-national actors maintaining a presence in Brussels to facilitate effective lobbying. Usage of these channels of access will be regular and diversified depending on the respective policy field.[27]

Crucially, fusion approaches should not be seen as envisaging a uniform EU system, but rather one that places differentiation and sub-optimality at its core with national and sub-national actors wanting, and maintaining, varying degrees of presence in the 'diversified, atomized and complex political space' of Brussels.[28] As Bartolini may contend,[29] these latter MFT aspects are equivalent to European integration prompting a process of 'political restructuring', in which there will be innovative systemic interaction and alliances among political elites through participation in the EU policy process.

D. Synergy

Fusion approaches place less emphasis on understanding European integration in terms of 'levels'—be they supranational, national or sub-national. Fusion highlights the importance of *synergy* in interpreting the EU as a system of governance, whereby competencies of actors and institutions are fusing together so that accountability for and of them is now effectively blurred; thus making clearly enunciated distinctions between the supranational, national and sub-national levels of only limited intellectual value. There is then also a complementary emphasis in fusion on performance outcomes in defining support for European integration rather than accountability or legitimacy criteria.

Given that fusion 'thinks bigger' by highlighting synergies, rather than differences, among supranational, national and sub-national competencies and institutions, it also provides a synergetic perspective that can be applied across more that one field of study. Furthermore, today, the fusion literature since 2005 now incorporates three interconnected fields—linked by a strong thematic perspective of the EU as a stable evolving system of governance where competencies are fusing in a messy compound polity that reflects, and acts as a catalyst for, the transformation of the nation state. In essence, fusion literature provides insights into the following:

(i) The trajectory of European integration: *the macro-fusion thesis*. To

---

[27] W Wessels, above n 12, 283.
[28] *Ibid*, 284.
[29] S Bartolini, above n 5, 39–47.

recap, then, the MFT explains the process of European integration by which national and EU actors increasingly merge resources in joint institutions and complex procedures. It also provides insights on long-term evolution that is producing a stable, sub-optimal and diverse EU compound governance system of mixed intergovernmental and supranational features[30] in which differentiation is commonplace.

(ii) Adaptation within the Member States (and, to a limited extent, third countries) with a stress on elite-driven pressures and drivers that takes as its starting point the central tenets of the MFT. Notions of micro *institutional fusion* stress the link between European integration and Europeanisation and explain the 'reactions and adaptations to a challenge which is common to all—i.e. the policy-cycle of the Union'.[31]

(iii) Against the background of macro-MFT assumptions, fusion conceptualises how national and sub-national policy-makers interpret European integration from a policy perspective: *the (micro) fusion perspective*.[32]

Synergic understanding of relationships among supranational, national and sub-national actors and institutions provides greater freedom of manoeuvre, at least in academic terms. Synergic interpretations of fusion are able then to reconcile the importance of blurred competencies and praxis in making the European Union what it is today. Fusion, for instance, acknowledges the importance of *comitology*, where there is a 'specific form of administrative interaction at a crucial intersection between the national and EC administrations'[33] that also attracts little public awareness.[34] Hence, the synergic strengths of fusion approaches provide scholars with insights into understanding not only the trajectory of the EU, but also the practical realities of how the EU does business.

E. Scenarios

With its emphasis on stability, sub-optimality, systemic linkages and synergies, fusion offers the potential to provide scenarios to interpret future EU evolution as a system of governance. In particular, the MFT accommodates two important contemporary trends affecting European integration since the 1990s: first, that European integration is driven, and accompanied by, a process of incremental socialisation of key political

---

[30] W Wessels, above n 12.

[31] W Wessels, A Maurer and J Mittag (eds), above n 24; and D Rometsch and W Wessels (eds), *The European Union and Member States: Towards Institutional Fusion?* (Manchester University Press, Manchester, 1996).

[32] See L Miles, above n 24; and M Lindh, L Miles, C Räftegård and H Lödén, above n 23.

[33] W Wessels, above n 14, 210.

[34] V Schmidt, *Democracy in Europe: The EU and National Politics* (Oxford, Oxford University Press, 2006) 27 & 39–43.

elites; and, secondly, that the logical implication of this process will be an increased emphasis by political elites on the merits of a differentiated Europe. As Wessels argues,[35] there is a continued shift of political attention and resources to the Brussels arena without always implying a direct communitarisation in strict legal terms.[36] It is then prudent to understand the Union's evolution in terms of a twin process—that of a *legal constitution* (legal treaty-making) alongside a process of mutually reinforcing learning (the so-called *living constitution*). Yet, a focus on a living constitution, prompted by fusion processes, helps further refine a quasi-constitution of sorts,[37] and provides the means whereby differentiated approaches are tested out in practice and thereby accepted by political elites. Fusion approaches are not incompatible with notions of differentiated integration; rather fusion approaches can provide a means to understand, and deliver differentiated, as well as uniform, arrangements.

If this is the case, fusion can provide insights into how the EU, as a system of governance, will develop in the future, with its mix of supranational and intergovernmental features, and accommodate the demands of a growing membership where differentiated routes to further integration are a practical reality of daily life in the EU system. Fusion approaches offer the potential to develop differing *fusion scenarios* for further EU development, while still accepting that clustering and differentiation have to be incorporated into such scenarios. Fusion's assumptions—that asymmetry and blurred accountability and workings are a normal part of the EU system—lend themselves to the refining of fusion scenarios—such as, *infusion, clustered fusion* and *de-fusion*—that explain the development of a fusing Europe in which there will be endemic levels of differentiated integration.[38]

V. FUSION: PRIMARY CHARACTERISTICS AND FUTURE SCENARIOS

Fusing concepts include three primary characteristics that explain aspects of the EU as a system of governance and, more specifically, why a fusing Europe can also incorporate notions of differentiation in the development

---

[35] W Wessels, 'Keynote Article: The Constitutional Treaty—Three Readings from a Fusion Perspective' in L Miles (ed), above n 2.

[36] E Regelsberger and W Wessels, 'The Evolution of the Common Foreign and Security Policy: a Case of an Imperfect Ratchet Fusion' in A Verdun and O Croci (eds), *The European Union in the Wake of Eastern Enlargement* (Manchester University Press, Manchester, 2005) 94.

[37] W Wessels, above n 11, 215.

[38] See JE Neve, 'The European Onion? How Differentiated Integration is Reshaping the EU' (2007) 29 *Journal of European Integration* 517.

of respective EU policy domains.[39] First, fusion approaches incorporate the central assumption that the *future EU evolution, as a system of governance, is performance- and output-related since the preferences of influential political elites are largely rational and state-centric.* Policy-makers have a pragmatic performance-related mentality (performance fusion[40]) that links European integration processes to the evolution of the nation-state and the effectiveness of the latter's decision-making apparatus and, thus, they conditionally accept the obligations of supranational European integration provided that the Union delivers political and economic results that are no longer available by using just national and sub-national strategies and policies. European integration is largely favoured, not out of some commitment to a vision of an integrated Europe, but rather because political elites perceive that there are discernible output benefits in being part of the Union and utilising supranational policy-making. In order to gain positive performance outputs, the nation-state and national and sub-national political elites will be fused into EU workings and transformed by them, although domestic support remains conditional upon the EU delivering performance outcomes.

Since performance orientations are at the heart of a beating fusing Europe, then this also explains the differentiation in national and sub-national positions, and the development of multi-speed and even multi-tier approaches in the EU, such as transitional periods, derogations, red-lines and opt-outs. The existence of these measures can be rationalised in fusion approaches as the combined outcomes of broader evaluations by political elites, who are also watchful of domestic considerations, of EU performance options, which, at the same time, are reconciled with their commitment to see the EU further evolve as a stable, largely supranational, integrationist platform. Fusion's performance characteristic lends easily to explanations of differentiated integration.

The second primary characteristic of fusion approaches is that they *accommodate a third way for European integration.* Assumptions on the kind of the path that the vast majority of (national and sub-national) policy-makers want the Union to take in its future evolution thus explain the *stability* and *sub-optimality* of the EU. Drawing on the MFT, political elites chart a path between the two disliked alternatives of: (i) the deficiencies of intergovernmental cooperation, which has limited effectiveness since the implementation of common decisions can be undermined by the lack of mechanisms to ensure universal compliance; and (ii) federal solutions that may have increased effectiveness, but also are perceived by

---

[39] See L Miles, 'Editorial: A Fusing Europe in a Confusing World?' in L Miles (ed), above n 2; above n 24; and 'Still a Fusing Europe in a Confusing World?' in A Haglund Morrissey and D Silander (eds), above n 2.
[40] *Ibid.*

national policy-makers to threaten the existing constitutional character of the Member States. Instead, they favour a 'third way' (identified as 'political fusion'[41]) between pure intergovernmentalism and federalism that is pro-integration and supranational—rejecting the limited effectiveness of pure intergovernmentalism and the negative, and largely politically symbolic, implications of constitutional federalism. The trajectory of a fusing Europe is explained by the behaviour and attitudes of policy-makers that are pro-supranational integration, yet are federo-sceptic since supranationalism is, correctly or incorrectly, perceived by policy-makers and the public alike as being more easily 'controlled', and certainly less politically risky than federal solutions. Such a third way preference enables political elites to develop the EU as 'a political system without a state',[42] and thereby 'continue to project traditional visions of national democracy'.[43]

Given that a 'third way' of a fusing Europe also encompasses an open *finalité politique*, European integration is not perceived to be automatic or linear (like neo-functionalism), nor to inevitably lead to a federal Europe or (perhaps) even a fully fledged constitutional Europe. The end result is up for grabs, yet will, most likely, be a sub-optimal, stable form of supranationalism that will co-exist in a mixed form with some vestiges of intergovernmentalism, underpinned by a pragmatic performance-orientated emphasis on a quasi-living constitution rather than a strictly applied and formally written legal one. The third way preference of pro-supranationalist, yet federo-sceptic, fusing EU is also compatible with differentiated integration, since there can be some intergovernmental cooperation and differing constellations of Member State participation depending on EU scepticism in political elite and domestic circles, while also pushing for supranational solutions and advanced fused competences in others.

The likely outcome will be a fusing 'Hub and Spokes Europe'[44] that reconciles the existence of a fusing Europe with differentiated integration (see Figure 1) and envisages the Union of 27 as essentially supranational in character, with all Member States subscribing to full membership status that has, at its heart, acceptance of the dynamics of the Single European Market (SEM). Within this broad supranational European construct that fuses together around the core SEM, the Member States of the euro-area form a core 'EMU Europe' *hub*, where, alongside even deeper levels of fusion, options of a federal Europe may also remain potentially viable.

---

[41] *Ibid.*
[42] L Tsoukalis, *What Kind of Europe?* (Oxford University Press, Oxford, 2005) 33.
[43] V Schmidt, above n 34, 3.
[44] L Miles, 'Editorial: Moving Towards a "Hub and Spokes Europe"?' in L Miles (ed), *The European Union: Annual Review 2002/2003* (Blackwell, Oxford, 2003); and 'Still a Fusing Europe in a Confusing World?' in A Haglund Morrissey and D Silander (eds), above n 2.

This euro-area hub is surrounded by a number of influential *spokes states*, which are also leading EU participants in coalitions (usually involving *euro-area hub states*) and championing certain policy issues in the EU supranational construct, such as the UK on crisis management issues, Sweden on environmental policy and Poland on economic and social cohesion. At all times, however, the SEM acts as the supranational glue holding the broader supranational EU together and providing rationales in performance, political and compound terms, for the further pan-EU fusion of political elites and their competencies.

Given that a dynamic euro-area hub remains the dominant integrative force (with higher levels of fusion), a European federation may (possibly) emerge out of agreement among the euro-area hub states. Yet, the spokes states will continue with a broader supranational European construct and fuse together in a more limited number of policy domains, reflecting the fact that there are a host of political elites in the Member States that regard the existing supranational structures as sufficient, support a continuing, but lower level of integration (and thereby some fusion), yet want to remain outside any constitutionally derived, European federation. According to this scenario, if a federal Europe is to emerge, it would be as a result of a merger of a limited number of euro-area hub states, rather than the entire supranational and fusing EU transforming itself *en bloc* into a pan-European federal framework (including the spokes)—in essence, the creation of a federal United States of Europe *as a member* of the broader, still fusing, supranational EU construct, rather than the entire fusing EU transforming wholesale into a federal Europe. In this scenario, the entire EU can fuse together in deeper forms of supranational integration, while still allowing for diversity on whether the future of Europe should, for some, be a federal one. In other words, a fusing Europe is fully compatible with and indeed, largely assumes, notions of differentiation.[45]

The third characteristic of fusion approaches revolves around an assumption that the EU, as a system of governance, represents compound arrangements and thus *a fusing Europe represents a compound polity*. The majority of political elites, consciously or unconsciously, envisage European integration ('compound fusion'[46]) as a process delivering political institutions that have fused their competencies on a broadening scale in a kind of politico-administrative system that works in conjunction with the nation states, with open and expanding access for intermediary groups to

---

[45]   L Miles, 'Still a Fusing Europe in a Confusing World?' in A Haglund Morrissey and D Silander (eds), above n 2.

[46]   See L Miles, above n 24; 'Domestic Influences on Nordic Security and Defence Policy: From the Perspective of Fusion' in AJK Bailes, G Herolf and B Sundelius (eds), *The Nordic Countries and the European Security and Defence Policy* (Oxford University Press, Oxford, 2006); and 'Still a Fusing Europe in a Confusing World?' in A Haglund Morrissey and D Silander (eds), above n 2.

Figure 1: A Fusing Supranational Hub and Spokes European Union

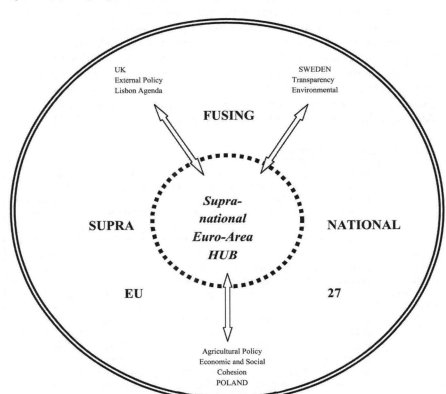

participate in EU decision-making. Yet, this is not just the perception of political elites, but also constitutes a preference that informs their behaviour. The EU as a compound polity is the choice preferred by national and sub-national policy-makers since they like the inclusive nature of compound fusion, with its growing array of committees, working groups and comitology. Political elites see, and advocate, an EU that does not correlate as a series of distinct 'levels' of supranational, national and sub-national competencies, but rather as a stable, sub-optimal and synergic EU compound, where public resources are merged.

Yet, the third primary characteristic of an open, yet rather messy, compound organisation of (mostly) supranational and intergovernmental features also lends itself to accommodating differentiation. Given that the compound system is designed to be open and inclusive, and is not based on uniformity, it offers groups from a diverse array of states, backgrounds and with many different preferences and views on EU configurations to partake in the EU system and develop a feeling of ownership of it. Political elites therefore define their own level of participation in this sub-optimal system, and in accordance with their diverse set of preferences, without necessarily requiring them to accept a uniform position on future trajectories of European integration. With these considerations in mind, it is possible to elaborate on the potential of fusion to offer scenarios into how the EU as a system of governance could develop in the future. In each scenario, there is compatibility with, and even a symbiotic relationship between, fusion and differentiation. Three possible scenarios seem obvious (see Table 1 below).

Table 1: Fusion Scenarios

	Micro-characteristic: performance fusion	Micro-characteristic: political fusion	Micro-characteristic: compound fusion	Macro-characteristic: fusion trajectory	Macro-characteristic: differentiation (hub and spokes)
Scenario A: infusing European Union	(+ performance perspective) Permissive comprehensive political elite consensus on EU performance	(+ supranational perspective) Preference for increasing supra-nationalism across all areas Intergovern-mentalism declining and rare	(+ polity perspective) Extensive supranational/national institutional fusion Extensive elite participation: multi-level players	(i) very stable; (ii) sub-optimal; (iii) uniform deepening of policy; (iv) strong synergies among sub-national, national and supra-national dimensions; (v) accelerated fused competencies	(i) strong euro-area hub; (ii) few spokes states; (iii) little use of opt-outs; (iv) differentiated integration approaches deemed undesirable and unnecessary

	Micro-characteristic: performance fusion	Micro-characteristic: political fusion	Micro-characteristic: compound fusion	Macro-characteristic: fusion trajectory	Macro-characteristic: differentiation (hub and spokes)
Scenario B: European Union of fusion clusters	(+/– performance perspective) Permissive, yet limited political elite consensus on EU performance Constrained to certain policy sectors	(+/– supranational perspective) Preference for clustered supranational extensions Preference for intergovern-mentalism for some policy fields	(+/– polity perspective) Clustered supranational/ national institutional fusion Selective elite participation; dependent on policy: few multi-level players	(i) stable, yet asymmetrical; (ii) sub-optimal; (iii) asymmetrical deepening; (iv) segmented synergies; (v) clustered fused competencies	(i) notable euro-area hub, yet strong spokes states in some clustered policy domains; (ii) Use of opt-outs in certain policy sectors; (iii) some usage of differentiated integration deemed necessary
Scenario C: defusing European Union	(– performance perspective) Resistant political elite consensus on EU performance Restrictive preference to clarity competencies	(– supranational perspective) Preference to resist supranational extensions Preference to retain and extend intergovern-mentalism	(– polity perspective) Little supranational/ national fusion; competencies clarified Reluctant elite participation: national performers	(i) unstable; (ii) sub-optimal; (iii) poor segmented deepening; (iv) weak synergies; (v) clarify competencies to limit supranational extensions	(i) weak euro-area hub; (ii) many spokes states; (iii) extensive use of opt-outs; (iv) application of differentiated approaches are the norm

A. Scenario A: Infusing European Union

In this scenario, the EU deepens extensively across a broad range of policy fields, including that of external relations. Political elites across the Member States, and in the EU institutions, share a common positive viewpoint on EU performance. A permissive political consensus on EU performance outcomes (performance fusion) is thereby created. There is strong political support among these respective actors for further, comprehensive extensions of the Union's supranational competencies (political fusion). At the same time, this productive political consensus does not extend fully to agreement on a full-blown and ambitious EU legal constitutional arrangement. The political consensus among the elites facilitates, and indeed advocates, the further development of the Union's compound polity (compound fusion).

Under these conditions, the Union progresses on a stable trajectory. EU Treaties are agreed and the EU further develops policy fields with the full participation of all Member States on a largely equal and comprehensive basis. The usage of opt-outs, 'red lines' and derogations are rare and multi-speed differentiated approaches are not usually deemed politically necessary. Alongside this, political elites readily fuse their competencies with those of the EU—leading to a kind of uniform infusion—in order to maximise impact of policy deliverables. In EU external relations policy, the usage of enhanced cooperation would be kept to a minimum. Further extensions of the supranational 'first pillar method' into the realms of foreign and security policy are agreed, with increased usage of qualified majority voting, and perhaps the eventual absorption of the CFSP into the 'first pillar method', with the universal support of the Member States.

B. Scenario B: European Union of Fusion Clusters

In this scenario, the EU further develops a narrower, yet still relatively extensive, range of policy fields, denoted by some asymmetrical extensions to EU competencies across those policies. There remains a majority of political elites, across the Member States and in the EU institutions, with similar positive viewpoints on EU performance. Yet, this is restricted to a smaller number of EU policy domains. There are discernible differences of support across the EU countries. There is a measured, sector-constrained political consensus on EU performance characteristics (performance fusion), and there is only a limited willingness among these respective parties to support further, usually comprehensive, extensions of the Union's supranational competencies (political fusion). Notable opposition among political elites remains in some Member States. The limitations of the political consensus rule out any kind of agreement on a full-blown and ambitious EU legal constitutional arrangement, although it does permit, and indeed advocates, the further development of the Union's sub-optimal compound polity (compound fusion) to cover some further policy areas.

Under these conditions, the Union evolves on a relatively stable trajectory. EU Treaties are agreed that enhance a limited array of policy portfolios. However, extensions to EU supranational functions remain clustered in small number of policy fields and the fusion of competencies among the political actors remains restricted to a smaller cluster of policy domains. There is also a wide variety of forms of participation of national and sub-national actors in those respective policy clusters and differentiation approaches are permitted even where fused clusters exist. The usage of opt-outs, red lines and derogations are more common. Multi-speed differentiated approaches are deemed politically necessary. In EU external relations policy, the usage of enhanced cooperation could be more common, and the participation of all Member States in the CFSP and ESDP on an equal basis would be more difficult. The extension of the Union's security and military competencies remains, albeit to a limited extent, controversial. There would, for example, be major differences across the Member States on the idea of the EU developing into a mutual defence pact and on the EU relationship to NATO. It is likely that extensions of qualified majority voting rules would be restricted or clustered to certain policy competencies. Preferences for retaining intergovernmental cooperation (and probably a distinct legal framework such as the current second pillar) as the normal *modus operandi* would exist for some CFSP/ESDP areas.

C. Scenario C: Defusing European Union

In this scenario, the EU develops a very limited range of policy fields, with notable asymmetry in its competencies across those policies.[47] There is an exceedingly small number of political elites across the Member States and in the EU institutions that share a common positive viewpoint on EU performance and, even here, the consensus is restricted to a very small number of EU policy domains. There are also highly discernible differences in the degree of support across the EU countries. Rather the tendency is for the political elites to have a largely negative assessment of the EU performance capacities (little/negative performance fusion). Consequently, there is little political will among these respective parties to support further and comprehensive extensions of the Union's supranational competencies (little/negative political fusion). Controversies and opposition to the EU are commonplace among political elites in the Member States. The limitations of the political consensus rule out any kind of agreement on a full-blown and ambitious EU legal constitutional arrangement. Instead, there would probably be extensive efforts to try and restrict the development of the Union's compound polity by seeking to agree explicit measures that clarify and restrict EU competencies (little/negative compound fusion).

[47] Eg A Johnson, above n 17.

Under these conditions, the Union evolves, yet the fusion of political elites and their competencies are halted. In some instances, a process of *de-fusion* may be evident, whereby political elites seek to clarify supranational, national and sub-national division of competencies in order to explicitly restrict those of the EU and possibly 're-nationalise' some EU policy domains. There is a wide variety of forms of participation of national and sub-national actors that include extensive usage of opt-outs, red lines and derogations in the EU. Multi-speed differentiated approaches are deemed politically necessary. In EU external relations policy, the usage of enhanced cooperation will be possible. There is a high degree of asymmetry as regards the participation of Member States in the CFSP and ESDP. Usage of unanimity ruling in certain external relations policy field would be essential in order to retain any semblance of support. Discussions on extending the Union's security and military competencies would be highly controversial. There would, for example, be major differences, and largely a negative assessment, across the Member States on the idea of the EU developing into a mutual defence pact and on the EU relationship to NATO. Intergovernmental cooperation (and probably a distinct legal framework based on the existing second pillar) as the normal *modus operandi* would be the dominant preference.

VI. INTERPRETING THE EUROPEAN UNION: A FUSION APPROACH

A. Reform Treaty: From a Political Strategy of Explicit to Implicit Constitutionalism

Although at the time of writing, ratification of the Treaty of Lisbon 2007 is not completed, it can be argued that, from a political science perspective, several interpretations can be drawn that are important for this discussion of fusion.

First, in political terms, governing political elites in the EU have, rightly or wrongly, interpreted that the emphasis on explicit constitutionalism in the Treaty establishing a Constitution for Europe 2004[48] was a tactical mistake, and a major reason for the Constitutional Treaty's downfall.[49] Although, in many respects, the EU continued to operate as 'business as

---

[48]   See W Wessels, above n 35.
[49]   See L Miles, 'Still a Fusing Europe in a Confusing World?' in A Haglund Morrissey and D Silander (eds), above n 2, 31; and P Taggart, 'Keynote Article: Questions of Europe—The Domestic Politics of the 2005 French and Dutch Referendums and their Challenge for the Study of European Integration' in U Sedelmeier and AR Young (eds), *The JCMS Annual Review of the European Union in 2005* (Blackwell, Oxford, 2006).

usual',[50] the fate of the Constitutional Treaty and the lessons drawn that shaped its 2007 successor can be interpreted as a failure of one political strategy that attempted explicit EU constitutionalisation; which, for some, was also regarded as opening the door to a European super-state and a substantial reduction in national autonomy.[51]

From this, the majority of EU leaders have deemed that the Reform Treaty will only be fully ratified across all of the Member States if the political elites do not take political risks and engage their respective publics through openly formulated constitutional orientated debates on the EU. As the Presidency Conclusions of the European Council meeting on 21 to 22 June 2007 stated: 'The constitutional concept, which consisted of repealing all existing Treaties and replacing them by a single text called "Constitution" is abandoned'.[52] For the near future, the strategy will be (to return to) that of incremental integration based around revisions of existing treaties. Again, the Presidency Conclusions are specific. The revised Treaty of European Union (TEU) and the Treaty on the Functioning of the European Union (TFEU, ie the revised EC Treaty) 'will not have a constitutional character',[53] while the final Treaty of Lisbon does not include reference to many EU constitutional-inspired symbols, such as anthems, and abandons the explicit language of an EU constitution. All of this suggests that the Treaty of Lisbon represents a strategy for delivering the continuation of a fusing Europe.

Secondly, the Reform Treaty reflects attempts by governing political elites to manage the impacts of *plebiscitary politics on EU agendas*. The championing, for example, by French President Sarkozy of a 'simplified amending Treaty' in the weeks before the June 2007 summit was an attempt by the president to build a consensus around a stipulation that any Treaty would, normally, require ratification merely by parliamentary vote. Even the German Presidency came to terms with the fact that it could not resurrect the original EU constitution, reflecting a new realism of what was possible in ratification terms. The temptation is for governments to continue with intergovernmental conferences (IGCs) as the 'safer', elite-driven format to produce treaties, since the constitutional convention approach resulted in a Constitutional Treaty that could not be ratified.

---

[50]   U Sedelmeier and AR Young, 'Editorial: Crisis, What Crisis? Continuity and Normality in the European Union in 2005' in U Sedelmeier and AR Young (eds), above n 49.

[51]   L Miles, 'Still a Fusing Europe in a Confusing World?' in A Haglund Morrissey and D Silander (eds), above n 2.

[52]   European Council Presidency Conclusions (21–22 June 2007), Annex 1, 11177/07, 15.

[53]   *Ibid*, 15.

B. Reform Treaty: Evidence of Fusion-Compatibility

The 2007 Reform Treaty incorporates many of the policy features of the previous 2004 Constitutional Treaty, yet these also highlight that the EU has an agreed format of *institutional and/or policy innovations that (subject to ratification) will reflect, and reinforce, a fusing Europe*. Reform Treaty innovations, such as a streamlined EU Commission and a new 'permanent' European Council President, as well as developments that improve EU external relations capabilities, are seen by elites as performance-driven EU vote-winners. The Presidency Conclusions of the European Council meeting on 21 to 22 June 2007 again stressed that the drawing up of a new Treaty was done 'with a view to enhancing the efficiency and democratic legitimacy of the enlarged Union, as well as the coherence of its external action'.[54] In this respect, the EU embraces selective institutional and policy innovation and the EU external relations portfolio represents one of the key sectors of innovation in the Treaty of Lisbon. On this basis, it is a key area pushing forward a fusing Europe; not least because the Reform Treaty envisages the delivery of institutional and policy action while simultaneously downplaying, in political terms, constitutional symbolism.

Moreover, there are aspects of the Reform Treaty, like the Constitutional Treaty before it, that are fusionist in tone. There are, for example, institutional innovations in the Reform Treaty that are designed to develop fused competencies among EU institutions, and of EU and national actors. In particular, the creation of a *High Representative (HR) of the Union for Foreign Affairs and Security Policy may represent one of the clearest pieces of evidence of fusion approach*. Wessels regarded the creation of such an EU Foreign Minister (the post was previously labeled in the old Constitutional Treaty) as not only a notable innovation, but one that can be seen as 'an ideal-typical case of fusion' given that the proposed 'double-hat' position merges the roles of High Representative (HR) for the CFSP (representing the intergovernmental second pillar) and a Vice-President in the European Commission (representing the supranational first pillar).[55] The translation of the EU Foreign Minister (in the 2004 Constitutional Treaty) into the re-named 'High Representative of the Union for Foreign Affairs and Security Policy' (in the Treaty of Lisbon 2007) was accompanied by no notable changes in institutional design or role, and therefore can continue to be viewed as an institutional innovation designed to deliver increasingly fused EU competencies.[56]

---

[54]   *Ibid.*
[55]   W Wessels, above n 35, 26.
[56]   See Art 19 of the revised TEU.

The HR is designed to enable the EU to perform better in external relations (performance fusion). The HR will have at his or her disposal an array of supranational and intergovernmental mechanisms that compliment the Member States (political fusion) and represent a fused compound of EU and national competencies in foreign affairs, with the HR acting as both a Vice-President of the European Commission and the chief of the EU's continuing CFSP. Lines of accountability will remain blurred. In addition, the Reform Treaty provides for the HR to be supported by a European External Action Service[57] that implies—'in line with fusion theory—a pooling of national and community administrative resources'.[58] The Reform Treaty includes innovations that can also be taken as evidence of fusion-compatible perspectives of EU policy-makers; and, if ratified, will shape the EU, as a system of governance, in a form compatible with the macro-fusion thesis.

C. External Relations Policy: A Catalyst for Further Fusion?

External relations policies (including the CFSP/ESDP) are enhanced fields in the Treaty of Lisbon, partly because there is a consensus among EU political elites of the need to strengthen EU capacities to send clear messages to third countries in international affairs. Since the EU 'exists to a large extent to provide a buffer between the countries of Europe and the outside world',[59] changes to the EU external relations portfolio, as envisaged in the Reform Treaty, reflect the Union's ambition to be more coherent and ensure, largely using fusion-compatible innovations, that the Union has mechanisms that can make it a more forceful international actor.[60] Those ambitions will not dissipate and are largely performance-driven. The external relations innovations in the 2007 Treaty include an implicit, and increasingly explicit, acknowledgement of the blurred capabilities for handling external and internal security threats between the fields of CFSP (currently under the second pillar) and police and judicial cooperation in criminal matters (currently under the third pillar), as well as

---

[57] See Art 27 of the revised TEU.

[58] W Wessels, above n 35, 27; N Klein and W Wessels, 'A "saut constitutionnel" out of an intergovernmental trap? The Provisions of the Constitutional Treaty for the Common, Foreign, Security and Defence Policy' in L Rovná and W Wessels (eds), *EU Constitutionalisation: From Convention to the Constitutional Treaty 2002–2005: Anatomy, Analysis, Assessment* (EUROPEUM Institute of European Policy, 2006).

[59] E Jones and M Rhodes, 'Europe and the Global Challenge' in P Heywood, E Jones, M Rhodes and U Sedelmeier (eds), *Developments in European Politics 2* (Palgrave, Houndmills, 2006) 25–6.

[60] The 2007 Treaty includes, for example, changes to 'Enhanced Cooperation' that allow the Council to authorise enhanced cooperation provided at least nine states participate in it: see Art 20 of the revised TEU.

the differentiated participation of Member States in those arrangements (in particular, through various mechanisms for enhanced cooperation). This extends to security and defence policy, with the Treaty of Lisbon providing for enhanced security cooperation among Member States in defence matters, but still allowing for political elites to adopt differentiated approaches.[61] The external relations institutional and policy innovations in the 2007 Treaty are evidence that external rationales—labelled as 'the demands of a confusing world'[62]—provide explanatory reasons for the Union deepening further and, in this context, enhance the prospect of a fusing Europe.

VII. CONCLUSION

As a conclusion, improving the Union's external relations portfolio is universally perceived, and enjoys broad public support, as an area where the Union can implement further reforms in order to enhance its effectiveness, and will be the basis for further EU innovation. Although there are concerns over constitutional Europe, the Reform Treaty packaged the provisions relating to practical CFSP/ESDP cooperation so as to lessen the likelihood that they would be resisted by the European populations. The Treaty builds an EU external relations structure that is compatible with, and pushes forward, a fusing Europe, and represents a pragmatic balance of intergovernmental and supranational features and can easily incorporate differentiated approaches. It is appropriate then, once again, to call upon scholars to 'think bigger' and further consider fusion approaches in order to explain why the EU maintains a stable, often sub-optimal, path of integration where competencies are increasingly fused. The 2007 Reform Treaty, if ratified, may strengthen a *Union of fusion clusters*—especially in the EU external relations area—within the broader framework of a fusing, supranational 'hub and spokes' Europe.

---

[61] The 2007 Treaty introduces amendments to the TEU enhancing defence cooperation; yet they also ensure that Member States have safeguards for differentiated approaches (including references to 'not prejudice the specific character of the security and defence policy of certain Member States': see Art 42 of the revised TEU).

[62] See L Miles, 'Editorial: A Fusing Europe in a Confusing World?' in L Miles (ed), above n 2; and 'Still a Fusing Europe in a Confusing World?' in A Haglund Morrissey and D Silander (eds), above n 2.

3

Reflections on the Roles of Mutual Trust in EU Law

PER CRAMÉR

I. INTRODUCTION

THE CONCEPT OF social trust is a construction, which in general terms refers to an ideal situation where all actors in a society are able to make a stable prognosis of the benign behaviour of all other actors. Thus, it is a phenomenon based on reciprocity, or mutuality, which on an individualised level could be described as a situation where 'I believe that you can be trusted if I also believe that you believe that I can be trusted'.

In political science the concept of mutual social trust is commonly seen as a precondition for good governance and estimates of mutual trust are frequently used as a variable in comparative studies of governance.[1] Mutual trust between actors in a society has furthermore been viewed as an important factor enhancing economic growth and international competitiveness. With the terminology of Douglass North, it constitutes an important informal institution of society.[2] In theories of international relations, the concept of mutual trust between states has gained importance as a precondition for creating international stability transcending the logic of the 'balance of power'. In this sphere of thinking, mutual trust refers to a situation where all states have stable expectations about all other states' peaceful, or benevolent, manners.[3] In the European political/legal debate, mutual trust has been brought up with increased frequency. It has even

---

[1] See, as an example, B Rothstein and D Eek, *Political Corruption and Social Trust—An Experimental Approach*, QCG Working Paper Series 2006:1 (available at <http://www.qog.pol.gu.se> accessed 2 September 2008).

[2] DC North, 'Where have we been and where are we going?' in A Ben-Ner and L Putterman (eds), *Economics Values and Organization* (Cambridge, Cambridge University Press, 1998).

[3] Compare the theory on security communities developed in KW Deutsch, *Political Community in the North Atlantic Area* (Princeton, Princeton University Press, 1957) 5–9 &

been hailed to be *at the heart of EC law*.[4] I believe that there is a certain truth to this observation. More specifically, I believe that analysing the functions of mutual trust in the European integration process has the potential to be a fruitful endeavour that might further our understanding of the development and functioning of EU law.

The purpose of this chapter is to present a number of tentative reflections on the various roles played by mutual trust in EU law. It is clear that, within the European legal system, the construction of mutual trust operates on different levels and in different perspectives. In the following sections, I will therefore make a rather unsophisticated separation between a principal constitutional level and a level of material Community law related to market integration. I will also separate mutual trust between Member States from mutual trust between Member States and the supranational Community institutions. The ideas presented are tentative and somewhat rhapsodic. Nevertheless, I hope that they will give an input to creative discussions on the functioning of the European legal structure.

II. MUTUAL CONSTITUTIONAL TRUST BETWEEN MEMBER STATES

Even if the European Union Treaties have been endowed with certain constitutional functions and characteristics, the fundamental intergovernmental character of a treaty structure has not been abandoned and the operations of the Union are based on powers attributed to it from the Member States.[5] Thus, the Member States of the European Union retain their constitutional sovereignty; the Member States as a collective can amend the 'constitution" of the European Union, while the latter cannot directly amend the national constitutions of the Member States. The Member States' retention of constitutional sovereignty may be seen as a fundamental principle for the structure of the European Union. From this principle follows a duty of mutual constitutional respect between the Member States and the Common institutions[6] as well as between the Member States themselves.

However, this constitutional respect between Member States has to be deserved and continuously reconfirmed by the mutual constitutional trust between the Member States. This in turn establishes limits on the national constitutional sovereignty.

Mutual constitutional trust between the Member States could be seen as an essential principle not only of EU law, but also of the EU itself. All

---

115–16. Internally, the EU could be described as such a security community where stability between the Member States is based on mutual trust rather than balance of power.

[4] 'Editorial' [2006] *European Constitutional Law Review* 1.
[5] Art 5 TEU; and Art 5 EC.
[6] Compare Art 6(3) TEU.

Member States have to have a stable trust that all other Member States uphold a set of basic common values, most importantly, democracy and effective safeguards for fundamental human rights and freedoms. Such trust is a necessary prerequisite for establishing an acceptance that legislative decisions may be taken by qualified majority in the Council, and that Community law is applied as the supreme 'law of the land' in all Member States.[7] The flip side of this coin is that, in order to uphold such acceptance, all Member States must show respect to the constitutional systems of all other Member States, so long as they abide to democratic principles.

These interrelated principles of respect and trust have of course been operating since the genesis of the integration project. However, primarily as a precautionary measure with a view to enlargement into central and eastern Europe, a codification took place through the Amsterdam Treaty that explicitly lays down a duty for the Member States to comply with the common principles of the Union, listed in Article 6(1) of the Treaty of European Union (TEU): liberty, democracy, respect for human rights and fundamental freedoms, and the rule of law. Within the Union framework, action against a Member State that has been found to seriously and persistently violate these principles could be taken in accordance with Article 7 TEU, the ultimate sanction being suspension of certain rights deriving from the Treaty.[8]

Thus, the Amsterdam Treaty amendments constituted a radical change to the extent that, instead of just confirming the democratic character of the systems of government of the Member States, the Union was vested with its own independent fundamental principles to which the Member States have to abide.[9] This development underlines the importance of the principle of mutual constitutional trust, but could also be seen as a sign of mistrust among the then present Member States concerning the future constitutional stability of the incoming Member States.[10]

The importance of stable mutual constitutional trust between the Member States was illustrated by the so-called 'Haider affair' in 2000, where 14 of the then 15 Member States, acting outside the Union, introduced diplomatic sanctions against Austria as a reaction to the creation of a

---

[7] JHH Weiler, 'The Function and Future of European Law' in V Heiskanen and K Kulovesi (eds), *Function and Future of European Law* (Helsinki, Forum Juris/KATTI, 1999) 9–22.

[8] Art 7(3) TEU.

[9] Compare Art F TEU: 'The Union shall respect the national identities of its Member States, whose systems of government are founded on the principles of democracy'.

[10] Compare N Neuwahl and S Wheatley, 'The EU and Democracy—Lawful and Legitimate Intervention in the Domestic Affairs of other States?' in A Arnull and D Wincott (eds), *Accountability and Legitimacy in the European Union* (Oxford, Oxford University Press, 2002).

coalition government including the far rightwing Freedom Party. By introducing these sanctions with reference to a situation that was in full compliance with the Austrian Constitution and with no signs of concrete infringements of human rights, the 'Group of XIV' ended up in a legally twilight position when a coalition government including the Freedom Party was formed. This inconvenient situation had to be solved through the appointment of an ad hoc monitoring committee by the President of the European Court of Human Rights. On the basis of a positive report on the human rights situation in Austria, the sanctions could be lifted without a loss of political face for the Group XIV. The experiences of this affair led to an amendment of Article 7 TEU through the Nice Treaty, according to which Member States can take precautionary action if they determine that there exists a *clear risk* of a serious breach by a Member State of the principles mentioned in Article 6 TEU.[11] The threshold for instigating such actions is considerably lower than for an action on the determination of the existence of a clear and persistent breach. Thus, a structure for preventive monitoring, through intergovernmental peer review, of compliance with the values laid down in Article 6 TEU was established.

The development of Articles 6 and 7 TEU could also be seen as an outflow of a regulatory trend with an increased focus on conditionality related to fundamental human rights values that commenced within the sphere of EC external relations in the 1990s, most importantly in connection with the pre-enlargement process.[12] Internally, this development introduced something new; what was earlier taken for granted now became codified and a price for non-compliance was established. Some commentators have described this development as the end of a true community of values,[13] and it could be argued that the pre-existing informal presumption of constitutional trust was done away with through the Amsterdam Treaty and substituted by the conditionality spelled out in Article 7 TEU.

The logic of system is, however, clear: mutual constitutional respect and trust between the Member States constitute fundamental prerequisites for the functioning of the Union. In order to enhance the stability of the process of integration, and against the background of the enlargement and deepening processes of the Union that commenced after the fall of the

---

[11] Art 7(1) TEU. On the legal repercussions of the Haider Affair, see P Cramér and P Wrange, 'The Haider Affair Law and European Integration' [2001] *Europarättslig Tidskrift* 28.

[12] It should be noted that, through the Amsterdam Treaty, the fulfilment of the fundamental principles listed in Art 6(1) TEU was formally codified as a precondition for accession to the EU: see Art 49 TEU.

[13] J Klabbers, 'On Babies, Bathwater and the Three Musketeers, or the Beginning of the End of European Integration' in V Heiskanen and K Kulovesi (eds), *Function and Future of European Law* (Helsinki, Forum Juris/KATTI, 1999) 275–81.

Berlin wall, an increasing need to safeguard the existence of such a situation was perceived. The instrument chosen to meet this need is a formalised system of intergovernmental peer review and the ultimate threat of sanctions in form of suspension. Such a decision on suspension is political, not judicial. To make use of this system inevitably leads to a confrontation between Member States on issues of fundamental constitutional values, and the political costs to make use of this system are likely to be very high. It could be questioned if the system could be applied other than in extreme situations, such as the collapse of a democratic regime. Accordingly, it should primarily be seen as a deterrent measure.[14]

Perhaps the most important result of this development has been the establishment of the European Union Human Rights Agency, which includes a network of independent human rights experts with the task of monitoring and reporting on the human rights situation in the Member States.[15] If efficient, this soft monitoring structure has the potential to contribute to constitutional stability within the Member States, thereby enhancing mutual trust between them.

III. CONSTITUTIONAL TRUST BETWEEN THE MEMBER STATES AND THE COMMON INSTITUTIONS

The principle of supremacy of Community law over national law, including national constitutional law, has been restated and elaborated by the European Court of Justice (ECJ) in numerous decisions. Most importantly, the Court in its 1970 decision in the case *Internationale Handelsgesellschaft* reaffirmed the supremacy of Community law over national constitutional law.[16] The development of the doctrine of supremacy, taken together with the framing of the doctrines of direct effect and pre-emption, amounted to a constitutionalisation of Community law. This was a road that was consciously and deliberately chosen by the judges. In a commentary published in 1989, Judge Mancini summed up these developments:

---

[14] According to Art 7(2) TEU, a determination of the existence of a serious and persistent breach in a Member State of the fundamental principles mentioned in Art 6(1) TEU requires unanimity in the Council, not taking into account the vote of the Member State in question. Concerning the limited possibility to apply Art 7 TEU, see A Williams, 'The Indifferent Gesture: Article 7 TEU, The Fundamental Rights Agency and the UK's Invasion in Iraq' (2006) 31 *EL Rev* 3; and A Verhoeven, 'How Democratic need European Union Members be?' (1998) 23 *EL Rev* 217.

[15] See Regulation 168/2007 [2007] OJ L53/1. Presidency Conclusions of the Brussels European Council, 12–13 December 2003, para 27.

[16] Case 11/70, *Internationale Handelsgesellschaft* [1970] ECR 1125, para 3.

The main endeavour of the Court of Justice has precisely been to reduce or remove the differences [between the EC Treaty and a federal constitution]. In other words, the Court has sought to 'constitutionalize' the Treaty, to fashion a constitutional framework for a quasifederal structure in Europe.[17]

The Member States have tacitly accepted the legal doctrines developed by the Court. In day-to-day affairs, national public authorities accept the jurisdiction of the ECJ and the principles of direct effect and supremacy are applied with a high degree of loyalty. However, the Member States tend to underline the Union's basic character as a structure based on the principles of international law; they recognise supremacy, not as an outflow of the inherent character of the treaties as pronounced by the ECJ, but rather by reference to national laws on accession.[18] Based on this reasoning, the constitutional courts in a number of Member States have retained a right to review secondary Community law in exceptional situations. This conditional acceptance of the principle of supremacy has been demonstrated in a number of well-known cases, most importantly the *Brunner* judgment of the *Bundesverfassungsgericht*.[19]

In general terms, two different lines of reasoning on conditionality may be observed: conditionality specifically related to national constitutional safeguards for fundamental rights; and conditionality related to the scope of the competences conferred upon the common European institutions.

Essentially, the conditional acceptance of the doctrine of supremacy means that Member States, with reference to their national constitutional sovereignty, have reserved for themselves a right to revolt against the

---

[17]   GF Mancini, 'The Making of a Constitution for Europe' (1989) 26 *CML Rev* 595, 596. Also published in RO Keohane and S Hoffman (eds), *The New European Community* (Boulder, San Francisco, Oxford, Westview Press, 1991).

[18]   Neil MacCormick has described this constitutional tension in the following way: '... the point of view of the European Court of Justice does not match that of the courts in the member states ... For them, the ultimate validating ground is found in the domestic constitutional law, whereas in the view of the ECJ, the Community has its own constitutional charter to whose validity in its own right the ECJ is necessarily committed according to its own longstanding doctrine': see N MacCormick, *Questioning Sovereignty: Law, State and Practical Reason* (Oxford, Oxford University Press, 1999) 101–2.

[19]   Cases 2BvR 2134/92 and 2153/92, *Manfred Brunner v the European Union Treaty*, 89 BverGE 155; reported in English at [1994] 1 CMLR 57. For general overviews of the national case law on this issue, see A Oppenheimer (ed), *The Relationship between European Community Law and National Law: The Cases* (Cambridge, Cambridge University Press, Vol I 1994 and Vol II 2003); AM Slaughter, A Stone Sweet and JHH Weiler (eds), *The European Courts and National Courts—Doctrine and Jurisprudence* (Oxford, Hart Publishing, 1998); and M Kumm, 'Who is the Final Arbiter of Constitutionality in Europe?' (1999) 36 *CML Rev* 356. It should be noted that Central and Eastern European Constitutional Courts have been profoundly influenced by the judicial reasoning of the German Constitutional Court. For an account of the development of relevant case law from the Constitutional Courts in the Czech Republic, Estonia, Hungary, Latvia and Poland, see A Albi, 'Supremacy of EC Law in the New Member States: Bringing Parliaments into the Equation of "Co-operative Constitutionalism"' [2007] *European Constitutional Law Review* 25.

exclusive competence to adjudicate on the validity of secondary Community law claimed by the ECJ.[20] The competing and incommensurable claims of the power to adjudicate have, however, never flared up into outright confrontation, but have rather resulted in mutual deterrence. Thus, a *modus vivendi*, based upon the idea of balance of power—a variation of the doctrine of Mutual Assured Destruction—has been established.[21] This balance of power could be seen as a logical outflow of the system of dual constitutionalism that constitutes a hallmark of the Union construction.

In concrete terms, this has led to a polycentric adjudication of constitutional issues within the Union that has forced the ECJ into a cooperative relationship with its national counterparts.[22] This balance of constitutional power has furthered the dynamic development of the integration process and contributed to ameliorating certain deficiencies in the legal system of the Union. The clearest example of this is the integration of principles for the protection of fundamental rights into the body of Community law through interpretation by the ECJ and subsequent codification in the form of the Union's Charter of Fundamental Rights.[23] This process was sparked off by the *Bundesverfassungsgericht*, which pushed the ECJ into a position where it had to take rights more seriously in order to retain legitimacy for the principle of supremacy.[24]

---

[20]   Case 314/85, *Firma Foto-Frost v Hauptzollamt Lübeck-Ost* [1987] ECR 4199, paras 15–20.

[21]   Compare JHH Weiler, UR Haltern and FC Mayer, 'European Democracy and its Critique' (1995) 18 *West European Politics* 4.

[22]   Compare S Weatherill, 'The Modern Role of the Court in Constitutional Law' in S Weatherill (ed), *Law and Integration in the European Union* (Oxford, Oxford University Press, 1995) 210–20. See also A Stone Sweet, *Governing with Judges: Constitutional Politics in Europe* (Oxford, Oxford University Press, 2000) 178.

[23]   [2000] OJ C364/1.

[24]   It should be noted that, during the early period of European integration, the ECJ took a restrictive position with regard to safeguards for individual rights. A good illustration of this is found in the judgement in Case 1/58, *Friedrich Stork v High Authority* [1959] ECR 17, para 4. The integration of safeguards for human rights into the body of Community law commenced during the late 1960s through the judgment in Case 29/69, *Erich Stauder v City of Ulm Sozialamt* [1969] ECR 419. This doctrine was thereafter successively restated and refined in a number of judgments, such as Case 4/73, *J Nold KG v Commission* [1974] ECR 491 and Case 44/79, *Liselotte Hauer v Land Rheinland-Pfalz* [1979] ECR 3727. Fundamental principles safeguarding human rights and fundamental freedoms were codified in Art 6(2) TEU and Art 13 EC through the Amsterdam Treaty in 1995. On 7 December 2000, the European Parliament, the Council and the Commission adopted a politically, but not legally, binding Charter of Fundamental Rights of the European Union [2000] OJ C364/1. For a critical analysis of the ECJ's role in this development, see J Coppel and A O'Neill, 'The European Court of Justice: Taking Rights Seriously' (1992) 29 *CML Rev* 669. For different perspectives, see D Keeling and F Mancini, 'Democracy and the European Court of Justice' (1994) 57 *MLR* 175; and JHH Weiler and N Lockhart, '"Taking Rights Seriously" Seriously: the European Court and its Fundamental Rights Jurisprudence' (1995) 32 *CML Rev* 51, 579.

It could be argued that the conditional acceptance of supremacy relating to the scope of the conferred competences has, to some degree, pushed the ECJ to also take competences more seriously. Developments on this issue are certainly not unambiguous, but the ruling in the *Tobacco Advertising Directive* case[25] has been perceived by several commentators to enhance the credibility of the ECJ as a guardian of the scope of competences conferred upon the Common institutions.[26] The importance of this single decision by the ECJ should, however, not be overemphasised.[27]

Thus, through an organic process, a situation in which constitutional tensions between the Union and its Member States are eased through horizontal negotiations, rather than vertical adjudication, has been created.[28] In a general context, it is not a daring hypothesis to suggest that the relative responsiveness of the Union institutions has furthered the loyalty of national institutions and strengthened the legitimacy of the Union structure at large within the Member States—while a situation of mutual constitutional trust between the actors has been established. This situation is, however, not without its risks. It has been argued that the combination of the increase in number of national constitutional actors that follows from enlargement, the increased use of qualified majority voting and the expanded scope of conferred competences will lead to Member States increasingly seeking to justify a selective application of Union law with reference to national constitutional rules.[29]

I do not believe that the risk for such abusive behaviour by Member States should be exaggerated. Mutual constitutional trust between the common supranational institutions and the Member States is a fundamental prerequisite for the functioning of the Union. Such trust can only be built on mutual constitutional respect. It is evident that a beneficial

---

[25]   Case C-376/98, *Germany v Parliament and Council* [2000] ECR I-8419.

[26]   See, eg S Douglas Scott, *Constitutional Law of the European Union* (London, Longman, 2002) 165–9. See also the casenote by JA Usher, (2001) 38 *CML Rev* 1519.

[27]   Consider the contribution by D Wyatt in this volume.

[28]   Compare the discussion concerning a structured and ongoing, intra-judicial dialogue between the national constitutional courts and the ECJ, in A Stone Sweet, 'Constitutional Dialogues in the European Community' in A-M Slaughter, A Stone Sweet and JHH Weiler (eds), *The European Court and National Courts—Doctrine and Jurisprudence* (Hart Publishing, Oxford, 1998).

[29]   In a study published in 2004, Kumm and Comella have observed this potential future area of contention: 'There is an increasing risk that, as the EU increasingly abandons unanimity voting and moves towards qualified majority voting in an ever expansive number of areas, the defeated States will play the jurisdictional "constitutional" card at home; they will choose to protect their interests, against the enforcement of EU norms they have voted against, through an appeal to their Constitutions and their courts. Moreover, since the claim that an EC norm is *ultra vires*, if true for one Member State, must be true for the rest of States, and the number of Member States is going up to 25, there is a special risk if the national courts subject EU law to this kind of review': see M Kumm and VF Comella, *Altneuland: The EU Constitution in a Contextual Perspective*, Jean Monnet Working Paper 5/04 (New York, NYU School of Law, 2004) 18.

constitutional balancing act presupposes that decision-makers on both the Union and the national levels act responsibly and avoid abusing their respective powers and there is certainly a limit to the constitutional divergences that could be handled within the system. However, it has to be presumed that the Member States, and certainly the supranational institutions of the Union, perceive European integration as basically good. Thereby a system of mutual deterrence will be operating: the striking down of an act of Union law by a national court would certainly be extremely detrimental to the functioning of the Union, from both a short- and medium-term perspective. Conversely, a pronouncement by the ECJ that a norm of national constitutional law could not be applied in the light of Union law would certainly lead to an erosion of the legitimacy of integration process among the Member States and thereby place the integration process into jeopardy.[30] Continued indeterminacy, ie whereby the crucial question of who is the final constitutional arbiter remains unanswered, thus seems to enhance mutual constitutional trust between the Member States and the common supranational institutions.

IV. THE ROLE OF MUTUAL TRUST IN MARKET INTEGRATION BASED ON THE PRINCIPLE OF MUTUAL RECOGNITION

Within the sphere of market integration, the question of mutual trust between the Member States is of essential importance when it comes to the possibilities for application of the principle of mutual recognition. This principle, as developed by the ECJ in its decision in *Cassis de Dijon* with regard to the free movement of goods,[31] has the power to do away with technical barriers to trade within the common market while maintaining regulatory diversity among the Member States. In essence, it means that all Member States must have trust in all other Member States' product-related regulations, professional requirements, etc. Each Member State has to believe that such regulations in other Member States, even the most lenient, may not be the same, but are at least essentially equivalent to its own requirements. However, this presumption of equivalence based on mutual trust functions only up to a certain threshold, a fact that was recognised by the ECJ already in its judgment in *Cassis de Dijon*. Here, the

---

[30]   P Cramér, 'Does the Codification of the Principle of Supremacy Matter?' (2004–2005) 7 *CYELS* 57. Kumm has argued for the likeliness of a 'Pangloss scenario', in which the Member States would only rarely strike down a piece of secondary Community law, and do so for good reasons: see M Kumm, 'The Jurisprudence of Constitutional Conflict: Constitutional Supremacy in Europe before and after the Constitutional Treaty' (2005) 11 *ELJ* 262, 291–2.

[31]   Case 120/78, *Rewe Zentrale v Bundesmonopolverwaltung für Branntwein* [1979] ECR 649, para 14. Concerning the application of the principle of mutual recognition with regard to establishment and the free movement of services, see Directive 2005/36 on the recognition of professional qualifications [2005] OJ L255/22.

Court formulated the principles for a dynamic safety valve, supplementing the Treaty provisions on derogations: the doctrine of mandatory requirements.[32] Thus, there exists a limited scope for residual host state control where mandatory interests of a non-economic character are at issue. This possibility for justified deviations from the principle of mutual recognition is limited by the principles of necessity and proportionality, under the final control of the ECJ.

When mutual trust is at hand, equivalence is presumed and harmonisation is not needed for the functioning of the internal market. Accordingly, the Commission can focus on developing proposals for harmonisation measures in areas where a Member State has successfully invoked a right to host state control under the doctrine of mandatory requirements or explicit Treaty provisions on derogation.[33] Harmonisation becomes the dynamic systemic reaction to a situation of mistrust between Member States that has been accepted as justified by the ECJ. This means that Member States may strategically trigger a process of harmonisation by showing mistrust, ie not accepting the presumption of equivalence.[34]

Nevertheless, the principle of mutual recognition constitutes a fundamental principle for market integration that requires the maintenance of mutual trust. A pre-condition for maintaining this trust is that its limits are negotiable. Mutual trust, and a presumption of equivalence, in 'normal' situations is enhanced by the mere existence of the possibility to exercise host state control in exceptional situations. Mutual trust between the Member States is also enhanced by obligations on transparency and the notification of national technical regulations, as established by Community law.[35] The functioning of the principle of mutual recognition is thereby facilitated and the need for harmonisation decreases. A similar function is

[32]   Case 120/78, *ibid*, para 8. Concerning the free movement of persons, see Case C-55/94, *Reinhard Gebhard v Consiglio dell'Ordine degli Avvocati e Procuratori di Milano* [1995] ECR I-4165, paras 36–7; and Case C-330/03, *Colegio de Ingenierieros de Caminos y Puertos v Administración del Estado* [2006] ECR I-801, para 21.

[33]   Compare C Barnard, *The Substantive Law of the EU* (Oxford, Oxford University Press, 2007) 589–91.

[34]   An illustrative example of this dynamic reflexive mechanism is found in the development of harmonised rules concerning packaging and packaging waste. In Case 302/86, *Commission v Denmark* [1988] ECR 4607, the ECJ ruled that a Danish law requiring that beverages could only be marketed in reusable containers constituted an infringement of the principle of mutual recognition that could be justified with the reference to the doctrine of mandatory requirements. After the judgment, the Commission started to develop a proposal for a harmonising measure that was adopted in December 1994: Directive 94/62 on packaging and packaging waste [1994] OJ L365/10. Following harmonisation, the Danish legislation had to be adapted to the directive and the full functioning of the internal market was re-established within this specific sphere.

[35]   See, eg Directive 98/34 laying down a procedure for the provision of information in the field of technical standards and regulations [1998] OJ L204/37.

to some extent played by the so-called open method of coordination, through a reflexive process of experimentation and learning within ongoing policy dialogues.[36]

Finally, it has to be underlined that mutual trust when it comes to national product-related regulations and professional requirements presupposes that the regulatory differences between the participating states are not too great; all states must be able to accept a presumption of equivalence even with regard to the most lenient national regulation. Increased regulatory divergences between the participating states would inevitably lead to increased strains on mutual trust and make a presumption of equivalence unacceptable. Therefore, the principle of mutual recognition could only be applied in market integration between states with limited regulatory divergences.[37]

V. APPLICATION OF HARMONISED RULES AND MUTUAL TRUST BETWEEN MEMBER STATES

Harmonisation through the adoption of acts of secondary Community law decreases regulatory diversity by establishing regulatory unity.

Even if the Community lacks the administrative structure for the general enforcement of its legislation, Member States usually comply with the Treaty obligations and apply secondary Community law with a high degree of efficiency and loyalty. However, the efficient application of Community rules is based on a situation of mutual trust: that all Member States trust that all other Member States implement and apply Community law efficiently. If it was not at hand, the efficiency of the common legal system would most certainly be undermined. Accordingly, all Member States have a self-interest to comply in order to safeguard the stability of the system. This pull towards compliance is thus based on mechanisms we usually find in theories of public international law, primarily the principle of reciprocity.[38]

---

[36] See Presidency Conclusions of the Lisbon European Council (23–24 March 2000). It should be noted that the Open Method of Coordination primarily has been used with regard to flanking policies within the framework of the Lisbon process. Nevertheless, there is a potential scope for wider application. See further: CM Radaelli, *The Open method of Coordination: A New Governance Architecture for the European Union?* (Stockholm, SIEPS, 2003).

[37] From this it follows that, with the existing regulatory divergences on a global level, the principle of mutual recognition could not be accepted as a general principle for trade on the multilateral level of regulation. This is illustrated by the Agreement on Technical Barriers to Trade that is annexed to the WTO Treaty. According to Art 2.7, the Members of the WTO are encouraged to conclude bilateral agreements on mutual recognition.

[38] Compare RO Keohane, 'Reciprocity in International Relations' (1986) 40 *International Organization* 1; and L Henkin, *How Nations Behave, Law and Foreign Policy* (New York, Columbia University Press, 1979) 39–87.

Against this background, it might at first glance seem paradoxical that the ECJ has denied the principle of reciprocity a legal status in EC law. In its decision in *Hedley Lomas*, the Court argued that a Member State may not unilaterally adopt, on its own authority, corrective or protective measures designed to obviate any breach by another Member State of rules of Community law.[39] Taking into account the exclusive competence entrusted to the ECJ to interpret Community law, and to adjudicate on questions of infringements, this conclusion is logical.[40] However, the Court followed up by adding that Member States must rely on trust in each other to implement their obligations under EC law.[41] What the ECJ did not emphasise in its argumentation is that the Member States, denied the possibility to act unilaterally in a harmonised policy area, because they ought to trust each other, as a last resort, have to trust the effectiveness of the system for enforcement before the ECJ. Accordingly, if this enforcement system does not meet the demands of the Member States, the strain on mutual trust between Member States would increase and the unity of the Community legal order would be threatened. The existence of an efficient supranational system for the adjudication of alleged infringements constitutes a means to maintain mutual trust between Member States.

In this connection, the importance of the role played by the national courts and their loyalty to the Community legal order could not be underestimated. This loyalty is in its turn dependent on the mutual trust between the Member States and the common supranational institutions.

---

[39] Case C-5/94, *R v Ministry of Agriculture, Fisheries and Food, ex p Hedley Lomas* [1996] ECR I-2553, para 20. See also the decision in Case 232/78, *Commission v France* [1979] ECR 2729, para 9.

[40] Compare the early argumentation by the ECJ in the Joined Cases 90 & 97/63, *Commission v Luxembourg and Belgium* [1964] ECR 625: 'The Treaty is not limited to creating reciprocal obligations between the different natural and legal persons to whom it is applicable, but establishes a new legal order which governs the powers, rights and obligations of the said persons, as well as the necessary procedures for taking cognizance of and penalizing any breach of it. Therefore, even where a Community institution has failed to carry out its obligations, except where otherwise expressly provided, the basic concept of the Treaty requires that Member States shall not fail to carry out their obligations and shall not take the law into their own hands.' See further: Hallström, 'The European Union—from Reciprocity to Loyalty' (2000) 39 *Scandinavian Studies in Law* 79.

[41] Case C-5/94, above n 39, para 19. The importance of mutual trust in this perspective is referred to by the ECJ in several cases, eg Case 46/76, *WJG Bauhuis v The Netherlands* [1977] ECR 5, para 22; Case C-230/98, *Amministrazione delle Finanze v Schiavon Silvano* [2000] ECR I-3547, para 53; Case C-124/95, *R, ex p Centro-Com v HM Treasury and Bank of England* [1997] ECR I-81, para 49; and Case C-73/06, *Planzer Luxembourg Sárl v Bundeszentralamt für Steuern* [2007] ECR I-5655, para 38.

It should be noted that supplementary measures, such as the adoption of common rules on administrative cooperation, have been enacted as instruments to maintain and enhance mutual trust between the Member States in the effective application of harmonised regulation by national administrative authorities.[42]

VI. A SPECIAL CASE: MUTUAL TRUST AND THE EUROPEAN ARREST WARRANT

During the last five years, the debate on mutual trust in EU law has largely been focused on the Council Framework Decision on the European Arrest Warrant (EAW) that was adopted on 13 June 2002.[43] Its overall objective is to facilitate extradition procedures between the Member States by the application of the principle of mutual recognition for an EAW issued by a Member State. Such a warrant is defined as a decision issued by a Member State with the view to the arrest and surrender by another Member State of a requested person, for the purposes of conducting a criminal prosecution or executing a custodial sentence or detention order.[44]

As has been discussed above, the application of a principle of mutual recognition requires the existence of mutual trust between the participating actors. Implicitly, the EAW Framework Decision presupposes that all Member States have mutual trust in each other in order to establish a presumption of equivalence concerning the quality of judicial decisions and procedural standards.

In the preamble of the Framework Decision, it is explicitly stated that the system established presupposes a *high level of confidence* between Member States. It is furthermore stated that its implementation may be suspended only in the event of a serious and persistent breach by one of the Member States of the principles set out in Article 6(1) TEU, as determined by the Council pursuant to Article 7(1) TEU, with the consequences set out in Article 7(2) TEU.[45] According to this formulation, it is presumed that mutual confidence, or mutual trust between the Member States, should be

---

[42] See, eg Regulation 515/97 on mutual assistance between the administrative authorities of the Member States and cooperation between the latter and the Commission to ensure the correct application of the law on customs and agricultural matters [1997] OJ L82/1. The importance of administrative cooperation as an instrument to enhance mutual trust, or mutual reliance, between Member States has been underlined the ECJ on several occasions, eg Case C-230/98, *Amministrazione delle Finanze v Schiavon Silvano* [2000] ECR I-3547, para 53; and Case C-432/92, *R v Minister of Agriculture, Fisheries and Food, ex p S Anastasiou (Pissouri) Ltd* [1994] ECR I-3087, paras 38–40.

[43] Council Framework Decision 2002/584 on the European arrest warrant and the surrender procedures between Member States [2002] OJ L190/1.

[44] *Ibid*, Art 1(1).

[45] *Ibid*, 10th recital in the Preamble.

at hand until a decision on the existence of a serious and persistent breach of the Union's fundamental values against a Member State that requests the surrender of an individual. Accordingly, the threshold for suspension of the Framework Decision is extremely high. Moreover, with reference to Article 6 TEU, it is clearly stated that nothing in the Framework Decision should be interpreted as prohibiting the refusal of surrender when there are reasons to believe, on the basis of objective elements, that an EAW has been issued *for the purpose of prosecuting* a person on the grounds of sex, race, religion, ethnic origin, nationality, language, political opinion or sexual orientation. Furthermore, derogations are possible referring to constitutional rules relating to due process, freedom of association, freedom of the press and other media, death penalty, torture and other inhuman treatment.[46] These possibilities to justify a refusal to surrender a person all relate to extreme situations where the fundamental rights of the concerned individual are at stake.

In addition, the EAW Framework Decision lists a number of mandatory and optional grounds for non-execution.[47] These listings are meant to be exhaustive.[48] Implicitly, by not listing them as mandatory or optional grounds for non-execution of arrest warrants, the EAW Framework Decision obliges Member States to surrender their own nationals. Moreover, no exceptions can be made for political offences or non-execution on humanitarian grounds. In sum, the EAW Framework Decision includes only limited possibilities for negotiating the limits of mutual trust on sensitive areas of national criminal policy.

Furthermore, the requirement of double criminalisation, which traditionally has constituted a fundamental principle for agreements on extradition, has been dropped for 32 categories of offences.[49] This creates what could be described as a paradox of trust. On the one hand, it is explicitly stated that the mechanism of the European Arrest Warrant is based on the existence of a high level of confidence between the Member States. On the other hand, the principle for extradition of double criminalisation has been abandoned for a large number of crimes. As has been pointed out by Tomuschat, this abandonment constitutes an expression of mutual mistrust between the Member States.[50] It assumes that one or several Member States have not been zealous enough in criminalising certain behaviour. The system gives primacy to the interest of prosecution and punishment in

---

[46]   *Ibid*, 12–13th recitals in the Preamble.

[47]   *Ibid*, Arts 3 and 4.

[48]   Compare 'Second evaluation report on the state of transposition of the Framework Decision on the European arrest warrant and the surrender procedures between Member States', MEMO/07/288 (Brussels, 11 July 2007) 2.

[49]   Art 2(2) Framework Decision 2002/584.

[50]   C Tomuschat, 'Inconsistencies—The German Federal Constitutional Court on the European Arrest Warrant' [2006] *European Constitutional Law Review* 209, 225.

a requesting state over a conscious choice of lenience in a requested state. Accordingly, a Member State's political decision against criminalisation is mistrusted. It could be argued that this is an inherent effect of the application of the principle of mutual recognition: regulatory diversity must be accepted and a presumption of equivalence based on mutual trust established. This method has been successfully applied to product-related regulation, but could it be transplanted into a sphere that concerns fundamental individual rights, such as criminal law, without the risk of repulsion? The situation becomes certainly problematic when the lifting of the requirement of double criminality is not restricted to acts committed within the territory of the requesting state. Thus, an EAW could be issued for an act not punishable in the Member State where the act is committed. This situation certainly does not enhance the mutual trust necessary for applying the principle of mutual recognition to criminal matters.

Even if the EAW today is widely used in order to secure arrests and surrender between the Member States, the Framework Decision has been frequently criticised and there are clear signs that the 'high level of confidence' on which the decision is formally based cannot be reconfirmed by references to reality.

Expressions of mistrust have been expressed in the public debate of several Member States. The standard argumentation follows the line that it is simply not acceptable to surrender a national to the authorities in another Member State whose police, judiciary and penal authorities we do not trust. Furthermore, the lack of presupposed mutual trust has also been demonstrated in a number of cases before national constitutional courts where implementation legislation has been found to infringe national constitutional provisions.[51] Moreover, in certain Member States, refusal grounds not mentioned in the EAW Framework Decision have been added into the relevant national implementation legislation. All of these signs have been noted and criticised by the Commission in its evaluation report on the implementation of the Framework Decision.[52] The legality of the

---

[51] Concerning Poland, see Judgment of 27 April 2005 in Case P1/05, Wyrok z dnia 27 kwienia 2005 r. Sygn. Akt. P1/05 nyr. A summary in English is available at <http://www. trybunal.gov.pl/eng/summaries/summaries_assets/documents/P_1_05_GB.pdf> accessed 6 October 2008. For commentary, see A Lazowski, 'Constitutional Tribunal on the Surrender of Polish Citizens Under the European Arrest Warrant' [2005] *European Constitutional Law Review* 569. Concerning Germany, see BVerfG, 2 BvR 2236/04 of 18 July 2005, available at <http://www.bverfg.de/entscheidungen/rs20050718_2bvr223604en.html> accessed 2 September 2008. For commentary, see C Tomuschat, 'Inconsistencies—The German Federal Constitutional Court on the European Arrest Warrant' [2006] *European Constitutional Law Review* 209. Concerning Cyprus, see Judgment by the Supreme Court of Cyprus of 7 November 2005. A summary in English may be found at <http://www.supremecourt.gov.cy/Judicial/SC. nsf/All/1F76458C67091E86C2257348004BC6B6?OpenDocument&print> accessed 2 September 2008.

[52] This situation has been observed by the Commission in the 'Second evaluation report on the state of transposition of the Framework Decision on the European arrest warrant and the

EAW Framework Decision has furthermore, unsuccessfully, been indirectly challenged before the ECJ, where the referring national court asked if the deletion of the requirement for double criminality is in conformity with Article 6(2) TEU, more specifically the principles of legality, equality and non-discrimination. The ECJ found that the examination of the questions submitted had not revealed any factor capable of affecting the validity of the Framework decision. In its argumentation the ECJ, in a declaratory manner, referred to the high degree of trust and solidarity between the Member States.[53]

Thus, there are indications that the ambition of deeper integration in this case, where the mutual trust required for the application of the principle of mutual recognition is not at hand, has strained mutual constitutional trust between the Member States and the common supranational institutions. Thereby, a judicial/political constitutional dialogue that will continue probably for some time has been triggered. Finally, it should be noted that, as would be expected, the clear expressions of mistrust that have been expressed have generated arguments for harmonisation of rules on procedural rights in criminal proceedings.[54]

VII. FINAL COMMENTS

From the observations presented above, a number of tentative conclusions could be made.

It seems clear that the building and maintenance of mutual trust between the actors within the European Union is a fundamental prerequisite for the process of European integration and for the functioning of EU law. Mutual trust is not a principle of law, but a fragile reflexive social situation that

---

surrender procedures between Member States', MEMO/07/288 (Brussels, 11 July 2007). See also E van Sliedregt, 'The European Arrest Warrant: Between Trust, Democracy and the Rule of Law' [2007] *European Constitutional Law Review* 244.

[53]   Case C-303/05, *Advocaten voor de Wereld VZW v Leden van de Ministerraad* [2007] ECR I-3633, para 57: 'With regard, first, to the choice of the 32 categories of offences listed in Article 2(2) of the Framework Decision, the Council was able to form the view, on the basis of the principle of mutual recognition and in the light of the high degree of trust and solidarity between the Member States, that, whether by reason of their inherent nature or by reason of the punishment incurred of a maximum of at least three years, the categories of offences in question feature among those the seriousness of which in terms of adversely affecting public order and public safety justifies dispensing with the verification of double criminality.'

[54]   See, eg the speech held in Berlin on 20 February 2007 by the European Commissioner responsible for Justice, Freedom and Security (Franco Frattini), entitled 'Common Standards in Criminal Proceedings to Strengthen Mutual Trust in the European Union: the need to balance security and Freedom', SPEECH/07/91. Available at <http://europa.eu/rapid/pressReleasesAction.do?reference=SPEECH/07/91&format=HTML&aged=0&language=EN&guiLanguage=en> accessed 2 September 2008.

has to be built organically through contacts between actors. It takes time to establish, but could easily erode. It cannot be taken for granted and cannot be established through decrees.

Within EU law mutual trust operates on different levels and in different perspectives, where different methods to enhance mutual trust and to handle situations of mistrust are applied.

On the constitutional level, mutual trust between the Member States is based on compliance with a set of common normative values that have been reconfirmed in codification as fundamental principles of the European Union. Compliance is upheld under the shadow of a theoretical risk of suspension and, perhaps more importantly, by the risk of facing political costs as a result of 'naming and shaming' when common constitutional values are infringed. The supranational common institutions play a marginal role in the process of maintaining mutual constitutional trust between the Member States. The power to decide to instigate a monitoring procedure concerning a specific Member State, or determining the existence of a serious and persistent breach of the Union's fundamental principles, lies primarily with the Member States. Within such an intergovernmental decision-making procedure, there is implicitly a possibility for negotiating the threshold for action and thus the limits of trust.

Mutual constitutional trust between the Member States and the common supranational institutions, most importantly the ECJ, is upheld by a sophisticated balance of constitutional power. Through the conditional acceptance of the doctrine of supremacy, the Member States, with reference to their constitutional sovereignty, have reserved a right to revolt in exceptional cases against the exclusive competence to adjudicate on the validity of secondary Community law claimed by the ECJ. The competing and incommensurable claims to the power to adjudicate have, however, never flared into outright confrontation, but rather resulted in mutual deterrence. In concrete terms, this has led to a polycentric adjudication of constitutional issues within the Union that has forced the ECJ and the national constitutional courts into a cooperative relationship. Constitutional tensions between the Union and its Member States are thus eased through horizontal negotiations rather than vertical adjudication. Mutual constitutional trust between the Member States and the common institutions has thereby been established and strengthened over time. The mutual constitutional trust established in this context is thus based on mutual constitutional respect and a mutual willingness to negotiate on the limits of this trust.

Mutual recognition has been developed into a fundamental principle for market integration. It is based on a presumption of equivalence of national regulation that presupposes mutual trust between the Member States. However, the Community legal system recognises that this trust cannot be absolute. This has resulted in the development of formalised safety valves under the control of the ECJ. The limits of trust are negotiable and derogations possible in exceptional situations. This flexibility undoubtedly contributes to the maintenance of mutual trust in normal situations. The systemic reaction to a situation where a Member State has justified a derogation from the principle of mutual recognition, a justification of mistrust, is the adoption of measures for harmonisation in order to re-establish the functioning of the internal market. Formal obligations on transparency and notification of national regulation, in combination with ongoing cooperative dialogues, are used as means to enhance mutual trust in this perspective.

When harmonised rules have been established, the focus of mutual trust between Member States moves from trust in the quality of national regulations to trust in the efficient and fair application harmonised rules. Community law precludes unilateral actions by Member States, with reference to the principle of reciprocity, in a situation of mistrust. Therefore, mutual trust between Member States has to be supplemented by a trust in the efficiency of the system for compliance control before the ECJ. The limits of trust between Member States when it comes to the application of harmonised rules are not negotiable and, if mutual trust breaks down, the legal system of the Union will be at risk. As a means to enhance mutual trust between Member States in this perspective, structures for cooperation and information between national administrative authorities have been established.

The EAW Framework Decision provides an interesting illustration of mutual trust in that the different perspectives are interrelated; mistrust within one perspective may spill over to other perspectives. The system established by the Framework Decision is based on the principle of mutual recognition of judicial decisions in criminal proceedings. It presupposes the existence of mutual trust between the Member States concerning procedural standards in criminal law. In doing so, it explicitly relies on the system established for maintaining mutual constitutional trust between the Member States. The Framework Decision leaves only a very limited scope for negotiating the limits of trust between Member States. As a consequence, it has been challenged by Member States through expressions of constitutional mistrust in relation to the common supranational institutions.

Against the backdrop of this brief presentation, I believe that further investigations of mutual trust between actors within the EU in relation to the functioning of EU law has the potential to provide us with insights that may enhance our ability to understand the dynamics of EU law and European integration at large. As has been shown, different perspectives of mutual trust in the legal structure of the Union are interrelated. Deterioration of mutual trust within one perspective of relations may spill over to other perspectives. This does not contradict that mistrust in one perspective could be compensated by trust in another.

Mutual trust can never be absolute. It is enhanced by mutual willingness to negotiate on the limits of this trust. In order to sustain it, there has to be a continuing bargaining process over the limits of such trust at any given time. Therefore, the regulatory structure has to make such bargaining processes possible. Mutual trust could furthermore be enhanced through the establishment of structures for information and open dialogue between the concerned actors. From this, it follows that mutual trust could be undermined by increased regulatory ambitions on the Union level. It is also clear that larger regulatory divergence between the Member States strains mutual trust. Accordingly, the necessity to maintain mutual trust in all perspectives accounted for above establishes dynamic limits for the process of integration.

As a final reflection, I think it appropriate to point out that there might be a risk that recurrent declarations of the importance for mutual trust between actors could lead to a situation of distorted perceptions of reality. This is because trust could be seen as a virtue, not just a belief. A virtue is a kind of social norm that we endorse for ourselves and for others. The risk with such a norm is that it could lead to self-deception: it could tell us to change our belief so as to think better of others than they deserve, in order to avoid the costs of deviating from the norm by showing mistrust. Trust should be presumed, but it has to be deserved.

4

The European Community's Federal Order of Competences—A Retrospective Analysis

ROBERT SCHÜTZE

I. INTRODUCTION: THE THREE DIMENSIONS OF LEGAL POWER

HAVING ENUMERATED THE 'tasks', 'activities' and 'institutions' of the Community,[1] the Treaty of Rome did *not* enumerate the Community's 'competences'. The Treaty had pursued a different legal technique: it attributed legal power for each and every Community activity in the respective Treaty title. Each policy area would contain a provision—sometimes more than one—on which Community action could be based.[2] These 'legal bases' defined the material scope within which the Community could become active, the legal instrument(s) that could be used for that purpose, and the legislative procedure to follow. Each legal base within the Treaty would be characterised by these three dimensions: competence, instrument and procedure. The three parameters determine the degree of legal 'power' enjoyed by the Community.[3]

---

[1] These were enumerated in Arts 2, 3 and 4 EEC respectively. This chapter will be confined to the EC legal order and not deal with the nature of EU competences under the second and third pillars. For an analysis of the specific nature of CFSP competences, see P Eeckhout, *External Relations of the European Union* (Oxford, Oxford University Press, 2004). As regards third pillar competences, see S Peers, *EC Justice and Home Affairs* (Oxford, Oxford University Press, 2006).

[2] The only exception to that logic is Art 3(1)(u) EC. However, Art 308 EC would be an available competence.

[3] The EC Treaty linguistically acknowledges the concept of competence and power, but leaves both notions undefined. The relation between the two concepts suggested here is that 'competence' represents an aspect of 'power'. This definition contrasts with that offered by V Constantinesco, *Compétences et pouvoirs dans les Communautés Européennes* (Pichon & Durand-Auzias, 1974). Diagnosing a 'dialectical relationship' between the two notions, Constantinesco attributed two meanings to the concept of power. First, '*le pouvoir au sens organique*' that is '*l'organe chargé de la mise en œuvre de la compétence*'. Power is here defined in an *institutional* sense as well as referring to the 'competences' of that organ.

This chapter will analyse the first dimension of legal power. The federal quality of this dimension emerged in the Community legal order after the European Court of Justice (ECJ) declared that the Community enjoyed 'real powers stemming from a limitation of sovereignty or a transfer of powers from the States to the Community, the Member States have limited their sovereign rights, albeit within limited fields, and have thus created a body of law which binds both their nationals and themselves'.[4] But what was the nature of these 'real powers'? Would their nature reveal the 'essence' of the Community?[5] Were there, perhaps, different types of federal power? This chapter will explore the various competence formats that have emerged, actually or rhetorically, in the European legal order in the past 50 years. Beforehand, we shall briefly investigate the relationship between the concept of competence and the instrumental and procedural dimension of power.

II. THE CONCEPT OF COMPETENCE

Thanks to their sovereignty, states are regarded as legally omnipotent. The Community's legal ability was, on the other hand, constitutionally *limited* by its charter: the E(E)C Treaty. The Community had been set up to fulfil only *certain* tasks and objectives and the EEC Treaty had not originally provided the Community with a general competence to fulfil all its tasks.[6] The Community cannot legally act on the basis of a task alone. It must find a 'competence' in the Treaty. Tasks and competences are, thus, distinct constitutional concepts. Tasks precede and inform competences.[7]

The Treaty employs the notion of competence in various provisions. Nevertheless, there is no positive definition of the concept. The Community legal order, therefore, requires hermeneutic assistance from legal

Secondly, '*le pouvoir au sens matériel*' was defined as '*la manifestation matérielle de la compétence*', that is, the totality of all legal acts based on the competence (82–6).

[4] Case 6/64, *Costa v ENEL* [1964] ECR 585.

[5] In this enthusiastic sense, see M Nettesheim, 'Kompetenzen' in A Von Bogdandy (ed), *Europäisches Verfassungsrecht* (Berlin, Springer, 2003) 415.

[6] A Dashwood, 'The relationship between the Member States and the European Union/European Community' [2004] 41 *CML Rev* 355, 358: 'No general empowerment was, or is, to be found in the EC Treaty for action by the institutions with a view to performing the tasks which are entrusted to the Community by Article 2, or to carrying on the activities of the Community identified by Article 3 (and, since the Treaty of European Union (TEU), also by Art.4).' However, while it is truly difficult to imagine the authors of the Treaty giving such a role to Art 308 EC, this competence has become just such a general competence—see R Schütze, 'Organized change towards an "ever closer union": Article 308 EC and the limits to the Community's legislative competence' [2003] 22 *Yearbook of European Law* 79.

[7] R Stettner, *Grundfragen einer Kompetenzlehre* (Duncker & Humblot, 1983) 35.

theory. Legal competences refer to 'legal ability'.[8] Competences are, thus, potentialities. There are no 'potential competences'.[9] The concept of competence is distinct from and broader than the totality of legal acts emanating from it.[10] So what does it refer to? The definition here chosen is the following: a competence is the *material field* within which an authority is entitled to exercise power. This definition allows us to distinguish between 'competence', 'instrument' and 'procedure' as three separate dimensions of legal power.

A. Competences and Instruments

The Treaty of Rome distinguished various legal instruments. The typical Community instruments, now listed in Article 249 EC, seemed character-ised by a distinct normative format. The original Treaty did, as a rule, 'leave the Community institutions with no choice as regards the legal form which their acts take; on the contrary, for each enabling rule they prescribe the form in which the required provisions must appear'.[11] In the early Community law literature, the debate on Community instruments was thus conducted in terms of legal *competence*:

> To obtain a precise view on the sharing out of legislative competence between the Community and its Member States, one must, however take account, apart from the factors determining substantive attributions, of how the various legislative instruments placed at the Community's disposal are allotted between these subject matters. The means available are not shared out equally. Far from it: the allotment depends closely upon the objective sought to be achieved in each sphere. This needs to be explained in more detail. The grant of the Community of a power to make a regulation is an indication that there is a 'transferred legislative competence'. Here the Community itself fixes the legal rules which are binding in the Member States without any intervention or the legislative or even

---

[8] LJ Constaninesco, *Das Recht der Europäischen Gemeinschaften* (Nomos, 1977) 234. The ability to act may be exercised legally or illegally. Hence, the question of competences needs to be distinguished from the question of substantive illegality. For the Community legal order, this distinction is suggested by Art 230 EC, which separates competence pleas from substantive illegality pleas. For the opposite view, see FC Mayer, 'Die drei Dimensionen der Europäischen Kompetenzdebatte' [2001] 61 *Zeitschrift für ausländisches öffentliches Recht und Völkerrecht* 577, 584: 'Es gibt grundsätzlich niemals eine Kompetenz zur Setzung rechtswidriger Akte.'

[9] The concept of 'potential competence'—known in the German legal order—is a pleonasm. For an analysis of the intellectual tensions within German competence federalism, see R Schütze, *From Dual to Cooperative Federalism: The changing Structure of the legislative Function in the European Union* (EUI Thesis, 2005) ch 3.

[10] V Constantinesco, above n 3, 78.

[11] E Grabitz, 'The sources of Community law: acts of the Community institutions' in EC Commission (ed), *Thirty Years of Community Law* (EC Commission, 1981) 81, 88.

the executive national authority ... On the other hand, resort to the medium of the directive and the decision is an indication of a 'retained legislative competence' on the part of the Member States.[12]

Early commentators would thus distinguish between 'regulation competences' and 'directive competences' of the EEC.[13] The debate on legal instruments was consequently embedded in discussions of the enumeration principle. The Community would act ultra vires—this is: beyond its legal *competence*—if it adopted a regulation on a legal basis that only granted a power to pass directives. The competence reading of the legal instruments was shared by the European Court.[14] Neither teleological interpretation nor implied powers could be used to change the instrumental aspect of a Community power.[15]

---

[12]   P Pescatore, *The Law of Integration: Emergence of a new Phenomenon in International Relations, based on the Experience of the European Communities* (Sijthoff, 1974) 62–3.

[13]   Eg HJ Rabe, *Das Verordnungsrecht der europäischen Wirtschaftsgemeinschaft* (Appel, 1963); as well as W Schmeder, *Die Rechtsangleichung als Integrationsmittel der Europäischen Gemeinschaft* (Heymann, 1978) referring to 'Richtlinienkompetenzen' (52) and 'Verordnungskompetenzen' (53).

[14]   Eg Case C-91/92, *Faccini Dori v Recreb* [1994] ECR 1-3325.

[15]   G Nicolaysen, 'Zur Theorie von den implied powers in den Europäischen Gemeinschaften' (1966) 1 *Europarecht* 129. In two cases on the Community doctrine of implied powers, the European Court of Justice used the doctrine to justify the binding character of Community measures. However, in Joined Cases 281, 283, 284, 285 & 287/85, *Germany v Commission (Migration Policy)* [1987] ECR 3203, the Court had to deal with a Commission decision based on (pre-SEA) Art 118 EEC that set up a communication and consultation procedure on migration policy. The Member States claimed that the Community had no power to adopt binding provisions under this competence. The latter only stated that for the task of promoting closer cooperation between the Member States in the social field, the Commission would be entitled to act 'by making studies, delivering options and arranging consultations'. The question was whether or not the third type of act included binding measures. The court did find that Art 118 EEC 'must be interpreted as conferring on the Commission all the powers which are necessary in order to arrange the consultations. In order to perform that task of arranging consultations the Commission must necessarily be able to require the Member States to notify essential information'. 'Indeed, the collaboration between Member States required by Article 118 [EEC] is only possible within the framework of organised consultations.' Yet, the court was eager to point out that 'the power which the Commission seeks to exercise under Article 118 [EEC] is simply a procedural one' (paras 28–30). In Case 242/87, *Commission v Council (Erasmus)* [1989] ECR 1425, the Commission claimed that the Erasmus Programme could be based solely on (pre-SEA) Art 128 EEC, which allowed the Commission to 'lay down general principles for implementing a common vocational policy'. The question arose whether binding measures were among the acts the Commission could lay down. The Council argued that 'the measures planned under the Erasmus Programme go beyond the powers conferred on the Council by Article 128 [EEC]', because 'the provision in question is of a programmatic rather than instrumental character' (paras 7–8). The Court sided with the Commission's argument that the power to adopt general principles entailed the power to adopt legally binding measures. Only that interpretation would ensure the effectiveness of the provision (paras 9–11). Both rulings must be confined to the specificity of the legal bases that they interpret. In both cases, the Community was permitted to adopt a certain type of measure whose legal matrix was not defined in Art 249 EC. Both rulings ought not to be seen as manifestations of a 'wide formulation' of the doctrine of implied powers according to which 'the existence of a given objective or function implies the existence of any power reasonably necessary to attain it' (cf TC Hartley, *The*

However, two constitutional developments have eroded the traditional competence reading of the second dimension of Community power. Firstly, the doctrine of direct effect has—to a great extent—'harmonised' the instrumental formats of Community action enumerated in Article 249 EC.[16] Secondly, while the original EC Treaty only exceptionally listed competences that provided the Community with a choice between alternative legal instruments, this phenomenon has become today's constitutional rule. Successive Treaty reforms have 'decoupled' the two dimensions of power.[17] The neutrality of many legislative competences towards the choice of legal instrument is manifested in all those legal bases that entitle the Community to simply adopt the necessary 'measures'.[18] The choice of legal instrument has, thus, become part of the discretionary power of the Community legislator. The constitutional debate on the Community's instruments has, thence, shifted from the *existence* aspect to the *exercise* aspect of the Community's powers—from the enumeration to the subsidiarity principle.[19]

B. Excursus: The Community's Treaty-Making 'Powers'

The Treaty of Rome acknowledged the legal personality of the European Economic Community. However, this *capacity* to establish contractual links with third countries was not taken to imply a general treaty-making *power* for all matters falling within the scope of the Treaty. In 1958, the Community's express treaty-making powers were confined to international agreements under the Common Commercial Policy and Association Agreements with third countries or international organisations.[20] In the past five

---

Foundations of European Community Law (Oxford, Oxford University Press, 2003) 106). In both cases, the legal nature of the acts to be adopted (acts to 'arrange consultations' or 'general principles') was unclear and the court used the *topos* of the implied power doctrine to justify the inclusion of legally binding acts. Neither case should then be seen as an illustration that a separate instrument can be implied in a legal base.

[16] R Schütze, 'The Morphology of Legislative Power in the European Community: Legal Instruments and the Federal Division of Powers' [2006] 25 *Yearbook of European Law* 91.

[17] J Bast, *On the Grammer of EU Law: Legal Instruments*, Jean Monnet Working Paper 9/03, 3, available at <http://www.jeanmonnetprogram.org/papers/03/030901–05.html> accessed 2 September 2008.

[18] Eg Art 95 EC now generally allows for 'measures' for the approximation of national law. The same reference to measures can be found in Art 308 EC.

[19] For an analysis of this shift, see R Schütze, above n 16, 144–8: 'The Choice of Legal Instrument: From Strict Enumeration to Subsidiarity Control'.

[20] Eg Arts 113 and 238 of the original EEC Treaty.

decades, the European Courts have led—and won—a remarkable campaign to expand the Community's treaty-making powers through the doctrine of parallel external powers.[21]

Two theoretical conceptualisations evolved to explain the Community's implied external powers. The classic version of the doctrine of parallel powers argues that 'the *competence* of the EC to enter into international agreements should run in "parallel" with the development of its internal competence'.[22] Parallel powers are parallel *competences*.[23] This theory of implied external powers introduces the idea of two distinct spheres of competences: beyond the internal sphere of Community competences exists a parallel legal universe of external competences. A second conceptualisation of the implied powers doctrine starts from the distinction between 'competence' and 'power': the former concept refers to the material policy field in which the Community can act, the latter corresponds to the legal instruments available to implement the policy objective.[24] Implied powers in the external sphere are not parallel competences, but parallel *instruments*. The 'competence'—in the sense of the legal entitlement to act in a material policy field—is thereby located in the 'internal' competence. This perspective finds strong support in the *ERTA* ruling, where the Court treated the Community's treaty-making power as a policy *measure*—an additional instrument to implement its competence under the common transport policy:

> According to [Article 70], the objectives of the Treaty in matters of transport are to be pursued within the framework of a common policy. With this in view, [Article 71(1)] directs the Council to lay down common rules and, in addition, 'any other appropriate provisions'. By the terms of subparagraph (a) of the same provision, those common rules are applicable 'to international transport to or from the territory of a Member State or passing across the territory of one or more Member States'. This provision is equally concerned with transport from or to third countries, as regards that part of the journey which takes place on Community territory. It thus assumes that the powers of the Community extend to relationships arising from international law, and hence involve the need in the sphere in question for agreements with the third countries concerned.[25]

---

[21]   R Schütze, 'Parallel External Powers in the European Community: From "Cubist" Perspectives Towards "Naturalist" Constitutional Principles?' [2004] 23 *Yearbook of European Law* 225.

[22]   D McGoldrick, *International Relations Law of the European Union* (Longman, 1997) 48.

[23]   D Wyatt, 'Competence of the Community internal and external' [1977] 2 *EL Rev* 47.

[24]   Within the context of international agreements, see T Tridimas and P Eeckhout, 'The External Competence of the Community and the Case-Law of the Court of Justice: Principles versus Pragmatism' [1994] 14 *Yearbook of European Law* 143, 144.

[25]   Case 22/70, *Commission v Council (ERTA)* [1971] ECR 263, paras 15–16 & 23–7. The instrument thesis equally gained strength from Opinion 1/75 (OECD Local Cost Standards) [1975] ECR 1355 in the context of the Community's express treaty-making powers. In exploring the Community's powers under the common commercial policy

While earlier jurisprudence thus gives support to the view that the Court originally considered implied external powers as parallel instruments to implement an 'internal' competence, recent jurisprudence betrays a judicial inclination in favour of the theory of parallel *competences*. The preference for this version of the parallelism doctrine is rooted in the way in which the Court conceptualises the exclusion of the Member States in the external sphere, where the Court has chosen to go down the 'subsequently exclusive' competence road.[26] This gives external competences of the Community a different constitutional *nature* to the Community's *shared* internal competences. In doing so, the Court has foreclosed the instrument thesis of parallel powers.

C. Competences and Procedures

Each legal base has its 'legislative' procedure.[27] The procedural dimension of power is expressly provided or implied.[28] Formally, European constitutionalism clearly distinguishes between the competence and procedural aspects of power in Article 230 EC. The substantive constitutional relation between competence and procedure is, however, less straightforward and three competing perspectives may be brought to the relationship.

First, the various legislative procedures could be seen to constitute a *competence* typology. The procedural dimension would thereby be read into the concept of competence. Such a competence typology would distinguish between 'consultation competences' or 'co-decision competences' and reflect the horizontal division of powers within the Community. In relation to the federal division of competences, that typology could distinguish between 'unanimity competences' and (qualified) 'majority competences' of the Community. The difficulty with such a federal competence typology is that it blurs the distinction between the Community and the Member States. It is after all not the Member States as such, but a Community institution—the Council—that is participating in the

---

provisions, the Court found the Community entitled 'pursuant to the powers which it possesses, not only to adopt internal rules of Community law, but also to conclude agreements with third countries', since a commercial policy was 'made up by the combination and interaction of *internal and external measures*' (emphasis added).

[26] For a longer discussion of this point, see Schütze, above n 21.

[27] Community constitutionalism has adopted the term 'legislative' procedure for all of the Community's 'decision'-making procedures. The concept was thus not tied to a specific 'decision-making' procedure, such as the co-decision procedure. Moreover, the notion was not to indicate that only legislative measures—in a functional sense of the term—could be adopted.

[28] In relation to the voting in the Council, Art 205(1) EC states: 'Save as otherwise provided in this Treaty, the Council shall act by a majority of its Members'.

legislative process.[29] A second perspective may thus view the legislative procedure as an aspect of the exercise of a *material* competence. Yet, this theory cannot explain why the Community will not be allowed freely to choose among its various legislative procedures. A third perspective, therefore, identifies legislative procedures with the 'author' of the act. Legislative procedures determine 'who' acts. This perspective would allow us to distinguish between different types of Community *legislators*.

III. THE COMPETENCES OF THE EC: A FEDERAL TYPOLOGY

The EEC Treaty did not specify the relationship between Community and national competences.[30] It betrayed no sign of a distinction between different types of competence. Two competing conceptions emerged in the early childhood of the Community legal order.[31] According to a first hypothesis, all competences mentioned in the Treaty were exclusive competences. The Member States had given up their sovereign rights to act within those policy fields because they had 'transferred' their powers to the European level.[32] The division of sovereign powers between the Community and the Member States was based on a strict separation of competences. The exclusivity thesis had been fuelled by early pronouncements of the ECJ.[33] An alternative second conception of the nature of the Community's competences also emerged in those early days: the Community's powers were shared powers.[34] In attributing powers to the supranational

---

[29]   On the question of authorship for Community acts, see Schütze, above n 16, 98–106.

[30]   JV Louis, 'Quelques Réflexions sur la Répartition des compétences entre la Communauté européenne et ses états membres' [1979] 2 *Revue d'intégration européenne* 355, 357.

[31]   For an early discussion of these two conceptions, see A Tizzano, 'The Powers of the Community' in Commission of the European Communities (ed), *Thirty Years of Community Law* (European Perspectives Series, 1981) 43, 63–7. Tizzano calls the first conception the 'federalist' view, the second conception the 'internationalist' view.

[32]   This is the term used in Case 6/64, *Flaminio Costa v ENEL* [1964] ECR 585: 'By creating a Community of unlimited duration, having its own institutions, its own personality, its own legal capacity and capacity of representation on the international plane and, more particularly, *real powers stemming from a limitation of sovereignty or a transfer of powers from the States to the Community*, the Member States have limited their sovereign rights, albeit within limited fields, and have thus created a body of law which binds both their nationals and themselves' (emphasis added). For an early critique of the 'transfer' theory, see LJ Constantinesco, above n 8, 237.

[33]   Eg Case 30/59, *De Gezamenlijke Steenkolenmijnen in Limburg v High Authority of the European Coal and Steel Community* [1961] ECR 1, para 22: 'In the Community field, namely in respect of everything that pertains to the pursuit of the common objectives within the Common Market, the institutions of the Community have been endowed with exclusive authority'.

[34]   Eg HP Ipsen, *Europäisches Gemeinschaftsrecht* (JCB Mohr, 1972) 432: 'Im übrigen verwendet die Abgrenzung zwischen ihnen und den Aufgaben der Mitgliedstaaten—anders als etwa das Grundgesetz—nicht das Mittel der Kompetenz*ausscheidung* nach *Sachgebieten* mit der Folge, daß diese jeweils ausschließlich oder alternativ-konkurrierend entweder nur der

level, the Member States had not intended automatically to renounce their powers within the scope of the Community's competences. Through the act of creation, the Member States had *attributed*—not transferred—legislative powers to the Community. Member States would only renounce their exclusive right to act within their territory by permitting an international organisation to share in the exercise of certain powers.

The constitutional development of the Community legal order was to take place between these two extreme conceptions. Different types of Community competence were 'discovered' in the course of the 1970s and, thence, Community constitutionalism moved from abstract speculation on 'the' nature of the Community's legislative competences to the credo of the new era: 'il n'y a pas *une* notion de la compétence communautaire mais *plusieurs* acceptations possible'.[35]

What was the purpose of having different types of competence? Where a competence typology exists, different types of competence constitutionally pitch the *relative degree of responsibility of public authorities* within a material policy field. The respective differences are of a relational kind: exclusive competences 'exclude' the other authority from acting within the same policy area, while shared competences permit legal co-existence. Importantly, if competences are *constitutional* phenomena, different competence types must transmit different genetic constitutional codes to 'their' legal acts. (A competence typology will only make sense where a particular competence constitutionally influences the legal nature of the emanated legal act.) The various competence categories are, therefore, mutually exclusive: each competence must belong to only one category.

What were the categories developed in the E(E)C legal order? Early on, the distinction between exclusive and non-exclusive competences had emerged. Since the Treaty of European Union, the dichotomy has become part of the official vocabulary of the constitutional charter of the European Union. While never 'officialised', a variety of power constellations has also been suggested for the Community's non-exclusive competences: shared, complementary, coordinating and parallel competences. These types all have one characteristic in common: they allow both the Community and the Member States to act independently within the same area and at the same time. Joint competences, by contrast, appear to tie the exercise of the Community's competence to that of the Member States. Lastly, the

Gemeinschaft oder aber nur den Mitgliedstaaten zur Regelung zustünden. Die Verträge folgen vielmehr einem System kumulativ-konkurrierender Zuständigkeit'.

[35] V Constantinesco, *Compétences et pouvoirs dans les Communautés européennes: Contribution a l'étude de la nature juridique des Communautés* (Pichon & Durand-Auzias, 1974) 248.

Community legal order has been said to acknowledge 'negative competences'; that is, competences that exclude the Community altogether from
an aspect of a policy area so as to protect a nucleus of national exclusive
powers.

Let us discuss each competence category and its treatment by the ECJ.

A. The Exclusive Competences of the EC

The Treaty establishing the European Economic Community contained no
verbal reference to the concept of exclusivity. While this silence could have
meant that all Community competences were exclusive of the Member
States, this thesis was soon rejected. All Community competences thus
appeared to be shared with the Member States. The emergence of constitutional exclusivity in particular policy areas dates from the 1970s. These
powers were 'discovered' by the ECJ. The Court has distinguished originally exclusive and subsequently exclusive competences.

1. Originally Exclusive Competences

Exclusive powers are constitutionally guaranteed monopolies. Only one
governmental level is entitled to act autonomously. Exclusive competences
are thus double-edged provisions. Their positive side entitles one authority
to act, while their negative side 'excludes' anybody else from acting
autonomously within its scope. In the context of the Community legal
order, exclusive competences have been defined as follows: 'Exclusive
competence comprises powers which have been definitely and irreversibly
forfeited by the Member States by reason of their straightforward transfer
to the Community.'[36]

What are the policy areas of constitutional exclusivity? The Court has
accepted a number of competences to qualify for this type.[37] The first
classification was made for the Common Commercial Policy (CCP) in
Opinion 1/75:

> Such a policy is conceived in that Article in the context of the operation of the
> common market, for the defence of the common interest of the Community,
> within which the particular interests of the Member States must endeavour to
> adapt to each other. *Quite clearly, however, this conception is incompatible with
> the freedom to which the Member States could lay claim by invoking a*

---

[36] K Lenaerts and P van Nuffel, *Constitutional Law of the European Union* (Thomson,
Sweet & Maxwell, 2005) 5–022.

[37] For the emergence of *a priori* exclusivity in European constitutionalism, see R Schütze,
'Dual federalism constitutionalised: the emergence of exclusive competences in the EC legal
order' [2007] 32 *EL Rev* 3.

concurrent power, so as to ensure that their own interests were separately satisfied in external relations, at the risk of compromising the effective defence of the common interests of the Community. In fact any unilateral action on the part of the Member States would lead to disparities in the conditions for the grant of export credits, calculated to distort competition between undertakings of the various Member States in external markets. Such distortion can be eliminated only by means of a strict uniformity of credit conditions granted to undertakings in the Community, whatever their nationality.[38]

An second candidate appeared to lie in the Community's competences for the customs union. According to Article 23(1) EC, '[t]he Community shall be based upon a customs union which shall cover all trade in goods and which shall involve the prohibition between Member States of customs duties on imports and exports and of all charges having equivalent effect, and the adoption of a common customs tariff in their relations with third countries.' Did this provision create an independent exclusive competence of the Community in relation to customs matters? Two points are in order here. On the one hand, the competence to establish *intra*-Community customs has been 'abolished'.[39] Regarding the external aspect of the customs union competence, on the other hand, the adoption of a common customs tariff is already covered and, thus, absorbed within the CCP.

By contrast the conservation of biological resources of the sea has been identified as a second exclusive competence of the Community.[40] The Court also acknowledged the possibility of exclusive implied external powers.[41] Should one add monetary policy as an exclusive Community competence? The argument has been made, albeit in a restrictive format, that is: only in relation to the Member States participating in the single currency.[42] However, can an exclusive Community policy be subject to differential integration? This is not the case for differentiation under the mechanism of enhanced cooperation. Article 43(d) EU instructs us that:

Member States which intend to establish enhanced cooperation between themselves may make use of the institutions, procedures and mechanisms laid down

---

[38] Opinion 1/75 (Draft understanding on a local cost standard) [1975] ECR 1355, point 13 (emphasis added).

[39] One must conclude with V Michel that '*le dessaisissement des Etats n'implique pas une attribution corrélative et automatique d'une compétence similaire à la Communauté. Les impératifs de la libre circulation des marchandises, principe fondamental de la Communauté, s'impose avec la même force aux institutions communes, qui ne peuvent, comme les Etats, y porter atteinte ... La compétence perdue pas les Etats ne se retrouve donc pas à l'identique dans le chef de la Communauté*' (V Michel, *Recherches sur les compétences de la communauté européenne* (L'Harmattan, 2003) 175). On the concept of 'abolished competences', see D Simon, *Le système juridique communautaire* (Presses Universitaires de France, 1998) 83.

[40] Case 804/79, *Commission v United Kingdom* [1981] ECR 1045.

[41] Opinion 1/76 exclusivity emerges with Opinion 1/94 (Competence of the Community to conclude international agreements concerning services and the protection of intellectual property) [1994] ECR 5267.

[42] A Dashwood, 'States in the European Union' [1998] 23 *EL Rev* 201, 212.

by this Treaty and by the Treaty establishing the European Community provided that the proposed cooperation ... does not concern the areas which fall within the exclusive competences of the Community.

Is the existence of differential integration, therefore, conclusive evidence *against* exclusivity of a competence? Not necessarily so. Article 43(d) EU deals with differential integration that is hierarchically placed below the EC Treaty. The provision may, thus, not as such be applicable to the *constitutional* differentiation enshrined in the provisions on monetary union. However, there is an important objection to extending the concept of constitutional exclusivity to situations of differential integration. The fact that there is more than one public authority—the EC and the national authorities of the *non-participating* Member States—within Europe provides a strong theoretical argument against classifying monetary union as an exclusive competence *of the Community*.[43] As long as this Community policy is subject to a differential constitutional regime—not dissimilar to the mechanism of enhanced cooperation—it is difficult to speak of an exclusive power *of the Community* vis-a-vis its Member States.

2. Subsequently Exclusive Competences: Concurrent Competences

The ECJ has not only acknowledged a priori exclusive competences. For its implied external powers, it has also recognised the category of subsequently exclusive or concurrent powers. Once these powers are exercised, they transform themselves into exclusive powers.

The meaning of the term 'concurrent competence' has been significantly shaped by German constitutional thought, in particular Article 72(1) of the German Constitution: 'In the domain of concurrent competences, the States will be entitled to legislate so long as and as far as the Federation has not made use of its legislative competences.' This formulation represents the constitutional fountain of German 'competence federalism', according to which all competences should belong to only one level of government at one time.[44] To the extent that the federation has exercised its concurrent competences, the Member States *lose* their competences.[45] State laws that fall within an area in which the German legislator has acted will be considered 'ultra vires'. The *exercise* of a federal concurrent competence thus limits the very *existence* of state competences. Competence overlaps

---

[43] For the opposite view, see D Dittert, *Die ausschliesslichen Kompetenzen der Europäischen Gemeinschaft im System des EG-Vertrags* (Lang, 2001) 171.

[44] For an analysis of German dual federalism theory, see R Schütze, above n 9, ch 3.

[45] T Maunz, 'Artikel 72' in T Maunz and G Dürig (eds), *Grundgesetz Kommentar* (CH Beck, 1982) 8: '*Wenn der Bund zulässigerweise selbst Gesetze erläßt, verlieren die Länder ihr Gesetzgebungsrecht.*'

are thus ruled out.[46] The constitutional nature of concurrent competences originates in the philosophy of dual federalism: there must never be a shared or parallel exercise of the same competence by the federation and its components at the same time.

Has this dual federalism been imported into the Community legal order? An eminent early *German*(!) commentator argued this way:

> To the extent that the Member States have transferred powers to the Community and the Community has exercised these powers, the Member States lose their legislative competences. National legal acts adopted or to be adopted within the scope of this lost competence are *ultra vires* for lack of competence. The conflict of Community law and national law will, thus, not be solved through a supremacy principle (e.g.: Community law breaks national law), but at the level of competences.[47]

The theory of concurrent competences would indeed be accepted by the ECJ for the Community's external sphere. In Opinion 2/91, we thus find the Court interpreting the *ERTA* doctrine to mean that '[t]he exclusive or non-exclusive nature of the Community's competence does not flow solely from the provisions of the Treaty'. The *exercise* of an internal competence could lead to 'subsequent exclusivity' of the parallel external competence, since it will 'deprive the Member States of an area of competence which they were able to exercise previously on a transitional basis'.[48] With the legislative space occupied by the Community, the states would lose their very competence to conclude international agreements. In spite of some judicial pronouncements to the contrary,[49] this was the vocabulary of concurrent competences.

A number of constitutional objections may be advanced against seeing parallel external powers as concurrent or subsequently exclusive powers. First, concurrent competences necessitate field pre-emption. However, this black-and-white mechanism has long gone out of touch with the constitutional practice of cooperative federalism in the external sphere.[50] Secondly,

---

[46] Eg J Ipsen, *Staatsrecht I: Staatsorganisationsrecht* (Luchterhand, 2001) 129: '*Die konkurrierende Gesetzgebungszuständigkeit des Bundes bedeutet entgegen ihrer mißverständlichen Bezeichnung keineswegs, daß Bund und Länder nebeneinander zuständig sind . . . Die Zuständigkeiten bestehen vielmehr hintereinander, so daß man die konkurrierende Bundeszuständigkeit besser als subsidiäre Landeszuständigkeit bezeichnet*'.

[47] W Hallstein, 'Zu den Grundlagen und Verfassungsprinzipien der Europäischen Gemeinschaften' in W Hallstein and HJ Schlochauer (eds), *Zur Integration Europas—Festschrift für C.F. Ophüls* (CF Müller, 1965) 1, 14 (translation—RS).

[48] Opinion 2/91 (Convention No 170 of the International Labour Organization concerning safety in the use of chemicals at work) [1993] ECR I-1061, para 9 (emphasis added).

[49] The European Court has come to speak about 'shared' or 'joint' powers in its jurisprudence. See, eg Opinion 2/91, para 12, as well as Opinion 1/94 (WTO) [1994] ECR I-5267, para 98.

[50] 'A picture is thus emerging, not so much of concurrent competence in the sense of separate compartments for the Community and the Member States ... but rather of shared

the existence of constitutional pre-emption in the external sphere triggers the artificial division into an internal and external competence hemisphere. The classification of parallel external powers as concurrent competences requires thus a doubling of the Community's competences, since the same legal basis cannot be seen as a shared and concurrent competence *at the same time*.

So, why did concurrent competences emerge in the external sphere? This solution may have seemed safer at a time when the Community legal order had not yet solved its ambivalent relationship towards the international powers of the Member States.[51] However, with the supremacy of EC law over international agreements of the Member States now fully accepted, there is no longer need to fall back on the rationale of dual federalism. Today, the Court could confidently re-interpret its *ERTA* doctrine in terms of a legislative pre-emption rationale. That would allow transforming parallel external powers into (ordinary) shared powers and would permit international agreements to be seen as (implied) instruments adopted on the basis of the *internal* Community competence.

B. The Non-Exclusive Competences of the EC

While exclusive competences reserve the right to act to a *single* public body, non-exclusive competences allow *two* or more public authorities to act in the same area at the same time. Each competence holder enjoys the legal capacity to act *autonomously*. Are there distinct competence types within the Community's non-exclusive powers? There has been some degree of terminological dissonance in past attempts to define a competence typology for non-exclusive powers. The search for constitutional order has been fairly disorderly.[52] In a line of descending legal power, the

---

and even complementary competencies, an absence of exclusivity which will imply an overlapping of competence to make rules, subject to the overriding obligation on the part of the Member States (derived both from [Article 10] EC as well as explicit statements in the Treaty) that Member State action must be compatible with the Treaty' (M Cremona, 'External Relations and External Competence: The Emergence of an Integrated Policy' in P Craig and G de Búrca, *The Evolution of EU Law* (Oxford, Oxford University Press, 1999) 137, 158).

[51] On this (previously) ambivalent relationship, see R Schütze, 'EC Law and International Agreements of the Member States—An Ambivalent Relationship?' [2006–7] 9 *CYELS* 387.

[52] Let us concentrate on two recent conceptual typologies for the Community's non-exclusive competences. A von Bogdandy and J Bast distinguish between concurrent, parallel (or shared) and non-regulatory (or complementary) powers. According to their definitions, 'concurrent competences permit autonomous national legislation, provided the Union has not made use of its competence. If, however, the Union has taken action, a concurrent competence allows it to regulate the field exhaustively. In other words, the Member States retain their right autonomously to regulate a particular field only as long as the Union has not exercised its regulatory powers'. Following that definition, they classify Art 95 EC as a concurrent competence, but 'exclude from the concurrent competences those harmonizing competences

candidates for the various competence types have been: shared, complementary, coordinating and parallel competences. Let us discuss each
suggested type of non-exclusive power in turn.

1. Shared Competences

In the internal sphere, the Community legal order has never accepted the
theory of subsequently exclusive competences. Here, the exercise of a
Community competence will not limit the competences of the Member
States to act. However, to the extent that Community law comes into
conflict with national law, the former would 'disapply' the latter. The
Court of Justice chose this milder supremacy principle in *Simmenthal*.[53]
For shared powers, the supremacy of Community law would not render
existing national measures void.

---

that limit the Union to legislating minimum standards. Under those competences, there can be
no pre-emption' (A von Bogdandy and J Bast, 'The European Union's vertical order of
competences: the current law and proposals for its reform' [2002] 39 *CML Rev* 227, 242–3).
However, the authors remain ambivalent, whether a concurrent competence must, by
definition, lead to the adoption of an act that exhaustively regulates its field. If this is not the
case and concurrent competences only make exhaustive rules *possible*—such as Art 95 EC,
which also allows for the adoption of minimum harmonisation—then their concept of
concurrent competence would not leave a *constitutional* imprint on all legal acts adopted on
its base. This, as pointed out above, would undermine the purpose of a *competence* typology.
Moreover, as will be seen below, their definition of concurrent competences is at odds with
the present operation of the principles of supremacy and pre-emption within the EC
constitutional order. Parallel or shared competences are, by contrast, defined as a 'type of
competence including those enabling norms under which the Union and Member State
competences can be exercised alongside one another. In this case, the Union's competence
does *not* lead to Member States' being prohibited from acting autonomously in the same field'
(247). The third competence category, which is described as 'a subcategory of parallel
powers', is called non-regulatory or complementary competence. Under these competences the
EC is 'prevented from regulating' and 'the Member States retain primary legislative competence'. The authors defend this third type 'as a separate category since—*under normal
circumstances*—a conflict of norms cannot arise'. (Does that mean that in exceptional
circumstances conflicts can arise?) These competences would therefore (principally) 'not
require a coordination rule, which is different from parallel competences in the narrow sense',
such as in the areas of 'Employment, Education, Culture and Health' (248–9). V Michel, on
the other hand, has developed the following typology for the Community's non-exclusive
competences. She distinguishes between 'shared competences' and 'joint competences'. Within
the former category, she includes concurrent competences (eg implied external powers) and
parallel competences (eg competition law). Within the second category, there are joint
competences of a national penchant, such as 'coordinating competences (eg Art 99(1) EC:
economic policy coordination) and 'complementary competences' (eg environmental policy).
The second sub-category of joint competences has a Community penchant and is identified
with the Community's harmonisation competences (V Michel, *Recherches sur les compétences
de la communauté européenne* (L'Harmattan, 2003)).
  [53] Case 106/77, *Amministrazione delle Finanze dello Stato v Simmenthal SpA* [1978]
ECR 629.

The effect of the supremacy doctrine appeared originally stronger in relation to *future* national legislation.[54] Was this to mean that national legislators were no longer *competent* to adopt national laws that would run counter to *existing* Community legislation? Some authors have indeed advocated the 'non-existence' theory and considered national laws that violated prior Community rules to be void.[55] This competence reading of the doctrine of supremacy was explicitly rejected in *Ministero delle Finanze v IN.CO.GE.'90 Srl*.[56] Pointing out that *Simmenthal* 'did not draw any distinction between pre-existing and subsequently adopted national law', the incompatibility of the latter with Community law did not have the effect of rendering these rules non-existent.[57] National courts were only under an obligation to disapply conflicting national legislation—be it prior *or* subsequent to the coming into force of the Community rule. The supremacy principle of the Community legal order meant that the Member States would retain their legislative competences even after the Community had exercised its competence.

The adoption of Community legislation, therefore, will not negate the underlying competence of the Member States. Community law has never committed itself to this 'extreme monist' view within its internal sphere.[58] Thus, it is incorrect to state that '*[a]u fur et à mesure que l'acquis communautaire croissait, les compétences des Etats membres se réduisaient*'.[59] The *internal* competences of the Community are not concurrent competences.[60] The pre-emptive effect of Community law takes place at the legislative level. It *suspends* national legislation in conflict with Community law. Moreover, for shared powers, the doctrine of Community pre-emption is a relative doctrine that cannot be reduced to field preemption. It is at the discretion of the Community to determine whether, and to what extent, the Member States may continue to legally exercise their powers alongside the Community. There is 'no magic formula that applies to all areas of shared power that determines the precise delineation

---

[54] The *Simmenthal* Court had stated that the supremacy of Community law would 'preclude the valid adoption of new legislative measures to the extent to which they would be incompatible with Community provisions' (*Simmenthal*, para 17).

[55] Eg E Grabitz, *Gemeinschaftsrecht bricht nationales Recht* (L Appel, 1966) 133 ; and A Barav, 'Les effets du droit communautaire directement applicable' [1978] 14 *Cahiers de Droit Européen* 265, 275–6.

[56] Joined cases C-10–22/97, *Ministero delle Finanze v IN.CO.GE.'90 Srl* [1998] ECR 6307.

[57] *Ibid*, paras 20–1.

[58] A Dashwood, 'The Relationship between the Member States and the European Union/European Community' [2004] 41 *CML Rev* 355, 379.

[59] K Lenaerts and P van Ypersele, 'Le principe de subsidiarité et son contexte: étude de l'article 3B du Traité CE' [1994] *Cahiers de droit européen*, 3 at 4.

[60] HP Ipsen, *Europäisches Gemeinschaftsrecht* (JCB Mohr, 1972) 432.

of power in any specific area'.[61] More than that: power sharing *within the same area* may differ significantly over time.[62] Shared powers, therefore, leave the development of a policy area at the discretion of the Community legislator. It can freely establish its preferred federal philosophy.

2. Complementary Competences

With the Single European Act emerges a third type of competence. The newly introduced competences set constitutional limits to the powers of the Community legislator in two ways. First, for a number of policy fields, the Treaty mandated the Community legislator to set minimum standards only. The method of constitutionally fixing minimum harmonisation occurs for the first time in relation to environmental and social policy.[63] Subsequent Treaty amendments would extend it to the area of consumer protection,[64] the protection of public health,[65] and to visa and asylum matters.[66] The constitutional relationship between the Community and the national legislator is relatively straightforward: the characteristic nature of complementary competences appears to lie in their constitutionally limited 'pre-emptive' capacity.[67] The Treaty will guarantee the ability of the Member States to go beyond the Community floor by adopting *higher* national standards.

The central issue for this special type of legislative competence has been *how much* legislative space the Community must leave to the national level. The Court has so far eschewed the question of whether complementary competences will prevent the Community from ever adopting measures that totally pre-empt national action. This 'hard' constitutional solution appears preferable in the light of the theoretical function of competence typologies: the genetic code of complementary competences should be found *in every single legal act adopted under it*. The legal matrix of the act would be the result of the very structure of the legal base.

With the Maastricht Treaty, a second group of competences appears. They limit the Community to 'complement', 'support' or 'coordinate' national action. The contours of this competence type are still largely unexplored by jurisprudence, especially as some of these competences

---

[61] P Craig, 'Competence: clarity, conferral, containment and consideration' [2004] 29 *EL Rev* 323, 333.
[62] R Schütze, above n 9, chs 7–8.
[63] See Arts 175–6 and 137 EC respectively.
[64] See Art 153 EC.
[65] See Art 152 EC.
[66] See Art 63(1)–(2) EC.
[67] This does not mean that there cannot be any pre-emption. When A von Bogdandy and J Bast argue that '[i]t is the essence of minimum harmonisation that there is no pre-emption' (above n 52, 351), the two brilliant scholars still seem caught in the black-and-white logic of dual federalism and its reductionist limitation of pre-emption to field pre-emption.

introduce the concept of 'incentive measures' that excludes all harmonisation within the field.[68] (If that is interpreted to exclude the Community from setting a material standard, then these competences may be described as coordinating competences.)

We shall describe both variants as 'complementary competences', since a number of 'minimum harmonisation' competences expressly refer to making a contribution or supplementing national action. Article 153 EC that forms by itself Title XIV dealing with Consumer Protection provides a salient example.

3. Coordinating Competences

There was a configuration of power within the 1957 Treaty that could be considered a separate type of Community competence: coordinating competences. Writing in 1976, an eminent commentator even drew a red line between a sphere of integration and a sphere of coordination within the European project.[69] For matters falling into the latter, the European Community would lack all legislative powers and could only provide an elastic framework of orientations.[70] A number of competences in the original Rome Treaty qualified for this definition.[71] In the social policy field under Article 118 EEC, the Community's involvement was defined as follows:

> Without prejudice to the other provisions of this Treaty and in conformity with its general objectives, the Commission shall have the task of promoting close cooperation between Member States in the social field, particularly in matters relating to:
>
> —employment;
> —labour law and working conditions;
> —basic and advanced vocational training;

---

[68] See, eg Art 152(4)(c). Two interesting arguments in favour of the legal nature of incentive measures have been put forward by C Trüe, *Das System der Rechtsetzungskompetenzen der Europäischen Gemeinschaft und der Europäischen Union* (Nomos, 2002) 281: '*Wäre der Erlaß rechtlich verbindlicher Akte ausgeschlossen, so wäre auch nicht verständlich, weshalb ein aufwendiges formelles Rechtsetzungsverfahren, meist das Mitentscheidungsverfahren nach Art 251 (ex 189 b) EGV, vorgeschrieben ist. Art 251 (ex 189b) EGV gilt nach seinem Absatz 1 nur für die Annahme von Rechtsakten. Auch die Harmonisierungsverbote wären überflüssig, wenn "Fördermaßnahmen" rechtlich unverbindlich wären, denn dann wäre Harmonisierung schon durch die Beschränkung auf "Fördermaßnahmen" ausgeschlossen. . . . Die Verwendung des Wortes "Fördermaßnahme" bedeutet daher nicht mehr als einen zusätzlichen, bestärkenden Hinweis auf die inhaltliche Begrenztheit der Kompetenz, nicht eine Begrenzung der zur Verfügung stehenden Handlungsformen*'.
[69] Cf LJ Constantinseco, *Das Recht der europäischen Gemeinschaften* (Nomos, 1977).
[70] *Ibid*, 249.
[71] A number of provisions within the EC Treaty refer to the 'coordination' of the national legal systems, such as Art 34 or 46 EC. However, these legal bases allow for the harmonisation of national laws by means of binding legal measures.

—social security;
—prevention of occupational accidents and diseases;
—occupational hygiene;
—the right of association, and collective bargaining between employers and workers.

To this end, the Commission shall act in close contact with Member States by making studies, delivering opinions and arranging consultations both on problems arising at national level and on those of concern to international organizations . . .

While this competence seemed 'soft' as regards the substantive *policy* measures that the Community could take, it would still allow the Community to set up the institutional and procedural framework to fulfil its 'soft' coordination task. To create the legal mechanism for consultations, the doctrine of implied powers could be legitimately used.[72] Soft policy coordination is thus as old as the EC Treaty itself. Yet, it recently experienced a renaissance in the form of the Open Method of Coordination.[73] The 'most structured form' of this coordination process has been said to be the Community's employment policy,[74] in particular Article 128 EC:

1. The European Council shall each year consider the employment situation in the Community and adopt conclusions thereon, on the basis of a joint annual report by the Council and the Commission.

2. On the basis of the conclusions of the European Council, the Council, acting by a qualified majority on a proposal from the Commission and after consulting the European Parliament, the Economic and Social Committee, the Committee of the Regions and the Employment Committee referred to in Article 130, shall each year draw up guidelines which the Member States shall take into account in their employment policies. These guidelines shall be consistent with the broad guidelines adopted pursuant to Article 99(2).

3. Each Member State shall provide the Council and the Commission with an annual report on the principal measures taken to implement its employment policy in the light of the guidelines for employment as referred to in paragraph 2.

4. The Council, on the basis of the reports referred to in paragraph 3 and having received the views of the Employment Committee, shall each year carry out an examination of the implementation of the employment policies of the Member States in the light of the guidelines for employment. The Council, acting by a

---

[72] For the use of implied powers theory in this context, see above n 15.
[73] The literature is vast and polarised. For an admirably nuanced view, see P Craig, *EU Administrative Law* (Oxford, Oxford University Press, 2006) ch 6.
[74] G de Búrca, 'The constitutional challenge of new governance in the European Union' [2003] 28 *EL Rev* 814, 815.

qualified majority on a recommendation from the Commission, may, if it considers it appropriate in the light of that examination, make recommendations to Member States.

5. On the basis of the results of that examination, the Council and the Commission shall make a joint annual report to the European Council on the employment situation in the Community and on the implementation of the guidelines for employment.

The Member States are obliged to submit information in the form of annual reports and the OMC will, therefore, not be entirely voluntarist. However, the obligations imposed on the Member States appear to be only of a procedural type. The 'soft' Community involvement will not establish a Community *policy* and, as such, will not affect the material policy choices of the Member States. The Community competence is here not 'complementary' in a *substantive* sense. For areas where the Community had not been given legislative power, the existence of a coordinating competence would clarify that the Community is at least entitled to intervene in a *procedural* manner. However, this will not necessarily mean a strict separation between a sphere of integration and coordination, since one could view soft policy coordination in general—and the OMC in particular—as an *implied* power wherever the Community is entitled to adopt substantive policy measures. If that position is accepted, the Community's 'coordination sphere' would embrace its 'integration sphere': every legislative competence of the Community would entail the implied power to softly 'coordinate' national policies before 'hard' Community action follows.

4. Parallel (Internal) Competences

Can we find Community competences that do not interfere with the exercise of national powers at all—neither substantively nor procedurally? The term 'parallel competence' suggest exactly that. Two parallel competences should never meet, for '[e]n mathématique, deux droites sont parallèles quand, situées sur un même plan, elles ne se coupent pas'.[75] From that definition, we can deduce that there cannot be any parallel *legislative* powers: Community legislation, as supreme and directly effective norms, will always establish a 'Community standard' pre-empting the Member States from exercising their competences in conflict with it. For legislative powers, there is no 'zero' pre-emption.

However, can the same conclusion be drawn for the Community's *executive* powers? The most promising candidate for a parallel *executive*

---

[75] V Michel, *Recherches sur les compétences de la communauté européenne* (L'Harmattan, 2003) 133.

competence within the EC legal order has been competition law. Here, the Community legal order has established its own enforcement mechanism. Would Member States be able to execute their national competition laws in parallel with the Community executing EC competition law? In *Walt Wilhelm v Bundeskartellamt*,[76] parallel proceedings had been brought under Community and national anti-trust law. The question arose whether execution of the former would *ipso facto* pre-empt execution of the latter. The European Court disagreed:

> Community and national law on cartels consider cartels from different points of view. Whereas [Articles 81] regards them in the light of the obstacles which may result for trade between Member States, each body of national legislation proceeds on the basis of the considerations peculiar to it and considers cartels only in that context. It is true that as the economic phenomena and legal situations under consideration may in individual cases be independent, the distinction between Community and national aspects could not serve in all cases as the decisive criterion for the delimitation of jurisdiction. However, it implies that one and the same agreement may, in principle, be the object of two sets of parallel proceedings, one before the Community authorities under [Article 81] of the E[]C Treaty, the other before the national authorities under national law ...
>
> [However] this parallel application of the national system can only be allowed in so far as it does not prejudice the uniform application throughout the common market of the Community rules on cartels and of the full effect of the measures adopted in implementation of those rules ... Consequently, conflicts between the rules of the Community and national rules in the matter of the law on cartels must be resolved by applying the principle that Community law takes precedence.[77]

While the 'parallel applicability' of national and Community competition law would follow from the 'special system of the sharing of jurisdiction between the Community and the Member States with regard to cartels',[78] the Court hastened to add a series of conditions: national competition law standards could only be executed if they do not conflict with Community law, like a Commission decision to grant an exemption.[79] The Community's executive powers within the field of competition law were thus normal shared powers.

---

[76] Case 14/68, *Walt Wilhelm v Bundeskartellamt* [1969] ECR 1.

[77] *Ibid*, paras 3–6.

[78] The court spotted the tension between the parallel proceedings and the *ne bis in idem* principle and gave its answer to the natural justice claim in para 11.

[79] One could thus speak of the 'pre-emptive effect for exemptions *vis-à-vis* national measures of competition law enforcement', see M Waelbroeck, 'The Emergent Doctrine of Community Pre-emption—Consent and Re-delegation' in T Sandalow and E Stein, *Courts and Free Markets: Perspectives from the United States and Europe, Vol II* (Oxford, Oxford University Press, 1982) 528, 552–3.But what types of executive Community action would

Has this categorisation changed with the adoption of Regulation 1/2003? Has the long-awaited legislative clarification of the relationship between Community and national competition law finally established a system of 'parallel' executive competences?[80] Does Article 3(2) of the Regulation introduce parallel competences for unilateral restrictions, as the Member States 'shall not under this Regulation be precluded from adopting *and applying* on their territory stricter national laws which prohibit or sanction unilateral conduct engaged in by undertakings'?[81] The answer must be in the negative: the national executive powers are still subject to the supremacy principle. Article 16 of the Regulation codifies this for national courts as well as national competition authorities.[82] The Community's executive powers for competition law are, therefore, still not parallel, but (ordinary) shared powers.[83]

---

pre-empt the application of stricter national competition rules had long been a matter of speculation. The debate in the literature orbited around the meaning of 'positive, though indirect action' formula.

[80] The term 'parallel competences' is used by Regulation 1/2003. For example, in preamble 22 the Community legislator states that: '[i]n order to ensure compliance with the principles of legal certainty and the uniform application of the Community competition rules in a system of parallel powers, conflicting decisions must be avoided. It is therefore necessary to clarify, in accordance with the case-law of the Court of Justice, the effects of Commission decisions and proceedings on courts and competition authorities of the Member States. Commitment decisions adopted by the Commission do not affect the power of the courts and the competition authorities of the Member States to apply Articles 81 and 82 of the Treaty'. See also the Commission Notice on cooperation within the Network of Competition Authorities (2004 OJ C101/43), para 5: 'The Council Regulation is based on a system of parallel competences in which all competition authorities have the power to apply Articles 81 or 82 of the Treaty and are responsible for an efficient division of work with respect to those cases where an investigation is deemed to be necessary. At the same time each network member retains full discretion in deciding whether or not to investigate a case'.

[81] Emphasis added.

[82] The provision reads: '(1) When national courts rule on agreements, decisions or practices under Article 81 or Article 82 of the Treaty which are already the subject of a Commission decision, they cannot take decisions running counter to the decision adopted by the Commission. They must also avoid giving decisions which would conflict with a decision contemplated by the Commission in proceedings it has initiated. To that effect, the national court may assess whether it is necessary to stay its proceedings. This obligation is without prejudice to the rights and obligations under Article 234 of the Treaty. (2) When competition authorities of the Member States rule on agreements, decisions or practices under Article 81 or Article 82 of the Treaty which are already the subject of a Commission decision, they cannot take decisions which would run counter to the decision adopted by the Commission'.

[83] Two additional points may be made. First, the competences of the National Competition Authorities (NCAs) to apply their *national laws* will be true parallel competences: Regulation 1/2003 EC did regrettably not federally coordinate their exercise. Secondly, the competence of the NCAs to execute Community law is a concurrent competence, for Art 11(6) of the Regulation stipulates that '[t]he initiation by the Commission of proceedings for the adoption of a decision [by the Commission] shall relieve the competition authorities of the Member States of their competence to apply Articles 81 and 82 of the Treaty'. The provision grants a concurrent executive competence to the Commission as its exercise will eliminate the competence of the NCA to deal with the specific case.

Does this mean that there are no internal parallel competences of the Community? One could perhaps identify parallel competence with those legal bases that only allow for the adoption of acts that exclusively bind the Community institutions (for example, decisions *sui generis*). Other candidates, whereby 'the competences of the Community and the Member States are perfectly parallel',[84] have been said to be: development cooperation[85]; economic, financial and technical assistance to third countries[86]; as well as research and technological development.[87]

C. Joint Competences

The types of non-exclusive Community competence discussed so far all allowed the Community and Member States autonomously to develop a policy area. Joint competences, on the other hand, tie the exercise of the Community competence to that of the Member States. The Community can only act 'jointly' with the Member States. This category is, hence, not characterised by a sharing out of legal power between two levels. This type rather constitutionalises 'mixed' or 'joint' action.

There are a number of provisions in the Treaty which refer to 'joint' action. Article 35 EC states that 'provision may be made within the framework of the Common Agricultural Policy' through, inter alia, the '*joint* financing of projects and institutions' to help an effective coordination of efforts in the spheres of vocational training and agricultural research, as well as '*joint* measures to promote consumption of certain goods'.[88] Article 180 EC obliges the Community and Member States to coordinate their policies on development and cooperation. Within that process, '[t]hey may undertake *joint* action'.[89] However, the two competences do not constitutionally require joint action. They expressly mention

---

[84] D Wyatt and A Dashwood *et al*, *European Union Law* (London, Thomson, Sweet & Maxwell, 2006) 95.

[85] Arts 177–81 EC.

[86] Art 181(a) EC.

[87] Arts 163–73 EC. According to Art 163 EC, the Community 'shall have the objective of strengthening the scientific and technological bases of Community industry and encouraging it to become more competitive at international level'. In pursuing this objective, and complementing the activities of the Member States, the Community is permitted to have recourse to certain defined 'activities'. In the light of the activities mentioned, this competence may indeed run perfectly parallel to that of the Member States. However, Art 165 EC raises a shadow of a doubt by insisting—and thus acknowledging the opposite possibility—that 'national policies and Community policy are mutually consistent'. If that provision is seen to envisage possible conflicts—to be resolved in favour of Community law—then the competence would be a 'normal' complementary competence.

[88] Emphasis added.

[89] Art 180 EC (emphasis added).

the joint exercise of a shared competence as one *possibility*. The joint exercise of *shared* competences as a voluntary limitation has long characterised EC external relations, where mixed agreements have been partly responsible for the constitutional peculiarities of the external competence paradigm.[90] However, the *voluntary* mixed exercise will not render these competences 'joint competences'. In line with the essence of competence typologies, only those competences that *constitutionally require* joint action should be classed as joint competences.[91]

Do we find competences that constitutionally require the Community to exercise its competences always together with the Member States? In *Portugal v Council*,[92] the applicant had argued that pure Community cooperation agreements could not be based on Article 181 EC, for as soon as 'a matter included in a cooperation agreement falls within the scope of the Member States' own competence, their participation in the conclusion of that agreement is required'.[93] The Court rejected that argument. Finding that the 'framework' character of the Community agreement satisfied the constitutional format of the (complementary) competence under Article 181 EC, there was no obligation flowing from the legal base to act together with the Member States.[94]

One joint competence may, however, be found in the common commercial policy title. Article 133 (6) EC stipulates that wherever the Community wishes to conclude an agreement relating to trade in cultural and audiovisual services, educational services and social and human health services, it can only exercise its competence 'jointly' with the Member States. Did Nice consciously constitutionalise mixity in Article 133 (6) EC; or was this,

---

[90] R Schütze, above n 21, 265: 'Excursus: "Mixed up" in the Luxembourg Compromise—Shared Powers versus Mixed Agreements'. For an excellent analysis of mixed agreements in the Community legal order, see: J. Heliskoski, *Mixed Agreements as a Technique for Organizing the International Relations of the European Community and its Member States* (The Hague, Kluwer 2001).

[91] This approach differs to that of the 1995 Common Market Editorial. There joint competences were defined by reference to those situations where 'Member States *prefer* not to exercise the, as such available, Community competence, and to preserve their national competence', with the consequence that 'the Community external competence can only be exercised if the Member States exercise theirs' ('Editorial: The aftermath of Opinion 1/94 or how to ensure unity of representation for joint competences' [1995] 32 *CML Rev* 385, 386 & 389, emphasis added). However, the fact that the Council decides not fully to exercise a Community competence does *not* acknowledge the existence of an exclusive competence on the part of the Member States. C Tomuschat rightly points out that the term 'joint competence' as such is misleading: 'A treaty which regulates both areas of Community and national competence does not lead to any merger of these two different courses of foreign affairs jurisdiction. The separation of powers as defined in the Community treaties continues to exist' (C Tomuschat, 'How to Handle Parallel Treaty Making Powers of Member States and their Territorial Subdivisions' in J Bourgeois, *La Communauté européenne et les accords mixtes* (Presses Interuniversitaires Européennes, 1997) 65, 67.

[92] Case 268/94, *Portugal v Council* [1996] ECR 6177.

[93] *Ibid*, para 31.

[94] *Ibid*, paras 45–6.

perhaps, an 'editorial' mistake?[95] Moreover, will the Member States be forced to conclude their agreements jointly with the Community? Let us look at the issue. Take the example of a bilateral agreement between France and Canada on cinematographic cooperation. Will Article 133(6) EC require France to thus convince the Community authorities of the agreement's usefulness—granting the latter a veto power? The reason behind paragraph 6 lay in the Member States' perceived need to *protect* their cultural specificity.[96] From a teleological point of view, it would thus be absurd if Member States were no longer allowed autonomously to conclude culture agreements on their own.[97] The better 'federalist' approach is therefore to restrict the obligation of mixed action to those agreements where the Community as such is a signatory.

D. 'Negative' Competences: Constitutional Saving Clauses

The competences of the EC are 'attributed' powers: each legal act must find a legal basis within the Treaty. The Community has no inherent competences drawn from the—metaphysical—idea of sovereignty. Nevertheless, the scope of the Community's competences has been controversial. In the past, the Community has—within certain *political* limits—determined the extent of its own competences.[98] It goes without saying that for policy areas outside the scope of the Treaty, the Member States remain exclusively competent. Yet, can we also find matters that fall within the scope of the EC Treaty, but are constitutionally guaranteed to remain within the exclusive competence of the Member States?

From the beginning of the European project, certain provisions within the Treaty could be read as constitutional guarantees for national exclusive

---

[95] After all Art 133(6) EC speaks of the 'shared competence of the Community and its Member States'.

[96] 'This provision does not merely preserve a residual competence for Member States while granting the Community competence to negotiate alone. Rather, the Treaty insists on shared competence in the sense of the joint negotiation and conclusion of agreements by Community and Member States in certain areas. It is clear from this subparagraph that the Community alone will not be able to conclude agreements in these sectors.' *Cf* M Cremona, 'A Policy of Bits and Pieces? The Common Commercial Policy after Nice' [2002] 4 *Cambridge Yearbook of European Legal Studies* 61, 84.

[97] For the opposite view, see CW Herrmann, 'Common Commercial Policy after Nice: Sisyphus would have done a better Job' [2002] 39 *CML Rev* 7, 22: '[T]he wording of paragraph 6 subparagraph 2 indicates that the obligation to conclude agreements jointly in those fields lies upon the Member States as well. Autonomous action on their part will hence be ruled out in the future'.

[98] The Community's power of auto-interpretation has included the doctrine of implied powers and the method of teleological interpretation, especially applied to Art 308 EC. On whether this resembles—at least partly—the concept of *Kompetenz-Kompetenz*, see R Schütze, above n 6.

powers. Apart from the mysterious Article 295 EC,[99] one of the more prominent candidates was Article 30 EC. The provision allows states to justify a violation of the free movement of goods on grounds of, *inter alia*, public morality, public policy and public security. Had these policy fields, therefore, remained within the exclusive powers of the states? The European Court gave short shrift to that argument in *Simmenthal*.[100] Pointing out that Article 30 EC was 'not designed to reserve certain matters to the exclusive jurisdiction of Member States',[101] the Member States could not insist on their stricter national standards where Community harmonisation measures provide for the necessary protection of the interests mentioned in Article 30 EC.

Reacting to this early defeat, the Member States have used subsequent Treaty amendments to increasingly insert provisions that aim to 'reserve' national exclusive powers within the Treaty. This intergovernmental redefinition of EC competences is illustrated within the area of social policy. Article 137 (4) and (5) EC safeguards the Member States' right in the following manner:

4. The provisions adopted pursuant to this article:

—shall not affect the right of Member States to define the fundamental principles of their social security systems and must not significantly affect the financial equilibrium thereof,

—shall not prevent any Member State from maintaining or introducing more stringent protective measures compatible with this Treaty.

5. The provisions of this article shall not apply to pay, the right of association, the right to strike or the right to impose lock-outs.

Article 152(5) EC, to give another example of general validity,[102] allows the Community to adopt measures in the field of public health, but

---

[99] The provision reads: 'This Treaty shall in no way prejudice the rules in Member States governing the system of property ownership'.

[100] Case 35/76, *Simmenthal v Italian Minister of Finance* [1977] ECR 1871; as well as Case 5/77, *Tedeschi v Denkavit* [1977] ECR 1555.

[101] *Simmenthal*, para 14. However, for a judicial 'slip of tongue', see Case 265/95, *Commission v France* [1997] ECR 6959, paras 32–3: 'Article [28] therefore requires the Member States not merely themselves to abstain from adopting measures or engaging in conduct liable to constitute an obstacle to trade but also, when read with Article [10] of the Treaty, to take all necessary and appropriate measures to ensure that that fundamental freedom is respected on their territory. In the latter context, the Member States, which retain exclusive competence as regards the maintenance of public order and the safeguarding of internal security, unquestionably enjoy a margin of discretion in determining what measures are most appropriate to eliminate barriers to the importation of products in a given situation.'

[102] The EC Treaty also acknowledged specific constitutional guarantees; see, eg Protocol (No 7) annexed to the Treaty on European Union and to the Treaties establishing the European Communities (1992), which states that '[n]othing in the Treaty on European Union, or in the Treaties establishing the European Communities, or in the Treaties or Acts modifying or supplementing those Treaties, shall affect the application in Ireland of Article

commits the Community to 'fully respect the responsibilities of the Member States for the organisation and delivery of health services and medical care' and in particular excludes any measures affecting 'national provisions on the donation or medical use of organs and blood'. What is the constitutional nature of these 'respect' and 'shall-not-affect' clauses? These clauses are not unknown in the international law of treaties.[103] They have also emerged in US constitutionalism. Known as 'express savings' clauses, they indicate the federal authority's intention to leave the states' powers within a certain field untouched.[104] The Community law provisions, mentioned above, appear to elevate these 'express saving' clauses to the constitutional level. If the Court decides to endorse that view, Community action could not 'pre-empt' any national action within the areas enumerated.

Could these fields then be seen as exclusive 'police powers' of the Member States? Would these 'savings clauses' also *limit* the Community's *other* competences? Apart from principled reasons against such a view,[105] the European Court has already expressed a negative inclination in *Germany v Parliament and Council (Tobacco Advertising)*.[106] The case concerned the 'express savings' clause of Article 152(4)(c) EC. The provision allows the Community to adopt incentive measures 'excluding any harmonisation of the laws and regulations of the Member States'. However, the Community had not acted on the basis of this material competence. Instead, it had chosen its general harmonisation competence under Article 95 EC and, as the Court admitted, '[t]he national measures *affected* [were] to a large extent inspired by public health policy objectives'.[107]

Could this be done? Would Article 152(4)(c) EC negatively limit Article 95 EC? Was there a 'negative competence' that prohibited the Community from ever harmonising national laws that protect and improved human health? The Court disagreed. Article 152(4)(c) EC did 'not mean that harmonising measures adopted on the basis of other provisions of the

---

40.3.3 of the Constitution of Ireland'. For an analysis of the 'Irish abortion' protocol, see D Curtin, 'The Constitutional Structure of the Union: A Europe of Bits and Pieces' [1993] 30 *CML Rev* 17, 47–9.

[103] A Aust, *Modern Treaty Law and Practice* (Cambridge, Cambridge University Press, 2006) 176–7.

[104] 'Savings clauses typically command that "nothing [herein] shall be constructed as pre-empting" certain state laws or that "nothing [herein] shall be constructed as authorizing" conduct forbidden by state law' (Note, 'A Framework for Preemption Analysis' [1978–79] 88 *Yale Law Journal* 363, 366).

[105] The view may compromise the *'acquis communautaire'*. For an analysis of this concept, see C Delcourt, 'The Acquis Communautaire: Has the Concept had its day?' [2001] 38 *CML Rev* 829.

[106] Case C-376/98, *Germany v Council (Tobacco Advertising)* [2000] ECR I-8419.

[107] *Ibid*, para 76 (emphasis added).

Treaty cannot have any impact on the protection of human health'.[108] '[T]he Community legislature cannot be prevented from relying on that legal basis on the ground that public health protection is a decisive factor in the choices to be made.'[109] The express saving clause would thus not operate as a constitutional *Querschnittsklausel*. Where Community legislation serves an internal market objective, the Community legislator can enter into these fields. Article 152(4) did not represent an absolute constitutional border protecting a nucleus of exclusive national powers.[110] However, the Court conceded that these saving clauses did have some constitutional significance: the Community must not use its general competences 'to circumvent the express exclusion of harmonisation laid down in [Article 152 (4) (c)] of the Treaty'.[111] Where the centre of gravity of a Community measure thus fell on the side of the public health competence under Article 152 EC, intervention that harmonises must be excluded. (Even in this case Community action may still be possible under Article 308 EC. However, this remains controversial.[112])

To sum up: the EC Treaty only provides a *relative* constitutional guarantee for national powers falling within the scope of the Treaty. These saving clauses are no constitutional recognition of exclusive national powers. They do not completely 'negate' the competence of the European Community.[113] Their limiting effect will not go beyond the scope of the legal base of which they form part. These policy areas are only 'pseudo-exclusive'. The Community legal order still has not committed itself to constitutionally safeguard a 'nucleus of sovereignty that the Member States can invoke, as such, against the Community'.[114]

---

[108] *Ibid*, para 78.

[109] *Ibid*, para 88.

[110] *Contra*, 'Hablitzel, Harmonisierungsverbot und Subsidiaritätsprinzip im europäischen Bildungsrecht' [2002] 55 *Öffentliche Verwaltung* 407, 409.

[111] *Germany v Council (Tobacco Advertising)*, para 79.

[112] For the two opposing views, see K Lenaerts, 'Education in European Community Law after 'Maastricht' (1994) 31 *CML Rev* 7; and M Niedobitek, 'Die kulturelle Dimension im Vertrag über die Europäische Union' (1995) 30 *Europarecht* 349, 363. The Lisbon Treaty would settle the issue, for Art 352 TFEU—the equivalent of Art 308 EC—clarifies in its third paragraph that '[m]easures based on this Article shall not entail harmonisation of Member States' laws or regulations in cases where the Treaties excludes such harmonisation'.

[113] The concept of 'negative competence' (FC Mayer, 'Die drei Dimensionen der Europäischen Kompetenzdebatte' [2001] 61 *Zeitschrift für ausländisches öffentliches Recht und Völkerrecht* 577, 583) will thus not perfectly fit these 'constitutional saving clauses'.

[114] K Lenarts, 'Constitutionalism and the Many Faces of Federalism' [1990] *American Journal of Comparative Law* 205, 220.

IV. CONCLUSION: REFORM AVENUES AFTER 50 YEARS OF
CONSTITUTIONAL *BRICOLAGE*

The legal bases of the Community are characterised by three dimensions: competence, instrument and procedure. Having defined competence as the legal power to act within a material policy field, we have seen that these three dimensions are independent of each other. A federal *competence* typology relates to the division of power between the Community and the Member States within a policy area. What are the advantages of competence typologies? Competence typologies classify power relationships. They define—and thus clarify—the respective roles of each level in a federal order. Since this definition is achieved at the constitutional level, the recognition of various competence types only makes sense if each type transmits a genetic federal code to 'its' legal acts.

The 1957 Treaty did not specify the relationship between the Community competence and the national competence. In the last five decades, a number of constitutionally qualified relationships have emerged. Exclusive competences emerged in the 1970s. These competences are double-edged: they are constitutional entitlements for the Community and *constitutional* prohibitions for the Member States. The Community has recognised original and subsequently exclusive competences. The latter have only been accepted for the Community's implied treaty-making powers. Non-exclusive competences represented the normal power-sharing mode within the EC legal order. Non-exclusive competences allow both the Community and Member States to legislate within the same policy field at the same time. The constitutional pre-emption, developed for implied *external* powers, has not been extended into the Community's internal sphere. Here, the operation of supremacy and pre-emption only lead to the national measure being *disapplied* to the extent that it conflicts with Community law.

After 50 years of growth, the EC legal order acknowledges a number of power-sharing formats within the umbrella category of shared powers. Complementary competences constitutionally guarantee a certain degree of legislative or executive responsibility for the Member States. Community action is restricted to setting a minimum standard or to support national action. Where the complementary role of the Community is limited to *procedural* matters, one could speak of coordinating competences. While the existence of parallel competences remains doubtful, the EC legal order has acknowledged one instance, where the Community must exercise its competence jointly with the Member States. Finally, 'negative competences'—or, better, constitutional savings clauses—are only relative phenomena. Exclusive national competences only exist outside the scope of the EC Treaty.

In the light of this retrospective analysis, was the Community's vertical order of competences in need of 'better divisions and definition of competences'?[115] Some have claimed there was no need for *structural* reform.[116] This may be true for the EC legal order. However, there existed 'reform' avenues to *enhance* its constitutional clarity and elegance. First, since the original ambivalences between EC law and the international agreements of the Member States have been resolved, there was no constitutional need for subsequently exclusive competences in the external sphere. The Community's parallel external powers could thus simply be 're-conceived' as shared competences. Secondly, complementary competences would only be a clear competence type once the Court opts for the 'hard' constitutional solution.[117] Thirdly, parallel competences are theoretically possible, but hardly needed.[118] Fourthly, joint competences are a constitutional nuisance, for they may seriously compromise the ability of the Community level—if not, worse, that of the national level—to act independently. In conclusion, with the assistance of Ockham's razor, enhanced constitutional clarity could have been gained by shaving off unnecessary competence types. Will the Lisbon Treaty go in this direction and improve the federal competence typology? It could be said that the *Laeken* mandate to enhance constitutional clarity has been missed—but this prospective analysis is a different argument.[119]

---

[115]   Laeken Declaration on the Future of the European Union.

[116]   A von Bogdandy and J Bast, 'The European Union's vertical order of competences: the current law and proposals for its reform' [2002] 39 *CML Rev* 227, 267.

[117]   R Schütze, 'Cooperative federalism constitutionalised: the emergence of complementary competences in the EC legal order' [2006] 31 *EL Rev* 167, 172 et seq.

[118]   HD Jarass, 'Die Kompetenzverteilung zwischen der Europäischen Gemeinschaft und den Mitgliedstaaten' [1996] 121 *Archiv des öffentlichen Rechts* 173, 190: '*Ingesamt besteht daher kein Bedarf für parallele Kompetenzen als eigenständige Kompetenzkategorie*'.

[119]   *Cf.* R. Schütze, Lisbon and the Federal Order of Competences: A Prospective Analysis, [2008] 33 *EL Rev* 709

5

Community Competence to Regulate the Internal Market

DERRICK WYATT QC

I. INTRODUCTION

THIS CHAPTER EXPLORES the development of the Community's competence to regulate the internal market before and since the landmark ruling in the *Tobacco Advertising* case.[1]

It will be argued that the claim of the Court of Justice in the *Tobacco Advertising* case that the Community institutions lack a general competence to regulate the internal market does not withstand critical examination. The *Tobacco Advertising* case contained both competence restricting and competence enhancing elements. The principal competence restricting elements were that: (i) obstacles to trade could be addressed by removal of the obstacles, but not by a ban on the subject matter of the trade; (ii) harmonisation could only be justified by distortions of competition if those distortions were appreciable; and (iii) in principle all provisions of a contested internal market measure must contribute to the internal market aims of the measure in question. The principal competence enhancing element was the proposition that a measure which makes some contribution to the internal market may be adopted as an internal market measure even if its main aim is public health protection; despite the fact that harmonisation of public health requirements is in principle ruled out by the Treaty. A further competence enhancing element was that the Court adopted an impressionistic approach to assessment of the requirement that distortions of competition must be appreciable if they were to justify harmonisation, leaving open the possibility that this requirement might be relaxed or sidestepped by the law-making institutions.

The competence restricting elements of the *Tobacco Advertising* case have been contradicted or eroded by subsequent case law, such as the *British American Tobacco* case and the *Swedish Match* case. After the

---

[1] Case C-376/98, *Germany v Parliament and Council* [2000] ECR I-8419.

latter case, obstacles to trade can be addressed by simply banning the trade. After the *British American Tobacco* case, it seems that hypothetical obstacles to trade, resulting from disparities between national labelling rules, can be addressed by eliminating the disparities in question, even if this makes no contribution to cross-border trade in the products in question. In the *Leitner* case, the Court confirms that its approach to the requirement adopted in *Tobacco Advertising*, that distortions of competition must be appreciable in order to justify harmonisation, will be an impressionistic one. Furthermore, in *Rundfunk*, the Court considers that as long as a measure makes a contribution to the internal market, it is legitimate for that measure to regulate situations which have no link at all with freedom of movement—something of a retreat from the *Tobacco Advertising* case, but in line with case law dating from the 1960s which gives a wide reading to competence to coordinate national social security rules in order to provide freedom of movement for workers.

II. DENIAL BY THE COURT THAT THE COMMUNITY INSTITUTIONS HAVE A GENERAL POWER TO REGULATE THE INTERNAL MARKET IN THE *TOBACCO ADVERTISING* CASE

In the *Tobacco Advertising* case, the Court of Justice denied that Article 95 EC bestowed upon the Community legislature 'a general power to regulate the internal market', and insisted that the measures referred to in that Article 'are intended to improve the conditions for the establishment and functioning of the internal market'.[2] The Court added that if 'a mere finding of disparities between national rules and of the abstract risk of obstacles to the exercise of fundamental freedoms or distortions of competition liable to result therefrom were sufficient to justify the choice of Article [95 EC] as a legal basis, judicial review of compliance with the proper legal basis might be rendered nugatory'.[3] Whatever the position after the *Tobacco Advertising* case, it must be said that prior to that case, the practice of the Community institutions had been to treat Treaty competences to regulate the common market/internal market as if they were indeed a 'general power to regulate' that market, and the mere 'abstract risk' of obstacles to the exercise of fundamental freedoms or

---

[2]   Case C-376/98, *ibid*, paras 83 and 84. In this case, Germany challenged the validity of Directive 98/43 on the approximation of the laws, regulations and administrative provisions of the Member States relating to the advertising and sponsorship of tobacco products, [1998] OJ L213/9. See also Case C-74/99, *R v Secretary of State for Health, ex p Imperial Tobacco Ltd* [2000] ECR I-8599, a reference from the English High Court on the validity of the same Directive. The two cases were joined for the oral hearing and the Opinion of AG Fennelly deals with both cases.

[3]   Case C-376/98, above n 1, para 84.

distortions of competition had been treated as a sufficient basis for recourse to, in particular, Articles 94 or 95, and/or Article 308 EC.

III. COMMUNITY INSTITUTIONS APPEAR TO CLAIM A 'GENERAL POWER TO REGULATE' THE COMMON MARKET/INTERNAL MARKET PURSUANT TO RELEVANT TREATY ARTICLES

A. A Broad View of Competence to Regulate the Common Market is Taken Prior to the Single European Act

Even before any reference to legislative competence in the field of the environment appeared in the EEC Treaty, the Community institutions had adopted ambitious legislation for the protection of the environment on the basis of Article 100 EEC (now Article 94 EC, and hereafter generally referred to as such), in conjunction with Article 235 EEC (now Article 308 EC and hereafter generally referred to as such).[4] The preamble of Directive 76/160 on the quality of bathing water, adopted on the basis of the latter Articles, stated that 'there exist in this area certain laws, regulations or administrative provisions in Member States which directly affect the functioning of the common market'.

No indication is given of how such laws might affect the functioning of the common market, nor how harmonisation might remedy such effects. The first reasoned recital of the preamble states that '... in order to protect the environment and public health, it is necessary to reduce the pollution of bathing water and to protect such water against further deterioration ...'. We are thus left in no doubt as to the real aim of the Directive. In truth, the Directive is adopted on the basis of an *assumption* that laws in Member States regulating (or not regulating) the quality of bathing water not only affect, but *directly* affect, the functioning of the common market. It might be objected that the Community legislature does not rely solely upon Article 94, but also upon Article 308. The latter Article has two essential preconditions to its application: one is that action by the Community should prove necessary to attain one of the objectives of the Community, and the other is that this necessity arises in the course of operation of the common market.[5] The preamble of Directive 76/160 justifies reliance on Article 308 as follows:

---

[4] See, notably, Directive 76/160 on the quality of bathing water, [1976] OJ L31/1 (Arts 100 and 235 EC); and Directive 80/778 on the quality of drinking water, [1980] OJ L229/11(Arts 100 and 235 EC).

[5] 'If action by the Community should prove necessary to attain, in the course of the operation of the common market, one of the objectives of the Community and the Treaty has

... surveillance of bathing water is necessary in order to attain, within the framework of the operation of the common market, the Community's objectives as regards the improvement of living conditions, the harmonious development of economic activities throughout the Community and continuous and balanced expansion.

The objectives are indeed objectives of the Community, set out in the text of Article 2 of the EEC Treaty as it stood at the time. However, the statement that the surveillance of bathing waters is necessary to attain the objectives referred to 'within the framework of the operation of the common market' is not explained, and it is not easy to see how it might be explained, except on the basis of the 'abstract risk' of obstacles to freedom of movement or of distortion of competition.[6]

The fact that decision making was at the time by unanimity (either because the Treaty so provided or by virtue of the practice subsequent to the Luxembourg accords) no doubt contributed to the tendency of the Member States to acquiesce in a broad reading of Treaty provisions conferring Community competence, and in particular Articles 94 and 308 EC, which provided an opportunity to legislate in areas for which at the time no specific Treaty base existed. The present writer accepts that most legislation adopted under Article 94 EC could be justified on the ground that it removed obstacles to the free movement of goods or persons and made a contribution to the common market. However, the fact remains that the practice of the Community institutions, prior to the adoption of the Single European Act, was to treat competence to legislate for the common market on the basis of Articles 94 and 308 EC as a very wide competence indeed,[7] which required no detailed justification as regards effects on the functioning of the common market.

---

not provided the necessary powers, the Council shall, acting unanimously on a proposal from the Commission and after consulting the European Parliament, take the appropriate measures.'

   [6] Weatherill is right to observe that the reference in Art 308 EC to the 'course of the operation of the common market' has 'exerted little if any restriction on legislative resort to Article 308 ...': see S Weatherill, 'Competence creep and competence control' (2004) 23 *YEL* 1, 28.

   [7] For reference to the debate in the House of Lords on 4 July 1978 on the 22nd and 35th Reports of the House of Lords Select Committee on the European Communities, in which criticism was levelled at over-extensive use of Arts 100 and 235 EC in the environmental and consumer protection fields, and for a defence of the Community's harmonisation policy in this regard, see G Close, 'Harmonisation of Laws: Use or abuse of the Powers under the EEC Treaty' (1978) 3 *EL Rev* 461. See also the reference to controversy over the issue at this time in J Usher's discussion of the *Tobacco Advertising* case at (2001) 38 *CML Rev* 1519, 1527.

B. The Adoption of a Generous Approach to Competence to Regulate the Internal Market

This generous conception of Community competence to regulate the common market survived the entry into force of the Single European Act, and was applied to the regulation of the internal market under Article 95 of the Treaty. The Unfair Contract Terms Directive is an example.[8] The purpose of the Directive is to harmonise the laws of the Member States relating to unfair contracts concluded between a seller or supplier and a consumer.[9] The Directive is based on Article 95 EC. The preamble records that:

> Whereas the laws of Member States relating to the terms of contracts between the seller or supplier of services, on the one hand, and the consumer of them, on the other hand, show many disparities, with the result that the national markets for the sale of goods and services to consumers differ from each other and that distortions of competition may arise amongst the sellers and suppliers, notably when they sell and supply in other Member States.

This recital appears to be based simply upon the assumption that disparities between national laws can be equated with differences in the national markets, and that the resulting risk of distortions of competition justifies European wide legislation based on Article 95 EC. But the preamble adds a further consideration:

> Whereas, generally speaking, consumers do not know the rules of law which, in Member States other than their own, govern contracts for the sale of goods or services; whereas this lack of awareness may deter them from direct transactions for the purchase of goods or services in another Member State ...

Reducing uncertainty for consumers contemplating cross-border purchases is presented as a basis for harmonisation. This recital has been described as foreshadowing the 'confidence-building' rationale for harmonisation of consumer law articulated in the preamble of Directive 99/44 on certain aspects of the sale of consumer goods and associated guarantees.[10] Cross-border purchases of goods and services amount in principle to

---

[8] Directive 93/13 on unfair terms in consumer contracts, [1993] OJ L95/29.

[9] *Ibid*, Art 1.

[10] Directive 99/44 on certain aspects of the sale of consumer goods and associated guarantees, [1999] OJ L171/12. See S Weatherill, 'Constitutional Issues—How Much is Best Left Unsaid?' in S Vogenauer and S Weatherill (eds), *The Harmonisation of European Contract Law: Implications for European Private Laws, Business and Legal Practice* (Hart Publishing, 2006). It is to be noted that the third recital of Directive 99/44 also refers to disparities of laws leading to distortion of competition between sellers.

transactions covered by Article 28 or 49 EC.[11] The above recital would support the proposition that internal market rules might properly be adopted at European level under, for example, Article 95 EC, whenever natural or legal persons might be deterred, by uncertainty created by disparities between national rules, from cross-border transactions which would—if carried out—amount to the exercise of a fundamental freedom. As indicated above, however, the legal uncertainty rationale did not stand alone in the preamble to the Unfair Contract Terms Directive, but supplemented a reference to disparities between national laws leading to distortions of competition.

Analogous considerations relating to legal uncertainty resulting from disparate national laws have been invoked to justify Community measures adopted to make it possible to facilitate cross-border cooperation and establish legal persons pursuant to Article 308 EC, and to justify the adoption of Directives harmonising national provisions of company law under Article 44(2)(g) EC. The proposition that recourse to internal market measures might be justified by the need to eliminate legal uncertainty might also be been as an aspect of a broader proposition, to the effect that internal market measures might generally be justified by the need to *facilitate* the exercise of fundamental freedoms by, for example, providing appropriate language teaching for the children of migrants.[12]

The extent to which internal market measures may be adopted in order to facilitate the exercise of fundamental freedoms, without necessarily removing obstacles to the exercise of such freedoms *stricto sensu*, or eliminating distortions of competition, is discussed further elsewhere.[13]

C. Eliminating Restrictions on the Free Movement of Products by Banning Products or Components of Products

It is explained below that the Court of Justice in the *Tobacco Advertising* case suggests that failure of a Community measure to guarantee free movement for products complying with harmonised requirements casts doubt on the contribution of that measure to the operation of the internal market. It is accordingly significant that legislative practice prior to the latter case had recognised a wide competence to determine whether particular products could or could not be placed on the market.

---

[11]   See, eg Case C-362/88, *GB-INNO-BM v Confédération du commerce luxembourgeois* [1990] ECR I-667 (cross-border shopping by Belgian residents in Luxembourg falls within the scope of Art 28 EC).

[12]   Directive 77/486 on the education of children of migrant workers [1977] OJ L199/32.

[13]   See the final section of an extended version of this article; Oxford Legal Studies Research Paper No 9/2007, <http://ssrn.com/abstract=997863> accessed 26 October 2008.

In the first place, the Community had acted to prohibit the use of additives in products where disparities between national laws might lead to the latter products being denied access to some markets. An example is Directive 88/146 prohibiting the use in livestock farming of certain substances having a hormonal action.[14] The preamble of the Directive noted that the administration to farm animals of certain substances having a hormonal action was regulated in different ways in the Member States, and that such divergence distorted the conditions of competition and was a serious barrier to intra-Community trade. It seems clear that Community legislation which determines which additives may or may not be added to products such as foodstuffs may have the effect of removing obstacles to the free movement of such products which would otherwise result.

Different considerations arise when Community rules prohibit a particular 'free standing' product from being placed on the market, or require a product to be withdrawn from the market. Here the product is not a component of another product, as in the example above, but a product in its own right. Directive 88/378 on the approximation of the laws of the Member States on the safety of toys aims to remove the obstacles to trade which would result from continuing disparities between national rules on toy safety.[15] The Directive establishes essential safety requirements to be satisfied by all toys if they are to be placed on the market.[16] It also provides that Member States shall take all appropriate measures to withdraw from the market toys which are found to fall short of the specified standard.[17] In a case such as this, both the prohibition on placing on the market products which do not comply with the specified safety standards, and the withdrawal from the market of products found to be non-compliant, comprise mechanisms to ensure that only products which comply with the relevant safety standard are placed on the market, or remain on the market. Similar considerations apply as regards Council Directive 92/59 on general product safety.[18] As the Court observed in *Germany v Council*:

> The free movement of goods can be secured only if product safety requirements do not differ significantly from one Member State to another. A high level of protection can be achieved only if dangerous products are subject to appropriate measures in all the Member States.[19]

---

[14] [1988] OJ L70/16.
[15] [1988] OJ L187/1 (as amended by Directive 93/681 [1993] OJ L220/1).
[16] For essential safety requirements, see Arts 2 and 3 and Annex II.
[17] Art 7 of the Directive.
[18] Amended and replaced by Directive 2001/95 [2002] OJ L11/4.
[19] Case C-359/92, [1994] ECR I-3681, para 34. See AG Fennelly in Case C-376/98, above n 1, point 86 of the Opinion.

Analogous considerations may apply as regards certain services. The Directives on Misleading Advertising[20] and Comparative Advertising[21] might be justified on the basis that they remove obstacles to, for example, cross-border movement of media such as newspapers, periodicals or radio and television broadcasts which carry advertisements. They do this by prohibiting those features of advertisements with respect to which national rules differ. The effect is to permit advertisements compliant with Community rules to 'move freely' within the Community.

There are some circumstances, however, where the prohibition by Community rules of a particular 'free-standing' product does not appear to make a contribution to the common market/internal market. An example is 'tobacco for oral use', banned by Directive 92/41 amending Directive 89/622 on the approximation of the laws, regulations and administrative provisions of the Member States concerning the labelling of tobacco products.[22] The preamble indicates that the law-maker sees the very existence of disparities between national rules and the existence of sales bans in certain Member States as providing a justification for a ban on tobacco for oral use, without, however, articulating how such a ban would contribute to the requirements of the internal market. It will be recalled that Article 14(2) EC provides that the 'internal market shall comprise an area without internal frontiers in which the free movement of goods, persons, services and capital is ensured in accordance with the provisions of this Treaty'. The ban on tobacco for oral use does not appear to make any contribution to the free movement of goods—unlike the bans on additives, unsafe toys and other products referred to above.

D. Summary of Position Prior to the Court's Judgment in the *Tobacco Advertising* Case

In light of the above, it appears that, prior to the judgment of the Court of Justice in the *Tobacco Advertising* case, 'a mere finding of disparities between national rules and of the abstract risk of obstacles to the exercise of fundamental freedoms or distortions of competition liable to result therefrom' could indeed suffice, in the eye of the Community law-maker, to justify measures of harmonisation based on one or more of the Treaty's provisions relating to the operation of the internal market or the common

---

[20] Directive 84/450 relating to the approximation of the laws, regulations and administrative provisions of the Member States concerning misleading advertising, [1984] OJ L250/17.

[21] Directive 97/55 amending Directive 84/450 concerning misleading advertising so as to include comparative advertising, [1997] OJ L290/18. The Directives are now codified in Directive 2006/114 [2006] OJ L376/21.

[22] [1992] OJ L158/30.

market. In addition, harmonisation could also, it seemed, be justified by the need to combat disparities between national laws which might create legal uncertainty and/or 'psychological' difficulties which might in turn deter individuals from cross-frontier activities or transactions. Moreover, where disparities between national rules created obstacles to the free movement of goods, it appeared that one solution, from the point of view of the internal market, was to ban the product rather than remove the obstacles. In what respects did the judgment of the Court of Justice in the *Tobacco Advertising* case suggest that the position thereafter would be any different?

IV. THE JUDGMENT OF THE COURT OF JUSTICE IN THE *TOBACCO ADVERTISING* CASE[23]

A. The Legal Basis, Rationale and Main Provisions of Directive 98/43 Prohibiting the Advertising and Sponsorship of Tobacco Products

The contested Directive was based on Articles 100a EC (now 95 EC), 57(2) EC (now 47(2) EC) and 66 EC (now 55 EC). According to the first recital to the preamble of the Directive, differences existed between national laws on the advertising and sponsorship of tobacco products. Since such advertising and sponsorship transcended national borders, the differences in question were likely to give rise to barriers to movement of products which serve as the media for such activities (such as newspapers and periodicals) and freedom to provide services in that area (advertising services and services relating to sponsorship), and to cause distortions of competition.[24] According to the second recital to the preamble, it was necessary to eliminate such barriers and, to that end, to approximate the rules relating to the advertising and sponsorship of tobacco products, while leaving Member States the possibility of introducing, under certain conditions, such requirements as they might consider necessary in order to guarantee protection of the health of individuals.

The Directive prohibited all forms of advertising and sponsorship of tobacco products and prohibited any free distribution having the purpose or effect of promoting such products.[25] The Directive did not, however,

---

[23] Case C-376/98, above n 1. The case provoked a number of notes and articles: see, eg T Hervey, (2001) 26 *EL Rev* 101; and (2001) 38 *CML Rev* 1421; C Hillion, (2001) *CLJ* 486; G Tridimas and T Tridimas, (2002) 14 *European Journal of Law and Economics* 171; J Usher, (2001) 38 *CML Rev* 1519; G de Búrca, *University of Cambridge Centre for European Legal Studies, Occasional Paper No 5*, 5–17; and D Wyatt, *University of Cambridge Centre for European Legal Studies, Occasional Paper No 5*, 19–32.

[24] The court summarises the Directive in paras 90–5 of its judgment.

[25] Arts 3(1) and (4).

prohibit communications between professionals in the tobacco trade, advertising in sales outlets or in publications published and printed in third countries not principally intended for the Community market.[26] The Directive prohibited (with certain exceptions) the use of the same names for tobacco products and for other products and services, and provided (with certain exceptions) that tobacco products must not bear the brand name, trade mark, emblem or other distinctive feature of any other product or service.[27] The rationale of prohibiting such 'diversification products' was to prevent tobacco product manufacturers advertising their products indirectly by marketing and advertising products such as clothing bearing the same trade mark as a tobacco product.

B. Principal Arguments of Germany to the Effect that the Directive was Invalid

Germany challenged the validity of the Directive under Article 230 EC. The principal arguments advanced by the German Government to establish the invalidity of the Directive were as follows. First, recourse to Article 95 EC is not possible where the 'centre of gravity' of a measure is focused not on promoting the internal market, but on protecting public health.[28] Secondly, a measure adopted under Article 95 EC must actually contribute to the internal market.[29] Thirdly, the Directive makes no such contribution. It does not promote trade in advertising media for tobacco products and freedom to provide services in that area, since the Directive requires, in practice, a total ban on tobacco advertising.[30] Fourthly, there is no contribution to the internal market as regards the 'diversification' products covered by the Directive, ie products carrying the same name or trademark as a tobacco product so as to indirectly advertise the latter through the former, since the Directive contains no 'free trade' clause guaranteeing access for compliant products.[31] Fifthly, any obstacles to trade or distortions of competition must be appreciable to justify recourse to Article 95 EC. If the Community legislature were permitted to harmonise national legislation even where there was no appreciable effect on the internal market, it could adopt directives in any area whatsoever and judicial review of the legislation's compliance with Article 95 would become

---

[26]   Art 3(5).
[27]   Arts 3(2) and 3(3)(a).
[28]   Case C-376/98, above n 1, paras 32–4.
[29]   *Ibid*, para 23.
[30]   *Ibid*, para 24.
[31]   *Ibid*, para 18.

superfluous.[32] No appreciable obstacles to trade or distortions of competition existed to justify the measure in question.[33] Finally, trade in so-called 'static' advertising media (such as posters, cinema advertising and advertising for the hotel and catering sector, for example, via parasols and ashtrays) between Member States is practically non-existent and has to date not been subject to any restrictions.[34]

C. The Court's Findings on Germany's Objections to Validity

1. The 'Centre of Gravity' Argument

Germany argued that the Court's case law indicated that 'the Community may not rely on Article [95] when the measure to be adopted only incidentally harmonises market conditions within the Community'.[35] Both the legislative history of the Directive in issue, and its content and purpose, according to Germany, showed that the 'centre of gravity' of the measure was public health protection.[36] Furthermore, harmonising measures in the field of public health were expressly prohibited by Article 152(4)(c) EC.[37]

This appeared to be at the very least a plausible argument, both in principle, and as regards the Directive in issue. The Court of Justice had held that Directive 91/156 on waste[38] could not be based on Article 95 EC, since the Directive's main object was environmental protection, and it had only the incidental effect of harmonising market conditions within the Community.[39] One of the Court's reasons for finding that the latter Directive could not be adopted on the basis of Article 95 EC was that the Directive could not be regarded as intended to implement the free movement of waste within the Community.[40] The Court did appear to accept in that case, however, that the harmonisation of conditions of competition as regards waste disposal and recovery, which would put an end to advantages enjoyed by economic operators in Member States with relatively less strict regimes for waste regulation, affected the functioning of the internal market. It is to be noted that Germany's 'centre of gravity'

---

[32] *Ibid*, paras 29–31.
[33] *Ibid*, para 31.
[34] *Ibid*, para 15.
[35] Germany cited Case C-70/88, *Parliament v Council* [1991] ECR I-4529, para 17; Case C-155/91, *Commission v Council* [1993] ECR I-939, para 19; Case C-187/93, *Parliament v Council* [1994] ECR I-2857, para 25; and Case C-84/94, *United Kingdom v Council* [1996] ECR I-5755, para 45.
[36] Case C-376/98, above n 1, para 4.
[37] *Ibid*, para 35.
[38] [1991] OJ L78/32.
[39] Case C-155/91, above n 35, paras 18 and 19.
[40] *Ibid*, para 15.

proposition involves two aspects, reflected in the case law it cited. The first is that, in order to adopt a measure on the basis of Article 95 EC, internal market aims must comprise the main object of that measure; the second is that its internal market aims must not be merely incidental to other aims.

As regards the 'centre of gravity' argument, the Court's judgment is at first sight a little difficult to fathom. The Court makes no mention of that argument as such, nor of any of the passages in the case law cited by Germany, and discussed at length by the Advocate General. The Court notes that the Directive in issue harmonises national measures which are 'to a large extent inspired by public health policy objectives'.[41] The Court notes that Article 129(4) EC (now 152(4)(c)) 'excludes any harmonisation of laws and regulations of the Member States designed to protect and improve human health', but adds that 'that provision does not mean that harmonising measures adopted on the basis of other provisions of the Treaty cannot have any impact on the protection of human health'.[42] On the other hand, the Court cautions that '[o]ther articles of the Treaty may not, however, be used as a legal basis in order to circumvent the express exclusion of harmonisation laid down in Article 129(4) of the Treaty'.[43] This seems to represent a different approach from that of the Advocate General. It suggests that account is to be taken of the latter express exclusion when reviewing the compatibility of a Community measure with the Treaty provision upon which it claims to be based. The Court declares that the measures referred to in Article 95(1) EC 'are intended to improve the conditions for the establishment and functioning of the internal market',[44] and that it follows that, in considering whether Article 95 EC was the correct legal basis, the Court 'must verify whether the measure whose validity is at issue in fact pursues the objectives stated by the Community legislature'.[45] The Court adds that 'provided that the conditions for recourse to Articles 100a, 57(2) and 66 [now 95, 47(2) and 55] as a legal basis are fulfilled, the Community legislature cannot be prevented from relying on that legal basis on the ground that public health protection is a decisive factor in the choices to be made'.[46] After summarising the contents of the Directive, the Court concludes that it is 'therefore necessary to verify whether the Directive actually contributes to eliminating obstacles to the free movement of goods and to the freedom to provide services, and to removing distortions of competition'.[47] Despite the fact that the Court

---

[41]   Case C-376/98, above n 1, para 76.
[42]   *Ibid*, paras 77 and 78.
[43]   *Ibid*, para 79.
[44]   *Ibid*, para 84.
[45]   *Ibid*, para 85. The court states that the same considerations apply to Art 47(2) EC, read in conjunction with Art 55 EC: see para 87.
[46]   *Ibid*, para 88.
[47]   *Ibid*, para 95.

does not mention the 'centre of gravity' argument advanced by Germany, the passages referred to above amount to rejection of that argument. The Court does *not* insist that the *main objective* of the Directive be to improve the conditions for the establishment and functioning of the internal market. The Court does not even in terms rule out the possibility that a contribution to the internal market which is merely incidental might nevertheless manifest an intention to improve the conditions for the establishment and functioning of the internal market. While the Court rejects the proposition that Article 95 EC vests in the Community legislature a general power to regulate the internal market, by its silence the Court implies that even if the main aim of a measure of harmonisation adopted under Article 95 EC (or any other Treaty base relating to the internal market) is health protection, it will nevertheless be valid provided that it makes *some* contribution to internal market aims.[48] This aspect of the Court's judgment is strongly supportive of Community competence to regulate the internal market, rather than the contrary. Despite the Court's insistence that Treaty articles such as Article 95 EC may not be used to circumvent the exclusion of harmonisation of health measures provided for by Article 152(4)(c) EC, the Court's approach leaves little obvious room for this principle to find expression, even if we are to infer that if a measure of harmonisation had only the 'marginal'[49] or 'incidental'[50] effect of harmonising market conditions, this would not suffice to justify recourse to Article 95 EC, and the circumvention of Article 152(4)(c) EC would thereby be avoided.

2. Germany's Argument that a Directive Adopted Under Article 95 EC Must Actually Contribute to the Internal Market

Germany made a number of submissions about the scope of Article 95 EC, and about the factual characteristics of the market for tobacco advertising. One submission which was to prove highly significant was to the effect that, since the Directive constituted, in practice, a total prohibition of tobacco advertising, instead of promoting trade in advertising media for tobacco products and freedom to provide services in that area, the Directive almost entirely negated those freedoms.[51] In other words—a Directive cannot be said to promote trade in tobacco advertising services by abolishing such services.

---

[48] D Wyatt, 'Constitutional Significance of the Tobacco Advertising Judgment of the European Court of Justice', *The ECJ's Tobacco Advertising Judgment*, CELS *Occasional Paper, No 5* (Cambridge, Cambridge University Press, 2001) 22.

[49] Case C-187/93, above n 35, para 25.

[50] Case C-70/88, above n 35, para 17.

[51] Case C-376/98, above n 1, para 24.

Germany also argued that Article 95 should only be available as a legal basis in cases where obstacles to the exercise of fundamental freedoms and distortion of competition were considerable.[52] Germany argued that if the Community legislature were permitted to harmonise national legislation even where there was no appreciable effect on the internal market, it could adopt directives in any area whatsoever and judicial review of the legislation's compliance with Article 95 would be superfluous.[53]

According to Germany, the factual characteristics of the tobacco advertising market supported these submissions. Tobacco product advertising was essentially an activity whose effects did not extend beyond the borders of individual Member States. Germany argued that trade in so-called 'static' advertising media (such as posters, cinema advertising and advertising for the hotel and catering sector, for example, via parasols and ashtrays) between Member States was practically non-existent and had to date not been the subject of restrictions. The only significant form of 'non-static' advertising media, in economic terms, was the press. Magazines and daily newspapers served as advertising media for tobacco products, but intra-Community trade in such products was very limited. Considerably fewer than 5 per cent of magazines were exported to other Member States and daily newspapers were used to a much lesser extent than magazines for carrying tobacco advertising. In Germany, in 1997, the share of total advertising revenue of daily papers accounted for by tobacco products advertising was 0.04 per cent.

3. The Court's Conclusion Regarding Elimination of Obstacles to the Free Movement of Goods and Freedom to Provide Services

Germany's argument that harmonisation was only justified to remove considerable or appreciable obstacles to trade was more or less accepted by Advocate General Fennelly, who noted that it was 'at least arguable that harmonising action should relate to national rules which have more than trivial effects on trade', but he did not pursue the point because he did not think that it arose in the present case.[54] The Court did not suggest any such limitation on competence to address obstacles to trade, and rejected Germany's arguments as regards advertising in periodicals, magazines and newspapers. It was true that no obstacles at present existed to their

---

[52]   *Ibid*, para 29.

[53]   *Ibid*, citing Case 91/79, *Commission v Italy* [1980] ECR 1099, para 8 ('Provisions which are made necessary by considerations relating to the environment and health may be a burden upon the undertakings to which they apply and if there is no harmonization of national provisions on the matter, competition may be *appreciably* distorted' (emphasis added)); and Case C-300/89, *Commission v Council (Titanium Dioxide)* [1991] ECR I-2867, para 23 (citing the previous judgment).

[54]   AG Fennelly in Case C-376/98, above n 1, point 104 of the Opinion.

importation into Member States which prohibited tobacco advertising. However, that situation might not continue:

> ... in view of the trend in national legislation towards ever greater restrictions on advertising of tobacco products, reflecting the belief that such advertising gives rise to an appreciable increase in tobacco consumption, it is probable that obstacles to the free movement of press products will arise in the future.[55]

It followed that in principle a Directive prohibiting the advertising of tobacco products in periodicals, magazines and newspapers could be adopted on the basis of Article 95 EC with a view to ensuring the free movement of press products 'on the lines of Directive 89/552, Article 13 of which prohibits television advertising of tobacco products in order to promote the free broadcasting of television programmes'.[56]

However, for numerous types of advertising of tobacco products, the Directive's prohibition could not be justified by the need to eliminate obstacles to the free movement of advertising media or the freedom to provide services in the field of advertising. That applied 'in particular, to the prohibition of advertising on posters, parasols, ashtrays and other articles used in hotels restaurants and cafés, and the prohibition of advertising spots in cinemas, prohibitions which in no way help to facilitate trade in the products concerned'.[57] It will be recalled that Germany had argued that restrictions on advertising on posters and parasols, etc made no contribution to the internal market along the same lines that it had argued that restrictions on press advertising made no contribution to the internal market—because trade was practically non-existent and no obstacles existed in practice. This might be part of the explanation of the Court's conclusion. Yet the Court's approach seems based on the broader contention advanced by Germany, to the effect that a total ban on advertising makes no contribution to trade in advertising media or advertising services; removing obstacles to trade in a good or service by banning the good or service is not, it seems, an option available to the Community law-maker.[58]

The Court thus draws a distinction between banning tobacco advertisements in newspapers or television broadcasts, which is an option available to the Community law-maker in order to remove obstacles to the free

---

[55] Case C-376/98, para 97.
[56] *Ibid*, para 98.
[57] *Ibid*, para 99.
[58] Disparities between national rules on poster advertising and filmed advertisements in cinemas would seem apt to comprise obstacles to trade—no doubt capable of justification— under Art 28 EC. Prohibiting the use of a product for its main purpose, or one of its main purposes (such as posters advertising cigarettes, or filmed advertisements for showing in cinemas) amounts to a restriction on imports: see Case C-473/98, *Kemikalienspektionen v Toolex Alpha AB* [2000] ECR I-5681.

movement of newspapers or television broadcasts, and banning advertisements on posters, parasols and ashtrays, etc, where no such option is available. It is perhaps significant that in these latter cases the advertising element of the product and the product itself are inextricably linked, since the products will be produced to order, bearing the relevant advertising material, and it could not be assumed that banning tobacco advertising would lead to increased cross-frontier trade in ashtrays, posters or parasols. Similarly, the prohibition of advertising spots in cinemas will make no contribution to the free movement of media products, viz, filmed tobacco advertisements for showing in cinemas. Banning the advertisements bans the products concerned and makes no contribution to the free movement of other products or services of which the banned product is a component. This explanation of the above statement by the Court is supported by the immediately following paragraphs of the Court's judgment.

The Court goes on to say that a measure adopted under Article 95 EC or 47(2) EC may incorporate provisions which do not contribute to the elimination of obstacles to the exercise of fundamental freedoms provided that they are necessary to ensure that certain prohibitions imposed in pursuit of that purpose are not circumvented. The Court concluded however, that '[i]t is, however, quite clear that the prohibitions mentioned in the previous paragraph do not fall into that category'.[59] In principle, then, measures of harmonisation which claim to eliminate obstacles to the exercise of fundamental freedoms must do so, and they must do so by eliminating the obstacles rather than eliminating the subject matter of the exercise of the fundamental freedom. The Court reinforces its point about elimination of obstacles to trade in media products with the further observation that 'the Directive does not ensure free movement of products which are in conformity with its provisions'.[60] The Court concludes that in such circumstances, the Community legislature cannot rely on the need to eliminate obstacles to the free movement of advertising media and the freedom to provide services in order to adopt the Directive on the basis of Articles 95, 47(2) and 55 EC.

4. Elimination of Distortion of Competition

Advocate General Fennelly in principle favoured the test advanced by Germany, to the effect that any distortion of competition to be remedied by a harmonising measure must be appreciable, although he considered that a definite conclusion on the point was not necessary for the purposes of his

---

[59]   Case C-376/98, above n 1, para 100.
[60]   *Ibid*, paras 101–4. The court repeats the point that the Directive contains no provision ensuring the free movement of products which conform to its provisions in para 104.

analysis.[61] The Court accepted the argument that, where a harmonising measure purports to eliminate the distortion of competition, that distortion must be appreciable.[62] In the absence of such a requirement, the Court considered that the powers of the Community legislature 'would be practically unlimited', since national laws often differ regarding the conditions under which the activities they regulate may be carried on, and this impacts directly or indirectly on the conditions of competition for the undertakings concerned.[63]

The Court proceeded to apply the 'appreciable distortion of competition' test to the Directive in issue. As regards advertising agencies and producers of advertising media, the Court noted that undertakings established in Member States which impose fewer restrictions on tobacco advertising are unquestionably at an advantage in terms of economies of scale and increase in profits. However, the Court insisted that the effects of such advantages on competition were remote and indirect and did not constitute distortions which could be described as appreciable. They were not comparable to the distortions of competition caused by differences in production costs such as those which prompted the Community legislation in issue in the *Titanium Dioxide* case.[64] Some differences between national rules on tobacco advertising were, however, capable of giving rise to appreciable distortions of competition. Therefore, the fact that sponsorship was prohibited in some Member States and authorised in others gave rise to certain sports events being relocated, with considerable repercussions on the conditions of competition for undertakings associated with such events.[65] While such distortions could be a basis for recourse to Article 95 EC in order to prohibit certain forms of sponsorship, they were not such as to justify the use of that legal basis for an outright prohibition of advertising of the kind imposed by the Directive.[66]

The Directive did not claim to address distortions of competition in the market for tobacco products, as opposed to the market in tobacco advertising services, and in advertising media products, and Germany argued that it did not cover such distortions. The Court nevertheless indicated that the Directive was likewise not apt to eliminate appreciable distortions of competition in that sector. The Court's reason for this conclusion was that imposing a wide-ranging prohibition on the advertising of tobacco products would generalise a restriction of forms of competition by limiting, in all of the Member States, the means available

---

[61]   AG Fennelly in Case C-376/98, above n 1, point 90 of the Opinion.
[62]   Case C-376/98, para 106.
[63]   *Ibid*, para 107.
[64]   *Ibid*, para 109.
[65]   *Ibid*, para 110.
[66]   *Ibid*, para 111.

for economic operators to remain in the market.[67] This reasoning is consistent with the Court's conclusion, referred to above, to the effect that elimination of trade in advertising services or advertising media products could not be regarded as a means of eliminating *obstacles* to that trade. A total ban on advertising tobacco products cannot be regarded as eliminating distortions of competition in that market, since such a ban reduces competition between economic operators in the sector in question. However, the Court does accept, as we have seen, that appreciable distortions of competition resulting from disparate rules on sponsorship may be addressed by eliminating sponsorship as a means of advertising. In the Court's scheme of things, a ban on a service or product must, in order to be justified as making a contribution to the internal market, either make a positive contribution to cross-frontier trade, or eliminate appreciable distortions of competition.

V. DID THE *TOBACCO ADVERTISING* CASE REALLY PLACE RESTRICTIONS ON THE 'GENERAL POWER TO REGULATE THE INTERNAL MARKET'?

A. Community Measures Regulating the Internal Market Must Make a Positive Contribution to the Internal Market

It has already been noted that the reason for the Court's conclusion that, for numerous types of advertising of tobacco products, the Directive's prohibition could not be justified by the need to eliminate obstacles to the free movement of advertising media or the freedom to provide advertising services, was that in such cases (advertising on posters, parasols, etc), the prohibition would not help to facilitate trade in the advertising media products concerned. The Court adopted a similar conclusion as regards diversification products, in light of the absence of a 'free movement' clause for compliant products, and the same reasoning is reflected in its rejection of the proposition that a ban on tobacco advertising could be justified by the need to eliminate distortion of competition in the tobacco products market. This reasoning leads inexorably to the conclusion that a ban on a service or a product must, in order to be justified as making a contribution to the internal market, either make a positive contribution to cross-frontier trade, or eliminate appreciable distortions of competition. While this conclusion would not affect the legal basis for measures discussed earlier in this chapter, such as Directive 88/378 on the safety of toys, or Directive 92/59 on general product safety, it certainly calls into question the internal

---

[67]   *Ibid*, para 113.

market justification of a ban on free-standing products, such as the oral tobacco products referred to in section III of this chapter.

The requirement that measures of harmonisation which make a contribution to the internal market through eliminating distortions of competition do so only in respect of distortions of competition which are *appreciable* represents, on the face of it, a major departure from the basis upon which common/internal market legislation had hitherto been adopted in the environmental and consumer protection fields, as is clear from the examples given in section III of this chapter. The Court accepts the fact that advertising agencies in Member States which impose fewer restrictions on tobacco advertising have an advantage in terms of economies of scale and profits, but describes the effects of these advantages on competition as too remote and indirect to constitute appreciable distortions of competition. Such disparities accordingly do not justify measures of harmonisation.

What is less clear is how to distinguish situations when relative advantages and disadvantages have only remote and indirect effects on competition, from those in which the effects of relative competitive advantage are appreciable. We are given two examples in the *Tobacco Advertising* case. One is that offered by the *Titanium Dioxide* case, where the Directive in issue addressed appreciable distortions of competition caused by differences in production costs resulting from disparities between national rules relating to control of pollution arising from waste from the titanium dioxide industry. No quantitative criteria are suggested by the Court. The example is of limited assistance. Does it follow that, where disparities in national rules affect the production costs of a product, it can automatically be assumed that an appreciable distortion of competition is present which justifies harmonisation? Or is it necessary to examine whether existing disparities (and potential disparities?) *actually* create *appreciable* distortions? A conclusion that such disparities actually lead to appreciable distortions of competition presumably depends on the nature of the disparities between national rules and the actual effects on relative costs of the disparities in question.

By way of contrast, as is noted above, the Court makes it clear that an appreciable distortion of competition does not result from the fact that a particular service (*in casu* advertising services to promote tobacco products) may be offered by advertising service providers in one Member State, but not in another. It would seem to follow, by parity of reasoning, that an appreciable distortion of competition does not result from the fact that a *product* may be lawfully marketed by operators in one Member State, but not in another. One clear indication of the existence of an appreciable distortion of competition is given by the Court—where disparities between national rules give rise to service providers (*in casu* the organisers of sponsored sporting events) relocating their activities in other Member States. As a rule of thumb, it seems that, where disparities between national rules are apt to lead to the relocation of economic activities, such disparities create appreciable distortions of competition which may be harmonised. That does not mean, however, that such potential for relocation is an essential characteristic of an appreciable distortion of competition. Monitoring compliance with the Court's conclusion that distortion of competition must be appreciable to justify harmonisation is not without difficulty, not least because the Court customarily allows the Community institutions a large measure of discretion in the exercise of their law-making functions.

The Court's ruling in this regard is potentially of some significance, since the mere existence of disparities between national rules cannot be regarded in itself as leading to the conclusion that distortions of competition exist which justify harmonisation. Yet in the absence of recourse to quantitative assessment of any kind, the requirement of appreciable distortions of competition may be relaxed or sidestepped by the Community institutions or the Court of Justice itself.

B. Scrutiny of a Harmonisation Measure to Determine Whether It Makes a Contribution to the Internal Market

The Court of Justice in the *Tobacco Advertising* case upheld the competence of the Community to prohibit the advertising of tobacco products in newspapers and periodicals, as a means of eliminating obstacles to the free movement of advertising media and the freedom to provide services. However, the Court held that this could not be said 'for numerous types of advertising of tobacco products', in particular 'advertising on posters, parasols, ashtrays and other articles used in hotels, restaurants and cafes, and the prohibition of advertising spots in cinemas'.[68] Similarly, the Court upheld the competence of the Community to prohibit certain forms of sponsorship, in order to eliminate appreciable distortions of competition, but held that this could not be said 'for an outright prohibition of advertising of the kind imposed by the Directive'.[69] Rejecting partial annulment on the ground that amendment of the Directive was a matter for the Community legislature, the Court annulled the Directive in its entirety.

It seems that a general provision such as 'all forms of advertising and sponsorship shall be banned in the Community' (Article 3(1) of the Directive) will only be regarded as valid to the extent that specific applications of that general provision can be regarded as making a contribution to the internal market. The Court accepted that a measure

---

[68] *Ibid*, para 99.
[69] *Ibid*, para 111.

adopted on the basis of Articles 95, 47(2) and 55 EC might incorporate provisions which do not contribute to the elimination of obstacles to exercise of fundamental freedoms 'provided that they are necessary to ensure that certain prohibitions imposed in pursuit of that purpose are not circumvented',[70] but considered that that was not the position in the instant case. The Court's approach might be described as competence restrictive and might seem to imply that the substantive provisions of the Directive must, in all their applications, make a contribution to the internal market, save for those provisions which do not, but which are justified by the need to avoid circumvention of those that do.

This approach may be contrasted with the Court's interpretation of the scope of Article 42 EC, which provides that the Council shall 'adopt such measures in the field of social security as are necessary to provide freedom of movement for workers ...'. The Court has interpreted the latter competence as having 'a considerably wider scope than Article [39 EC on freedom of movement for workers]',[71] and upheld the application of Community social security measures to a German national who had an accident in France, despite the fact that he was not a migrant worker and was on holiday in France.[72] The Court has also upheld the application of such measures to stateless persons and refugees.[73] As Advocate General Jacobs has noted, despite the fact that the aim of the Community social security measures is to provide for freedom of movement for workers, those measures apply to civil servants, who are excluded from the scope of the provisions on freedom of movement.[74] One reason advanced by the Court for upholding the competence of the Community to adopt social security rules applying to persons who do not fall within the scope of the provisions on freedom of movement has been that it would be impracticable to adopt any other course,[75] and the Court described the category of stateless persons and refugees as 'that very restricted category of persons' which would have necessitated a parallel regime designed solely for them.[76] In the *Tobacco Advertising* case, the Court of Justice made no attempt to uphold the general application of the prohibitions in issue on grounds of practicability, and seems to exclude that possibility in principle. The Court maintained its extensive interpretation of Article 42 EC after the judgment

---

[70] *Ibid*, para 100.
[71] AG Jacobs in Case C-95/99, *Mervett Khalil* [2001] ECR I-7143, point 56 of the Opinion.
[72] Case 44/65, *Maison Singer* [1965] ECR 965.
[73] Case C-95/99, above n 71.
[74] AG Jacobs in Case C-95/99, point 55 of the Opinion (the learned Advocate General is no doubt referring to those civil servants excluded by Art 39(4) EC by virtue of their specific responsibilities).
[75] Case 44/65, above n 72, 971.
[76] Case C-95/99, above n 71, para 57.

in the *Tobacco Advertising* case,[77] possibly suggesting a more restrictive approach to competence under Articles 95 and 47(2) EC than under Article 42 EC. It is suggested below that more recent case law suggests that measures adopted under Article 95 EC may cover situations which have no connection with free movement.

C. Conclusion—the Court's Judgment Contains Both Competence Restrictive and Supportive Elements

The Court's judgment in *Tobacco Advertising* contains both elements which are restrictive of Community competence to regulate the internal market, and elements which are supportive of such competence. Two elements fall squarely in the former category—the requirement that Community measures regulating the internal market make a *positive contribution* to the internal market, and the requirement that measures which make such a contribution through eliminating distortions of competition do so only in respect of distortions of competition which are *appreciable*. The Court's ruling in this latter regard is of potential significance. The mere existence of disparities between national rules cannot be regarded in itself as leading to the conclusion that distortions of competition exist which justify harmonisation. The weakness of the test is the lack of any objective criteria for its application.

A further element in the Court's judgment which might be said to be competence restrictive is the willingness of the Court to annul the Directive on the ground that it prohibited tobacco advertising in situations which made no contribution to the internal market despite the fact that the prohibition in issue did make such a contribution in other situations, viz, as regards advertising in newspapers and periodicals, and as regards eliminating appreciable distortions of competition in the sponsorship of sporting events, etc.

Other elements of the Court's judgment are, however, strongly supportive of Community competence to regulate the internal market. In this category falls the Court's conclusion that a measure of harmonisation may be based on Article 95 EC if it makes *some* contribution to the internal market, even if that contribution does not comprise the main objective of the measure in question. Also in this category falls the implicit rejection by the Court of the argument that measures of harmonisation may only be adopted to remove obstacles to trade if those obstacles are appreciable. The Court held that recourse to Article 95 EC was possible if the aim was to prevent the emergence of future obstacles to trade resulting from multifarious development of national laws, although the emergence of such

---

[77] Case C-95/99 was decided in the year following the *Tobacco Advertising* case.

obstacles must be likely and the measure in question must be designed to prevent them. However, the Court did not refer to any requirement that the obstacles to trade must be substantial.

VI. THE COURT'S APPROACH IN SUBSEQUENT CASES HAS LARGELY REVERSED THE COMPETENCE RESTRICTING EFFECTS OF THE *TOBACCO ADVERTISING* CASE

A. The *Tobacco Advertising* Judgment—a False Dawn?

Perhaps the most important question posed by the *Tobacco Advertising* case was and is the extent to which it represents a foretaste of the approach which the Court will take to reviewing the competence of the Community legislature to adopt internal market measures, and thus comprise a credible deterrent to excessive claims to competence by the Community institutions. Was the Court's judgment the beginning of a line of cases coherently defining and limiting the scope of Community competence to regulate the internal market? Or was it the exception which proves the rule; the rule being that the Community legislature *does* enjoy a general competence to regulate the internal market, and the role of the Court is for the most part to enhance and support that competence rather than to limit it? The present writer considers that the signs so far support the latter conclusion.

B. The *Swedish Match* Case

Reference was made above to 'tobacco for oral use', banned by Directive 92/41 amending Directive 89/622 on the approximation of the laws, regulations and administrative provisions of the Member States concerning the labelling of tobacco products.[78] Directive 89/622 was repealed and replaced by Directive 2001/37, Article 8 of which reproduced the ban on tobacco for oral use. In *Swedish Match*,[79] the Court of Justice considered a reference on the question of the validity of Article 8 on a number of grounds, including the adequacy of Article 95 EC as a legal base. The Court referred to the *Tobacco Advertising* case for the proposition that, while a mere finding of disparities between national rules is insufficient to justify having recourse to Article 95, it is otherwise where there are differences between the laws of the Member States which are such as to

---

[78] [1992] OJ L158/30.
[79] Case C-210/03, *R, on the application of: Swedish Match AB and Swedish Match UK Ltd v Secretary of State for Health* [2004] ECR I-11893. See also Case C-434/02, *Arnold André GmbH & Co KG v Landrat des Kreises Herford* [2004] ECR I-11825.

obstruct the fundamental freedoms and thus have a direct effect on the functioning of the internal market.[80] The latter case was also cited for the proposition that, while recourse to Article 95 EC as a legal base is possible if the aim is to prevent future obstacles to trade resulting from the heterogeneous development of national laws, the emergence of such obstacles must be likely and the measure in question must be designed to prevent them.[81] The Court added that, where the conditions for recourse to Article 95 EC as a legal basis are fulfilled, the Community legislature cannot be prevented from relying on the legal basis on the ground that public health protection is a decisive factor in the choices to be made.[82] The Court emphasised this latter point by reference to Articles 152(1) and 95(3) EC as follows.

> It should also be noted that the first subparagraph of Article 152(1) EC provides that a high level of protection of public health is to ensured in the definition and implementation of all Community policies and activities, and that Article 95(3) EC expressly requires that, in achieving harmonisation, a high level of protection of human health should be guaranteed.[83]

All of this is indeed consistent with the judgment in the *Tobacco Advertising* case, but in the following passages there is a distinct departure from the reasoning in the latter case.

> It follows from the foregoing that, where there are obstacles to trade or it is likely that such obstacles will emerge in future because the Member States have taken or are about to take divergent measures with respect to a product or a class of products such as to ensure different levels of protection and thereby prevent the product or products concerned from moving freely within the Community, Article 95 EC authorises the Community legislature to intervene by adopting appropriate measures, in compliance with Article 95(3) EC and with the legal principles mentioned in the Treaty or identified in the case-law, in particular the principle of proportionality.

> Depending on the circumstances, those appropriate measures may consist in requiring all the Member States to authorise the marketing of the product or products concerned, subjecting such an obligation of authorisation to certain conditions, or even provisionally or definitely prohibiting the marketing of a product or products (see, in the context of Council Directive 92/59/EEC on product safety, Case C-359/92 *Germany v Council* [1994] ECR I-3681, paragraphs 4 and 33).[84]

---

[80] Case C-210/03, *ibid*, para 29.
[81] *Ibid*, para 30.
[82] *Ibid*, para 31.
[83] *Ibid*, para 32.
[84] *Ibid*, paras 33–4.

The reference of the Court of Justice in *Swedish Match* to paragraphs 4 and 33 of the judgment of the Court in *Germany v Council*[85] to support its conclusion that a ban on products is an appropriate means of removing obstacles to trade in such products is unconvincing. These paragraphs do indeed refer to the provisions of the product safety directive which permit withdrawal of dangerous products from the market. However, as paragraph 34 of the Court's judgment in the latter case indicates, the rationale of these provisions is to ensure the free movement of goods.[86] As noted above, the rationale of withdrawal from the market of non-compliant products is to enforce application of the relevant safety standard, and contribute to the elimination of disparities between national rules and their application, and thereby to the free movement of goods between the Member States. Prohibiting non-compliant products as a means of enforcement of a safety standard, application of which facilitates the free movement of compliant products, is quite different from outright prohibition of a product.

The Court goes on to apply the reasoning quoted above to the prohibition on oral tobacco products. It notes that it was common ground that, at the time the ban was introduced, there were differences between the laws of Member States; two Member States had banned such products, and a third had adopted provisions which, while not yet in force, had the same object. Those prohibitions contributed to 'a heterogeneous development' of the market in tobacco products and 'were therefore such as to constitute obstacles to the free movement of goods'.[87] Article 8 of Directive 2001/37 was adopted in a context which was no different, from the point of view of obstacles to the free movement of goods, from that which existed when the ban was originally introduced.[88] The Court concluded that it followed from the foregoing that the prohibition on oral tobacco products in Article 8 of Directive 2001/37 could be adopted on the basis of Article 95 EC.

The Court's conclusion that Article 95 EC provides an adequate legal basis for a ban on a free-standing product contradicts the reasoning on the elimination of obstacles to trade contained in the *Tobacco Advertising* judgment. The basis for the Court's annulment of Directive 98/43 was in large part the failure of that Directive to make any contribution to cross-frontier trade in advertising services and media products, and diversification products. The prohibition of advertising on posters, parasols, ashtrays and other articles used in hotels, restaurants and cafes, and the

---

[85] Case C-359/92, above n 19.
[86] The court states that: 'The free movement of goods can be secured only if product safety requirements do not differ significantly from one Member State to another.'
[87] Case C-210/03, above n 79, paras 37 and 38.
[88] *Ibid*, para 40.

prohibition of advertising spots in cinemas, did not help to facilitate trade in the products concerned. One reason that the prohibition did not help to facilitate trade was because it simply prohibited the subject matter of the trade in question.[89] It was certainly the latter approach which led the Court to its conclusion that the Directive's ban on diversification products did not contribute to the free movement of goods. The Court makes it clear that the fact that the Directive does not ensure the free movement of products which are in conformity with its provisions is inconsistent with contentions that the Directive removes obstacles to the free movement of diversification products.

Swedish Match adopts a completely different approach. If obstacles exist to trade in a product (certain oral tobacco products), as a result of the fact that some Member States prohibit the product, and others do not, recourse to Article 95 EC is permissible to prohibit the product in all of the Member States, thereby removing the obstacles to trade by prohibiting the product. It is instructive to compare the treatment of the ban on oral tobacco products with the ban on diversification products contained in Directive 98/43. The latter stood condemned for lack of a free movement clause; the former was upheld. Moreover, a comparison might be made between the posters and filmed cinema advertisements advertising tobacco products, referred to in the *Tobacco Advertising* case. The Court held that prohibiting advertising on the posters and in the cinemas did not facilitate the free movement of the advertising media concerned. Yet disparities between national laws on the permissibility of such advertising would seem capable of restricting trade in the media concerned. Prohibiting the use or the main use of a product (such as posters or films advertising tobacco products) amounts to a restriction on imports, although one no doubt capable of justification.[90] On the *Swedish Match* analysis, Article 95 EC would provide a Treaty base for a Community-wide ban on the products concerned. This is clearly a different approach from that of the Court in the *Tobacco Advertising* case.

The same conclusion is reached if one considers posters and filmed cinema advertisements from the point of view of the provision of services. It will be recalled that in *Gourmet International*,[91] the Court considered a ban on advertising of alcoholic beverages on TV and radio and in periodicals and other publications other than publications distributed solely at point of sale. It held that this ban was a restriction under Article

---

[89] It is noted above that the court might have accepted Germany's argument that no obstacles to trade existed as regards the media products referred to.

[90] Case C-473/98, above n 58.

[91] Case C-405/98, *Gourmet International Products AB (GIP)* [2001] ECR I-1795. See A Arnull, A Dashwood, M Dougan, M Ross, E Spaventa and D Wyatt, *Wyatt and Dashwood's European Union Law*, 5th edn (London, Sweet & Maxwell, 2006) para 19–029.

49 EC because it restricted the right of providers of advertising space to offer that space to potential advertisers in other Member States.[92] It would seem to follow that national rules preventing those offering billboard space for poster advertising from accepting tobacco products advertising would amount to restrictions on the provision of services to potential customers in other Member States.

The same analysis would apply to national rules preventing cinemas showing tobacco products advertisements. It is true that the Court observed in *Gourmet* that a measure such as that in issue 'even if it is non-discriminatory, has a particular effect on the cross-border supply of advertising space, given the international nature of the advertising market in the category of products to which the prohibition relates', but the tobacco products would seem to resemble the alcoholic beverages market as regards the international nature of the relevant advertising market, and in any event, it is difficult to read the Court's observation in *Gourmet* as placing much in the way of a limit on the general proposition that, where a national rule can be shown to prevent a potential in-state service provider from supplying a potential out-of-state customer, Article 49 EC applies.

Given that national rules restricting advertising on posters and in cinemas amount in principle to restrictions on the freedom to provide services, the approach of the Court in *Swedish Match* would suggest that one appropriate response to the existence of such restrictions would be to ban the services in question. Yet, as noted above, this was not the approach in the *Tobacco Advertising* case. Furthermore, the Court in the latter case rejected the proposition that Article 95 EC could provide the basis for a measure prohibiting tobacco products advertising on the ground that disparities between national rules amounted to distortions of competition, since such disparities would not be appreciable. Yet this consideration seems no longer of practical significance in light of the *Gourmet* judgment, since even if the disparities between restrictions in different Member States do not appreciably distort competition, the existence of advertising restrictions in some Member States undoubtedly leads to the provision of services to customers in other Member States being restricted, and thereby, on the basis of the *Swedish Match* approach, provides the basis for a Community-wide ban on the services in question. It is difficult to avoid the conclusion that the reasoning of the Court of Justice in *Swedish Match* could be used to justify the general ban on advertising of tobacco products rejected by the Court in *Tobacco Advertising*.

This is a regrettable conclusion. The Community law-maker has no legitimate interest in the banning of free-standing products. Member States

---

[92] Case C-405/98, *ibid*, paras 37–8. The court held that the restriction could be justified on grounds of public health, subject to the principle of proportionality, which was a matter for the national court: see paras 40–1.

are best placed to decide whether or not to permit or prohibit free-standing products such as the oral tobacco products in issue in *Swedish Match*. Action at the Community level makes no contribution to the internal market in fact; it simply asserts Community competence for the sake of an abstract principle—the principle that, in a single market, it is the central authority which decides which products or services may be placed on that market.

This outcome also seems inconsistent with the principle of subsidiarity. It is true that subsidiarity concerns the exercise of competence rather than the scope of competence. Yet, although the Court insists that the principle of subsidiarity applies where the Community legislature makes use of Article 95 EC,[93] it has treated the objective of eliminating the barriers raised by disparities between national laws as being an objective which cannot be sufficiently achieved by the Member States acting individually and an objective which can be better achieved at Community level.[94] This approach would seem to lead to the conclusion that, although internal market measures are subject to the requirements of subsidiarity, they automatically meet the requirements of subsidiarity.

It has been pointed out that this approach is flawed, since it is based on the proposition that, in the case of an internal market measure, the only objectives relevant for determining the appropriate level for action are those objectives of the measure which are internal market objectives. Yet it has already been made clear that the objectives of an internal market measure may be predominantly public health objectives. The Court indeed recognises that the public health objectives of an internal market measure may be of significance in determining the proportionality of such a measure.[95] In assessing compliance with the principle of subsidiarity of a measure pursuing both internal market and public health objectives, the latter as well as the former should be taken fully into account.[96]

If such an analysis is applied to the ban on oral tobacco products in issue in *Swedish Match*, it is difficult if not impossible to avoid the conclusion that all the objectives of the internal market provision in issue can be achieved by Member States acting individually. The objective of making a contribution to the internal market is no more nor less than an objective of banning oral tobacco products; as pointed out above, there are no improvements in trade or competition which flow from this. The objective of banning oral tobacco products can clearly be achieved by those Member

---

[93] Case C-491/01, *R v Secretary of State for Health, ex p British American Tobacco (Investments) Ltd and Imperial Tobacco Ltd* [2002] ECR I-11453, para 179.

[94] *Ibid*, paras 181–3.

[95] *Ibid*, paras 122–41.

[96] For a critical assessment of subsidiarity, and discussion of its application where internal market measures pursue public health aims, see A Arnull *et al*, above n 91, paras 4–018–21.

States which wish to impose such a ban. It is true that not all Member States might wish to impose such a ban. However, the provision in issue did not even have the objective of making such a ban universal, since it did not apply to all the Member States.[97] The approach of the Court in the *Swedish Match* case extends internal market competence to subject matter which makes no contribution to the internal market, and which appears to fail the demands of subsidiarity.

C. *Tobacco Advertising (No 2)*

Directive 2003/33 was adopted by the European Parliament and the Council of the European Union following the annulment by the Court of Directive 98/43 in the *Tobacco Advertising* case. In accordance with the latter judgment, the Directive prohibits tobacco product advertising in the press and other printed publications, with certain limited exceptions,[98] and in radio broadcasts.[99] The Directive also prohibits 'sponsorship of events or activities involving or taking place in several Member States or otherwise having cross-border effects'.[100] The Directive provides that Member States 'shall not prohibit or restrict the free movement of products or services which comply with this Directive'.[101] Germany challenged the Directive under Article 230 EC on the ground, inter alia, that Article 95 EC did not comprise an appropriate legal basis.[102] Germany's challenge failed, and that failure was perhaps unsurprising given the terms of the earlier judgment of the Court relating to Directive 98/43. However, one aspect of the Court's judgment is worthy of remark. Its reasoning incorporates the formulation adopted in *Swedish Match*, to the effect that Article 95 EC authorises the Community legislature to respond to obstacles to trade by adopting appropriate measures, which may consist in requiring all the Member States to authorise the marketing of the product or products concerned, subjecting such an obligation or authorisation to conditions, *or even provisionally or definitively prohibiting the marketing of a product or products.* It is somewhat ironic that this reasoning is included in this judgment of the Court. If such reasoning had been adopted in the first *Tobacco Advertising* case, the Court would have upheld Directive 98/43, for the reasons given above.

---

[97] The ban did not apply in Sweden: see Case C-210/03, above n 79, para 11.
[98] Art 3 of the Directive.
[99] Art 4 of the Directive.
[100] Art 5 of the Directive.
[101] Art 8 of the Directive.
[102] Case C-380/03, *Germany v Parliament and Council* [2006] ECR I-11573.

D. The *British American Tobacco* Judgment

It will be recalled that in the *Tobacco Advertising* case the Court of Justice denied that Article 95 EC bestowed on the Community legislature 'a general power to regulate the internal market', and insisted that the measures referred to in that Article 'are intended to improve the conditions for the establishment and functioning of the internal market'.[103] The Court stated that if:

> ... a mere finding of disparities between national rules and of the abstract risk of obstacles to the exercise of fundamental freedoms or distortions of competition liable to result therefrom were sufficient to justify the choice of Article [95 EC] as a legal basis, judicial review of compliance with the proper legal basis might be rendered nugatory.[104]

Yet in the *British American Tobacco* case,[105] decided only two years later, the Court upheld labelling requirements concerning health warnings which could make no practical contribution to the free movement of packaged tobacco products, on the sole ground that a recital to the relevant directive refers to the existence of different national laws with respect to the presentation of such warnings.

In order to understand the significance of the Court's ruling in this case, it is necessary to refer briefly to relevant legislation and case law by way of context.[106] In the *Schwarzkopf* case,[107] the Court acknowledges that the rationale of common labelling rules at the European level is the possibility of multilingual labelling, which enables a product to be placed on the market in a number of Member States, and indicates that a directive laying down common labelling rules which does *not* facilitate multilingual labelling would be invalid for inconsistency with Article 28 EC. The Court indicates that common labelling rules must not make it 'excessively difficult for ... products having the same get-up to be marketed in several Member States'. 'Several' means more than two, and it seems that in the *Schwarzkopf* case it was, according to Advocate General Mischo, 'possible to print the warning, in three languages, on the tube and corresponding packaging'.[108]

In the case of common rules for the labelling of tobacco products, internal market aims appear to have been lost sight of both by the Community law-maker and the Court of Justice itself. The preamble of

---

[103]   Case C-376/98, above n 1, paras 83 and 84.
[104]   *Ibid*, para 84.
[105]   Case C-491/01, above n 93.
[106]   The following issues are discussed in A Arnull et al, above n 91, paras 21–026–9.
[107]   Case C-169/99, *Hans Schwarzkopf GmbH & Co KG* [2001] ECR I-5901.
[108]   *Ibid*, point 96 of the Opinion.

Council Directive 89/622 on the labelling of tobacco products[109] referred to differences between national rules on labelling of products and to the fact that those differences were likely to constitute barriers to trade. Provision was made for all unit packets of tobacco products to carry, 'on the most visible surface, the following general warning in the official language or languages of the country of final marketing: "Tobacco seriously damages health"'.[110] With regard to cigarette packets, the 'other large surface of the packet shall carry, in the official language or languages of the country of final marketing' various specific warning selected from the Annex and alternating as specified.[111] On cigarette packets the warnings referred to must cover 'at least 4% of each large surface of the unit packet'.[112] In the United Kingdom, the Directive was implemented by the Tobacco Products Labelling (Safety) Regulations 1991,[113] which provided that the warnings were to cover 'at least 6%' of the relevant surface area for *domestic products*.[114]

In the *Gallaher* case,[115] various tobacco companies challenged the latter provisions on the ground that all Member States were bound to implement the Directive by providing that warnings cover 'at least 4%' of the relevant surface area, rather than 'at least 6%'. The effect of the rules adopted by the United Kingdom was that domestically produced cigarettes were required to carry larger health warnings than imported cigarettes. The issue was referred to the Court of Justice, before which the Commission and the United Kingdom advanced the argument that the reference in the Directive to 'at least 4%' gave Member States a discretion to require that the warnings cover a larger surface area if they so wished, in the case of domestic products. The Advocate General pointed out that a similar issue had arisen before the Court in the *Ratti* case,[116] in which the Court had interpreted Directive 73/173 on the classification, packaging and labelling of dangerous preparations. In that case, the Court had held that Member States were not entitled to maintain, parallel with the rules laid down by the Directive for imports, *different rules* for the *domestic market*. The rules laid down by the Directive included a provision that the label must be 'at least' a certain dimension. Advocate General Lenz argued:

---

[109] [1989] OJ L359/1.

[110] Art 4(1).

[111] Art 4(2).

[112] Art 4(4). This percentage was increased to 6% for countries with two official languages and to 8% for countries with three official languages.

[113] SI 1991/1530.

[114] Regs 5(2)(d) and 6(3)(b).

[115] Case C-11/92, *The R v Secretary of State for Health, ex p Gallaher Ltd, Imperial Tobacco Ltd and Rothmans International Tobacco (UK) Ltd* [1993] ECR I-3545.

[116] Case 148/78, *Pubblico Ministero v Ratti* [1979] ECR 1629.

That which is valid in this regard for Directive 73/173 must *a fortiori* also be valid for the present Directive, as it must be borne in mind that the Community legislature would have been aware of the Ratti judgment when it adopted Directive 89/622.[117]

Mr Lenz concluded that 'at least 4%' meant that all Member States must adopt the rule that warnings must cover at least 4 per cent of the unit packet and that there was no discretion in Member States to prescribe a larger warning for domestic products. He reasoned as follows:

42. This conclusion is consistent with the objective pursued by the Directive both with regard to the easing of restrictions on the movement of goods and the approximation of conditions of competition.

As the applicants in the United Kingdom proceedings correctly argued, a manufacturer wishing to export his produce from Member State A, which imposes a more stringent spatial requirement than that laid down by the Directive, to Member State B, which has the same official language as Member State A, would have to change his packaging if Member State B treats a spatial requirement of 4% as adequate. Although the product labelled in accordance with the provisions of Member State A would also be marketable in Member State B (if one subscribes to the views expressed by the Commission and the United kingdom), those imports would be placed at a commercial disadvantage vis-à-vis domestic goods produced in Member State B if the manufacturer were not to adapt to the less stringent requirements existing in the latter State. The liberalization of trade and the approximation of conditions of competition, as objectives of the Directive, would here be placed in equal jeopardy.

43. ... This conclusion is all the more justified when one considers that the Directive (if understood as laying down a minimum limit) does not specify any maximum limit for the percentage which may be imposed by Member States. Consequently, that figure could—theoretically—lie anywhere between 5% and 100%. I cannot imagine that those who drafted the Directive intended to bring about such a position in law.

The Court of Justice, however, appeared to conclude that such a position could indeed have been intended. It took the view that the expression 'at least' was to be interpreted as giving to Member States a discretion to decide that the indications and warnings are to cover a greater surface area than 4 per cent. It noted that in the *Ratti* case the Court had not had to rule specifically on the labelling provision, but on 'other provisions of that directive and on the nature of its provisions in general'.[118] The Court accepted that this interpretation of the Directive's provisions 'may imply less favourable treatment for national products in comparison with imported products and leaves in existence some inequalities in conditions

---

[117] Case C-11/92, above n 115, point 26 of the Opinion.
[118] *Ibid*, para 21.

of competition', but regarded these consequences as being 'attributable to the degree of harmonisation sought by the provisions in question, which lay down minimum requirements'.[119] The difficulty with the Court's conclusion is that it deprives the Directive of virtually all useful effect as regards removing obstacles to trade or eliminating distortions of competition, as the Advocate General so clearly demonstrates. It was noted above that the chief benefit of common labelling rules at the European level is that they make possible multilingual labelling. Certainly a '4% rule' applicable in the way suggested by the Advocate General would make multilingual labelling possible; a packet of cigarettes could be labelled for the UK, France and Belgium with health warnings covering only 16 per cent of the large surface areas. Yet as the Advocate General points out, the Court's interpretation would allow a Member State to require such a large size label for sale of domestic production on its own market that it would be impossible in practice to label for other Member States as well.

The provisions on labelling of tobacco products were amended by Article 5(2) of Directive 2001/37 of the manufacture, presentation and sale of tobacco products.[120] Each unit packet of tobacco products must carry a general warning, on the most visible surface of the unit packet, and an additional warning, on the other most visible surface. The general warning 'shall cover not less than 30% of the external area of the corresponding surface of the unit packet ... on which it is printed. That proportion shall be increased to 32% for Member States with two official languages and 35% for Member States with three official languages'. The additional warning 'shall cover not less than 40% of the external area of the corresponding surface of the unit packet of tobacco on which it is printed. That proportion shall be increased to 45% for Member States with two official languages and 50% for Member States with three official languages'.[121] Member States are furthermore entitled to stipulate that the warnings referred to are to be accompanied by a reference, outside the box for warnings, to the issuing authority.[122]

A challenge to the validity of the Directive by various tobacco companies in the English High Court led to a reference to the Court of Justice.[123] The applicants argued that Article 5 of the Directive was invalid because, contrary to the requirements of the *Schwarzkopf* case, that provision made it, at the very least, excessively difficult for tobacco products complying with the labelling rules in question to be marketed in several Member

[119] *Ibid*, para 22.
[120] [2001] OJ L194/26.
[121] Art 5(5) Directive 2001/37.
[122] Art 5(8) Directive 2001/37.
[123] *R on the Application of (British American Tobacco (Investments) Ltd, Imperial Tobacco Ltd v The Secretary of State for Health, HM Attorney General*, 2001 WL 1676838.

States, to the extent that parallel imports would in practice be excluded, and tobacco products would continue to be labelled exclusively for the Member State in which they are to be marketed.[124] The Court simply does not address these points. It refers to its judgment in the *Gallaher* case for the proposition that 'some provisions contained in the Community harmonisation measures already adopted merely laid down minimum requirements leaving the Member States a degree of discretion to adapt them'.[125] It also refers to the fact that certain recitals in the preamble 'refer to the fact that different Member States have different laws with regard to the presentation of warnings'.[126] The Court goes on to note that the Directive guarantees the free movement of products which comply with its requirements,[127] and concludes that 'the Directive genuinely has as its object the improvement of the conditions for the functioning of the internal market'.[128] This reasoning is at a level of generality which does not engage with the argument referred to above to the effect that the size requirements for the warning labels make it impossible or excessively difficult for a commercial operator to label for 'several Member States'. Furthermore, the Court says nothing to indicate that the reasoning adopted in the *Gallaher* case and referred to above does not apply to the Directive under consideration. The references in Article 5(2) to warnings covering 'not less than' 30 per cent, etc, would seem capable of being construed as minimum standards still allowing to Member States a discretion to require larger labels for domestic products. Yet quite apart from this, the labelling requirements in Article 5, far from facilitating cross-frontier trade in tobacco products, ensures that such trade is close to impossible. The internal market aims claimed by the Directive appear to have been wholly subordinated to public health aims. More than that, however, the Court does not even attempt to demonstrate that the terms of Article 5 of the Directive remove obstacles to trade. The Court's reference to disparities between national laws, and the assertion that the Directive genuinely has as its aim the improvement of the conditions for the functioning of the internal market, are entirely formalistic. The only conclusion which can be drawn is that the fact that harmonisation of labelling rules *in principle* may contribute to the free movement of goods provides a justification for labelling rules which *in fact* make no such contribution. That would seem to amount to judicial endorsement of the very general power to regulate the internal market so emphatically denied by the Court of Justice in the

---

[124]   Report for the Hearing, paras 73–5.
[125]   Case C-491/01, above n 93, para 66.
[126]   *Ibid*, para 72.
[127]   *Ibid*, para 74.
[128]   *Ibid*, para 75.

Tobacco Advertising case. The present writer finds the conclusion unfortunate. The Community law-maker has no legitimate interest in specifying the labelling of a product where the specification will make no contribution to the internal market and is accordingly solely of interest from the point of view of public health, which is in principle a matter reserved for the Member States. Moreover, for similar reasons, the provisions in question do not comply with the principle of subsidiarity. Since free movement in packaged tobacco products is not ensured by the labelling requirements, the internal market objective of the provisions is purely nominal, and the predominant objective—public health protection—is one which can be sufficiently achieved by the Member States acting individually.[129]

E. Is the Court Adopting a Low Threshold for the Concept of 'Appreciability' of Distortions of Competition?

It is argued above that the *Tobacco Advertising* judgment contains elements which are competence restrictive, and that one such element is the requirement that measures which make a contribution to the internal market through eliminating distortions of competition do so only in respect of distortions of competition which are *appreciable*. It was suggested earlier in this chapter that the Court's ruling in this regard is of significance, since it means that the mere existence of disparities between national rules cannot be regarded in itself as leading to the conclusion that distortions of competition exist which justify harmonisation. Yet this conclusion is qualified by the observation that the lack of any reference to quantitative assessment by the Court could make it possible for the Community legislature and the Court of Justice to sidestep or relax the requirement of appreciability if they so desired.

Some indication that the latter concern may be justified is given by the judgment in the *Simone Leitner* case,[130] in which the Court of Justice was called upon to interpret Article 5 of Directive 90/314 on package holidays, which provided for liability to consumers for the proper performance of the obligations arising under a contract for a package holiday. The question referred to the Court of Justice was whether the latter Article was to be interpreted as meaning that compensation is in principle payable in respect of claims for compensation for non-material damage. The context of the reference was a claim for compensation in national proceedings in

---

[129] For a critical assessment of subsidiarity, and discussion of its application where internal market measures pursue public health aims, see A Arnull *et al*, above n 91, paras 4–018–21.

[130] Case C-168/00, *Simone Leitner v TUI Deutschland Gmbh & Co KG* [2002] ECR I-2631.

respect of a package holiday in the course of which the claimant had suffered food poisoning which had continued beyond the duration of the holiday. Her claim was for pain and suffering, and for non-material damage caused by loss of enjoyment of the holiday. The Court of Justice stated:

> It is not in dispute that, in the field of package holidays, the existence in some Member States but not in others of an obligation to provide compensation for non-material damage would cause significant distortions of competition, given that, as the Commission has pointed out, non-material damage is a frequent occurrence in that field.

> Furthermore, the Directive, and in particular Article 5 thereof, is designed to offer protection to consumers and, in connection with tourist holidays, compensation for non-material damage arising from the loss of enjoyment of the holiday is of particular importance to consumers.[131]

Neither the Court nor the Advocate General thought it necessary to define the expression 'non-material damage'. Normally, the term 'material damage' refers to pecuniary loss, resulting from an adverse effect on the economic situation of a claimant, and is to be contrasted with the term 'moral damage', which covers non-pecuniary loss, and refers to those losses which cannot immediately be calculated, as they do not amount to a tangible or material economic loss.[132] As is indicated above, the non-material damage in issue was loss of enjoyment of a holiday. The Court's readiness to accept that the existence in some Member States but not in others of an obligation to provide compensation for non-material damage would cause *significant* distortions of competition, suggests that the threshold for an *appreciable* distortion of competition, regarded by the Court in the *Tobacco Advertising* case as justifying measures of harmonisation, is to be assessed impressionistically.

The Court's observation in *Leitner* indicates that if the sole disparity between the laws of Member States on the subject matter of package holidays had been the possibility in some states but not in others of securing damages for loss of enjoyment of the holiday, that specific aspect of the law of contract could have been harmonised. This is a far cry from the appreciable distortion of competition identified in the *Tobacco Advertising* case itself; disparities between the laws of Member States on the

---

[131]   *Ibid*, paras 21 and 22.

[132]   See, eg the Explanatory Report on the Council of Europe Civil Law Convention on Corruption, para 38, referring to the concept of 'damage' in Art 3 of the Convention: <http://conventions.coe.int/Treaty/EN/Reports/Html/174.htm> accessed 3 September 2008. Anzillotti contrasts moral damage with material damage, and describes the latter as 'economic or property damage in the true sense of the word', see P-M Dupuy, 'Dionisio Anzilotti and the Law of International Responsibility of States' (1992) 3 *European Journal of International Law* 139, 142.

question of sponsorship of sporting events by tobacco companies, which could have the effect of determining in which Member State certain sporting events would take place. That is not to say that awards under the head of loss of enjoyment of the holiday might not be substantial, relative to the price of the holiday concerned. One of the cases cited by the Advocate General as an example of current national rules on the question of non-material damage was *Jarvis v Swan Tours*,[133] in which the Court of Appeal awarded compensation for loss of enjoyment equal to twice the price of the holiday concerned.

Providing against the risk of such liability certainly comprises part of the cost of doing business as a tour operator. However, the cost could only be regarded as significant as regards the relative competitive position of economic operators in different Member States if the risk was likely to materialise sufficiently frequently for the cost of provision against the risk to increase the *price* of holidays to a degree which consumers would *regard* as appreciable. The Court was ready simply to assume that the existence of the disparity could have this effect, based on the impressionistic approach that non-material damage is a frequent occurrence in the package holiday business. If the Court of Justice is willing to come to such conclusions on such a basis, what is probably the sole surviving competence restrictive aspect of the *Tobacco Advertising* case is unlikely to provide much deterrence to the Community legislature if it is minded to adopt Community rules on public health or consumer protection as internal market measures justified by the need to address 'appreciable' distortions of competition. The present writer has no objection to the conclusion of the Court of Justice in the *Leitner* case. That conclusion appears to be correct, for one of the reasons advanced by Advocate General Tizzano, who considered inter alia that the Directive should be interpreted as laying down a high level of protection for consumers, in accordance with Article 95(3) EC.[134]

However, it is unfortunate that the Court chose to base its conclusion on an argument which could undermine an otherwise potentially promising competence-restricting element of the *Tobacco Advertising* case. The requirement that distortions of competition be appreciable to justify harmonisation should be assessed by reference, in principle, and where possible, to quantitative criteria. That is to say, the Community institutions should, in principle, and where possible, address potential distortions of competition in quantitative terms. This is not an unreasonable approach. Indeed, it is consistent with the principle of subsidiarity, and would even seem to be required by it. The Protocol on Subsidiarity and Proportionality

---

[133] [1973] 1 All ER 71; [1972] 3 WLR 954.
[134] Case C-168/00, above n 130, point 26 of the Opinion.

lays down guidelines for compliance with the principle of subsidiarity. One guideline indicates a possible need for Community action where actions by Member States alone or lack of Community action would conflict with the requirements of the Treaty as regards the need to correct distortion of competition.[135] The Protocol furthermore states that 'the reasons for concluding that a Community objective can be better achieved by the Community must be substantiated by qualitative, or, *wherever possible, quantitative indicators*' (emphasis added).[136] The impressionistic approach in *Leitner* quite simply sends the wrong signals to the law-making institutions.

F. Recourse to Article 95 EC as a Legal Basis

It was suggested above that the Court's approach in the *Tobacco Advertising* case implied that the substantive provisions of the Directive must in all their applications make a contribution to the internal market, save for those provisions which do not, but which are justified by the need to avoid circumvention of those that do. This approach was described by the present writer as being competence restrictive, and contrasted with the broader approach of the Court to competence under Article 42 EC to adopt such social security measures as are necessary to ensure the free movement of workers. More recently, the Court of Justice has been willing to endorse provisions of internal market measures adopted on the basis of Article 95 EC which do not themselves make a contribution to the internal market on the ground that use of Article 95 EC as a legal basis does not presuppose an actual link with free movement in every situation covered by the measure concerned. In the context in which the Court asserts this principle in *Tobacco Advertising No 2*, it is uncontroversial. It upheld Community competence to prohibit tobacco advertising in periodicals, magazines and newspapers, since such a ban made a contribution to ensuring the free movement of those goods. It rejected Germany's argument that the Directive applied to advertising media of a local or national nature which lack cross-border effects, on the ground that '[r]ecourse to Article 95 EC as a legal basis does not presuppose the existence of an actual link with free movement between the Member States in every situation covered by the measure founded on that basis'.[137] In context, this is correct. Where disparities between national rules lead to harmonisation to remove obstacles to trade, it is self-evident that not all products to which the internal market rules relate will actually be traded across

---

[135] Protocol, at para 5.
[136] Protocol, at para 4.
[137] Case C-380/03, n 102 above, para 80.

national frontiers! If it is objected that the degree to which trade is liberalised does not justify the adoption of Community-wide product specifications, such an objection finds more appropriate expression in the principle of proportionality.[138]

The Court relied for the principle articulated in this case on recent case law concerning the legal basis of Directive 95/46 on the protection of individuals with regard to the processing of personal data and on the free movement of such data,[139] viz, the *Rundfunk* and *Lindqvist* cases.[140] *Rundfunk* concerned national rules requiring a state body to collect and transmit data on income for the purpose of publishing the names and incomes of employees of a broadcasting organisation governed by public law. The Court noted that Directive 95/46 was adopted on the basis of Article 95 EC, and was intended to ensure the free movement of personal data between Member States through the harmonisation of national provisions on the protection of individuals with regard to the processing of such data.[141] The Court observed that since any personal data can move between Member States, Directive 95/46 requires in principle compliance with the rules for protection of such data with respect to any processing of data.[142] Submissions made to the Court argued that application of the Directive to the facts of the national proceedings could have at best only remote and indirect effects on freedom of movement (*in casu* free movement of workers), and that that called in question the application of an internal market measure such as the Directive.[143]

The Court's response to this argument was that recourse to Article 95 EC as a legal basis for the Directive did not presuppose the existence of an actual link with free movement between Member States in every situation referred to by the measure founded on that basis. What *was* essential, said the Court, citing the *Tobacco Advertising* case, was that the Directive be actually intended to improve the conditions for the establishment and functioning of the internal market, but the Court noted that that was not

---

[138] Germany did indeed also allege breach of the principle of proportionality. The court held that it was not possible for the Community legislature to adopt, as a less restrictive measure, a prohibition on advertising from which publications intended for a local or regional market would be exempted, since such an exception would have rendered the field of application of the prohibition 'unsure and uncertain, which would have prevented the Directive from achieving its objective of harmonisation of national law on the advertising of tobacco products': see Case C-380/03, above n 102, para 149.

[139] [1995] OJ L281/31.

[140] Joined Cases C-465/00 and 138 & 139/01, *Rundfunk* [2003] ECR I-4989; and Case C-101/01, *Lindqvist* [2003] ECR I-12971.

[141] Joined Cases C-465/00 and 138 & 139/01, *ibid*, para 39.

[142] *Ibid*, para 40.

[143] *Ibid*, para 37.

in dispute.[144] That being the case, the Court emphasised that the applicability of Directive 95/46 could not depend on whether the specific situations at issue in the main proceedings have a sufficient link with the exercise of the fundamental freedoms guaranteed by the Treaty, such as *in casu*, the free movement of workers,[145] since:

> ... a contrary interpretation could make the limits of the field of application of the directive particularly unsure and uncertain, which would be contrary to its essential objective of approximating the laws ... of the Member States in order to eliminate obstacles to the functioning of the internal market deriving precisely from disparities between national legislations.[146]

The Court considers that this conclusion is confirmed by the wording of Article 3(1) of the Directive, which defines its scope in very broad terms, not making the application of the rules on protection depend on whether the processing has an actual connection with freedom of movement between Member States. Article 3(1) provides:

> This Directive shall apply to the processing of personal data wholly or partly by automatic means, and to the processing otherwise than by automatic means of personal data which form part of a filing system or are intended to form part of a filing system.

The Court argues that its conclusion that the application of the Directive cannot depend on a link with freedoms of movement is confirmed by the terms of various exceptions to the scope of the Directive, which the Court considers would have been worded differently if the Directive were applicable exclusively to situations where there is a sufficient link with the exercise of freedoms of movement.[147]

One of the exceptions referred to by the Court in this connection is contained in Article 3(2), and excludes from the scope of Article 3(1) of the Directive processing 'in the course of a purely personal or household activity'. Another is that contained in Article 8(2)(d), which provides an exception to Article 8(1) of the Directive.

Article 8(1) requires Member States to prohibit the processing of personal data revealing racial or ethnic origin, political opinions, religious or philosophical beliefs, trade union membership and the processing of data concerning health or sex life. Article 8(2) provides that paragraph 1 shall not apply where:

---

[144]   *Ibid*, para 41.
[145]   The reference to free movement of workers seems inappropriate, since Art 95(2) EC excludes from its scope provisions relating to the free movement of persons and to the rights and interests of employed persons. Recourse by implication to Art 40 EC is perhaps possible, which could justify regulation of data processing likely to adversely affect the free movement of workers. However, the court in *Rundfunk* refers only to Art 95 EC.
[146]   Joined Cases C-465/00 and 138 & 139/01, above n 140, para 42.
[147]   *Ibid*, para 43.

... processing is carried out in the course of its legitimate activities with appropriate guarantees by a foundation, association or any other non-profit-seeking body with a political, philosophical, religious or trade-union aim and on condition that the processing relates solely to the members of the body or to persons who have regular contact with it in connection with its purposes and that the data are not disclosed to a third party without the consent of the data subjects.

The line of argument being adopted by the Court is worthy of remark. Its point about the wording of the exceptions is that, if the scope of the Directive were confined to situations connected with freedom of movement, it would not be necessary to exclude processing such as that in the course of a purely household activity, or processing by non-profit-seeking bodies with aims of a political or philosophical nature, etc.

It is certainly the case that bodies such as those referred to in Article 8(2)(d), set out above, do not themselves fall within the scope of the provisions of the Treaty on freedom of establishment and to provide services—non-profit-making bodies are excluded from the scope of the chapters on establishment and services by Articles 48 and 55 EC. Moreover, data processing by such bodies, or by any natural or legal persons, for that matter, would seem to fall within the scope of the internal market only to the extent that the relevant data processing could be regarded as the provision of a service normally provided for remuneration within the meaning of Article 49 EC.[148] The Court is thus right to assume—as by implication it does—that the carrying out of data processing by such bodies is unlikely to fall within the scope of the free movement provisions of the internal market.

Yet it is to be noted that Article 8(2)(d) nevertheless *regulates* processing by such bodies, albeit less rigorously than would be required pursuant to Article 8(1), for Article 8(2)(d) excludes from Article 8(1) only processing carried out 'with appropriate guarantees', while imposing the condition of consent on release of data to third parties. Moreover, Article 8(1) would prohibit (subject to national exemptions pursuant to Article 8(4)) the processing of data of the kind referred to in that paragraph even where the processing were carried out, otherwise than for remuneration, by non-profit-seeking bodies, which could not, however, bring themselves within the scope of Article 8(2)(d), because of not pursuing aims falling within the scope of that provision. For example, a parents' voluntary group for the

---

[148] It is the case that 'goods' for the purposes of the provisions relating to the free movement of goods include objects of no commercial value, but only where they are 'shipped across a frontier for the purposes of commercial transactions': see Case C-2/90, *Commission v Belgium* [1992] ECR I-4431, para 26.

protection of local children, seeking to compile data on the local where-abouts of convicted sex offenders, would fall within the scope of both Article 8(1) and 8(5) of the Directive.[149]

It follows from the foregoing that the Directive applies to a number of situations where the data processing regulated by the Directive does not fall within the scope of Article 95 as an activity relating to the free movement of goods or services, since it is provided by a non-profit-making-body and does not amount to the provision of a service for remuneration. Nor does it seem possible to justify regulation by the need to eliminate appreciable distortions of competition, since no relevant economic activity is involved in the situations in question. Justification by reference to the free movement of workers is the possibility raised in argument in *Rundfunk*, but is difficult to square with the choice of Article 95 EC as Treaty base, which does not apply to the free movement of person,[150] and with the terms of the preamble of the Directive.

The preamble refers to the free movement of persons only in the context of a reference to the internal market in which the free movement of goods, persons, services and capital is ensured.[151] Article 1(1) of the Directive refers to protecting the fundamental rights and freedoms of natural persons, in particular their right to privacy, but this appears to be a reference to the European Convention on Human Rights and Fundamental Freedoms, and this is confirmed by Article 1(2), which provided that Member States shall neither restrict nor prohibit the free flow of personal data between Member States for reasons connected with the protection afforded under paragraph 1. The core definition of the internal market 'mischief' at which the Directive is aimed appears in recital (7) of the preamble, which states that the different levels of privacy protection for individuals in different Member States may prevent the inter-state trans-mission of data, and this difference 'may therefore constitute an obstacle to the pursuit of a number of economic activities at Community level, distort competition and impede authorities in the discharge of their responsibilities under Community law'. It would seem to follow that Directive 95/46 on data protection applies to a number of situations which fall outside its stated internal market rationale.

The approach of the Court in *Rundfunk* seems to differ from that in the *Tobacco Advertising* case. In the latter case, the Court condemned a

---

[149]   Art 8(5) provides that '[p]rocessing of data relating to offences, criminal conviction … may be carried out only under the control of official authority …'.
[150]   As noted above, Art 95(2) EC excludes from its scope provisions relating to the free movement of persons and to the rights and interests of employed persons. However, recourse by implication to Art 40 EC as a supplementary legal basis of the Directive is perhaps possible, which could justify regulation of data processing likely to adversely affect the free movement of workers.
[151]   Preamble, recital 3.

general prohibition on tobacco advertising because it could be demonstrated that it applied to 'numerous' situations in which such application could not make a contribution to freedom of movement. In *Rundfunk*, the Court endorses general coverage of the Directive on data protection on the ground that it is not necessary for there to be an actual link with free movement in every situation referred to by the measure founded upon that basis. What the Court might mean is simply that providing 'specifications' for all data processing of a particular type is necessary to achieve, for example, freedom to provide services in connection with data processing of that particular type, even if not all data processing of that particular type will be connected with cross-frontier service provision. That is the basis on which *Rundfunk* is cited in *Tobacco Advertising No 2*.

However, it does not seem that the Court's observations can be so limited, not least because the Court cites in support of its approach a provision of the Directive which both creates an exception to the strict requirements of the Directive for bodies apparently regarded by the Court as having no links with freedom of movement, nor with the provision of data processing services for remuneration, but which nevertheless subjects data processing by those bodies to regulation under the Directive. In truth, the approach of the Court of Justice in *Rundfunk* seems closer to that of the Court in its case law on the scope of Article 42 EC, which has been discussed above. That case law allows the possibility that a Treaty basis for social security measures to ensure the free movement of workers may apply to persons who *are* workers, but who are *not* engaged in free movement for the purposes of their work, and may apply even to persons who are not workers at all, on the ground that an alternative conclusion would be impracticable. *Rundfunk* appears similarly to allow the possibility that a Directive adopted under Article 95 EC to regulate data processing as a means of removing obstacles to cross-frontier economic activities and eliminating distortions of competition may apply data processing carried out inter alia for non-economic reasons by non-profit making bodies, on the ground that an alternative conclusion would make the limits of application of the Directive 'particularly unsure and uncertain'.

VII. CONCLUSIONS

The picture painted by the present writer is of an expansive approach to competence on the part of the Community law-making institutions and the Court of Justice. It is not contended that the approach of either should be unduly restrictive. However, what the present writer would contend is that putting some outer limits on Community competence to regulate the internal market is necessary. The competence to regulate the internal market currently enjoyed by the Community law-maker, in part de jure, in part de facto, amounts to a competence to regulate society, provided that the measures in question make some contribution to the internal market. Adopting internal measures solely on the basis that such measures are necessary in order to reduce legal uncertainty for those contemplating cross-frontier activities, or generally to facilitate freedom of movement, could lead to the increased use of such measures as instruments of general governance. This would not be consistent with the spirit of system based upon attribution of competences,[152] nor with a scheme in which decisions are to be taken 'as closely as possible to the citizen'.[153]

---

[152]   Art 5(1) EC.
[153]   Art 1 of the Treaty of European Union.

6

New EU Governance: The Case of Employment Policy

SAMANTHA VELLUTI

I. INTRODUCTION

IN THE LAST decade the European Union (EU) has seen the emergence of new approaches to governance other than supranational legal regulation in different policy domains, with techniques and enforcement mechanisms ranging from relatively 'hard' to 'soft'.[1] The use of soft law instruments and policy coordination to advance the European integration process is not a new phenomenon.[2] Soft law encompasses a variety of processes, the common feature of which is that 'while all have normative content they are not formally binding'.[3]

Forms of governance based on policy coordination processes have increased significantly in importance in the EU and have been given formal recognition in recent constitutional reforms of the Union. The defunct Constitutional Treaty recognised a new category of 'supporting, coordinating and complementary' competence,[4] although this was expressed as supplementary to the specific competence of coordinating economic and employment policies.[5] Similarly, the Lisbon Treaty includes these two categories of policy coordination and distinguishes between economic and employment policy coordination as a separate category of competence from that to 'support, coordinate or supplement' the actions of Member States.[6]

---

[1] J Scott and D Trubek, 'Mind the Gap: Law and New Approaches to Governance in the European Union' (2002) 8(1) *European Law Journal* 1.

[2] L Senden, *Soft Law in European Community Law* (Oxford, Hart, 2004).

[3] D Trubek, P Cottrell and M Nance, 'Hard and Soft Law in European Integration' in J Scott and G De Búrca (eds), *New Governance and Constitutionalism* (Oxford, Hart, 2006) 65.

[4] Pt III, Title III, Chapter V.

[5] Arts III-179 and III-206.

[6] Arts 2(5), 5 and 6 TFEU.

This chapter looks at the emergence and proliferation of new forms of regulation and associated legal instruments and governance techniques in the EU. The focus of analysis is on the Open Method of Coordination (OMC) and its application to the field of employment policy. The first section provides a framework of analysis by situating the study of the European Employment Strategy (EES) in the context of New Governance and constitutionalism debates. The second section looks at the historical background and origins of the EES, examining the main reasons leading to its creation and launch. This analysis provides a first important insight into the strengths and weaknesses of the strategy. The third and fourth sections critically discuss the structure, operation and effectiveness of the EES and its main regulatory tool, the OMC, at the levels of policy formulation, implementation and enforcement. There is a particular focus on its main features and objectives in order to identify elements of continuity and break from previous modes of regulation.

The investigation takes place on two levels of enquiry: a substantive level, that is, a social/employment policy level; and a governance/ constitutional level. This analytical approach will enable the chapter to meet its threefold objective. First, to unfold the different reasons which explain the emergence of experimental modes of governance such as the EES. Secondly, to explore in what way, and to what extent, they can be defined as 'new' in comparison to the more traditional instruments used in the Community Method. Thirdly, from the perspective of effectiveness, to examine critically the level of convergence in terms of policy objectives and the degree of open participation that they purport to ensure. This analysis is important because it helps us to unravel and discuss the implications for EU social governance and what these regulatory techniques may signify for social rights.

II. NEW GOVERNANCE AND EU CONSTITUTIONALISM: FRIENDS OR FOES?

The EU and its evolving integration process rest upon a complex and dynamic balance between intergovernmental and supranational forces, co-existing within its regulatory framework. One of the key challenges to the EU system is finding ways to maintain its capacity to operate and function efficiently and adapt its policy and decision-making system to the changing conditions of its regulatory framework.

The current EU is a highly institutionalised template for integration, equipped with a whole spectrum of different modes of regulation ranging from 'hard' to 'soft' which, particularly in recent years, have been pragmatically combined to develop a hybrid and multi-tiered EU system: recourse to a single process of integration, based on a single structure, has been made untenable by several waves of enlargement and the typology of new competencies which have required an increase in the diversity and flexibility of both policy and legal responses.

As a consequence, there is a constantly growing tension between the traditional sectors and modes of integration, where the Community Method is applied, and new policy areas, where experimental forms of integration are being developed and applied.[7] Tellingly, the 'dramatic expansion of the EU governance tool-kit and hybridization of the objectives and internal structures of these EU governance tools'[8] have relied on a non-clearly identifiable mix of legal and policy instruments. These changes in EU governance pose a challenge to the rule of law and its main tenets and do not sit well with the European Court of Justice (ECJ). Szyszczak aptly defines these changes as entailing a shift from 'court-watching' to 'agenda-watching'.[9]

These new approaches to EU governance force European scholars to rethink the way in which the EU system operates and the way in which Europeanisation is being pursued. Any attempt to situate 'New' Governance within well-defined theoretical frameworks becomes a challenging enterprise, as the processes falling under this umbrella term and, in particular, their definition, modes of operation and effectiveness, are not undisputed.[10] As Armstrong points out, new forms of governance pose a challenge to EU constitutionalism because they occupy an unsettled constitutional space. This space is characterised by a range of possible encounters between constitutionalism and governance.[11] Armstrong 'characterize[s] these as involving "accommodation"—an ability of one to co-exist with the other without change to either—"adaptation"—an encounter which alters in a limited manner one and/or the other—and "transformation"—a more fundamental change to either governance or constitutionalism—as well as "antagonism"—manifested as either incompatibility or irritation'.[12]

The OMC provides a good ground of analysis as it has rapidly become a Community mode of governance in its own right and has been employed in different policy domains other than the social field. The chapter's point of

---

[7] J Zeitlin, 'Social Europe and Experimentalist Governance: Towards a New Constitutional Compromise?' in G De Búrca (ed), *EU Law and the Welfare State: In Search of Solidarity* (Oxford, Oxford University Press, 2005) 213.

[8] C Kilpatrick, 'New EU Employment Governance and Constitutionalism' in G De Búrca and J Scott (eds), *Law and New Governance in the EU and the US* (Oxford, Hart, 2006) 121.

[9] E Szyszczak, 'The Evolving European Employment Strategy' in J Shaw (ed), *Social Law and Policy in an Evolving European Union* (Oxford, Hart, 2000) 197, 218.

[10] K Armstrong and C Kilpatrick, 'Law, Governance, Or Governance? The Changing Open Method of Coordination' (2007) 13(3) *Columbia Journal of European Law* 649.

[11] K Armstrong, 'Governance and Constitutionalism after Lisbon' (2008) 46(2) *Journal of Common Market Studies* 415, 416.

[12] *Ibid.*

departure is that the OMC, beyond any definitional issue, should be viewed as another form of European integrative experiment without entailing a 'systemic change to the underlying constitutional settlement of 1957'.[13]

Further, the OMC represents a response to a variety of regulatory shortcomings of the EU and is part of a broader redesign of the EU. As Weiler emphatically predicted in one of his seminal papers back in 1991, 'Today's Community is impelled forward by the dysfunctioning of its current architecture'.[14] The 'invention' of the OMC should be seen as part of the ongoing search for new forms and methodologies of integrative policy-making and rule-setting in the context of the EU's evolving nature and ability to mutate and adapt itself constantly to external and internal change.[15]

III. THE BACKGROUND AND ORIGINS OF THE EES

The creation and further development of the Single Market added to calls for a complementary emphasis on social issues. As Scharpf explains, the course of European integration from the 1950s onward generated a fundamental asymmetry between market efficiency and market correcting policies due to the Communitarisation of economic policies which reached its apex with the creation of the Economic and Monetary Union (EMU) whilst, at the same time, social and labour policies remained the domain of national decision-making.[16] Prior to the Social Policy Agreement annexed to the EC Treaty in 1992, there was no firm legal basis for EU social policy proposals and thus no clear scope of Community intervention in this area.

Further, the Maastricht Treaty with its emphasis on economic convergence and controls on the recourse Member States could make to fiscal, monetary or exchange rate policies, strengthened such arguments as the creation of a *euro-zone*, entailed a reconfiguration of macroeconomic policy instruments available to Member States and forced a rethinking and

---

[13] E Szyszczak, 'Experimental Governance: The Open method of Coordination' (2006) 12(4) *European Law Journal* 486, 487. See also S Velluti, 'Towards the Constitutionalisation of New Forms of Governance: A Revised Institutional Framework for the European Employment Strategy' (2003) 22 *Yearbook of European Law* 353, 358.

[14] J Weiler, 'The transformation of Europe' (1991) 100 *Yale Law Journal* 2403, 2483.

[15] *Ibid.*

[16] F Scharpf, 'The European Social Model: Coping with the Challenges of Diversity' (2002) 40(4) *Journal of Common Market Studies* 645.

rationalisation of national social security systems[17] and demands to recreate a 'level playing field' by Europeanising social policies as well.[18]

The origins of the EES, therefore, may be traced back to the immediate post-Maastricht period. Although concerns over high unemployment levels throughout the EU already existed towards the end of the 1980s and proposals for having some degree of EU competence in the social arena had already been put forward, it was during the early 1990s that high employment and job creation became top priority on the Community agenda.

In the White Paper on *Growth, Competitiveness and Employment*,[19] considered as the watershed document for the Community's approach to unemployment,[20] the Commission provided an array of different solutions to tackle unemployment and strategies to enhance job creation. This White Paper was particularly significant since it not only launched an overall debate on the coordination of economic and employment policies at European level, but also brought the issue of employment on to the Community's top agenda. The White Paper was also innovatory in the way that it aimed at reforming labour markets by introducing flexibility and promoting atypical forms of work and drew on the conclusions of the Green Paper on *European Social Policy*,[21] which called for new responses and measures to address technological and structural change in world economy.

While employment has been a main feature of post-Treaty of European Union (TEU) debates on social policy, the issue crystallised as a priority with the conclusions of the European Council at Essen in 1994. Five key priority areas for tackling unemployment emerged in the conclusions of that summit with a mix of deregulatory and active labour market policies.[22] These priorities included increasing the intensity of employment growth through more flexible organisation of work and reduction of non-wage labour costs, together with the promotion of investment in vocational training and active labour market policies.

From a procedural perspective, the most salient aspect of the Essen Council was that it set out a multi-annual programme of guidelines and

---

[17] I Begg, 'EMU and EMPLOYMENT. Social models in the EMU: Convergence? Co-existence? The role of economic and social actors', Working Paper 42/02, *One Europe or Several?*, 4. Available at <http://www.sbu.ac.uk/euroinst/oneeurope/papers.html> accessed 5 June 2008.

[18] Scharpf, above n 16.

[19] COM(93) 700 final, White Paper on Growth, Competitiveness and Employment.

[20] C Barnard, 'EC Social Policy' in P Craig and G De Búrca (eds), *The Evolution of EU Law* (Oxford, Oxford University Press, 1999) 479, 487.

[21] COM(93) 551, Green Paper on European Social Policy.

[22] Presidency Conclusions of the Essen European Council (9–10 December 1994), available at <http://europa.eu/european_council/conclusions/index_en.htm> accessed 3 September 2008.

reports in relation to employment and job creation, drawing its inspiration from economic coordination procedures,[23] which was to be the blueprint for the subsequent employment chapter and operation of the EES.

The 'Essen Strategy' failed to develop into a Community employment policy process.[24] This was due to a major and significant limitation to the Europeanisation of social and employment policy, which, as will be shown, also besets the EES, undermining its effective operation. The main problem with such strategies is that they are constrained a priori by the diversity of national welfare states, differing not only in levels of economic development, but also in their normative and socio-philosophical aspirations and institutional structures.[25] Hence, while the option of uniform European employment legislation has been ruled out in favour of a soft coordination process with the specific aim of addressing national diversity, the creation of a 'European' strategy nevertheless presupposes a 'European' model and thus a 'European' solution to be applied to common problems at national level. The solution to this conundrum has been the development of a strategy that is not a reality in the sense in which we think of national welfare state measures, but rather a governance tool that remains highly aspirational, incorporating a broad set of ideals, objectives and parameters to which all European welfare states may loosely conform.

This is an intrinsic weakness in strategies such as the EES and shows how social and employment policy relate not to the provision of social services, but are designed to prevent, mitigate or alleviate the negative effects of economic development within the EU on the social sphere, due also to the fact that the EU is currently not an 'optimum currency area'.[26] This situation is aggravated by the fact that the EMU has itself internal contradictions because the economic dimension of monetary union has been instrumental in the creation of the EMU and, more broadly, in the European project rather than being the reason for having the EMU.[27] This

---

[23] C De La Porte, 'Is the Open Method of Co-ordination Appropriate for Organising Activities at European Level in Sensitive Policy Areas?' (2002) 8(1) *European Law Journal* 38.

[24] For a critical analysis of the 'Essen Priorities', see D Meulders and R Plasman, 'European Economic Policies and Social Quality' in W Beck, F van der Maesen, Thomése and A Walker (eds), *The Social Quality of Europe* (The Hague, Kluwer Law International, 1997) 3, 31–3.

[25] Scharpf, above n 16.

[26] G Tavlas, 'The "New" Theory of Optimum Currency Areas' (1993) 16 *World Economy* 663; and L Navarro, 'As the euro prepares for take off: a critical review of the first three years of EMU' (2001) 9 *Groupement D'Etudes et De Recherches Notre Europe* 12. For a theory of the 'optimum currency area', see R Mundell, 'A Theory of Optimal Currency Area' (1961) 51 *American Economic Review* 657; and R McKinnon, 'Optimum Currency Areas' (1963) 53 *American Economic Review* 717.

[27] P De Grauwe, *The Economics of Monetary Union* (Oxford, Oxford University Press, 1997). See also RM Lastra, 'The Independence of the European Central Bank' (1992) 33 *Harvard Journal of International Law* 475.

has led to a primacy of monetary convergence over real convergence, with significant negative spill-over effects on national welfare systems.

At the 1997 Amsterdam Summit, a new Title on Employment was inserted in the Treaty, Title VIII,[28] and amendments were made to the old Title VIII, on Social Policy, Education, Vocational Training and Youth, which became the new Title XI.[29] The latter Title, as revised, finalised the establishment of the European Social Dialogue. Title VIII is to be read together with Title VII on Economic and Monetary Policy: the combined effect of these two titles is a strategy to promote employment based on the coordination of Member States' macroeconomic policies and structural reforms. Article 126 EC obliges Member States to pursue their employment policies in a way that is consistent with the broad guidelines of the economic policies of the Member States and of the Community.

The EES was immediately fast-tracked by the Luxemburg Extraordinary European Council Meeting on Employment, the 'Luxemburg Process',[30] before the ratification of the Treaty of Amsterdam. While Title XI may be said to consolidate horizontally accepted judicial and political practice, Title VIII on the other hand may be said to consolidate political and proactive thinking in the social field elaborated by the Commission through the use of ad hoc soft law instruments.[31] These changes have greatly contributed to the further development of a European social and employment policy departing from the narrow guise of labour law and labour market regulation, with major repercussions on Member States' competence in this area. Since then, EC employment policy has gradually taken on an independent identity and has helped to revive and re-conceptualise the European Social Model.[32]

When it was set up and in its first years of implementation, the EES was greeted with great enthusiasm by those who advocated a stronger 'Social Europe'. The EES was considered to represent a sea change in the EU law-making process both at national and European levels,[33] owing to its

---

[28] Arts 125–30 EC.

[29] Arts 136–43 EC.

[30] Presidency Conclusions of the Extraordinary Luxembourg European Council Meeting on Employment (20–21 November 1997). Available at <http://europa.eu/european_council/conclusions/index_en.htm> accessed 3 September 2008.

[31] Szyszczak, above n 9, 197–8.

[32] The 'European Social Model' concept is reflected through three basic principles: (i) the recognition of social justice as a policy target; (ii) the acceptance of the productive role of social policy and its contribution to economic efficiency; and (iii) the development of a process of high level bargaining between the social partners. For a detailed analysis of the European Social Model, see M Jepsen and A Serrano Pascual, 'The European Social Model: An Exercise in Deconstruction' (2005) 15(3) *Journal of European Social Policy* 231.

[33] S Régent, 'The Open Method of Coordination: A New Supranational Form of Governance?' (2003) 9(2) *European Law Journal* 190.

reliance on iterative processes, *bottom-to-top* policy-making and deliberative forms of democracy. Further, it was touted as entailing a shift from
'social law and legislative initiatives, towards soft law, or rather policies
aimed at employment creation, which for the most part eschew legislation'.[34]

However, most of these initial evaluations of the EES were limited in
scope since they focused chiefly on the procedures employed in the EES
and policy formulation rather than on its real impact in terms of the
content of national policies and policy outcomes. In the years that
followed, both theoretical analyses and empirical studies have revisited and
assessed more critically the 'newness' of the EES and its regulatory tool, the
OMC, and their much claimed participatory nature, and have highlighted
their failure to meet initial expectations, particularly in terms of policy
results.[35] The examination of the EES and its implementation through the
OMC, which follows in the next two sections, benefits from this copious
literature and builds upon some of these more recent empirical accounts of
the functioning and efficiency of the EES and the OMC.

IV. STRUCTURE, MODE OF OPERATION AND OBJECTIVES OF THE EES

A. Structure and Functioning of the EES

The EES is a cyclical and multi-level governance process involving several
steps[36]:

(i) adoption of a joint annual report; employment guidelines; national
     reports on employment;
(ii) definition of indicators, identification and exchange of best practices;

---

[34] D Ashiagbor, *The European Employment Strategy. Labour Market Regulation and New
Governance* (Oxford, Oxford University Press, 2005) 317.
[35] See, eg *ibid*, D Chalmers and M Lodge, 'The Open Method of Coordination and the
European Welfare State', Paper No 11 (ESRC Centre for Analysis of Risk and Regulation,
London School of Economics and Political Science, 2003); M Barbera (ed), *Nuove Forme di
Regolazione: Il Metodo Aperto di Coordinamento delle Politiche Sociali* (Milano, Giuffrè,
2006); M Buechs, *New Governance in European Social Policy: the Open Method of
Coordination* (Basingstoke, Palgrave Macmillan, 2007); K Jacobsson and A Vifell, 'New
Governance Structures in Employment Policy-Making' in I Linsenmann, O Meyer and W
Wessels, *Economic Government of the EU A Balance Sheet of New Modes of Policy
Coordination* (Basingstoke, Palgrave Macmillan, 2007); J Zeitlin, P Pochet and L Magnusson,
*Open Method of Coordination in Action: The European Employment and Social Inclusion
Strategies* (Brussels, P.I.E-Peter Lang, 2005); and F Beveridge and S Velluti (eds), *Gender and
the Open Method of Coordination—Perspectives on Law, Governance and Equality in the
EU* (Aldershot, Ashgate, 2008).
[36] Arts 128–30 EC.

(iii) monitoring and peer review; and

(iv) adoption of recommendations and incentive measures.

Initially, it was based on a four-'pillar' structure, with a series of employment guidelines centred around these pillars:

(i) to improve employability;

(ii) to create a new culture of entrepreneurship;

(iii) to promote and encourage the adaptability of firms and their workers; and

(iv) to strengthen equal opportunities policies.

The main objectives were: higher employment participation, increasing active unemployment systems, the number of highly skilled workers and employment intensive growth indicators, helping maintain the lower skilled workers in employment, striking a balance between flexibility and security, supporting and promoting the start up of smaller companies and entrepreneurship and promoting gender equality.[37]

Although the pillars and guidelines have a clear Treaty basis in Title VIII, they pertain to the sphere of soft law since they are not produced in the form of legally binding instruments such as directives or regulations. Despite their 'soft' nature, these guidelines have important implications for policy and law-making within the Member States. In addition, the EC Treaty provides that legislation and regulation is still a matter for Member States. Articles 127 EC and 129 EC make it clear that Member States' competence in the field of employment must be respected and that measures taken by the Council to promote employment shall not include harmonisation of the laws and regulations of the Member States. Moreover, there are no legal sanctions to be imposed on any Member State that fails to comply with the employment guidelines.

Following an impact evaluation report in 2002 and key communications in which the Commission outlined a redesign of the EES,[38] the strategy was simplified with the employment guidelines reduced to 'ten commandments', streamlined with the economic coordination process and transformed into a three-year policy cycle, the focus being on full employment, quality and productivity of work and cohesion and inclusion. The EES was subject to another significant revision in 2005 following the re-launch of

---

[37] D Trubek and J Mosher, 'New Governance, Employment Policy and the European Social Model' in J Zeitlin and D Trubek (eds), *Governing Work and Welfare in a New Economy: European and American Experiments* (Oxford, Oxford University Press, 2003).

[38] COM(2002) 416 final, Taking Stock of Five Years of the European Employment Strategy; COM(2002) 487 final, Annual Economic and Employment Policy Coordination Cycles; and COM(2003) 6 final, The Future of the European Employment Strategy.

the Lisbon Strategy pursuant to the recommendations of the Kok Report.[39] This new process sees the adoption of Integrated Guidelines for Growth and Jobs (2005–2008). Reduced from 10 to eight, the employment guidelines are now part of the package of 24 guidelines of the Lisbon Strategy. The guidelines are presented in conjunction with the macroeconomic and microeconomic guidelines (previously named 'Broad Economic Policy Guidelines') for a period of three years.

Despite these changes, the employment guidelines have maintained the same principles on which they were originally based. Apart from the guidelines concerning equal opportunities, all of the other guidelines form part of a supply-side strategy that focuses on the structural problems of unemployment, in line with a neo-liberal conception of economic integration.[40] Theoretically, they are a combination of neo-liberal policy objectives stressing deregulation and individual responsibility for training and labour market mobility, and neo-corporatist strategies which envisage collective solutions to the reconciliation of flexibility and security. However, their 'accent' remains strongly neo-liberal. These guidelines are the basis for the Community Lisbon Programme and the National Reform Programmes, to be delivered at the end of the three-year cycle. During the three-year cycle, Joint Employment Reports and National Implementation Reports from the Member States continued to be submitted by the end of each year.

In the years that followed, EC employment policy still gathered momentum. The employment situation improved considerably in the year 2000. Growth increased and unemployment declined steadily in most European countries. It was this positive economic and social scenario that propelled the political drive for the launch of the Lisbon Strategy. At the Lisbon Summit,[41] Member States agreed a new overarching and strategic goal for the Union for the next decade: to make the EU the most competitive knowledge-based economy in the world, establishing a nexus between employment, economic reform and social cohesion, the main aim being to put the EU on an equal footing with the US and Japan.[42]

The key achievement of the Lisbon Summit was to provide a clear and positive link between social, employment and economic issues and to place the renewal of the European Social Model at the heart of an integrated

---

[39] W Kok *et al*, *Facing the Challenge: The Lisbon Strategy for Growth and Employment*, Report from the High Level Group (Luxembourg, OOPEC, 2004).

[40] Scharpf, above n 16, 654–5.

[41] Presidency Conclusions of the Lisbon European Council, 23–24 March 2000, available at <http://europa.eu/european_council/conclusions/index_en.htm> accessed 3 September 2008.

[42] The Lisbon goal of becoming the most competitive and dynamic economy in the world has now been abandoned.

economic and employment strategy.[43] In particular, Lisbon emphasises a fundamental transformation of the European Social Model from merely activating the unemployed, to the Adult Worker Model goal of promoting employment for all adults.[44] This entails increasing economic activity rates overall, getting all adults—including those conventionally excluded from the labour market—into employment and ensuring adequate levels of social protection.[45]

B. The Creation of the OMC as a Governance Template for Building 'Social Europe'

The Lisbon Presidency Conclusions provided a detailed list of new actions, initiatives and measures confirming that social policy remained firmly on the Community agenda with the further implementation of the EES and formalisation of its regulatory tool, the OMC. The latter refers to a mode of governance which relies on the use of soft law techniques and methods used either in areas in which there has traditionally been a very narrow margin of opportunity for action at European level, or in areas that have never been in the remit of Community decision-making. In particular, it was decided that the priority areas in the framework of the OMC were to be employment, social protection, social security and education. Hence, the rigid traditional procedures of the Community Method were replaced by a softer approach to policy-making in which the employment, economic reform and macro-economic reform processes became increasingly coordinated.

The OMC, launched at the Lisbon Summit, has its origins in the Treaty provisions of the EMU and, in particular, in the 'hard' EC fiscal procedures and the 'soft' coordination processes of national economic policies.[46] The same definition of this novel regulatory tool as an 'open method of coordination' signifies the decision to include different policy areas of EU law and actors into the EES.[47] In addition, it also refers to targets being mostly not quantified. This process, defined in general terms by the European Council, structured in more detail by the Commission and the Council and implemented under the supervision of the Commission and in most cases ad hoc EU committees, relies upon peer pressure. The constraint

---

[43]   Ashiagbor, above n 34.
[44]   C Annesley, 'Lisbon and Social Europe: Towards a European "Adult Worker Model" Welfare System' (2007) 17 *Journal of European Social Policy* 195.
[45]   COM(2005) 141 final, Integrated Guidelines for Growth and Jobs, 28.
[46]   De La Porte, above n 23, 40–1.
[47]   M Telò, 'Governance and Government in the European Union. The Open Method of Co-ordination' in MJ Rodriguez (ed), *The New Knowledge Economy in Europe* (London, Elgar, 2001).

on Member States is not a legal one, since the OMC lacks any system of sanctions and enforcement procedures; it is rather a moral or political constraint. It was also agreed that a fully decentralised approach would be applied in line with the principle of subsidiarity in which the EU, the Member States, the regional and local levels, as well as the social partners and civil society, would be actively involved, using variable forms of partnership.

The Lisbon Summit was particularly significant for EC social policy in that it provided a new constitutional architecture for expanding Community competence in the area of social policy.

C. The Objectives of the EES

The EES has been conceived with the aim of developing a social dimension to the activities of the EU. The EES trades off the legal force of traditional regulations in order for the EU to deal with some key areas of social policy that, until 1997, were solely reserved to the Member States.[48]

The EES does not cover all policies related to employment. Important areas such as monetary, fiscal and wage policy, concerning economic and employment growth in the EU, are not included in the EES. This explains why the EES has been streamlined with the economic coordination process and then subsequently subsumed into the Lisbon Strategy to form Integrated Guidelines.

A limitation to the effective functioning of the EES is that the way in which it operates does not challenge the *acquis* of the Internal Market and the EMU, which remain the paramount objectives of the Community. Even when responding to the guidelines, therefore, Member States continue to operate under exactly the same legal and economic constraints of economic integration, limiting their policy choices whenever they act individually. Moreover, the stress on working flexibility and the role of entrepreneurship in creating jobs embody the 'Third Way' emphasis on overcoming dependency and show acceptance of the need to promote risk-taking and adapt social protection to the business needs for flexibility. Nonetheless, the EES foresees an important role for the state and for the social partners: it presumes that the core of the welfare state will remain in force and does not envisage major changes in the organisation of industrial relations. Moreover, the EES is a strategy that looks at reform and re-calibration in the short term, with a gradual shift towards major restructuring in the long term.

---

[48] Ashiagbor, above n 34.

In addition to developing a social dimension to the EU, the EES aims at achieving six other major objectives[49]:

(i) legitimacy of Community action;
(ii) promotion of transnational forms of governance whilst maintaining a certain degree of convergence;
(iii) efficiency of policy-making at European and national level;
(iv) increase of policy coordination among all levels of governance;
(v) promotion of greater interaction between different policy areas; and
(vi) promotion of policy learning.

The first four objectives have always been pursued by the EC institutions in the difficult achievement of further promoting the European integration process. Hence, from this perspective, the EES does not represent an entirely new mode of governance. Rather, it may be defined as constituting a *tertium genus*, that is, a middle way, in that it presents elements of continuity with previous methods of policy-making in the field of social law and, at the same time, represents an innovative and qualitative break with the past, chiefly *in the way* in which these objectives are pursued.

An innovative feature of the EES that may be said to be 'new' is that it integrates separate policy domains (objective 5). The four pillars and related guidelines cover a variety of different issues, although some areas such as fiscal and wage policy are not covered by the strategy. This explains why the EES has been streamlined with the economic coordination process and then included in the Lisbon Strategy to form Integrated Guidelines. The EES has also brought changes to the objectives of the EU social agenda. In comparison with previous EU social measures, the EES focuses on issues that directly affect national employment and industrial relations systems. However, as explained earlier, the EES operates within the overarching framework of the Internal Market and the EMU, which limit its effective functioning.

Another innovative objective of the EES is the promotion of policy learning (objective 6). Easterby-Smith, Crossan and Nicolini have listed various regulatory mechanisms which enhance policy learning, such as mechanisms that reconfigure policy networks, foster cooperation between different policy areas, promote multi-tiered forms of policy-making, promote decentralisation, produce information on innovation, foster the

---

[49] Trubek and Mosher, above n 37; and J Goetschy, 'The European Employment Strategy, Multi-level Governance and Policy Co-ordination: Past, Present and Future' in J Zeitlin and D Trubek (eds), *Governing work and welfare in a new economy: European and American experiments* (Oxford, Oxford University Press, 2003).

exchange and benchmarking of best practices, or promote deliberative modes of governance for problem solving.[50]

The EES presents most of these features: its iterative process consisting of the adoption of guidelines, national reports and recommendations aims at introducing change at national level in the way in which welfare issues are conceived and measures adopted. Moreover, the strategy aims at creating partnerships between different stakeholders and levels of authority, exemplifying the deliberative nature of the strategy. There are also several benchmarking mechanisms and to this end structural indicators have been developed. The existence of these mechanisms fostering policy learning clearly shows that the EES does aim at promoting policy learning and innovation, although these mechanisms need to be implemented more effectively. Empirical studies show that such changes have only concerned the stage of policy formulation entailing the adoption of new guidelines and amendments to the national reports, which have remained programmatic. Moreover, where change has occurred at national level it has been difficult to identify a causal link between the EES and the new measures adopted at domestic level. Hence, data on operational and institutional change at national level has either been tentative or speculative.

V. ACHIEVEMENTS AND SHORTCOMINGS OF THE EES

While the political-institutional structure of social solidarity in Europe has remained national, its substance has changed. In this context, the EES within the Lisbon Strategy plays an important role in changing the policy rationales and discourses on which labour and employment measures adopted at domestic level are premised.

The EES is consistent with its attempts to create an active welfare state in the context of 'competitive solidarity',[51] replacing protectionist social protection systems with a focus on measures that improve employment and earning capacity and remove the disincentives for activity, either within or outside the formal labour market.

Embedded in a policy environment which has removed their control over traditional instruments of macroeconomic policy, the EES is an attempt to reduce

---

[50]   M Easterby-Smith, M Crossan and D Nicolini, 'Organisational Learning: Debates Past, Present and Future' (2000) 98(2) *Columbia Law Review* 267.
[51]   W Streeck, 'Competitive Solidarity: Rethinking the "European Social Model"' in K Hinrichs *et al* (eds), *Kontingenz und Krise: Institutionenpolitik in kapitalistischen und postsozialistischen Gesellschaften* (Frankfurt am Main, Campus, 2000) 245.

the willingness of national governments and politicians to condone high unemployment and inactivity, and strengthen their resolve to engage in reform.[52]

According to Visser, by focusing on the employability of workers in combination with adaptability policies, the supply-side egalitarianism on which the EES is premised would make ex post political redistribution less pressing.[53] However, as explained below, the EES has fallen short of reaching these initial expectations.[54]

Among the most salient features used in the EES there are what Jacobsson has defined as 'discursive regulatory mechanisms', which although not unique to this method are herein employed systematically.[55] In particular, the EES provides a common cognitive framework for understanding and describing problems in national labour markets and for identifying workable solutions that are adaptable to the different socio-economic context of different welfare systems. Thus, concepts and categories developed in the context of the iterative process of the EES are increasingly used in national labour market policy discourse and have had at least a symbolic impact nationally.[56] Moreover, peer review and critique is now seen by the Member States as a legitimate exercise and has been institutionalised as a governance procedure to take place on a regular basis.[57] Similarly, Ashiagbor talks about the emergence of a common discourse among elite actors. She argues that we can identify a transfer effect generated by the EES via the OMC, which, although less coercive than the one resulting from traditional hard law measures, may change policy discourse within Member States, altering the boundaries of what is considered an acceptable range of policy choices for Member States.[58] Particularly with the Lisbon Strategy, a policy paradigm emphasising prevention, activation and lifelong learning has clearly been established. It follows that the legal significance of national reports lies *in the way* in which Member States interpret and use the concepts developed in the EES, as well as how the Commission and Council use the information and

---

[52] J Visser, 'Is the European Employment Strategy the Answer?' Paper Prepared for the NIG Workshop 'Governability in Post-Industrial Societies: The European Experience', Utrecht School of Governance, 26–27 April 2002.

[53] *Ibid.*

[54] By contrast, see the Commission's recent evaluation report of the EES: European Commission, 'Ten Years of the European Employment Strategy (EES)', Directorate-General for Employment, Social Affairs and Equal Opportunities Unit D.2 Manuscript completed in July 2007. Available at <http://ec.europa.eu/employment_social/publications/2007/ke7807329_en.pdf> accessed 3 September 2008.

[55] K Jacobsson, 'Soft Regulation and the Subtle Transformation of States: The Case of EU Employment Policy' (2004) 14(4) *Journal of European Social Policy* 355.

[56] *Ibid.*

[57] See, eg <http://www.mutual-learning-employment.net/> accessed 3 September 2008.

[58] Ashiagbor, above n 34, 233.

knowledge gathered in transforming them into standards and structural indicators that Members States then use to develop their labour and employment policies.

However, the EES has also been disappointing on several grounds. With regard to participatory democracy and social partnership, the studies showed that even where the implementation of the employment guidelines appear to be most influential, such as in Sweden and Denmark, the EES had little direct relation with decisions made within the domestic labour-market policy process, and the apparent success of the EES was mainly due to similar objectives. Moreover, the whole process has been mainly administered at ministerial level and in most countries parliamentary bodies have been excluded from the EES process, without the possibility of any decision-making input in the preparation of national reports. Knowledge about the EES is generally not well diffused in the national or sub-national labour market administrations or in civil society.[59] In particular, the involvement of social partners has been more formalistic and passive, that is, more a matter of information than real consultation or negotiation with governments. Recent studies show greater participation, although the degree of the social partners' contribution varies according to the area taken into consideration and also depends on which management or labour representatives have been involved in the process.[60]

However, on the whole, the role of the social partners in the EES remains unsatisfactory. Casey argues that the strategy's contribution to the development of a social partnership approach has been disappointing. In his study, he explains how this approach has not succeeded in depoliticising employment-related problems from national contingencies.[61] Furthermore, the EES illustrates the elitist nature of social partnership in practice by including certain organisations and excluding others, which may have hindered necessary reformulation of employment policy.

Hence, the EES has various weaknesses, most of which are inherent in its soft law nature. For the purposes of this chapter, those which hinder its potential ability to be a workable mode of governance will be highlighted. First, the very nature of the EES as a non-binding legal instrument does not allow for accurate assessment of the results achieved, given that national measures may not be based on the employment guidelines to be adopted and that many elements of the EES are already part of national policy programmes. Secondly, the subordination of EES implementation to the economic situation and political vagaries at national level does not guarantee its further development in moments of economic recession or

---

[59] Jacobsson and Vifell, above n 35.
[60] *Ibid.*
[61] B Casey, 'Building Social Partnership? Strengths and Shortcomings of the European Employment Strategy' (2005) 1 *Transfer* 45.

political instability. Further, developing a transnational system of target-setting, benchmarking and peer review with limited enforcement powers may allow Member States to reduce the possibility of unexpected and unwanted consequences, that is, of real structural changes in areas where the OMC is implemented.[62] In addition, the absence of any clear definition of the distribution of competence, particularly at national level, and, finally, the lack of any system of legal or formal sanctions in the event of non-alignment of a given Member State with the employment guidelines, seriously undermine the legitimacy and effectiveness of the strategy.

There is one further problem concerning the EES and the OMC and their relationship with constitutionalism: given that Title VIII provides a legal framework whereby the soft law discourse may be translated into binding normative rules, what are the implications that these experimental and non-binding regulatory techniques may have for social rights? Or more simply, what should their relationship be? One can view this relationship either as one where fundamental social rights, conceived as substantive rights, have a corrective or limitative function in relation to New Governance or, following a more Habermasian approach that considers fundamental social rights as procedural or participatory rights, as one in which New Governance and, in particular, the OMC becomes a means to implementing fundamental social rights.

Andronico and Lo Faro identify one main reason for coupling the OMC with fundamental rights. They maintain that while the OMC is said to guarantee diversity, fundamental rights are meant to ensure unity. In other words, 'fundamental rights constitute the element of indispensable hierarchy which corrects the unsustainable heterarchy of an otherwise excessively 'open' method of coordination'.[63] Ashiagbor points out that coordination processes such as the OMC need to be underpinned by a European-level core of fundamental rights and principles to counterbalance the dominance of the economic policy rationale over discourses of social justice and solidarity.[64]

Independently of how we conceive of the relationship between fundamental social rights and New Governance, namely the OMC, it is questionable whether—although highly desirable—this would ever be possible without entailing a drastic change in the nature of the OMC (for example, there may be a risk of returning to the same substantive regulatory rationality of *command* and *control* or 'hard' law from which

---

[62]   Chalmers and Lodge, above n 35.

[63]   A Andronico and A Lo Faro, 'Defining problems: The Open Method of Coordination, Fundamental Rights and the Theory of Governance' in S Deakin and O De Schutter (eds), *Social Rights and Market Forces: the Implementation of Fundamental Social Rights in the European Single Market* (Bruylant, Bruxelles, 2005) 93.

[64]   Ashiagbor, above n 34.

the OMC is said to depart). It must not be forgotten that the EES and its regulatory tool, the OMC, were deliberately conceived with an economic context as their overarching framework of implementation. Unanimous consensus by the Member States over the EES and subsequently the OMC as a constitutional architecture for 'Social Europe' could have been attainable only on these grounds, not on discourses of social justice and solidarity, which are much too controversial concepts to be easily accepted by all Member States.

It should also be recalled that the OMC was conceived as a governance technique eschewing the classic *integration by law* approach and it mainly serves the purpose of providing a common cognitive framework in order to help Member States identify the best path for solving labour market problems at domestic level. The OMC has not been conceived as a legal instrument or, put simply, as a 'provider and enforcer of legally justiciable social rights', precisely because this function belongs to legally binding norms. Moreover, the OMC, although centrally coordinated at EU level, is mostly intergovernmental. Rather than attempting to 'transplant' enforcement rules pertaining to the sphere of hard law into the arena of soft law and to render soft Community acts justiciable, it would perhaps be easier to transpose any claim or challenge against these acts within the iterative process of the OMC, which does not exclude but actually conceives of change as being an intrinsic part of the coordination process. Hence, guidelines may be and have been changed over the years, reflecting the Member States' desire to review the content of the guidelines. On the other hand, the chances of litigation arising from them is more complex and in this context we can envisage two scenarios.

In the case of legal disputes between Member States or between Member States and either the Commission or the Council or between the latter and the European Parliament, whether the ECJ will be able to consider the legality of New Governance processes is open to debate, and lawyers are divided on the matter.[65] There is a series of legal and technical problems

---

[65] M Barbera, 'Nuovi Processi Deliberativi e Principio di Legalità nell'Ordinamento Europeo' in M Barbera (ed), *Nuove Forme di Regolazione: Il Metodo Aperto di Coordinamento delle Politiche Sociali* (Milano, Giuffrè, 2006) 299; G De Búrca, 'The Constitutional Challenge of New Governance in the European Union' (2003) 28(6) *EL Rev* 814; V Hatzopoulos, 'A (More) Social Europe: A Political Crossroad or a Legal One-Way? Dialogues Between Luxembourg and Lisbon' (2005) 42 *CML Rev* 1599; and D Strazzari, 'Tra Soft e Hard Law: Prime Riflessioni in Favore della Giustiziabilità degli Atti Emanati nell'Ambito del Metodo Aperto di Coordinamento' in M Barbera (ed), *Nuove Forme di Regolazione: Il Metodo Aperto di Coordinamento delle Politiche Sociali* (Milano, Giuffrè, 2006) 317. In terms of case law, see also Case 113/75, *Frecassetti v Amministrazione delle Finanze dello Stato* [1976] ECR 983; Case 90/76, *Van Ameyde v UCI* [1977] ECR 1091; and Case C-322/88, *Grimaldi v Fonds des Maladie professionelles* [1989] ECR 4407. In Case C-188/91, *Deutsche Shell AG v Hauptzollamt Hamburg-Hamburg* [1993] ECR I-363, the Court held that even though a measure of Community law has no binding effect, it does not preclude the Court from ruling on its interpretation in proceedings for a preliminary ruling

needing to be taken into consideration should a case be brought before the Court. There is also another scenario to be considered, as guidelines may lead to the adoption of binding measures at national level. In this case, public or private applicants who feel that certain social rights may have been infringed by a domestic measure adopted pursuant to the Integrated Guidelines will need to follow the judicial rules of standing at national level.

The above analysis showed how New Governance techniques have intrinsic weaknesses that may undermine their credibility as a workable means of EU integration. One solution could be to strengthen the complementarity between New Governance and constitutionalism by creating a positive dialogue between them rather than seeing them as opposites. In a similar vein, Hatzopoulos maintains that:

> ... the Lisbon objectives and recourse to the OMC constitute the supplement, in the form of (soft) positive integration, to the (hard) negative integration already achieved by the Community judiciary ... Seen from this perspective, the lack of legitimacy and the absence of judicial control of the Lisbon process, appears far less dramatic.[66]

VI. CONCLUSION

This chapter has sought throughout to identify the extent to which and the ways in which the EES and its regulatory tool, the OMC, may be said to be 'new', in order to consider subsequently some of the most salient governance and constitutionalism implications of their differences, in comparison with the classic Community Method. In turn, this has helped the analysis by better contextualising the examination of the question of New Governance's effectiveness and what this may mean for social rights.

The EES and OMC cannot be defined merely as being either 'new' or 'old' or, to use Kilpatrick's expression, it may be more appropriate to talk about 'limited newness'.[67] In particular, the OMC, as a regulatory tool, has long-standing antecedents. Indeed, the success of the Community Method may be said to have been the creation of a *sui generis* constitutional order intertwined with flexibility and differentiation, even within the Common

---

under Art 177 EC (now 234 EC) and added that, although soft law measures cannot confer upon individuals rights which they may enforce before national courts, the latter are nevertheless obliged to take them into consideration in order to resolve disputes submitted to them and may thus be included in the 'acts' under Art 177(1)b EC. For comment, see J Kenner, *EU Employment Law. From Rome to Amsterdam and Beyond* (Oxford, Hart, 2003) 203; and Velluti, above n 13, 387.

[66] Hatzopoulos, *ibid*, 1633.

[67] C Kilpatrick, 'New EU Employment Governance and Constitutionalism' in G De Búrca and J Scott (eds), *Law and New Governance in the EU and the US* (Oxford, Hart, 2006) 121.

Market 'core'.[68] Like many other socio-economic processes currently taking place in the EU, the EES presents elements of continuity with the past, namely, a concern for improving employment and the social situation in the EU while, at the same time, presenting innovatory elements particularly in terms of governance techniques.

The chapter has shown the limited success of the EES as a governance tool for furthering the European integration process in the social field. This may be explained by different factors, among others, the unbalanced and conflictual relationship between its two basic rationales centered on a deregulatory agenda and a social justice and solidarity discourse.

The EU has often been portrayed as a one-eyed man, solely preoccupied with its economic objectives and forgetful of the social dimensions of Europeanisation.[69] The purpose of the EES was to counter this criticism by showing that the EU could actively fight unemployment. However, far from counter-balancing the excessive restrictions imposed on growth by the EMU, the EES on the contrary limits its action in this pre-defined framework. Thus, the existence and purpose of the EES remains anchored to making the labour markets function more efficiently and this has become even more evident since the Lisbon Strategy.

Despite what some scholars say—that the main achievement of the Lisbon Strategy has been to synthesise competing ideological perspectives, by urging that economic reform and market liberalisation could co-exist with the European Social Model and, in particular, that social policies were a necessary element of successful economic performance—a careful analysis of the Lisbon Strategy and its components seems to reveal that employment and social coordination remain instrumental to the pursuit of economic objectives. The EES, therefore, even after two re-launches, still remains very much a limited strategy: a weak centralised coordination of national employment policies and 'facilitative' rather than 'prescriptive'.[70]

However, the EES has had an important contribution to the development of a 'social Europe': it has fostered a cognitive and normative consensus around common challenges, objectives and policy approaches, and the language and outlooks developed in the context of the EES increasingly seem to colour national policy discourse.[71] In this sense, it may be argued

---

[68]   G De Búrca, 'Differentiation within the Core: The Case of the Common Market' in G De Búrca and J Scott (eds), *Constitutional Change in the EU: From Uniformity to Flexibility?* (Oxford, Hart, 2000).

[69]   G Raveaud, 'The European Employment Policy: From Ends to Means?' in R Salais and R Villeneuve (eds), *Europe and the Politics of Capabilities* (Cambridge, Cambridge University Press, 2005).

[70]   C Barnard and S Deakin, 'A Year of Living Dangerously? EC Social Rights, Employment Policy, and EMU' (1999) 30(4) *Industrial Relations Journal: European Annual Review 1998* 355.

[71]   Jacobsson, above n 55, 366.

that even though the immediate effects of the EES and the OMC on Member States' national labour market policies have been unsatisfactory thus far, they may, nevertheless, have a more long-term impact. However, due to the limitations inherent in soft law strategies and governance techniques such as the EES and OMC, respectively, this impact may only be ideational and cognitive. A more workable solution seems to be a stronger dialogue between 'soft' and 'hard' regulatory mechanisms, that is, between New Governance and constitutionalism, leading to a hybridised multi-level governance regime in which all governance tools are aimed at achieving the same set of goals.

7

Common Foreign and Security Policy: Looking Back, Thinking Forward

PANOS KOUTRAKOS

I. INTRODUCTION

THE ROLE OF the European Union as a global player has been at the very core of all the debates about the Union's reform in the last five years. It was one of the main parameters within which the debate about the drafting and acceptance of the Treaty Establishing a Constitution for Europe was carried out: in the Laeken Declaration on the Future of European Union,[1] the European Council wondered: '[d]oes Europe not, now that it is finally unified, have a leading role to play in a new world order, that of a stabilising role worldwide and to point the way ahead for many countries and peoples?'.[2] It was also one of the starting points for the inception and drafting of the Lisbon Treaty. Launching the Intergovernmental Conference, which let to the adoption of the Lisbon Treaty, the European Council stated that '[i]n order to secure our future as an active player in a rapidly changing world and in the face of ever-growing challenges, we have to maintain and develop the European Union's capacity to act'.[3]

To discuss the development and future of the Common Foreign and Security Policy is to delve into one of the main constitutional idiosyncrasies of the European Union. This is the starting point for this chapter: the CFSP rules are different in so far as their normative qualities and underpinning political sensitivity set them apart from the Community legal framework and the model of integration which has been developed within it in the last 50 years. The prevailing role of unanimity, the provision for special

---

[1] Adopted on 15 December 2001.
[2] See p 2.
[3] Presidency Conclusions of the Brussels European Council (21–22 June 2007), para 2.

instruments (joint actions, common positions, common strategies),[4] the sharing by the Commission of legislative initiative with the Member States, the considerably reduced role of the European Parliament, the express exclusion of the jurisdiction of the European Court of Justice,[5] all define a set of rules fundamentally distinct from the Community legal order. As for the scope of CFSP, this is described in very broad terms in Article 11 of the Treaty of European Union (TEU): it covers 'all areas of foreign and security policy'.

The aim of this chapter is twofold: on the one hand, to describe the development of CFSP since its inception by focusing on its main characteristics, a task necessary in order to appreciate the practical implications of the normative distinctiveness of its rules; on the other hand, to identify some trends which characterise its current conduct, a task necessary in order to gauge the future direction of the Union's external policy.

II. LOOKING BACK

The genesis of CFSP is attributed to a variety of factors, two of which are the most prominent, namely the spill-over effect of the cooperation carried out within the EC legal framework and the expectation by third parties and international organisations that the Member States would act as a combined force on the international scene. In other words, the genesis of the CFSP was not a top-down operation, it was not part of a grand plan about the role of the Union on the international scene. Instead, it emerged rather slowly and gradually from the existing political circumstances while all the actors involved had one paramount consideration in mind: to ensure that the cooperation between the Member States in the area of high politics would not emulate the model of integration followed under EC law—it could draw upon it, but should not follow it.

This gradual emergence of cooperation in the area of foreign policy underpinned the development of the relevant legal framework. It has been characterised by three main features.[6] The first one is its incremental development. There was no specific model against which a common foreign policy was structured. Instead, it consisted of ad hoc arrangements, each one based on and further developing those already in operation. For about 15 years, the principles on the basis of which the Member States cooperated were laid down in three reports adopted by their Foreign

---

[4] Arts 13–15 TEU.
[5] Art 35 TEU.
[6] See also P Koutrakos., 'Constitutional Idiosyncrasies and Political Realities: The Emerging European Security and Defence Policy of the European Union' (2003) 10 *Columbia Journal of European Law* 310.

Ministers in the period between 1970 and 1981.[7] These reports formed the basis of the precursor to CFSP, namely European Political Cooperation.[8] Providing for procedures which would enhance closer consultation between the Member States, these reports set out the non-binding framework within which the Member States gradually fostered a culture of cooperation. Then, these rules were incorporated in primary law for the first time in the Single European Act. However, they were a distinct part of the Treaty, clearly intergovernmental in nature and rather aspirational in their effect.[9] The subsequent amendments at Maastricht, Amsterdam and Nice saw this part become the second pillar of the European Union with much tighter legal duties imposed on the Member States.[10] Therefore, the current legal framework developed gradually from a set of informal arrangements to a set of loose principles and, finally, to a Treaty-based legal framework.

The second feature of the development of the CFSP has been its *sui generis* nature. It became apparent over the years that the foreign policy developed by the EU was distinct from both national models and international mechanisms of the conduct of foreign policy. For instance, following the dissolution of Yugoslavia in the very early 1990s, the Member States sought to adopt a common approach as regards recognition of the emerging states: they created a procedural framework within which they would recognise the new states.[11] It was interesting how recognition, a traditional public international law act, was instrumentalised by the Member States in a way which would shape a distinct European foreign policy response to a crisis. This is in stark contrast to the approach of the EU to the issue of recognition of Kosovo, which proclaimed its independence more recently. In its conclusions of 18 February 2008, the Council 'note[d] that Member States will decide, in accordance with national practice and international law, on their relations with Kosovo'.[12] Whilst

---

[7] These were the Luxembourg, Copenhagen and London Reports adopted in 1970, 1973 and 1981 respectively: see *European Political Co-operation (EPC)*, 5th edn (Bonn, Press and Information Office of the Federal Government, 1988).

[8] See S Nuttall, *European Political Cooperation* (Oxford, Clarendon Press, 1992); P de Schoutheete de Tervarent, *La Coopération Politique Européenne*, 2ème edn (Brussels, Editions Labor, 1986).

[9] For instance, Art 30(1) SEA provided that: 'The Member States shall endeavour to jointly formulate and implement a European foreign policy'.

[10] According to Art 24 TEU post-Lisbon, 'the common foreign and security policy is subject to specific rules and procedures'.

[11] See DH Bearce, 'Institutional Breakdown and International Cooperation: the European Agreement to Recognize Croatia and Slovenia' (2002) 8 *European Journal of International Relations* 471; and R Kherad, 'La Reconnaissance des Etats Issus de la Dissolution de la Republique Socialiste de Yugoslavie par les Membres de l'Union Européenne' (1997) 101 *Revue Générale de Droit International Public* 663.

[12] General Affairs and External Relations Council Conclusions (18 February 2008).

this approach may be viewed as a retrograde step,[13] it indicates that, its broad scope as defined in primary law notwithstanding, the CFSP would deal with international challenges in a decidedly ad hoc manner.

A third main feature of the development of CFSP has been its distinct and somewhat unhealthy focus on procedures. So strong has the desire of the Member States been to stress that the locus of power of this policy lies with them that unanimity has always been the rule. The exceptions to this principle are only very minor.[14] On the other hand, this constant theme of the need for unanimity has been attacked very heavily by many proponents of the Union's role on the world scene—it has been viewed as the main obstacle to the development of a truly effective foreign policy. This tension over the years developed into a rather tiresome obsession with procedures, especially every time an intergovernmental conference was about to discuss a reform of the relevant rules. One almost felt that, had it not been for the prevailing role of unanimity, the Union would have assumed its rightful place at the very centre of the world scene.

This focus on procedures and the obsession with unanimity is unhealthy, for it ignores the element of political solidarity. The emergence of political solidarity lies firmly beyond the legal sphere of foreign affairs. It develops on the basis of the progressive and subconscious outcome of a number of diverse and subtle developments, based on factors as indeterminate as cultural developments, economic progress, social advancement, to a certain extent legal developments and, ultimately, time. The role of political solidarity as a *conditio sine qua non* for an effective CFSP became abundantly clear in the incidents about Imia, between Greece and Turkey, and the Parsley islands, between Spain and Morocco. In both cases, a Member State felt that its territorial integrity was under threat by a third state; in both cases, the Union institutions failed to support Greece and Spain; furthermore, in both cases, the tension was solved due to an intervention by the US State Department.[15] In the light of the above, unanimity in the area of CFSP should be viewed as the inevitable indicator of the distinct position which foreign policy, security and defence have in the multi-level EU constitutional legal order. Even the provision of majority voting would not alter the nature of that policy and would not shift the political underpinnings which define it, therefore rendering this procedure irrelevant at a time of crisis.

---

[13]   This is despite the fact that the Slovenian Foreign Affairs Minister, speaking on behalf of the Presidency, stated that 'The EU once again survived this test of unity': *Financial Times*, 19 February 2008, 10.

[14]   Art 23(1)–(2) TEU.

[15]   J Monar, 'The CFSP and the Leila/Perejil Island Incident: The Nemesis of Solidarity and Leadership' (2002) 7 *European Foreign Affairs Review* 251.

III. MOVING FORWARD

The CFSP is now at the centre of all of the debates regarding the reform and development of the EU. This may be explained by a number of factors, such as the gradual entrenchment of a culture of cooperation amongst the Member States, the increasing economic weight of the Union, and the growing demand for a more multi-polar international order following the unilateralist tendencies of the American administration in the last eight years. However, another factor of a different nature is that of popular support. The Eurobarometer poll results published in December 2007 show a 68 per cent score for support for the CFSP and ESDP in the whole EU.[16] This enthusiasm for the development of an effective CFSP appears to be shared by the EU institutions which have dedicated considerable energy in this area of activity. This becomes apparent by the adoption, as well as the content, of the European Security Strategy, which states that '[a]n active and capable European Union would make an impact on a global scale. In doing so, it would contribute to an effective multilateral system leading to a fairer and more secure world'.[17]

It is noteworthy that the fate of the Constitutional Treaty and the ensuing two-year period of 'group therapy' which the Union underwent by no means impeded the development of CFSP. The following sections will focus on three separate but interlinked themes which underlie current developments, namely the quest for coherence, the progress in the area of security and defence policy, and the increasing emphasis on flexibility.

IV. THE QUEST FOR COHERENCE

As was pointed out above, the CFSP is somehow 'different'. And yet, the relevant rules, set out in Title V TEU, are not part of a free-standing system within which the EU is to operate, as if in a legal and political vacuum. Whilst legally distinct from the Community legal order, they are also interrelated to it. Article 3 TEU states that 'the Union shall ... ensure the consistency of its external activities as a whole in the context of its external economic relations, security, economic and development policies'. Under the same provision, 'the Council and the Commission shall be responsible for ensuring such consistency and shall cooperate to this end'. On the other hand, the interaction between the pillars cannot impinge upon the integrity

---

[16] Available at <http://ec.europa.eu/public_opinion/archives/eb/eb68/eb68_first_en.pdf> accessed 3 September 2008.

[17] See p 16. The European Security Strategy was approved by the European Council in December 2003. Available at <http://www.consilium.europa.eu/uedocs/cmsUpload/78367.pdf> accessed 3 September 2008.

of the Community legal order. Article 47 TEU provides that 'nothing in this Treaty shall affect the Treaties establishing the European Communities'.

This ambiguous relationship between the CFSP and EC legal frameworks may appear convoluted and a potential source of conflict. Whilst the logic of the status of the CFSP rules is clear, namely to draw upon the culture of cooperation fostered between the Member States under EC law and, yet, ensure that its institutional sophistication and expertise, the pace of cooperation as well as its substantive content are distinct, problems are inevitable. Timothy Garton Ash argues that:

> ... Europe has a hundred left hands and none of them know what the right hand is doing. Trade, development aid, immigration policy, education, cultural exchanges, classic diplomacy, arms sales and anti-proliferation measures, counter-terrorism, the fight against drug and organized crime: each European policy has an impact, but the effects are fragmented and often self-contradictory.[18]

The quest for coherence in the EU's international relations was at the very core of the process of the drafting of the Lisbon Treaty. In its Draft Intergovernmental Conference Mandate, the Brussels European Council stated in its very first paragraph that '[t]he IGC is asked to draw up a Treaty ... amending the existing Treaties with a view to enhancing the efficiency and democratic legitimacy of the enlarged Union, as well as the coherence of its external action'.[19]

This section will focus on three dimensions of coherence which underpin the development of CFSP in the recent years.

A. Substantive Coherence

The first dimension is about substantive coherence. Ensuring that the various external policies of the EU are part of a whole which makes sense and is devoid of contradictions appears to be increasingly on the agenda of the EU institutions. In order to appreciate the role this plays within the context of the multi-layered system of EU external relations, two initiatives from the two opposite ends of the policy spectrum are worth mentioning. Originating in the Community legal framework, development policy is an obvious example of external action which straddles economic, political and security polices. An effort to bring the different strands of this policy within a common overall set of objectives is illustrated by a Joint Statement

---

[18]   T Garton Ash, *Free World* (Penguin, 2005) 218.
[19]   June 2006.

adopted in November 2003 by the Council, the Representatives of the Governments of the Member States meeting within the Council, the European Parliament and the Commission. Entitled 'The European Consensus on Development',[20] this document seeks to outline the vision of the development policy to be pursued by the Union and its Member States. It stresses the various dimensions of development policy and puts considerable emphasis on insecurity and violent conflicts as two of the biggest obstacles to achieving the Union's Millenium Development Goals. This Statement was welcomed by the European Council in December 2005.[21]

A similar document was adopted by the Council, the Representatives of the Governments of the Member States meeting within the Council, the European Parliament and the Commission in the area of humanitarian aid in January 2008.[22] Entitled 'The European Consensus on Humanitarian Aid', this document is drafted in similar terms to those of the 'European Consensus on Development'[23] and sets out common principles and good practice for the EU's humanitarian policy. Coherence and complementarity constitute two focal points of the statement. For instance, it is stated that:

> ... the EU commits to ensuring policy coherence, complementarity and effectiveness by using its influence and the full range of tools at its disposal to address the root causes of humanitarian crises. In particular, humanitarian aid and development cooperation, as well as the various instruments available to implement stability measures, will be used in a coherent and complementary fashion especially in transitional contexts and situations of fragility, in order to use the full potential of short- and long-term aid and cooperation.[24]

The statement also comprises a section dealing specifically with Community humanitarian aid policy.

It remains to be seen whether the above two initiatives are no more than an outline of some general principles of rhetorical significance. At this juncture, suffice it to point out that, as initiatives undertaken by all of the EU institutions and the Member States, they suggest an awareness of the vital role of coherence in a multi-level and multi-centred legal system. In fact, defining a common point of reference for policies whose very core straddles diverse sets of rules and involves a wide range of actors is welcomed in so far as it provides the first step towards a more concrete application of the requirement of coherence on specific policy areas. This trend towards a more formalised, and yet policy-specific and practice-oriented, approach is illustrated not only by the adoption of the above statements, but also their content in terms of their application. Both

---

[20]   [2006] OJ C646/1.
[21]   Presidency Conclusions of the Brussels European Council (15–16 December 2005).
[22]   [2008] OJ C25/1.
[23]   To which it refers expressly, *ibid*, para 22.
[24]   *Ibid*, para 30.

statements refer to further specific measures enhancing their effectiveness. The Statement on Humanitarian Aid, for instance, states that the Commission 'will present an action plan for practical measures to implement it, in close consultation with other relevant stakeholders and with due consideration of the respective roles and competences of all the actors involved in the provision of EU humanitarian aid'.[25]

At the other end of the spectrum, in the area of foreign, security and defence policy, there is the 'European Security Strategy'. Drafted under the responsibilities of the CFSP High Representative Javier Solana and approved by the European Council in December 2003, this is a document which has become a point of reference for the Union's ambition 'to assert its identity on the international scene' and the ways in which this may be fulfilled. This document defines the international role of the EU in the area of security as one which straddles traditional divisions between distinct policy areas. It states that the Union needs to '[be] more active, more coherent and more capable'.[26] And the way to do this is by relying upon 'the full spectrum of instruments for crisis management and conflict prevention at our disposal, including political, diplomatic, military and civilian, trade and development activities. ... We need to develop a strategic culture that fosters early, rapid, and when necessary, robust intervention'.[27]

The 'European Security Strategy' has been the subject of considerable academic debate.[28] For the purpose of this analysis, suffice it to say that it suggests a concrete effort to define the charter of the EU's security policy, a set of principles and objectives which set out to define the threads of the EU's external actions and shape its coherent development. As such, it is in line with the other initiatives outlined in this section and set out to enhance coherence in specific policy areas.

B. Normative Coherence

Another dimension of coherence, which is also central to the effectiveness of the EU external action, is normative. This is concerned with the relationship between the CFSP and the Community legal order, as defined by the requirement for consistency set out in Article 3 TEU and the principle that the EC Treaty does not be affect CFSP actions, as set out in

---

[25] *Ibid*, para 100.
[26] See p 11.
[27] *Ibid*.
[28] S Duke, 'The European Security Strategy in a Comparative Framework: Does it Make for Secure Alliances in a Better World?' (2004) 9 *European Foreign Affairs Review* 459; and A Toje, 'The 2003 European Union Security Strategy: A Critical Appraisal' (2005) 10 *European Foreign Affairs Review* 117.

Article 47 TEU. In an increasingly interdependent international environment, the Union is called upon to act in ways which would not necessarily reflect its complex constitutional arrangements.

Some of the ambiguities have been addressed by the Court of Justice. In a case about sanctions imposed on Yugoslavia, for instance, it set out the main principle underpinning the relationship between CFSP and EC: whilst foreign policy falls within the domain of the Member States, in acting within that area they must comply with their obligations under EC law.[29] Clearly suggesting that the dividing line between the Union's external economic and foreign policies is not as rigid as it might have appeared, the question which then arose is who is the ultimate arbiter as to where the dividing line actually lies. Again, this has now been addressed by the Court of Justice. In its judgment in *Airport Transit Visa*,[30] it made it clear that it was within its jurisdiction to ensure that action taken beyond the EC legal order should not have been undertaken under the EC legal framework. Following the judgments in *Environmental Crimes*[31] and *Maritime Pollution*[32], where the Court actually annulled Framework Decisions about a number of environmental offences in relation to which Member States would be required to introduce criminal penalties, the message has now been underlined.

An interesting twist in the story of managing the normative coherence in the EU's external relations has appeared in the case law of the Court of First Instance (CFI) on smart sanctions freezing assets of specific individuals as a matter of EU law following a UN Security Council Resolution. In a series of judgments,[33] starting with *Yusuf*[34] and *Kadi*,[35] the CFI held that Article 308 EC could not provide the legal basis for the adoption of measures which are necessary for the fight against international terrorism. This is one of the objectives of the EU, rather than the EC, and to rely upon Article 308 EC would be to impinge upon the CFSP and to undermine 'the constitutional architecture of the Union'.[36] Whilst the Court of Justice annulled the relevant EC measures on appeal, it sanctioned this specific argument.[37] However, it is an interesting development to see the Community judiciary assume the role of the guardian of the integrity of the legal rules which lie beyond the Community legal order.

---

[29] Case C-124/95, *Centro-Com* [1997] ECR I-81, paras 24–5.
[30] Case C-170/94, *Commission v Council (re: Airport Transit Visas)* [1998] ECR I-2763, para 16.
[31] Case C-176/03, *Commission v Council* [2005] ECR I-7879.
[32] Case C-440/05, *Commission v Council* (judgment of 23 October 2007).
[33] Case T-49/04, *Hassan* (judgment of 12 July 2006) (now on appeal in Case C-399/06 P); and Case T-253/02, *Ayadi* [2006] ECR II-2139 (now on appeal in Case C-403/06 P).
[34] Case T-306/01, *Yusuf* [2005] ECR II-3533 (now on appeal in Case C-415/05 P).
[35] Case T-315/01, *Kadi* [2005] ECR II-3649 (now on appeal in Case C-402/05 P).
[36] *Ibid*, para 120.
[37] Joined Cases C-402/05P and Case C-415/05P *Kadi* and *Al Barakaat*, judgment of 3 September 2008, not yet reported, para 202.

Finally, another aspect of the normative requirement of consistency between the various aspects of EU international relations is the encouragement which seems to permeate the relevant case law directed towards the Member States—this is encouragement to rely upon the Community procedures and mechanisms. This became apparent in the area of exports of dual-use goods, ie products which may be of both civil and military application. Adjudicating in this area, which clearly straddles trade and foreign policies, the Court of Justice held that the foreign policy objective of trade measures may not render them beyond the scope of EC law.[38] However, in cases where Member States feel that they need to protect their security by deviating from such rules, the Court acknowledged that they enjoy wide discretion to do so. In addition, it pointed out that it was for the national courts to ascertain whether, in exercising their discretion, national authorities comply with the principles of necessity and proportionality.

It becomes apparent from the above that the role of the Court of Justice has been central in ensuring that the practical implications of the requirement of coherence would not affect the EU constitutional order as defined in primary law. Its role becomes even more prominent in the light of recent disputes about the relationship between development and foreign policy. In the *Philippines Borders* case,[39] the Court was asked to determine whether the Commission had the authority to adopt a decision providing funding for the security of the Philippines border in the context of development policy. Its judgment is underpinned by a distinct effort to ensure that development policy would not be construed so broadly as to impinge upon areas which are not covered by the EC legal order. Responding to the Commission's argument that borders safety would contribute to building up the institutional capacity necessary for economic cooperation, the Court pointed out the absence of any indication in the contested measure as to how the objective pursued by the project could contribute effectively to making the environment more conducive to investment and economic development. It then proceeded to conclude that the Commission's decision was not a development measure which could have been funded by the Community budget and annulled it.

Another case where the delineation between the Community's external relations and the Union's foreign policy was in issue was the *ECOWAS* case.[40] The Commission challenged a CFSP measure adopted by the Council that provided financial assistance to the Economic Organisation

---

[38]   Case C-367/89, *Richardt* [1991] ECR I-4621; Case C-83/94, *Leifer* [1995] ECR I-3231; and Case C-70/94, *Werner* [1995] ECR I-3189.

[39]   Case C-403/05, *European Parliament v Commission* (judgment of 23 October 2007).

[40]   Case C-91/05, *Commission v Council* , judgment delivered on 20 May 2008, not yet reported. See J Heliskoski, 'Small Arms and Light Weapons within the Union's Pillar structure: An Anlysis of Article 47 of the EU Treaty' (2008) 33 *ELRev* 898.

of West African States (ECOWAS) in the field of Small Arms and Light Weapons. As the control of small arms and light weapons had been the subject of EC, as well as CFSP, action, the Commission argued that the Council Decision and the section of the Joint Action which it implemented should have been adopted under EC law.

In its judgment, the Court interprets Article 47 TEU broadly and holds that 'a measure having legal effect adopted under Title V of the EU Treaty affects the provisions of the EC Treaty within the meaning of Article 47 EU whenever it could have been adopted on the basis of the EC Treaty, it being unnecessary to examine whether the measure prevents or limits the exercise by the Community of its competence'.[41] It then points out that, on the basis of its aim and content, the contested Decision contributed to the elimination or reduction of obstacles to the development of the ECOWAS Member States, which is an objective of the EC development policy, as well as the preservation of peace and the strengthening of the international security, the latter being a CFSP objective. As both these form the main components of the measure in question, the latter should have been adopted pursuant to the EC Treaty development provisions because 'the Union cannot have recourse to a legal basis falling within the CFSP in order to adopt provisions which also fall within a competence conferred by the EC Treaty on the Community'.[42] The broad interpretation of Article 47 TEU in *ECOWAS*, its implications for the construction of the Community's development policy as well as the substance of policies adopted under Title V TEU illustrate the significance of adjudicating upon the dividing line between EC and CFSP rules.

The various issues that the normative dimension of coherence has raised for the EU institutions and the Member States, the increasing reliance upon litigation as a means to address them and the assertiveness of the EU Courts' approach to them suggest an increasingly prominent role for the EU judiciary in the conduct of CFSP. This follows not only from the distinct legal character of the CFSP rules and the inevitable inter-pillar interactions envisaged under primary law, but also the assertive nature of the EU's foreign policy and the broadening of the scope of its operations. The central position of the EU judiciary is not likely to be affected by the new constitutional arrangement envisaged under the Lisbon Treaty, for, whilst it removes the pillar structure, the latter does not do away with the fundamentally distinct character of the CFSP rules.

The outcome of the actions mentioned above will, hopefully, bring some clarity in the delineation of competence between the EC external relations and the EU foreign policy. However, the increasingly prominent role of the

[41] Para 60.
[42] Para 77.

Court is unlikely to produce certainty in the delineation and management of the EU's external powers. The inter-institutional disputes which have dominated the EC external relations, the ad hoc approach followed in the delineation of policy areas and the alarming lack of clarity in the ensuing case law are phenomena which may well arise in the context of the CFSP.[43]

C. Administrative Coherence

Another dimension of coherence deals with the specific practical arrangements which the EU institutions deem necessary for the effective conduct of CFSP. An interesting illustration is provided by the Commission's Communication entitled 'Europe in the World—Some Practical Proposals for Greater Coherence, Effectiveness and Visibility'.[44] This proposal tackles the relationship between the Commission, the Council and the CFSP High Representative. It suggests ways in which these actors may interact in strategic planning and develop joint assessments, joint strategies and joint action. It tackles the issue of coordination between the Commission services and the Council Policy Unit, but also with the Member States. For instance, it suggests an enhanced programme of exchange of personnel with diplomatic services of the Member States and staff of the Council Secretariat.

This document is noteworthy because it is quite specific and practical in its focus and minimalistic in its approach. It adopts a bottom-up approach which is concerned with the practicalities of the day-to-day conduct of external relations. To be sure, in itself, it bears the hallmarks of its drafters: its emphasis is on the ways in which the Commission may contribute, in various ways and at various levels, in policy planning and information assessment. Nonetheless, it is significant as it is focused on practical ways of ensuring improved coherence at all possible levels of management and decision-making. In this respect, this is not an isolated example of a policy approach. In the areas of sanctions, for instance, the Council approved a set of guidelines on the implementation and evaluation of sanctions regimes in the CFSP framework.[45] These guidelines have a similarly practical focus and are geared towards the management of sanctions rather than the overall process leading to their adoption.

---

[43] For an analysis in the context of EC external relations, see P Koutrakos, 'Legal Basis and Delimitation of Competence' in M Cremona and B de Witte (eds), *EU Foreign Relations Law: Constitutional Fundamentals* (Oxford, Hart Publishing, 2008) 171.

[44] COM(2006) 278 Final (Brussels, 8 June 2006).

[45] Council Conclusions 15535/03 (PESC 356) of 8 December 2003. See P Koutrakos, *EU International Relations Law* (Oxford, Hart Publishing, 2006) 446–8.

V. A FOCAL POINT EMERGING: EUROPEAN SECURITY AND DEFENCE POLICY

The European Security and Defence Policy (ESDP) is an area where considerable developments have rendered it at the centre of the EU's external relations and have also brought about significant initiatives in the Community legal order. The significance of this policy for the EU in general is illustrated by the European Security Strategy. As already noted, this is a document drawn up by EU High Representative Solana and approved by the European Council in December 2003. Setting out the strategic priorities for the EU's external actions, its main premise is expressed as follows: 'a union of 25 states with over 45-million people producing a quarter of the world's ... GNP, the European Union is, like it or not, a global actor; it should be ready to share in the responsibility for global security'.[46]

In the area of ESDP in particular, the range of operations carried out by the EU is quite considerable and covers military operations,[47] police,[48] rule of law,[49] border assistance[50] and security sector[51] missions. The EU has also sent a planning team to Kosovo regarding a future crisis management operation in the area of the rule of law.[52] In the context of these operations, it has also concluded a number of international agreements with third countries,[53] to a large extent addressing the problem of whether the Union possesses international legal personality, which would be addressed for good by the Lisbon Treaty.[54]

---

[46] *European Security Strategy*, 2.

[47] At the time of writing, EUFOR-Althea in Bosnia-Herzegovina (under Council Decision 2004/57/CFSP, [2004] OJ L252/10), EUFOR TCHAD/RCA in Chad and the Central African Republic (under Council Decision 2007/677/CFSP, [2007] OJ L279/21).

[48] At the time of writing, EUPM in Bosnia Herzegovina (under Council Joint Action 2002/210/CFSP, [2002] OJ L70/1, continued under Council Joint Action 2007/749/CFSP, [2007] OJ L303/40), EUPOL COPPS in the Palestinian Territories (under Council Joint Action 2005/797/CFSP, [2005] OJ L300/65 and implemented by Council Decision 2008/134/CFSP, [2008] OJ L43/38), EUPOL AFGHANISTAN in Afghanistan (under Council Joint Action 2007/369/CFSP, [2007] OJ L139/33, amended by Council Joint Action 2007/733, [2007] OJ L295/31), EUPOL RD CONGO in Congo (under Council Joint Action 2007/405/CFSP, [2007] OJ L151/46 amended by Council Joint Action 2008/38/CFSP, [2008] OJ L9/18).

[49] At the time of writing, Eujust Lex in Iraq (under Council Joint Action 2005/190/CFSP, [2005] OJ L62/37 last amended by Council Joint Action 2007/760/CFSP, [2007] OJ L305/57).

[50] At the time of writing, EU BAM Rafah at Rafah Crossing Point in the Palestinian territories (under Council Joint Action 2005/889/CFSP, [2005] OJ L327/28 last amended by Council Joint Action 2007/359/CFSP, [2007] O L 133/51).

[51] At the time of writing, EUSEC RD Congo in Congo (under Council Joint Action 2007/406/CFSP, [2007] OJ L151/52).

[52] At the time of writing, EUPT Kosovo (under Council Joint Action 2006/304/CFSP, [2006] OJ L112/19, last amended by Council Joint Action 2007/778/CFSP, [2007] OJ L312/68).

[53] See the analysis in A Sari, 'The Conclusion of International Agreements by the European Union in the Context of the ESDP' (2008) 57 *ICLQ* 53.

[54] Art 1(55) of the Lisbon Treaty, [2007] OJ C306/1.

It is interesting that the fate of the Treaty Establishing a Constitution for Europe has not affected the development of the ESDP. In fact, quite the contrary seems to have been the case: the process of deliberating on the content of the Constitutional Treaty at the Convention, drafting it and then debating on it during the ratification process and its aftermath seem to have built up considerable momentum for the development of ESDP. A reason for this is the focus of the external relations provisions of the Constitutional Treaty on ESDP, also suggested by its renaming as Common Security and Defence Policy.[55]

The range of ESDP operations undertaken by the Union and the increasing emphasis on its role in the international geopolitical constellation has drawn attention to the practical prerequisites for an effective security and defence role, namely defence industries. Their central function becomes apparent even with a mere reference to the ambition of the ESDP:

> ... [the Member States] will be able to agree to deploy rapidly and then sustain forces capable of the full range of Petersberg tasks as set out in the Amsterdam Treaty, including the most demanding, in operations of up to corps level (up to 15 brigades or 50,000–60,000 persons). These forces should be militarily self-sustaining with the necessary command, control and intelligence capabilities, logistics, other combat support services and additionally, as appropriate air and naval elements. Member States should be able to deploy in full at this level within 60 days, and within this to provide smaller rapid response elements available and deployable at very high readiness. They must be able to sustain such a deployment for at least one year. This will require an additional pool of deployable units (and supporting elements) at lower readiness to provide replacements for the initial forces.[56]

One of the reasons for which this objective has yet to be achieved is the seriously fraught state of the defence industries in the EU. Suffering from fragmentation, divergence of capabilities, excess production capability in certain areas and shortages in others, duplication, short production runs, reduced budgetary resources, and failure to engage in increasingly costly research, the defence industries have not made it easy for the EU to carry out its ESDP objectives in so far as its problems slow down the ability of multinational forces to assemble and engage in rapid deployment. In addition, the practical arrangements for the effective deployment of multinational forces become extremely difficult to manage and research and development, which is essential for an effective and ambitious defence policy, is hampered.

---

[55] See, inter alia, H Briobosia, 'Les nouvelles formes de flexibilité en matière de défense' in G mato, H Bribosia and B De Witte (eds), *Genèse et destine de la Constitution européenne* (Bruylant, 2007) 835; and Koutrakos, above n 43 at 481–506.

[56] Finnish Presidency Progress Report to the Helsinki European Council, annexed to the Presidency Conclusions (10–11 December 1999).

However, the political, practical and economic imperative for the rationalisation and consolidation of the defence industries in EU has traditionally met a legal obstacle, namely Article 296 EC, and its political (mis)interpretations. This rather obscure and badly drafted EC Treaty provision[57] enables Member States to deviate from the entire body of EC law in so far as the production of or trade in arms, munitions and war material is concerned in cases where this is necessary for the protection of the essential interests of national security. This 'wholly exceptional' provision[58] was interpreted for a long time as offering Member States a *carte blanche* to exclude defence industries in their entirety from the scope of EC law, an attitude largely tolerated by the EU institutions.[59]

In an initiative undertaken in the late 1990s, the European Commission put forward a comprehensive approach to the restructuring and consolidation of the defence industries of the Member States. Based on an assessment of the economic problems and challenges facing their fragmented state in an increasingly globalised market,[60] it adopted a document entitled 'Implementing European Union Strategy on Defence Related Industries'.[61] This suggested a detailed set of legal measures which was comprehensive in scope and covered areas such as public procurement, defence and technological development, standardisation and technical harmonisation, competition policy, structural funds, export policies and import duties on military equipment. This document articulated the need for a wide synergy of Community, EU, national and international measures whilst affirming the link between their subject matter and the core of national sovereignty.

However, this initiative was not taken up by the Member States. In response to a request by the European Parliament, the Commission returned to the issues raised by the need for the consolidation of the defence industries in 2003 and reiterated the need for a coherent cross-pillar approach to the legal regulation of defence industries with special

---

[57] Art 296 EC reads as follows: '1. The provisions of this Treaty shall not preclude the application of the following rules: (a) no Member State shall be obliged to supply information the disclosure of which it considers contrary to the essential interests of its security; (b) any Member state may take such measures as it considers necessary for the protection of the essential interests of its security which are concerned with the production of or trade in arms, munitions and war material; such measures shall not adversely affect the conditions of competition in the common market regarding products which are not intended for specifically military purposes. 2. The Council may, acting unanimously on a proposal from the Commission, make changes to the list, which it drew up on 15 April 1958, of the products to which the provisions of paragraph 1(b) apply'.

[58] Case 222/84, *Johnston* [1986] ECR 1651, para 27.

[59] See P Koutrakos, *Trade, Foreign Policy and Defence in EU Constitutional Law* (Hart Publishing, 2001) ch 8; and M Trybus, *European Union Law and Defence Integration* (Hart Publishing, 2005) ch 5.

[60] COM(96) 10 Final, The Challenges facing the European Defence-Related Industry. A Contribution for Action at European Level, adopted on 24 January 1996.

[61] COM(97) 583 Final, adopted on 12 November 1997.

emphasis on standardisation, intra-Community transfers, competition, procurement, exports of dual-use goods and research.[62] In addition, the Commission also underlined the need to focus on research and development in the area of security.[63] The main tenet of its proposal is the development of a coherent security research programme at EU level which would be 'capability-driven, targeted at the development of interoperable systems, products and services useful for the protection of European citizens, territory and critical infrastructures as well as for peacekeeping activities' whilst also directly linked to 'the good functioning of such key European services as transport and energy supply'.[64] Four different areas are targeted: consultation and cooperation with users, industry and research organisations under the umbrella of a European Security Research Advisory Board; the establishment of a European Security Research Programme implemented as a specific programme with its own set of procedures, rules for participation, contracts and funding arrangements; cooperation with other institutional actors established under the CFSP and ESDP framework and especially the European Defence Agency; the establishment of a structure which would ensure the flexible and effective management of the European Security Research Programme.

Whilst underlining the problems of defence industries and making suggestions for addressing them, the above initiatives were met with indifference. It has only been in the last three years that a more tangible shift in the EU's institutions' approach has become apparent. Whilst a detailed analysis of them is beyond the confines of this chapter,[65] they may be summarised as follows. First, in December 2006, the Commission adopted the 'Interpretative Communication on the application of Article 296 of the Treaty in the field of defence procurement'.[66] In this document, it puts forward a restrictive interpretation of Article 296 EC: it should apply only to products of a purely military nature and purpose which are included in the Article 296(1)(b) EC list and only in cases where a deviation from EC law is necessary in order to protect the essential security interests of the dtate. In cases where it deems that these conditions are not met, the Commission is determined to initiate proceedings under Article 226 EC.[67] The Commission describes its role as follows:

---

[62]   COM(2003) 113 Final, European Defence—Industrial and Market Issues. Towards an EU Defence Equipment Policy, adopted on 11 March 2003.

[63]   COM(2004) 590 Final, Security Research: The Next Step.

[64]   *Ibid*, 4.

[65]   See P Koutrakos, 'The Application of EC Law to Defence Industries-Changing Interpretations of Article 296 EC' in O Odudu and C Barnard (eds), *The Outer Limits of Community Law* (Hart Publishing, 2009, forthcoming).

[66]   COM(2006) 779 Final, adopted on 7 December 2006.

[67]   For the only case where this has happened, see Case C-414/97, *Commission v Spain* [1999] ECR I-5585. See the analysis in M Trybus, *European Union Law and Defence Integration* (Hart Publishing, 2005) 152–4.

It is not for the Commission to assess Member States' essential security interests, not which military equipment they procure to protect those interests. However, as guardian of the Treaty, the Commission may verify whether the conditions for exempting procurement contracts on the basis of Article 296 TEC are fulfilled.

In such cases, it is for Member States to provide, *at the Commission's request*, [emphasis in the original] the necessary information and prove that exemption is necessary for the protection of their essential security interests ...

Therefore, when the Commission investigates a defence procurement case, it is for the Member State concerned to furnish evidence that, under the specific conditions of the procurement at issue, application of the Community Directive would undermine the essential interests of its security. General references to the geographical and political situation, history and Alliance commitments are not sufficient in this context.

Secondly, a year later, in December 2007, the Commission adopted the so-called 'defence package'. This consists of three documents which go further than any previous initiative undertaken in the area. The first document is a Communication on the competitiveness of the defence industry[68] and outlines a number of measures which would strengthen the European defence market, including the promotion of the use of common standards, the development of an EU-wide system on security of information, and the possibility of a common control system of strategic defence assets. In addition, it outlines a number of measures aimed at improving the overall coordination between national authorities in the process of defence planning and investment.

The most important feature of the 'defence package', however, is the two legislative proposals put forward by the Commission. The first consists of a proposal for a Directive on public procurement of arms, munitions, war material, and related works and services.[69] Following from a long period of consultation,[70] this proposal is based on the principles of transparency and flexibility. On the one hand, it introduces common procedures and criteria for the award of public contracts in relation to defence products which fall beyond the scope of Article 296 EC, the latter understood strictly. On the other hand, it acknowledges the specific requirements of defence procurement 'in terms of complexity, security of information or security of supply'.[71] To that effect, Member States are granted with considerable flexibility in the process of the negotiation of all aspects of the

---

[68]   COM(2007) 764 Final (5 December 2007).

[69]   COM(2007) 766 Final (5 December 2007).

[70]   In COM(2004) 608 Final, the Commission had outlined the main parameters of an envisaged EC Directive in the area and launched a public consultation process the results of which were presented in December 2005 in COM(2005) 626 Final, Communication on the results of the consultation launched by the Green Paper on Defence Procurement and on the future Commission initiatives.

[71]   See above n 67, para 25.

award as well as to impose specific clauses in order to ensure the confidentiality of sensitive information. The second legislative proposal consists of a Directive on intra-Community transfers.[72] It covers the existing divergent national licensing regimes and outlines a system ensuring their simplification and harmonisation.

These initiatives undertaken by the Commission are welcome in so far as they constitute the first tangible step to address a practical parameter which is a *sine qua non* for the effective development of the ESDP.[73] Their significance becomes more apparent in the broader context of the increasingly strong focus of the EU on defence industries as illustrated beyond the Community legal order. It is recalled that the Constitutional Treaty provided for the establishment of the European Defence Agency to be specialised in the area of defence capabilities development, research, acquisition and armaments.[74] This provision, which remains in the Lisbon Treaty, states that the Agency 'shall identify operational requirements, shall promote measures to satisfy those requirements, shall contribute to identifying and, where appropriate, implementing any measure needed to strengthen the industrial and technological base of the defence sector, shall participate in defining a European capabilities and armaments policy, and shall assist the Council in evaluating the improvement of military capabilities'.[75]

In a clear illustration of the momentum created by the process of drafting and debating the Constitutional Treaty, the Agency was established in July 2004, before the process of ratification which signalled the death of the Constitutional Treaty.[76] The analysis of the function of the Agency is beyond the scope of this chapter.[77] Suffice it to point out that in November 2005, a voluntary code of conduct on defence procurement was agreed upon and entered into force on 1 July 2006.[78] This code covers contracts worth more than €1 million which are covered by Article 296 EC (and therefore would not be covered by the proposed Directive on defence procurement) and establishes a single online portal provided for by the

---

[72]   COM(2007) 765 Final, 5 December 2007.
[73]   See Editorial, 'The Commission's "Defence Package" (2008) 33 *European Law Review* 1.
[74]   Article I-41(3), subpara 2.
[75]   Art 28A(3) TEU as amended by the Lisbon Treaty (this reproduces Art I-41(3), subpara 2 of the Constitutional Treaty). Further, see Art 28D TEU as introduced by the Lisbon Treaty.
[76]   2004/551/CFSP, [2004] OJ L245/17. See also Council Decision 2003/834/EC creating a team to prepare for the establishment of the agency in the field of defence capabilities development, research, acquisition and armaments, [2003] OJ L318/19.
[77]   See M Trybus, 'The New European Defence Agency: A Contribution to a Common European Security and Defence Policy or a Challenge to the Community *Acquis?*' (2006) 43 *Common Market Law Review* 667.
[78]   <http://ue.eu.int/ueDocs/cms_Data/docs/pressData/en/misc/87058.pdf> accessed 3 September 2008.

Agency itself, hence publicising procurement opportunities.[79] It introduces objective award criteria based on the most economically advantageous solution for the particular requirement and provides for debriefing, whereby all unsuccessful bidders who so request are given feedback after the contract is awarded. At the time of writing, all Member States participating in the Agency,[80] except for Bulgaria and Romania, also participate in this intergovernmental regime.

VI. FLEXIBILITY

In a Union of ever-widening membership, its ability to act on the international scene becomes more easily compromised. Therefore, a degree of flexibility is inevitable and it may be either formalised or non-formalised. Non-formalised flexibility has been present in the development of the CFSP all along. For instance, for years in the past the Prime Ministers of the United Kingdom, Germany, Italy, Spain and France used to hold regular meetings with the Turkish Prime Minister, meetings which set the tone of the EU's relationship with Turkey. A more recent example of flexibility is the engagement of the so-called EU 3, namely the United Kingdom, Germany and France, with Iran and their effort to negotiate an agreement over Iran's nuclear facilities.[81]

Such activities operate clearly beyond the CFSP formal institutional set-up. To a certain extent they are inevitable, because of the nature of the CFSP and of the international crises that may occur. To a certain extent they may also be desirable—the negotiations with Iran have worked quite smoothly, as far as the projection of the EU's position is concerned. However, a note of caution is necessary in relation to their function: to rely overly upon such flexible arrangements would be to gradually undermine the role and effectiveness of the institutional system set up under the CFSP rules. This became quite clear in the case of the negotiations with Iran, when the EU 3 gradually brought the CFSP High Representative into the fold, involving him in some of the negotiations. In fact, it is interesting how his involvement was seen as complementary to that of the EU 3. The British Minister for Europe, Geoff Hoon, for instance, stated that the EU 3 'have set out a negotiating framework for [Solana] to deliver'.[82] Eventually, they also started informing the Council regularly over the progress of their negotiations with Iran. This was surely the right thing to do—and it could

---

[79] <http://www.eda.europa.eu/ebbweb/> accessed 3 September 2008.

[80] That is all Member States except Denmark.

[81] See E Denza, 'Non-proliferation of Nuclear Weapons: The EU and Iran' (2005) 10 *European Foreign Affairs Review* 289.

[82] House of Lords Paper 228, 'Current Developments in European Foreign Policy', Minutes of Evidence, 5.

have happened earlier, in fact it *should* have happened earlier, to make it clear that the EU 3 were not acting beyond the EU framework.

In terms of formalised flexibility, there was considerable resistance to its introduction in the CFSP area for a long time. For instance, in successive IGCs, the call for the introduction of a flexibility clause in the second pillar was ultimately turned down by the Member States. This changed at Nice[83] in relation to matters implementing a joint action or a common position and, in any case, does not apply to matters with security and defence implications. It is indicative of the maturity of the CFSP system, and the deeply entrenched nature of the culture of cooperation developed in the last 40 years that the Member States should have felt confident enough to introduce flexibility in the formal CFSP framework, a position further developed by the Constitutional Treaty[84] and the Lisbon Treaty.

This has become apparent in the area of security and defence policy, where there is no exception to the principle of unanimity. Within this area, formalised flexibility may take various forms: Member States which together establish multinational forces might make them available to the common security and defence policy[85]; a group of Member States might assume the role of implementing a defence task in order to 'protect the Union's values and serve its interests'[86]; a mechanism of permanent structured cooperation would be established in order to allow Member States to deal with 'the most demanding missions'.[87]

It is entirely proper that flexibility mechanisms should be viewed as a necessary component of an effective security and defence policy. In an entity as diverse in not only membership but also defence capacity as the European Union is, flexibility would enhance its ability to assert its identity on the international scene. What is noteworthy in the mechanisms set out in the Lisbon Treaty and originating in the Constitutional Treaty is the increasing tendency in the EU towards not only an expansion of the scope of flexibility, but mainly its formalisation.

VII. CONCLUSION

In December 2001, the Laeken Declaration referred to 'the governance of globalisation' and stressed that the European Union should shoulder its

---

[83]   Art 27(a)–(e) TEU.

[84]   See the analysis in Koutrakos, above n 43, 499–504. See also J Howorth, 'The European Draft Constitutional Treaty and the Future of the European Defence Initiative: A Question of Flexibility' (2004) 9 *European Foreign Affairs Review* 483.

[85]   Art 49(c)(3) of the Lisbon Treaty.

[86]   Art 49(c)(5) of the Lisbon Treaty. The execution of the tasks would be governed by Art 28C.

[87]   Art 49(c)(6) of the Lisbon Treaty. The execution of the tasks would be governed by Art 28E.

responsibilities.[88] In the light of political circumstances (the incidents on September 9, 2001, the unilateralist tendencies of the American administration, the opportunity offered by the drafting of and debate about the Constitutional Treaty, and the period of reflection which followed), the practical implications of this statement emerged by the focus of EU, as well as national, decision-makers on CFSP.

Having highlighted the incremental, *sui generis* and the heavily focused on procedures emergence of CFSP, this chapter outlined three main aspects of this policy which appear to shape its current state and future development. The first is the increasing focus of the EU institutions on coherence in terms of its substantive content, normative ramifications and administrative management. In the light of the EU's multi-faceted and cross-pillar international profile, the central role of coherence has given rise, on the one hand, to an increasingly prominent role for the EU judiciary and, on the other hand, an emphasis by the EU institutions on the elaboration of practical mechanisms which would enhance the management of coherence between the various strands of CFSP. The emerging ESDP and the increasing emphasis on formalising flexibility were the other two aspects of the current state of the EU's foreign policy examined in this chapter.

The above trends which underpin the current conduct of CFSP may appear to be paradoxical: on the one hand, the EU is keen to provide broad sets of principles and objectives aiming to bring disparate strands of its foreign policy under a common policy framework whilst, on the other hand, it focuses on the elaboration of specific, practical, almost minimalistic mechanisms aiming to manage this framework. In essence, these approaches are complementary and have a common origin: the realisation of the impossibility of the quest for uniformity in EU foreign policy and the need to focus on the coherence of the different threads of this policy and the management of their relationship. Quite how this will be achieved in the constitutional constellation emerging from the Lisbon Treaty saga is the challenge for the EU in the years to come.

---

[88] It has also sought to highlight the contribution of the Lisbon Agenda in enhancing the EU's position in a globalised order: COM(2007) 581 Final, The European Interest: Succeeding in the age of globalization, 3 October 2007.

8

The International Legal Personality of the European Community and the European Union

DOMINIC MCGOLDRICK

I. INTRODUCTION

THIS CHAPTER PRINCIPALLY examines the legal implications of Article 47 of the Lisbon Reform Treaty (2007).[1] This provides: 'The Union shall have legal personality'. Part II considers the requirements that different legal orders set for legal personality. Part III looks 'back' at the evolution of legal personality during the period from the establishment of the EC through to the establishment of the European Union in the Maastricht Treaty of European Union (1992). Part IV looks at the development of the issue of the EU's international personality from 1992 through to the single international personality provided for in the Lisbon Reform Treaty (2007). Part V looks 'forward' to life after Lisbon. What emerges is a classic tale of pragmatic factual and conceptual evolution which makes a 'before and after' analysis rather artificial. As with many other occasions in the EC/EU reform-making process, the latest Treaty largely encapsulates what had already arguably become a legal reality with respect to legal personality of the EU. Nonetheless, it is submitted that the express recognition of EU personality, and its succession to the EC's personality, are significant. The former confirms a legal reality, provides helpful legal clarification and carries symbolic significance. The latter necessitates a wider assessment of the legal and practical implications of the EU's single international personality. Legal personality is a technical question, but it is also about the coherence of external international identity and action, representativeness, the promotion and protection of

* I am grateful to Steve Peers (Essex University) for his comments on a draft of this chapter. The usual disclaimer applies.

[1] [2007] OJ C306/01. It retains the same number in the consolidated TEU: see Consolidated versions of the Treaty on European Union and the Treaty on the functioning of the European Union, [2008] OJ C115/1.

European interests and values at the global level, speaking with a single voice, and being able to operate more effectively internationally.[2] For third parties it is more about determining responsibility for breach of international obligations.

This chapter considers how the legal personality and related provisions captured in the Lisbon Treaty would have been and may yet be given effect. The Lisbon Treaty captured a moment in the constitutional and historical evolution of the idea of Europe. The fate of the Treaty, as such, is uncertain after the vote against it in the Irish referendum in June 2007. However, although it was discussed, according international personality to the EU did not appear to be in any way central to the Irish debate. It seems likely that the substance of the provisions of the Lisbon Treaty discussed here will subsequently appear, although it may have to be in a different treaty signed in a different European city.

II. LEGAL ORDERS AND LEGAL PERSONALITY

A. Legal Orders

Broadly speaking, there are at least three different views as to the nature of the EC/EU legal order.[3] In *Van Gend En Loos*, it was famously described by the European Court of Justice (ECJ) as 'a new legal order of international law'.[4] In later formulations, the reference to 'of international law' was subsequently dropped leaving it simply as a new legal order. On a second view the legal order is *sui generis*, and on a third it is a development on national states' constitutional systems.[5] The resistance to the first view—as a specific of international law—was based on the perceived limitations of the latter, in particular, its state centricity, dependence on state consent and the optional nature of international judicial jurisdiction. The EC (principally through the ECJ) has made remarkable progress in its

---

[2] See Art 3 of the revised TEU (Art 2 of the current TEU on the objectives of the Union). As always, there are also significant inter-institutional elements.

[3] See TC Hartley, 'International Law and the Law of the European Union—A Reassessment' (2001) 2 *British Yearbook of International Law* 1.

[4] Case 26/62, *Van Gend En Loos* [1963] ECR 1, para 12.

[5] '... the Treaty has created a municipal order of transnational dimensions, of which it forms the "basic constitutional charter"': AG Maduro in Case C-402/05 P, *Yassin Abdul Kadi v Council of EU and Commission of EC* (point 21 of the Opinion delivered 16 January 2008), citing Case 294/83, *Les Verts* [1986] ECR 1339, para 23. See also the discussion in Joined Cases C-402/05 and 415/05 P, *Kadi and Al Barakaat International Foundation v Council*, paras 278–330 (judgment of 3 September 2008); Case C-91/05 *Commission v Council* not yet reported, para 65 (on the exercised of community powers in the observance of the undertakings given in the context of the United Nations and other international organisations). On a fourth view, it could be some combination of the first three views.

attempt to escape these limitations in its internal order. However, when the EC sought to act externally, it necessarily had to seek an accommodation with the legal order of public international law (PIL). The most pertinent examples are precisely the issues of the international legal personality of the EC and EU respectively. As the external competences of the EC expanded, it inevitably came into closer relations with the PIL system.[6] Following the establishment of the European Union in the Maastricht Treaty of European Union (TEU) in 1992, this external role has substantially increased and deepened, particularly with the formal advent of the EU's common foreign and security policy. Thus, consideration of the inter-relationship between the EU and PIL legal orders has become more frequent and complex.[7] Inevitably, perhaps, there has been some level of discord.[8]

B. International Legal Personality

An entity which has international personality possesses rights and duties in PIL.[9] A claim of international legal personality is a claim for a personality in the sphere of PIL; therefore, the claim has to satisfy the requirements of that system of law.[10] PIL determines the requirements of an international

[6] See M Koskenniemi (ed), *International Legal Aspects of the European Union* (The Hague, Kluwer, 1997). Art 3(5) of the post-Lisbon TEU makes express reference to the EU contributing to the 'protection of human rights, in particular the rights of the child, as well as to the strict observance and the development of international law, including respect for the principles of the United Nations Charter'. See also the references to international law in Art 21 (principles which guide the EU's action on the international scene) and Art 214 (humanitarian aid) of the revised TEU.

[7] See V Kronenberger (ed), *The European Union and the International Legal Order: Discord or Harmony?* (The Hague, TMC Asser Press, 2001) and n 7 below.

[8] A notable example has been in the context of the listing of individuals and organisations in the context of anti-terrorism measures which results in the freezing of their assets in the EU or travel restrictions. See Case T-253/02, *Zubeyir Aydar on behalf of Kongra-Gel v Council of the European Union* [2004] OJ C262/28; Case T-315/01, Case C-402/05 P, *Kadi v Council and Commission* [2005] ECR II-3649; Case T-306/01, *Yusuf v Council and Commission* [2005] ECR II-3353; and AG Maduro's Opinion in Case C-402/05 P *Yassin Abdul Kadi v Council of EU and Commission of EC* (delivered 16 January 2008). AG Maduro strongly asserts that it is for the Community courts to determine the effect of international obligations within the Community legal order by reference to conditions set by Community law: para 23. Case T-228/02, *OMPI v Council* [2006] ECR II-4665; P Eeckhout, 'Community Terrorism Listings, Fundamental Rights, and UN Security Council Resolutions. In Search of the Right Fit' (2007) 3 *European Constitutional Law Review* 183; and J Almqvist, 'A Human Rights Critique of European Judicial Review: Counter-Terrorism Sanctions' (2008) 57 *ICLQ* 303.

[9] See JE Nijman, *The Concept of International Legal Personality, An Inquiry into the History and Theory of International Law* (TCM Asser/Cambridge University Press, The Hague, 1994).

[10] D Akande, 'International Organisations' in M Evans (ed), *International Law*, 2nd edn (Oxford, Oxford University Press, 2006) 277. See also E Benvenisti, 'The Conception of

organisation and of the rights, powers and duties that international personality engages for it.[11] The original model of public international law conceived of it as a purely rule-generating, inter-state, normative system. The theoretical structure was composed of a number of autonomously acting spheres of influence/supremacy/jurisdiction called states. The PIL system was simply made up of the accumulation of rules which operate to organise their relations *inter se*. Modern conceptions of international law are much more sophisticated as to the range of international actors and the values and processes of international law.[12] PIL has determined that both states[13] and international organisations can possess international personality.[14] As there are in excess of 100 intergovernmental organisations, this is of enormous significance to the theory and practice of the system.[15]

The leading PIL precedent on the international personality of public international law institutions is the advisory opinion of the International Court of Justice (ICJ) in the *Reparation for injuries suffered in the service of the United Nations* case (1949).[16] In September 1948, Count Bernadotte was the Chief UN Truce Negotiator in Jerusalem. Jerusalem was at the time in Israeli possession. He was killed, allegedly by a gang of private terrorists. The UN General Assembly sought an advisory opinion from the ICJ. It asked, inter alia, whether the United Nations, as an organisation, had the capacity to bring an international claim against the responsible de jure or de facto government with a view to obtaining reparation due in respect of the damage caused to the UN, and to the victim or to persons entitled through him? The ICJ analysed the provisions of the Charter as a whole. It noted in particular that the Charter established organs charged with various tasks, established various obligations for the members in relation to the UN, gave the UN legal capacity and privileges and immunities in the territory of each of its Member States, and contained provisions for the conclusion of agreements between the UN and its members which had been acted on in practice. It concluded that the UN was intended to exercise and enjoy functions and rights which could only

International Law as a Legal System' (2008) *Tel Aviv University Law Faculty Papers*, Paper 83. Available at <http://law.bepress.com/taulwps/fp/art83> accessed 3 September 2008.

[11] 'To say that an entity has international personality is to say that the entity is a bearer of rights and duties *derived* from international law': D Akande, 'International Organisations' in M Evans (ed), *International Law*, 2nd edn (Oxford, Oxford University Press, 2006) 281. On the consequences which flow from the possession of international legal personality by an international organisation, see *ibid*, 282–3.

[12] See V Lowe, *International Law* (Oxford, Oxford University Press, 2007).

[13] See C Warbrick, 'States and Recongnition in International Law' in Evans, above n 10, 217–75.

[14] See R Jennings and A Watts, *Oppenheim's International Law*, 9th edn (Longman, Essex, 1996) 16–22.

[15] See generally N White, *The Law of International Organisations*, 9th edn (Manchester, Manchester University Press, 2005).

[16] Advisory Opinion, ICJ Reports, 1949, 174.

be explained on the basis of the possession of a large measure of international personality and the capacity to operate upon an international plane. It was not a state, but it was an international person:

> Whereas a State possesses the totality of international rights and duties recognised by international law, the rights and duties of an entity such as the organisation must depend upon its purposes and functions as specified in its constituent documents and developed in practice.[17]

The UN therefore possessed a right of functional protection in respect of its agents. A second question arose from the fact that Israel was not at the relevant time a member of the United Nations.[18] The ICJ could have stated that the UN existed as an international person in respect of the Member States of the UN only, that is, 'subjective international personality'. This would have been consistent with a view that the Member States of the UN had, by becoming parties to the UN Charter, consented to the functional degree of international personality necessary for the international organisation which they created to exercise its functions. However, the ICJ went further:

> 50 States, representing the vast majority of the members of the International Community, had the power, in conformity with international law, to bring into being an entity possessing *objective international personality* and not merely personality recognised by them alone, together with capacity to bring international claims . . .

This international law principle of 'objective legal personality' means that entities can exist within a system even in relation to other entities which have not consented to their existence within that system. There is, therefore, an 'objective' element to the functioning and existence of the PIL system that cannot be denied by other actors within that system.

The precedent of the *Reparations* case could have been limited in that the Opinion related to an organisation created by a number of states which represented the 'vast majority of members of the International Community' at that time. Subsequently, however, practice has greatly reduced the strict requirements that could have been drawn from that statement.[19] There is now little doubt that international organisations can have objective international personality even when brought into existence by only a limited number of states.

---

[17] *Ibid*, 180.
[18] It joined in May 1949.
[19] See Akande, above n 10, 284.

C. Determining International Legal Personality: Subjective, Objective or both?

There has been a conceptual debate in PIL as to whether international personality depends, at least in the first instance, on the subjective will (or intention) of those who create (and those who deal with) an international organisation or on the satisfying of objective conditions relating, for example, to permanence, organs, powers and functions.[20] Both elements were discussed in the *Reparations* case. The debate becomes particularly important when (as was the case with the EU from 1992 to 2007) the relevant international provisions do not make express provision and so it must be determined whether such personality is implied or inherent.[21] That an international organisation has international personality does not determine what rights and duties it has in PIL (sometimes referred to as 'capacities' or 'competencies'). However, inherent in the very idea of a legal personality separate from that of the Member States of the organisation must be that the organisation has at least some rights and obligations that are distinct from those of the Member States.[22] If so, then to some degree it must also be inherent in the idea of international personality that it can bring a claim in PIL to maintain those rights (some of which may take the form of privileges or immunities) and be the subject of a claim in PIL for non-fulfillment of its obligations, that is, it can bear international responsibility as a matter of PIL.[23] An international person must be able to enter into relationships with other international persons (right of intercourse).[24] An international organisation could have international personality but not possess treaty-making power, although in practice, the most important attribute of legal personality under international law is a treaty-making power. The right of legation (ie to send and receive diplomatic envoys) has traditionally been restricted to full sovereign states, but in principle that right could be extended to an international organisation.[25] The longer the organisation exists the greater is the potential evidential basis for its

---

[20]   See N White, above n 15, 35–40.

[21]   P de Schoutheete and S Andoura, 'The Legal Personality of the European Union' (2007) 1 LX *Studia Diplomatica*. Available at <http://www.irri-kiib.be/papers_eur.html> accessed 3 September 2008.

[22]   Related to this is the question of a how the separate will of the international person can find expression.

[23]   See C Tomuschat, 'The International Responsibility of the EU' in E Cannizzaro (ed), *The EU as an Actor in International Relations* (Kluwer, The Hague, 2002) 177.

[24]   See M Rama-Montaldo, 'International Legal Personality and Implied Powers of International Organisations' (1997) 44 *British Yearbook of International Law* 111.

[25]   See E Denza, The Intergovernmental Pillars of the European Union (Oxford, OUP, 2002) 85–6, 164–6; Jennings and Watts, above n 14, 1056–8.

practice, for example with respect to making claims, accepting international responsibility, treaty-making and legation, to found a claim of international personality. In Parts III to IV below, we examine the practices of the EC and the EU in these respects. As we shall see, the substantial degree of uncertainty to date has not been occasioned by the requirements of PIL. Rather, they have been due to the uncertainty as to the intentions of the Member States with respect to the international personality of the EU.

III. LOOKING BACK: LEGAL PERSONALITY OF THE EC

A. Municipal Legal Personality of the EC

Since the original EEC Treaty, Member States have had to grant the Community 'the most extensive legal capacity accorded to legal persons under their laws'.[26] The EC may, in particular, acquire and dispose of moveable property and be a party to legal proceedings.[27] To this end, the EC was represented by the Commission.[28] A 1965 Protocol on the privileges and immunities of the EC to the Merger Treaty (1957) made provision for the privileges and immunities of the EC in the Member States.[29]

B. The International Legal Personality of the EC

Consideration of this issue requires an examination of the provisions of the EC Treaty which are relevant to the EC's external relations.[30] On any analysis of those provisions, the EC clearly satisfied the functionalist test of the ICJ in the *Reparations* case, even more so than the UN. Moreover, this is strongly supported by the EC's extensive international practice.[31] The original Article 210 EEC (later Article 281 EC) was clear and precise: 'The Community shall have legal personality'. This was an assertion of personality in international law and not just personality in each of the Member

---

[26] Originally Art 211, then Art 282 EC.

[27] *Ibid.*

[28] See Case T-451/93, *San Marco Impex Italiana SA v Commission* [1994] ECR II-1061; and Case C-257/90, *Italsolar SpA v Commission* [1990] ECR I-3841.

[29] [1967] OJ 152. See Case C-88/92, *van Rosendaal v Staatssecretaris van Financien* [1993] ECR I-3315. For a rare judicial decision on the immunities of an international organisation, see *Entico v UNESCO and Secretary of State for Foreign and Commonwealth Affairs* [2008] EWHC 531 (Comm), upholding UNESCO's immunity claim in the UK in the face of a human rights challenge.

[30] See I Macleod, ID Hendry and S Hyett, *The External Relations of the European Communities* (Oxford, Oxford University Press, 1996) 29–36.

[31] *Ibid.*

States.[32] The ECJ interpreted this as entailing acknowledgment of the external capacity of the EC to establish contractual links with non-Member States in all policy areas falling within its competence.[33] The EC thus had the power to conclude and negotiate agreements in line with its external powers, to become a member of an international organisation and to have delegations (but not technically diplomats) in non-member countries. While Member States happily accepted the international personality of the EC (and also of Euratom and the ECSC), there were long and complex internal battles in terms of competence, external negotiation and representation.[34] There has also been some resistance from other states against any perception that the EC should receive any privileged treatment. This ranged from non-recognition[35] to demands for clarity as to competence and voting rights. International treaties to which the EC was allowed to become a party commonly required that it deposit an explicit statement of its competence with respect to that treaty.[36] This is particularly evident where the EC has actually taken over the competence of its Member States in certain respects.[37]

1. International Agreements

A number of Articles of the EC Treaty made express provision for the EC to enter into international agreements. The principal ones related to the common commercial policy (Article 133 EC), what become known generically as association agreements (Article 310 EC), the environment (Article 174 EC) and development cooperation (Article 181 EC). Moreover, the ECJ also established that the EC had a treaty-making capacity that went much wider than these express powers, because there could be an implied external competence as a result of the taking of certain internal measures.[38] In addition there were more limited and specific powers relating to monetary or foreign exchange regime matters (Article 111 EC), education,

---

[32] See Part III, A above.

[33] Case 22/70, *Commission v Council (AETR)* [1971] ECR 263, para 14.

[34] DR Verwey, *The European Community, The European Union And The International Law Of Treaties: A Comparative Legal Analysis Of The Community And Union's External Treaty-Making Practice* (The Hague, TMC Asser Press, 2004); T Delreux, 'The EU in International Environmental Negotiations: A Legal Perspective on the internal decision-making process' (2006) 6 *International Environmental Agreements* 231; *Opinion 1/94 re WTO Agreement* [1994] ECR I-5267; and *Opinion 2/00 re Cartagena Protocol on Biosafety* [2001] ECR I-9713.

[35] This was the initial position of the then USSR as regards the EC.

[36] See A Aust, *The Modern Law of Treaties*, 2nd edn (Cambridge, Cambridge University Press, 2007) 140.

[37] Eg trade policy, fisheries or agriculture. See, eg Arts 305–7 of the UN Law of the Sea Convention (1982).

[38] See *AETR Case*, above n 33; and P Koutrakos, *EU International Relations Law* (Hart, Oxford, 2006) 77.

vocational training and youth (Articles 149(3) and 150 EC), culture (Article 151 EC), public health (Article 151 EC), and the EC's multi-annual framework programme on research and technological development (Article 170 EC).[39]

Article 300 EC made provision for the procedures to be followed for the 'conclusion of agreements between the Community and one or more States or international organisations'.[40] The Commission negotiated on the basis of authorisation by the Council. The Council concluded the agreements. The EC developed a very substantial international treaty practice on this basis. For example, it is a party to over 50 UN multilateral agreements. It is solely party to some treaties, while for others it is a party alongside some or all of the Member States.[41] In certain circumstances, although only Member States may be parties to a treaty, they are effectively acting as trustees for the EC. This arises when the EC has competence over certain matters, but it cannot be a member of a particular organisation because membership is limited to states. The International Labour Organisation is an example, where the EC has only observer status.[42]

2. Sanctions

Economic sanctions could be imposed under Article 133 EC, as part of the common trade policy following the adoption of a decision by Member States within European Political Cooperation. The first use of such sanctions in 1982 was directed against the then Soviet Union, following the declaration of martial law in Poland.[43] After the Maastricht Treaty, the relevant legal basis became Article 301 EC, and/or Article 60 EC for financial sanctions, following a common action or joint position under the CFSP.

---

[39] Other international agreements were also foreseen in the EC Treaty. Art 293 (ex Art 220) EC provided for the Member States to enter into negotiations with each other with a view to securing certain specified benefits for their nationals. After the TEU (considered below), Member States had a choice between an Art 293 EC Convention and one under the third pillar of the TEU (dealing with justice and home affairs). Since the Treaty of Amsterdam (1997), the use of Conventions has effectively been phased out. See S Peers, *EU Justice and Home Affairs Law*, 2nd edn (Oxford, Oxford University Press, 2006) 31.

[40] See P Eeckhout, *Relations of the European Union* (Oxford, Oxford University Press, 2004) 169.

[41] See Koutrakos, above n 38, 137–81.

[42] See Opinion 2/91 (*ILO Convention*) [1993] ECR I-1061.

[43] Regulation 877/82 [1982] OJ L72/15. See Koutrakos, above n 38, 428–41; and Eeckhout, above n 40, 424–53.

3. Relations with International Organisations and Institutions[44]

The EC Treaty provided for the Commission to ensure the maintenance of all appropriate relations with the UN, its Specialised Agencies, the General Agreement on Tariffs and Trade (now World Trade Organisation (WTO)) and all international organisations.[45] This related to arrangements at the administrative level. Two other international organisations are singled out, although with reference to the Community rather than the Commission. The Community was to establish 'all appropriate forms of cooperation with the Council of Europe'[46] and 'close cooperation with the Organisation for Economic Cooperation and Development'.[47]

4. Membership of, or Participation In, International Organisations[48]

The EC Treaty contained no express authority for EC membership of other international organisations. Nonetheless, in Opinion 1/76, the ECJ clearly recognised that the EC had the competence to participate in the establishment of international organisations and to be a member of such organisations.[49] In practice, the EC has had to fight a series of battles with Member States and with international organisations in order to gain recognition, or partial recognition, of its role and so be able to obtain membership or participation.[50] These conflicts with Member States, and with third parties, partly explain the substantial variations in the rights of the EC, and the different modes of representation, found in the different organisations. After the TEU, Article 300 EC referred to the conclusion by the EC of 'agreements establishing a specific institutional framework by organising cooperation procedures'.

As of October 2008, the EC was only a member of three general international organisations or institutions. These are the UN Food and Agriculture Organisation (FAO),[51] the European Bank for Reconstruction

---

[44] See Macleod, Hendry and Hyett, above n 30, 165–207.

[45] Art 302 EC.

[46] Art 303 EC.

[47] Art 304 EC. The details were to be determined by common accord.

[48] See Eeckhout, above n 40, 199–225. Also <http://ec.europa.eu/external_relations/organisations/index_en.htm> accessed 3 September 2008.

[49] Opinion 1/76 [1977] ECR 741.

[50] See J Sack, 'The EC's Membership of International Organisations' (1995) 33 *CML Rev* 1227; and E Denza, 'The Community as a Member of International Organisations' in N Emiliou and D O'Keeffe (eds), *The European Union and World Trade Law* (Chichester, Wiley, 1996) 3.

[51] See R Frid, 'The EEC: A Member of a Specialised Agency of the UN' (1993) 4 *European Journal of International Law* 239.

and Development (EBRD)[52] and the WTO.[53] The terms of membership varies enormously between the three institutions.[54] Membership of the FAO was a major breakthrough in political and legal terms. Possibilities for future membership are the International Labour Organisation (ILO), the International Civil Aviation Organisation (ICAO) and, with the single currency established, the International Monetary Fund (IMF).[55] The EC is also a member of over 60 international organisations which have been created under the terms of an international treaty to deal with a specific matter. Such organisations are sometimes referred to as treaty organs, to distinguish them from the more general international organisations. They mainly concern fisheries, environmental protection and commodity agreements under the UN Conference on Trade and Development (UNCTAD).[56] Some of them can be of major importance. Since 2007, the EC has been a member of the Hague Conference on Private International Law, which works for the progressive unification of the rules of private international law.[57]

The EC has sometimes been treated, in terms of membership or participation, simply as any other international organisation would be.[58] Increasingly, however, it has been treated in a unique way by a specific provision on the EC,[59] or by a reference to 'regional economic integration organisations'.[60] Although this appears to be a general formulation, it is defined in such a way as to only cover the EC. This formulation acknowledges that the EC is a unique entity in terms of its competence. Some treaties have required the EC, and sometimes its Member States, to

---

[52] See D McGoldrick, 'A New International Economic Order for Europe' (1992) 12 *Yearbook of European Law* 434, 448–56.

[53] See Opinion 1/94 *re WTO Agreement* [1994] ECR I-5267, discussed in Eeckhout, above n 40, 26–35 & 74–81; M Matsushita, TJ Schoenbaum and PC Mavroidis, *The World Trade Organisation* (Oxford, Oxford University Press, 2006) 95–9; and A Qureshi, *The World Trade Organisation* (Manchester, Manchester University Press, 1996) 164–91.

[54] See Frid, above n 51.

[55] EMU countries remain individual members of the IMF. Since the IMF's Articles of Agreement confine membership to countries, the euro area as such is not able to appoint a governor or appoint or elect executive directors in the IMF. In December 1998, the ECB was granted observer status at selected Executive Board meetings.

[56] On environmental negotiations, see Delreux, above n 30. The 'Group of 77', representing the developing countries in the UN, supported EC participation in commodity agreements. It is now composed of 130 states.

[57] See A Schulz, 'The Accession of the EC to the Hague conference on Private International Law' 56 ICLQ (2007) 939–50.

[58] See Art 305(1)(f) and Annex IX of the LOSC; and KR Simmonds, 'The Communities Declaration Upon Signature of the UN Convention on the Law of the Sea' (1986) 23 *CML Rev* 521.

[59] As in the WTO Agreement.

[60] See the UN Framework Convention on Biological Diversity (1992).

make 'declarations' of competence and to update them.[61] The EC is also an observer at a significant number of international organisations, including the UN General Assembly,[62] its Economic and Social Council,[63] and most of its Specialised Agencies, including the ILO, the WHO and UNESCO.[64] The more active role of the UN since the end of the Cold War has enhanced the importance of these links.[65] So too with the Organisation for Security and Cooperation in Europe (OSCE), where the EC is also an observer. The EC has close cooperation with, but not the formal status of observer at, the Council of Europe.[66] A Memorandum of Understanding was signed between the EU and the Council of Europe in May 2007.[67]

5. Diplomatic Recognition/Representation

Diplomatic recognition and representation are important indicators of the recognition of the international personality of an international entity.[68] As of October 2008, over 170 states and territories were accredited to the EC. After the TEU, many of them have adopted the designation of 'Mission to

---

[61] See, eg Art II(4) of the FAO Constitution, as amended. Article 44(1) of the UN Disability Convention provides, 1. 'Regional integration organization' shall mean an organization constituted by sovereign States of a given region, to which its member States have transferred competence in respect of matters governed by this Convention. Such organizations shall declare, in their instruments of formal confirmation or accession, the extent of their competence with respect to matters governed by this Convention. Subsequently, they shall inform the depositary of any substantial modification in the extent of their competence.

[62] See GA Resolution 3208 (XXIX) of 11 October 1974. The same resolution also governs the status of the EC at UN conferences, the number and importance of which is rising. For the UN Conference on Environment and Development in 1992, the GA granted the EC the enhanced role of 'full participant status', GA Resn 6/470 of 12 April 1992. In practical conference of representation, participation in committees and working groups, debating and submitting amendments, this took the EC close to the status of participating states, except that it could not vote or submit procedural motions. The EC assumed a leadership and mediation role at different times in the conference. Since then the EC/EU has often sought such a status.

[63] This extends to its Regional and Functional Commissions. The latter include the former Commission on Human Rights (now the Human Rights Council, see GA Resolution 60/251, 3 April 2006) and the Commission on Sustainable Development. On the latter, see GA Resolution 47/191 of 23 January 1993 providing for the full participation of the EC within its areas of competence but without the right to vote; Bull-EC, 6–1992 on the principles governing the EC's participation. See also Art 19 TEU on Member states who are members of the Security Council.

[64] For full details, see Macleod, Hendry and Hyett, above n 30, 195–207.

[65] An exchange of letters regulates day-to-day contacts with the UN Secretariat.

[66] In the context of Opinion 2/94, on *EC accession to the European Convention on Human Rights*, the EC did not propose to join the Council of Europe. See point 6 of the Opinion. This is still the case.

[67] <https://wcd.coe.int/ViewDoc.jsp?Ref=CM(2007)74&Language=lanEnglish> accessed 3 September 2008. The first meeting under the Memorandum took place in October 2007. See also the 'Agreement between the Council of Europe and the EC concerning co-operation between the Council of Europe and the EU Agency for Fundamental Rights, CM (2008) rev 6.

[68] See Macleod, Hendry and Hyett, above n 30, 208–25.

the EU' to reflect the wider scope of the EU's activities, but this was not considered to have legal significance. Around 18 international organisations or entities have established '*bureaux de liaison*' in Brussels. The EC has a massive and growing diplomatic presence around the world.[69] It maintains over 130 delegations or offices in third states or territories, involving over 5,000 staff.[70] Technically, these are 'Commission Delegations' based on the Commission's powers to establish its own departments,[71] rather then EC delegations based on international diplomatic law. This is because it is not yet accepted that international organisations can send and receive diplomats.[72] In practice, however, the EC maintains the equivalent of a worldwide diplomatic presence. That presence operates in close cooperation with the missions of Member States to third countries and international organisations and with the Presidency, which also plays a significant role.[73] They also play an important role in the ensuring compliance with and implementation of the CFSP. Commission delegations have also been established to a number of international organisations.[74]

6. International Responsibility

If an entity has international personality, then it may both bring international claims and have claims brought against it.[75] Some international treaties make specific provision for the EC, for example, the WTO Agreement.[76] The EC may bear joint or separate responsibility with the

---

[69] By contrast, some Member States are reducing their diplomatic representation around the world as a cost-saving exercise. There are only three states in the world where all Member States have diplomatic representation: China, the Russian Federation and the US. See Diplomatic and Consular Protection of Union Citizens in Third Countries, European Commission, Green Paper, COM(2006) 712 final.

[70] European Commission, 'Taking Europe to the world—50 years of the European Commission's External Service' (Luxembourg, Office for Official Publications of the European Communities, 2004).

[71] See the Opinion of AG Tesauro in Case C-327/91, *France v Commission* [1994] ECR I-3641, point 28.

[72] See Macleod, Hendry and Hyett, above n 30, 208–9. Cf Oppenheim, above n 14, which is more equivocal on this issue.

[73] See BR Bot, 'Cooperation in the Missions of the EC in Third Countries: European Diplomacy in the Making' (1984) 1 *Legal Issues of European Integration* 149; and Art 17 of the post-Lisbon TFEU (currently Art 20 EC) on Union citizenship.

[74] Eg UN, FAO, UNESCO, OECD, IAEA and UNIDO.

[75] See J Groux and P Manin, *The European Communities in the International Order* (European Commission, Brussels, 1985) 141. It may face procedural limitations in certain dispute settlement forums.

[76] See Matsushita *et al*, above n 53. About half of the GATT/WTO Panel Reports have concerned the EC. Cases have been brought against the EC and or Member States, but they have been defended by the EC.

Member States.[77] The ECJ has accepted that the EC is subject to customary international law[78] and that the ECJ itself can be bound by a decision of an international tribunal under the terms of an international agreement to which the EC is a party.[79] A particular problem for the EC is where the practical exercise of its international personality is limited because the relevant procedure or system does not permit the EC to have recourse to it. For example, the EC cannot be a member of the UN because this is limited to states. For the same reason, the EC could not be a party to contentious proceedings before the ICJ.[80] The system under the European Convention on Human Rights does not apply directly to the EC because it is not a party.[81] Indeed, it could not become a party unless the ECHR was amended to permit this—although in any event, in its Opinion 2/94, the ECJ had concluded that, '[a]s Community law now stands, the Community has no competence to accede to the ECHR'.[82]

The EC is then something less than a state, but something much more than an international organisation. Hence it is often, although not necessarily very helpfully, described as *sui generis*.

IV. THE INTERNATIONAL LEGAL PERSONALITY OF THE EUROPEAN UNION

A. Municipal Legal Personality of the EU

Under Article 335 of the post-Lisbon TFEU, the substantive provision of the EC Treaty on municipal personality is repeated, but it will be the EU which enjoys the personality. The EU shall be represented by the Commission. However, the EU 'shall be represented by each of the institutions, by

---

[77] See Case C-316/91, *European Development Fund: EP v Council, Re* [1994] ECR I-625, para 29 on the joint liability of the EC and the Member States under the Lome IV Convention. See also Case 327/91, *France v Commission* [1994] ECR I-3641; and Macleod, Hendry and Hyett, above n 30, 158–9.

[78] See Case C-286/90, *Anklagemyndigheden v Poulsen and Diva Navigation* [1992] ECR 6019; Case C-432/92, *R v Ministry of Agriculture, Fisheries and Food, ex p Anastasiou* [1994] ECR I-3087; and the cases in n 8 above. See also V Lowe, 'Can the EC Bind the Member States on Questions of Customary International? Law?' in Koskenniemi (ed), above n 6, 149.

[79] Opinion 1/92 (*First EEA Opinion*) [1991] ECR 6079, points 39–40.

[80] Art 34 of the Statute of the ICJ. Nor, under Art 96 of the Statute, could the EC be authorised by the UN to request an advisory opinion.

[81] The European Court has had to determine the limits of its jurisdiction to review EC matters; see *Matthews v UK* (1999) 28 EHRR 361; and *Bosphorus Hava Yollari Turizm v Ireland* (2006) 42 EHRR 1. See C Costello, 'The *Bosphorus* Ruling of the European Court of Human Rights: Fundamental Rights and Blurred Boundaries in Europe' (2006) 6 *Human Rights Law Review* 87.

[82] Opinion 2/94 (ECHR) [1996] ECR I-1759.

virtue of their administrative autonomy, in matters relating to their respective operation'. Article 343 TFEU provides that: 'The Union shall enjoy in the territories of the Member States such privileges and immunities as are necessary for the performance of its tasks, under the conditions laid down in the 1965 Protocol'. Protocol No 7 annexed to the revised treaties specifically addressed the privileges and immunities of the European Union.[83]

B. The International Legal Personality of the EU: From Maastricht (1992) to Lisbon (2007)

Given the broad objectives of the EU stated in Article B of the original TEU, some Member States feared that, if the EU did have international personality, then it would be very wide ranging. Indeed, it would come very close to having all of the international personality of a state. That was no doubt an important factor for those states that opposed international personality for the EU. However, those that supported EU personality argued that it was possible for provisions to be drafted that would allow the EU rather than the EC to be party to international agreements without altering the principles on competence in the EC pillar.

International organisations that have international personality are normally intergovernmental in nature. In that sense, the EU fits more naturally into the mould of international personality than the EC (with its supranational personality).[84] Those internal and external battles on EC international personality partly explain why some Member States have resisted the explicit recognition of EU personality. They feared that such recognition would reinforce the supranational character of the entity with personality, however named. Most international organisations are created for specific purposes and are functionally limited. There can be some degree of functional evolution, as there has been with the North Atlantic Treaty Organisation. By contrast, the history of the European project has been one of consistent functional growth and enhancement. It was from that perspective that according recognition of the EU's personality could be seen to give the appearance of taking the EU closer to having the character and status of a federal state in its own right.[85] Legally, this perspective is inaccurate. International personality acknowledges a *capacity* to act in the

---

[83] It deals, inter alia, with Property, Funds, Assets and Operations of the European Union, Communications and *Laissez-Passer*, Members of The European Parliament, Representatives of Member States Taking Part in the Work of the Institutions of the European Union, Officials and Other Servants of the European Union, Privileges and Immunities of Missions of Third Countries Accredited to The European Union.

[84] White, above n 15, 66.

[85] A 'United States of Europe' as it were.

international sphere, but it does not determine the circumstances in which the relevant actor has the *competence* to act. That depends on its constituent texts and varies, therefore, from one organisation to another. Nonetheless, the European Community/Union has historically sought to push its competences to the limit and in politics perceptions are important. Acknowledging its international personality could be interpreted as encouraging the EU to gradually replace Member States on the international stage as a political actor,[86] in the same way that the EC has done in some contexts where it enjoys competence.[87] In that context, the issue of international personality becomes one of high political importance.

As we shall see, there has been substantial disagreement over whether the EU, at least as initially established, satisfied the criteria of the ICJ in the *Reparations* case.[88] Consideration of this issue requires an examination of the provisions of the TEU which are relevant to the EU's external relations and an analysis of subsequent international practice of the EU, Member States, non-Member States and other international organisations.

1. The Treaty on European Union (1992)

The European Union was created in the Maastricht Treaty of 1992, but there was no express provision on international personality.[89] Given the existence of Article 210 EC, that was clearly deliberate. From the outset, there was some degree of studied ambiguity about what exactly it was, if indeed it was anything at all. The two Communities (EC and Euratom) making up the EU each had legal personality.[90] However, the TEU did not contain any provisions on the Union's legal personality, even though the Union comprised the two communities and two areas of intergovernmental cooperation, namely common foreign and security policy (CFSP) and what later became Justice and Home Affairs (JHA). The reasoning against the EU having legal personality, as it stood on the entry into force of the Treaty in November 1993, was as follows. First, there was no express provision in the TEU on international personality. Secondly, various functions that one would expect the Union to exercise, if it did have such personality, were in fact exercised by the Community (all the provisions on concluding external

---

[86] See T Thlikainen, 'To Be or Not to Be? An Analysis of the Legal and Political Elements of Statehood in the EU's External Identity' (2001) 6 *European Foreign Affairs Review* 223, who considers the extent to which the EU was beginning to be vested with the key elements of statehood and how its external identity is based on well-known principles of sovereignty and territoriality.

[87] For example, at the WTO.

[88] See P Gautier, 'The Reparation for Injuries Case Revisited: The Personality of the European Union' (2000) 4 *Max Planck Yearbook of the United Nations* 31.

[89] For the view that the TEU created a new legal system, see R Wessels, 'Revisiting the International Legal Status of the EU' (2000) 5 *European Foreign Affairs Review* 507, 508–9.

[90] As does the European Central Bank.

treaties were in the EC Treaty and provided for the Community to conclude such treaties). There were no such powers given to the Union, in the CFSP or elsewhere. Similarly, citizenship was in the Community section. Thirdly, the Union did not occupy a position of sufficient detachment from the Member States. The latter had a dominant role in the CFSP. In particular, the execution of the CFSP was left almost entirely to Member States, with Council playing an essentially procedural role. Fourthly, with respect to the CFSP, systematic cooperation and joint actions were processes for engaging the Member States, not as instruments of the Union as such. Fifthly, there was no provision for the conclusion of international agreements by the EU. Sixthly, the evidence of the (unpublished) *travaux preparatoires* revealed a clear intention during negotiations *not* to confer legal personality. The question was raised, and the Dutch Presidency said firmly that the Union would not have legal personality. They were supported by the Director General of the Council Legal Service. The Director General of the Commission Legal Service took the same view in evidence to the European Parliament.[91]

There were arguments in response to each of these points, so that none of them appeared conclusive. On the basis of the functional approach of the ICJ in the *Reparations* case, there was a tenable argument that the EU could have had international personality. First, international personality does not have to be express, but could be inherent or potential in the EU on a functional basis. Secondly, if the Union had sought to make or be a party to international agreements as part of the CFSP, or relating to Justice and Home Affairs, and if it was accepted by other international actors, then it could have been recognised as being capable of possessing international personality. However, not until 2001, that is after the entry into force of the Treaty of Amsterdam (1997), did the EU become a party to an international agreement.[92] Thirdly, although citizenship is in the Community part of the Treaty, it was citizenship of the Union, not of the Community. Moreover, there were international aspects to that citizenship.[93]

However, it was strongly asserted, and seemingly accepted, that the EU did not have international personality. Ultimately what seemed to be the most convincing explanation was the clear subjective intention of the Member States for the EU not to have international personality. This negatived any implied or inherent basis for such personality. In its ruling of

[91] See MR Eaton, 'Common Foreign and Security Policy' in D O'Keeffe and P Twomey (eds), *Legal Issues of the Maastricht Treaty* (Chichester, Wiley, 1994) 224.

[92] See below n 111.

[93] See Art 8 TEU. See now Arts 20–24 of the post-Lisbon TFEU, particularly Art 23 TFEU.

12 October 1993, the Federal German Constitutional Court, in constitutional proceedings against the Treaty on European Union, stated that:

> ... the treaty of Union nowhere points to any shared resolve of the contracting parties to institute, with the Union, an independent legal subject that would be endowed with powers in its own right. In the opinion of the Federal Government, the Union does not possess, either in relation to the European Communities or to the Member States, a distinct legal personality.[94] ... the Maastricht Treaty construes the Union as a name for the Member States acting in concert, not an independent legal entity. It is the Member States which, through the Treaty, provide the means and set the objectives for the Union.[95]

The UK similarly took the view that the Union did not have international legal personality.[96]

Among the practical consequences of the EU's lack of legal personality were that it could only act through Community institutions; it had no budget of its own, but was dependent on that of the EC; and that the Union used Community funds to secure positions or actions adopted.

2. The Amsterdam Treaty (1997) Amending the TEU

In its submissions to the 1996 IGC, the European Parliament (EP) called for the Union to be given international personality.[97] This would suggest that the EP accepted that it did not have it at that stage. The Commission also appeared to accept this view.[98] This opinion was confirmed by the statement of Mr Dewost, then Director-General IV, Political and Institutional Affairs Division, during the IGC, that 'the TEU does not conceive of the Union, in this connection, as an autonomous subject in law, but as a designation for the Member States acting in concert. Under the Treaty, it is the Member States that confer on the Union its objectives and means'.[99] The majority of academic opinion also supported this view.[100]

The question of the EU's international personality was discussed in the Reflection Group for the 1996 IGC. Its Final Report records that:

---

[94] (1994) 33 *ILM* 388 (judgment of 12 October 1993).

[95] *Ibid*, 428–9.

[96] See the Memorandum from the Foreign and Commonwealth Office in *Europe Beyond Maastricht*, House of Commons, Foreign Affairs Committee (1992). In evidence to the HL Select Committee on the European Communities, Martin Eaton stated that ' . . . we do not believe that the Union will constitute an international organisation with a separate international legal personality. It would be better characterised as an association of Member States which, for certain purposes described in the Treaty, act in common', Session 1992–93, 3rd Report, HL paper 10, para 129.

[97] EP's Report to the 1996 IGC, para 14(ii).

[98] See Commission's Report to the 1996 IGC, 64.

[99] Cited in EP Briefing, Intergovernmental Conference Briefing No 20, 'Legal Personality Of The Union' (1 July 1997).

[100] See A Sari, 'The Conclusion of International Agreements by the EU in the Context of ESDP' (2008) 57 *ICLQ* 53. On the issue before the Amsterdam Treaty, see J Klabbers,

A majority of members points to the advantage of international legal personality for the Union so that it can conclude international agreements on the subject-matter of Titles V and VI concerning the CFSP and the external dimension of justice and home affairs. For them, the fact that the Union does not legally exist is a source of confusion outside and diminishes its external role. Others consider that the creation of international legal personality for the Union could risk confusion with the legal prerogatives of Member States.[101]

The Amsterdam Treaty, which entered into force in May 1999, added a new Article 24 in Title V TEU (provisions on a common foreign and security policy). This provided:

> When it is necessary to conclude an agreement with one or more States or international organisations in implementation of this Title, the Council, acting unanimously, may authorise the Presidency, assisted by the Commission as appropriate, to open negotiations to that effect. Such agreements shall be concluded by the Council acting unanimously on a recommendation from the Presidency. No agreement shall be binding on a Member State whose representative in the Council states that it has to comply with the requirements of its own constitutional procedure; the other members of the Council may agree that the agreement shall apply provisionally to them.
>
> The provisions of this Article shall also apply to matters falling under Title VI.[102]

On the face of it, this was the first strong piece of empirical evidence that pointed towards the international personality of the EU.[103] The Treaty also introduced a number of changes which could be interpreted as increasing the sense of the EU's detachment from the Member States. For example, the EU bears sole responsibility for defining and implementing the CFSP. However, as so often with the EU, things were not that simple. Much turns on the conflicting interpretations of Article 24 TEU. Agreements are concluded by the Council, but is it acting as a European institution or as a joint body of the Member States?[104] Moreover, Article 24 TEU does not clarify on whose behalf the Council concludes agreements—the EU, or the Member states, or both. Opinion was split between those who considered that Article 24 TEU was simply a procedure for the collective conclusion of agreements by the Member States, and those who considered that Article

'Presumptive Personality: The EU in International Law' in M Koskenniemi (ed), above n 6, 231–53; and RA Wessels, 'The International Legal Status of the European Union' (1997) 2 *European Foreign Affairs Review* 109.

[101] 'Report by the Reflection Group: A Strategy for Europe', pr. 150 (Brussels, 5 December 1995). Available at <http://www.europarl.europa.eu/enlargement/cu/agreements/reflex2_en. htm> accessed 3 September 2008.

[102] Provisions on police and judicial cooperation in criminal matters.

[103] See Editorial, 'The EU—A New International Actor' (2001) 38 *CML Rev,* 825, reflecting on the first use of Art 24 TEU.

[104] See S Marquardt, 'The Conclusion of International Agreements under Article 24 of the TEU' in Kronenberger, above n 7, 333.

24 TEU implicitly recognised the treaty-making capacity of the EU as such, and thus its international personality.[105] That 'no agreement shall be binding on a Member State whose representative in the Council states that it has to comply with the requirements of its own constitutional procedure' suggests that the agreement bound the Member States rather than the Union. There were also conflicting interpretations of Declaration No 4 to the TEU which stated that Article 24 TEU 'shall not imply any transfer of competence from the Member States to the European Union'.[106]

Again, there was a strong argument that the evidence from the *travaux preparatoires* supported the view that there was no agreement to endow the EU with international personality. The issue was specifically considered. Proposals were put to that effect by the Dutch and Irish Presidencies in turn, but they were not adopted because of the lack of unanimity.[107] It is difficult to interpret Article 24 TEU to achieve an effect that was clearly not acceptable to some states.

3. The Nice Treaty (2001)

The Nice Treaty of February 2001 entered into force in February 2003. It added two modalities to Article 24 TEU, which then read:

1. When it is necessary to conclude an agreement with one or more States or international organisations in implementation of this title, the Council may authorise the Presidency, assisted by the Commission as appropriate, to open negotiations to that effect. Such agreements shall be concluded by the Council on a recommendation from the Presidency.

2. The Council shall act unanimously when the agreement covers an issue for which unanimity is required for the adoption of internal decisions.

3. When the agreement is envisaged in order to implement a joint action or common position, the Council shall act by a qualified majority in accordance with Article 23(2).

4. The provisions of this Article shall also apply to matters falling under Title VI. When the agreement covers an issue for which a qualified majority is required for the adoption of internal decisions or measures, the Council shall act by a qualified majority in accordance with Article 34(3).

---

[105] For an excellent analysis, see Sari, above n 100, and the literature cited there.
[106] *Ibid*, 75.
[107] *Ibid*, 75–7. See Council Doc CONF 2500/96, 'A General Outline For A Draft Revision Of The Treaties, Dublin II', 88–90 (5 December 1996). In June 1997, Tony Blair, then Prime Minister of the UK, stated in Parliament that '[w]e have also ruled out other potentially damaging proposals. For example, others wanted to give the European Union explicit legal personality across all the pillars of the treaty. At our insistence, that was removed', Hansard HC vol 296 col 314.

5. No agreement shall be binding on a Member State whose representative in the Council states that it has to comply with the requirements of its own constitutional procedure; the other members of the Council may agree that the agreement shall nevertheless apply provisionally.

6. Agreements concluded under the conditions set out by this Article shall be binding on the institutions of the Union.[108]

Thus, Article 24(3) TEU provided for the possibility of the Council approving an agreement by qualified majority rather than by unanimity when the agreement was envisaged in order to implement a joint action or common position. It is logically difficult to see how a Member State which votes against a decision adopted by qualified majority voting (QMV) could be considered to have concluded an agreement. However, it is equally difficult to see the need for Article 24(5) TEU and its reference to national 'constitutional procedure' and the provisional application of treaties if the agreements did not bind Member States. Article 24(6) TEU provided that agreements concluded bind the 'institutions of the Union', but that is not necessarily the same as binding the EU as such. Thus, the Nice amendments added to the ambiguities rather than clarifying them.[109]

4. *International Practice*

It is now common for decisions on the interpretation of international treaties to be strongly determined by subsequent practice in relation to them.[110] It is necessary to have regard to the subsequent practice of EU itself, of the Member States and of third parties.[111] In practice, the need soon arose for the EU to act. During the 1990s, there were a number of Memorandum of Understandings relating to missions and administration in the Former Yugoslavia. However, these referred to the party on the EU side as the 'Member States of the European Union acting within the framework of the Union'. In April 2001, there was the first agreement concluded in the name of the EU and on the basis of Article 24 TEU, a status of mission agreement between the EU and the Former Republic of Yugoslavia.[112] Others quickly followed.[113] Since 2001, in the context of European Security and Defence Policy, the EU has concluded over 70

---

[108] Consolidated TEU after Nice: see [2002] OJ C325.
[109] See Sari, above n 100; Wessels, above n 89; and N Neuwahl, 'Legal Personality of the European Union—International and Institutional Aspects' in Kronenberger, above n 7.
[110] See Art 31(3)(b) Vienna Convention on the Law of Treaties (1969); and Aust, above n 36.
[111] See Verwey, above n 34; and Sari, above n 100.
[112] [2001] OJ L125/2.
[113] A Sari, 'Status of Forces and Status of Mission Agreements under the ESDP: The EU's Evolving Practice' (2008) 19 *European Journal of International Law* 67.

agreements on the basis of Article 24 TEU.[114] There have been three broad categories of agreement: (i) status of forces agreements; (ii) agreements with third states contributing personnel and assets to ESDP operations; and (iii) agreements regulating the exchange of classified information between the EU and third parties.

As noted, Article 24(3) TEU provided that its provisions 'shall also apply to matters falling under Title VI' (the third pillar concerning police and judicial cooperation in criminal matters). However, there has been very little practice under Article 24 in this field. In 2003, two agreements based on Article 24 TEU were signed between the EU and the US on extradition and mutual legal assistance.[115] However, the US insisted on including a provision that the EU ensure that its Member States confirm in written agreements exchanged between themselves and the US, the undertakings entered into by the EU in the two agreements. It took three years to get these confirmations of acceptance from the Member States. This provision evidences equivocation on the US's part about its negotiating partner. In 2007, there was a controversial EU–US agreement on the Processing and Transfer of passenger name record data by air carriers to the United States Department of Homeland Security.[116] There have been two agreements between the EU and other international organisations, viz, NATO and the International Criminal Court.[117] There have been treaties to which both the EC and EU were parties. The Schengen association agreements with Switzerland in 2004 were an example. It was an agreement between the EU, the EC and the Swiss Federation. In 2006, a Protocol on the accession of Liechtenstein to that agreement was initialled. On the other hand, the Schengen association treaty with Norway and Iceland in 1999 was concluded by the Council of the European Union, Iceland and Norway.

The evidence derived from the EU's international treaty practice is equivocal.[118] Although all concluded in the name of the EU, negotiated by and signed by the Presidency in order to bind the EU, there are few examples of where the agreements appear to grant rights or impose duties on the EU separately from its Member States. The agreements generally sought to avoid proceedings and claims involving the EU directly. Any

---

[114]   See Sari, above n 100. See also R Gosalbo Bono, 'Some reflections on the CFSP legal order' (2006) 43 *Common Market Law Review* 337.

[115]   See [2003] OJ L181/27 (extradition) and [2003] OJ L181/34 (MLA).

[116]   [2007] OJ L204/18. In Joined Cases C-317 & 318/04, *European Parliament v Council* [2006] ECR I-4721, the ECJ had annulled Council Decision 2004/496 on the approval by the EC of the previous Agreement (on the processing and transfer of PNR data by air carriers to the US Administration), as well as Commission Decision 2004/535 (the so-called Adequacy Decision), which was closely linked to it. The Court annulled these decisions on the grounds that they did not fall within the competence of the EC.

[117]   See EU-NATO, 14 March 2003, [2003] OJ L80/35; and EU-ICC, 10 April 2006, [2006] OJ L115/50.

[118]   See Sari, above n 100, 80.

disputes related to the international agreements were to be resolved by diplomatic means rather than judicial or arbitral decisions. Any claims were to be met by Member States, the EU institutions or third states, but not the EU itself. However, what may have changed is that Member States are more content with accepting the idea that the EU has a degree of functional personality.[119] As we shall see, this has been the case with the United Kingdom.

5. The Convention on the Future of Europe (European Convention)

When the European Convention met in Brussels in the spring of 2002, one of its first decisions was to create a Working Group on Legal Personality, chaired by Giuliano Amato, which delivered its final report in October 2002.[120] It considered that the situation with respect to legal personality often led to confusion regarding the European system, both in relations with states which are not members of the Union and among Europeans themselves. Its main conclusion was 'that there was a very broad consensus (with one member against) [known to be the UK] that the Union should in future have its own explicit legal personality. It should be a single legal personality and should replace the existing personalities'.[121] By becoming a subject of international law, the European Union would technically be able to represent Europe, sign treaties, go to and be summoned to court, and become a member of international organisations. The result could be greater clarity in relations with the rest of the world, increased effectiveness and legal certainty and more effective action.[122] The Working Group recommended that the EU be given a single legal personality that would replace the existing personalities.[123]

> A single legal personality for the Union is fully justified for reasons of effectiveness and legal certainty, as well as for reasons of transparency and a higher profile for the Union not only in relation to third States, but also vis-à-vis European citizens. The latter will be encouraged to identify more closely with the Union, which will undertake to respect their fundamental rights and those arising from European citizenship.[124]

It stated that giving the Union a legal personality additional to those that existed would not go far enough in providing the clarification and

---

[119] *Ibid.* Academic opinion has moved more strongly in favour of the EU having international personality: see Eeckhout, above n 40, 154; and Koutrakos, above n 38, 406.

[120] 'Final report of Working Group III on Legal Personality', The European Convention, Doc CONV 305/02, WG III 16, Brussels, 1 October 2002.

[121] *Ibid*, para 2.

[122] *Ibid*, para 19.

[123] The Working Group noted that this was supported by the Legal Services of the EP, Council and Commission.

[124] 'Final Report', above n 120, Recommendation 2.

simplification necessary in the Union's external relations. It underlined that explicit conferral of a *single* legal personality on the Union did not per se entail any amendment, either to the current allocation of competences between the Union and the Member States or to the allocation of competences between the current Union and Community.[125] Nor did it necessarily involve amendments to institutional powers and procedures relevant to international agreements, although it accepted that some simplification could be achieved. More generally, the Working Group concluded that merger of the TEU and EC Treaty would be a logical consequence of merger of the EU's personality with that of the EC.

6. The Treaty Establishing a Constitution for Europe (2004)

Article I-7 of the 2004 Constitutional Treaty contained an express grant of international legal personality: 'The Union shall have legal personality'.[126] The positioning of this technical provision in the first part of the Treaty establishing a Constitution for Europe was explained by its perceived constitutional status.

7. The Lisbon Treaty (2007)

Once the Brussels European Council in June 2007 deconstitutionalised the Constitutional Treaty into the Draft Reform Treaty, the issue of legal personality returned more to the lower political realms occupied by legal technicalities.[127] Express provision for the EU's international personality was more acceptable once it was clearer that the 'F' (Federal) and 'C' (Constitution) words and concepts had been dropped. Although Eurosceptics and anti-federalists opposed the granting of legal personality, particularly because of its symbolic significance, for Member States it was no longer seen as an issue of principle.[128] The Treaty of Lisbon reflects a reassertion of state primacy over the evolution of the EU system.

It was particularly significant that the UK changed its position on the question of EU personality, given that it had been the strongest objector. The UK Government's White Paper on the Reform Treaty commented that, when it acted in the CFSP and some third pillar matters, the EU already had a 'degree of "functional" legal personality by virtue of its power to make international agreements' and added that conferring a single legal personality 'will be simpler than the existing situation and will therefore

---

[125] *Ibid*, para 20.
[126] Treaty Establishing a Constitution for Europe, published at [2004] OJ C310/01.
[127] 'Presidency Conclusions', Brussels, Council of the European Union, Doc 11177/07 (June 2007).
[128] See the evidence to HL Committee, below n 132, by Peers, Chalmers, Jacobs, Donnelly and Edward.

allow the EU to act in the international arena in a more coherent way' and that this 'should lead to streamlined procedures for negotiating agreements throughout the EU'.[129] Member States would decide the negotiating mandate and approve any final agreement on the same basis. The method of tasking the EU to negotiate on behalf of the Member States would not change under the Reform Treaty. Single legal personality would be simpler than the existing situation and would therefore allow the EU to act in the international arena in a more coherent way. This should lead to streamlined procedures for negotiating agreements through the EU and this would be reflected in a declaration. International personality would not impact on the independence of Member States' foreign policies. The IGC Mandate also included a Declaration stating that nothing in the Treaty affected the responsibilities and powers of Member States in foreign policy.[130] Arguably, this was rewriting the history of international personality a little, but as long as all of the Member States were agreed, then precisely when the EU acquired this functional personality was not of great concern in the absence of any claims. .

The then Minister for Europe, Jim Murphy, explained that the government's position had changed because it was able to secure the distinct treaty status for the CFSP in the revised TEU, retaining the CFSP's special intergovernmental status. Thus, it was argued that, 'with the retention in a separate Treaty [the TEU as opposed to the TFEU] of CFSP, what this single legal personality does to the Union, the Government feels, is confirm the existing practice'.[131] The House of Lords' Select Committee on European Union similarly concluded that:

[T]he European Union implicitly has had legal personality to the extent that it has the power to enter into international agreements under Articles 24 and 38 of the current TEU. Conferring legal personality expressly on the Union will have the effect that the other attributes of such status, such as the ability to join international organisations or to take, or be subject to, proceedings in international tribunals, will apply to the EU in the areas currently covered by the second and third pillars.[132]

In the mandate that provided the exclusive basis and framework for the work of the 2007 IGC, it was to:

---

[129] *The Reform Treaty: The British Approach to the European Union Intergovernmental Conference* (Cm 7174, 2007). See also House of Commons, European Scrutiny Committee, 'European Union Intergovernmental Conference', Thirty-fifth Report of Session 2006–07, HC1014, 9 October 2007.

[130] *Ibid.*

[131] Minister for Europe, Evidence to HL Committee, below n 132, Q S242.

[132] The House of Lords, Select Committee on European Union, Tenth Report, 'The Treaty of Lisbon: an impact assessment', HL 62-I (March 2008), para 2.58.

... contain two substantive clauses amending respectively the Treaty on the European Union (TEU) and the Treaty establishing the European Community. (TEC). The TEU will keep its present name and the TEC will be called Treaty on the Functioning of the Union, *the Union having a single legal personality*. The word 'Community' will throughout be replaced by the word 'Union' it will be stated that the two Treaties constitute the Treaties on which the Union is founded and that the *Union replaces and succeeds the Community*. Further clauses will contain the usual provisions on ratification and entry into force as well as transitional arrangements. Technical amendments to the Euratom Treaty and to the existing Protocols, as agreed in the 2004 IGC, will be done via Protocols attached to the Reform Treaty.[133]

It was stated that: 'There will in particular be an Article on the legal personality of the Union'.[134] When the Lisbon Reform Treaty emerged, however, the wording had remained exactly the same: 'The Union shall have legal personality'. The intent is that the EU has the legal personality of an international organisation. However, *sub-silentio*, it does not have the powers of a state. This is evidenced by the Declaration that the Brussels Council stated that the IGC would agree on: 'The Conference confirms that the fact that the European Union has a legal personality will not in any way authorise the Union to legislate or to act beyond the competences conferred upon it by the Member States in the Treaties'.[135] This supports the view that there is no reason to suppose that an express legal personality increases the EU's competence as regards the Member States.[136]

However, it is particularly important to note that the Lisbon Treaty states that the EU 'shall replace and succeed the European Community' (Article 1 of the revised TEU), and inserts the new Article 47 on the Union's legal personality into the final provisions of the revised TEU.[137] This idea of succession was carried over from the 2004 Constitution, but a detailed Article dealing with institutions, their acts and the case law of the Community courts was not.[138] The effect is that a single legal personality is thereby extended to the whole of the Union, ie the current Community plus the current second (CFSP) and third pillars (police and judicial cooperation in criminal matters). The replacement of the EC with the EU could not have been done without the EU being accorded international personality. To have done otherwise would have been to 'remove the Community's

---

[133] IGC Mandate, para 2.
[134] *Ibid*, para 16.
[135] This became Declaration No 24, 'Declaration concerning the legal personality of the European Union', *Consolidated TEU*, 438.
[136] S Peers, Evidence to HL, Select Committee, above n 132, S151.
[137] See Secretariat, The European Convention, 'Note on the effects of Making Union legal personality explicit and on the merger of Union and community legal personalities', Working Group III 'Legal Personality', 13 June 2002, WG III, WD 01.
[138] See Art IV-438 on 'Succession and Legal Continuity'.

existing treaty-making power, as well as disabling the Union from exercising its existing power'.[139] The end result is that the EU has very wide treaty-making powers, as it must at least have all the EC's and the EU's powers. The historical experience would suggest that the EU will push its treaty-making powers to the limit. It is important to recall that the ECJ will not have jurisdiction with respect to treaties concluded within the field of the CFSP. The Court of Justice does not have jurisdiction with respect to these provisions in the field of CFSP, with the exception of its jurisdiction to monitor the compliance with Article 40 of the revised TEU,[140] and to review the legality of certain decisions as provided for in Article 275(2) of the post-Lisbon TFEU.[141]

V. LOOKING FORWARD: THE TEU AND TFEU AFTER LISBON

The change from EC to EU will necessitate legislative or even constitutional changes in some states.[142] The single personality of the EU will help it in building an external identity. It will erase the terminological confusion that the EC/EU split has always engendered and should end arguments as to what the EU actually is when acting on the international stage. With a single legal personality, the EU may strengthen its actual or perceived negotiating power, making it even more effective on the world stage and a more visible partner for third countries and international organisations.

International personality is a necessary, but not determinative, criterion of statehood.[143] However, after Lisbon the Member States are comfortable that the destiny of the EU is not statehood. Keeping CFSP as intergovernmental is central to this. To the extent that the pillar structure of the TEU was problematic, the substantial collapse of Pillar Three (police and judicial cooperation in criminal matters) into Pillar One (the current Community pillar), so that both will now be under the TFEU, should contribute to a more coherent and effective external identity.[144] The reform

---

[139] Sir Francis Jacobs, Evidence to HL, Select Committee, above n 132, S148.

[140] This provides: 'The implementation of the common foreign and security policy shall not affect the application of the procedures and the extent of the powers of the institutions laid down by the Treaties for the exercise of the Union competences referred to in Articles 3 to 6 of the Treaty on the Functioning of the European Union. Similarly, the implementation of the policies listed in those Articles shall not affect the application of the procedures and the extent of the powers of the institutions laid down by the Treaties for the exercise of the Union competences under this Chapter'. See also Art 275(1) of the post-Lisbon TFEU.

[141] This provides that the Court shall also have jurisdiction to rule on proceedings, reviewing the legality of decisions providing for restrictive measures against natural or legal persons adopted by the Council on the basis of Chapter 2 of Title V of the TEU (Specific Provisions on the CFSP).

[142] See UK's European Union (Amendment) Act (2008), s 3 and Sch 1.

[143] See Thlikainen, above n 86.

[144] The UK, Denmark and Ireland had opt outs.

can also be viewed as the abolition of the pillar system, but with different rules on decision-making and ECJ jurisdiction being retained for the CFSP. Affording single international personality to the EU does not eliminate the EU's lack of a common identity. However, it gives the appearance of a clearer common identity and that can be politically and symbolically important. To an extent, it removes an obstacle to 'political actorness'.[145] Other reforms—the establishment of a President of the European Council, the creation of the High Representative of the Union for Foreign Affairs and Security Policy,[146] the establishment of the European External Action Service—all contribute to the potential cohesiveness of the EU as an international actor.[147] With the EU's constitutional and personality arguments behind it, the CFSP may deepen and become more 'common'[148] and the Member States may be more comfortable with the EU assuming a more proactive international role:

> The Reform Treaty will develop the Union's capacity to act by bringing together Europe's external policy tools, both in policy development and policy delivery. It will give Europe a clear voice in relations with our partners worldwide, and sharpen the impact and visibility of our message. It will also bring more coherence between the different strands of EU external policy—such as diplomacy, security, trade, development, humanitarian aid, and international negotiations on a range of global issues. This will mean an EU able to play a more responsive and effective part in global affairs.[149]

For example, in the context of ensuring the settlement of the status of Kosovo in 2007, the EU agreed on the deployment of an ESDP Policing and Rule of Law Mission (EULEX) consisting of 2,200 international personnel. This will be the largest civilian ESDP mission to date. An EU Special Representative to Kosovo (Pieter Feith) was appointed in February 2008.[150] The EU agreed to make a major contribution to the international

---

[145] '... in external relations the EU has almost covertly achieved a set of capacities which raises its international actorness above that of Member States', Thlikainen, above n 86, 241.

[146] The High Representative will chair the Foreign Relations Council.

[147] See M Martin and I Lirola, 'External Action of the European Union after the Constitutional Setback' (2006) 2 *European Constitutional Law Review* 358. See also the positive appraisal in *Opinion of the European Commission on the Conference of representatives of the governments of the Member States convened to revise the Treaties*, Council of the European Union, Brussels, 13 July 2007, Doc 11625/07.

[148] See E Denza, 'Lines in the Sand: Between Common Foreign Policy and Single Foreign Policy' in T Tridimas and P Nebbia (eds), *EU Law for the Twenty-first Century* (Hart, Oxford, 2004) 259.

[149] See Commissions's *Opinion*, above n 147. See also *The EU in the World—The Foreign Policy of the European Union*, European Commission, Directorate-General for Communication (June 2007).

[150] See Council Joint Action 2008/124/CFSP of 4 February 2008, on the European Union Rule of Law Mission in Kosov EULEX KOSOVO, Official Journal of the European Union, L 42/92, 16 Feb 2008; Political and Security Committee Decision EULEX/1/2008 of 7 February 2008, concerning the appointment of the Head of Mission (2008/125/CFSP), Official Journal

civilian office which will oversee settlement implementation. It also committed itself to the promotion of Kosovo's economic and political development. The Commission will use Community instruments (although the latter will not be so designated in the future) to take this forward and is planning to organise a donors conference.

It may become easier to discern an identifiable corpus of EU international law practice[151] that can be differentiated from that of the Member States.[152] Under the Lisbon Treaty, the EU 'shall accede' to the ECHR.[153] This appears to create an obligation to do so. Protocol 14 to the ECHR has already made provision for this on the Council of Europe's side.[154] Such accession shall not affect the EU's competences as defined in the Treaties.[155] However, the EC's and EU's competences have continued to evolve and the former will be wholly succeeded to by the EU.[156] The EU will be the only party to the ECHR that is not a state. On 30 March 2007, the EC ratified the UN Convention on the Rights of Persons with Disabilities (2007).[157] This is the first UN human rights treaty to be ratified by the EC on the basis of shared competence in a number of areas covered by the Convention. This may presage ratification of other international human rights conventions as EU accession to the major international human rights conventions is going to be increasingly on the international agenda.[158]

As for the specific effects internationally, it is helpful to outline the essential elements of the EU's international personality as it will be (or would have been) expressed after the entry into force of the Lisbon Treaty.

of the European Union, L 42/99, 16 Feb .2008. As of October 2008, the EU had ten Special Representatives (EUSRs) in different regions of the world.

[151]   There could perhaps be a *Yearbook of European Union International Law.*

[152]   Eg the EU's different practice under SOFA's of affording the same status as diplomats to members of missions. See Sari, above nn 100 and 113.

[153]   Art 6(2) of the revised TEU. See also Protocol No 8 relating to Art 6(2) of the Treaty on European Union on the Accession of the Union to the European Convention on the Protection of Human Rights and Fundamental Freedoms. The EU will have to contribute to the budget of the ECHR control mechanism.

[154]   All members of the Council of Europe have ratified Protocol 14 except Russia. The Russian Parliament (Duma) has so far refused to approve of ratification despite great diplomatic pressure being exerted on it to do so.

[155]   Art 6(2) of the revised TEU.

[156]   See D McGoldrick, 'The European Union after Amsterdam: An Organisation with General Human Rights Competences?' in D O'Keeffe and P Twomey (eds), *Legal Issues of the Amsterdam Treaty* (Hart, Oxford, 1999) 249.

[157]   <http://www.un.org/disabilities/default.asp?navid=12&pid=150> accessed 3 September 2008. The Convention entered into force in May 2008. See R Kayess and P French, 'Out of Darkness into Light? Introducing the Convention on the Rights of Persons with Disabilities' (2008) 8 *Human Rights Law Review* 1.

[158]   See A Rosas, 'The EU and International Human Rights Instruments' in Kronenberger, above n 7, 53.

A. International Agreements

All existing EU agreements will continue. For all existing EC agreements, the EU will succeed the EC. Presumably the repositories of the relevant treaty will be so informed. In as much as it is simply a change of name, there is no reason to believe that any other party, be it state or international organisation, could or would object.[159] The scope of international agreements is being pushed wider. For example, the Cotonou Agreement of 2000, the Partnership Agreement between the members of the African, Caribbean and Pacific Group of States (ACP), of the one part, and the European Community and its Member States, of the other part, was revised in 2005 to cover a wide range of issues, including provisions for enhanced political dialogue and references to the fight against terrorism, cooperation in countering the proliferation of weapons of mass destruction and the International Criminal Court.[160] In the future there will not be arguments about legal personality, but there will continue to be arguments about competence and decision-making.[161] All future international agreements will be concluded by the EU, but their legal basis will be under the revised TEU, the TFEU or both. Under Article 8 of the revised TEU, the EU shall develop a special relationship with neighbouring countries, aiming to establish an area of prosperity and good neighbourliness, founded on the values of the Union and characterised by close and peaceful relations based on cooperation. Article 8 of the revised TEU does not appear to be a specific and separate legal base. Rather, for these purposes the Union may conclude specific agreements with the countries concerned. Under Article 37 of the revised TEU (currently Article 24 TEU), the Union may conclude agreements with one or more states or international organisations in areas covered by the CFSP.

There are a number of new or revised legal bases for treaty-making which it is useful to highlight. Under Article 79(3) of the post-Lisbon TFEU, the EU may conclude agreements with third countries for the readmission to their countries of origin or provenance of third-country

---

[159] There have been a few instances of states changing their names outside of territorial changes. In May 1997, Zaire changed its name to the Democratic Republic of the Congo.

[160] See S Smis and SS Kingah, 'The Utility of Counter-Terrorism and Non-Proliferation of WMD Clauses under the EU-ACP Revised Cotonou Agreement' (2008) 57 *ICLQ* 149, who note that 'that agreement is a noteworthy departure from the approach of restricting essential elements to the respect of human rights and democratic processes' (151).

[161] In relation to what were Title IV EC matters (ie police and judicial cooperation in criminal matters), see Declaration No 25 on the entitlement of Member States to conclude agreements with third countries and international organisations in these areas, in so far as such agreements are consistent with Union law. *Quaere* whether the shift in responsibility for existing EC treaties to the EU could also entail a shift in competence for those existing treaties, ie to the extent that those existing treaties were 'mixed' because of provisions on policing/criminal law and foreign policy.

nationals who do not or no longer fulfil the conditions for entry, presence or residence in the territory of one of the Member States. This explicit legal base for readmission agreements simply confirms the status quo, ie that readmission agreements are already adopted on the basis of the EC's implied powers. Under Article 209 TFEU, the EU may conclude with third countries and competent international organisations any agreement helping to achieve the objectives referred to in Article 21 of the revised TEU (General Provisions on the Union's External Action) and in Article 208 TFEU (development cooperation). This shall be without prejudice to Member States' competence to negotiate in international bodies and to conclude agreements. Article 214 TFEU is an entirely new provision on humanitarian aid. The previous practice was to adopt humanitarian aid rules as part of development policy. Under Article 214(4) TFEU, the EU may conclude with third countries and competent international organisations any agreement helping to achieve the humanitarian objectives referred in Article 214(1) TFEU and in Article 21 TEU. Again, this is without prejudice to Member States' competence to negotiate in international bodies and to conclude agreements.

The general provision on the conclusion of international agreement is now in Article 216 TFEU. Under Article 216(1) TFEU, the EU may conclude an agreement with one or more third countries or international organisations where the Treaties so provide or where the conclusion of an agreement is necessary in order to achieve, within the framework of the Union's policies, one of the objectives referred to in the Treaties, or is provided for in a legally binding Union act or is likely to affect common rules or alter their scope. Article 216(1) TFEU is new, but attempts to summarise the current case law regarding the existence of external competence within EC law. Importantly, these principles will now apply across the EU (ie to what were the three 'pillars', including foreign policy). Article 216(2) TFEU provides that: 'Agreements concluded by the Union are binding upon the institutions of the Union and on its Member States'. This is taken from Article 300(7) of the existing EC Treaty and Article 24(6) of the current TEU (which governs foreign policy treaties). However, as we noted above, the latter had not specified that agreements are binding on the Member States. This clause does not concern the nature of EU international agreements, that is, whether competence in question is exclusive to the EU or shared between the EU and its Member States.[162] The reference to implied competence in Article 216 of the post-Lisbon TFEU is notable.

---

[162] See Art 3(2) TFEU which does concern that issue. It provides: 'The Union shall also have exclusive competence for the conclusion of an international agreement when its conclusion is provided for in a legislative act of the Union or is necessary to enable the Union to exercise its internal competence, or in so far as its conclusion may affect common rules or

Under Article 217 TFEU, the EU may conclude with one or more third countries or international organisations agreements establishing an association involving reciprocal rights and obligations, common action and special procedure (association agreements). This Article now applies to the old second and third pillars. In practice, EU association agreements have for a number of years included provisions on EU foreign policy, policing and criminal law matters. Article 207 TFEU makes detailed provision for the procedures for the conclusion of agreements in the context of the common commercial policy. The scope of the 'EU' part of association agreements might now be broader, with the inclusion of the second and third pillars.

Article 218 TFEU sets out the procedures for the negotiation and conclusion of agreements between the Union and third countries or international organisations. It is without prejudice to Article 207 TFEU (common commercial policy). The Council shall authorise the opening of negotiations, adopt negotiating directives, authorise the signing of agreements and conclude them. The Commission, or the High Representative of the Union for Foreign Affairs and Security Policy where the agreement envisaged relates exclusively or principally to the common foreign and security policy, shall submit recommendations to the Council, which shall adopt a decision authorising the opening of negotiations and, depending on the subject of the agreement envisaged, nominating the Union negotiator or the head of the Union's negotiating team. The Council may address directives to the negotiator and designate a special committee in consultation with which the negotiations must be conducted. The Council, on a proposal by the negotiator, shall adopt a decision authorising the signing of the agreement and, if necessary, its provisional application before entry into force. The Council, on a proposal by the negotiator, shall adopt a decision concluding the agreement. Except where agreements relate exclusively to the common foreign and security policy, the Council shall adopt the decision concluding the agreement, after obtaining the consent of the European Parliament in a number of specified cases. The Council shall act by a qualified majority throughout the procedure. However, it shall act unanimously when the agreement covers a field for which unanimity is required for the adoption of a Union act as well as for association agreements and the agreements referred to in Article 212 with the states which are candidates for accession. The Council shall also act unanimously for the agreement on accession of the Union to the ECHR; the decision

alter their scope'. *Quaere* what about the implications of also applying Art 3(2), the exclusive competence rule, to the second and third pillar?

concluding that agreement shall enter into force after it has been approved by the Member States in accordance with their respective constitutional requirements.

Article 218 of the post-Lisbon TFEU merges the current Article 300 EC with the current Article 24 TEU, which concerns foreign policy treaties (and in effect also Article 38 TEU, which concerns criminal law and policing treaties). There are still separate rules within this Article for CFSP treaties, but Third Pillar treaty rules will now largely be covered by the general non-CFSP rules (the old Article 37 TEU on third pillar representation during international conferences was deleted). Negotiating mandates and signature and conclusion of treaties would be adopted in the form of normal 'decisions' (confirming the case law permitting these measures to be subject to the jurisdiction of the Court of Justice). The European Parliament (EP) would have assent power whenever the co-decision procedure or assent procedure apply to internal legislation (not just where legislation adopted by co-decision would have to be amended) and for accession to the ECHR, and would have information rights throughout. The Council must be unanimous to agree accession to the ECHR (and the accession treaty must also be ratified by Member States), whereas in the old Constitutional Treaty, QMV applied. Due to the expansion of co-decision and QMV as regards internal EU policies, the assent power of the EP (to be called the 'consent' power in the revised treaties) and the use of QMV to negotiate and conclude EU agreements will also increase. The EP retained its other existing assent powers over the conclusion of treaties.

Finally, Article 219 of the post-Lisbon TFEU makes provision for negotiations and conclusion of international agreements concerning economic and monetary union. Future EU treaties could in reality be mixed in as much as they are joint EU/Member States agreements, but they could also be 'doubly mixed', that is, based on TEU (for EU) and TFEU (for old Pillars 1 and 2) and Member State agreements.

It is not uncommon now for the EU to adopt a leading role with 'like-minded states' in international negotiations. For example, this has been the case with environmental treaties,[163] and with respect to the establishment of the International Criminal Court.[164]

---

[163] See Delreux, above n 34.

[164] See D McGoldrick, 'Legal and Political Responses to the ICC' in D McGoldrick, P Rowe and E Donnelly (eds), *The Permanent International Criminal Court* (Hart, Oxford, 2006) 392–4.

B. Sanctions

Under Article 301 EC, economic sanctions could be taken by the EC following a common position or joint action relating to the CFSP.[165] Under the Lisbon Treaty, Article 215 TFEU provides a wider legal base for sanctions against third countries, now including non-state entities and individuals.[166]

C. Relations with International Organisations and Institutions

Under Article 220 TFEU, the EU shall establish all appropriate forms of cooperation with the organs of the UN and its specialised agencies, the Council of Europe, the OSCE and the Organisation for Economic Cooperation and Development. The EU shall also maintain such relations as are appropriate with other international organisations. The High Representative of the Union for Foreign Affairs and Security Policy and the Commission shall be instructed to implement this Article. Compared to the existing provisions, the new one applies to the subject matter of all three pillars, and includes a role for the High Representative as regards foreign policy alongside the Commission. The reference to the OSCE is also new.

D. Membership of, or Participation In, International Organisations

The EU is not a member of any international organisations, but it will automatically succeed to those where the EC has been a member. The EU (but to date technically the EC) has already been a major player in the WTO.

E. Diplomatic Recognition/Representation

All overseas missions Commission delegations will become Union delegations and they will represent the Union.[167] They are placed under the

---

[165]   See Koutrakos, above n 43.

[166]   Cf the discussion of legal base in Case T-315/01 *Kadi v Council and Commission* [2005] ECR II-3649. The decision was upheld in Cases C-402/05 P and 415/05 P, *Kadi v Council* and *Al Barakaat International Foundation v Council*, paras 121–236 (Judgment of 3 September 2008). *Quaere* whether the JHA legal base regarding anti-terrorism measures would also cover sanctions against international terrorists, as that legal base is not limited in scope to domestic terrorists.

[167]   Art 221 of the post-Lisbon TFEU. See Art 32 of the revised TEU (currently Art 16 TEU) on Union delegations in third countries and at international organisations, and Art 35

authority of the High Representative of the Union for Foreign Affairs and Security Policy.[168] Under Article 27 of the revised TEU, in fulfilling his or her mandate, the High Representative shall be assisted by a European External Action Service. This service shall work in cooperation with the diplomatic services of the Member States and shall comprise officials from relevant departments of the General Secretariat of the Council and of the Commission, as well as staff seconded from national diplomatic services of the Member States.[169] All diplomatic missions to the EU will now be accredited to the EU.[170]

F. International Responsibility

The Convention Working Group on Legal Personality had noted that the Union was increasingly adopting instruments liable directly or indirectly to affect the rights of individuals. It cited the cases of an officer who invoked Union liability for bodily injury sustained in Bosnia and Herzegovina; a company invoking the Union's non-contractual liability for damages sustained as a result of sanctions against the Former Republic of Yugoslavia; and Yugoslav citizens invoking Union liability for damages sustained as a result of the visa ban on the basis of a Council joint action.[171] The Lisbon Treaty makes it possible for the EU to be held formally accountable. Where it succeeds to the EC, this is only a name change. However, where treaties are concluded in the name of the EU, it may struggle to maintain its strategies of avoiding judicial or arbitral resolution of disputes and avoiding direct financial liability.[172] Future debates will be less about personality and more about responsibility and accountability. A striking recent example of this was the decision of the Grand Chamber of the European Court of Human Rights that it did not have jurisdiction over actions by states parties to the ECHR performed as part of UN peacekeeping operations in Kosovo.[173] Individuals affected by those actions

---

of the revised TEU (currently Art 20 TEU) on Union delegations in third countries and international conferences, and their representations to international organisations.

[168] Art 221 of the post-Lisbon TFEU. In practice, the Commission delegations represent the EC and were subject to the Commission's authority. See 'Taking Europe to the world: 50 years of the European Commission's External Service' (Office for Official Publications of the European Communities, Luxembourg, 2004), available at <http://ec.europa.eu/external_relations/library/publications/07_50_years_broch_en.pdf> accessed 3 September 2008.

[169] See also Declaration Nos 13–15, *Consolidated TEU*, 434–5.

[170] In the past, some were so designated, but this was technically wrong.

[171] See 'Final Report', above n 120.

[172] R Wessels, 'The EU as a party to International Agreements: Shared Competencies? Mixed Responsibilities' in A Dashwood and M Maresceau (eds), *Law and Practice of EU External Relations* (Cambridge, Cambridge University Press, 2008) 152–87.

[173] A Sari, 'Jurisdiction and International Responsibility in Peace Support Operations: The *Behrami* and *Saramati* Cases' (2008) 8 *Human Rights Law Review* 151.

would have to seek remedies from the UN as an international organisation. This approach has clear implications for the extensive number of EU peace-keeping and humanitarian missions overseas. The principles governing the international responsibility of international organisations have been on the agenda of the UN's International Law Commission since 2000.[174] A consistent problem for the ILC has been the insufficient availability of practice in respect of the responsibility of international organisations.[175] The EU is relatively transparent as compared to other international organisations. Part of the value of the EU's separate international personality may be that it leads to a better knowledge and understanding of the practices of international organisations with respect to their international responsibility.

VI. CONCLUSION

As noted in the introduction to this chapter, legal personality is a technical legal question, but it is concerned with the EU's external international identity, visibility, action, coherence and representativeness. The uncertain and ambiguous personality of the EU has seen it critiqued from all of these perspectives. With the seeming resolution of the issue at the time of the Lisbon Treaty in 2007, the EU can look forward to focusing its single personality on the promotion and protection of its interests and values and on being able to operate more effectively internationally. However, with clarity on the EU's international personality will come even greater demands from other international actors. Two contemporary examples are instructive. First, there has been concern over what are termed 'disconnection' clauses such as that in Article 43(3) of the Council Of Europe Convention on The Protection of Children Against Sexual Exploitation and Sexual Abuse,[176] which provides that:

> Parties which are members of the European Union shall, in their mutual relations, apply Community and European Union rules in so far as there are Community or European Union rules governing the particular subject concerned

---

[174]   The ILC's Special Rapporteur is Mr Giorgio Gaja. See 'International Law Commission, Report on the work of its fifty-ninth session' (7 May—5 June and 9 July—10 August 2007) Ch. VIII, General Assembly, Official Records, Sixty-second Session, Supplement No. 10 (A/62/10); and the ILC's 2008 Report, A/63/10, Ch VII. An interesting issue discussed in 2008 was whether the Member States of an international organisation can take countermeasures against it.

[175]   *Ibid*, 2007 Report, para 331. Art 2 of the ILC's Draft Articles on the Responsibility of International Organisations uses the term 'international organisation' to refer to an 'organisation established by treaty or other instrument governed by international law and possessing its own international legal personality', ILC Report, *ibid*, 2008 Report, p 299.

[176]   CETS 201 (25 October 2007).

and applicable to the specific case, without prejudice to the object and purpose of the present Convention and without prejudice to its full application with other Parties.

The EU's policy is to request the inclusion of such a clause in any draft convention which might affect the community *acquis*, particularly any convention not open to accession by the EU//EC. The objective is to take account of the institutional structure of the EU and in particular the transfer of sovereign powers. However, other states have been concerned that the use of such clauses can erode the object and purpose of standard-setting treaties. While such provisions may be legally valid, the EU is under pressure to be more transparent in terms of such treaties by providing more details on the respective competencies of the EU and the Member States. Secondly, there will be more pressure on the EU for it to accept clearly that it, as such, can bear international responsibility for breach of international law obligations and for it to demonstrably have at its disposal the relevant financial, legislative and political measures to provide the appropriate international remedies.[177] The EU's international actions will also be subject to the same kinds of ethical critiques as are directed at states.[178]

---

[177] See e.g Joined Cases C-120/06 P and C-121/06 P, *FIAMM and Georgio Fedon & Figli v Council and Commission* (9 September 2008) (no community liability for damages stemming from EC non-compliance with WTO law. For criticism see A Alemanno, 'European Court Rejects Damages Claim From Innocent Bystanders in the EU-US "Banana-War"' 12(21) *ASIL Insight* (2008) http://www.asil.org/insights081022.cfm (last visited 22 October 2008).

[178] For an excellent example of this see U Khaliq, *Ethical Dimensions of the Foreign Policy of the European Union: A Legal Appraisal* (Cambridge, Cambridge University Press, 2008).

9

The Future of the Area of Freedom, Security and Justice

ELEANOR SHARPSTON*

I. INTRODUCTION

THE 'AREA OF freedom, security and justice' (AFSJ) is a relatively new legal 'brand' within European Union law, launched in 1999 with the entry into force of the Treaty of Amsterdam. It is a combination of the new (the competences and institutional possibilities put in place by that Treaty) and the old (the legacy of the pre-Amsterdam years).

Let us begin by looking at the old. In the pre-Amsterdam world, there were essentially informal arrangements[1] in the field of justice and home affairs, negotiated (if I may put it this way) in the shadow of the EEC Treaty framework. The pre-Amsterdam *acquis* was located in large part within the original 'third pillar' (justice and home affairs or JHA) that was introduced into the (then new) EU Treaty framework by the 1992 Maastricht Treaty.[2] There was also a wider, more diverse corpus of arrangements, *outside* the EU structure, between particular Member States

---

* The views expressed are personal and inevitably partly speculative. They are intended by the author to stimulate discussion and criticism and do not bind the institution in which she serves. She would like to thank her colleague in chambers, Dr Geert de Baere, for his helpful comments on a draft of this chapter.
[1] Eg the Working Group on Immigration, the Trevi Group, the Working Group on Judicial Cooperation, the Customs Mutual Assistance Group and, from 1989, the Group of Coordinators on free movement of persons.
[2] The 1992 TEU was immediately likened to a Grecian Temple with three 'pillars': a central 'first pillar' (the EEC, now rechristened EC) and two flanking pillars of 'areas of common interest' (the second pillar comprising the Common Foreign and Security Policy (CFSP) and the third pillar on JHA).

(most notably, the Schengen agreements of 1985 and 1990)[3] and a variety of Council of Europe instruments in the area of mutual legal assistance.[4]

The first (and indeed the most obvious) question to ask is whether the AFSJ is a coherent topic that can be studied and whose future can be predicted—whether coherence is defined as 'internal coherence' (the AFSJ as a distinctive legal field) or as 'external coherence' (the AFSJ in its social and political context)?[5]

Beyond the bare AFSJ label, there is not much internal coherence of a thematic, historical or institutional kind that is immediately apparent. Perhaps there is some degree of policy coherence (in the sense of an attempt to construct a new policy whole out of diverse parts).[6] Even here, however, the coherence is only partial. Certainly there are overlapping strands between two of the main topics that the AFSJ straddles (migration control and police and judicial cooperation in criminal matters). It is, however, rather more difficult to see how policy considerations associated with the programme put forward by the special Tampere European Council (1999)[7] to develop a common policy field within and across four general headings ('A Common EU Asylum and Migration Policy'; 'A Genuine European Area of Justice'; 'A Union-wide Fight against Crime'; and 'Stronger External Action')[8] have much in common with another important part of the AFSJ, namely judicial cooperation in civil matters (as specified in Article 65 EC).

A broader, social science question might be whether developments in JHA (and subsequently in the AFSJ) have been proactive or merely reactive. Certainly it is characterised simultaneously by multiple (often rather ambitious) initiatives and by failed projects and cut-down or stalled proposals. As one commentator nicely puts it:

[3] Agreement between the Governments of the States of the Benelux Economic Union, the Federal Republic of Germany and the French Republic on the gradual abolition of checks at their common borders, [2000] OJ L239/13; and Convention implementing the Schengen Agreement of 14 June 1985 between the Governments of the States of the Benelux Economic Union, the Federal Republic of Germany and the French Republic on the gradual abolition of checks at their common borders, [2000] OJ L239/19.

[4] Eg the 1959 Council of Europe Convention and the 1978 Protocol on Mutual Assistance in Criminal Matters.

[5] See, eg N Walker, 'In search of the area of Freedom, Security and Justice: A Constitutional Odyssey' in N Walker (ed), *Europe's Area of Freedom, Security and Justice* (Oxford, Oxford University Press, 2004).

[6] See, generally, Walker, above n 5.

[7] Tampere Special European Council held in October 1999: see <http://www.consilium. europa.eu/ueDocs/cms_Data/docs/pressData/en/ec/00200-r1.en9.htm> accessed 25 October 2008.

[8] The rhetoric in this field is replete with initial capitals, as well as with timetables and 'milestones'.

... for all its institutional restlessness and abundant incrementalism, it would be inaccurate to see the history of FSJ as one of remorseless integration. Alongside the record of expansion, there have been many examples of frustration and blocked ambition. Each institutional initiative has left some parties disappointed with its modesty, each new initiative (as in Amsterdam) has been preceded by a critique of the ineffectiveness of the old, and each resumé of progress (as in the Tampere mid-term report by the Belgian presidency in 2001) has produced an indictment of the conditions impeding progress.[9]

Behind (or perhaps beneath) both questions is the fundamental (and generally recognised) issue of the ideological fault-line between what is supranational and what is intergovernmental. An intergovernmental approach implies that priority continues to be accorded to national (ie sovereign Member State) authority within the AFSJ structure. A supranational approach, in contrast, stresses the importance of transferring a significant measure of such national authority to within the EU structure. That said, it is possible for Member States that are unreceptive to the overall concept of deeper integration nevertheless to support certain areas of AFSJ cooperation. Such cooperation can legitimately be both perceived and presented as an enlightened *defence* of their national sovereignty in an increasingly interconnected world, rather than as the undesirable *pooling* of national sovereignty within a post-nation state universe.[10]

Permission for JHA to join the supranational 'core' was purchased at the cost of a new *internal* distinction *within* the renamed AFSJ between those matters 'promoted' to Title IV, Part Three EC of the first pillar and those remaining in a residual third pillar. It has been argued that:

... regardless of their 'pillar' domicile, *all* aspects of FSJ moved in a more or less 'communitarized' direction at Amsterdam, and just as newly supranational elements in the area of initiative, intensity of measures, and—to a limited extent—justiciability and oversight were invested in the residual third pillar, so too some significant 'intergovernmental' elements, especially as regards the key issue of unanimity in adoption, were retained in Title IV.[11]

So much for the background. Providing a comprehensive overview of what has happened so far in AFSJ would require a volume in itself. It would be inappropriate for me to try to offer a wide-ranging prophetic analysis of the likely hotspots for the future and how precisely the Court is going to

---

[9] Walker, above n 5, 15.

[10] It may also be suggested that the previous sharp distinction between the 'intergovernmentalism' of JHA (third pillar) and the 'supranationalism' of the core components (EC first pillar) did not, realistically, survive the reform of the Maastricht TEU at Amsterdam.

[11] Walker, above n 5, 17. Writing before the check to the constitutional process caused by the French and Dutch referenda, Walker concluded that 'the effective dismantling of the new internal distinction introduced at Amsterdam appears a foregone conclusion'. Writing during the process of ratification for the Treaty of Lisbon, I have no intention of tempting fate in the same way.

deal with them. I shall therefore focus exclusively on the part that the Court in which I have the honour to serve is likely to find itself contributing to the future development of the AFSJ. What is the extent of the role that the Member States have entrusted to the Court; and how is it likely to approach that role?

II. EXTENT OF THE COURT'S ROLE

It is trite to observe that the questions put to the Court by national courts seeking preliminary rulings under Article 234 EC have been a major driving force in the development of EC law, within an overall system of judicial overview that includes (in particular) provision for actions by the Commission against defaulting Member States,[12] applications for annulment of Community acts,[13] and claims for damages against the Community institutions.[14] Both Title IV, Part Three EC and Title VI TEU contain provisions delineating the Court's jurisdiction. How do these compare with the familiar arrangements for 'mainstream' EC law? The process is familiar and yet significantly different.

A. Title IV, Part Three EC: Visas, Asylum, Immigration and Other Policies Related to Free Movement of Persons

Article 68 EC applies the reference procedure contained in Article 234 EC to Title IV, Part Three EC matters with certain significant limitations. First, only courts of last resort may make such references.[15] Secondly, the Court 'shall not have jurisdiction to rule on any measure or decision taken pursuant to Article 62(1) relating to the maintenance of law and order and the safeguarding of internal security'. Thirdly, a novel possibility was created for the Council, the Commission or a Member State to request the Court to give an interpretative ruling on matters falling within Title IV, Part Three EC,[16] with the express rider that 'the ruling given by the Court … in response to such a request shall not apply to judgments of courts or tribunals of the Member States which have become *res judicata*'.

The process of giving answers to any question involving Title IV, Part Three EC is complicated (I mean that term in a purely technical sense) by

---

[12]   Art 226 EC.
[13]   Art 230 EC.
[14]   Art 235 EC read with Art 288 EC.
[15]   The wording mirrors Art 234(3) EC.
[16]   Ie on the provisions of Title IV, Part Three EC itself and on acts of the institutions based thereon.

the fact that, whilst the Schengen *acquis* has now been integrated into the EU framework,[17] specific arrangements apply to the United Kingdom and to Ireland.[18]

B. Title VI TEU: Provisions on Police and Judicial Cooperation in Criminal Matters

Article 35 TEU gives the Court jurisdiction to give preliminary rulings on the validity and interpretation of: (i) framework decisions; (ii) decisions on the interpretation of conventions established under Title VI; and (iii) measures implementing such conventions. This is an 'opt-in' arrangement. Article 35 TEU applies only if a Member State makes a declaration accepting the Court's jurisdiction. Any Member State may, however, intervene in an Article 35 TEU reference, whether or not it has accepted jurisdiction.[19]

Article 35 TEU confers jurisdiction on the Court to hear two separate, additional categories of action. The Court may review, on classic 'judicial review' grounds,[20] the legality of framework decisions in actions brought by a Member State or the Commission.[21] It may also rule in disputes between Member States concerning the interpretation or application of *any* measure adopted under Article 34(2) TEU,[22] if the dispute cannot be sorted out by the Council within six months of referral, and in disputes between the Commission and a Member State regarding the interpretation or application of a convention adopted under Article 34(2)(d) TEU.

Like Article 68 EC, Article 35 TEU includes an express 'hands off' provision. Article 35(5) TEU provides that the Court shall have no jurisdiction to review the validity or proportionality of operations carried out by the police or other law enforcement services of a Member State or the exercise of the responsibilities incumbent on Member States with regard to the maintenance of law and order and the safeguarding or internal security.

---

[17] Protocol (No 2) integrating the Schengen *acquis* into the framework of the European Union (1997).

[18] See Protocol (No 3) on the application of certain aspects of Art 14 of the Treaty establishing the European Community to the United Kingdom and to Ireland and Protocol (No 4) on the position of the United Kingdom and Ireland.

[19] An updated list of which Member States have accepted the court's jurisdiction under Art 35 TEU, together with an indication of whether they have done so in respect of all courts or only courts of last resort, is to be found on the court's website at <http://curia.europa.eu/en/instit/txtdocfr/txtsenvigueur/art35.pdf>.

[20] The arrangements in Art 35(6) EC here closely resemble Art 230 EC.

[21] But not, it seems, by other privileged applicants, still less by non-privileged applicants.

[22] Ie common positions, framework decisions, other decisions and conventions.

C. So: What Is Covered and What Is Not?

So far as the procedure for preliminary rulings is concerned, the possibility of making a reference is either limited to courts of last resort (for matters arising under Title IV, Part Three EC) or dependent upon the Member State concerned having decided to accept the Court's jurisdiction to answer such questions at all (for Title VI TEU).

So far as 'direct actions' are concerned, since Title IV, Part Three EC is an integral part of the EC Treaty, the normal avenues to judicial scrutiny are open: infringement proceedings, applications for annulment, and so on. The position in respect of Title VI TEU is (unsurprisingly) much more restricted. The only direct actions contemplated are those expressly listed in Article 35 TEU. They are confined to specific questions and specific (privileged) players.

An important omission is that there is no equivalent, in Title VI TEU, to the standard Article 226 EC procedure whereby the Commission can bring infringement proceedings against a Member State. Thus, for example, it was impossible for the Commission to act against Germany when the *Bundesverfassungsgericht* (German Constitutional Court) struck down the implementation of the framework decision on the European Arrest Warrant in that Member State.[23]

Significantly, under both Title IV, Part Three EC and Title VI TEU, the Member States have clearly fenced-off certain sensitive matters from scrutiny by the Court, namely any ruling on 'any measure or decision taken pursuant to Article 62(1) [EC] relating to the maintenance of law and order and the safeguarding of internal security' (Title IV, Part Three EC)[24]; and any review of 'the legality or proportionality of operations carried out by the police or other law enforcement services of a Member State or the exercise of the responsibilities incumbent upon Member States with regard to the maintenance of law and order and the safeguarding of internal security' (Title VI TEU).[25]

All that said, it is perhaps permissible to speculate that questions may at some point arise that will (unaccountably) fail to respect the neat boundaries that have been put around (some parts of) AFSJ (by some Member States) to delineate AFSJ from mainstream EC law.

---

[23]   Judgment of 18 July 2006, *Europäischer Haftbefehl*, 2 BvG 2236/04.
[24]   Art 68(2) EC.
[25]   Art 35(5) TEU.

III. PARAMETERS WITHIN WHICH THE COURT IS LIKELY TO OPERATE

The starting point, I suggest, is the Court's clear understanding (which derives directly from the operating mandate given to it at its foundation) that its job is to ensure that 'the law is observed'.[26] To make the same point in a slightly different way, the Court's belief that it is there to uphold the rule of law is hardwired into the system.

A second (perhaps equally obvious) point is that the Court will work with the texts that the legislators have put in place. The initiative as to how far the AFSJ advances, how rapidly, and in what general direction, therefore lies (and will correctly and necessarily lie) with the Member States.

That said, the Court will, however, always seek to give an *effective* meaning to the text, notwithstanding that the text may be opaque. Possibly, the text may even deliberately have been left ambiguous in order to secure agreement at a particularly protracted meeting. If, however, the Court is asked directly what meaning is to be ascribed to a particular provision, the time for ambiguity comes to an end.

In relation to the AFSJ (as indeed in other areas of the Court's jurisdiction), the general proposition holds good that the Court does not pick fights, but it does have to deal with the cases with which it is seized. There is no docket control. In consequence, once the question is raised the Court has in principle to give an answer, however 'hot' or awkward the issue. This is particularly true of issues that come to the Court via a request for a preliminary ruling. These may sometimes involve questions that the Commission might well *not* have chosen to bring to the Court's attention in infringement proceedings (at that moment, or possibly at all). Nevertheless, if the national court refers the problem, the Court has to deal with it.[27]

Finally, the Court is generically aware of the importance of protecting individual rights and the core legal values that are common to our legal constitutional traditions and that lie at the very heart of the rule of law. I believe that this is particularly important in any area in which concerns for 'security' and protecting perceived collective interests may very easily overshadow the niceties of (for example) due process or access to justice for an (unpopular) individual.[28]

---

[26] The text that started life as Art 164 EEC has proved remarkably impervious to change: see now Art 220 EC.

[27] Occasionally, a reference is so fragmentary that it can be dismissed as inadmissible. Occasionally, the court can choose to answer the questions in a particular order that means it does not have to answer them all. Nevertheless, the general proposition holds good.

[28] Walker, for example, recognises the danger that 'a reactive, security-centred approach carries within it a tendency to marginalize familiar constitutional constraints such as the

IV. THE IMMEDIATE CURRENT CHALLENGE: THE NEW URGENT PRELIMINARY RULING PROCEDURE

References involving Title IV, Part Three EC are likely to raise new questions of EC law that will be both sensitive and complicated. At the same time, they may very well require urgent treatment.[29] In 2006, the Court produced two discussion documents, which it sent to the Council,[30] outlining possible ways of handling this conundrum. On 1 March 2008, the amended Rules of Procedure making provision for an urgent preliminary ruling procedure came into effect.[31] The Court has just given judgment in the first *procédure préjudicielle d'urgence* (PPU): *Rinau*, a dispute involving child abduction that required the interpretation of six questions concerning the Brussels IIa Regulation.[32]

The PPU references pose obvious challenges for the Court. As *Rinau* shows, they raise complicated issues in uncharted territory. The Court is under (obvious) pressure to get the answer out fast. It also needs to get the answer right. In achieving that (intrinsically awkward) combination, it will have to provide as much clear and helpful information and careful reasoning as possible for the national courts. If it achieves speed at the cost of being too short and Delphic in its rulings, the result will be confusion

---

proper balancing of fundamental values, the primacy of democratic decision, due process in individual cases and a robust system of separation and diversification of powers and of institutional checks and balances' (above n 5, 13). In his Opinions in Case C-402/05 P, *Kadi v Council and Commission* (16 January 2008) and Case C-415/05 P, *Al Barakaat International Foundation v Council and Commission* (23 January 2008), AG Poiares Maduro made a powerful argument for effective access to the courts and judicial supervision in precisely such a sensitive area. The Court's judgment in those two cases (3 September 2008) annulled the Council regulation imposing specific restrictive measures on persons suspected of association with Usama bin Laden, the Al-Qaeda network and the Taliban insofar as it concerned the appellants: a notable triumph for the rule of law that has probably created a number of real, practical headaches for the Council.

[29] Eg in cases involving deprivation of liberty, or where a matrimonial dispute includes child abduction.

[30] Discussion papers of 25 September 2006 (available at <http://register.consilium.europa.eu/pdf/en/06/st13/st13272.en06.pdf>) and 14 December 2006 (available at <http://register.consilium.europa.eu/pdf/en/06/st17/st17013.en06.pdf>).

[31] Available at <http://curia.europa.eu/en/instit/txtdocfr/txtsenvigueur/txt5.pdf>. The English acronym (presumably 'UPRP') seems more than usually unpronounceable. Within the court, the new procedure is universally referred to as the 'PPU' (*'procédure préjudicielle d'urgence'*).

[32] Case C-195/08, *Rinau* (judgment of 11 July 2008). Because of their urgency, the court gives judgment in such cases 'having heard the Advocate General' (that is, without delivery of a formal opinion that would, necessarily, have to be translated into French and the language of procedure before it could be presented to the court). The court has yet to decide whether to publish the Advocate General's *'prise de position'* after the judgment has been handed down and the urgency has therefore ceased to exist. The European Parliament's Rapporteur, commenting on the draft rules of procedure, was firmly in favour of such transparency: see the report of the European Parliament's Committee on Legal Affairs 2007/0812(CNS), published on 22 October 2007 and available at <http://www.europarl.europa.eu/meetdocs/2004_2009/documents/pr/691/691242/691242en.pdf>.

and legal uncertainty. National courts may respond by sending more cases for clarification that have to be handled as PPUs. Conversely, they may react by refraining from using the reference mechanism. Neither outcome would be particularly desirable.

Moreover, there is at present very little indication how many references will need to be handled under the PPU. For the moment, the limitation in Article 68 EC (that only 'final' courts may refer) gives a degree of protection to the ECJ at the expense of restricting national courts' ability to ask for assistance and, arguably, at the expense of the individual claimant's access to justice. If or when the Treaty of Lisbon 2007 is ratified, the power to make references under Title IV, Part Three EC would be extended to all national courts. It is virtually inevitable that, to the extent that one case is handled with extreme urgency under the PPU, that is done at the expense of causing some delay to the handling of other cases by the same chamber of judges and the same Advocate General.[33] It is therefore unclear what the implications will be, in the longer term, for the handling of the Court's overall workload.

V. CONCLUSION: STANDING BACK AND LOOKING FORWARD

Let me conclude by (unashamedly) looking at the future of the AFSJ through the Court's spectacles.

It seems a safe prediction that the Member States will put forward more texts (in the guise of different legal instruments, with differing ostensible degrees of legal effect). They remain firmly in the driving seat. Primarily through the reference procedure, the Court will be asked to rule on the meaning of some proportion of those texts. In so doing, the Court will have to grapple with issues that link through directly to mainstream Community law and that raise, essentially, the same kinds of question. What right(s) are/are not being conferred? Are there duties as well as rights? Where is the balance to be struck between individual rights and collective interests? How (and by whom) are rights to be guaranteed effective protection? The Court's decisions will likewise go to, and affect, structural issues within EU law, such as the nature of the preliminary reference procedure, the nature (and practical operation) of cooperation

---

[33] The PPU was created as a new procedure precisely because experience with the accelerated procedure had shown that its use produced serious delay to other cases being treated. However, even under the new PPU procedure it remains (unfortunately) true that the same judges and Advocate General cannot be reading documents, sitting in an extended hearing and drafting their respective contributions with the assistance of their *référendaires* in the PPU *literally at the same time* as they are getting on, without pause, with their existing normal workload.

between the ECJ and the national courts, and the respective roles played by the ECJ and the national courts in interpreting and applying EU law.

In dealing with AFSJ cases, the Court will have to develop the expertise and vision to put an appropriate shape on the new areas of law that are placed within its jurisdiction. For a court that, historically, has dealt with economic substantive law, that is a significant challenge. It is to be hoped that the Member States will make full use of their right to intervene in preliminary references to place the issues, as they see them, squarely before the Court. It would be unfortunate—to put it mildly—if they failed to intervene and then expressed their dissatisfaction with the Court's judgment after the event.

The global challenge will, however, remain the same—albeit within different parameters—as the challenge that the Court has faced since its inception. Ensuring that the European Union is and remains subject to the rule of law should be at the core of future development, above all in the AFSJ. The Court will have to respond to its new role in a way that reconciles the imperative need for a single, consistent, authoritative and uniform interpretation of EU law with the need to maintain effective judicial process. That is going to be an interesting challenge to try to meet.

10

From Complainant to 'Private Attorney General': the Modernisation of EU Competition Enforcement and Private Antitrust Actions Before National Courts

I. INTRODUCTION

COUNCIL REGULATION 1/2003, on the implementation of the rules on competition laid down in Articles 81 and 82 of the Treaty, introduced key changes to the manner in which Articles 81 and 82 of the EC Treaty are applied.[1] By establishing a framework for the decentralised enforcement of the Treaty antitrust rules on the part of National Competition Authorities (NCAs) and of national courts, and by abolishing the monopoly of the Commission in the application of the exemption clause contained in Article 81(3) EC, the Modernisation Regulation sought to pursue the objective of allowing the Commission to regain control of its 'enforcement agenda'[2] and be able to target 'more serious' antitrust infringements.

---

* Heartfelt thanks are owed to Professor Alison Jones, of the School of Law, King's College, London, for her feedback on an earlier draft of this chapter. The author is solely responsible for any errors or omissions.

[1] [2003] OJ L1/1.

[2] Commission White Paper on Modernisation of the rules implementing Articles 85 and 86 [now 81 and 82] of the EC Treaty (hereinafter referred to also as 'the 1999 Modernisation White Paper'), Brussels, 28 April 1999, paras 12–13. For commentary, inter alia, CD Ehlermann, 'The Modernisation of EC Competition policy: a legal and cultural revolution' (2000) 37 *CML Rev* 537; T Calvani, 'Representing clients after the modernisation of EC competition law' (2003) 14 *International Company and Commercial Law Review* 335; CD Ehlermann and I Atanasiu, 'The Modernisation of EC antitrust law: consequences for the future role and function of the EC courts' (2002) 23 *European Competition Law Review* 72;

In the light of the features and objectives of the 2003 reforms, it is clear that the role of individuals and especially of the victims of antitrust breaches has changed. Whereas in the context of public enforcement they are regarded, in their capacity as complainants, as a fundamental source of information and evidence,[3] in that of private enforcement they are invited to adopt a more active role before national courts, so that judicial proceedings can effectively complement the action of the administrative agencies in this area.[4] Plaintiffs are therefore called not only to pursue their individual claims to protect their own rights, but also to seek the wider public interest of maintaining genuine competition in the Common Market, as 'quasi private attorney generals'.[5]

This chapter will examine the development of the role of individuals in competition proceedings, from complainants in administrative proceedings to plaintiffs in private antitrust actions both pre- and post-modernisation. It will concentrate on the efforts made by the Commission and some of the NCAs[6] to encourage private lawsuits concerning the application of Articles 81 and 82 EC and examine key developments in the area of competition damages, in particular the *Courage* and *Manfredi* judgments.[7]

Thereafter, the chapter will assess the effectiveness of private enforcement in the context of the 'modernised' enforcement framework. It will speculate on the prospects of reform in the light of the debate sparked by the Commission Green Paper on damages actions for breach of the EC antitrust rules[8] (hereinafter, 'the 2005 Green Paper') as well as of the proposals made in the 2008 White Paper on damages actions for breach of the EC antitrust rules[9] (hereinafter, 'the 2008 White Paper').

K Holmes, 'The EC White Paper on Modernisation' (2000) 23 *World Competition* 51; M Paulweber, 'The end of a success story? The European Commission's White Paper on the Modernisation of EC Competition law' (2000) 23 *World Competition* 3; and J Venit, 'Brave new world: the modernisation and decentralisation of the enforcement under Articles 81 and 82 of the EC Treaty' (2003) 40 *CML Rev* 545.

  [3] See, inter alia, 1999 Modernisation White Paper, paras 117–18.

  [4] *Ibid*, paras 99–100. See, inter alia, AP Komninos, 'New prospects for private enforcement of EC Competition law: *Courage v Crehan* and the Community right to damages' (2002) 39 *CML Rev* 447.

  [5] 1999 Modernisation White Paper, para 27.

  [6] See, eg Office of Fair Trading (OFT), 'OFT consults on competition law modernisation documents', 7 April 2004, Press release 66/04, available at <http://www.oft.gov.uk/news/press/2004/66–04> accessed 23 September 2008. See also 'Understanding competition law: Modernisation', available at <http://www.oft.gov.uk/shared_oft/business_leaflets/competition_law/oft442.pdf> accessed 23 September 2008.

  [7] Case 453/99, *Courage Ltd v Crehan* [2001] ECR I-6297; and Joined Cases C-295–298/04, *Manfredi v Lloyd Adriatico SpA* [2006] ECR I-6619.

  [8] Commission Green Paper—Damages actions for breach of the EC antitrust rules, COM(2005) 0672 Final, SEC (2005) 1732, hereinafter referred to as 'the 2005 Green Paper'.

  [9] Commission White Paper on Damages actions for breach of the EC antitrust rules, COM(2008) 165, hereinafter referred to as 'the 2008 White Paper'.

This chapter will argue that although the EU institutions have repeatedly expressed their commitment to strengthening the role of the enforcement of the Community competition rules by domestic courts, this endorsement has not so far been reflected in an actual increase in the number of claims being lodged. Consequently, it will be suggested that the 'agenda for change' enshrined in the 2008 White Paper constitutes a turning point, since it paves the way for future targeted action in this area through the enactment of legislative measures seeking to promote private antitrust actions in a manner which is consistent with the objective of creating a level playing field for business and consumers alike across the EU.

II. GENERAL REMARKS: THE ENFORCEMENT OF ARTICLES 81 AND 82 EC AFTER THE MODERNISATION REGULATION

The genesis of the Modernisation Regulation has been widely discussed elsewhere and the limited purvey of this work does not allow for the examination of its features.[10] Suffice to say that Council Regulation 1/2003 sought the decentralised application of the Community competition rules across the Member States through the abolition of the Commission's monopoly in applying the 'exemption clause'. It also aimed to encourage the decentralised application of the Treaty competition rules by NCAs and the national courts.[11]

Article 5 of Council Regulation 1/2003 empowers national courts and the administrative competition agencies to apply Articles 81 and 82 EC in their entirety to cases of allegedly anti-competitive behaviour, subject to the requirement of 'effect on inter-state trade' being fulfilled.[12] In this context, national courts enjoy parallel jurisdiction[13] and are empowered to ask the Commission's assistance with respect to individual judicial proceedings, without prejudice to their ability to ask the ECJ to provide a preliminary ruling in accordance with Article 234 EC. The Commission and the NCAs, on their part, can intervene as *amici curiae* before domestic courts, subject to the applicable national procedural rules.[14]

---

[10] See, inter alia, R Wesseling, 'The draft regulation modernising the competition rules: the Commission is married to one idea' (2001) 26(4) *EL Rev* 357; Ehlermann and Atanasiu, above n 2; S Kingston, 'A new division of responsibilities in the proposed regulation to modernise the rules implementing Articles 81and 82 EC? A warning call' (2001) 22(8) *European Competition Law Review* 340; Paulweber, above n 2; and Venit, above n 2.

[11] Arts 3 and 5, Council Regulation 1/2003 [2003] OJ L1/1; see also 1999 Modernisation White Paper, paras 6, 12 and 70–71.

[12] Art 5, Council Regulation 1/2003; see recital 4, 6–7 of the Preamble to the Regulation.

[13] See, inter alia, Case 127/73, *BRT v SABAM* [1974] ECR 313, paras 15–16.

[14] Arts 15 and 16(1), Regulation 1/2003; see 1999 Modernisation White Paper, paras 100 and 107.

The limited scope of this work does not allow further comment on the implications of the enforcement framework established by Council Regulation 1/2003. Nonetheless, it is clear that its enactment has had profound consequences on the manner of exercise of the powers enjoyed by EU and domestic agencies, including the judiciary of the Member States, and ultimately on the position of the individuals affected by anti-competitive behaviour.[15]

The following sections will therefore address the question of whether the enactment of the Modernisation Regulation has in fact encouraged the development of the individual's position from one of 'complainant' to that of European 'private attorney general', which has been borne out by the practical experience of the application of the Treaty competition rules in national courts.

III. COMPLAINTS IN EC COMPETITION PROCEEDINGS AND ENFORCEMENT PRIORITIES: THE *AUTOMEC* JUDGMENT

The enforcement of the EC competition rules has constantly relied on the flow of information provided to the Commission by complainants, which is thus regarded as a 'very valuable means of detecting infringements of the competition rules'.[16] According to the 1999 White Paper, prior to 1998 around 30 per cent of new investigations had been launched upon a formal complaint and the majority of proceedings initiated on the Commission's own motion were based on evidence provided informally.[17] In 2005, more than 50 per cent of new cases had arisen from formal complaints,[18] which, accordingly, amount to perhaps the most significant source of information, leading to new cases, for the Commission.[19]

Making a complaint has undeniable attractions for third parties alleging to have suffered an injury to their interests resulting from anti-competitive conduct, in view of the wide powers of investigations granted to the Commission and, perhaps most importantly, to the fact that the complainant does not bear the obligation to pay costs in the event of the allegations being unfounded.[20] However, due to its nature of administrative authority

---

[15]   Inter alia, Ehlermann, above n 2, 588–9.

[16]   1999 Modernisation White Paper, para 117.

[17]   *Ibid.*

[18]   European Commission, 'Report on Competition Policy 2005', SEC(2006) 761 final, 85, available at <http://ec.europa.eu/comm/competition/annual_reports/2005/en.pdf> accessed 23 September 2008.

[19]   See, inter alia, *ibid*, 24–5.

[20]   Inter alia, M Friend, 'Rights of complainants in EC competition proceedings' (1994) 110 *LQR* 209.

charged with upholding the public interest and to the limited resources at its disposal, the Commission is under no obligation to pursue each and every complaint.[21]

In the *Automec* judgment,[22] the Court of First Instance (CFI) held that the Commission was entitled to set 'priorities within the limits prescribed by the law' as regards which cases it should pursue.[23] In the light of its 'general supervisory task',[24] unless the latter was acting within its exclusive competence, complainants could not therefore claim a right to obtain a decision on the merits.[25] They would therefore only be entitled to have their complaint thoroughly examined[26] and, if the Commission wished to reject it, to submit observations and, eventually, to obtain a decision formally turning down the complaint, which they could challenge in court.[27]

The Court acknowledged that the Commission could refer to the lack of 'Community interest' as one of the grounds for rejecting the complaint,[28] so long as it had 'set out the legal and factual considerations which led it to conclude that there was insufficient Community interest to justify investigation of the case',[29] it had examined the factual and legal circumstances of the case and had 'balance[d] the significance of the alleged infringement ... the probability of establishing [its] existence ... and the scope of the investigation required'.[30] In that context, the Court considered especially relevant the circumstance that the facts at issue in the complaint already constituted the subject matter of judicial proceedings before the national courts and thus held that for 'reasons of procedural economy and sound administration of justice',[31] the case should be dealt with by the competent domestic judge.[32]

The CFI stated that, since these norms produced direct effects,[33] the jurisdiction to enforce Articles 81(1) and 82 EC was shared between the Commission and the national courts, in accordance with the duty of loyal cooperation imposed on the EC and national authorities by Article 10 of the Treaty.[34] It was held that the domestic courts, despite not being

---

[21] Case T-24/90, *Automec v Commission* [1992] ECR II-2223, para 74.
[22] *Ibid.*
[23] *Ibid*, para 77.
[24] *Ibid*, para 74.
[25] *Ibid*, para 76.
[26] *Ibid*, para 78.
[27] *Ibid*, paras 79–80.
[28] *Ibid*, para 85.
[29] *Ibid.*
[30] *Ibid*, para 86.
[31] *Ibid*, para 88.
[32] *Ibid.*
[33] *Ibid*, para 90.
[34] *Ibid.*

empowered to impose financial penalties on the infringers,[35] could find a violation of Article 81(1) EC and, unless it fell within the scope of a block exemption regulation, apply the sanction of nullity to the agreement in question.[36] Furthermore, if doubts arose on the interpretation or validity of the applicable EC law, they could raise a preliminary reference to the ECJ under Article 234 EC.[37] Therefore, the Court concluded that, in the circumstances of the case, the Commission had been entitled to reject the complaint on the ground of absence of Community interest.[38] The fact that it had thoroughly assessed the extent of the protection available to the complainant's interests before the domestic courts represented an essential factor confirming the validity of the decision.[39]

The importance of the *Automec* judgment for the position of individuals affected as 'interested parties' by competition proceedings cannot be understated. The CFI, by relying on established principles such as the direct effect of the EC competition rules (with the exception, at the time of the third paragraph of Article 81 EC)[40] and by recognising the concurrent jurisdiction enjoyed by the Commission and by the national courts,[41] appeared to look with favour at the domestic judicial protection as an 'adequate alternative' to lodging a complaint with the Commission.

The fact that the 1993 Notice on Cooperation with National Courts[42] restated the position adopted by the CFI in this decision may be interpreted as evidence of the Commission's commitment to boosting the private enforcement of the EC competition rules and thereby being able to target 'serious' cases of anti-competitive conduct.[43] It could also be read as inviting a gradual shift in the position of individuals allegedly aggrieved by the consequences of anti-competitive conduct from 'sources of information' for the Commission to active players in the enforcement of the EC competition rules.[44]

However, the lack of recognition, at the time, of a legal basis for the cause of action that individuals could bring before domestic courts to obtain that compensation constituted a major obstacle for lodging new claims.[45] Consequently, it could be argued that until the *Crehan* judgment,

---

[35]   *Ibid*, para 93.
[36]   *Ibid*, para 92.
[37]   *Ibid*.
[38]   *Ibid*, para 96.
[39]   *Ibid*, para 94.
[40]   Case 127/73, above n 13, paras 15–16.
[41]   Case C-234/89, *Delimits v Henninger Brau AG* [1991] ECR I-935, paras 44–5.
[42]   [1993] OJ C39/6, paras 14–16.
[43]   Inter alia, J Shaw, 'Competition complainants: a comprehensive system of remedies?' (1993) 18 *EL Rev* 427, 440–41.
[44]   See also 1999 Modernisation White Paper, para 46.
[45]   See Case T-24/90, above n 21, para 50: 'Article 85(1) prohibits certain anti-competitive agreements or practices. Among the consequences which an infringement of that prohibition

the emergence of 'private attorney generals' in competition enforcement envisaged in *Automec* remained an aspiration.[46] The next section will therefore address the implications of the ruling in *Crehan* for private enforcement and the position of aggrieved individuals.

IV. FROM DIRECT EFFECT TO *COURAGE V CREHAN*: THE IMPACT OF AN EC LAW CAUSE OF ACTION FOR ANTITRUST DAMAGES

A. EC Antitrust Claims before *Crehan*: Between Direct Effect and National Autonomy

The previous sections illustrated how enhancing private actions concerning the application of Articles 81 and 82 EC before national courts had already been recognised by the European Courts as an indispensable complement to the public enforcement of the competition rules on the part of the Commission and of the NCAs.

In the very terse *BRT v SABAM* preliminary ruling,[47] the ECJ held that both Articles 'tend by very nature to produce direct effects in relations between individuals', and conferred on them 'rights ... which the national courts must safeguard'.[48] They were therefore empowered to apply these provisions to disputes pending before them in order to protect these rights[49] and in that context, were allowed to raise a preliminary reference to Luxembourg concerning the interpretation of the Treaty antitrust rules.[50] In the later *Delimitis* ruling,[51] the ECJ expressly recognised that the national courts shared with the Commission the power to apply Articles 81(1) and 82 EC to individual cases.[52] Similarly, in the *Masterfoods* decision,[53] the Court stated that, by virtue of that parallel jurisdiction, national courts retained the power to rule over disputes relating to the

---

may have in civil law, only one is expressly provided for in Article 85(2), namely the nullity of the agreement. The other consequences attaching to an infringement of Article 85 of the Treaty, such as the obligation to make good the damage caused to a third party or a possible obligation to enter into a contract ... are to be determined under national law. Consequently, it is the national courts which, where appropriate, may, in accordance with the rules of national law, order one trader to enter into a contract with another.' See also European Commission, Notice on cooperation between the national courts and the Commission in applying Articles 85 and 86 of the EEC Treaty [now Articles 81 and 82 EC] [1993] OJ C39/6, para 17. See, inter alia, Komninos, above n 4, 451.

[46] Case 453/99, above n 7.
[47] Case 127/73, above n 13.
[48] *Ibid*, para 16.
[49] *Ibid*, para 17.
[50] *Ibid*, para s 20, 23.
[51] Case C-234/89, above n 41.
[52] *Ibid*, para 45.
[53] Case C-344/98, *Masterfoods Ltd v HB Ice Cream Ltd* [2000] ECR I-11369.

application of the Treaty antitrust rules even after the Commission had commenced individual proceedings as regards the same practice.[54]

However, the ECJ did not go as far as to state that Community law provided a legal basis for antitrust damages' claims.[55] Although in the later *Guerin* decision,[56] the Court had hinted at the possibility that an undertaking whose grievances have been dismissed by the Commission could, if it considered that it had 'suffered damages as a result of restrictive practices', rely on the Treaty competition rules in proceedings before national courts, on the ground that these provisions were directly effective.[57] It was not until the *Courage* preliminary ruling that the ECJ recognised a right to obtain compensation for damages arising from the consequences of anti-competitive conduct.

In the light of the above analysis, it can be concluded that, although until the 2001 preliminary ruling in *Crehan* the ECJ had not expressly recognised a legal basis for claims for antitrust damages as a matter of EC law, it had acknowledged the role of private enforcement as complementing the action of the Commission.[58] The next section will therefore examine the genesis and development of a Community right to antitrust damages and discuss its impact on the role of individuals in the context of competition enforcement.

B. '*Courage v Crehan*': A 'Private Attorney General' in EC Competition Law?

As is well known, the dispute between Mr Crehan and Courage Ltd (now Inntrepreneur Pub Co Ltd) concerned payment of some £15,000 in respect of the supply of beer by the brewery to the defendant, one of the plaintiff's tenants. Mr Crehan, however, challenged that claim by alleging that the 'beer tie' in which he had entered was void in as much as it infringed Article 81(1) EC and filed a counterclaim seeking compensation for the damages he had supposedly suffered as a result of the agreement.[59]

On a reference from the English Court of Appeal, the ECJ reiterated that Article 81(1) EC produced direct effects and conferred rights which the

---

[54]   *Ibid*, para 47.
[55]   Case T-24/90, above n 21, para 50. Cf, *mutatis mutandis, Garden Cottage Foods Ltd v Milk Marketing Board* [1984] AC 130, *per* Lord Diplock, p 141.
[56]   Case C-282/95, *Guerin Automobiles v Commission* [1997] ECR I-1503.
[57]   *Ibid*, para 39. See also, *mutatis mutandis*, Case C-128/92, *Banks & Co Ltd v British Coal Corp* [1994] ECR I-1209, *per* AG Van Gerven, para 42.
[58]   See C Jones, *Private enforcement of antitrust law in the UK, the EU and the USA* (Oxford, Oxford University Press, 1999) 77–8.
[59]   *Courage Ltd v Crehan* [1999] ECC 455 (CA), para 1.

national courts must protect.[60] As a result, it was held that the effectiveness of Article 81(1) of the Treaty would be jeopardised if an individual could not rely on its violation[61] to claim compensation for the damages he or she had suffered as a result of an anti-competitive practice.[62] The availability of this remedy 'strengthen[ed] the working of the Community competition rules and discourag[ed] ... practices which are frequently covert', thus contributing 'to the maintenance of effective competition' across the Common Market.[63]

The ECJ then moved to the issue of whether EC law did provide a legal basis for an action to claim antitrust damages. It acknowledged that, according to the principle of national autonomy, national courts should not be precluded from applying domestic rules designed to prevent the unjust enrichment of the parties aggrieved by the consequences of anti-competitive behaviour, provided that the principles of effectiveness and equivalence were satisfied.[64] The ECJ added that these rules could prevent individual applicants 'found to bear significant responsibility for the distortion of competition'[65] from claiming compensation wholly or in part.[66] Regard should be had to the 'economic and legal context', their 'respective bargaining power' and their conduct in the course of their commercial relations.[67]

The ruling in *Courage* was welcomed as providing an express legal basis in EC law for antitrust damages' claims in national courts. Commentators observed that, although the ECJ did not 'explicitly extend its earlier case law on Member State liability to cover the liability of individuals', it relied on substantially the same arguments and principles, namely the need to preserve the *effet utile* of the Treaty competition rules and to promote the achievement of conditions of genuine competition in the Common Market.[68]

In addition, the express reference to the role of antitrust damages actions as a means to increasing the efficacy of the competition rules in achieving the goals of the Treaty appears consistent with their function of necessary complement to public enforcement of Articles 81 and 82 EC.[69] As a result, individual claimants would 'pursue their Community rights in the national

---

[60] Case C-453/99, above n 7, paras 19 and 23.
[61] *Ibid*, para 24.
[62] *Ibid*, para 26.
[63] *Ibid*, para 27.
[64] *Ibid*, para 30.
[65] *Ibid*, para 31.
[66] *Ibid*, para 32.
[67] *Ibid*.
[68] V Milutinovic, 'Private enforcement: upcoming issues' in G Amato and CD Ehlermann (eds), *EC Competition Law: A Critical Assessment* (Oxford, Hart, 2007) 727.
[69] Komninos, above n 4, 464.

courts', and thus directly protect their individual interests[70] and 'indirectly ... act in the Community interest',[71] thus assuming a 'private attorney general role ... in antitrust cases'.[72] Their action, in other words, would fulfil a twofold function, namely to secure compensation for the loss suffered as a result of anti-competitive conduct as well as to correct 'the "enforcement gap" generated by the perceived inability of public enforcement to deal with all attention-worthy cases'.[73]

In the later *Manfredi* decision,[74] the ECJ confirmed these principles and expressly stated that the wording 'any individual' should be read as allowing any party to bring an action for damages provided that the plaintiff could demonstrate the existence of a causal link between the invalid agreement or practice and the harm suffered,[75] thus extending the cause of action it had established in its 2001 ruling to all claims for damages satisfying that requirement of causation.[76]

In the light of the standing conditions established by the *Manfredi* preliminary ruling, it is suggested that a shift may already be taking place in respect of the role of individuals in the context of competition enforcement, from mere 'sources of intelligence' for the Commission and the NCAs to that of 'quasi private attorney generals' in the context of the enforcement framework.[77] The circumstance that in its recent White Paper on antitrust damages the Commission confirms the existence of a right to damages for 'any individual' who could demonstrate to have suffered loss arising from the consequences of anti-competitive conduct[78] is thus consistent with the complementary function of private antitrust claims as a means to provide redress for the damages suffered by the applicant, as well as to uphold the effectiveness of the Treaty rules and the Community competition policy.[79]

Against this background, it is also clear that the existence of an efficient framework for bringing these actions is vital for the achievement of these objectives, since a higher detection rate for anti-competitive conduct would result from individuals having access to 'effective legal mechanisms to

---

[70]   *Ibid.*
[71]   *Ibid*, 464–5.
[72]   *Ibid.*
[73]   *Ibid*, 458.
[74]   Joined Cases C-295–298/04, above n 7.
[75]   *Ibid*, paras 61–3.
[76]   See also, *mutatis mutandis*, European Commission, Notice on the Handling of Complaints by the Commission under Articles 81 and 82 of the EC Treaty [2004] OJ C65, paras 34 and 36–8.
[77]   Milutinovic, above n 68, 730–31.
[78]   *Ibid*; see also White Paper, Commission Working Document SEC(2008) 404 (hereinafter referred to as 'the 2008 Working Document'), paras 27 and 37.
[79]   See Komninos, above n 4, 486–7. See also 2008 Working Document, paras 2 and 15.

bring infringements of competition law before civil courts'.[80] Accordingly, the 2008 White Paper argued that without any of these mechanisms being in place, the overall effectiveness of the EC antitrust rules would be jeopardised, especially in respect of those breaches that escape the net of public enforcement.[81]

On this point, it could be argued that the Modernisation Regulation, with its drive towards a more proactive decentralised enforcement, had sought to encourage this transition. At the same time, however, it should be reminded that Council Regulation 1/2003, just as the *Courage* and *Manfredi* decisions, did not establish any condition governing these actions, but, instead, reaffirmed the principle of national autonomy.[82] Consequently, the issue of whether the exercise of the function of 'private attorney generals' by individuals can act in practice as an effective complement to the enforcement of Articles 81 and 82 EC remains open to question and will be investigated in the following section.

V. PRIVATE ANTI-TRUST CLAIMS IN THE MODERNISATION FRAMEWORK: AN EFFECTIVE COMPLEMENT TO PUBLIC ENFORCEMENT?

A. Private Enforcement of the Competition Rules in Europe: An 'Underdeveloped' Mechanism for the Application of Articles 81 and 82 EC?

> The European Court of Justice has been clear: the right to damages is necessary to guarantee the useful effect of the EC competition rules. But even in Member States with advanced national antitrust rules, there is little evidence that consumers and business customers are fully exercising their right to damages for harm. That means that many injuries are left uncompensated, with society and the economy left to absorb that loss. This situation is clearly unjust, incompatible with our Community of law, and at odds with our shared competitiveness objectives.[83]

Arguably, this statement from a 2007 speech given by Neelie Kroes, the current EU Commissioner for Competition, paints a fairly accurate picture

---

[80] 2008 Working Document, para 38; see also 2008 White Paper, para 1.2.
[81] *Ibid.*
[82] Case C-453/99, above n 7, para 29. Joined Cases C-295–298/04, above n 7, para 62.
[83] Neelie Krooes, 'Reinforcing the fight against cartels and developing private antitrust damages actions: two tools for a more competitive Europe', speech given at the Commission/ IBA Joint Conference on EC Competition Policy, Brussels, 8 March 2007, SPEECH 07/128, available at <http://europa.eu/rapid/pressReleasesAction.do?reference=SPEECH/07/ 128&format=HTML&aged=0&language=EN&guiLanguage=en> accessed 23 September 2008.

of the state of private antitrust damages claims in the Common Market. According to the Ashurst Report, commissioned by the DG Competition in 2004 to investigate the matter, despite the strong emphasis on the role of private actions as a means to complement public enforcement of Articles 81 and 82 EC, the state of private enforcement in the EU offers a 'picture ... of astonishing diversity and total underdevelopment'.[84]

In light of these findings, the Commission argued that the underlying cause of the under-development of private antitrust enforcement in Europe was in the existence of an 'information asymmetry' between the two parties of a given dispute.[85] In other words, 'the uncertainty of the outcome' of the dispute would not allow the plaintiff to balance the potentially high costs against 'correspondingly good prospects of recovery', due to the complexity of these cases, their fact-intensive nature and the resulting possibility that unpredictable outcomes could result.[86]

Consequently, the Commission called for the introduction of incentives to readjust the 'risk/reward balance' in antitrust claims, which is currently 'skewed against bringing actions',[87] and thus to encourage individual litigants to seek redress of their antitrust injuries before national courts, for the purpose of creating a 'level playing field' across the Member States.[88] In respect of the gathering of evidence, the 2005 Green Paper had argued that the lack of rules facilitating plaintiffs in this task constituted a major obstacle to the bringing of damages actions.[89] It was noted that in the majority of the Member States, the powers of the competent courts to order the production of that evidence were extremely limited and, except in a few jurisdictions, there are no general obligations to disclose documents in advance of the trial.[90]

In addition, the administrative decisions of the NCAs are not usually binding on domestic judges, a factor making 'follow-on actions', namely civil claims brought against undertakings that have already been found to be responsible for a competition infringement by administrative agencies,

---

[84] D Waelbroeck, D Slater and G Even-Shoshan, 'Study on the conditions of claims for damages in case of infringement of the EC competition rules', 31 August 2004, available at <http://ec.europa.eu/comm/competition/antitrust/actionsdamages/comparative_report_clean_en.pdf> accessed 28 March 2008 (hereinafter referred to as 'the Ashurst Report'), Comparative Report, para 1.

[85] Commission Staff Working Paper, Annex to the Green Paper, COM/2005/0672, final (hereinafter referred to as 'the 2005 Staff Working Paper'), para 45.

[86] *Ibid.*

[87] *Ibid.*

[88] *Ibid*, para 10.

[89] Waelbroeck *et al*, above n 84, 61–2.

[90] 2005 Staff Working Paper, para 34.

potentially as difficult as 'stand-alone' claims, ie claims brought without a competition authority first having found a violation of the competition rules.[91]

The Ashurst Report also found that certain conditions imposed by the laws of some Member States to establish liability could constitute an obstacle to antitrust damages claimants, such as the requirement to prove that the defendant was at fault in addition to the proof of the infringement.[92] Although the Commission recognised that in those legal systems where this evidence was necessary, proof of negligence was normally sufficient to establish liability,[93] it accepted that this condition may discourage applicants.[94]

The rules on causation and the quantification of damages also emerged as obstacles to an effective private antitrust enforcement. The 2004 Report demonstrated that differing standards concerning the establishment of a causal link between the infringement and the loss allegedly incurred by the plaintiff, compounded by the 'case-by-case' approach to the issue prevailing in many Member States, constituted yet another factor 'tipping the scale' against bringing an antitrust damages action.[95]

With respect to the quantum of damages available to a successful plaintiff, the Ashurst Report found that the restrictions in the amount of compensation, present in the laws of some Member States, and the varying rules concerning interest constituted an additional obstacle to the likelihood of these actions, as well as being inconsistent with the need to ensure full compensation to successful applicants.[96] The Commission also queried whether the introduction of 'treble damages' could encourage fresh actions.[97] The burden of costs and legal fees associated with the legal proceedings in national courts represented another considerable difficulty for prospective claimants. The 2004 Report found that in the majority of the Member States fees have to be paid upfront, which in itself constitutes a considerable deterrent factor vis-à-vis new claims being lodged.[98]

With respect to legal costs, the analysis of the laws of the Member States indicates that the award of costs generally follows the 'loser pays'

---

[91]   *Ibid*, para 36.
[92]   *Ibid*, para 32.
[93]   *Ibid*, para 103.
[94]   *Ibid*, paras 109–12.
[95]   2005 Working Paper, para 37; see Ashurst Report, 72.
[96]   *Ibid*, 82 and 84–5; see also 2005 Working Paper, paras 40–41.
[97]   2005 Working Paper, paras 120–21.
[98]   Ashurst Report, 92. See also 2005 Working Paper, para 203.

principle,[99] which has constantly been regarded as a factor considerably discouraging these actions, especially when they are brought by small claimants, such as consumers.[100]

Finally, domestic rules governing the burden and standard of proof in civil proceedings were also regarded as a possible obstacle to the effective private enforcement of the antitrust rules.[101] It was argued that, especially in less 'clear-cut' cases, where economic analysis inevitably plays a decisive role and the applicable legal standards are consequently more fluid, the plaintiff may be faced with considerable technical difficulties in proving their case to the required standard.[102]

The above analysis highlighted a number of, albeit not exhaustive, factors jeopardising the emergence of an effective system for the application of Articles 81 and 82 EC to individual disputes in national courts. On this point, it is particularly telling that in its 2008 White Paper the Commission substantially confirmed the finding that, although since the publication of the 2004 Report, the awareness of the importance of individual antitrust actions increased, the shortcomings identified by the 2005 Green Paper had remained by and large unaffected.[103]

Accordingly, it was argued that correcting this 'clear deficit in terms of corrective justice',[104] which results in very few victims being actually compensated,[105] was indispensable also to secure 'other beneficial effects' stemming from private enforcement, namely an increased deterrence and detection of anti-competitive conduct that would otherwise escape any form of sanction.[106] The following section will therefore illustrate the options proposed to address these obstacles and examine the wider general issues arising from the discussion in this area.

B. Boosting Private Anti-Trust Enforcement: Debating the Perspectives for Change

The previous section illustrated the principal obstacles to the efficient private antitrust enforcement existing in the laws of the Member States.[107] Having regard to the issues concerning the admissibility of evidence and

---

[99] Ashurst Report, 92 and 94–5; see also 2005 Staff Working paper, para 213.
[100] 2005 Staff Working Paper, paras 213–14.
[101] *Ibid*, paras 89, 95–6 and 98.
[102] *Ibid*, para 83–94 and 99; see T Eilmansberger, 'The Green Paper on damages action for breach of the EC antitrust rules and beyond: reflections on the utility and feasibility of stimulating private enforcement through legislative action' (2007) 44 *CML Rev* 431, 456.
[103] 2008 Working Document, para 11.
[104] *Ibid*, para 37.
[105] *Ibid*, para 34.
[106] *Ibid*, para 38.
[107] Ashurst Report, Executive Summary, 1–9.

the burden of proof imposed on plaintiffs, in view of the 'information asymmetry' existing between the litigants in individual cases,[108] the Commission 2005 Green Paper argued that ad hoc measures to facilitate the acquisition of that evidence, for instance by introducing some form of 'pre-trial' disclosure in the laws of the Member States[109] and by conferring on individual litigants the right to seek access to the evidence held by the NCAs.[110]

The Green Paper also suggested that the burden of proof of competition infringements should be alleviated to allow plaintiffs to establish a successful claim when some factual evidence has been disclosed which would reveal the likelihood of a violation and the defendant cannot rebut that evidence[111] or when an administrative decision finding a breach has already been given, by making that decision in fact binding on the national court as regards the finding of an infringement of the competition rules.[112] It was also suggested that especially in 'novel' or more 'controversial' cases, limiting the burden of proof of an infringement to the establishment of a prima facie case could provide a considerable incentive to new antitrust damages actions.[113]

Despite attracting support in the course of the Commission inquiry,[114] these proposals were criticised as potentially resulting in unmeritorious litigation and, more generally, as threatening the coherence of the procedural rules of individual legal systems.[115] It was added that the proposed amendments could eventually result in the over-deterrence of 'less serious' antitrust breaches, such as vertical anti-competitive practices.[116]

The 2004 Ashurst Report was also critical of the requirement to prove that the defendant had been at fault in addition to establishing the infringement of the EC competition rules.[117] Consequently, the Commission proposed that similar national rules should either be abolished or limited to cases in which the defendant had failed to prove that he or she had committed an 'excusable error of law or fact'.[118] However, commentators were sceptical as to whether totally eliminating the requirement of

---

[108] 2005 Staff Working Paper, paras 56–7.
[109] *Ibid*, paras 56–7 and 90–91.
[110] *Ibid*, paras 73–4.
[111] *Ibid*, paras 81–2 and 97.
[112] *Ibid*, paras 85–6 and 98.
[113] Eilmansberger, above n 102, 456.
[114] *Ibid*.
[115] *Ibid*, 457. See, inter alia, Jones, above n 58, 207–8.
[116] 2005 Staff Working Paper, paras 139–40.
[117] 2004 Ashurst Report, para 32.
[118] *Ibid*, paras 109–12.

fault would conform to the complementary function of private enforcement and argued that a similar change could 'have an over-deterring effect and encourage unmeritorious' litigation.[119]

In respect to the rules governing the quantification of damages, it has been queried whether the introduction of some form of 'damages multiplier' could be desirable to encourage new lawsuits.[120] Jones has argued that, despite not being essential to encourage antitrust claims,[121] punitive damages constitute a considerable incentive for individual plaintiffs by ensuring a better chance of 'full compensation' for the injury sustained.[122]

Nonetheless, other commentators question whether this could, on its own, be an adequate and convincing justification for the introduction of multiple damages and express doubt that their punitive nature could be sustainable in the light of the general principles governing the award of compensation.[123] It was added that the majority of the Member States considered 'double' or 'treble' damages inconsistent with the 'compensation-restitution' rationale of non-contractual liability.[124] On this point, it is noteworthy that according to the High Court in England and Wales the absence of the award of exemplary damages would not be contrary to the principle of effectiveness of the rights conferred by EC law to individuals.[125]

The High Court held in the *Devenish* judgment that a 'damage multiplier' in private antitrust actions fulfilled a punitive and deterrent function[126] and that therefore double or treble damages could not be awarded against defendants who had already been fined by the Commission in respect of the same finding of a breach of the Treaty competition rules.[127] Consequently, it was concluded that as a matter of Community law, plaintiffs would only be entitled to compensatory damages and could seek exemplary damages only if the latter were available for similar actions grounded in domestic law.[128]

Finally, in relation to the costs associated with bringing these actions, the 2004 Ashurst Report and the Commission Working Paper found that the

---

[119]   Eilmansberger, above n 102, 452.
[120]   2005 Staff Working Paper, para 121.
[121]   Jones, above n 58, 228.
[122]   *Ibid*, 231–2.
[123]   Eilmansberger, above n 102, 450–51.
[124]   Ashurst Report, 84; see 2005 Staff Working Paper, paras 112, 114–15 and 120.
[125]   *Devenish Nutrition Ltd v Sanofi Aventis* (Ch) [2008] ECC 4, paras 34 and 36. See also Case C-453/99, above n 7, Opinion of AG Mischo, points 58–9.
[126]   *Devenish Nutrition Ltd v Sanofi Aventis* (Ch) [2008] ECC 4, *per* Lewinson J, paras 47–8.
[127]   *Ibid*, para 52.
[128]   *Ibid*, para 37.

application of the 'loser pays' principle to antitrust disputes could discourage these actions even further.[129] Accordingly, the Commission Working Paper called for the introduction of measures designed to mitigate the adverse impact of cost and fees' rules on the likelihood of single claimants to lodge damages actions.[130] With respect to lawyers' fees, the Commission argued in the 2005 Working Paper that the introduction of contingency fee agreements, despite being allowed only in a limited number of Member States,[131] could have a positive impact since it would 'split the risk' associated with these actions between the plaintiff and his or her legal adviser.[132]

Having regard specifically to claims brought by individual consumers and small businesses, the possibility of introducing some form of collective action was regarded as an appropriate response to the need to facilitate the access to justice of individual claimants, while at the same time limiting the number of lawsuits actually lodged before the courts and grounded on 'common issues of law and fact'.[133] Accordingly, the Commission envisaged the introduction of standing for collective organisations, such as consumers associations, along with specific rules governing the quantification and distribution of damages, to encourage especially small purchasers.[134] It argued that similar actions were already available in several Member States and,[135] although it recognised that their introduction could involve a considerable inroad in the principle of national autonomy,[136] it would in any event be desirable to boost these actions, streamline court proceedings and avoid forum shopping.[137]

So far, this section has considered, albeit not exhaustively, a number of options for reform aimed at improving the conditions governing antitrust enforcement in domestic courts and has examined a number of more general issues concerning private enforcement. The 2004 Green Paper and the ensuing consultation illustrated that there may be convincing justifications for introducing legislation facilitating private enforcement of the Community antitrust rules. In fact, due to the paucity of the actions currently being lodged and the inherent difficulties faced by individual applicants, at this stage and without ad hoc legislative intervention, the

---

[129] See Ashurst Report, 92 and 94–5; and 2005 Staff Working Paper, paras 213–14.
[130] Eilmansberger, above n 102, 448.
[131] *Ibid*, 449.
[132] 2005 Staff Working Paper, para 218.
[133] Milutinovic, above n 68, 751.
[134] 2005 Staff Working Paper, paras 198–9.
[135] *Ibid*, para 197.
[136] *Ibid*.
[137] Milutinovic, above n 68, 754–5.

role of individuals in the overall context of competition enforcement is unlikely to 'progress' to a more proactive one of litigants and 'private attorney generals'.

The next section will therefore analyse the proposals made by the Commission in its 2008 White Paper with a view to assessing whether the 'agenda for reform' set by the Commission is capable of fostering the 'transition' to an effective system for the application of the Treaty antitrust rules in national courts.

C. The 2008 White Paper: A Legislative Proposal for the Efficient Judicial Enforcement of the Treaty Anti-trust Rules

The previous sections explored a number of possible alternatives aimed at the creation of a more effective and coherent framework for the application of Articles 81 and 82 EC by national courts. It was argued that in spite of the strong judicial affirmations of the existence of a right to seek compensation for damages caused by anti-competitive behaviour, the current state of the law does not provide individual applicants with concrete and effective means of redress of their rights before domestic courts.

The 2008 White Paper on antitrust damages proposes the enactment of a set of legislative measures aimed at establishing a set of minimum standards governing competition damages actions to ensure full compensation to aggrieved litigants, improve awareness and deterrence of competition enforcement as a whole, facilitate the access to justice, promote efficient use of the civil justice system and eventually contribute to a more level playing field across the EU for both businesses and consumers.[138]

The White Paper envisages a right to bring a claim for damages for 'any individual' who suffered harm arising form the consequences of anti-competitive behaviour.[139] Accordingly, both direct and indirect purchasers would be entitled to seek compensation.[140] To encourage new claims by consumers and small businesses, the White Paper also proposes the introduction of a combination of means of collective redress, in the form of representative actions and opt-in collective actions, namely actions in which the alleged victims of unlawful practices 'decide to combine their individual claims ... into one single action'.[141]

Having regard to the access to evidence, the White Paper was clearly aware of the need to rebalance the information asymmetry existing

---

[138]   2008 Working Document, para 4.
[139]   2008 White Paper, para 2.1. See Joined Cases C-295–298/04, above n 7, para 61.
[140]   2008 White Paper, para 2.1.
[141]   *Ibid*, para 2.1.

between the plaintiff and the defendant in these actions, while at the same time avoiding abuses of process[142] and showing concern for the interests of defendants, who may be forced to settle perhaps not entirely meritorious claims just to avoid the damaging consequences of orders imposing wide disclosure obligations.[143]

For this reason, the White Paper suggests introducing a 'minimum level' of *inter partes* disclosure subject to specific requirements of fact pleading and to the strict control of the trial court.[144] That disclosure would be granted only if the applicant presented the Court with all the facts and evidence that are 'reasonably available to him' and showed that 'plausible grounds' existed to suspect that he or she suffered damage from the alleged antitrust infringement.[145] The claimant must satisfy the trial judge that he or she is unable, 'applying all the efforts that can reasonably be expected', to obtain that evidence by any other means.[146] The request must indicate 'sufficiently precise categories'[147] of evidence and explain to the satisfaction of the Court that the measure applied for is 'both relevant to the case and necessary and proportionate'.[148]

The 2008 White Paper was also in favour of conferring binding legal effect to decisions adopted by NCAs on national courts in respect of the finding of an antitrust infringement, provided that the decision is final and relates to the same parties and practices as those at issue before the trial court[149] and regardless of the jurisdiction in which the civil action is brought.[150] To safeguard the independence of the judiciary, the White Paper added that this proposal would not prejudice the national courts' powers and obligations under Article 234 of the EC Treaty,[151] especially when 'serious doubts as to the legal correctness of the interpretation of Articles 81 or 82 by the NCA' arose.[152]

Furthermore, the Commission sought to avoid the effectiveness of leniency programmes in force throughout the EU being jeopardised by the bringing of private antitrust claims. It thus suggested in the White Paper that the corporate statements made by leniency applicants would not be

---

[142] *Ibid*, para 2.2. See 2008 Working Document, paras 87–8.
[143] 2008 White Paper; and 2008 Working Document, para 93.
[144] 2008 White Paper; and 2008 Working Document, paras 94–6.
[145] *Ibid*.
[146] 2008 Working Document, paras 95–6.
[147] *Ibid*, para 98.
[148] *Ibid*.
[149] 2008 White Paper, para 2.3.
[150] 2008 Working Document, paras 143–4.
[151] *Ibid*, para 148.
[152] *Ibid*, para 145.

open to *inter partes* disclosure[153] even after the adoption of the administration decision on the part of either the Commission or an NCA.[154]
Although, in principle, the parties to a dispute should not be able to object
to the discovery of 'unfavourable evidence' before the trial court,[155] the
White Paper was clearly concerned with providing 'adequate protection' to
the confidentiality of documents submitted by actual or potential whistle-
blowers, regardless of whether or not they are successful.[156]

However, the Commission rejected calls for the lowering of the standard
of proof and for the shifting of the burden of proof in antitrust damages
cases,[157] since it considered these proposals as carrying too high a risk of
judicial error and of abuses of process on the part of individual plaintiffs,
and also as encouraging unmeritorious litigation.[158]

Having regard to the conditions governing liability and to the requirement to prove that the defendant be 'at fault', in addition to the proof of a
breach of the EC antitrust rules,[159] the White Paper suggested that a
defendant should be presumed to be 'at fault' if the claimant could
establish that the practice in question was contrary to the EC antitrust
rules[160] and unless the defendant demonstrated that the breach was owed
to a 'genuinely excusable error'.[161] An error would, however, be 'excusable' only if it could be shown that 'a reasonable person, applying a high
standard of care, could not have been aware that conduct restricted
competition',[162] having regard, inter alia, to the type of conduct, to any
official statements made by 'competent public entities' and the nature—
whether novel or not—of the legal issues involved.[163] Therefore, it could
be expected that this requirement would be read narrowly.[164]

In respect of the damages available, one of the White Paper's objectives
was to ensure full compensation for the harm suffered by winning
plaintiffs, in the measure of both the actual loss and the reduction in
profits resulting from losses in sales caused by the anti-competitive
conduct.[165] In accordance with the ECJ case law, the plaintiff should also

---

[153]   2008 White Paper, para 2.2. See also 2008 Working Document, para 117.
[154]   2008 White Paper, para 2.9; see 2008 Working Document, paras 272–3 and 292–3.
[155]   2008 Working Document, para 120.
[156]   *Ibid.*
[157]   *Ibid*, paras 91–2.
[158]   *Ibid*, para 92.
[159]   See, eg 2008 Working Document, para 67.
[160]   2008 White Paper, para 2.4. See 2008 Working Document, paras 170–71.
[161]   2008 White Paper. See also 2008 Working Document, para 176.
[162]   *Ibid*, para 177.
[163]   *Ibid*, para 179.
[164]   *Ibid.*
[165]   2008 White Paper, para 2.5. See 2008 Working Document, para 180.

be entitled to the payment of interests accrued on the amount of compensation from the date on which the damage occurred.[166] However, the Commission rejected the calls for the introduction of forms of punitive damages.[167] It took the view that although punitive damages were not incompatible with EC law and should be available to claimants if they were already provided by national law in respect to similar actions grounded in domestic law,[168] successful plaintiffs should be entitled in principle only to single damages.[169]

To respect the compensatory nature of this award and avoid the unjust enrichment of winning plaintiffs, the defendant should also be able to plead that the successful claimant had 'passed on' any overcharge he or she had suffered and, as a result, had succeeded in offsetting his or her loss by reflecting it in the prices charged to his or her own customers, so as to reduce the extent of liability.[170] Similarly, indirect purchasers should be allowed to rely on the passing-on argument to bring an action against a supplier found to have infringed the EC competition rules in respect of the harm they had suffered due to having been overcharged.[171]

In respect to the costs arising from antitrust damages actions, the White Paper suggested a number of measures aimed at reducing the impact of the relevant domestic rules, including encouraging the non-judicial resolution of disputes, both out-of- and in-court[172] and designing the rules on courts' fees so as to prevent them placing a disproportionate burden on claimants, perhaps by setting them as a percentage on the value of the dispute, to improve their predictability.[173]

The Commission, however, declined to derogate from the 'loser pays' principle, in view of its 'filtering' function of unmeritorious claims.[174] Consequently, it only proposed that Member States should consider allowing their courts the power to 'grant protection from cost recovery' even when the plaintiff is not successful.[175] That decision should be subject to the discretionary assessment of, inter alia, the financial situation of the

---

[166] 2008 White Paper; and 2008 Working Document, para 187; see, inter alia, Case C-271/91, *Marshall v Southampton and West-Hampshire AHA* [1993] ECR I-4367, para 31.

[167] 2008 Working Document, para 181.

[168] *Ibid*, para 190. See Joined Cases C-295–298/04, above n 7, para 93.

[169] 2008 White Paper, para 2.5; see also 2008 Working Document, paras 190–91.

[170] 2008 White Paper, para 2.6; see 2008 Working Document, paras 201 and 210.

[171] 2008 White Paper; and 2008 Working Document, para 215.

[172] 2008 White Paper, para 2.8; see 2008 Working Document, paras 247 and 250.

[173] 2008 Working Document, paras 262–3.

[174] *Ibid*, paras 252–3.

[175] *Ibid*, para 255.

parties, the value of the claim, the circumstances of the case,[176] and of considerations of 'fairness, reasonableness and equity'.[177]

Finally, in respect to the interaction of private enforcement with leniency programmes, the White Paper proposed that the joint liability of successful applicants vis-à-vis other cartel members be removed in respect of the damages arising from the unlawful practice,[178] so that they would be exposed only to those damages arising from their direct action, whilst ensuring full compensation for the winning plaintiffs.[179]

At this stage, it is premature to attempt to gauge the implications of the White Paper. However, a few general points can be made. First, in respect to the question of whether taking legislative action at EU level in this field would be justified, the Commission strongly argued that the lack of EU-wide action in this area would maintain the 'marked inequality in the level of judicial protection' of the rights of individuals aggrieved by anti-competitive conduct, as a result of which the 'competitive environment for business' would remain inconsistent.[180]

Legislative action at EU level in this area would therefore be appropriate, in accordance with the principle of subsidiarity, because it would give individuals a 'clear picture of their basic rights', provide Member States with a framework of 'minimum standards' for their protection and increase the overall awareness and deterrence of private antitrust enforcement, thus contributing 'to a European level playing field for both claimants and defendants'.[181] It would also be necessary in the light of the 'public policy' nature of the prohibitions enshrined in Articles 81 and 82 EC, to the transnational nature of EU competition breaches and to the complexity of the legal and economic analysis involved, as well as to the information asymmetry between the parties.[182]

Secondly, with respect to the nature and function of antitrust damages, the White Paper takes the view that the award should only seek to compensate successful plaintiffs fully for the loss suffered as a result of anti-competitive conduct, and should not, therefore, constitute an 'additional punishment' for illegal practices, especially when the latter have already been detected by the Commission or NCAs.[183]

---

[176]   See 2008 Working Document, paras 256–8.
[177]   *Ibid*, para 259. See European Commission, Impact Assessment Report SEC(2008) 405 of 2 April 2008 (hereinafter referred to as '2008 Impact Assessment document'), para 157, table 18.
[178]   2008 Working Document, para 280.
[179]   *Ibid*, para 305.
[180]   See, eg Case C-453/99, above n 7, paras 28–9. See 2008 Impact Assessment document, para 165.
[181]   2008 Working Document, para 320.
[182]   See *ibid*, paras 313–15.
[183]   See 2008 Working Document, paras 319–20.

In the light of the above analysis, it can be concluded that the White Paper, by focusing on the ability of private enforcement to boost both the awareness and deterrence of the EU antitrust rules, fosters the evolution of the position of individuals aggrieved by the consequences of anti-competitive practices from complainants to 'private attorney generals'.[184] However, until these proposals are formally debated through the legislative process, the status quo as regards the viability of private enforcement remains unchanged. The final section will therefore conduct a brief 'reality check' on the state of judicial antitrust proceedings in the UK, to assess whether the current rules already allow the emergence of a European 'private attorney general' on antitrust matters.

VI. PRIVATE ANTI-TRUST ENFORCEMENT BETWEEN POLICY EXPECTATIONS AND REALITY CHECK: WHAT FUTURE FOR A EUROPEAN 'PRIVATE ATTORNEY GENERAL'? TENTATIVE CONCLUSIONS

The analysis conducted so far indicates that, although both the case law of the ECJ and the Modernisation Regulation have actively sought to encourage private enforcement actions in the field of competition law in order to boost detection, provide redress to the rights of those aggrieved by anti-competitive conduct and as a result, to contribute to the deterrence of future unlawful conduct, significant obstacles remain with respect to the emergence of a 'European private attorney general'.[185] In the light of these concerns, the proposals of the 2008 White Paper should be welcomed since they provide a strong restatement of the importance of private enforcement of the EC antitrust rules and offer practical options aimed at making these actions an effective complement to the administrative activity in this area.

However, it is undeniable that, until such time as they are put into a legislative proposal and the latter is thrashed out through the legislative process, it is unclear whether the existing principles governing antitrust damages actions afford, at least for the time being, adequate protection to the rights of aggrieved individuals and thus ensures that private enforcement can fulfil its auxiliary role vis-à-vis the activity of the Commission and the NCAs.

On this point, the recent study conducted by Rodger in relation to private antitrust claims lodged in the United Kingdom appears to reinforce

---

[184] See *ibid*, para 320; also 2008 Impact Assessment document, para 165.

[185] 2008 Impact Assessment document, section 5.1, fn 82 and accompanying text. See 2004 Ashurst Report, paras 3–9.

the view that the answer to this question remains negative.[186] Rodger examined cases launched both under Articles 81 and 82 EC and the UK Competition Act 1998 in years between the 1970s and 2004 in the light of factors such as their actual number, the type of issues raised and their success rate.[187]

The study found that 90 'competition cases' had been lodged before British courts in this time frame[188] and identified a 'peak' in 1999, namely after the entry into force of the 1998 Act. However, Rodger pointed out that a similar increase did not occur in 2005, the year after the full entry into force of the Modernisation Regulation.[189] In terms of their success rate, the study found that of 90 cases, only 16 were 'successful' and seven 'partially successful', with the highest number of instances in which the competition law pleas had been allowed being concentrated in the 1980s.[190]

Although, given the limited scope of this work, it is not possible to comment any further, it is suggested that, on the basis of its findings, the expected increase in the number of private enforcement claims after the entry into force of the Modernisation Regulation does not appear to have materialised.[191] By contrast, Rodger emphasises how a 'considerable number' of claims were lodged in the 1970s and 1980s, 'an era of more limited awareness of Community law generally and competition law in particular'.[192] On the basis of this study, it could be argued that, at least in the United Kingdom and up until 2004, the objective of boosting private competition enforcement had not been achieved to the extent envisaged by the Commission and Community legislature.[193]

These conclusions are also consistent with the evidence concerning the activity of the Competition Appeal Tribunal between 2005 and 2007. According to the CAT Annual Reviews, no actions for antitrust damages grounded in either the 1998 UK Competition Act or Articles 81 and 82 EC were lodged in either Session 2004/05 or 2005/06.[194] It was not until Session 2006/07 that some activity before the CAT in respect to private

---

[186] B Rodger, 'Competition law litigation in the UK' (2006) 27(5) *European Competition Law Review* 235; (2006) 27(6) *European Competition Law Review* 279; (2006) 27(7) *European Competition Law Review* 341.

[187] *Ibid*, Part I (2006) 27(5) *European Competition Law Review* 241.

[188] *Ibid*, 244.

[189] *Ibid*.

[190] *Ibid*, 245.

[191] *Ibid*, 349.

[192] *Ibid*.

[193] *Ibid*.

[194] See Competition Appeal Tribunal, 'Annual Review and Accounts', session 2004/05, 20; and session 2005/06, 35.

antitrust enforcement was recorded. The Annual Review for that period shows three such cases pending before the Tribunal.[195]

In the light of the above considerations, it can be concluded that the 'reality check' on the viability of the expectation of the emergence of a 'private attorney general' in the field of antitrust law has not led to overall encouraging results. Nonetheless, it is clear that the 2008 White Paper, despite not being entirely ground-breaking, provides a momentous opportunity to discuss and bring forward effective reforms in this area. Although it is perhaps too early to fully appreciate its implications, the White Paper appears to go beyond simply reflecting the Commission's continuing commitment to the effective civil enforcement of the EU antitrust rules. In fact, it sets forward a clear agenda aimed at laying down the conditions for the adequate and timely redress of the rights enjoyed by the parties aggrieved by anti-competitive behaviour, for the purpose of ultimately ensuring a level playing field for business and consumers alike within the EU.

---

[195] See Competition Appeal Tribunal, 'Annual Review and Accounts', session 2006/07, 36–7.

11

Energy: Efficiency, Security and the Environment

PETER D CAMERON

I. INTRODUCTION

T HE CHALLENGE I have been set by the editors is to reflect on the
role of 'energy' in relation to the European Treaties and to 'think
forward'. It is an exciting time to do so.[1] After almost a quarter of a
century, energy has returned to the top of public policy concerns, driven by
volatile oil prices, concerns over the availability of petroleum supplies for
an energy-thirsty European bloc and the tabling of proposals to revive
nuclear power. This time, however, 'energy' is inextricably linked to the
challenge of climate change mitigation, one that has been largely created
by energy use in the modern age. Now, as has been the case so often
before, the dilemma for the Community institutions is to identify a
Community dimension which gives energy policy a role distinct from the
one it already has in each of the 27 Member States. In this challenging
context, the question arises: to what extent do the Treaties help or hinder
the development of a Community dimension in energy?

If one relies upon the debates and conclusions on the proposed Constitutional Treaty,[2] and subsequently the Treaty of Lisbon,[3] it appears that
there is a strong body of opinion that the founding Treaties, even when
amended up to the Treaty of Nice, are unsatisfactory in their treatment of

---

[1] Eventually, this excitement may reach the authors of EU law textbooks, which so far
have largely ignored energy issues. Two recent examples of this are the book by D Chalmers,
C Hadjiemmanuil, G Monti and A Tomkins, *European Union Law* (Cambridge, Cambridge
University Press, 2006), which contains three very brief references, two of them to Euratom,
in 1154 pages; and A Arnull, A Dashwood, M Dougan, M Ross, E Spaventa and D Wyatt,
Wyatt and Dashwood's European Union Law (London, Sweet & Maxwell, 2006), which has
two references, both of them to Euratom, in 1191 pages. In the past, a notable exception has
been PJG Kapteyn and P Verloren van Themaat, *Introduction to the Law of the European
Communities* (The Hague, Kluwer, 1998), but the English version of this text is very much
out of date by now.

[2] Section 10, Energy (Art III-256) CT: [2004] OJ C310/1.

[3] Title XXI, Energy (Art 194) TFEU: see consolidated texts of the revised Treaties
published at [2008] OJ C115/1.

energy issues. The European Coal and Steel Community Treaty came to an end in 2002 and no successor was thought necessary. The European Atomic Energy Treaty (Euratom) has attracted much criticism over the years and an attempt was made to absorb it into a consolidated Treaty in 2002. The absence of specific provisions on energy in the European Economic Community Treaty and its successors has attracted critical comment over the years and has led to the inclusion of an energy chapter, first in the proposed Constitutional Treaty, and more recently in the Treaty of Lisbon. Yet, whatever the lack of precision in Community competences in the Treaties,[4] it can hardly be doubted that enormous steps have been taken in the development of energy policy and, particularly in the last 12 years, in the introduction of a body of European energy law designed to achieve Community policies of greater competition, enhanced security and environmental protection. Perhaps the neatness sought by the proposed Constitutional Treaty and now by the Treaty of Lisbon by including an energy chapter is not so vital to further progress in these areas after all.

Independently of the proposed energy chapter in the Treaty of Lisbon, the Council has argued strongly that a European energy policy is now essential and has adopted an Action Plan to take this forward.[5] A comprehensive programme of secondary legislation on energy and climate change has also been proposed by the Commission,[6] and in some form appears likely to be adopted by the Council and Parliament.[7]

---

[4] In this context, I note there are two other Treaties concerning energy to which the Community is a party: the Energy Charter Treaty [1998] OJ L69/1; and the Energy Community Treaty [2006] OJ L198/18. They both date from the aftermath of communism in Central and East Europe and are designed principally to forge links with the former communist states that were not members of the EU at the time of their signature. Since this book is about the European Treaties that date from the 1950s, I have not considered these later Treaties in any detail, although the EU was decisive in bringing them into being. The fact that they have been concluded, however, does not refute my argument.

[5] Presidency Conclusions of the European Council meeting of 8–9 March 2007: 7224/1/07 REV1 (2 May 2007).

[6] Proposal for a Directive of the European Parliament and of the Council amending Directive 2003/54/EC of the European Parliament and of the Council of 26 June 2003 (the Electricity Directive) COM(2007) 548; Proposal for a Regulation of the European Parliament and of the Council amending Regulation 1228/2003/EC (the Electricity Regulation) COM(2007) 531; Proposal for a Directive of the European Parliament and of the Council amending Directive 2003/55/EC of the European Parliament and of the Council of 26 June 2003 (the Gas Directive) COM(2007) 529; Proposal for a Regulation of the European Parliament and of the Council amending Regulation 1775/2005/EC (the Gas Regulation) COM(2007) 532; Proposal for a Regulation of the European Parliament and of the Council establishing an Agency for the Cooperation of Energy Regulators COM(2007) 530; Proposal for a Directive of the European Parliament and of the Council on the promotion of the use of energy from renewable sources COM(2008) 30 Final; Proposal for a Directive of the European Parliament and of the Council on the geological storage of carbon dioxide and amending Council Directives 85/337/EEC, 96/61/EC, Directives 2000/60/EC, 2001/80/EC, 2004/35/EC, 2006/12/EC and Regulation 1013/2006/EC COM(2008) 18 Final, and Proposal

In this chapter, I will examine the three policy drivers that have shaped the provisions on energy matters in the Treaties, with respect to each of the three founding Treaties. I shall conclude that, with or without a clear expression of Community competences in Treaty form, the pressures for a common approach to the solution of European energy problems have led to a pragmatic use of the existing legal instruments already available to the Community institutions. In addressing the heightened concerns about 'energy security' and climate change, this pragmatic approach is likely to continue.

II. THREE PRIORITIES AND THREE TREATIES

Throughout the Community's history, three priorities have had a recurring but varying degree of importance in its deliberations on law-making and policy formation in the energy sector.[8] These priorities have been expressed differently in Community documents over the years, but in substance have showed a remarkable degree of continuity: the pursuit of economic efficiency, in particular by the promotion of competition within the framework of an internal market; the achievement of energy security, usually interpreted to mean availability of energy supplies and their regular delivery at reasonable prices; and finally the development of energy laws and policies that are compatible with the Community's environmental sustainability goals.[9] The environmental goal was the latest to join in this triumvirate, but since the 1990s has figured prominently. In different ways, these priorities all figure in the three main Community Treaties that have evolved over the past 50 years: the Coal and Steel Community Treaty (now expired), the Euratom Treaty and the Treaty establishing the European Community. They have figured too in the now defunct Constitution and in the Treaty of Lisbon.

The three priorities are evident in a recent document, the Community's Energy Policy for Europe (EPE), an integrated climate and energy policy

for a Directive of the European Parliament and of the Council amending Directive 2003/87/EC so as to improve and extend the greenhouse gas emission allowance trading system of the Community COM(2008) 16 Final.

[7] Council of the European Union, 'Transport, Telecommunications and Energy', Press Release No 10310/08 (6 June 2008).

[8] By the 'energy sector', I understand the part of the European economy that involves the management and utilisation of coal, oil, gas, electricity, renewable sources such as wind, wave and solar power, and nuclear power.

[9] These are defined slightly differently in the Council's 2007 Energy Policy for Europe, which is to pursue the following three objectives: increasing security of supply; ensuring the competitiveness of European economies and the availability of affordable energy; and promoting environmental sustainability and combating climate change: see the Presidency Conclusions of the European Council meeting of 8–9 March 2007: 7224/1/07 REV1 (2 May 2007), para 28.

with the strategic objective of limiting the global average temperature increase to not more than two degrees Centigrade above pre-industrial levels. Energy production and use are the main sources of greenhouse gas emissions, so an integrated approach is thought essential. The EPE which the Council adopted in March 2007 has three distinct objectives: to increase security of supply; to ensure the competitiveness of EU economies and the availability of affordable energy; and to promote environmental sustainability and combat climate change. It is integrated in another sense too: the EPE combines action at the European and the Member State levels. The so-called Action Plan is intended to be reviewed annually and updated following reports from the Commission.

This is a triangular structure, with the three elements—security, competitiveness and sustainability—sometimes referred to by Commission officials without apparent irony by place names: respectively, Moscow, Lisbon and Kyoto. The green light was given to the Commission to bring forward proposals for legislation in a number of these areas. This is the first time the EU has developed something like a common energy policy and, importantly, it is one that is expressly linked to an environmental policy.

The interplay between the various priorities can be revealing and merits a few observations before we proceed to consider the Treaties themselves.[10] Energy has always been an area of economic activity in which Member States have been very reluctant to cede national control to Community institutions. The justification for this approach has usually been couched in terms of some defensive notion of 'security'. For specific reasons, coal and nuclear power were limited exceptions to this. It was only in the late 1980s that arguments for a Community energy strategy based on gains in economic efficiency appeared and gained support. Even then, they benefited strongly from the drive for a wider single market programme at the time and were focused almost exclusively on two sectors, the provision of electricity and gas. The benefits of greater competition in these network-bound sectors found many advocates at a time of very low oil and gas prices, and negligible fears about supply. It coincided with a period of intellectual enthusiasm about the benefits of competition in networks generally, especially in telecommunications and to some extent railways.[11] As a result, the Member States agreed (albeit slowly and in some cases most reluctantly) to the adoption of a body of directives and regulations that have changed these utilities markets irreversibly. The final stages of

---

[10]   This matter is examined in a comprehensive way in P Cameron, *Competition in Energy Markets: Law and Regulation in the European Union* (New York, Oxford University Press, 2007), particularly chs 17 and 18 dealing with environmental protection and energy security (respectively).

[11]   See, eg DM Newbery, *Privatization, Restructuring and Regulation of Network Utilities* (Cambridge, MIT Press, 2000).

this process coincided with a revived interest in energy security triggered initially by concerns about gas supplies from Russia and then by high and volatile oil prices.

III. THE COAL AND STEEL COMMUNITY TREATY

For a period of 50 years until 24 July 2002, the principal rules of European law applicable to the coal sector were those set down in the Treaty establishing the European Coal and Steel Community (ECSC), signed on 18 April 1951 by six states (Belgium, France, Germany, Italy, Luxembourg and the Netherlands).

The general aim of the ECSC Treaty was to establish a common market with common institutions. The Treaty provided a framework of production and distribution arrangements for coal and steel in six signatory states and set up an autonomous institutional system to manage it. It entered into force on 23 July 1952 and expired on 23 July 2002. The principles of a market economy were accorded a central role in Article 4 of the ECSC Treaty, but the potential for regulatory intervention in cases of need such as crisis or shortage was extensive.[12]

When the Treaty was due to expire, there appeared to be no compelling reason to seek its continuation. Coal had been in long-term decline in the Community and had acquired a negative reputation as a high-polluting and environmentally damaging source of energy. The regulation of the coal sector is now governed by a general rather than a sector specific legal instrument, the EC Treaty, and until 2010 by a new scheme for state aids, Council Regulation 1407/2002.[13] The latter expressly provides that aid covering costs for the period of 2002 prior to its entry into force may continue to be subject to the rules and principles laid down in Decision 3632/93,[14] with the exception of rules on deadlines and procedures. This is activated by a request by a Member State. In terms of procedure, aid to the coal industry is now subject to special rules of notification, appraisal and authorisation as set out in the state aid regime under the Regulation.

Regulation 1407/2002 aims to make coal respond to the energy and sustainable development needs of the EU in the twenty-first century. In Article 1, it emphasises that the rules for the grant of state aid to the coal industry have the aim of contributing to the restructuring process, but will

---

[12] For an overview of the ECSC Treaty provisions with respect to competition, see P Roth, *Bellamy and Child's EC Competition Law*, 5th edn (London, Sweet & Maxwell, 2001) 1176–99.

[13] [2002] OJ L205/1.

[14] [1993] OJ L329/12.

also take into account the social and regional aspects of this process and the need to maintain—as a precautionary measure—a minimum quantity of indigenous coal production for security of supply purposes. The latter point highlights the energy security aspect of the contemporary coal industry in the Community.

Although no new Treaty was considered necessary, the long-term decline in overall coal production within the EU constituted a driver for the design of a successor regime.[15] There are now only a few Member States that have significant production from indigenous sources of hard coal: Germany, Spain, the UK, Poland, the Czech Republic and, to a lesser extent, Hungary.[16] Large quantities of brown coal or lignite are also produced, mostly from Germany, Greece and Spain, but also from the Czech Republic, Hungary, Poland, Slovakia and Slovenia. The majority of the remaining coal mines are not competitive against imported coal. Consumption of coal has also been in decline. The driver for change has been competition from other sources of energy, particularly oil products, natural gas and to some extent from nuclear power. The impact of liberalisation in electricity markets has accelerated a shift from coal to gas for electricity generation. Gas is also regarded as less environmentally damaging than coal. Nonetheless, the picture is not uniformly bleak. Virtually all of the Member States consume coal as part of their energy mix, and its advantages in terms of security of supply have been acknowledged by the EC. As the Commission has stated: 'The production of coal on the basis of economic criteria has no prospect ... in the European Union ... Its future can only be maintained within the framework of the European Union's security of supply.'[17] In addition, the operation of the EU Emissions Trading Scheme may work to the advantage of the coal sector by allowing coal plants to purchase emissions allowances and continue to operate.

Environmental pressures on coal use are nonetheless considerable. The Large Combustion Plant Directive, for example, requires that any coal-fired power stations not equipped to extract SOx emissions from flue gases by 2008 face a maximum operational life of 20,000 hours until 2015.[18] After this date, compulsory closure is to be made.

---

[15] There are a variety of reasons behind the high costs of production in EU Member States. The reserves nearest the surface have been depleted so that, if mining is to continue, it must be done at greater depths and requires more costly infrastructure. In some cases, this is compounded by the poor quality of the deposits that result from complex, irregular, geological structures and a low density of reserves compared with those of the main non-EU coal exporters: see L Piper, 'State Aid to the European Union coal industry' (1994) 23 *Energy in Europe* 22.

[16] IEA Clean Coal Centre, 'Profiles: Coal in an Enlarged European Union' (June 2004).

[17] Green Paper, Towards a European Strategy for the Security of Supply, COM(2000) 769 Final, section II.B(d) on security of energy supply.

[18] Art 4(4)(a) Directive 2001/80 on the limitation of emissions of certain pollutants into the air from large combustion plants [2001] OJ L309/1.

A major task for the current legal regime is therefore to continue the social and economic adaptation of the EU coal sector to this long-term trend towards decline, and to ensure that the resulting grant of state aids is subject to strict control. What may be a new element in EU policy towards the coal sector is the notion that a minimum level of coal production is a significant contributor to energy security in the EU. This security consideration has been used to justify the maintenance of a coal-producing capability supported by state aid, and is therefore a source of constraint on the operation of the market mechanism.[19] As the Commission has stated in a decision allowing the grant of aid to the coal sector of a Member State[20]:

> The world political situation brings an entirely new dimension to the assessment of geopolitical risks and security risks in the energy sector and gives a wider meaning to the concept of security of supplies ... It is therefore necessary, on the basis of the current energy situation, to take measures which will make it possible to guarantee access to coal reserves and hence a potential availability of Community coal. Strengthening the European Union's energy security therefore justifies the maintenance of coal-producing capability supported by State aid.

IV. EURATOM

The second of the Treaties to concern itself with energy is the Treaty Establishing the European Atomic Energy Community (Euratom), which was signed on 17 April 1957.[21] However, in contrast to Article 97 of the former ECSC Treaty, Euratom has no built-in time limit and remains in force. Indeed, it has endured long periods of unpopularity, so as now to benefit from a renewed interest in many Member States in the potential for nuclear power in the overall fuel mix.

At the time of its adoption, the Treaty's overall aim was to act both as a vehicle for the promotion of nuclear energy for civil purposes and as a means of regulating the emerging nuclear industry. This goal of promotion is spelled out in Article 1 of the Treaty, which states that:

> It shall be the task of the [Atomic Energy] Community to contribute to the raising of the standard of living in the Member States and to the development of relations with the other countries by creating the conditions necessary for the speedy establishment and growth of nuclear industries.

---

[19] Recital 7 and Art 1 Regulation 1407/2002 on state aid to the coal industry [2002] OJ L205/1.

[20] Commission Decision on grant of aid to Hungary, N92/2005, point 40; similar wording was used in the grant of aid to Poland, N571/2004.

[21] For a comprehensive overview of the Treaty, see J Grunwald, *Das Energierecht der Europaeischen Gemeinschaften* (Berlin and New York, De Gruyter, 2003) 193–308.

The origins of this goal lay in the perception of nuclear energy as an alternative safe source of energy for European countries. At the time it was drafted, the growing dependence upon imported sources of oil from the Middle East and the uncertainties following the Suez crisis, plus the limited growth potential of coal and geographical constraints on hydro-power, all combined to reinforce that perception. At the same time, the very considerable investment that would be required to fund the development of the nuclear fuel cycle was beyond the financial means of individual European countries and this too provided an impetus to cooperation in a Community structure. The latter goal has since fallen into abeyance, partly due to the lack of consensus on nuclear energy among the Member States, and partly because the nuclear industry is well established and needs little of this kind of support from the EU. Perceptions of nuclear energy use have also diverged with significant questions arising about its overall cost, and most of all the legacy of radioactive waste it leaves behind.

With respect to competition, a key difference between Euratom and the EC Treaty was evident at the outset. Euratom was designed to promote a highly specialised industry which at the time of signature was virtually non-existent in Europe. The EC Treaty had as its main aim a general economic integration by means of fairly strict legal rules. The aim of those rules was to ensure competition in all of the industrial and economic sectors of the signatory states which were deemed to have already reached a level of maturity.

Euratom sets out a number of goals, including the promotion of research, establishment of safety standards, facilitation of investment, ensuring all users receive a regular and equitable supply of ores and nuclear fuels, and ensuring that nuclear materials are not diverted to purposes other than the peaceful ones they were intended for (non-proliferation).[22] Among these goals was the creation of a nuclear common market in the goods and products involved in the use of nuclear energy.[23] To this end, Article 93 Euratom provides for an abolition of all customs duties on imports and exports, charges with equivalent effect, and all quantitative restrictions in imports and exports in internal trade. Article 96 Euratom provides for free movement of workers with specialist skills in the nuclear energy sector.

Significant efforts have been made to achieve the goal of establishing uniform safety standards to protect the health of workers and the general public and ensuring that they are applied.[24] The Commission (the implementing agency under Euratom) has the power to require Member States

---

[22] Art 2 Euratom.
[23] *Ibid*, Art 2 and Ch IX.
[24] *Ibid*, Arts 2(b), 30 and 31.

to implement safety directives and to ensure that they are enforced.[25] Some Member States have been reluctant to allow the Commission to regulate nuclear power in a comprehensive way. Health and safety are covered only to a very limited extent under Euratom, but efforts have been made by the Commission to use Chapter III as a legal base for a number of measures and proposals on basic safety standards.

Legislative development under Euratom has been extensive. Directives have been made to lay down radiation standards for health protection.[26] The aim of these Directives has been to ensure that Community citizens are adequately protected to internationally agreed levels, and that all exposures are adequately regulated and kept as low as is reasonably achievable (the ALARA principle). Radioactivity levels are monitored by the EC through national reporting.[27] More recent measures include ones proposed for the setting of standards for operational safety, radioactive waste management and rules on the funding of decommissioning.[28]

Safety is, however, only one of the eight tasks listed in Article 2 Euratom. Other tasks include facilitating investment, and ensuring that all users in the Community receive a regular and equitable supply of ores and nuclear fuels. This interventionist role for the Community is one of several potentially market-distorting features in Euratom. Another example is the tax exemptions that may be enjoyed by joint undertakings which receive a special status under Euratom (Chapter V and Annex III). The name is misleading, since the Treaty does not require that these are to be 'joint ventures' involving two or more Member States.

There are a number of institutional features that also require comment. A key feature of the Treaty is the degree of control in law-making exercised by the Council and the Commission in relation to the European Parliament. There is no co-decision procedure for its operational functions. Under Article 31 Euratom, the Council only has to request the opinion of the Parliament. In this sense, the competence structure is very different from that of the EC Treaty, where Parliament and the Council have the leading role in law-making, with the Commission taking the role as initiator of legislation. The institution that has the key decision-making role remains the Council of Ministers.

---

[25] *Ibid*, Arts 33 and 38.

[26] Directive (Euratom) 76/579 [1976] OJ L187/1; Directive (Euratom) 79/343 [1979] OJ L83/18; Directive (Euratom) 80/836 [1980] OJ L246/1; and Directive (Euratom) 84/467 [1984] OJ L265/4.

[27] Art 34 Euratom.

[28] Amended Proposal for a Council Directive (Euratom) COM(2004) 526 laying down basic obligations and general principles on the safety of nuclear installations, and on the safe management of the spent nuclear fuel and radioactive waste. The Accession Treaties with Central and East European states included commitments to close down eight nuclear reactors in three of the new Member States as well as nuclear safety. They were: Bulgaria, Lithuania and Slovakia. In each case, EU financial assistance was provided.

Another notable feature is the establishment of a Euratom Supply Agency (ESA) under the Treaty, supervised by the Commission. Its task is to ensure a regular and equitable supply of ores and nuclear fuels for all EU users. It has a combination of market and planned economy characteristics, and is required to pursue the aim of long-term security of supply through a diversification of supply sources and avoidance of excessive dependence upon any one source. In a context of liberalised electricity markets and fair trade, it is required to ensure that the viability of the European nuclear industry is maintained.[29] At the time of its creation, the US Government had ownership of fissile material and a monopoly on the offer of nuclear materials and services, and there was strict governmental control over the nuclear industry with few commercial applications. In this context of perceived scarcity of source material, the ESA was to be the European 'owner' and supplier to EU users, as a counterweight to US dominance. Now, however, there is a relatively open commercial market for the European nuclear industry, with support and monitoring by the ESA over the contractual landscape of the fuel cycle operations.

The continuation of Euratom might seem surprising. There have been considerable changes since Euratom was drawn up, in terms of attitudes to nuclear energy, experience with its use, the enormous increase in concern with environmental goals in the Community since that time and in terms of EU membership. Questions have indeed been raised about its continued relevance, at least in its present form. At present, the absence of provision for decommissioning under Euratom or for the management of high-level radioactive waste means that there are important—and costly—subjects to be tackled by Member States themselves in a way that avoids the market distorting impacts of subsidies or other support schemes. This level of control at the Member State level is a limit on Euratom, but also underlines the reluctance of the Member States concerned to give up any of their powers over their domestic nuclear industries.

Many of the doubts about Euratom coalesced at the time when the Convention on the Future of Europe (established by the Laeken European Council) was formulating its proposals for reform of the Union's primary law. Various arguments were advanced to have Euratom abolished, or absorbed into a new Constitution for the Union, or into the existing EC Treaty,[30] but they were not successful. Had they been, they would have increased the scope for Parliamentary scrutiny of Euratom, in line with the

---

[29] ESA, Advisory Committee Task Force on Security of Supply, 'Analysis of the Nuclear Field Availability at EU', Final Report of the Task Force (June 2005) 6.

[30] See, eg the Contribution to the European Convention by Ms Marie Nagy, Ms Renee Wagner and Sir Neil MacCormick, alternate members of the Convention: 'The Future of the Euratom Treaty in the Framework of the European Constitution', CONV 563/03 (18 February 2003).

competence of the European Parliament over environmental issues that has grown in recent years. They might also have ensured that the considerable importance played by environmental and sustainability considerations in all EC policy-making, including energy, was reflected in the Community's approach to nuclear energy, especially with respect to the legal framework for the long-term management of high-level radioactive waste,[31] a matter that will require at least some elaboration of the current Treaty provisions.

V. THE TREATY ESTABLISHING THE EUROPEAN COMMUNITY

Of the three founding treaties, the more general instrument of integration was the Treaty establishing the European Economic Community. It was entered into between the six original Member States in 1957, and subsequently renamed the European Community Treaty (EC Treaty). The scope of the EC Treaty was much broader than the other two treaties. Article 2 EC described the task of the Community as one in which, by establishing a common market and 'progressively approximating the economic policies of the Member States', it would:

> ... promote throughout the Community a harmonious development of economic activities, a continuous and balanced expansion, an increase in stability, an accelerated raising of the standard of living, and closer relationships between the States belonging to it.

The Treaty contained specific provisions dealing with the establishment of the common market, although none specifically providing for a common energy policy.[32] Some provisions of the EC Treaty are highly relevant to energy activities, and especially to the electricity and gas businesses. The rules falling under Articles 28 to 31 EC and those falling under Article 86 EC are of particular relevance.

However, there was no explicit grant of a 'special' status to the energy sector under the EC Treaty, exempting it from the ambit of some or all of its provisions. There are at least two possible interpretations of this lacuna. First, it may be argued that the intention was to treat energy no differently

---

[31] This has, however, been addressed at the multilateral level in the Joint Convention to which the EC and its Member States are parties: see P Cameron, 'Joint Convention on the Safety of Spent Fuel Management and on the Safety of Radioactive Waste Management' in NLJT Horbach (ed), *Contemporary Developments in Nuclear Energy Law: Harmonising Legislation in CEEC/NIS* (The Hague, Kluwer Law International 1999), 117–28. Some of the UK aspects of this are discussed in P Cameron, 'The Revival of Nuclear Power: An Analysis of the Legal Implications' (2007) 19 *Journal of Environmental Law* 71.

[32] Cf *Rapport des Chefs de Delegations aux Ministères des Affaires Étrangères* (Secretariat of the Inter-Governmental Conference, Brussels, 21 April 1956 (the Spaak Report)). The report had identified energy and especially oil as an area for urgent attention, but this was not taken further. A widely held view at the time, which led to non-action in this area, was that oil companies were well equipped to deal with issues in this sector.

from any other economic sector in the integration process. Had the authors of the Treaty sought to set the industry apart in any way, they would have been well aware of the means by which this could have been done—but they did not.[33] After all, explicit provisions were inserted into the Treaty, especially Article 33(1) EC, at a time when, with the aim of stabilising markets, actions were envisaged to ensure security of supplies (including energy products) or to guarantee access to the market to consumers at reasonable prices.

For example, production of and trade in agricultural products was excluded from the application of the competition rules under Article 37 EC to the extent determined by the Council. Where special circumstances were deemed to exist—as in the sectors of coal and nuclear energy—legal instruments had already been concluded and were in force. Moreover, the European Court of Justice (ECJ) has expressly ruled that electricity is a 'good' and falls within the scope of the competition rules.[34] In addition, there was no doubt about the status of other sources of energy—such as oil and gas—which were classifiable as goods.

An alternative view is that the energy sector has unique characteristics and a special importance in the EU, so that provision for it should be made in the primary law itself. The absence of a systematic provision in the EC Treaty was therefore a mistake. To a large extent, this lay behind the design of a new Energy Chapter in the proposed Treaty establishing a Constitution for Europe, and subsequently the Treaty of Lisbon (discussed below). Indeed, the most important sources of energy in the EU today—oil, natural gas and electricity—received little or no express treatment in the original three founding legal instruments. The only energy subjects expressly covered by law were coal, nuclear energy and, at a time of emergency in supply, oil.[35] One commentator has concluded that this situation was 'a failure of vision' on the part of the progenitors of the Community.[36] Another has described the patchwork treatment of energy policy in the EC

---

[33] This view is expressed in CD Ehlermann, 'The Role of the European Commission as Regards National Energy Policies' (1994) 12 *Journal of Energy Natural Resources* 342. For a historical review of the early period, see T Daintith and L Hancher, *Energy Strategy in Europe: The Legal Framework* (Berlin and New York, De Gruyter, 1986).

[34] Case 6/64, *Costa v Enel* [1964] ECR 1251. At a later date, this was reinforced by Case C-393/92, *Almelo Gemeente v NV Energiebedrijf Ijsselmij* [1994] ECR I-1477 and Joined Cases C-157–160/94, *Commission v Netherlands, Italy, France and Spain* [1997] ECR I-5699 et seq.

[35] There have been attempts to enlarge Community competences during crises in oil supply in the 1970s and during the Gulf War: see Security of Supply, the Internal Market and Energy Policy, Working Paper of the Commission of the EC (1990) SEC(90) 1248; and later in the definition of common energy objectives.

[36] N Green, 'The Implementation of Treaty Policies: the energy dilemma' (1983) 8 *EL Rev* 186, 189.

Treaty as 'astonishing'.[37] The effect of this lacuna has been that, for many years, measures on energy have been adopted on the basis of powers conferred for other purposes, such as the internal market, competition matters, the environment or external relations.[38]

Whatever assessment one may make of the treatment of energy in the primary legislation of the EC Treaty, it is certainly true to say that, for many years, the application of those provisions relevant to the network-bound energy sector (that is, the transportation and distribution of electricity and gas) was virtually non-existent. Even for the European Commission, state monopolies of a commercial character 'were not perceived as an obstacle to the establishment of the first stages of the Common Market'.[39]

A key factor behind this state of affairs was the close relationship between Member State governments on the one hand and public undertakings in energy networks on the other. Throughout the Community's history, Member States have been reluctant to cede control over energy policy to the European institutions. If the absence of a systematic approach to energy constituted a flaw, it nevertheless received tacit approval from the majority of Member States, wishing to retain maximum control over their national energy regimes.[40] Moreover, given the diversity of aims of national energy policies, the instruments designed to achieve them, the industry structure as well as the resource base of each Member State and, not least, the strategic character of energy supplies for any modern state, this resistance to a centralised approach to energy policy was understandable.

The chapter on energy in the Treaty of Lisbon might be seen, then, as an innovation, but in fact the idea that energy should have express recognition in the fundamental legislation of the EU has a long history. Looking back

---

[37] J Schwarze, 'European Energy Policy in Community Law' in EJ Mestmäcker (ed), *Natural Gas in the Internal Market: A Review of Energy Policy* (London, Graham & Trotman, 1992) 155.

[38] The main powers are to: adopt measures for the approximation of provisions concerned with the establishment and functioning of the internal market (Art 95 EC); establish a common commercial policy (if the measure relates to trade in raw materials, eg oil or coal) (Art 133 EC); adopt research and development programmes and agreements (Title XVIII EC); adopt measures relating to the environment (Title XIX EC); take measures or conclude agreements in the area of development cooperation policy (Title XX EC), if they are part of the Community's cooperation with less developed countries; encourage the establishment and development of trans-European networks, if the measure concerns energy infrastructures (Title XV EC); and conclude association agreements under Art 238 EC, that provide, inter alia, for energy cooperation. Also relevant is Art 308 EC, where no other powers can be found and where the proposed measure meets the criteria in this article.

[39] CD Ehlermann, above n 33.

[40] The close connection between energy policies and national interests as a limit to integration in the EU energy sector at the time is explored in T Daintith and S Williams, *The Legal Integration of Energy Markets* (Berlin and New York, De Gruyter, 1987).

to the Single European Act of 1986 or the Treaty on European Union, it is notable that there is no reference to an energy policy or other energy provision, in spite of the fact that there were proposals for their inclusion—they were made and were rejected. This underlined the Member States' wish to retain their competence over energy. Article 3 EC as amended by the Maastricht Treaty had introduced a specific provision, albeit in rather vague terms: 'the activities of the Community shall include ... measures in the spheres of energy, civil protection and tourism'. Subsequently, the Commission carried out its task according to Declaration No 1 of the Maastricht Treaty, producing a proposal for an energy chapter which would either have consolidated the provisions of the three Treaties or have introduced a new chapter pursuing the completion of the single market, environmental protection and measures to improve security of supply.[41] Although the proposal was noted by the Council of Ministers in May 1996, no action was taken or encouraged. Two months prior to the Amsterdam Inter-Governmental Conference, the Commission issued a further document.[42] It also had no effect.

An alternative approach adopted by the Commission was to advocate a greater coordination of existing EU competences.[43] The impetus to both of these initiatives was the absence of a clear competence on energy matters which led to a dependence upon a number of EU competences that have a bearing upon energy policy: for example, the single market rules including technical and tax harmonisation and public procurement; environment, regional, and competition policy; and the trans-European networks policy. However, it is very questionable whether these competences are so inadequate that a new Treaty chapter is required. At a later date, during the discussions on the Treaty of Nice text, the Portuguese Presidency noted that an 'issue to be addressed' was whether the repeated use of Article 308 EC in areas such as energy, external competence and the establishment of decentralised agencies justified the creation in the EC Treaty of a specific legal basis requiring a qualified majority.[44] However, the proposal was dropped.

The proposed Treaty established a Constitution for Europe and took a bolder step in this direction, declaring that energy is a 'shared competence' between the Union and the Member States.[45] This meant that under Article

---

[41] COM(1996) 496 Final. There was an earlier report by the Commission for the Reflection Group chaired by Carlos Westendorp in May 1995 prior to the EC Inter-Governmental Conference in 1996.

[42] European Commission, An Overall View of Energy Policy and Actions, COM(1997) 167.

[43] Towards an EU Energy Policy, COM(1995) 682 Final (the White Paper).

[44] Conference of the Representatives of the Governments of the Member States (22 February 2000) CONFER 4711/00.

[45] [2004] OJ C310/1

I-12(2) CT, the Union and Member States may legislate and adopt legally binding acts in that area. The Member States were to exercise their competence to the extent that the Union had not exercised or had decided to cease exercising its competence. The relevant provision, Article III-256, fell within Chapter III concerned with 'Policies in Other Areas' (than, say, economic or monetary policy). Although the Constitution initiative failed, the text on energy was repeated in almost identical form in the Treaty of Lisbon text.[46] Article 194 TFEU reads as follows:

1. In the context of the establishment and functioning of the internal market and with regard for the need to preserve and improve the environment, Union policy on energy shall aim in a spirit of solidarity between Member States, to:

(a) ensure the functioning of the energy market;

(b) ensure security of energy supply in the Union; and

(c) promote energy efficiency and energy saving and the development of new and renewable forms of energy; and

(d) promote the interconnection of energy networks.

2. Without prejudice to the application of other provisions of the Treaties, the European Parliament and the Council, acting in accordance with the ordinary legislative procedure, shall establish the measures necessary to achieve the objectives in paragraph 1. Such measures shall be adopted after consultation of the Economic and Social Committee and the Committee of the Regions.

Such measures shall not affect a Member State's right to determine the conditions for exploiting its energy resources, its choice between different energy sources and the general structure of its energy supply, without prejudice to Article 192(2)(c).

3. By way of derogation from paragraph 2, the Council, acting in accordance with a special legislative procedure, shall unanimously and after consulting with the European Parliament, establish the measures referred to therein when they are primarily of a fiscal nature.

The short provision would make energy a 'policy' alongside existing policies such as 'environment', 'social policy', 'agriculture and fisheries' and 'trans-European networks'. There would be a shared competence between the Union and Member States.[47] It would give formal recognition to a situation that has already emerged in practice, with the adoption of a comprehensive sector-specific energy law regime and specialist regulatory institutions for electricity and gas. However, in dealing with the long-standing question of competence, it would also place energy into a horizontal zone of policies in which no clear priority exists, and in dealing

---

[46] [2008] OJ C115/1.
[47] Art 4(2)(i) TFEU.

with any particular issue, a balancing of policy priorities is required: a situation that has already occurred with respect to competition and environmental policies.

VI. THE USE OF EXISTING COMPETENCES

This review of energy developments in the context of the three founding treaties would be highly incomplete if the story ended with the proposal to include a new chapter on energy in the Treaty of Lisbon. In fact, there have been parallel legal developments occurring in a very robust way over the past decade or more. For the most part, these legal measures have been based on the internal market competence in the EC Treaty, and they have resulted in the establishment of a comprehensive body of energy law in the EU for the first time in its history, all achieved without an express treaty competence in energy.

This development began almost 20 years ago with the attempt to accelerate the establishment of an internal market. Energy was included in the programme, but the focus was largely on the electricity and gas sectors. Little attempt was made to innovate in the oil and gas exploration and production markets in the name of competition, largely because there already appeared to be an open market. The result of this legislative activity has been a battery of first, second and soon third generation directives and regulations, and a number of decisions, supplemented by an institutional dimension, as the legislation required the establishment of national energy regulators in every Member State.

At the very outset of the internal energy market programme, choices were made about its design and the appropriate instruments to achieve it. Given the then political sensitivities about market reform in the electricity and gas sectors, the Community institutions and Member States decided to introduce directives under Article 95 EC, in preference to relying upon the existing powers based on EC competition law, and to do so according to a generous timetable that would allow Member States and incumbent utilities to adapt to the pressures of a 'liberalised' market. Once these choices were made, the Community legislative process aimed at the introduction of *new, sector-specific* rules for the promotion of competition.

Many years later, a body of law exists in the form of framework directives and regulations that sets out the requirements of an internal market in energy, particularly in the electricity and gas sectors.[48] This body

---

[48] In particular, Directive 2003/54 concerning common rules for the internal market in electricity and repealing Directive 96/92 [2003] OJ L176/37; and Directive 2003/55 concerning common rules for the internal market in natural gas and repealing Directive 98/30 [2003] OJ L176/57. For detailed analysis, see P Cameron, above n 10, chs 5 and 6.

of law has been enforced by a variety of agencies. First, specialist energy regulators have been established with a minimum set of powers in EU law. They exist in every Member State and are part of a new regulatory culture that has accompanied the liberalisation process in energy and other industries in recent years. Secondly, the competition authorities in the Member States and the Commission itself have been active in ensuring that energy is not treated as having exceptional status (as it was de facto for many years). The Commission too has been active in encouraging cooperation between the national authorities and in ensuring a peaceful co-existence with the specialist regulators, with whom there is sometimes overlapping competence. Thirdly, there are the national courts, the Court of First Instance (CFI) and the ECJ. The judgment of the ECJ in the Dutch interconnector case was an important one in deciding against the preferential treatment of electricity generating firms under pre-liberalisation or legacy contracts.[49] At the national level, companies have been active in the courts of Spain and Germany in protesting against proposed mergers involving Endesa and Ruhrgas.[50]

However, this project remains an uncompleted one. Clear and unequivocal evidence of anti-competitive practices has emerged combined with a continued segmentation of EU energy markets, and from some quarters there have been instances of national protectionism, suggesting that at least a renewed legislative effort is required to bring about genuine competition in EU energy markets. The Commission's Energy Directorate commented in its annual benchmarking report that 'meaningful competition does not exist in many Member States' and noted that no less than 34 infringement procedures have been launched against 20 Member States for violation and non-transposition of the internal market legislation.[51] Based on a detailed analysis of conditions in 25 of the 27 Member States, it concluded that 'the persistent nature of these infringements ... clearly demonstrates the insufficiencies and shortcomings of the current EC legal framework arising from the directives'. The context has also become less favourable to continuing market reform as Member States' concerns about their energy security have grown. Some—as in France—have talked openly about the need for national champions to provide the necessary security.

Looking to the future, the existing legislation will be significantly revised in the coming two years to enhance the powers of national regulators and

---

[49] Case C-17/03, *Vereniging voor Energie, Milieu en Water, Amsterdam Power Exchange Spotmarket BV, Eneco NV v Directeur van de Dienst uitvoering en toezicht energie* [2005] ECR I-4983.

[50] P Cameron, above n 10, 384–9.

[51] Commission of the European Communities, Prospects for the internal gas and electricity market, COM(2006) 841 Final; and Implementation Report, SEC(2006) 1709, an accompanying document to the Communication: <http://ec.europa.eu/energy/energy_policy/doc/10_internal_market_country_reviews_en.pdf> accessed 23 September 2008, 2 and 6.

to promote a more extensive form of corporate 'unbundling' (separation of activities such as transmission from generation and supply within vertically integrated entities). The final form of this, however, will only be the result of a protracted debate. Two comments may be made. First, each package of legislative measures aimed at promoting competition in EU energy markets has led to a wave of mergers and acquisitions in the sector. If this were to happen again, and early indications are that it will, an even more concentrated market will emerge, leaving less scope for competition. However, in the recent GdF/Suez proposed merger, the Commission tried to impose a new pro-competitive corporate structure as a condition of the merger going ahead.[52] Secondly, non-EU companies are increasingly interested in entering this market: Gazprom (Russia) and Sonatrach (Algeria) are two examples. Prospective buyers of EU energy utilities from the Middle East may also become involved. In its Presidency Conclusions of March 2007, the European Council invited the Commission 'to assess the impact of vertically integrated energy companies from third countries on the internal market and how to implement the principle of reciprocity'.[53] The idea behind the single market—in energy at least—was that EU companies would become more competitive as a result, not that the liberalised market, once created, would become a playground for non-EU-based monopolies from countries in which EU companies may not compete de facto or de jure.

VII. THINKING AHEAD

In a sense, the internal energy market programme has already been overtaken by events. The vision for energy in the EU is now shaped not only by the goal of economic efficiency, but also by external relations issues, and by the Council's view that energy policy has to be integrated into a climate change policy. This 'opening up' of the EU's programme for the energy sector is only hinted at in the energy provisions proposed by the Treaty of Lisbon and requires some comment.

Essentially, the Council, guided by the Commission, has identified a number of problems that require a common response, since they cannot be resolved by the Member States acting alone. What makes the current situation unusual (since this would not be an unusual position for the *Commission* to take) is the growing awareness by Member States of their inter-dependence on energy matters. The UK provides a vivid example of

---

[52] *Competition Policy Newsletter*, spring 2007, 83–91.
[53] Presidency Conclusions of the European Council meeting of 8–9 March 2007: 7224/1/07 REV1 (2 May 2007) 17.

the sea-change at work.[54] For many years, it resisted a common approach to energy policy except on issues of market opening, in which it was already well ahead of most of its neighbours. In the past three years or so, it has accepted (and encouraged) both the proposed Treaty provisions on energy and a common EU energy policy. As the UK becomes more import dependent, it has a strong interest in the openness of its neighbours' markets and a growing concern about import dependence on fossil fuels from Russia, for example. It can also not make significant progress in its domestic climate change policy without ensuring that the EU scheme—the ETS—actually works.

Security issues have risen rapidly up the energy policy agenda. The long period of low oil prices from the mid-1980s through to the 1990s muted concerns about import dependence for fossil fuels. During this period, two important developments occurred in the security of EU energy supplies, which have reversed this complacency.

First, there was a rapid increase in the use of gas for power generation instead of coal and, to a lesser extent, oil. Gas appeared clean and abundant. For several Member States, most notably Germany, this led to a significant increase in its dependence on Russian supplies of gas, which remains an important feature of the EU energy mix today. This trend has appeared less sensible when transit states have interrupted the supply of gas in the context of disputes with Russia. Much more importantly, it has come to appear a risky option given the trend in recent years towards an authoritarian state in Russia itself. Both the transit risk—which may prove temporary as new pipelines are constructed to the north and south which will bypass these states—and the political risk expose the difficulty the EU has in developing an external policy to the East. Until very recently, the EU has preferred to deal with its neighbour suppliers, especially Russia, on a bilateral basis, with governments supporting their national champions. Occasionally, and with very limited success, it has relied upon the Energy Charter Treaty in its diplomacy. The resulting sense of vulnerability is reflected in the wording of the Treaty of Lisbon's new Energy Chapter, which refers to Member States attempting to achieve their energy policy goals 'in a spirit of solidarity'.[55] This new emphasis on solidarity reflects a view that the era of bilateral, government-to-government deals has limits in the modern EU and reflects the influence of new Member States in Central Europe, which have tended to be the losers from such bilateral deals with Russia.

---

[54] For a comprehensive account and analysis of this process, see P Cameron, 'From Producer to Consumer: the UK's Changing Energy Strategy in the EU' in P Andrews-Speed (ed), *International Competition for Resources: The Role of Law, the State and of Markets* (Dundee, University of Dundee Press, 2008) 45–69.

[55] Art 194(1) TFEU.

A second development that occurred during the 1990s, and has continued since, is the liberalisation of the EU electricity markets. When a number of more or less severe interruptions to electricity supply occurred in 2003–2004—one of them led to a black-out of the entire electricity supply in Italy, caused initially by an accident in Switzerland—the question was raised whether this was a consequence of energy market liberalisation introduced through the EU internal market programme. In the era of state monopolies, the obligation to ensure an uninterrupted supply of electricity had been part of the deal whereby the incumbents obtained exclusive or special rights from the state. In the more complex environment of liberalised markets, the responsibility for various security tasks has to be explicitly fixed on certain parties or they will not act for 'social' ends.

There is indeed an issue here, and it is one familiar to the UK as the laboratory of energy market liberalisation since the 1980s. In the period before liberalisation, large-scale investment was carried out either directly through the state or indirectly through national monopolies in most countries in the EU. The legacy of this period was a very extensive infrastructure that provided the foundation for market opening in the 1990s and after. However, the trend was to squeeze as much value out of existing infrastructure as possible—sometimes called 'asset sweating'. It has become clear in recent years that ageing networks need to be expanded and sometimes replaced entirely. Left to market forces, there are few companies which are likely to invest in spare or redundant capacity in the interests of providing some slack for the network as a whole, for use during an emergency that may never occur. This kind of problem has led to a Directive on Electricity Supply Security and other support measures in the internal energy market legislation.[56] However, the long-term solution has to lie in greater coordination of electricity networks across the EU, perhaps initially on a regional basis. A number of transmission system operators and regulators have already taken steps in this direction. The same point applies, although with less emphasis, for gas pipeline networks. So, an outcome of this situation is a growing awareness of interdependence among EU Member States, some more than others. An addition to the Energy Chapter of the Lisbon Treaty text was therefore agreed upon: a new point (d) of Article 194(1) TFEU was included on the interconnection of energy networks.

In line with the radically increased concerns about 'security' (and there are many definitions of this), there are equally strong developments in perceptions about sustainability and energy policy. The likely impact on energy policy in the coming years can hardly be exaggerated. On one view,

---

[56] Directive 2005/89 concerning measures to safeguard security of electricity supply and infrastructure investment [2006] OJ L33/22.

we have a new energy paradigm in which the goal of carbon mitigation will dominate all other priorities and shape energy policy for decades to come.[57] Indeed, the EPE is inseparable from the EU's commitment to achieve at least a 20 per cent reduction of greenhouse gas emissions by 2020 compared to 1990, as its contribution to a global and comprehensive post-2012 agreement. The aim of this is to build upon and broaden the Kyoto Protocol architecture.

However, ensuring that environmental goals are compatible with internal market ones is not a new challenge. Even before the EPE was adopted, during the period when the Community has been making efforts to establish an internal market in energy, environmental policy has been strongly influenced by the EU's commitments to achieve substantial reductions in carbon emissions and increase the share of renewable energy. The result has been the design and adoption of measures that have actual and potential impacts upon the opening of electricity and gas markets to competition,[58] but are intended to be consistent with such opening. In particular, these are the measures to promote the use of renewable sources of energy under Directive 2001/77 (the Renewables Directive),[59] the Directive establishing the European Emissions Trading System[60] and the taxation of energy uses.[61]

The design of these environmental measures has been made with an eye to their compatibility with the Community's commitment to competition and to the goal of developing an internal market in energy. Indeed, the authors of the environmental measures could hardly have been unaware of the high price paid in the past by the perceived negative implications of

---

[57] D Helm, *The New Energy Paradigm* (Oxford, Oxford University Press, 2007).

[58] Other measures have been adopted that impact upon the energy sector (and have impacts on the achievement of carbon reduction) but have less evident actual or potential impacts upon competition: eg the body of energy efficiency legislation comprising Directive 2003/66 on energy labelling of household electric refrigerators, freezers and their combinations [2003] OJ L170/10; Directive 2002/91 on the energy performance of buildings [2003] OJ L1/65; Directive 2005/32 establishing a framework for the setting of ecodesign requirements for energy-using products [2005] OJ L191/29; and Directive 2006/32 on the promotion of end-use efficiency and energy services [2006] OJ L114/64. Measures concerning environmental impact assessment also have implications for the energy sector, specifically: Directive 85/337 on the assessment of the effects of certain public and private projects on the environments [1985] OJ L175/40 (as amended in 1997 and 2003).

[59] Directive 2001/77 on the promotion of electricity produced from renewable energy sources in the internal electricity market [2001] OJ L283/33.

[60] Directive 2003/87 establishing a scheme for greenhouse gas emission allowance trading within the European Community and amending Directive 96/91 [2003] OJ L275/32.

[61] Elements of Directive 2004/8 on the promotion of cogeneration based on a useful heat demand in the internal energy market [2004] OJ L52/50 may also be noted in this respect: 'the development of cogeneration contributes to enhancing competition'; '[i]t is therefore necessary to take measures to ensure that the potential is better exploited within the framework of the internal energy market' (recitals 2 and 1, respectively).

proposals for competitiveness.[62] The Community's failure to secure an EU energy tax in the 1990s was only one example of this. As a result, the recent environmental measures have shown a high degree of market sensitivity in both design and implementation. The emissions trading scheme (ETS) is a particularly vivid illustration of this. While, in the past, the overall environmental aims of the EU might have been seen as a source of constraint upon the development of an internal energy market, the declared aim is now to create opportunities for synergy. Nonetheless, their potential for market distortion remains.

As the Renewables Directive recognises,[63] the rules of Articles 87 and 88 EC apply with respect to public support schemes. The Guidelines on State Aid for Environmental Protection are applicable to such support. In practice, the Commission has interpreted the Guidelines liberally and approved no fewer than 60 state aid schemes between 2001 and 2004 that provided some support for renewable energy schemes.[64] Its decisions appear to have been driven by the consideration that the use of renewables is a priority in the Community and that the beneficial effects of such support schemes are greater than their distorting effects on competition. In practice, a plethora of mechanisms to support renewable energy sources have been adopted among the Member States. They include green certificates, investment aid, tax exemptions or reductions, tax refunds or direct price support, and have the effect of creating advantages for renewable sources in energy markets. The Renewables Directive does not attempt to harmonise the many support schemes; instead, it attempts to monitor them by means of extensive reporting requirements. As a result, it permits considerable discrepancies among the various schemes to continue, and may create difficulties for an eventual harmonisation of the schemes. No attempt at harmonisation appears likely in the near future, partly due to the wide differences and trends among the current systems, and also due to the possibility that short-term changes 'might potentially disrupt certain markets and make it more difficult for Member States meeting their targets'.[65]

---

[62] A Cosbey, 'Climate Change and Competitiveness: A Survey of the Issues', unpublished background paper to an experts' workshop, *Climate Change, Trade and Competitiveness* (Chatham House, London, 30 March 2005).

[63] Recital 12, Directive 2001/77 [2001] OJ L283/33.

[64] European Commission, The Support of Electricity from Renewable Energy Sources, COM(2005) 627 Final, 10.

[65] European Commission, The Support of Electricity from Renewable Sources, COM(2005) 627 Final, 11. The Commission explained elsewhere that '[t]he situation would be very different if wind energy performed across the Community at the level achieved in Denmark, Germany and Spain, if biomass heating was as dynamic everywhere as it is in Finland or if geothermal energy managed at the level of development being achieved in Sweden and Italy': Commission Communication, Report in accordance with Article 3 of

One of the most important instruments for achieving significant emissions reductions is the emissions trading scheme. It is the EU's most ambitious effort yet to give companies incentives to invest in low carbon electricity generation and measures to save electricity. In 2003, a Directive was adopted which establishes a Community scheme for greenhouse gas emission allowance trading within the Community.[66] It is based on Article 175(1) EC, as the appropriate legal basis for actions with an environmental aim under Article 174 EC. Its declared goal is to promote reductions of greenhouse gas emissions in a cost-effective and economically efficient manner.[67] In contrast to the Kyoto Protocol, however, it concerns itself with only one of these gases: carbon dioxide or CO_2 (carbon), partly because it is the most harmful and partly because it is easy to monitor. In practice, a number of Member States had already begun such initiatives on an individual basis (for example, the UK, the Netherlands and Denmark), but a Europe-wide scheme was justified on the grounds that it could accommodate a level playing field and provide a uniform price for allowances traded in the EU. The measure is relevant to the energy sector, and particularly electricity markets, although it is directed at a wide range of non-energy industries. It has implications for both competition and energy policies, with respect to state aid and market distortion issues, and proposals for its amendment and extension are well underway.

VIII. CONCLUSIONS

The greatest challenge for the Community in dealing with its new European energy policy will lie in ensuring that the three corners of its triangular policy—which reflect elements that have a long history—co-exist amicably. The bold linkage of energy to climate change policy should not detract from the fact that progress in establishing competition in EU energy markets has been slow and difficult. As competition in EU energy markets begins to bite, there is a risk of national protectionism reviving under the guise of 'security' concerns, and of market distorting measures being introduced under an environmental sustainability flag through large-scale subsidies for renewable sources of energy. Increasingly, energy lies in a horizontal zone of policies in which no clear priority exists. The innovation of a new chapter on energy in the Treaty of Lisbon will not

Directive 2001/77/EC, evaluation of the effect of legislative instruments and other Community policies on the development of the contribution of renewable sources in the EU and proposals for concrete actions, COM(2004) 366 Final.
   [66]   Directive 2003/87 establishing a scheme for greenhouse gas emission allowance trading within the Community and amending Council Directive 96/61 [2003] OJ L275/32.
   [67]   *Ibid*, Art 1.

resolve this. The potential for tension will remain, although this need for a balancing of policies and values is hardly new in the Community's history.

For many years, the growing importance of energy law in the EU has made little evident impact on the various high-level schemes to modify and expand the scope of the Treaties. Ironically, amidst the turmoil of the debate on the Constitutional Treaty and its near-successor, the Treaty of Lisbon, a formal recognition has emerged of the current importance of energy in the EU legal order. Perhaps it is a case of too little, too late. In the meantime, the growing body of EU energy law continues to develop on the back of other, more established legal competences. Both developments are driven by the appreciation of the scale of the problems that lie ahead and the need to develop common solutions if progress is to be made at all.

12

New Frontiers in EU Labour Law: From Flexicurity to Flex-Security

JEFF KENNER

I. INTRODUCTION

ONE OF THE starkest dilemmas facing the European Union, looking forward, arises from the sheer velocity of change in the organisation and functionality of work in the wake of technological development, globalisation of production and services, privatisation, outsourcing and the vertical disintegration[1] of companies. As the composition of the workforce changes,[2] workers have become increasingly mobile and adaptable and subject to ever more diverse contractual arrangements. These developments have brought about a huge, and almost certainly irreversible, shift towards casual or intermittent employment, part-time working, contracting out and agency placements involving multiple employing entities. As 'flex' working[3] increases, the essential elements of the employment relationship are being transformed and so too are the expectations of employers and workers about security. In response, European labour law is undergoing a process of 'modernisation'[4] at the

---

[1] This term has been applied to the break up of monolithic or 'Fordist' company structures induced by contracting out, diffusion and 'downsizing'. In some cases workers excluded from the original employing entity are deemed to be independent contractors. See H Collins, 'Independent Contractors and the Challenge of Vertical Disintegration to Employment Protection Law' (1990) 10 *OJLS* 353–80.

[2] There has been a significant increase in the number of women and older workers in the EU in recent years. See European Commission, Employment in Europe (Brussels, 2007): <http://www.ec.europa.eu/employment_social/publications/2007/keah07001_en.pdf> accessed 23 September 2008.

[3] In the Netherlands, these groups are collectively known as 'flexworkers'. See further, T Wilthagen, F Tros and H van Lieshout, 'Towards "flexicurity"? Balancing Flexibility and Security in EU Member States' (2004) 6 *European Journal of Social Security* 113–36.

[4] See the Commission's Green Paper on Modernising Labour Law, COM(2006) 708 Final. For a critique of the use of 'modernisation' as an 'ambivalent' and 'non-legal' concept, see S Sciarra, 'EU Commission Green Paper "Modernising labour law to meet the challenges of the 21st century"' (2007) 36 *Industrial Law Journal* 375.

forefront of which is the main issue addressed in this chapter, namely, what steps should be taken to extend the scope of employment protection legislation to include all those in diverse 'non-standard' but dependent working relationships? This leads us to an even larger question about the boundaries of labour law and its future viability as an effective means of redressing the personal and economic subordination of the worker in the employment relationship.[5]

In Part II, this chapter will evaluate the concept of 'flexicurity', one of the central features of the Green Paper on *Modernising Labour Law*[6] and subsequent policy development,[7] and assess its potential contribution to the process of reshaping the contours of labour law to help bring about a less segmented and more inclusive labour market that is also more flexible.[8]

Part III assesses the prospects for extending the personal scope of employment protection laws in the EU by removing, as far as possible, uncertainties with regard to employment status both in individual and multiple forms of employment relationships. It assesses the strengths and weaknesses of three possible scenarios or pathways towards this end. The first scenario would require utilisation of the open method of coordination (OMC) to encourage an incremental extension of the reach of labour law based on sharing of best practice, strategic guidance and monitoring. In the second scenario, perhaps in tandem with the first, a directive could be proposed to establish a common legal definition of a 'worker' applicable horizontally to all EU labour law directives. In a third alternative scenario, the EU would issue a framework directive setting out common approaches towards establishing the existence of an employment relationship with reference to international guidance. Under each scenario, the effectiveness of the method as a means of broadening the scope of labour law will be assessed. In addition to sources of law, the content of legal definitions and common approaches, specific problems will be addressed, not least, how should labour law encompass not only non-standard workers with a single employer, but also temporary workers in triangular working relationships with employment agencies and end users?

Following on from analysis of these possible scenarios, the conclusion reflects, in a concise fashion, on the main themes of the chapter in the context of evolving labour law. Predicated on the basis that the scope of employment protection law in the EU can be extended by pursuing one or

---

[5] For a stimulating collection of essays on this theme, see G Davidov and B Langille (eds), *Boundaries and Frontiers of Labour Law* (Oxford, Hart, 2006).

[6] See n 4 above.

[7] See, especially, the Commission's Communication, Towards Common Principles of Flexicurity: more and better jobs through flexibility and security, COM(2007) 359 Final.

[8] Green Paper, above n 4, 7.

more of the three scenarios referred to above, it will seek to evaluate the reasonable expectation of protection that should be offered to the European worker engaged in the less dependant, more autonomous employment relationships[9] that we see today in flexible firms.[10] Does 'flexicurity' provide a useful device in which greater flexibility for the employer to restructure or relocate is traded off for the offer of security to the worker by an employer or the state? Does it necessarily follow that employment protection laws should be 'moderated' as the price to be paid for inclusiveness?[11]

II. FLEXICURITY—MORE THAN A SLOGAN?

... [W]hile much has been written about the need for flexibility of the labour market and its regulation, much less has been said about the need for *flexibility and security* in the workplace ...[12]

'Flexicurity', the EU's latest neologism,[13] has a long lineage. Over the last 15 years, from the launch of the 'Growth, Competitiveness, Employment' White Paper,[14] the EU's leaders have sought to reconcile the highly contested concepts of employment security and labour market flexibility[15] by advancing a third way or middle path to overcome conventional bipolar thinking.[16] On the one side, it is argued, against the backdrop of an influential report of the Organisation for Economic Cooperation and

---

[9] The importance of worker autonomy has been advanced by Supiot who has sought to focus debate on the subjective experience of the worker in his or her working life and advanced the notion of a continuum between working time and leisure time. See A Supiot, *Beyond Employment: Changes in Work and the Future of Labour Law in Europe* (Oxford, Oxford University Press, 2001).

[10] The term 'flexible firm' is used to describe rapid change in company organisation from fixed systems of production ('Fordist') to flexible open-ended processes of organisational development in which, ideally, workers will have greater job satisfaction, higher skills and long-term employability. See European Commission, Partnership for a New Organisation of Work: Green Paper, Bull EU Supp 4/97, paras 18 and 31.

[11] See COM(2007) 359 Final, above n 7, 15–16.

[12] Partnership for a New Organisation of Work, above n 10, para 3. Emphasis added.

[13] Hans Adriannsens, a Dutch sociologist, is credited with introducing the term in the mid-1990s. For a concise history, see M Keune and M Jepsen, *Not Balanced and Hardly New: The European Commission's Quest for Flexicurity*, European Trade Union Institute Working Paper 2007.01, available at <http://www.etui-rehs.org/research/content/download/2736/17963/version/2/> accessed 23 September 2008.

[14] European Commission, Growth, Competitiveness, Employment: the Challenges and Ways Forward into the 21st Century, Bull EC Supp 6/93, 3.

[15] See, eg the declaration at the Essen European Council of 9/10 December 1994, in favour of a 'more flexible organisation of work in a way which fulfils the wishes of employees and the requirements of competition': Bull EU 12/94.

[16] See J Kenner, 'The EC Employment Title and the Third Way: Making Soft Law Work?' (1999) 15 *International Journal of Comparative Labour Law and Industrial Relations* 33.

Development (OECD),[17] that high unemployment and slow job creation are caused by 'rigidities' in the labour market. Rules deemed restrictive and hidebound might discourage employers from taking on new workers. Such rigidities, it is suggested, can only be removed by deregulation of labour laws and modernisation of social protection systems to create more flexibility in order to attract entrepreneurs into the Single Market.[18] Taken to its logical conclusion, this type of flexibility would arrogate to employers power to hire and fire at will for economic reasons. On the other side, it is argued that flexibility should not be a byword for deregulation, but rather it should be understood as including workers' need for flexibility and security throughout their working life. Flexible work organisation entails work to be adapted to the worker who is able to work more autonomously, and balance work and family responsibilities. In this conception of flexibility, the worker has more flexible working time, the opportunity to work part-time, to be a parent and/or carer, and to have flexible leave arrangements.[19] It follows that labour markets and social welfare systems should be adapted through active measures designed to ensure economic stability and high levels of employment.[20] For the antagonists, there is little compromise to be found in the language of security = rigidity / flexibility = deregulation.

Flexicurity has been lampooned as 'a classic piece of sophistry',[21] but it offers a 'valuable corrective'[22] to what has become a rather sterile debate. It is more than a convenient amalgamation of divisive terms. Rather, it signifies, in its elaboration, a genuine attempt to develop 'an integrated

---

[17]   *Labour Market Flexibility*, Report by a High Level Group of Experts (Paris, OECD, 1986).

[18]   See H Siebert, 'Labor Rigidities: at the Root of Unemployment in Europe' (1997) 11 *Journal of Economic Perspectives* 43. For a critique, see S Deakin and H Reed, 'The Contested Meaning of Labour Market Flexibility: Economic Theory and the Discourse of European Integration' in J Shaw (ed), *Social Law and Policy in an Evolving European Union* (Oxford, Hart, 2000) 71–99.

[19]   Partnership for a New Organisation of Work, above n 10, paras 48–54. On flexibility of working time, see J Kenner, 'Regulating Working Time—Beyond Subordination?' in S Weatherill (ed), *Better Regulation* (Oxford, Hart, 2007) 195–217.

[20]   See M Rhodes, *Globalisation, Labour Markets and Welfare States: A Future of 'Competitive Corporatism'*, EUI Working Paper No 97/36 (Florence, EUI, 1997) 5. See also S Deakin and F Wilkinson, 'Rights vs Efficiency: The Economic Case for Transnational Labour Standards' (1994) 23 *Industrial Law Journal* 289.

[21]   In the sense that it will mean whatever the Commission or the Member States choose it to mean. See P Reid, 'Why EC Paper Turns me Green', *People Management*, 8 March 2007, available at <http://www.peoplemanagement.co.uk> accessed 23 September 2008.

[22]   See the Memorandum by A Bogg annexed to the House of Lords EU Committee's 22nd Report of Session 2006–07, 'Modernising European Union labour law: has the UK anything to gain?', 118, available at <http://www.publications.parliament.uk/pa/ld/ldeucom.htm> accessed 23 September 2008.

strategy to enhance, at the same time, flexibility and security in the labour market'.[23] As the Kok Report explained:

> Flexibility is not just in the interest of employers; it also serves the interest of workers, helping them to combine work with care and education, for example, or to allow them to lead their preferred lifestyles. On the other hand, security does not just mean employment protection, but encompasses the capacity to remain and progress in work.[24]

Building on earlier attempts to enhance the quality of working life and employability of the workforce,[25] and focused on reviving the Lisbon Strategy of 'more and better jobs',[26] flexicurity draws on the International Labour Organisation's (ILO's) conception of 'decent work'[27] and is being developed through procedural methods in the form of 'common principles' and 'pathways' to be taken forward and put into practice at national level.[28] The worker is offered security in employment throughout their working life, but not security in a particular job or job function. The imperative of flexicurity is that the worker should be able, and indeed empowered, to adapt to rapid change within the work organisation (internal flexicurity), to retrain and be re-employed or become self-employed. It is implicit that restructuring and possible redundancy are a normal facet of modern working life. To prepare for such an eventuality, and to seize new opportunities, 'transitions' can be made in working life—the 'lifecycle' approach (external flexicurity)—to offer 'safe' moves from one job into another, backed up by benefits if needed.[29] The first of four 'common principles' of flexicurity in the Commission's June 2007 Communication is most relevant for the future of EU labour law. It calls for:

> ... *flexible and reliable contractual arrangements* (from the perspective of the employer and the employee, of 'insiders' and 'outsiders') through modern labour laws, collective agreements and work organisation ...[30]

---

[23]   See COM(2007) 359, above n 7, 4.

[24]   'Jobs, Jobs, Jobs: Creating More Employment in Europe', Report of the Employment Taskforce, November 2003, 9. Available at <http://www.ec.europa.eu/employment_social/employment_strategy/pdf/etf_en.pdf> accessed 23 September 2008.

[25]   See Partnership for a New Organisation of Work, above n 10; Modernising the Organisation of Work, COM(98) 592; and the Social Policy Agenda, COM(2000) 379.

[26]   See Lisbon European Council, Presidency Conclusions, 23–24 March 2000, available at <http://www.europa.eu/european_council/index_en.htm> accessed 23 September 2008.

[27]   See 'Decent Work', Report of the Director General to the 87th session of the International Labour Conference, Geneva 3 (1999), available at <http://www.ilo.org/public/english/standards/relm/ilc/ilc87/rep-i.htm> accessed 23 September 2008.

[28]   COM(2007) 359, above n 7.

[29]   COM(2007) 359, above n 7, 7.

[30]   COM(2007) 359, above n 7, 5. The other three common principles are more familiar, namely: comprehensive lifelong learning strategies; effective active labour market policies; and modern social security systems.

The 'insider/outsider' dichotomy had earlier been developed in the Kok Taskforce Report and the Labour Law Green Paper. Under these proposals,[31] Member States and the social partners are urged to examine the degree of security for 'non-standard'[32] or 'flex' workers who work under alternative forms of contracts to 'standard' open-ended contracts. In order to tackle contractual segmentation, non-standard workers would be brought within the coverage of labour law while, at the same time, there is a hint that 'overly protective terms and conditions'[33] afforded by legislation to workers on standard contracts should be weakened.[34] It is implicit that the 'insiders' have benefited from the full force of regulated labour standards at the expense of the 'outsiders',[35] who are often trapped in 'a succession of short-term, low quality jobs with inadequate social protection leaving them in a vulnerable position'.[36] Under the 'flexicurity pathways', it is suggested that the position of non-standard workers within contractual arrangements should be improved alongside a complementary 'tenure track' approach, whereby workers would be offered open-ended contracts at the beginning of the employment relationship with 'a basic level of protection, and protection would build up during job tenure, until "full" protection is achieved'.[37] In seeking to develop the flexicurity idea, the Commission has lauded the example set by the Netherlands and Denmark, both of which have benefited from high skills and high levels of employment over the last 10 years.[38]

The Dutch Flexibility and Security Act 1999 is based on a package deal negotiated by the social partners containing three main elements: (i) limiting the consecutive use of fixed-term contracts to three (the next contract being open-ended); (ii) eliminating obstacles for temporary agencies; and (iii) recognition of fixed-term and temporary agency contracts in the labour code and introducing minimum protection and payment.[39]

---

[31] See n 24 above. Green Paper, above n 4, 3.

[32] This has been defined as 'those forms of work which depart from the model of the "permanent" or indeterminate employment relationship constructed around a full-time continuous work week'. See B Burchill, S Deakin and S Honey, *The Employment Status of Individuals in Non-standard Employment* (UK, Department of Trade and Industry, 1999) URN 98/943, available at <http://www.delni.gov.uk/employment_status_consultation_document.pdf> accessed 23 September 2008.

[33] Green Paper, above n 4, 5. The Commission suggests that such terms can deter employers from hiring during economic upturns.

[34] For a denial of this point, see COM(2007) 359, above n 7, 7.

[35] See the Memorandum by D Ashiagbor, above n 22, 111.

[36] Green Paper, above n 4, 8.

[37] COM(2007) 359, above n 7, 28. This suggestion came from the Wilthagen Report: 'Flexicurity Pathways: turning hurdles into stepping stones', Expert Group Report on Flexicurity (Brussels, European Commission, June 2007).

[38] In 2006, the employment rate was 74% in the Netherlands and 77% in Denmark, well above the Lisbon targets. See COM(2007) 359, above n 7, 36–7.

[39] COM(2007) 359, above n 7, 37.

There is a mandatory legal presumption that an employment contract exists where work has been carried out for another person in return for pay on a weekly basis, or where there is at least 20 hours' work per month during three consecutive months.[40] The success of the Netherlands in activating its unemployed labour by increasing opportunities for 'flex' workers is often described as the 'Dutch miracle', although its critics have concerns about the sufficiency of social protection.[41]

Danish-style flexicurity is based on a 'golden triangle' of high mobility (numerical security), an active labour market policy (better skills for job transitions), and a generous support scheme (social security).[42] High mobility is due, in part, to relatively low job security for individual workers. 30 per cent switch their jobs yearly and most workers expect to change jobs several times in their working life.[43] Labour market policy is based on a mix of incentives and sanctions with an emphasis on mandatory upskilling or 'activation' schemes.[44] Significantly, women have almost as high a labour market participation rate as men, in part due to high quality public care for children and the elderly.[45] Most distinctively, general taxation funds high unemployment benefits for 150,000 people set at 'wage-replacement' levels payable for four years.[46] Wage levels are comparatively high and, therefore, even though there is little protection against economic dismissals, surveys suggest that Danish workers feel generally safe and content.[47] Essentially, the Danish model is the outcome of a 'trade off' between flexible employment laws and strong social security,[48] but it has been constructed, going back to 1899,[49] by historical compromises between the social partners and a strong consensus about the role of taxation in funding social security.

---

[40] Green Paper, above n 4, 11.

[41] See W van Oorschot, 'Balancing work and welfare: activation and flexicurity policies in The Netherlands, 1980–2000' (2004) 13 *International Journal of Social Welfare* 15.

[42] Opinion of the European Economic and Social Committee on Flexicurity: the case of Denmark (2006/C 195/12), [2006] OJ C195/48, para 3.2.

[43] *Ibid*, para 1.5.

[44] *Ibid*, para 1.7.

[45] 73.1% to 79.4%. See further LL Hansen, 'From Flexicurity to FlexicArity? Gendered Perspectives on the Danish Model' (2007) 3 *Journal of Social Sciences* 88.

[46] EESC Opinion, above n 42, para 3.3, containing a useful diagram of the 'golden triangle'.

[47] EESC Opinion, above n 42, para 1.5.

[48] See generally, PK Madsen, *The Danish Model of "Flexicurity": A Paradise with Some Snakes* (Dublin, European Foundation for the Improvement of Living and Working Conditions, 2002), available at <http://www.eurofound.europa.eu/ewco/employment/documents/madsen.pdf> accessed 23 September 2008.

[49] This was when the world's first ever general agreement between national social partners—the 'September compromise'—was struck between the Danish national social partners. See EESC Opinion, above n 42, para 4.2.

In summary, security under the Dutch and Danish models is engendered *either* through strong job security based on a presumption of an employment contract *or* strong social security equivalent to a living wage. The circumstances that have brought about the relative success of these particular variants of flexicurity are unique to each country and not easily replicated in other systems. Ultimately, what flexicurity offers is the opportunity for mutual learning and, through soft law, procedural implementation backed up by monitoring under the OMC. We will discuss the potential effectiveness of this approach in the next part, but how evenly balanced is the Commission's approach to security and flexibility?

Although the Commission has endorsed these models, it has been strongly criticised for downplaying the importance of security in the job. Despite an assurance that flexicurity 'does not mean "hire and fire"; nor does it imply that open-ended contracts are a thing of the past', the Commission relies heavily on economic analysis of the OECD,[50] which favours 'moderate' employment protection law and regards protection against economic dismissal as 'overly strict' because, it is alleged, it encourages companies to take on new temporary workers instead of permanent employees.[51] Commissioner Špidla has asserted that flexicurity is geared more to the protection of people than the protection of jobs and, using the unfortunate analogy of a sinking ship, has suggested that 'the most important thing is not to save the ship but to save the people on board'.[52] Not surprisingly, these comments have incurred the wrath of critics in the trade unions who argue that the Commissioner's interpretation of flexicurity would negate traditional contractual arrangements at the point where workers are most vulnerable and would lead to 'more unstable employment and less tangible guarantees'.[53] Flexicurity has also been criticised for taking insufficient account of the reality of working life, especially for part-time and agency workers. These workers are predominantly female, often dependent on flexible working and, having to juggle work and care—the 'dual burden'—are in the most precarious position at the edge of the protective framework of labour law.[54]

Flexicurity is proving to be just as contentious a word as flexibility, at least in its interpretation, but it has fostered a much needed debate about

[50]   *Boosting Jobs and Income* (Paris, OECD, 2006). See COM(2007) 359, above n 7, 16.
[51]   COM(2007) 359, above n 7, 15 (in a box marked 'What is "employment protection legislation?"').
[52]   Informal Ministerial Meeting, Villach (Austria), 20 January 2006.
[53]   See Keune and Jepsen, above n 13, 13–14. The employer's organisation, Business Europe, is equally unhappy with the Commission's interpretation of flexicurity, which they believe presents 'an unjustifiably negative picture' of flexible forms of work. See Business Europe, Position Paper (6 March 2007), available at <http://www.businesseurope.eu> accessed 23 September 2008.
[54]   See S Fredman, 'Women at Work: The Broken Promise of Flexicurity' (2004) 34 *Industrial Law Journal* 299.

fundamental issues of labour law, not only concerning the depth of employment protection, but also its width. For flexicurity to be meaningful, it has to be more than a slogan. It has to be an inclusive concept for the most vulnerable workers and, to pursue our research question, it is to this issue—and most particularly the means to pursue it—that we now turn.

III. EXTENDING THE PERSONAL SCOPE OF EU LABOUR LAW

A. What is Labour Law and Who is it for?

In its opening statement, the Labour Law Green Paper purports to challenge the status quo by asserting that[55]: 'The *original purpose* of labour law *was* to offset the inherent economic and social inequality within the employment relationship'.

This statement draws from Kahn-Freund's classic definition of the employment relationship as 'a condition of subordination' derived from the 'inequality of bargaining power which is inherent' between the contracting parties.[56] According to Kahn-Freund, it is only through labour law, acting as a 'countervailing force', that this inequality is counteracted.[57] The foundational basis of labour law is being, somewhat obliquely, challenged by the Commission's statement, if we interpret it as suggesting either that the 'original purpose' of labour law no longer holds good or, more likely, that it has ceased to operate effectively as a mechanism to offset inequality. If it is the former, the Commission stands rightly accused of ignoring the continuing relevance of the 'emancipating role of labour law'.[58] If we accept the latter, it follows that the thesis in the Green Paper is that labour law is malfunctioning and, moreover, that the employment relationship is now more unequal than it was at the time of the Treaty of Rome, because it redistributes power primarily to those who have 'employee' status under national law,[59] and thus limits or wholly excludes from protection almost 40 per cent of the EU workforce, whose working

---

[55] Green Paper, above n 4, 8. Emphasis added.

[56] P Davies and M Freedland, *Kahn-Freund's Labour and the Law*, 3rd edn (London, Stevens, 1983) 18. The notion of 'inequality of bargaining power' is challenged by some, mainly American, economists. For analysis of this debate, see G Davidov, 'The Reports of my Death are Greatly Exaggerated: "Employee" as a Viable (Though Over-used) Legal Concept' in Davidov and Langille, above n 5, 133–52.

[57] Davies and Freedland, *ibid*.

[58] See the European Economic and Social Committee's Opinion, Modernising Labour Law, SOC/246 (30 May 2007), available at <http://www.eesc.europa.eu> accessed 23 September 2008.

[59] On the redistributive function of labour law, see H Collins, *Employment Law* (Oxford, Oxford University Press, 2003) 13–14.

arrangements differ from the 'standard contractual model'.[60] Non-standard or atypical workers in multi-segmented workforces[61] include, inter alia, casual or intermittent workers, 'zero hours' workers, home workers, outworkers, on-call workers, temporary agency workers, gang workers, trainees and consultants.[62] These workers are more likely to be female and working on part-time or fixed-term contracts with different employers in multiple locations. There has been a rapid increase in the number of workers in three-way relationships, both agency workers and in chains of sub-contracting. Other workers, the most precariously placed—often third-country migrants—are carrying out undeclared work wholly outside the bounds of labour law.[63] Labour law is 'in flux' even if its inherent purpose remains unchanged.[64]

The origins of the two-tier labour market can be traced to the bargain struck in Rome that each Member State would be able to retain its own stratified system of personal work or employment relationships in the Common Market. Such distinctiveness in the field of labour law was not regarded as inimical to the goals of market integration.[65] There was a consensus that the personal scope of labour law in the Member States was broadly a fit for the standard European worker, who was usually male, typically working full time on a permanent basis for the same employer without a career break and carrying out the same or similar job function in a single location throughout his working life.[66] The standard worker was personally and economically dependent on the employer and had limited decision-making powers. The labour market was relatively homogenous and thus the protective net of labour law stretched wide, *but there were outsiders*, especially women,[67] part-time workers and the self-employed.

---

[60]   Green Paper, above n 4, 7, based on the 'EU Labour Force Survey', 2005. This figure includes those who are dependent on an employer for work and the self-employed.

[61]   See H Collins, 'Multi-segmented Workforces, Comparative Fairness, and the Capital Boundary Obstacle' in Davidov and Langille, above n 5, 317–36.

[62]   See M Freedland, 'From the Contract of Employment to the Personal Work Nexus' (2006) 35 *Industrial Law Journal* 1, 9.

[63]   For evidence of EU concern about undeclared work because of its distorting effect on inter-state competition, see the Council Resolution on transforming undeclared work into regular work [2003] OJ C260. Similar concerns have been raised in the US: see KVW Stone, 'Rethinking Labour Law: Employment Protection for Boundaryless Workers' in Davidov and Langille, above n 5, 155–79.

[64]   For a stimulating analysis, see S Fredman, 'Labour Law in Flux: The Changing Composition of the Workforce' (1997) 26 *Industrial Law Journal* 337.

[65]   See the 'Ohlin Report' on 'Social Aspects of European Economic Co-operation' (1956) 74 *International Labour Review* 99.

[66]   See U Mückenberger, 'Non-standard Forms of Work and the Role of Changes in Labour and Social Security Regulation' (1989) 17 *International Journal of the Sociology of Law* 381.

[67]   Prior to the Equal Treatment Directive 76/207 [1976] OJ L39/40, it was common practice in several Member States for national law to permit the dismissal of women when they married or had children. The UK maintained a policy of automatically dismissing

The contract of employment between the employer and the employee is the central institution of individual labour law and is therefore the reference point for employment protection legislation. Even though there is considerable diversity of labour law norms throughout the Member States, the contract of employment is a feature of both civil law and common law systems. Within civil law systems there is what Freedland and Kountouris aptly describe as a 'standardised contract typology' constructed on the basis of systematic principles, such as the superimposition of terms of collective agreements and codified law on the agreement of the parties.[68] Common law systems[69] offer less certainty of protection because the contract of employment is, formally at least, 'self-designed'[70] by the parties, but it operates within a protective framework provided by a mix of judge-made law and statute. The prevailing logic, until the early 1990s, was that there was no need for the Community to intervene on the issue of employment status because national systems of employment regulation were performing a broadly protective function for the benefit of the predominant group of workers within their ambit.

It followed that when the Community first adopted a legislative strategy in the area of social policy in the mid-1970s, it did not interfere with the internal organisation of national systems for determining terms such as 'employee', 'worker', 'contract of employment' or 'employment relationship'. It was left to each Member State to demarcate who would benefit from the minimum standards of employment protection laid down in labour law directives. For example, the Transfers of Undertakings Directive has a standard clause that defines an 'employee' as 'any person who, *in the Member State concerned*, is protected as an employee under national law'.[71] Only those defined as 'employees' in the state where the transfer takes place fall within the scope of protection and have a guarantee that their rights will be safeguarded by the new employer. Other workers, typically casual workers, who are in a direct or indirect employment relationship with the original employer or an associated employer may fall outside the national definition of 'employee' and are excluded.

In EU health and safety legislation, the broader term 'worker' is preferred to 'employee', but again there is deference to national definitions

---

pregnant women from the armed forces until August 1990 when it was reversed following the Court of Justice's rulings that dismissals of this kind are directly discriminatory and violate Directive 76/207: Case C-177/88, *Dekker* [1990] ECR I-3941; and Case C-179/88, *Hertz* [1990] ECR I-3979. See further, A Arnull, 'EC Law and the Dismissal of Pregnant Servicewomen' (1995) 24 *Industrial Law Journal* 215.

[68] M Freedland and N Kountouris, 'Towards a Comparative Theory of the Contractual Construction of Personal Work Relations in Europe' (2008) 37 *Industrial Law Journal* 49, 62.

[69] Specifically the UK and Ireland from the point of accession to the Community in 1973.

[70] Freedland and Kountouris, above n 68, 62.

[71] Art 2(1)(d) Directive 2001/23 [2001] OJ L82/16 (emphasis added).

based on a standard-type employment contract.[72] Even more inclusive measures stemming from concerns about the need to protect 'atypical workers' and promote more flexibility and security in the labour market,[73] such as the directives concerning part-time and fixed-term work, are subject to the rules of interpretation of Member States.[74] Legislative deference has been reinforced by the social provisions of the EC Treaty, as revised, which provide that the Community and Member States shall implement measures 'which take account of the diverse forms of national practices, *in particular in the field of contractual relations*'.[75] Moreover, the Charter of Fundamental Rights, which purports to offer 'every worker' the right to protection against unjustified dismissal, adds the rider that this right must be interpreted 'in accordance with Union law and national laws and practices'.[76]

The personal scope of EU labour law is therefore subject to a strong form of vertical subsidiarity which leads to a lack of legal coherence and contrasts with the development by the Court of Justice of a horizontal application of the concept of a 'worker' for the purposes of establishing the personal scope of core free movement provisions in the EC Treaty and, more recently, sex equality law.

In the context of free movement of workers, the rationale for a Community conception of a 'worker' is based on the transnational dimension of work as economic activity under Article 39 EC. The Court of Justice in *Hoekstra*[77] rejected a unilateral interpretation of 'worker' by each Member State precisely because it would undermine free movement by allowing national laws to exclude certain groups, such as public

---

[72] See, eg Art 2(1) Young Workers Directive 94/33 [1994] OJ L216/12, which provides that: 'This Directive shall apply to [under 18s] having an employment contract or an employment relationship defined by the law in force in a Member State and/or governed by the law in force in a Member State'. There is no specific definition of a 'worker' in the Working Time Directive 2003/88 [2003] OJ L299/9, but recital 4 of the preamble makes it subject to the general framework Directive 89/391 on the Safety and Health of Workers at Work [1989] OJ L183/1, where a 'worker' is defined in Art 3(a) as 'any person employed by an employer, including trainees and apprenticeships but excluding domestic servants'.

[73] For the original proposals, see COM(90) 228 published in [1990] OJ C224/4.

[74] See Clause 2(1) of the Framework Agreement annexed to the Fixed-term Work Directive 1999/70 [1999] OJ L175/43, which limits its scope to 'fixed-term workers who have an employment contract or employment relationship as defined in law, collective agreements or practice in each Member State'. A similar clause is contained in Clause 2(1) of the Framework Agreement annexed to the Part-time Work Directive 97/81 [1998] OJ L14/9.

[75] Art 136 EC (emphasis added).

[76] Art 30 of the Charter, as revised [2007] OJ C303. Under Art 52(6): 'Full account shall be taken of national law and practices as specified in this Charter'. This clause has been added 'in the spirit of subsidiarity' according to the explanations annexed to the Charter. See further, J Kenner, 'Economic and Social Rights in the EU Legal Order: The Mirage of Indivisibility' in T Hervey and J Kenner (eds), *Economic and Social Rights under the EU Charter of Fundamental Rights: A Legal Perspective* (Oxford, Hart, 2003) 1–25.

[77] Case 75/63, *Hoekstra (née Unger) v Bestuur der Bedrijfsvereniging voor Detailhandel en Ambachten* [1964] ECR 177, 184.

officials,[78] from the scope of protection. In *Lawrie-Blum*, the Court ruled that the concept of a 'worker' for the purpose of Article 39 EC must be defined in accordance with objective criteria that distinguish the 'employment relationship' by reference to the rights and duties of the persons concerned, the essential feature of which is that 'for a certain period of time a person performs services for and under the direction of another person in return for which he receives remuneration'.[79] Evidence of a relationship of both personal and economic subordination is required, although it is for a national court to decide whether a relationship of subordination exists.[80]

Until 2004, the legal question of 'worker' status under Community law had been confined to free movement of workers, but, in *Allonby*,[81] the Court was asked whether a college lecturer whose work had been sub-contracted and was now designated as self-employed under national law could, nonetheless, be a 'worker' and fall within the provisions of Article 141(1) EC on equal pay between men and women. In its ruling, the Court noted that 'there is no single definition of worker in Community law: it varies according to the area in which the definition is to be applied'.[82] However, the Court suggested a clear rationale for adopting a uniform interpretation in relation to equal pay based on the objectives of the EC Treaty, namely that Article 141(1) EC constitutes 'a specific expression of the principle of equality for men and women, which forms part of the fundamental principles protected by the Community legal order'.[83] It follows that Article 141(1) EC has evolved into a foundational principle of Community law[84] and must be given a Community meaning that cannot be interpreted restrictively.[85] The Court proceeded to apply the *Lawrie-Blum* test[86] and held that, even if Ms Allonby was defined as self-employed under national legislation, she could be a 'worker' for the

---

[78] See Case 152/73, *Sotgiu v Deutsche Bundespost* [1974] ECR 153, para 5. This can be compared with the deferential approach of the Court in respect of labour law directives: see Case C-343/98, *Collino and Chiappero v Telecom Italia SpA* [2000] ECR I-6659, in which telecommunications workers in Italy fell outside the personal scope of the Transfers of Undertakings Directive, above n 71, because they had public law status under national law and were not 'employees'. The Court held that the Directive could be relied on only by persons who were protected as 'employees' under national labour law regardless of the tasks they performed.

[79] Case 66/85, *Lawrie-Blum v Land Baden Württemberg* [1986] ECR 2121, para 17.

[80] Case C-337/97, *Meeusen v Hooffddirectie van de Informatie Beheer Groep* [1999] ECR I-3289, paras 15–16.

[81] Case C-256/01, *Allonby v Accrington and Rossendale College* [2004] ECR I-873.

[82] *Ibid*, para 63, applying Case C-85/96, *Martínez Sala* [1998] ECR I-2691, para 31.

[83] *Ibid*, para 65, applying Joined Cases C-270 & 271/97, *Deutsche Post* [2000] ECR I-929, para 57.

[84] *Ibid*, para 65, applying Case 43/75, *Defrenne v Sabena (No 2)* [1976] ECR 455, para 12.

[85] *Ibid*, para 66.

[86] See n 79 above.

purpose of Article 141(1) EC, so long as she was in a relationship of subordination with respect to the sub-contractor.[87] In particular, this would be the case if the worker's independence were 'merely notional', thereby disguising an employment relationship.[88] In this regard, account could be taken of any limitation on a worker's freedom to choose his or her timetable, and the place and content of work. The fact that no obligation was imposed on an individual to accept a teaching assignment was thus of no consequence.[89]

The significance of *Allonby* in this context is twofold. First, it applies the 'worker' test in free movement law to equal pay law and hence the social provisions of the Treaty, but only on the basis of the special status of the sex equality principle in EU law. The application of *Allonby* is thus limited to equalities and anti-discrimination law[90] and does not extend to labour law derived from Article 137 EC in general, although there is a minor overlap.[91] Secondly, by applying the *Lawrie-Blum* test broadly, the Court of Justice is requiring national courts to examine the issue of subordination objectively without reference either to the labels placed on the employment relationship under national law or to overly restrictive tests for employment status based on the obligation to accept work. The Court's reference to an 'obligation' to accept work relates to the law on employment status in the United Kingdom from where *Allonby* derived. In the UK, the courts have adopted a 'mutuality of obligation' test as the basis for establishing a contract of employment, or dependent 'employee' status.[92] The legal test for broader 'worker' status under UK law also requires a degree of mutuality of obligation between the parties in order to distinguish the quasi-dependant 'worker' under a duty to perform work personally from

---

[87]   *Allonby*, above n 81, para 68.
[88]   *Allonby*, above n 81, para 71.
[89]   *Allonby*, above n 81, para 72.
[90]   In Case C-313/02, *Wippel v Peek & Cloppenburg GmbH & Co KG* [2004] ECR I-9483, the Court held, at paras 31 and 36, that a worker with an employment contract was entitled to rely on the Equal Treatment Directive 76/207 [1976] OJ L39/40, on the basis that the Directive provided for equal treatment between men and women in respect of 'working conditions' and would apply to such a worker. No direct reference was made to the test in *Allonby*. As the anti-discrimination directives based on Art 13 EC are similarly drafted and in line with the revised Equal Treatment Directive 2002/73 [2002] OJ L269/15, it is submitted that it follows, by analogy that a Community meaning consistent with *Allonby* should be given to the terms 'employment and working conditions' contained in each of those directives.
[91]   Art 137(1)(i) EC provides a legal basis for directives in the field of 'equality between men and women with regard to labour market opportunities and treatment at work', but this seems superfluous given the broad legal basis for such equal treatment measures in Art 141(3) EC.
[92]   Employment Rights Act 1996, s 230(1), based on the common law. See *O'Kelly v Trusthouse Forte Plc* [1983] IRLR 369.

the non-dependent self-employed person running a business.[93] The distinction is important because, as Anne Davies notes, in the UK the 'self-employed get almost no protection, workers get some protection, and employees get all the protection the law has to offer'.[94] If the 'worker' concept in UK law was to be subject to a broad Community meaning based on the *Allonby* formula, there would potentially be a clearer divide between those who are substantively and economically dependent on an employer,[95] including some self-employed people who are not running their own businesses, and those who are wholly autonomous business owners.

What then are the possibilities for the development of a parallel judicial approach to worker status under EU labour law? As outlined above, a literal interpretation of definitional clauses in labour law directives would close the door on this option, but should the Court of Justice adopt a more inclusive interpretation of their personal scope when the aim of the measure in question is to protect vulnerable workers from exploitation? The Part-time Work Directive, which seeks to establish a general framework for eliminating discrimination against part-time workers,[96] is a case in point. The personal scope of the Directive was tested in *Wippel*,[97] an Austrian case that highlights the problems arising from a formalistic approach to interpreting clauses on employment status. Ms Wippel, a part-time casual worker, was seeking to rely on the Directive to claim equal treatment with full-time workers carrying out a similar job function and employed by the same employer. She had a 'work on demand' or 'zero-hours' contract in the retail clothing business under which she had no fixed working hours. The length of her working time and job placement were determined by agreements that she made with her employer on a job-by-job basis. This employment was her main source of income, but she could accept or refuse a job placement offered without giving a reason. Significantly, Austria had not taken advantage of a clause in the Directive permitting it, 'for objective reasons', to 'exclude wholly or partly ... part-time workers who work on a casual basis'.[98] The Court ruled that workers on demand such as Wippel would come within the scope of the Directive where they have a contract of employment under national law,

---

[93] Employment Rights Act 1996, s 230(3). See *Byrne Bros v Baird* [2002] IRLR 96.
[94] ACL Davies, *Perspectives on Labour Law* (Cambridge, Cambridge University Press, 2004) 89.
[95] See *Byrne Bros v Baird* [2002] IRLR 96, 101.
[96] Directive 97/81 [1998] OJ L14/9, recital 11 of the preamble.
[97] See n 90 above.
[98] Directive 97/81 [1998] OJ L14/9. Clause 2(2) of the annexed Framework Agreement. This derogation can only be applied subject to national law and consultation with the social partners. Member States relying on it must review such exclusions periodically 'to establish if the objective reasons for making them remain valid'.

work fewer hours than a comparable full-time worker, and Austria had not excluded casual workers pursuant to the derogation.[99]

The Court's ruling on this point creates a presumption that casual workers fall within the scope of the Directive where the Member State has not taken advantage of the derogation. However, formally protecting casual workers only serves to emphasise the hierarchy of employment status at national level as buttressed by a distinction contained in the Directive whereby, in order to claim equal treatment under the Directive, part-time workers must have the '*same type of contract or relationship*' as a 'comparable' full-time worker in the same establishment engaged in the same or similar work.[100] In the absence of a comparable full-time worker or applicable collective agreement, the comparison must be 'in accordance with national law'.[101] Notwithstanding its earlier more inclusive reasoning, the Court ruled narrowly that full-time workers at the same establishment did not have the 'same type of contract' as Wippel and were not comparable full-time workers because they had fixed working hours and wages and were unable to refuse work.[102] The Court's overly formalistic approach ignores the fact that both groups of workers were in the same relationship of economic dependency and the work on demand workers, who were more likely to be female, had a different type of contract because they often had caring responsibilities. Ultimately, cases such as *Wippel* reveal that, although the part-time and fixed-term work directives were intended to achieve 'comparative fairness' between different groups of workers,[103] they are difficult to adapt to the reality of a multi-segmented workforce, an issue that is highlighted also in *Allonby*,[104] where it was not possible for the contracted-out lecturers to compare their pay with their male colleagues in direct employment.

Wippel neatly highlights the way in which, in the absence of a harmonised approach to employment status, EU labour law, far from combating the two-tier labour market, may inadvertently serve to reinforce segmentation and social exclusion. It demonstrates the need to counter the risks of excluding workers without 'employee' status from basic entitlements and reducing the enforceability of labour law, as identified by the report of the expert group on labour law.[105] The Green Paper's call for an end to uncertainty with regard to the law is welcome. As the Commission notes,

---

[99]   *Wippel*, above n 90, para 40.
[100]   Clause 3(2) Directive 97/81 (emphasis added).
[101]   *Ibid.*
[102]   *Wippel*, above n 90, para 61.
[103]   See Collins, above n 5, 319–24.
[104]   *Allonby*, above n 81. See also Case C-320/00, *Lawrence v Regent Office Care* [2002] ECR I-7325. For a critique, see Fredman, above n 54.
[105]   S Sciarra, *The Evolution of Labour Law (1992–2003)*, Vol 1, General Report (Luxembourg, OOPEC, 2005).

'the binary distinction between "employees" and the independent "self-employed" is no longer an adequate depiction of the economic and social reality of work'.[106] Those who are in 'economically dependent work' occupy a 'grey area' between labour law and commercial law,[107] quite separate from the issue of disguised self-employment.[108] However, rather than put forward concrete proposals, the Green Paper, as Sciarra observes,[109] understates the issue by simply asking rhetorically whether 'greater clarity is needed in *Member States' legal definitions* of employment and self-employment'.[110]

The Green Paper also addresses a whole section to the thorny problem of how to protect workers and clarify responsibilities in triangular relationships under which a temporary worker (A) is contracted out by an employment agency (B) to a user company (C), often for an uncertain period of time, thus creating a 'dual employer' situation which 'adds to the complexity of the employment relationship'.[111] Typically A performs work for C under C's control, but retains a contractual relationship with B, who may be responsible for paying wages and determining arrangements for sick leave or holidays. Such arrangements lack legal certainty because they do not fit with the inherently two-sided nature of the contract of employment in which there is mutuality of obligation arising from the wage/work bargain struck between the employer and employee. Without a clearly defined employer with responsibility under labour law, such workers are ripe for exploitation. This is a particular problem in the UK, where there are over 600,000 agency workers and mutuality of obligation is regarded as essential at common law.[112] The mutuality of obligation requirement makes it difficult for the courts to place responsibility on the end user and, even in an arrangement lasting for more than a year, it is only possible to imply a contract between a worker and an end user at common law if there is evidence of a pre-existing agreement between them sufficient to take precedence over any agreement with the agency.[113]

---

[106]   Green Paper, above n 4, 10.

[107]   Green Paper, above n 4, 11.

[108]   Green Paper, above n 4, 10–11. Disguised self-employment refers to misclassification where an employee's status is hidden unlawfully to avoid taxes and social security contributions. The Commission advises that this issue should be dealt with primarily by the Member States.

[109]   Sciarra, above n 4, 381.

[110]   Green Paper, above n 4, 12. Emphasis added.

[111]   Green Paper, above n 4, 12–13.

[112]   See F Reynolds, 'Will the Real Employer Please Stand Up? Agencies, Client Companies and the Employment Status of the Temporary Worker' (2006) 35 *Industrial Law Journal* 301.

[113]   *James v Greenwich Borough Council* [2008] IRLR 302 (Court of Appeal), distinguishing its more expansive ruling in *Dacas v Brook St Bureau* [2004] IRLR 354.

The proposed directive on temporary agency work, as amended,[114] would recognise the temporary agency as the employer for the period during which the worker is 'posted' to the end user,[115] although it would leave the national definition of a 'worker' untouched.[116] During the period of posting, the temporary worker would be entitled to equal treatment in terms of 'at least' the basic working and employment conditions 'that would apply if they had been recruited directly by that enterprise to occupy the same job'.[117] The draft directive has the potential partially to redress the problem, but it has become mired in political disagreement at the Council over the length of the transitional period before it would enter into effect.[118] In the absence of agreement, the Green Paper once again seeks guidance on whether there is a need to clarify the law on the status of temporary agency workers.[119]

B. Three Scenarios for Broadening the Scope of Labour Law in the EU

How best then to proceed towards an overarching EU-wide legal framework for the employment relationship, applicable to all those who are economically dependent on another for work, regardless of the type of contract and the agency/end-user divide? Such a development would have the potential to increase certainty for the parties and would also put into effect the ILO's 'decent work' agenda based on guaranteeing a core of labour rights for all those with a 'durable employment relationship'.[120] Let us consider three possible scenarios for the EU to pursue should it wish to bring those outside or at the edge of labour law in from the cold. These scenarios, which are not intended to be either/or choices, are as follows:

1. Using the open method of coordination (OMC) to encourage Member States to broaden the scope of personal employment protection through exchange of best practice and cyclical surveillance.
2. Launching a proposal for a horizontal directive applicable to specified EU labour law directives where, at present, the definition of an 'employee' or 'worker' is left to national law and practice. The scope of protection under these directives would be extended to all those who have 'worker' status as defined in the proposed measure, but

---

[114] COM(2002) 701 Final, amending COM(2002) 149 Final.
[115] *Ibid*, Art 2(1).
[116] *Ibid*, Art 3(1)(a).
[117] *Ibid*, Art 5(1).
[118] See C Barnard, *EC Employment Law*, 3rd edn (Oxford, Oxford University Press, 2006) 483–4.
[119] Green Paper, above n 4, 13.
[120] See *Decent Work*, above n 27. See also, question 8 of the Green Paper, above n 4, 12.

employment status for the purposes of national labour and social security law would otherwise be left untouched.

3. Revising Directive 91/533 on an employer's obligation to inform employees of conditions applicable to the contract or employment relationship.[121] The revised measure would act as a framework directive on the existence of an employment relationship applicable to each national system on the basis of indicators of dependency derived from national laws and the ILO Employment Relationship Recommendation No 198.[122] If present, these indicators would create a presumption of entitlement to employment protection. It is envisaged that this presumption would be applied over time to all economically dependent workers, including those in casual, home or agency work.

1. Convergence Through the OMC

The first scenario, pursuing a soft law solution, is the natural choice of Member States, the EU institutions and the social partners so long as there is a broad consensus that social policy objectives can be fulfilled without requiring legislative harmonisation.[123] Binding EU labour law within the confines of conferred Treaty powers is permissible as the ultimate guarantee of the enjoyment of social rights,[124] but it has become the method of last resort in the age of subsidiarity.[125] Increasingly, the form of action, its level and intensity, is recognised as being less important than its effectiveness measured by the quality of the *outcome* rather than the process or instrumentation. The OMC as a systematised soft law technique is capable of facilitating convergence between national policies and procedures and has been an effective tool for developing cyclical policy surveillance. Examples include the European Employment Strategy, the Integrated Guidelines for Growth and Jobs,[126] and an OMC addressing social security and pension issues, all of which underpin the Lisbon Strategy.[127] Post the Green Paper, the OMC forms the centrepiece of the common principles and 'pathways' of flexicurity to be developed in the Member States.[128] It offers a pragmatic method for unpicking intractable problems that lie at,

---

[121]   [1991] OJ L288/32.

[122]   Adopted at the 95th session of the International Labour Conference in June 2006, available at <http://www.ilo.org/ilolex/cgi-lex/convde.pl?R198> accessed 23 September 2008.

[123]   See the Social Policy Agenda, COM(2000) 379, 7.

[124]   See the European Parliament's response to the Social Policy Agenda, A5–0291/2000.

[125]   See further, G de Búrca, *Reappraising Subsidiarity's Significance After Amsterdam*, Harvard Jean Monnet Working Paper 7/99, 4, available at <http://www.jeanmonnetprogram.org/papers> accessed 23 September 2008.

[126]   COM(2005) 141 Final.

[127]   See further J Kenner, *EU Employment Law: from Rome to Amsterdam and Beyond* (Oxford, Hart, 2003) 467–509.

[128]   COM(2007) 359, above n 7, 26.

or outside, the boundaries of Community competence and, as is often the case in matters of labour law, have caused divisions among the Member States and social partners. As a dynamic and inherently malleable process, the OMC can be adapted to broaden participation and input from the social partners and wider civil society. It draws on experiences and best practices in the Member States and allows for policy exchange and adaptation tailored for each national system. At its most effective, it has the potential to act as a kind of 'reflexive harmonisation'[129] that, by means of bespoke design, may have a wider and deeper impact on national law than ready-made minimum standards legislation weakened by political compromise, formalism and the straightjacket of hard Treaty-based legalism.

How suitable, then, is the OMC for broadening the scope of protection of labour law in the EU? The Green Paper points to several examples of best practice, not just the Dutch and Danish models discussed in Part 1 above. In other Member States, notably Germany, Italy and Spain, steps have been taken to include the economically dependent self-employed within the social security system.[130] In the UK, there is a kind of patchwork quilt system whereby superior employment protection is granted to those with 'employee' status, increasing with length of service, whereas lesser protection (for example, minimum wage, working time, anti-discrimination law, health and safety legislation) is afforded to others who are economically dependent, but have only 'worker' status.[131] There is the potential for this divide to be bridged by extending the scope of employment protection legislation to cover both groups equally, but this is a somewhat distant dream.

Under the Integrated Guidelines, the Member States are required to report explicitly on flexicurity strategies as part of their National Reform Programmes. This suggests that the first option for extending the scope of employment protection laws is already underway and, over time, there is considerable potential for mutual learning or benchmarking of best practice and cross-fertilisation between national systems of labour law. Given that legislative harmonisation of the national legal definitions of employment and self-employment is not on the agenda, the OMC may provide some momentum for integration without interfering with the distinction between labour law and commercial law.[132] Herein also lies the danger, for the OMC may serve only to highlight the differences between national approaches that are, in the main, deficient in protecting those who fall

---

[129] See generally, R Rogowski and T Wilthagen (eds), *Reflexive Labour Law* (Deventer, Kluwer, 1994).

[130] Green Paper, above n 4, 11.

[131] See the Memorandum by C Barnard and S Deakin, above n 22, 113–15.

[132] See the EESC's Opinion on the Green Paper, above n 58, para 3.7.1.

outside their own system for standardising work contracts which, with a few exceptions, exclude the most vulnerable and economically subordinate groups of workers. As outlined above, such differences are reinforced by the confusing and illogical state of EU labour laws with alternating protection for only 'employees' or 'workers', according to national definitions. Reliance solely on the OMC would leave this framework untouched and, without the prospect (or threat) of hard law to follow, may undermine the whole flexicurity agenda leading to a 'flexibility first, security second' approach, rather than mutual reinforcement.

2. Harmonising 'Worker' Status Across EU Labour Law Directives

Convergence through soft law has the potential, over time, to extend the scope and intensity of labour law in some Member States, but it does not offer a comprehensive EU-wide normative framework guaranteeing a core of labour rights applicable to all those in one or more working relationships of economic dependency, particularly casual workers, agency workers and other vulnerable groups.[133]

In the area of labour law, subsidiarity has been the guiding rule at least from 1989, when the Social Charter placed responsibility for implementation of the 'fundamental social rights of workers' on the Member States,[134] including the need to improve 'the living and working conditions of workers',[135] while leaving open the option of harmonisation measures as regards 'forms of employment other than open-ended contracts, such as fixed-term contracts, part-time working, temporary work and seasonal work'.[136] The Social Charter provided a launch pad for legislative proposals on part-time, fixed-term and temporary work, to be taken forward on the basis that Treaty objectives cannot be achieved sufficiently by the Member States and, consistent with subsidiarity, be better achieved at EU-level.[137] However, these measures have been primarily concerned with providing equal treatment for workers with the same type of contract under national law and have not addressed the question of who is a worker for the purposes of EU labour law in general. It is entirely compatible with subsidiarity for the next incremental development in relation to non-standard working relationships to be in the form of a horizontal directive to implement a commonly agreed definition of a 'worker', a status that would guarantee effective protection under EU labour law.

---

[133] See n 122 above, para 8 of the preamble.
[134] *Social Europe 1/90*, point 27.
[135] Art 136 EC.
[136] *Social Europe 1/90*, point 7.
[137] See Art 5 EC.

One legislative model for the Commission and the social partners to consider, should this scenario be played out, can be found in the Burden of Proof (Sex Discrimination) Directive.[138] This horizontal measure was adopted in order to effectively implement the principle of sex equality by identifying common objectives across four vertical directives and laying down rules on the establishment of the burden of proof,[139] including, for the first time in a directive, definitions of direct and indirect discrimination[140] applicable, in the jurisdictions of the Member States, to each of those directives and Article 141 EC.[141] Significantly, the Directive was designed to increase transparency and hence effectiveness, even though it trespasses into national juridical processes. The Burden of Proof Directive was justified on the basis of codifying existing case law of the Court of Justice. There is not an exact comparison with EU labour law, because case law has arisen in a different Treaty context, and the introduction of new definitions at EU level to complement or replace national law would be a more radical step. However, there is a strong case, based on grounds of transparency and effectiveness, for a horizontal directive on the employment relationship to improve the quality of the law, to provide legal certainty and, to apply Freedland's term, to 'construct fairness'.[142] This might be achieved by laying down a set of rules to clarify and update the law on the definition of a 'worker' and to extend the scope of those labour law directives presently limited only to 'employees', as part of the EU's established process of legislative review based on simplification and modification of the law.[143] Further, it can be asserted that because such a recasting of the law would clarify the rules for employers and workers alike, including those in three-way relationships, it would not hinder competition and would be consistent with the prevailing 'better regulation' agenda.[144]

What would such a legislative proposal entail? We might wish to name it the 'Worker Status (Interpretation) Directive'. The aim of the legislation would be to provide a single definition of a 'worker' applicable only to a list of core EU labour law and health and safety directives falling within Article 137 EC as the appropriate legal basis.[145] In the preamble, one

---

[138] Directive 97/80 [1998] OJ L14/9.

[139] *Ibid*, Art 3(1).

[140] *Ibid*, Art 2.

[141] *Ibid*, Art 4.

[142] M Freedland, 'Constructing Fairness in Employment Contracts' (2007) 36 *Industrial Law Journal* 136.

[143] See COM(93) 545, 8 and the report of the expert 'Molitor' Group, COM(95) 288.

[144] See further, Weatherill (ed), above n 19.

[145] Specifically, Transfers of Undertakings Directive 2001/23, above n 71; Insolvency Protection Directive 80/987 [1980] OJ L283/23; Framework Safety and Health Directive 89/391, above n 72—extending to all subsidiary directives; Employee Information Directive 91/533 [1991] OJ L288/32; Pregnancy and Maternity Directive 92/85 [1992] OJ L348/1;

might expect to find references to the need to clarify and simplify the law, and to ensure transparency, coherence and consistency as to the scope of the listed directives. This proposal ought to only apply to the definitions of 'worker' or 'employee' contained in those directives and, in accordance with subsidiarity and proportionality, would not affect the definitions of those terms, or the establishment of a contract of employment, for the purposes of domestic labour or social security law. Additional sources might include the Social Charter, the Lisbon Strategy, the Integrated Guidelines, the Common Principles on Flexicurity, and ILO Recommendation No 198. Social inclusion would be its principal rationale, with emphasis on protecting vulnerable workers, equality of treatment under the law, and the need 'to achieve the required balance between flexibility and security'.[146] An additional clause might be included to stress that, for the purposes of equal treatment in respect of part-time, fixed-term and temporary work, all those falling within the unified definition of a 'worker' would be treated as having the same type of contract. This would overcome the problem created by the ruling in *Wippel*,[147] and complement the proposed directive on temporary agency work.[148]

Turning to the content of the definition, a starting point would be to look to *Lawrie-Blum*, where a 'worker' is defined as a person who 'for a certain period of time … performs services for and under the direction of another person in return for which he receives remuneration'.[149] This definition is relatively straightforward and would not be limited to workers with standard open-ended contracts. It might be suggested that it would be for the Court of Justice to ensure, through teleological interpretation, that casual workers and agency workers are included. However, the term 'under the direction of another person' is somewhat problematic as it may exclude more autonomous workers not under the day-to-day control of an employer, but also not independently self-employed. It might also be interpreted, narrowly, as requiring evidence of 'mutuality of obligation' between the contracting parties, although this was not regarded as a requirement in *Allonby*.[150] For this reason, a broader definition of a

Young Workers Directive 94/33, above n 72; Part-Time Work Directive 97/81, above n 74; Collective Redundancies Directive 98/59 [1998] OJ L225/16; Fixed-Term Work Directive 1999/70, above n 74; Working Time Directive 2003/88 [2003] OJ L299/9; and Framework Information and Consultation Directive 2002/14 [2000] OJ L80/29.

[146] See also recital 6 of Fixed-Term Work Directive 1999/70, above n 74. Similar language can be found in recitals 5, 6 and 12 of Part-Time Work Directive 97/81, above n 74.

[147] See n 90 above.

[148] See n 114 above.

[149] *Lawrie-Blum*, above n 79, para 17.

[150] See n 81 above, para 72.

worker, intended to include all those except genuine independent contractors, would be preferable. The UK's statutory definition would provide a
useful starting point:

> ... an individual who has entered into or works under ...
>
> (a) a contract of employment, or
>
> (b) any other contract, whether express or implied and (if it express) whether
> oral or in writing, whereby the individual undertakes to do or perform work
> personally any work or services for another party to the contract whose status is
> not by virtue of the contract that of a client or customer or any profession or
> business undertaking carried on by the individual ...[151]

Adoption of this provision, or a variation thereof, would have a number of
advantages. First, it is clearly designed to cover employees and workers
alike within a single definition of a dependent 'worker'. Secondly, if
interpreted broadly, it would include all casual workers, agency workers
and home workers on the basis that only independent contractors are
excluded from its scope. However, to avoid the risk of a narrow interpretation, these groups might be specified as included within the definition.
Thus, although a degree of economic dependency is required, it would not
be essential to show control or an obligation to accept offers of work,
contrary to the narrow interpretation placed on it by the UK courts.[152] It
may be necessary to specifically add a sentence stating that 'mutuality of
obligation' is not a pre-requisite of worker status. Alternatively, we might
substitute a different test, drawn from South African law, that a 'worker' is
a person who is 'economically dependent on the other person for whom
that person works or renders services'.[153]

Further clarification would also be needed on the issue of who is an
'employer' in order to fully protect, in respect of the coverage of EU labour
law, both agency workers in triangular relationships and workers involved
in extended chains of contracting where it is unclear who the principal
parties to the contract are. In the case of agency workers, their legal status
might be clarified by express incorporation of the definitional provisions of
the draft directive on temporary agency work, although placing responsibility wholly on the agency may not be an accurate reflection of the reality
of the employment relationship. An alternative would be to add a further
sentence stating that 'the person only works or renders services to one

---

[151] Employment Rights Act 1996, s 230(3).
[152] See part III.1 above.
[153] Labour Relations Act 1995 and Basic Conditions of Employment Act 1995, ss 83A
and 200A. For discussion, see the reply by Catherine Barnard to the Green Paper at
<http://www.ec.europa.eu/employment_social/labour_law/green_paper_responses_en.htm>
accessed 23 September 2008.

person'. Such a provision, also from South African law,[154] would guarantee that the employment relationship is treated as bilateral, but leave it to national courts to determine whether the agency or the end user is the other party. If this provision was included it would not be necessary to give a separate meaning to an 'employer', although this term is defined quite broadly in the Framework Safety and Health Directive.[155]

The problem of chains of sub-contracting, or vertical disintegration,[156] is identified as an issue in the Green Paper, which discusses the option of making principal contractors responsible for the obligations of their sub-contractors under a system of joint and several liability.[157] It is difficult to see how this complex problem can be satisfactorily addressed in what would need to be a straightforward directive on 'worker' status. Simply to determine that only one person is liable for each worker would not address the fundamental problem of comparability between different groups of workers working for different contractors, as highlighted in *Allonby*,[158] and would go beyond the bounds of EU labour law. It would require a separate measure to attempt to resolve this issue by determining exactly who is liable as the 'employer' in these situations. This would raise the most complex questions that extend well beyond the standard paradigm of bilateral relations between contracting parties.[159] Not surprisingly, the issue of regulating sub-contracting is highly divisive within the EU institutions and Member States, and arouses bitter opposition from employers concerned about 'restraints' that might obstruct free provision of services in the internal market.[160]

Even if each of these elements could be incorporated within a single definition of a 'worker' for EU labour law, it would be extremely difficult to reach political agreement in the present climate. Member States would need to be assured that such a proposal would not affect the fundamental status of the employment relationship under national law, and would not extend to areas such as wage-setting, collective bargaining and individual dismissal, except in cases involving a violation of a right contained in one of the directives. Moreover, by focusing on securing agreement on an inclusive conception of a 'worker' at EU level, the suggested directive would not address the binary divide between the dependent employee/

---

[154] *Ibid.*
[155] Directive 89/391, above n 72, Art 3(b): 'employer: any natural or legal person who has an employment relationship with the worker and has responsibility for the undertaking and/or establishment'.
[156] See Collins, above n 1.
[157] Green Paper, above n 4, 13.
[158] See n 104 above.
[159] For a stimulating discussion, see P Davies and M Freedland, 'The Complexities of the Employing Enterprise' in Davidov and Langille, above n 5, 273–93.
[160] Green Paper, above n 4, 13.

worker and the independent contractor, which is the basis for distinguishing labour law from commercial law. The strict legal dichotomy between
the employed and self-employed has been the subject of a powerful critique
by Mark Freedland,[161] who argues that the distinction is no longer
coherent because of the increasingly heterogeneous nature of work relationships. The introduction of the 'worker' concept, he suggests, has added
to this incoherence. Freedland proposes to end the binary divide and
replace it with a new concept of a 'personal employment contract' that
would also encompass independent or autonomous work relations.[162]
There is no question that labour law internationally is being reconceptual-
ised and Freedland's ideas have sparked a lively debate, but, for the time
being, the immediate task *at EU level* is to clarify the scope of existing
directives without traversing the known boundaries of labour law. Nevertheless, the launch of such a proposal, and its potential adoption, would
have a profound impact on the national debate about employment status
and, together with soft law, may act as a catalyst for change leading to a
broad convergence of the law and a possible end to employee/worker
distinction.[163]

3. Adopting a Framework Directive on the Existence of an Employment Relationship

As outlined above, pursuit of the second scenario would be the most direct
means to extend the scope of EU labour law, but it would not allow for
general harmonisation of national laws on the essential elements of an
employment relationship. The factors to be taken into account to determine the existence of a contract of employment vary between Member
States and reflect legal and cultural differences. Several Member States
have sought to broaden the coverage of labour law by introducing
indicators that, if present, lead automatically to the award, or presumption
of, 'employee' status and a full or partial package of employment rights.[164]
The adoption, in 2006, of ILO Recommendation No 198 concerning the
employment relationship, has provided an additional spur to action
because it addresses the difficulties of establishing whether or not an

---

[161] See especially, M Freedland, *The Personal Employment Contract* (Oxford, Oxford
University Press, 2003).
[162] For a concise analysis, see S Deakin, 'Does the "Personal Employment Contract"
Provide a Basis for the Reunification of Employment Law?' (2007) 36 *Industrial Law Journal*
68.
[163] For an alternative view, see Davidov, above n 56.
[164] For analysis, see E Marín, 'The Employment Relationship: The Issue at the International Level' in Davidov and Langille, above n 5, 339–54.

employment relationship exists, also based on indicators.[165] These developments tie in with the suggestions of the Expert Group on Flexicurity for an American-style 'tenure track' to provide a pathway into employment protection.[166]

The emergence of these ideas leads us to a third alternative scenario, which is more ambitious and yet fits with the current trend towards inclusion of those who have previously been in a precarious position, uncertain as to whether or not they have access to labour law. Under this scenario, the Commission would propose a general framework directive setting out common indicators to define the existence of an employment relationship. Choosing a framework directive offering a menu with a variety of choices, from which each Member State can select to suit their own palate, would be consistent with the general preference for broad measures that allow for flexibility of application and differentiated solutions to common problems. The social partners would have more incentive to negotiate a framework agreement around such proposals,[167] as a basis for a directive, if they were satisfied that the common framework that emerged would reflect the pluralistic nature of the employment relationship in the Member States.

One largely unheralded vehicle for such a framework measure might be the 1991 Employee Information (Contract or Employment Relationship) Directive.[168] It is far more straightforward to make a case to revise a directive as part of a technocratic process of review than to adopt a wholly new measure in the area of EU labour law. Any such review would need to refer to the original purpose of the Directive, which was to oblige an employer to issue every employee with a 'document constituting a form of *proof of the main terms of the employment relationship*'.[169] Based on a desire to end uncertainty in working relationships, the proposal has familiar echoes for those researching the origins of the flexicurity agenda. Under the proposal, the employer's document would provide detailed conditions and elements of the contract acting as declaratory written proof of a relationship already established under national law, even in the absence of a written contract.[170] The negotiated text was not as far-reaching. Crucially, it disaggregated the declaratory statement of the 'essential aspects of the contract or employment relationship', which was

---

[165]   See n 122 above, para 3 of the preamble.
[166]   See n 37 above.
[167]   Under the procedure in Arts 138–9 EC.
[168]   Directive 91/533 [1991] OJ L288/32. For analysis, see J Kenner, 'Statement or Contract?—Some Reflections on the EC Employee Information (Contract or Employment) Relationship Directive after *Kampelmann*' (1999) 28 *Industrial Law Journal* 205.
[169]   [1991] OJ C24/3, sixth recital of the draft preamble.
[170]   See the Explanatory Memorandum, COM(90) 563 Final, paras 11–12.

included,[171] from the element of 'proof of employment', which was discarded. Nevertheless, the Directive represented a small but important step towards transparency and added greater certainty as to the content of the employment relationship on the basis of a list of common features agreed at European level. Moreover, it created a presumption that casual workers or those with non-specific contracts would be included within its purview, which can only be rebutted by reference to 'objective considerations'.[172]

Any review of this Directive would be bound to take account not only of the flexicurity proposals for extending the scope of labour law, and the desire for enhanced transparency, but also of international guidance, such as ILO Recommendation No 198, which offers a framework upon which to base the core features of a suggested amended and renamed 'Framework Directive on the Existence of an Employment Relationship'.[173] It would contain additional provisions offering choices to Member States consistent with subsidiarity. This would provide a framework for economically dependent workers, complementary to scenario two above, to establish either immediately, or over time, the *existence of an employment relationship* upon which labour law rights would be attached. Provisions retained from the original directive would flesh out the detail of the *content of that employment relationship*.[174]

ILO Recommendation No 198 offers strategic guidance to national governments to ensure, through law and practice, that workers whose contractual position is uncertain are not deprived of the legal protection to which they are entitled.[175] It seeks to encourage transparency and effectiveness of laws concerning the existence of an employment relationship.[176] Member States are advised to make reference to a broad range of indicators to determine the existence of an employment relationship and to consider providing for 'a legal presumption that an employment relationship exists where one or more relevant indicators is present'.[177] These indicators are listed in point 13 and might include:

> (a) the fact that the work: is carried out according to the instructions and under the control of another party; involves the integration of the worker in the

---

[171] See n 168 above, Art 2.
[172] See n 168 above, Art 1(2)(b). Discussed by B Bercusson, *European Labour Law* (London, Butterworths, 1996) 432.
[173] The European Parliament has called for 'implementation' of the Recommendation. See European Parliament Report: A6–0247/2007 (25 June 2007). Green Paper follow-up: COM(2007) 627, 7. It is referenced by the Commission in a tucked away footnote in the Green Paper, above n 4, 11.
[174] See n 168 above, Art 2(2).
[175] See n 122 above, para 3 of the preamble.
[176] See n 122 above, point 4(a)–(g).
[177] See n 122 above, point 11(a)–(b).

organisation of the enterprise; is performed solely or mainly for the benefit of another person; must be carried out personally by the worker; is carried out within specific working hours or at a workplace specified or agreed by the party requesting the work; is of a particular duration and has a certain continuity; requires the worker's availability; or involves the provision of tools, materials and machinery by the party requesting the work;

(b) periodic payment of remuneration to the worker; the fact that such remuneration constitutes the worker's sole or principal source of income; provision of payment in kind, such as food, lodging or transport; recognition of entitlements such as weekly rest and annual holidays; payment by the party requesting the work for travel undertaken by the worker in order to carry out the work; or absence of financial risk for the worker.

The attraction of these indicators, as a basis for incorporation into the envisaged directive, lies with the fact that they are not prescriptive and allow for selection to fit national situations. Nonetheless, the indicators are targeted, by determining the existence of an employment relationship, at extending the scope of employment protection to all those in a position of economic subordination or dependency, regardless of the type of employment contract or the number of parties to it. It would also be possible to incorporate provisions from recent laws of Member States designed to extend protection to those in economically dependent relationships, notably Portugal, Italy and France.[178] Others, including Ireland, have developed indicators through a social partners' agreement. South Africa provides a model for indicators under national law that creates a presumption of a contract of employment.[179] Indicators can be designed specifically to identify the existence of a contract of employment for different groups of vulnerable workers. For example, they might include the presumption under the Dutch Flexibility and Security Act 1999, that a temporary employment agreement is an employment contract between the agency and the worker.[180]

Ultimately, the exact combination of indicators selected would be a matter of negotiation and there is always the possibility, nay likelihood, of a measure that is either too complex and/or insufficiently precise to bring about a significant increase in the numbers of workers protected under labour law. What such a directive would potentially offer, however, consistent with the flexicurity pathways, is a series of identifiable stepping

---

[178] In Portuguese labour legislation of 2004, this has been achieved through *contratos equiparardos*—that is treating contracts for the supply of services as comparable with formally subordinate employment contracts. Italian legislation of 2003 guarantees adequate employment protection for 'parasubordinates', autonomous workers without subordination. France assimilates economically dependent workers into a category of wage earners with entitlements to limited employment protection. See Marín, above n 166, 349.

[179] See Marín, above n 166, 346.

[180] See Wilthagen, Tros and van Lieshout, above n 3, table at figure 5. Both parties have some freedom in the first 26 weeks to enter or sever the employment relationship.

stones progressively building up to full employment protection under labour law along the lines of a 'tenure track'.[181]

IV. TOWARDS FLEX-SECURITY?

Labour law as a discipline has traditionally had, as its starting point, an asymmetrical relationship between two contracting parties in which the purpose of the law is to act as a corrective to the intrinsic problem of subordination. For the law to be effective as a regulator of the employment relationship, it has been necessary to mark out, as clearly as possible, a frontier between labour law and commercial law. Once the boundaries have been demarcated, entitlements are attached to essentially defensive, or 'protective', rights against unfair treatment in working life and arbitrary dismissal to those who fall within them. What this chapter has sought to demonstrate is that, paradoxically, those who are in the most unequal, complex and multifaceted relationships of work/wage dependency are often found at the borderline or outside the boundaries of labour law altogether, and yet they are increasing in number. It is therefore imperative that, if labour law is to remain true to its inherent purpose, it must occupy new, largely unmapped, territory in order to bring in those outsiders. The flexicurity dynamic, with its emphasis on finding pathways to inclusion, offers the EU an opportunity to act on this imperative.

Labour law is often portrayed, not only by its opponents, as rigid or 'overly strict'.[182] The examples discussed above, however, paint a quite different picture. What is remarkable is the sheer dexterity of labour law both in form and substance, not only at national level, as shown in the Dutch and Danish models, but also emanating from the EU, with its unique blend of soft law, social partner agreements, variants of harmonisation that allow Member States to maintain or introduce 'more stringent protective measures',[183] and framework directives that offer a range of solutions to be applied to suit diverse national systems. EU labour law has been a laboratory for conducting experiments to discover the most effective methods to supplement and complement national rules.[184]

---

[181] See COM(2007) 359, above n 7, 28.

[182] *Ibid*, 15.

[183] Art 137(4) EC.

[184] See Kenner, above n 19. Examples include the variety of methods open to Member States to 'prevent abuse arising from successive fixed-term employment contracts' under Clause 5 of the Fixed-Term Work Directive, above n 74, and the opportunities for variations to the calculation of working time and rest periods under the Working Time Directive, above n 72.

Each of the scenarios discussed in Part III offers a different approach to the problem of how best to broaden the scope of labour law in the EU. The purpose of presenting them, and playing them out somewhat speculatively, has been to identify how they might complement each other and assess their advantages and disadvantages as means of achieving this end. The first scenario, utilising the OMC, is already under way and will help to create a momentum to bring about changes, such as refashioning the contract of employment or reforming social security systems, which are beyond the competence of the EU. On its own, however, the OMC is not capable of achieving a common approach. Harmonising 'worker' status as the basis for extending the coverage and application of EU labour law directives, under the second scenario, would bring a degree of certainty to the law, providing there is consistent judicial interpretation, and ensure that most non-standard workers would have access to the substantive employment protection that EU law currently offers only to those with 'employee' or 'worker' status under national law. For this approach to be effective, it is essential that the definition of 'worker' is sufficiently wide and specific to include both those who would have difficulty showing 'mutuality of obligation' and also those who have more than one possible employer. Such an extension of protection would provide for equality of treatment, but it would not directly determine the existence of an employment relationship, the most essential element for employment protection. The third scenario, perhaps the one that would be the most difficult to achieve politically, would potentially be the most effective because it would address this fundamental issue by requiring Member States to apply specific indicators of an employment relationship that are best suited to their own system. This would allow for a legal presumption of an employment relationship to be established as a basis upon which to attach the right to employment protection under national law.

Extending the scope of labour law in the EU begs the question of what should be the reasonable expectation of protection for all those workers within its ambit? The 'tenure track' idea would be a positive step so long as it leads, within a reasonable period of time, to equality of treatment. There will, of course, continue to be significant variations in the protection offered under national labour laws, and no single 'European Social Model', but increasing the number of people who are protected under employment relationships does not provide a rationale for diluting core rights that remain essential as a corrective against inequality in the employment relationship. These include the right to, inter alia, a minimum wage, safe working conditions, paid holidays, non-discrimination, join a union and take collective action, and protection against arbitrary dismissal. Access to such core rights, and their retention, would correct the present imbalance between flexibility and security. Such a development—I will call it 'flex-security'—would be based on a conception of flexicurity that, contrary to the thrust of the Commission documents, recognises that widening the scope of labour law is a *sine qua non* and not a basis for trade offs that would undermine its inherent purpose.

13

Fifty Years of Avoiding Social Dumping? The EU's Economic and Not So Economic Constitution

CATHERINE BARNARD*

I. INTRODUCTION

SOCIAL DUMPING HAS been an issue for the EU since its inception.[1] It troubled Spaak, it has troubled the International Labour Organisation (ILO) and it has troubled the World Bank. Most of all, it has troubled trade unions and their members who see their jobs going east, to the near East (the Central and Eastern European countries (CEECs)) and to the far East. They blame forces of globalisation generally and, in the EU, the effects of market integration in particular for the decline in national industry. As soon as there is a sign of capital flight, they cry 'social dumping'.[2]

There is, of course, another side to this story: what is social dumping to the losers (richer Northern European states) is economic opportunity to the winners (poorer Eastern European states) who take advantage of their lower labour costs to gain a foothold on these new markets. Ultimately, this will lead to greater prosperity in these states, one of the objectives of the European Union ('the raising of the standard of living and quality of life'[3]). However, if richer states feel genuinely threatened by the challenge

---

* I am grateful for comments from Professor Rosa Greaves, the participants at the conference in Liverpool celebrating 50 years of the Treaty of Rome in July 2007 and the delegates at the Fordham conference, New York in February 2008 where I also presented a version of this chapter.

[1] A Guillén and S Alavarez, 'Southern European welfare states facing globalization: Is there social dumping?', paper presented to the Year 2000 International Research Conference on Social Security, Helsinki (25–7 September 2000).

[2] 'The idea that you replace an employee with a cheaper one coming from somewhere else'—per Mr Zitting, chairman of the FSU quoted by Gloster J in the High Court in *Viking* [2005] EWHC 1222, para 119.

[3] Art 2 EC.

posed by Eastern European states, they might decide to reduce labour standards in order to compete. If the Eastern European states respond, in turn, by cutting their labour standards, a race to the bottom may occur in which standards of living for all are lowered, not raised. This is not part of the EU's objectives.

The aim of this chapter is to examine the social dumping debate and the effect it has had on legislative and judicial policy in the EU (section III). It will argue that, despite the lack of concrete evidence that much actual social dumping is taking place within the EU, even since the 2004 enlargement, the *perception* has firmly taken hold that social dumping is occurring and that 'something must be done' to stop it. This perception has been used by various actors to argue for their particular agenda (section IV). In particular, we shall examine how the perception has shaped the debate surrounding four Directives, two originally intended to avoid social dumping, two seen as promoting social dumping. We shall also see how the Court's interpretation of the Treaty provision on the free movement of services has affected the original purposes of one of these measures, the Services Directive. The chapter concludes with an examination of an alternative method and rationale for social legislation (section V). First, however, we shall examine why the conditions for social dumping might arise.

II. THE CONDITIONS FOR SOCIAL DUMPING

A. Promoting Free Movement

The original EEC Treaty had as its task the establishment of a common market and the progressive approximation of the economic policies of the Member States.[4] According to the Spaak report, the creation of a single market '*permet, par la division accrue du travail, d'eliminer un gaspillage des ressources, et, par une sécurité accrue d'approvisionnement, de renoncer à des productions poursuivies sans consideration de coût*'.[5] Later, the Spaak report talks of the fusion of the markets leading to '*la repartition la plus rationelle des activités, au relèvement general du niveau de vie et à un rythme plus actif d'expansion*'.[6] Thus, the Treaty provisions on the four freedoms (goods, persons, services and capital), as well as the rules on competition law, were intended to open up the national markets to competition from elsewhere in the EU. They also permitted resources to move to the area where they could be most efficiently used: as Spaak put it,

---

[4]   Art 2 EEC.
[5]   Report of the Heads of Delegation to the Ministers of Foreign Affairs (Spaak Report), Brussels, 21 April 1956, 13.
[6]   *Ibid*, 53.

the free movement provisions should allow industries needing a lot of labour to locate to areas where labour is plentiful, those industries relying on heavy materials to locate near places where those materials are produced or delivered and those industries requiring heavy investment to locate in countries where capital is freely available and financial charges are lowest.[7] This virtuous circle should lead to salary levels and interest rates being equalised when the demand for labour or capital increases.[8] These ideas lie at the heart of the EU's *economic* constitution: the Treaty protects the economic freedoms (freedom of movement) in the same way as civil and political rights are traditionally protected in national constitutions.[9]

Of course, the aims of the EC Treaty are more complex than this, but the need to ensure the effectiveness of the four freedoms has been one of the driving forces behind the jurisprudence of the European Court of Justice. This has been demonstrated, in particular, in its use of the market access test (also known as the 'restrictions' or 'obstacles' approach) first signalled in *Säger*.[10] In the context of services, the Court said that Article 49 EC required:

> ... *not only* the elimination of all discrimination against a person providing services on the ground of his nationality *but also* the abolition of any restriction, even if it applies without distinction to national providers of services and to those of other Member States, when *it is liable to prohibit or otherwise impede* the activities of a provider of services established in another Member State where he lawfully provides similar services.[11]

The Court continued that any such restriction could be justified by imperative reasons relating to the public interest provided the steps taken are proportionate.[12] As we shall see in the next section, this test, while controversial, has proved an effective tool to cut through swathes of national rules which impede the creation of a single market.

---

[7] *Ibid*, 61.

[8] *Ibid*.

[9] D Gerber, 'Constitutionalizing the Economy: German Neo-Liberalism, Competition law and the "New Europe"' (1994) 42 *American Journal of Comparative Law* 25, 45–6; and M Streit and W Mussler, 'The Economic Constitution of the European Community—From "Rome" to "Maastricht"' (1995) 1 *ELJ* 5.

[10] Case C-76/90, [1991] ECR I-4221, para 12, emphasis added.

[11] Case C-19/92, *Kraus* [1993] ECR I-1663, para 32: '*liable to hamper or to render less attractive* the exercise by Community nationals, including those of the Member State which enacted the measure, of *fundamental freedoms* guaranteed by the Treaty'.

[12] Case C-76/90, [1991] ECR I-4221, para 15.

B. The 'Risks' of Free Movement: The Social Dumping Thesis

The ideal world envisaged by Spaak would come to pass only in situations of perfect competition. The real world is rather different. There has long been a fear, which Spaak also recognised, that capital may well be attracted to particular locations, not because of the abundance of the location's workforce or capital, but for other, less worthy reasons such as a more favourable social security regime for employers (ie the indirect costs are lower) and cheaper wage costs. Spaak tried to stamp on these 'malentendus'. For example, his report says that differences in social security burdens or public expenditure do not, by themselves, distort conditions of competition, being compensated for, in particular, by the rate of exchange.[13] Furthermore, differences in salary levels also do not need to be harmonised because they reflect differences in productivity.

Nevertheless, Spaak did list certain factors which could lead to distortions of competition, including direct and indirect taxation, some regimes for financing social security, some regulation of prices and different policies concerning credit. In the context of labour issues, Spaak noted that different pay for men and women and the rules regulating working time, overtime and paid holiday[14] might prompt companies to move to another Member State not because the production environment was better, but because, for example, women were being paid less than men and this difference in pay had nothing to do with productivity. This migration is often referred to (although not by Spaak) as *social dumping*. The social dumping thesis becomes possible because of the division of competence between EC and national law. While the free movement rules are set at the EC level and so benefit from the doctrine of primacy of EC law over national law, national social policy and employment law remain (and, by and large, continue to remain) regulated at national level.

Two central tenets of the Court of Justice's jurisprudence have served to reinforce fears about social dumping: mutual recognition and market access. In respect of mutual recognition, the fears about social dumping have taken two forms. First, there was a concern that countries with lower labour standards would be able to produce goods more cheaply and, benefiting from the principle of mutual recognition, these goods could be sold in other Member States at a cheaper price. This concern was exacerbated by the fact that companies in the 'higher standard' states might take advantage of their free movement rights in order to establish themselves in the 'lower standard' countries and also take advantage of mutual recognition. While goods were the early concern, similar issues

---

[13] Spaak, above n 5, 60.
[14] *Ibid*, 62–3.

arose in respect of the free movement of services: service providers (such as the infamous Polish plumber) could take advantage of the lower standards in the home state to provide cheaper services in the host state. What goods and services have in common is that they are essentially covered by the country of origin principle—or home state control.

The other principle which has raised fears about social dumping is the widespread use of the market access test by the Court of Justice to strike down host state social legislation. In the days when the non-discrimination model applied, national social legislation was immune from challenge by Community law, so long as it did not discriminate against migrants either directly or indirectly. Those days are now gone and national social legislation is subject to review under the market access test, as the high profile decisions in *Viking* and *Laval* show.[15] *Viking* concerned a Finnish company wanting to reflag its vessel, the Rosella, under the Estonian flag so that Viking could man the ship with an Estonian crew to be paid considerably less than the existing Finnish crew. The International Transport Workers' Federation (ITF) told its affiliates to boycott the Rosella and take other solidarity industrial action. Viking therefore sought an injunction in the English High Court, restraining the ITF and the Finnish Seaman's Union (FSU), now threatening strike action, from breaching Article 43 EC on freedom of establishment.

Laval concerned a Latvian company which won a contract to refurbish a school in Sweden using its own Latvian workers who earned about 40 per cent less than comparable Swedish workers. The Swedish construction union wanted Laval to apply the Swedish collective agreement, but Laval refused, in part because the collective agreement was unclear as to how much Laval would have to pay its workers, and in part because it imposed various supplementary obligations on Laval, such as paying a 'special building supplement' to an insurance company to finance group life insurance contracts. There followed a union picket at the school site, a blockade by construction workers, and sympathy industrial action by the electricians unions. Although this industrial action was permissible under Swedish law, Laval brought proceedings in the Swedish labour court, claiming that this action was contrary to *Community* law (in particular Article 49 EC on freedom to provide services).

Using the market access approach, the Court said that the collective action in both cases constituted a 'restriction' on free movement and so breached Articles 43 and 49 EC, even though it had recognised earlier in the judgment that the right to strike was a fundamental right which formed

---

[15] Case C-438/05, *Viking Line ABP v The International Tansport Workers' Federation, the Finnish Seaman's Union*, not yet reported; and Case C-341/05, *Laval un Partneri Ltd v Svenska Byggnadsarbetareförbundet*, not yet reported.

an integral part of the general principles of Community law.[16] On justification, the Court noted in *Viking* that the right to take collective action for the protection of workers was an overriding reason of public interest provided that jobs or conditions of employment were jeopardised or under serious threat. On the facts, the Court suggested this was unlikely because Viking had given an undertaking that no Finnish workers would be made redundant. If the trade unions could justify the collective action, the Court suggested that it would be proportionate only if it was taken as a last resort. In *Laval*, the Court also recognised that the right to take collective action for the protection of Swedish workers 'against possible social dumping' was a justification, but found on the facts that using collective action to force Laval to sign a collective agreement, whose content on central matters such as pay was unclear, could not be justified.

The unions greeted these rulings with dismay.[17] Addressing the European Parliament in February 2008, John Monks, General Secretary of the European Trade Union Confederation (ETUC), said:

> So we are told that the right to strike is a fundamental right but not so fundamental as the EU's free movement provisions. This is a licence for social dumping and for unions being prevented from taking action to improve matters. Any company in a transnational dispute has the opportunity to use this judgment against union actions, alleging disproportionality.

The ETUC has therefore called for the adoption of a social progress clause which would say that '[n]othing in the Treaty, and in particular neither fundamental freedoms nor competition rules shall have priority over fundamental social rights and social progress'. It adds: 'In case of conflict, fundamental social rights shall take precedence.'[18]

Similar concerns about social dumping prompted the inclusion of Article 119 EEC (now Article 141 EC) on equal pay for men and women, Article 120 EEC (now Article 142 EC) on paid holiday schemes and the third protocol on 'Certain Provisions Relating to France' on working hours and overtime[19] in the original EEC Treaty 50 years ago. In particular, these provisions were designed to protect French industry from attempts by Italy,

---

[16] *Viking*, para 44; and *Laval*, para 91. For criticism of the restrictions approach, see S Deakin, 'Regulatory Competition after *Laval*' (2007–8) 10 *CYELS* forthcoming.

[17] See, eg 'Dumping social: les syndicates européens "déçus" par la Cour de Justice', lemonde.fr (8 December 2007).

[18] ETUC's Resolution adopted on 4 March 2008: <http://www.etuc.org/IMG/pdf_ETUC_Viking_Laval_-_resolution_070308.pdf> accessed 23 September 2008.

[19] This provided that the Commission was to authorise France to take protective measures where the establishment of the Common Market did not result, by the end of the first stage, in the basic number of hours beyond which overtime was paid and the average rate of additional payment for overtime industry corresponding to the average obtaining in France in 1956. It does not seem that France has called upon this safeguard clause: M Budiner, *Le Droit de la femme l'Égalité de salaire et la Convention No. 100 de l'organisation internationale du travail* (Librairie Générale de Droit et de Jurisprudence, Paris, 1975).

which did not respect such standards, to attract French business.[20] The essentially protectionist function of these provisions was recognised by Advocate General Dutheillet de Lamothe in *Defrenne (No 1)*.[21] He said that although Article 141 EC had a social objective, it also had an economic objective,

> ... for in creating an obstacle to any attempt at 'social dumping' by means of the use of female labour less well paid than male labour, it helped to achieve one of the fundamental objectives of the common market, the establishment of a system ensuring that competition is not distorted.

He continued: 'This explains why Article [141] of the Treaty is of a different character from the articles which precede it in the chapter of the Treaty devoted to social provisions.'

The Court echoed these sentiments in its landmark judgment in *Defrenne (No 2)*,[22] where it famously said that the aim of Article 141 EC was to avoid a situation in which undertakings established in states which had actually implemented the principle of equal pay suffered a competitive disadvantage in intra-Community competition as compared with undertakings established in states which had not yet eliminated discrimination against women workers as regards pay. However, having recognised the economic purpose of Article 141 EC, the Court then blurred the economic focus of the provision when it said that Article 141 EC also formed part of the social objectives of the Community. This was the first time that the Court sought to find a balance between the economic and social dimension of the EU.

III. THE REALITY OF SOCIAL DUMPING

Despite John Monks' remarks, there is still remarkably little empirical evidence on the question of whether social dumping is a myth or reality.[23]

---

[20] According to (French) AG Dutheillet de Lamothe in Case 80/70, *Defrenne (No 1) v SABENA* [1971] ECR 445, 'It appears to be France which took the initiative, but the article [119] necessitated quite long negotiations'. However, the content of Art 119 EEC was strongly influenced by ILO Convention No 100 on equal pay. See C Hoskyns, *Integrating Gender* (Verso, London, 1996); and A Arnull, *The European Union and its Court of Justice* (Oxford, Oxford University Press, 2006), 534–40.

[21] Case 80/70, [1971] ECR 445. In Case 69/80, *Worringham and Humphreys v Lloyd's Bank* [1981] ECR 767, AG Warner again referred back to AG Dutheillet de Lamothe's statement in *Defrenne (No 1)* that the first purpose of Art 119 EEC was to 'avoid a situation in which undertakings established in Member States with advanced legislation on the equal treatment of men and women suffer a competitive disadvantage as compared with undertakings established in Member States that have not eliminated discrimination against female workers as regards pay'.

[22] Case 43/75, [1976] ECR 455. This was emphasised in Case C-50/96, *Deutsche Telekom v Schröder* [2000] ECR I-743, paras 53–5.

[23] This is discussed further in C Barnard, 'Social Dumping Revisited: Lessons from Delaware' (2000) 25 *EL Rev* 57.

Some of the most recent research has been carried out by Roberto Pedersini for the European Foundation for the Improvement of Living and Working Conditions.[24] His research comes with a number of caveats about the problems with the evidence on which his findings are drawn. Nevertheless, some of his conclusions suggest that the trade unions' fears may be well founded. For example, he says that Foreign Direct Investment (FDI) data seem to indicate that economic actors are increasingly interested in establishing control over foreign firms located in developing, formerly peripheral economies. This relates especially to locations in CEECs and China. Such investment flows are very likely to include transfers of production capacity to these areas. Furthermore, he says that survey results show a high interest in, and attention to, relocation of production among the business community. Relocation is mentioned as a concrete option, either realised or envisaged in the near future, by a significant and seemingly increasing number of firms.

On the other hand, Pedersini also points to the European Restructuring Monitor (ERM[25]), which suggests that cases of relocation still form a relatively small proportion of all restructuring cases (see Table 1 below).

Table 1: Cases of restructuring reported by ERM, by type, 2002–5

Type of restructuring	Redundancies (no)	%	Cases (no)	%
Internal restructuring	1,191,215	74.95	1,665	46.25
Bankruptcy/closure	215,203	13.54	659	18.31
Offshoring/delocalisation*	**72,635**	**4.57**	**208**	**5.78**
Merger/acquisition	58,833	3.70	125	3.47
Relocation*	22,052	1.39	71	1.97
Outsourcing	19,890	1.25	22	0.61
Other	8,577	0.54	17	0.47
Business expansion	950	0.06	833	23.14
Total	**1,589,355**	**100**	**3,600**	**100**

* According to ERM definitions, 'relocation' refers to transfers within national boundaries, while 'offshoring' covers transfers abroad.

Source: ERM (31 December 2005). Taken from Table 2 (Pederisini), emphasis added.

[24] 'Relocation of Production and Industrial Relations' (6 February 2006), available at <http://www.eurofound.europa.eu/eiro/2005/11/study/tn0511101s.htm> accessed 23 September 2008.

[25] European Restructuring Monitor run by the European Monitoring Centre on Change (EMCC).

The ERM data therefore suggests that offshoring/delocalisation accounts for only about 5 per cent of all redundancies.

This view is supported by the Commission in its publication 'Enlargement, two years after: an economic evaluation'.[26] Under the heading 'Fears of relocation not justified', it notes that the evidence indicates that FDI flows to the new Member States, while relevant for the recipient countries, have in fact been only a minor part of overall FDI outflows of the EU-15: within the latter, in 2004 the share of outflows to new Member States was 4 per cent against a corresponding share of 53 per cent for outflows to other Member States in the EU-15 and a 12 per cent share for flows to the US. It also says that a large part of the FDI by the EU-15 in the new Member States, particularly in the services sector where most of FDI is invested, has occurred in the context of privatisation programmes to capture fast-growing markets and does not involve the substitution of activities previously carried out in the home country. The Commission continues that different studies have tried to identify the impact of relocation on employment. It says that recent research for some EU-15 countries suggests that a 'mere 1–1.5% of the annual job turnover can be attributed to relocation, and that only a part concerns relocation to the new Member States'. Moreover, in many instances, outsourcing part of the production process to the new Member States has allowed firms in EU-15 to strengthen their competitive position with a net favourable impact on employment.

The Commission continues that, in the relocation debate, the argument has been advanced that relocation may be driven by differences in corporate tax rates between Member States. However, it says that international investment appears driven mainly by other factors, such as unit labour costs or agglomeration economies (geographical location advantages, market size, external economies, the general business environment, human capital) leading to spatial concentration. Elsewhere, the Commission has noted that:

> Studies confirm that relocation of companies from the old to the new Member States remains a marginal phenomenon. Moreover, Central and Eastern Europe is not the main destination for relocation, but rather Asia; it is not enlargement that mainly causes outsourcing and relocation but global competition.[27]

The Commission's conclusion is supported by earlier studies. For example, the OECD found that despite pressures on labour standards 'there is no compelling evidence that "social dumping" has occurred so far in OECD

---

[26] <http://ec.europa.eu/economy_finance/publications/publication7548_en.pdf> accessed 23 September 2008.

[27] Commission, 'Myths and facts about Enlargement', available at < http://ec.europa.eu/enlargement/questions_and_answers/myths_en.htm>, accessed 25 October 2008.

countries'.[28] Similarly, Schonfield's unpublished study on pay and collective bargaining for the Commission as part of its evaluation of the impact of the Single Market concludes '[t]he dangers of "social dumping" have been exaggerated with only isolated examples of competitive undercutting of pay and conditions by firms exploiting labour cost differences between countries'.[29] He did, however, add that there was evidence from Germany that companies were increasingly using the possibility of relocation as a bargaining counter to achieve changes in working practices at home.[30]

This opportunistic use of the threat of social dumping is not confined to employers. As we shall see in the next section, the Commission has not been averse to using the social dumping discourse to help legitimise its own legislative activity.

IV. THE LEGISLATIVE/EXECUTIVE RESPONSE TO 'SOCIAL DUMPING'

A. Introduction

In its influential White Paper on Social Policy of 1994,[31] the Commission said that 'the establishment of a framework of basic minimum standards, which the Commission started some years ago, provides a bulwark against using low social standards as an instrument of unfair economic competition and protection against reducing social standards to gain competitiveness'.[32] In other words, Community social legislation is necessary to stop social dumping, a view the Commission had expressed in the earlier Green Paper on European Social Policy, where it said 'a "negative" competitiveness between Member States would lead to social dumping, to the undermining of the consensus making process . . . and to danger for the acceptability of the Union'.[33] Indeed, the Commission is reported to have proposed extending the rules on worker consultation because 'there have been suspicions that different labour standards caused "social dumping"—

---

[28] OECD, 'Labour Standards and Economic Integration' in *Employment Outlook 1994* (OECD, 1994) 138.

[29] Reported by A Taylor, 'Wage Bargaining diversification under EU Single Market', *Financial Times* (7 April 1997).

[30] See, eg 'Siemens deal launches debate on longer working hours', available at <http://www.eurofound.europa.eu/eiro/2004/07/feature/de0407106f.htm> accessed 23 September 2008.

[31] COM(94) 333.

[32] *Ibid*, Introduction, para 19. See also Chapter III, para 1.

[33] COM(93) 551, 46. See also AG Jacobs' observations in Case C-67/96, *Albany International BV v Stichting Bedrijfspensioenfonds Textielindustrie* [1999] ECR I-5751, para 178, where he said that the 'main purpose of trade unions and of the collective bargaining process is precisely to prevent employees from engaging in a "race to the bottom" with regard to wages and working conditions'.

where some countries with lower standards can give companies a competitive edge—and there was a need for common rules'.[34]

These views are not confined to the Commission. In its Resolution on certain aspects for a European Union social policy,[35] the Council notes that 'Minimum standards ... meet the expectations of workers in the European Union and calm fears about social dismantling and social dumping in the Union'.[36] Even the Court, in *Commission v UK*,[37] recognised that the enactment of the Directives on Collective Redundancies and Acquired Rights[38] was justified by the need to ensure comparable protection for workers' rights in the different Member States and to harmonise the costs which such protective rules entail for Community undertakings.[39]

In the next section of the chapter, I will consider how the social dumping debate has shaped the legislative agenda. I am going to consider two Directives—the Posted Workers Directive and the Ferries Directive—which were intended to put a stop to fears about social dumping. I will then consider two further Directives—the Port Services Directive and the Services Directive—which have precipitated concerns about social dumping. I will also consider the impact of the Court's interpretation of Article 49 EC which may affect the understanding and purpose of these various Directives.

B. The 'Social Dumping' Avoidance Directives?

In this section I consider two Directives which have as their aim the need to combat social dumping. However, to understand the significance of the Directives we need to consider the Treaty environment against which they were adopted.

---

[34] C Southey, 'EU looks to extend laws on worker consultation', *Financial Times* (23 September 1996).

[35] Council Resolution of 6 December 1994 on certain aspects for a European Union social policy: a contribution to economic and social convergence in the Union [1994] OJ C368/4, para 10.

[36] See also the Resolution on the Commission's Communication on the impact of the third package of air transport liberalisation measures (Bull. EU 1/2–1998, para 1.3.188), where the Parliament expressed concern about the implications of relocation which 'leads to social dumping to the detriment of European employees'..

[37] Case C-382/92, *Commission v UK* [1994] ECR I-2435; and Case C-383/92, *Commission v UK* [1994] ECR I-2479.

[38] Directive 75/129 [1975] OJ L48/29 and Directive 77/187 [1977] OJ L61/27 (respectively, as they then were).

[39] Para 15.

1. The Posted Workers Directive

As we have seen, the wide market access approach to Article 49 EC, read in conjunction with the country of origin principle, created fears in Northern European states about social dumping. The facts of *Rush Portuguesa*[40] demonstrated the problem. A Portuguese company entered into a subcontract with a French company to carry out rail construction work in France. The Portuguese company used its own third-country national workforce to do the work,[41] thereby contravening French rules which provided that only the French *Office d'Immigration* could recruit non-Community workers. The Court ruled that Articles 49 and 50 EC:

> ... preclude a Member State from prohibiting a person providing services established in another Member State from moving freely on its territory *with all his staff* and preclude that Member State from making the movement of staff in question subject to restrictions such as a condition as to engagement *in situ* or an obligation to obtain a work permit.[42]

The Court said that the imposition of such conditions discriminated against guest service providers in relation to their competitors established in the host country who were able to use their own staff without restrictions. In *Vander Elst*,[43] the Court went one stage further: it confirmed that Articles 49 and 50 EC precluded the host state (France) from obliging guest service providers which lawfully and habitually employed nationals of non-Member States (in this case Moroccan workers legally resident in Belgium, holding Belgian work permits, covered by the Belgian social security scheme and paid in Belgium) to obtain and pay for work permits for those workers.[44]

In these cases, the Court appeared to be taking an important step towards opening up the market in services and allowing companies from countries with cheaper labour costs, primarily the southern and eastern European states, to profit from their comparative advantage to win contracts in other states (primarily the northern states with higher labour costs). The reason why they could afford to win contracts is that, under the Rome Convention (and soon under the Rome I Regulation), the conditions

---

[40]   Case C-113/89, *Rush Portuguesa v Office national d'immigration* [1990] ECR I-1417.

[41]   The workforce was actually Portuguese, but at the time the transitional arrangements for Portuguese accession to the EC were in place, which meant that the rules on freedom to provide services were in force but not those relating to the free movement of workers. Therefore, Portuguese workers did not enjoy the rights of free movement and so for our purposes the Portuguese workers constitute third-country nationals (see para 4 of the judgment).

[42]   Para 12 (emphasis added).

[43]   Case C-43/93, *Vander Elst v Office des Migrations Internationales* [1994] ECR I-3803.

[44]   However, the Court did accept that the host state was entitled to insist on TCNs having a short-stay visa permitting them to remain in France for as long as necessary to carry out the work (para 19), a so-called '*Vander Elst* visa' which was subsequently adopted by Germany.

of employment of temporary staff are usually governed by the labour law rules applicable in the country where the company is established and where the individual habitually carries out his or her work.

Germany and France were particularly concerned about the threat posed by the Treaty provision on services to their respective labour law systems.[45] In response, the Court added in *Rush Portuguesa* that:

> Community law does not preclude Member States from extending their legislation, or collective labour agreements entered into by both sides of industry, to any person who is employed, even temporarily, within their territory, no matter in which country the employer is established; nor does Community law prohibit Member States from enforcing those rules by appropriate means.[46]

Thus, in one (unreasoned) paragraph, the Court put a stop to a threat of social dumping[47]—without using this language—by allowing the host state to extend its labour laws and conditions to the staff employed by service providers working in its country apparently contrary to the Rome Convention.

In reaching this conclusion, the Court incidentally gave the green light to the enactment of the Directive 96/71 on Posted Workers.[48] As Vladimir Špidla, former EU Employment, Social Affairs and Equal Opportunities Commissioner bluntly put it, this Directive is a 'key instrument both to ensure freedom to provide services and to prevent social dumping'.[49] It aims to coordinate (not harmonise) the legislation in the Member States,

---

[45] See, eg the German response to threats of social dumping. Germany enacted the Arbeitnehmer-Entsendungsgestez (AEntG), which was approved by Parliament on 26 February 1996 (See May 1996 *EIRR* 268, 15). The legislation stipulates that all employers based outside the country and sending one or more employees to work in Germany must abide by provisions laid out in the relevant collective agreement, relating to minimum pay and certain conditions of employment, such as minimum holiday pay. These employers must also make payments into the relevant social security funds unless they are already paying into social security funds in their own country or have already done so. Employers with headquarters outside Germany but which are sending employees to work in the country must register in writing with the relevant local authorities in Germany before work commences. Employers must supply the name of the employee concerned, the commencement and expected duration of the employment and the location of the site where the work is to be carried out. These provisions are valid from the first day of employment in Germany. Employers who contravene this legislation are liable to fines of up to 100,000 DM (£43,800). The Ministry of Labour and customs offices are to be responsible for ensuring that employers comply with this law. As EIRR points out, this legislation puts Germany on a par with other EU countries, most notably France, which has national legislation on minimum pay and conditions for posted workers. In answer to written question E-2507/97, the Commission said that the German law was in accordance with Community law, provided that the checks carried out to ensure the compliance with the minimum wage were not discriminatory or disproportionate.

[46] Citing Joined Cases 62 & 63/81, *Seco SA* [1982] ECR 223.

[47] This was the overriding public interest subsequently offered by the Court to explain *Rush Portuguesa* in Case C-244/04, *Commission v Germany* [2006] ECR I-885, para 61.

[48] Directive 96/71 [1996] OJ L18/1. See P Davies, 'Posted Workers: Single Market or Protection of National Labour Law Systems' (1997) 34 *CML Rev* 571.

[49] IP/06/423.

laying down a 'nucleus of mandatory rules'[50] in Article 3(1) which the host state must apply to posted workers working in their territory. These include rules on working time, health and safety, equality and, most importantly for our purposes, pay, but only minimum rates of pay,[51] which *must* be respected by undertakings assigning their employees to work in another Member State.[52] In this way, the Directive goes further than *Rush Portuguesa*, which merely *permitted* Member States to extend certain rules to employees posted to their territory and did not specify which rules could be extended. It also reverses the rule in the Rome Convention that the home state rules should apply, with the result that workers employed by the out of state service provider will enjoy the same standards as national workers in respect of those matters listed in Article 3(1). In this way, the Directive appears to undermine the out-of-state service provider's competitive advantage by forcing it to comply with the employment laws of the host state in order to create a 'climate of fair competition'.[53]

However, the Court in *Laval* and subsequently in *Rüffert*[54] gave a strict reading to the Directive. One of the issues in *Laval* was that the Latvian company had to sign up to the 'special building supplement' and the other insurance premiums contained in the Swedish national collective agreement. These matters were not coordinated by the Directive and so the Court ruled that the Directive did not apply. Nevertheless, Sweden and the defendant trade unions pointed to Article 3(10) of the Directive, under which Member States can apply terms and conditions of employment on matters other than those referred to in Article 3(1) in the case of so-called 'public policy provisions'. However, said the Court, Member States had to positively opt to rely on Article 3(10), which Sweden had not done. And since trade unions were not a public body, they could not rely on Article 3(10) either.[55]

---

[50] 13th Recital of the Directive.

[51] *Laval*, para 70.

[52] Art 1(3) provides that the posting of workers can take one of three forms: first, posting under a contract concluded between the undertaking making the posting and the party for whom the services are intended (this was the situation in *Rush Portuguesa*); secondly, posting to an establishment or an undertaking owned by the group (this category, referred to as intra-firm or intra-group mobility, has been included to prevent an undertaking from opening a subsidiary in another Member State purely to place some of its workers there to carry out temporary assignments, and thereby to avoid the scope of the Directive); thirdly, posting by a temporary employment or placement agency (temp agency) to a user undertaking established or operating in the territory of another Member State, provided there is an employment relationship between the temp agency and the worker during the period of posting.

[53] Fifth Recital to the Directive.

[54] Case C-349/06, *Dirk Rüffert v Land Niedersachsen*, not yet reported. See also Case C-319/06, *Commission v Luxembourg*, not yet reported.

[55] Paras 83–4. See also Case C-319/06, *Commission v Luxembourg*, not yet reported, para 50, where the Court gave an extremely strict reading of the phrase public policy.

Article 3(7) of the Directive appears to contain a minimum standards clause,[56] suggesting that host states can apply terms and conditions which are more favourable to workers.[57] However, the Court in *Laval* came close to making Article 3(1) not a floor but a ceiling when it said that host states 'cannot make the provision of services in its territory conditional on the observance of terms and conditions of employment which go beyond the mandatory rules [in Article 3(1)] for minimum protection'.[58] So, once again, the Swedish trade unions could not rely on Article 3(7).

The matters listed in Article 3(1) must be laid down by (i) *law*, regulation or administrative provision; and/or (ii) in respect of activities referred to in the Annex (ie all building work relating to the construction, repair, upkeep, alteration or demolition of buildings), *collective agreements* or arbitration awards which have been declared universally applicable within the meaning of Article 3(8). If the national rules are not laid down in one of these ways, they cannot be applied to the posted workers.

Since there is no *law* on the minimum wage[59] in either Sweden or Germany, the Court in *Laval* and *Rüffert* focused on Article 3(8) dealing with collective agreements. Article 3(8) has two limbs. The first limb deals with those systems which have a doctrine of extension (also known as the *erga omnes* effect) of collective agreements. It says that collective agreements or arbitration awards which have been declared universally applicable are those which must be observed by all undertakings in the geographical area and in the profession or industry concerned. This limb of the definition was at issue in *Rüffert*. Germany has a system for declaring collective agreements universally applicable. However, on the facts, the collective agreement setting pay in the building industry had not been declared universally applicable,[60] and so the collectively agreed rules on pay rates could not be applied to the posted workers,[61] no matter that the German state law on the award of public contracts required contractors and their subcontractors to pay posted workers at least the remuneration prescribed by the collective agreement in force at the place where those services were performed.

The second limb of Article 3(8) deals with those industrial relations systems which do not have a procedure for extending collective agreements

---

[56] Confirmed in the 17th Recital.

[57] This was the view taken by AG Bot in Case C-349/06, *Dirk Rüffert v Land Niedersachsen*, not yet reported.

[58] Para 80. In para 81, the Court suggested that Art 3(7) of the Directive was confined to the situation of out-of-state service providers voluntarily signing a collective agreement in the host state which offered superior terms and conditions to their employees or where the home state laws or collective agreements were more favourable.

[59] Para 8. All other terms and conditions laid down by Art 3(1) of the Posted Workers Directive have been implemented by Swedish law: para 63.

[60] Para 26.

[61] Para 31. Cf AG Bot's Opinion.

to all workers (systems such as those in the UK and Sweden). It provides that in these situations *Member States* may, *if they so decide*, base themselves on collective agreements or arbitration awards which are generally applicable to all similar undertakings in the geographical area and in the profession or industry concerned, and/or collective agreements which have been concluded by the most representative employers' and labour organisations at national level and which are applied throughout national territory. Once again, as with Article 3(10), Member States must positively opt for this route. In the absence of a Member State actually taking advantage of the second paragraph of Article 3(8), the collective agreements will not apply to the posted workers. Since Sweden had not taken advantage of the second paragraph of Article 3(8),[62] the collective agreements could not be applied to Laval. And since there was a breach of the Directive, there was also a breach of Article 49 EC.

The effect of the decisions in *Laval* and *Rüffert* is that the Posted Workers Directive provides less solid protection for labour standards in Northern states than would first appear. Labour lawyers made a mistake in thinking of the Posted Workers Directive as a worker protection measure. Its legal basis (Articles 47(2) and 55 EC) is firmly rooted in the chapter on freedom to provide services, not social policy. This view is reinforced by the Court's observations in *Laval* that the Directive is 'firstly' intended to 'ensure a climate of fair competition between national undertakings and undertakings which provide services transnationally',[63] and that the mandatory rules for minimum protection prevent a situation from arising where the out-of-state provider competes unfairly against the host state.[64] Only 'secondly' does the Court refer to the worker protection element of the Directive.[65]

Thus, the effectiveness of the Posted Workers Directive, introduced as an anti-social dumping measure, has been reduced by the Court's narrow reading of the Directive's provisions, especially the rights in Article 3(1) and the 'derogations' in Articles 3(7) and (10), against the backcloth of a broad market access approach to the Treaty provisions on free movement of services. The Court's interpretation of the Directive in *Laval* has prompted the ETUC, in its Resolution adopted on 4 March 2008,[66] to call

---

[62]   Para 67.

[63]   Para 74.

[64]   Para 75.

[65]   Para 76. Cf AG Mengozzi who reverses the priority (para 171): 'Article 3 of Directive 96/71 has a twofold aim of providing minimum protection for posted workers and equal treatment as between service providers and domestic undertakings in similar circumstances. Those two requirements must be pursued concurrently'.

[66]   <http://www.etuc.org/IMG/pdf_ETUC_Viking_Laval_-_resolution_070308.pdf> accessed 23 September 2008.

for the revision of the Posted Workers Directive, including making mandatory what are currently only 'options' (ie Articles 3(7) and 3(10) of the Directive), ensuring that host country collective agreements can provide for higher than minimum standards, guaranteeing a broad scope for what can be considered 'public policy provisions' that Member States can apply in addition to the nucleus of minimum standards in Article 3(1)—and making clear that both legislative sanctions and social partner activity including collective action are available to enforce the standards. At present there appears little political appetite to make such changes.

We turn now to the second Directive intended to stop social dumping, the Manning Directive whose purpose was broadly to extend the Posted Workers Directive's principles to seafarers.

2. The Manning Directive

The terms and conditions of employment of those working on ferries has been a long running sore. There was particular concern about de-skilling and unemployment of 'Community seafarers on EU flagged vessels and the risk of social dumping in the industry'[67] as EU crew was being steadily replaced by non-EU crew. The Commission therefore proposed two measures 'to promote the employment of Community seafarers in regular passenger and ferry services between Community ports and to eliminate possible unfair competition that can arise from the employment of seafarers under third country conditions'.[68] The second of those measures, a Directive, defined a minimum standard of working conditions at Community level, applicable both to Community nationals and TCNs.[69]

The proposed Directive was to apply to nationals of Member States and to shipping companies established in a Member State which provided regular passenger and ferry services, including mixed passenger/cargo services, between ports situated in different Member States. It was also to apply to nationals of a Member State established outside the Community and to shipping companies established outside the Community and controlled by nationals of a Member State if their vessels were registered and flew the state's flag. The proposed Directive gave rights to TCNs employed on one of these boats. The basic rule, found in proposed Article 2(1), guaranteed that TCNs would enjoy the same terms and conditions (listed in Article 3 and broadly mirroring the equivalent list in Article 3(1) of the Posted Workers Directive[70]) applicable to the residents of the Member State of registration of the vessel.

---

[67] Commission Communication, 'Towards a new maritime strategy' and Bull. EU 4–1998 (1 February 1994).

[68] COM(98) 251.

[69] Bull. EU 4–1998 (1 February 1994).

[70] Art 1(2) of the Posted Workers Directive expressly states that '[t]his Directive shall not apply to merchant navy undertakings as regards seagoing personnel'.

Nevertheless, the proposal was withdrawn in 2004[71] due to concerns that such a measure might increase pressure on ship owners to consider registering their ships in third countries. Yet, trade unions continue to push for such a Directive, pointing to the Irish Ferries dispute as justification. In order to compete with low cost airlines like Ryan Air, Irish Ferries decided to replace 543 directly employed staff with Latvian agency staff, hired through a Cypriot agency, as well as reflagging its vessels in Cyprus. They hoped this would secure cost savings amounting to €11.5 million. As a result, SIPTU, the union representing ship officers, decided to take industrial action. This led to Irish Ferries' ships being delayed in Welsh and Irish ports for almost three weeks.[72] In August 2005, SIPTU and opposition Labour party politicians lobbied the Irish Government to push for an EU directive to combat 'social dumping' in the ferries sector. Eventually, an agreement was reached in December 2005 allowing Irish Ferries to maintain its changes, but to pay Irish minimum wage standards to the Latvian crew. In addition, it agreed to maintain the rates of pay for staff who continued to work for Irish Ferries and to offer reasonably generous severance packages for members of staff who left.[73]

Nevertheless, ITF is still concerned about 'social dumping in the Irish sea'. It found shipping firms 'employing EU nationals but treating them unfairly and discriminatedly [sic]'.[74] The Manning Directive would not have covered this situation, since it applied to TCNs only, but there are further moves to ensure that seafarers are not expressly excluded from Community legislation[75]: the European Transport Federation is lobbying for specific legal instruments on employment conditions to address '"social dumping" in the European ferry sector',[76] whereby owners look to use the cheapest EU or non-EU crews, which they argue is on the increase.[77] Employers are resistant:

> If the Commission was to insist on the interpretation of EU employment law whereby seafarers from one EU Member State, working on a ship registered with another, must be paid the same wage rates relevant to the flag state, then we believe this could be to the detriment of the employment of seafarers from

[71]　COM(2004) 542.

[72]　B Sheehan, 'Landmark Agreement reached at Irish Ferries', available at <http://www.eurofound.europa.eu/eiro/2006/04/articles> accessed 5 July 2007.

[73]　Further details can be found in 'Irish Ferries dispute finally resolved after bitter stand-off', available at <http://www.eurofound.europa.eu/eiro/2005/12/feature/ie0512203f.html> accessed 23 September 2008.

[74]　J Tweedie, 'ITF starts week of maritime action', *Morning Star* (5 June 2007).

[75]　Eg Art 1(2) Posted Workers Directive. Also the original Art 1(3) exclusion from the Working Time Directive 93/104 [1993] OJ L307/18.

[76]　H O'Mahoney, 'Seafarers and owners square up over EU employment rules: Maritime Green Paper documents expose great divide', *Lloyd's List* (14 December 2006).

[77]　'European maritime space initiative will save ferry jobs says transport union', *Lloyd's List* (8 November 2006).

accession countries and may increase pressure on shipowners to consider registering their ships in third countries.[78]

These are the very arguments that have been used to try to discourage the EU from legislating at all in the social field—the risk that the EU will price itself out of the market and there will be capital flight to the far East.

C. The 'Social Dumping' Facilitating Directives?

So far we have considered two Directives aimed at combating social dumping. Yet while one part of the Commission (DG Employment) is keen to advocate such regulatory measures, other parts of the Commission (for example, DG Internal Market) prefer to legislate to deregulate, thereby opening up the market to free trade—with all the implications this may have for national employment laws. We turn now to consider two Directives which appeared to do just that: the Port Services Directive and the Services Directive.

1. The Port Services Directive

Port services are services of a commercial nature that are provided, for payment, to port users.[79] They include cargo handling, piloting, towing and mooring services. Historically, port services have been provided within frameworks characterised by exclusive rights and/or legal or de facto monopolies of a public or private nature.[80] Sometimes, these monopolies have become abused, as the facts of *Porto di Genoa*[81] showed. Italian law conferred on an undertaking the exclusive right to organise dock work at the port of Genoa and required the company to have recourse to a dock work company formed exclusively of national workers. The company abused its monopoly by demanding payment for unrequested services, offering selective reductions in prices and refusing to have recourse to modern technology. The Court found a breach of Article 86 EC. While the outcome of the case was not surprising on the facts, the most striking

---

[78] H O'Mahoney, 'Seafarers and owners square up over EU employment rules: Maritime Green Paper documents expose great divide', *Lloyd's List* (14 December 2006).

[79] Commission Communication, Reinforcing Quality Service in Sea Ports: A Key for European Transport, COM(2001) 35, 3.

[80] *Ibid*, 4.

[81] Case C-179/90, *Merci Convenzionali Porto di Genova v Siderurgica Gabrielli* [1991] ECR I-5889. See also Case C-163/96, *Criminal Proceedings against Silvano Raso* [1998] ECR I-533; Decision of the Commission 97/744, *Italian Ports Employment Policy: The Community v Italy, Re* [1998] 4 CMLR 73.

feature of the Court's judgment was, as Deakin points out,[82] the almost complete disregard shown for social arguments which could have been made in favour of the dock labour monopoly. In particular, no reference was made to the need to combat casualisation of labour, the principal aim of ILO Convention No 137 on registered dock workers.

The Commission has been determined to liberalise the market in port services, noting that, because the markets have not been opened up, the supply of these services often represents a disproportionate cost factor to port users.[83] Therefore, as part of its Ports Package, the Commission proposed a measure to open up the market in port services.[84] Employment protection concerns were recognised in the Preamble to the draft Directive which said that 'Member States must ensure an adequate level of social protection for the staff of undertakings providing port services'[85]; and also in Article 15 of the draft Directive, which provided that '... Member States shall take the necessary measures to ensure the application of their social legislation'.

The basic premise of the proposed Directive was set out in Article 1: 'Providers of port services shall have access to port installations to the extent necessary for them to carry out their activities'. The draft Directive did allow states to require that a provider of port services be authorised providing that the criteria for granting the authorisation be transparent, non-discriminatory, objective, relevant and proportionate.[86] Most controversially, the draft Directive permitted 'self-handling',[87] ie 'a port user provides for itself one or more categories of port-services'.[88] In other words, 'ships could be unloaded by non-dockers, either ship's crew or personnel hired by the shipowners, with all the major safety risks and real danger of social dumping that implies'.[89] This proposal led to Europe-wide strike action.[90] It was also the subject of heated debate in two readings in the European Parliament and a subsequent conciliation procedure between Parliament and the Council. The compromise text agreed by the

---

[82] S Deakin, 'Labour Law as Market Regulation: the Economic Foundations of European Social Policy' in P Davies, A Lyon-Caen, S Sciarra and S Simitis (eds), *European Community Labour Law: Principles and Perspectives* (Oxford, Oxford University Press, 1996) 75.

[83] COM(2001) 35, 4.

[84] *Ibid*, 5.

[85] 27th Recital.

[86] Art 6.

[87] Art 11.

[88] Art 4(7).

[89] M Sapir, 'Harmonization vs Deregulation', HESA, ETUI-REHS (March 2006) 2.

[90] See, eg 'Strike action against proposed port services Directive', available at <http://www.eurofound.europa.eu/eiro/2001/09/inbrief/fi0109102n.html> accessed 23 September 2008.

Conciliation Committee[91] included revised provisions on self-handling which would be allowed only in cases where shipping companies deployed their *own* seafaring personnel. However, the European Parliament rejected this compromise by a narrow majority (by 209 votes to 229, with 16 abstentions). In 2004, the Commission controversially submitted a revised proposal,[92] whose basic structure and provisions followed the compromise text that had emerged from the conciliation procedure, albeit with some notable differences, including a now compulsory authorisation for all port services and the extension of self-handling to new circumstances as well as more prominent social provisions. However, the more robust provisions on social protection were counterbalanced by the newly introduced draft Article 7(6), which said that providers of port services had the right freely to choose the personnel to be employed.

This revised version of the Directive was universally unpopular, criticised by terminal operators, ship owners and trade unions alike, albeit for different reasons.[93] For our purposes, the concerns of the trade unions are most relevant. In particular, they feared that draft Article 7(6) would take jobs away from the present port workforce for the benefit of others and that the whole proposal was 'merely an attempt to undermine the trade unions in ports'. Trade unions also had health and safety concerns over the self-handling provisions: 'many accidents are attributable to poor manning and fatigue onboard, so seafarers should not be expected to take on more work'.[94] Once again, trade unions mobilised their members to protest about the revised draft Directive.[95] British parliamentarians were particularly vociferous in their opposition to the measure.[96] For example, Labour MEPs Glenys Kinnock and Eluned Morgan expressed concerns on behalf of workers that the revised draft Directive would have a detrimental impact on safety standards and bring job cuts as 'cheap labour from other

---

[91] Joint text 3670/2003—C5–0461/2003 and report on the joint text approved by the Conciliation Committee for a European Parliament and Council directive on market access to port services—European Parliament delegation to the Conciliation Committee—A5–0364/2003.

[92] COM(2004) 654. A discussion on the background can be found in 'How vengeful and deluded Eurocrats presided over this ports directive fiasco', *Lloyd's List* (19 January 2006).

[93] H Hill, 'Reworked port services directive comes under fire from all sides: conference hears shipping industry is united in its condemnation of directive. But is it enough to sink the Bill in Brussels?', *Lloyd's List* (17 June 2005). See also J Stares, 'Five good reasons to ditch the new EU port services directive', *Lloyd's List* (12 August 2005).

[94] Hill, above n 93.

[95] Eg B Erdogan, 'EU dockers down tools over port services directive', *Lloyd's List* (21 November 2005); and 'Dockers plot Strasbourg protest over port services', *Lloyd's List* (13 January 2006).

[96] 'British MEPs in Brussels fight over port services', *Lloyd's List* (12 January 2006); and J Stares, 'Barrot isolated as MEPs maul doomed ports directive', *Lloyd's List* (18 January 2006).

countries floods the market'.[97] Ms Morgan said that '[i]t could mean the loss of skilled labour as companies engage in a race to the bottom for cheap workers'. Eventually, the European Parliament rejected the 2004 version of the proposal in January 2006, by 532 votes to 120, and the Commission subsequently withdrew the measure.[98] Frank Leys, secretary of the ITF's dockers' section, is reported as saying: 'Chalk one up to common sense, to committed opposition by trade unions and to virtually the whole industry uniting in rejection of the package.'[99] However, ship owners urged the Commission 'not to be afraid' to continue to use the Treaty to take action against quayside monopolies.[100]

Therefore, extensive protest by trade unions and others managed to put a stop to a draft Directive that was perceived to lead to social dumping. Similar debates raged around the Services Directive.

2. The Services Directive

The Services Directive is the measure most directly associated with the social dumping debate. The original 'Bolkestein' draft[101] precipitated these fears, especially because of its provisions on temporary service provision, namely the country of origin principle (CoOP) in Article 16 and the provisions on worker protection. According to the CoOP, service providers would be subject only to the law of the country in which they are established; Member States would not be able to restrict services from providers established in another Member State. This CoOP principle, based on a strong notion of mutual recognition, was, however, to be accompanied by derogations which were either general, or temporary, or which could be applied on a case-by-case basis.

The ETUC was particularly concerned about the country of origin principle.[102] It argued that, while the CoOP might work where the service itself moved (as with television broadcasting), it did not and should not apply where the service *provider* moved. It argued that, when workers moved under Article 39 EC, the 'country of destination' principle applied, ie migrant workers were treated in the same way as own nationals (the non-discrimination model). It said the same should apply to service providers. The ETUC also argued that the country of origin principle is premised on unequal treatment of workers on the grounds of nationality since domestic workers and migrant service providers working side by side

---

[97] M Shipton, 'Euro-MPs to fight threat to dockers', *Western Mail* (18 January 2006).
[98] [2006] OJ C64/03.
[99] J Snares, 'Crushing "no" vote kills EU ports directive: Majority is larger than predicted and it spells the end for the controversial legislation', *Lloyd's List* (19 January 2006).
[100] *Ibid.*
[101] COM(2004) 2 Final/3.
[102] <http://www.etuc.org/a/384> (9 June 2004) accessed 23 September 2008.

in a Member State, State A, would be subject to different laws (domestic workers would be subject to the laws of their home state, State A, service providers subject to the laws of their home state, State B).[103]

The second controversial aspect of the Bolkestein draft of the Services Directive concerned the provisions on posted workers. Bolkestein provided that the Posted Workers Directive 96/71[104] should apply instead of the Services Directive. As a result, Article 17 of the original draft Services Directive contained a derogation from the country of origin principle in respect of posted workers. Specific provision was also made for the posting of third-country nationals (TCNs).[105] However, in order to facilitate the free movement of services and the application of Directive 96/71, the Bolkestein draft clarified the allocation of tasks between the country of origin and the Member State of posting. In particular, Article 24 of the proposed Directive removed certain administrative obligations concerning the posting of workers (such as notification and registration requirements with the host state authorities), while at the same time increasing the measures to reinforce administrative cooperation between states. The ETUC believed that 'the proposal places too many restrictions on the right of Member States to act against abuses of labour law and to protect migrant workers on their own soil'. It doubted that authorities in the country of origin would be able to carry out effective monitoring and control across borders.[106] As Claes-Mikael Jonsson, then legal adviser to the ETUC, put it: 'The problem with Article 24 (and certain parts of Article 16) was that many of the forbidden obligations mentioned are essential for enforcement and supervision of labour standards.'[107] The ETUC was also concerned that the exclusion of 'matters covered by the Posted Workers Directive' in Article 17 was sufficient to protect workers. It pointed out that Article 17 did not mention the Rome Convention, nor did the exclusion take the other Community *acquis* into account, such as Directive 91/383 on health and safety and Directive 80/987 on employer insolvency.[108] The Commission had also failed to consider what would happen, in circumstances such as those in *Laval*, where the Posted Workers Directive did not apply to the particular circumstance of the case.

[103] Speech given by Claes-Mikael Jonsson, legal adviser to the ETUC, 'Would the proposed Services Directive help or hurt cross-border workers?', European Institute of Public Administration (9–10 March 2006). On file with the author.

[104] [1997] OJ L18/1.

[105] Art 25.

[106] <http://www.etuc.org/a/436> (24 May 2004) accessed 23 September 2008.

[107] Speech given by Claes-Mikael Jonsson 'Would the proposed Services Directive help or hurt cross-border workers?', European Institute of Public Administration (9–10 March 2006). On file with the author.

[108] Directive 91/383 [1991] OJ L206/19 and Directive 80/987 [1980] OJ L283/23 (respectively).

It was the perceived dilution of the provisions on posted workers, read in conjunction with the country of origin principle, combined with the 2004 enlargement to the East that caused many on the left to argue that the Services Directive paved the way for social dumping.[109] For example, John Monks, General Secretary of the ETUC, described the country of origin principle as 'a gun to start the race to the bottom' in terms of social standards.[110] This concern coalesced around the figure of the Polish plumber who became the symbol of 'low cost, low standard, Eastern European Labour'[111] coming to provide services in the old Member States under the Services Directive. The fact that he was likely to be self-employed and thus not covered by host state employment laws got lost in the telling.[112] The 'Polish plumber' assumed particular importance in France,[113] where many French voters saw him and his kind as leading to the demise of the 'European social model'.[114] Some attributed the French

---

[109] See F Hendrickx, 'The Services Directive and Social Dumping: National Labour Law under Strain' in U Neergaard, R Nielsen and L Roseberry (eds), *The Services Directive—Consequences for the Welfare State an the European Social Model* (DJØF Publishing, Copenhagen, 2008).

[110] Quoted in 'Symbol of a European battleground', *The Independent* (15 February 2006).

[111] Eg N Watt, 'Unions protest as EU debates "plumbers" rule', *The Guardian* (15 February 2006). The Swedish trade minister, Thomas Ostros, was reported as saying, 'There cannot be a service directive, unless there is also a protection against social dumping': T Küchler, 'McCreevy locks horns with Swedish unions' *euobserver.com* (10 October 2005). See also J Flower, 'Negotiating the Services Directive' (2006–7) 9 *CYELS* 217, 224.

[112] This is discussed more fully in C Barnard, 'Employment Rights, Free Movement under the EC Treaty and the Services Directive' in M Rönnmar, *National Industrial Relations v. EU Industrial Relations* (Kluwer Law, 2008).

[113] This was not helped by the fact that Frits Bolkestein noted that he would like to hire a Polish plumber because he found it hard to get a good handyman for his second home in Northern France. See also C Mortished, 'March of EU economy's gravediggers', *The Times* (15 February 2006): 'The free market wreckers agitated. In France, they demonised Piotr, the mythical cut-rate Polish plumber, as a harbinger of an avalanche of "social dumping". No one asked whether Piotr's plumbing skills were useful, and far less whether he needed a job'.

[114] See the remarks made by Evelyne Gebhardt, Socialist MEP, with responsibility for steering the Services Directive through the EP. Writing in *Parliament Magazine* and reported in *EUPolitix.com* (4 October 2004), she said the Bolkestein proposal 'constitutes a threat to consumer protection, the European social model and public services'. The Prime Minister and then President of the European Council, Jean-Claude Juncker, said (<http://www.eu2005.lu> (24 March 2005) accessed 23 September 2008) that any new draft of the Directive's text will 'take into account the double imperative of the opening of the services market as well as respect for the European social model in accordance with the motto: Yes to the liberalisation of services, no to social dumping. Those who wish the services directive to be fashioned in such a way that employees lose all their rights, thereby bringing unhealthy pressure to bear on the level of salaries and diminishing employees' rights through the opening up of markets, are sadly mistaken'. For a fuller discussion on this issue, see House of Lords' Select Committee Sixth Report 2005–6, especially ch 7. See also Fourth Recital to the Services Directive, which talks of removing the legal barriers to the establishment of the internal market 'while ensuring an advanced social model'. For full discussion, see D Schiek, 'The European Social Model and the Services Directive' in U Neergaard, R Nielsen and L Roseberry (eds), *The Services Directive—Consequences for the Welfare State an the European Social Model* (DJØF Publishing, Copenhagen, 2008).

'no' vote in the referendum on the Constitutional Treaty in 2005 to French hostility to the proposed Services Directive,[115] or at least to their perception of the excessive economic liberalism which they saw the Services Directive as representing.[116]

The European Parliament was sympathetic to these concerns,[117] and proposed the removal of the country of origin principle. The Commission then drafted a revised proposal.[118] This 'McCreevy' draft—which was ultimately successfully adopted[119]—was narrower in scope than its Bolkestein predecessor. It was shorn of both the country of origin principle,[120] at least expressed in these terms,[121] and the provisions on Posted Workers.[122] The Commission did, however, issue a Communication on the Posted Workers Directive[123] aimed at strengthening the position of service providers wishing to use their own workforce to fulfil contracts in other Member States. The McCreevy draft also excluded labour law[124] and fundamental rights[125] from the scope of application of the Directive. In his speech to the European Parliament,[126] Mr McCreevy said that the decision

---

[115] Editorial Comments, 'The Services Directive Proposal: Striking a balance between the promotion of the internal market and preserving the European social model' (2006) 43 *CML Rev* 307, 308; and M Arnold, 'Polish plumber symbolic of all French fear about the Constitution', *Financial Times* (28 May 2005).

[116] Others argued that the Polish plumber embodied a serious challenge to citizenship, both national and European, because he was present on French soil, but not subject to French regulation, and operated under a more beneficial regime. Therefore, two plumbers (French and Polish), working side-by-side, would operate 'under different legal regimes with different rights, despite a shared EU citizenship' with its associated guarantees of equality: G Davies, 'Services, Citizenship and the Country of Origin Principle', *Mitchell Working Paper Series* 2/2007, 7.

[117] A6–0409/2005 FINAL.

[118] COM(2006) 160.

[119] Services Directive 2006/123 [2006] OJ L376/26.

[120] Only a year before, Commission President Barroso is quoted as saying that, 'The directive just wouldn't work without' the country of origin principle: 'The Services Directive and the European Constitution' *Euobserver.com* (21 March 2005).

[121] R Craufurd-Smith, 'Old Wine in New Bottles? From the "country of origin principle" to the "freedom to Provide Services" in the European Community Directive on Services in the internal market', *Mitchell Working Paper Series* 6/2007.

[122] Arts 24 and 25 of the original proposal were removed.

[123] 'Guidance on the posting of workers in the framework of the provision of services': COM(2006) 159. This is accompanied by a report SEC(2006) 439. It also issued a Communication, 'Social services of general interest in the European Union' COM(2006) 177. It is beyond the scope of this work to consider the latter issue.

[124] Art 1(6) provides: 'This Directive *does not affect* labour law, that is any legal or contractual provision concerning employment conditions, working conditions, *including* health and safety at work and the relationship between employers and workers, which Member States apply in accordance with national law which respects Community law. Equally, this Directive does not affect the social security legislation of the Member States.'

[125] Art 1(7) says: 'This Directive does not affect the exercise of fundamental rights as recognised in the Member States and by Community law. Nor does it affect the right to negotiate, conclude and enforce collective agreements and to take industrial action in accordance with national law and practices which respect Community law.'

[126] SPEECH/06/220 (4 April 2006).

to remove all interaction between the services proposal and labour law was one of the most important elements in creating a more positive atmosphere around this new draft. He continued that '[t]his has allowed us to move on from allegations of lowering of social standards and threats to the European social model', adding that '[w]hile this perception was wrong it did not go away and poisoned the debate'.

Yet while fundamental rights, including the right to take industrial action, are excluded from the Directive, they are not excluded from the scope of the Treaty, as *Viking* and *Laval* make clear: industrial action which the Court deems inconsistent with Community law—such as the situation identified in *Viking*, where strike action is taken even though no jobs are 'jeopardised or under serious threat'[127]—will be covered by the Services Directive and Article 49 EC.[128] And herein lies the rub. The Bolkestein draft of the Directive was seen as facilitating social dumping; under pressure from the ETUC and the European Parliament, labour law and fundamental rights were excluded from the Directive in an effort to stop attempts at social dumping. Yet these matters will still be covered by the Treaty and, as the decisions in *Viking* and *Laval* make clear, the application of Articles 43 and 49 EC can be potentially devastating to national employment laws, especially those concerning industrial action. This prompted John Monks, General Secretary of the ETUC, to say to the EP's Employment and Social Affairs Committee on 27 February 2008, that 'in the *Laval* case the European Court of Justice, by accident or design, has come close to challenging the European Parliament's compromise position on the Services Directive by ruling that the free movement of services can impede the exercise of trade union fundamental rights to demand equal treatment'.

V. ALTERNATIVE APPROACHES

As the previous section has shown, the language of social dumping is a powerful and emotive tool. It has been used to justify the adoption of social legislation (such as the Posted Workers Directive) and to dilute legislation (as with the Services Directive). It seemed that the loudest voices sing to the tune of the need to stop social dumping, not the need for social progress through trade, where states take advantage of the cheaper labour costs. This point was noted by Peter Mandelson, then EU Commissioner for External Relations, in a speech to the Polish Enterprise Council:

---

[127] Para 84.
[128] See also *Viking*, para 44: the right to strike may be 'subject to certain restrictions. As is reaffirmed by Article 28 of the Charter ... those rights are to be protected in accordance with Community law and national law'. For a full discussion, see chs 17–22 (2007–8) 10 *CYELS* forthcoming.

On issues like the services directive and worker mobility, EU governments too often indulge public fears about enlargement rather than explaining the benefits. The famous—or infamous—Polish plumber represents the competitive and flexible economic agent that enlargement and the single market have created. But he also represents for many the fear of that competitive challenge and the need to keep the door closed for as long as possible to internal migration.[129]

Pascal Lamy, the French former EU Commissioner, was more blunt: 'plumber phobia', he said, had been 'cunningly manipulated' in a way that reminded him of 'simple xenophobia'.[130]

So what are the benefits of enlargement? For the new entrants, their lower labour costs enable them to access the markets of other Member States as a means of bettering their economic and social position. For the old Member States, the cheaper labour means more competition, so cheaper goods and services in the EU-15, as well as new sources of labour to fill skills gaps. For example, in 2005 France was short of 6,000 plumbers; 150 of the legendary Polish plumbers helped fill that gap.[131] Further, the EU-15 now have bigger markets to trade in themselves. The *Financial Times* quotes Commission evidence that while 'France lost 6,500 jobs to companies moving operations to east Europe, [this figure was] dwarfed by the 150,000 jobs created in France by its trade surplus with these countries which more than doubled in 10 years to Euros 1.1bn'.[132]

Ultimately, labour costs will equalise between the West and the East and so the incentive to move purely for reasons of labour costs will reduce. There is already evidence of this happening. A report in the *Financial Times* shows that, with migration of skilled workers in the building industry from East to West, labour costs for locals have risen significantly, with a 30 per cent increase in nominal costs in Latvia in the year to September 2007, rises of more than 20 per cent in Romania, Estonia and Lithuania and 12 per cent in Poland.[133] However, wage differentials between West and East are still vast: hourly labour costs are about €28 in Germany compared to €8 in the Czech Republic, €7.50 in Poland and €4 in Romania.[134] On the other hand, in terms of labour productivity, Germany ranks eighth, while the Czech Republic is 29th, Poland 33rd and Romania

---

[129] 'The Polish Plumber and the Chinese textile worker: Europe's response to economic change' delivered 2 June 2006: < http://ec.europa.eu/commission_barroso/mandelson/speeches_articles/sppm104_en.htm> accessed 23 September 2008.

[130] Reported by M Arnold, 'Polish plumber symbolic of all French fear about the Constitution', *Financial Times* (28 May 2005).

[131] *Ibid.*

[132] *Ibid.*

[133] S Wagstyl, J Cienski, K Eddy and T Escritt, 'Gone west: why Eastern Europe is labouring under an abundance of jobs', *Financial Times* (16 January 2008).

[134] Cheaper labour costs in Romania help to explain why the Finnish firm Nokia is closing its plant in Bochum in Germany and moving it to Cluj in Romania where average pre-tax salaries are €450 a month, a seventh of the level in Bochum: 'Nokia finds Romania's labour

Figure 1: Growth in Real Wages

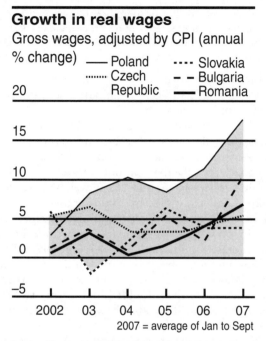

Growth in real wages
Gross wages, adjusted by CPI (annual % change)

— Poland   ···· Slovakia
······· Czech   – – Bulgaria
Republic   — Romania

Source: Vienna Institute for International Economic Studies. Reproduced in Wagstyl, Cienski, Eddy and Escritt, 'Gone west: why Eastern Europe is labouring under an abundance of jobs', *Financial Times*, 16 January 2008.

38th (see Figure 1). Furthermore, other factors influence location decisions, in particular the business environment, including taxation.[135]

With this in mind it seems that social dumping is not the strongest basis on which the EU can justify its social legislation—because of the highly contested nature of the argument about social dumping, because of the absence of political will to adopt legislation at a high enough level to rule out any possibility of social dumping, and because of the risk that any such legislation could be circumvented by the Court of Justice when interpreting the Treaty anyway. Is there another rationale and method of legislating?

---

force, closes German plants', available at <http://uk.reuters.com/article/technologyNews/idUKL2488834520080125> accessed 23 September 2008.

[135] See, eg H McRae, 'Corporate tax will keep falling if companies vote with their HQs', *Business & Money* (7 January 2007); 'Britain's outdated taxlaws fuel the corporate exodus', *The Business* (13 January 2007); and J Daley, 'FTSE directors warn on surge in corporate tax', *The Independent* (17 January 2007).

Here, I would return to a theme Simon Deakin and I have discussed elsewhere.[136] A more positive rationale for enacting social legislation would be to promote the efficient use of labour by ruling out low-productivity strategies of firms engaged in regulatory arbitrage between systems. Directives of this kind could set basic or minimum standards as a 'floor of rights' which Member States must not derogate from, but upon which they may improve by setting superior standards. These interventions can be thought of as implicitly encouraging a 'race to the top', while ruling out less socially desirable forms of competitive federalism. They encourage a process by which rules are selected not on the basis of the threat of exit by the factors of production, but through mutual learning by states: legislators may observe and emulate practices in jurisdictions to which they are closely related by trade and by institutional connections. This is sometimes described as 'reflexive harmonisation' by analogy to the idea of reflexive law.[137]

The essence of reflexive law is that regulatory interventions are most likely to be successful when they seek to achieve their ends not by direct prescription, but by inducing 'second-order effects' on the part of social actors. In other words, this approach aims to 'couple' external regulation with self-regulatory processes. The role for the law is to underpin and encourage autonomous processes of adjustment, in particular, by supporting mechanisms of group representation and participation, rather than to intervene by imposing particular distributive outcomes. This approach to regulation shows just how far the EU has come since Spaak. As Deakin argues,[138] Spaak's specific arguments against harmonisation in the labour law field no longer hold; the arrival of the euro has meant the end of exchange rate flexibility for a majority of the Member States, with most of the rest heading in the same direction, while the enlargement of the Union has meant that nominal cost levels are no longer closely aligned across national borders. However, 'Few now argue for the use of harmonising measures to put in place a comprehensive European labour code'. Reflexive law has been the EU's response.

Perhaps the best example of this reflexive approach can be seen in the Information and Consultation Directive 2002/14,[139] a measure introduced

---

[136] C Barnard and S Deakin, 'Market Access and Regulatory Competition' in C Barnard and J Scott (eds), *The Law of the Single European Market: Unpacking the Premises*, (Hart Publishing, 2002).

[137] See generally, G Teubner, *Law as an Autopoietic System* (Blackwell, 1993); and R Rogowski and T Wilthagen (eds), *Reflexive Labour Law* (Kluwer, 1994).

[138] S Deakin, 'Regulatory competition after *Laval*' (2007–8) 10 CYELS forthcoming.

[139] [2002] OJ L80/29. For full details, see M Hall, 'Assessing the Information and Consultation of Employees Regulations' (2005) 34 *ILJ* 103; and KD Ewing and G Truter, 'The Information and Consultation of Employees Regulations: Voluntarism's Bitter Legacy' (2005) 68 *MLR* 626.

to help make the labour market more productive. As the Green Paper on Partnership explained,[140] flexibility within organisations is to be encouraged by reinforcing mechanisms for employee participation at the level of the plant or enterprise: 'the role of workers in decision-making and the need to review and strengthen the existing arrangements for workers' involvement in their companies will . . . become essential issues'.[141] The Directive provides the minimum framework in which information and consultation can take place: all the detail is left to be worked out by the Member States or the national or subnational Social Partners. So, Article 1 says that the Directive's objective is to establish a general framework for informing and consulting employees in the EC. The Member States then have the choice to apply the Directive to undertakings employing at least 50 employees in any one Member State,[142] or establishments employing at least 20 employees in any one Member State. However, Member States are to determine the method for calculating the thresholds of employees employed. This is consistent with the overall aim of the Directive to ensure that it sits within the national industrial relations systems. This ethos is confirmed by Article 1(2), which provides that: 'The practical arrangements for information and consultation shall be defined and implemented in accordance with national law and industrial relations practices in individual Member States in such a way as to ensure their effectiveness.' The Directive identifies three possible outcomes of the negotiation process. These are referred to in the British implementation[143] as pre-existing agreements (PEAs),[144] negotiated agreements (NAs)[145] and standard or fall back arrangements. Only if there is neither a PEA nor an NA will the fall back provisions found in Article 4 apply. These are the carrot and stick for the social partners to reach an agreement independently. If they do not, the fall back provisions will apply. This flexibility has been much appreciated in the UK. For the first time, the Confederation of British Industry, Trade Union Congress and government sat round a table to hammer out a deal on how to implement the Directive. The results have been encouraging to

---

[140]   Green Paper on Partnership, COM(97) 127 final, Executive Summary.

[141]   *Ibid*, para. 44.

[142]   According to the Commission, this excludes 97% of companies in the EU with salaried employees.

[143]   The Information and Consultation of Employees (ICE) Regulations 2004 (SI 2004/3426).

[144]   PEAs are agreements existing on the date the Directive came into force (23 March 2005), as well as any subsequent renewals of such agreements.

[145]   Negotiated agreements are those negotiated by management and labour, at the appropriate level including at undertaking or establishment level, setting out the practical arrangements for informing and consulting employees.

the extent that the flexibility offered by the Directive and its implementation measures has allowed employers to adapt to information and consultation requirements. However, the effectiveness of the information and consultation mechanism depends much on the industrial relations culture in the workplace.[146]

VI. CONCLUSIONS

This chapter has argued that the need to avoid social dumping has been a persuasive rationale for the adoption of EC social legislation, but ultimately social dumping is a term which is so contested and a concept so lacking in a proper evidentiary base that its meaning and significance have become obscured. The chapter therefore concluded with an examination of an alternative basis and method for the Community adopting social legislation.

The social dumping thesis is premised on an opposition between the economic and the social. And in an economic constitution, the economic is likely to prevail, as *Viking* and *Laval* suggest. Would the Lisbon Treaty have made any difference? Possibly. In its statement of aims, Article 3 of the revised TEU says:

> The Union ... shall work for the sustainable development of Europe based on balanced economic growth and price stability, a highly competitive *social market economy*, aiming at full employment and social progress ... It shall combat social exclusion and discrimination, and shall promote social justice and protection, equality between women and men, solidarity between generations and protection of the rights of the child' (emphasis added).

The term 'social market economy' was introduced at the behest of Joschka Fischer and Dominique de Villepin to underline the link between economic and social development and to ensure greater coherence between economic and social policies.[147] It could be argued that this was reflected in the Court's observations in *Viking* and *Laval* that:

> Since the Community has thus not only an economic but also a social purpose, the rights under the provisions of the Treaty on the free movement of goods, persons, services and capital must be balanced against the objectives pursued by social policy, which include, as is clear from the first paragraph of Article 136 EC, *inter alia*, improved living and working conditions, so as to make possible

---

[146] See further A Koukiadaki, *Reflexive Regulation and the Development of Capabilities: The Impact of the 2002/14/EC Directive on Information and Consultation of Employees in the UK*, PhD examined July 2008.

[147] Working Group XI on Social Europe, CONV 516/1/03 REV 1, para 17.

their harmonisation while improvement is being maintained, proper social protection and dialogue between management and labour.[148]

In other words, social policy is no longer residual; it is as important as the economic policies of the Community.[149] Further, the proposed incorporation of the Charter of Fundamental Rights into the Treaty, including the Solidarity chapter (but subject to the 'opt-out' for the UK and Poland[150]) might help in the overall rebalancing process between the economic and social. However, as we saw in *Viking* and *Laval*, cases which, for the first time, give express recognition to the right to strike as a fundamental human right, do not lead to enhanced protection of that right and the talk of balance was largely that—talk. In reality, the economic constitution has taken firm hold and talk of social dumping will not easily be shaken off.

---

[148]   *Viking*, para 79; and *Laval*, para 105.
[149]   See also the earlier decision in Joined Cases C-270 & 271/97, *Deutsche Post AG v Elisabeth Sievers and Brunhilde Schrage* [2000] ECR I-929.
[150]   C Barnard, 'The "Opt-Out" for the UK and Poland from the Charter of Fundamental Rights: Triumph of Rhetoric over Reality?' in S Griller and J Ziller (eds), *The Lisbon Treaty: EU Constitutionalism without a Constitutional Treaty* (SpringerWien, New York, 2008).

14

Federalisation Versus Centralisation: Tensions in Fundamental Rights Discourse in the EU

ELEANOR SPAVENTA*

I. INTRODUCTION

THE DEBATE ABOUT fundamental rights in the European Union does not concern so much the identification of the values which should be considered at the very heart of our conception of humanity. After all, those values were identified in 1950 in the European Convention of Human Rights. Rather, the debate revolves around the identification of the *locus*, supranational or domestic, where it is appropriate to carry out the balancing exercise between these conflicting values; and also, on the identification of the institution, judicial or political, which should carry out such balancing exercise. This balancing exercise normally reflects deeply held societal preferences as to the respective strengths of the values enshrined in fundamental rights documents. In this respect, the Member States' acceptance to defer the balancing exercise, as a last resort, to the European Court of Human Rights was based on the assumption that the European Convention of Human Rights would represent a floor of rights; such a minimalist conception allowed the balance to oscillate considerably between different assessments of the respective force of conflicting values. In this way, the Convention, as interpreted by the European Court of Human Rights, served the double purpose of respecting the plurality of societal choices that characterises different polities, while at the same time enforcing a minimum level of protection which itself reacts to changes in social perception. As complex as the creation of an international human rights discourse might be, then, it is considerably

* I am grateful to the participants to the Liverpool conference on *50 Years of the European Treaties* for a very fruitful discussion. I am indebted to Lorenzo Zucca and Michael Dougan for their comments on an earlier draft. The usual disclaimer applies.

simpler than its supranational counterpart. In the international sphere, there is no ambition to harmonise the fundamental rights discourse beyond what is required by the minimum floor of protection. In the supranational sphere, on the other hand, and as we shall see in more detail below, the emergence of a fundamental rights discourse might require the imposition of a sole standard (sometimes lower and sometimes higher than the national counterpart) in the protection of fundamental rights.

In this sense, the fundamental rights discourse in the European Union reflects the evolution of, and the tensions inherent in, the Union's constitutional process. In particular, the debate about fundamental rights protection mirrors the tension between federalisation and centralisation, and the deep worries which we have seen expressed in relation to the recent constitutional process. At both political and judicial level, there are in fact two conflicting forces, centripetal and centrifugal, in relation to fundamental rights protection. The centripetal force attracts the fundamental rights discourse within the European Union project, first as an ancillary goal and then—more and more—as an aim in itself.[1] The centrifugal force, by contrast, seeks to pull away fundamental rights from the EU gravitational orbit.[2] The centripetal force reflects the development of the European Union in a more mature and comprehensive constitutional system, a system that has long stepped outside the confines of the internal market. The centrifugal force, on the other hand, reflects the desire to maintain a diversified and multifaceted constitutional system, where national sovereignty is seen as the source of the Union's own constitutional legitimacy.

This contribution seeks to explore these dynamics; in particular, it will be argued that if the fundamental rights discourse aims to serve a legitimising function, it must reflect these tensions and acknowledge that centralisation of fundamental rights is not always the answer. We will start by a short historical introduction of the development of fundamental rights discourse in the European Union, and then focus on the two forces at play, the centralising and the federalising force, in the case law of the European Court of Justice.

II. THE DEVELOPMENT OF FUNDAMENTAL RIGHTS IN THE EU: A HISTORICAL INTRODUCTION

As is well known, the original Treaty of Rome did not contain any reference to fundamental rights; but this lacuna in the Treaties was soon

---

[1] Eg the Treaty amendments and the proclamation of the Charter of Fundamental Rights, both discussed below.

[2] Eg the limited scope of the Charter of Fundamental Rights and the limited mandate of the EU Fundamental Rights Agency: see n 15 below.

filled by means of judicial interpretation. Thus, the European Court of Justice held that fundamental rights formed part of the general (unwritten) principles of Community law which bound the European institutions.[3] While we shall examine in the next sections the extent to which fundamental rights as general principles of Community law bind the Member States, the decision to include fundamental rights in the general principles of law which the European institutions must respect is, and was, not particularly controversial. Rather, it is unthinkable that either the national or the Community judiciary would have allowed the Member States to derogate, by means of an action at Community level, from that minimum floor of rights that they themselves had signed up to in the European Convention of Human Rights (not to speak about their national constitutions).[4] And indeed, a few years after the *Internationale Handelsgesellschaft* ruling,[5] the Council, the Commission and the European Parliament issued a joint declaration endorsing the case law of the Court and committing themselves to respecting fundamental rights as general principles of Community law.[6] Thereinafter, each Treaty revision included a fundamental rights 'element'. The preamble to the Single European Act referred to the Member States' determination 'to promote democracy' on the basis of fundamental rights as recognised in national constitutions and in the ECHR; the Treaty of Maastricht included an express obligation for the European Union to respect fundamental rights,[7] while the Treaty of Amsterdam introduced a mechanism to 'suspend' a Member State in the case of a serious and persistent breach of fundamental rights.[8] The Treaty of Nice established the Council's power to make recommendations to a Member State in the event of a clear risk of a serious breach of fundamental rights,[9] as well as providing the occasion for the institutions' joint proclamation of the Charter of Fundamental Rights.[10] And finally, the Treaty of Lisbon would

---

[3] Case 29/69, *Stauder v City of Ulm* [1969] ECR 419; Case 11/70, *Internationale Handelsgesellschaft* [1970] ECR 1125; and Case 4/73, *Nold v Commission* [1974] ECR 491.

[4] The Court has been accused of having been forced into this step by recalcitrant national constitutional courts, since in the earlier cases, it had failed to recognise fundamental rights: see Case 1/58, *Stork v High Authority* [1959] ECR 17, 26; Joined Cases 36–40/59, *Geitling v High Authority* [1960] ECR 425; and to a certain extent Case 40/64, *Sgarlata v Commission* [1965] ECR 215. However, the present writer does not share this criticism and believes that the way in which the questions had been phrased in these cases, referring to national constitutional rights, determined the ECJ's response. In Case 29/69, above n 3, the reference was phrased in relation to the general principles of *Community* law and the Court's answer was positive.

[5] Case 11/70, above n 3.

[6] Joint Declaration by the European Parliament, the Council and the Commission concerning the protection of fundamental rights and the European Convention for the protection of human rights and fundamental freedoms [1977] OJ C103/1.

[7] Art F TEU (Maastricht).

[8] Art 7 TEU (Amsterdam).

[9] Art 7 TEU (Nice).

[10] [2000] OJ C364/1.

give full legal effect to the Charter, as well as provide for the Union's competence to accede to the European Convention of Human Rights.[11]

The developments herein mentioned by no means exhaust the Union's activity in relation to fundamental rights protection.[12] Rather, they have been recalled for three reasons: first, because they constitute the expression at the highest political level of the emergence of a fundamental rights discourse in the Union's political and legal rhetoric; secondly, they illustrate well the dual dimension of such rhetoric, which seeks to impact on the European *and* on the national discourse; thirdly, they highlight the gradual process of transformation of the fundamental rights rhetoric from a political discourse to a legal one.

This process, then, can be seen from a historical perspective as one of the most tangible effects of the constitutional development of the European project. Even leaving aside the earlier reactions to the Court's case law, it is clear that the inclusion of what is currently Article 6 TEU in the Maastricht Treaty was deemed necessary to complement (and maybe to legitimise and support) the expansion of the European Communities'/Union's activities so as to include the Common Foreign and Security Policy and what was then Justice and Home Affairs. However, it should be noted that, while there cannot be any doubt that the obligations in the current Article 6 TEU were, and are, legally binding, the Treaty drafters excluded the jurisdiction of the Court. Therefore, the provision was of little direct relevance for citizens, who could not rely on it to challenge the acts of the institutions in the sphere of the second and third pillar. The impossibility of enforcing Article 6 TEU was, of course, a side effect of the very nature of Union competence in these fields: since Union acts needed implementation in national law in order to produce legal effects beyond the sphere of international law, the enforcement of fundamental rights could be guaranteed by means of national law. Thus, the importance of Article 6 TEU has never been merely symbolic: in creating a clear obligation for the Union institutions, it could arguably inform the interpretation and application of national legislation adopted to implement Union acts.

Moreover, the centrality of the values enshrined in Article 6 TEU for the Union project is later reinforced: the Treaty of Amsterdam extended the jurisdiction of the Court to the so-called third pillar (albeit on a voluntary basis); and made respect of Article 6 TEU both a precondition for accession to the Union, and the precondition for the full exercise of the prerogatives of Union membership. Thus, while the possibility of suspending voting rights for breaches of fundamental rights provided in Article 7

---

[11]   Art 6 of the revised TEU (see consolidated version published at [2008] OJ C115).
[12]   Eg the establishment of the European Human Rights Agency; Art 13 EC granting competence to fight discrimination on grounds other than nationality.

TEU can be cynically seen as a piece of empty rhetoric,[13] which is there to embellish the Union more than to ensure that a minimum standard of fundamental rights protection is maintained throughout the 27 Member States, its symbolic value cannot be underestimated. The effect of Article 7 TEU is to create a revolving door which links a 'bottom up' approach with a 'top down' approach. If fundamental rights as general principles of Union law are a by-product of national constitutional traditions, such general principles might bounce back in national law, so that any systematic derogation from those principles could, at least potentially, give rise to a reaction at the Union level. Even though the threshold for triggering the suspension mechanism is very high and the mechanism is politically extremely sensitive, its existence is significant in that it links the national and the Union fundamental rights discourses. In this sense, it could be argued that Article 7 TEU might help to legitimise the Court's enforcement of the general principles against Member States (which shall be examined in detail in the next section).

Finally, the gradual but constant evolution of the fundamental rights rhetoric from political to legal discourse again highlights the centrality of such rhetoric in legitimising the expansion of Union competences. Thus, the very idea of drafting a Charter of Fundamental Rights was also due to the need to provide greater legitimacy for the Union's action both in the field of foreign policy and in the field of cooperation in criminal matters. In relation to foreign policy, it was felt that a Union Charter of Fundamental Rights might help to provide legitimacy for the increased frequency in the use of human rights conditionality clauses.[14] As for cooperation in criminal matters, it is obvious that the existence of a clear catalogue of rights might reinforce not only the legitimacy of action taken in such a delicate field, but also the guarantees for individuals.

These progresses and their significance should not therefore be underestimated. And yet, the most important force behind the development of fundamental rights in the European Union is, unsurprisingly, the European Court of Justice. In this respect, while the political institutions attempted

---

[13] Eg the failure to use the Art 7 TEU procedure against Italy in relation to the excessive concentration of the media in the hands of Mr Berlusconi during his periods as prime minister: see generally, R Crauford-Smith, 'Rethinking European Union competence in the field of media ownership: the internal market, fundamental rights and European citizenship' (2004) 29 *EL Rev* 652 and references therein included. Also, the debate about the fingerprinting of Roma families in Italy (see Plenary session of the European Parliament, 8 July 2008).

[14] On the possible reasons that might have created the momentum for the decision to draft a Charter of Fundamental Rights, see E Paciotti, 'La Carta: i contenuti e gli autori' in A Manzella, P Melograni, E Paciotti and S Rodotà, *Riscrivere i diritti in Europa* (Il Mulino, Bologna, 2001).

to safeguard an element of national sovereignty over fundamental rights protection,[15] the case law, especially in the past 10 years, has seen strong centralising elements.

III. CONFLICTING FORCES IN THE CASE LAW OF THE ECJ: CENTRALISATION VERSUS FEDERALISATION

We have mentioned above that, in the early 1970s, the Court held that the European Communities were bound by fundamental rights as general principles of Community law.[16] As we have said, this step was not particularly controversial: it is natural that the benchmark for the European institutions should be that set by the European Court of Justice with reference to the general principles of Community law.

More controversial, however, is the decision to extend the application of fundamental rights as general principles of Community law to acts of the Member States. This step was first taken in relation to domestic acts which are adopted with a view to implementing a Community act.[17] The reasoning behind this intrusion in the national fundamental rights arena is simple enough. When the Member State implements Community law, it is acting as an 'agent' of the Community, and as such it cannot breach those rights which bind the Community legislature.[18] Furthermore, it is likely that this principle applies also in relation to framework decisions adopted pursuant to Title VI TEU (the third pillar),[19] although the extent to which fundamental rights might become directly effective through the medium of Union law is open to debate.[20]

In any event, in relation to acts of the Member States implementing Community/Union law, when there is a different standard between domestic and Community fundamental rights, and provided the Member State is exercising some discretion, the highest standard should prevail. Where it is

[15] Eg the Charter applies to the Member States only when they *implement* EU law, and not when they act within the field of EU law; the European Human Rights Agency [2007] OJ L53/1 is only concerned with Member States when they implement Community law, and has only 'reporting' powers.

[16] Case 29/69, above n 3; and more clearly Case 11/70, above n 3.

[17] Case 5/88, *Wachauf* [1989] ECR 2609; Joined Cases C-20 & 64/00, *Booker Aquaculture Ltd v Scottish Ministers* [2003] ECR I-7411; it should be noted that a link between free movement and fundamental rights had already been established in Case 36/75, *Rutili v Minister for the Interior* [1975] ECR 1219.

[18] On the confusion as to the extent of this obligation, see A Arnull, A Dashwood, M Dougan, M Ross, E Spaventa and D Wyatt, *Wyatt and Dashwood's EU Law*, 5th edn (London, Sweet & Maxwell, 2006), 267–8.

[19] Case C-105/03, *Pupino* [2005] ECR I-5285.

[20] On this point, see E Spaventa, 'Opening Pandora's Box: Some Reflections on the Constitutional Effects of the Ruling in Pupino' (2007) 3 *European Constitutional Law Review* 5; and 'Remembrance of Principles Lost: on Fundamental Rights, the Third Pillar and the Scope of Union Law' (2006) 24 *Yearbook of European Law* 153.

impossible to determine whether the national or Community standard is higher, for instance because the matter involves the balancing of conflicting rights, then the Community standard should apply and the ultimate arbiter would be the European Court of Justice. This approach has been codified in the Charter, which applies only to the acts of the Union institutions and to the acts of the Member States when they implement Union law.[21]

A. The *ERT* and *Familiapress* Case Law: Balancing Centralisation and Federalisation

A more problematic step is that of extending the application of fundamental rights as general principles of Community law to the actions of the Member States whenever the matter falls within the scope of Community law, and in particular, when the Member State is limiting one of the free movement rights. This case law originated with the *ERT* decision.[22] There, the Court held that, when a Member State relies on the Treaty to justify a derogation from one of the free movement rights, it has to respect fundamental rights as a matter of Community law. In *Familiapress*,[23] the same reasoning applied to situations in which the Member State is limiting (rather than derogating from) the free movement rights and is therefore relying on the mandatory requirements doctrine. Furthermore, it now appears that this case law should apply in the same way also to situations concerning limitations to one of the rights associated with Union citizenship.[24]

There are two concurring reasons why the extension of the field of application of the general principles of Community law is debatable. First of all, the effect of such case law is to render fundamental rights as general principles of Community law directly effective in the national system. In this respect, consider that fundamental rights scrutiny and the power to

---

[21] Art 51 of the Charter of Fundamental Rights of the European Union [2007] OJ C303/1.

[22] Case C-260/89, *Elliniki Radiophonia Tileorassi AE (ERT) v Dimotiki Étairia Pliroforissis (DEP)* [1991] ECR I-2925.

[23] Case C-368/95, *Vereinigte Familiapress Zeitungsverlags- und vertriebs GmbH v Heinrich Bauer Verlag* [1997] ECR I-3689.

[24] Arts 17 *ff* EC. There is no ruling on this specific point as yet. However, in Case C-413/99, *Baumbast and R v Secretary of State for the Home Department* [2002] ECR I-7091, the Court applied the 'general principle of proportionality to limitations to the right of residence', and there is therefore no reason why other general principles, including fundamental rights, should not be applicable. On this point, see M Dougan and E Spaventa, 'Educating Rudy and the (non-)English Patient: A Double-Bill on Residency Rights under Article 18 EC' (2003) 28 *EL Rev* 699. See also Case C-300/04, *Eman and Sevinger* [2006] ECR I-8055, which is on the principle of equality, but should apply a fortiori to all fundamental rights. In relation to deportation and the public policy derogation, the Court has already had the chance to uphold its fundamental rights jurisprudence also in relation to Union citizenship: see Joined Cases C-482 & 493/01, *Orfanopoulos and Olivieri* [2004] ECR I-5257.

strike down conflicting legislation, when at all available,[25] is usually reserved to specialised or higher courts. However, through the medium of Community law, any national court or tribunal acquires the power and the duty to scrutinise those rules which are deemed to fall within the scope of Community law as to their compatibility with fundamental rights.[26] Secondly, the constant extension of the scope of the Treaty, and the uncertain boundaries of the free movement provisions, render the *ERT/Familiapress* case law of pervasive constitutional impact.

And yet, the interpretation of the Court is entirely consistent with its premises. Indeed, it would seem peculiar if the Member State could legitimately invoke a Treaty derogation or justify a limitation to a free movement right if, in doing so, it breached not only the right to move of the claimant but also her fundamental rights. And even should one not adhere to Mr Jacobs' opinion that all migrant citizens should be reassured that moving will never entail a loss in fundamental rights protection,[27] one can well justify the Court's interpretation. After all, the hermeneutic principle driving the fundamental rights jurisprudence is exactly the same as that driving the proportionality assessment: limitations to the right to move must be proportionate because proportionality is a general principle of Union law. It would then be strange if proportionality were the only general principle to apply to such limitations. Therefore, the misgivings one could have about the Court's case law might really be with its extensive interpretation of what constitutes a barrier to movement: it is that interpretation which causes what, to some, might seem as undue interference with national autonomy in setting the fundamental rights standards in the domestic arena.[28]

Furthermore, it should be noticed that the centralising approach inherent in this case law is tamed, in both *ERT* and *Familiapress*, by the fact (first) that the assessment as to the balance between conflicting interests is left to the national court and (secondly) that, in any event, the Treaty rights are used to enhance the protection of fundamental rights and not to interfere with it. As a result, the standard of fundamental rights protection should again always be the highest between the national and Community law standards.

---

[25] In the UK there is no such power; rather according to s 4 of the Human Rights Act 1998, the national courts can only make a declaration of incompatibility which triggers an accelerated procedure for amendment of the legislation at stake (s 10). The European Court of Human Rights has declared such a remedy (for the time being) not effective: see, eg *Burden v UK* (Application no 13378/05).

[26] On this point, see E Spaventa, 'Seeing the Wood Despite the Trees? On the Scope of Union Citizenship and its Constitutional Effects' (2008) 44 *CML Rev* 13.

[27] Opinion in Case C-168/91, *Konstantinidis v Stadt Altensteig, Standesamt und Landratsamt Calw, Ordnungsamt* [1993] ECR I-1191.

[28] On this point, see E Spaventa, above n 26.

B. The Second Line of Case Law: Towards a More Centralising Approach

However, in a second stage, the Court seems eager to assess for itself the correct balance to be struck between competing interests when there is a Community element involved. The more interventionist approach is visible, for instance, in *Carpenter*,[29] where the assessment of the fundamental rights element appears to be predominant. Interventionism is also apparent in those cases where the Court instructs the national referring court to take into due account the fundamental rights of the claimant, even though it itself found no evidence of the existence of a barrier to intra-Community movement capable of bringing the matter within the scope of Community law.[30]

The more proactive approach towards fundamental rights protection, which might well reflect a change in the Court's perception of its own role, is visible also in the case of *Ferstersen*.[31] There, rather unusually as well as unnecessarily, the Court referred to the European Convention on Human Rights in scrutinising a residence requirement. In the case at issue, the question related to the compatibility with Community law of a requirement that those who purchased agricultural property took up fixed residence in the property. As is well known, a residence requirement always constitutes indirect discrimination[32]; as such it not only falls within the scope of the Treaty, but it is also difficult to justify, since territorial requirements go against the very idea of the freedom to move freely granted by Community law.[33] One could have well imagined then that any reference to Article 2 Protocol 4 ECHR on the right to move would be wholly unnecessary. This is especially the case since the right to move provided therein refers to intra-state movement and not inter-state movement, and that, in any event, one would think, the right to move in Community law goes far beyond the rights granted by the above-mentioned Protocol.

---

[29] Case C-60/00, *Carpenter v Secretary of State for the Home Department* [2002] ECR I-6279.

[30] Case C-109/01, *Secretary of State for the Home Department v H Akrich* [2003] ECR I-9607. For an attempt to justify the requirement of a fundamental rights review, see E Spaventa, Annotation of *Akrich* (2005) 42 *CML Rev* 225; Case C-71/02, *H Karner Industrie-Auktionen GmbH v Troostwijk GmbH* [2004] ECR I-3025; and F De Cecco, 'Room to Move? Minimum Harmonization and Fundamental Rights' (2006) 43 *CML Rev* 9.

[31] Case C-370/05, *Festersen* [2007] ECR I-1129.

[32] Consistent case law, eg Case 152/73, *Sotgiu* [1974] ECR 153; Case 33/74, *van Binsbergen* [1974] ECR 1299; and Case C-111/91, *Commission v Luxembourg* [1993] ECR I-817.

[33] In the case of the free movement of services, residence requirements are the 'very negation' of the freedom granted by the Treaty (see Case 205/84, *Commission v Germany* [1986] ECR 3755) and so are even more difficult to justify.

This case law signals a much more interventionist approach and as such demonstrates a willingness on behalf of the Court to engage with the fundamental rights discourse beyond what might be seen as required by the demands of the internal market. What is relevant from a constitutional law perspective is that, as a result of this centralising tendency, national courts are pre-empted in carrying out their own (national) fundamental rights assessment. However, and as mentioned above, this step is still constitutionally justified in that fundamental rights and Treaty freedoms concur in affording the most extensive protection to the individual, albeit at the expense of national regulatory autonomy.

C. The Third Line of Case Law: Fundamental Rights to Justify a Restriction to the Free Movement Provisions

A slightly different scenario occurs when the Member State relies on the need to protect fundamental rights, as guaranteed by national law, to justify a restriction to the free movement provisions. This possibility, already evident in *Familiapress*, was fully explored in *Omega*.[34] In that case, Germany sought to justify the prohibition on games mimicking the killing of people by relying on the need to protect human dignity as a value enshrined in the German Constitution. The Court accepted that the protection of a constitutionally enshrined value could fall within the scope of the public policy derogation. In this respect, the Court clarified that, in order to assess the proportionality and the necessity of the rules at issue, '[i]t is not indispensable ... for the restrictive measure issued by the authorities of a Member State to correspond to a conception shared by all Member States as regards the precise way in which the fundamental right or legitimate interest in question is to be protected'.[35] In *Omega*, it is made clear that the Community free movement provisions will not (necessarily) force upon Member States a 'levelling' down of fundamental rights protection. In other words, there is space for a departure from a minimum standard of fundamental rights. The standard in fundamental rights is supervised by the European Court of Justice, but is still left to the discretion of Member States. In this respect, the centralising effect is minimal, relating simply to a supervisory role of the Court, and the 'federalising' tendency appears predominant. This said, there is a fourth line of case law which, while at first sight appearing similar to the *Omega* case law, is more problematic.

---

[34] Case C-36/02, *Omega Spielhallen- und Automatenaufstellungs-GmbH v Oberbürgermeisterin der Bundesstadt Bonn* [2004] ECR I-9609.

[35] *Omega*, para 37.

IV. ASSESSING CONFLICT OF RIGHTS

The fourth, and in my opinion more complex development, is that relating to the *Schmidberger* case law.[36]

A. The Ruling in *Schmidberger*

It might be recalled that the *Schmidberger* case arose as a result of a previous ruling of the Court. In *Commission v France*,[37] the Court held that Member States could be in breach of their Treaty obligations if they fail to actively protect enjoyment of the Treaty rights. In *Schmidberger*, an environmental group staged a demonstration on the Brenner motorway to protest against a planned expansion of the motorway. Schmidberger, an international transport company, brought proceedings to claim *Francovich* damages against the Austrian authorities on the grounds that, by allowing the demonstration to proceed, they had failed to protect the claimant's rights under Article 28 EC. The Court held that the failure to prevent the demonstration was to be qualified as a measure having equivalent effect to a quantitative restriction on imports; and that it was justified having regard to the fundamental right of freedom of expression. At this point, it is useful to quote directly from the Court's judgment:

> 77. The case thus raises the question of the need to reconcile the requirements of the protection of fundamental rights in the Community with those arising from a fundamental freedom enshrined in the Treaty and, more particularly, the *question of the respective scope* of freedom of expression and freedom of assembly, guaranteed by Articles 10 and 11 of the ECHR, and of the free movement of goods, where the former are relied upon as justification for a restriction of the latter.

> 78. First, whilst the free movement of goods constitutes one of the fundamental principles in the scheme of the Treaty, it may, in certain circumstances, be subject to restrictions for the reasons laid down in Article 36 [now 30] of that Treaty or for overriding requirements relating to the public interest ...

> 79. Second, whilst the fundamental rights at issue in the main proceedings are expressly recognised by the ECHR and constitute the fundamental pillars of a democratic society, it nevertheless follows from the express wording of paragraph 2 of Articles 10 and 11 of the Convention that freedom of expression and freedom of assembly are also subject to certain limitations justified by objectives in the public interest, in so far as those derogations are in accordance with the

---

[36] Case C-112/00, *Schmidberger* [2003] ECR I-5659.
[37] Case C-265/95, *Commission v France* [1997] ECR I-6959.

law, motivated by one or more of the legitimate aims under those provisions and necessary in a democratic society, that is to say justified by a pressing social need and, in particular, proportionate to the legitimate aim pursued ...

80. Thus, unlike other fundamental rights enshrined in that Convention, such as the right to life or the prohibition of torture and inhuman or degrading treatment or punishment, which admit of no restriction, neither the freedom of expression nor the freedom of assembly guaranteed by the ECHR appears to be absolute but must be viewed in relation to its social purpose. Consequently, *the exercise of those rights may be restricted*, provided that the restrictions in fact correspond to objectives of general interest and do not, taking account of the aim of the restrictions, constitute disproportionate and unacceptable interference, impairing the very substance of the rights guaranteed ...

81. In those circumstances, the interests involved must be weighed having regard to all the circumstances of the case in order to determine whether a *fair balance was struck between those interests.*

82. The competent authorities enjoy a wide margin of discretion in that regard. Nevertheless, it is necessary to *determine whether the restrictions placed upon intra-Community trade are proportionate in the light of the legitimate objective pursued, namely, in the present case, the protection of fundamental rights.*

...

91. An action of that type usually entails inconvenience for non-participants, in particular as regards free movement, but the inconvenience may in principle be *tolerated* provided that the objective pursued is essentially the public and lawful demonstration of an opinion [emphasis added throughout].

At first sight, the *Schmidberger* ruling might appear both inoffensive and balanced. After all, the end result is exactly what one might have expected and desired. And yet, the case signals a move towards centralisation which is qualitatively different and greater, since the effect of the Court's interpretation is that of conferring upon itself the hermeneutic monopoly over the possible clash between a fundamental (non-economic) right and a Treaty right. Here, consider that there is a substantial difference between this case and *Omega*. In the latter, what was at stake was a *rule* which, while aimed at the protection of fundamental rights, also directly restricted the enjoyment of one of the Treaty freedoms. In *Schmidberger,* on the other hand, what is at stake is not a direct barrier imposed by the state, but rather the failure of the state to curtail a fundamental right.

In the writer's opinion, the effect of the Court's choice to define the legitimate exercise of fundamental rights as a barrier to Community movement is conceptually problematic. In particular, the following issues deserve closer attention.

First, even though the Court accepts that fundamental rights might prevail *even* over the Treaty rights, it seems to put the two on the same level. As a result, the language used by the Court is resonant of that used in relation to a clash of fundamental rights. And yet, one should be careful in accepting this premise as one which can be constitutionally justified. The Treaty rights might well be 'fundamental' to the achievement of European integration, and they might well be very important to Union citizens, but they are radically and qualitatively different from fundamental human rights recognised by the European Convention or in bills of rights across Europe. The Treaty rights are instrumental to the achievement of a political project; and they are rights which derive from a Treaty. Those rights would not, and do not, exist outside the Treaty providing for them. Furthermore, the constituency of right-holders is limited not only through the requirement of nationality; but also because those (Treaty) 'fundamental rights' are conditional upon movement and, in cases of mobility which is less transient in nature, also upon the satisfaction of given economic prerequisites, be those economic activity or economic independence.[38]

Fundamental rights, on the other hand, are those that we recognise, if not altogether inherent to, at least as being at the very core of our understanding of humanity. These rights do not necessarily need to be codified and are available to any person, regardless of nationality or wealth. They are not 'granted' by a legal document, but rather *recognised* in legal documents.[39] Without entering into the debate about the true nature of fundamental rights, this understanding of some rights as 'fundamental' is evident in the Union's own Charter of Fundamental Rights, which does not 'create' rights, but simply makes them more visible, and which recognises that some rights are available regardless of possessing Union citizenship.[40]

The use of the same terminology, that of fundamental rights, to identify two radically different types of rights is thus debatable; it suggests a homogeneity which is not conceptually sound and might lead to the classification of those 'spurious' conflicts of rights as *true* clashes of fundamental rights.[41] And this erroneous classification is not simply a matter of terminology: rather, it might deceive as to the respective strength

---

[38] Ie for stays of more than three months: see Art 7 Directive 2004/38 on the right of citizens of the Union and their family members to move and reside freely within the territory of the Member States [2004] OJ L229/35.

[39] This is certainly true for the European Community or else it would have been impossible for the Court to develop its general principles case law.

[40] We shall not enter into the debate as to whether the drafters' intention of avoiding a hierarchy of rights in the Charter has been fulfilled; in any event the scope of the rights in the Charter, and therefore the extent to which they can be protected, varies considerably from right to right. In this respect, consider also the distinction between 'principles' and 'rights' as drawn in Art 52(5) Charter (2007 version).

[41] On spurious conflicts, see L Zucca, *Constitutional Dilemmas. Conflict of Fundamental Legal Rights in Europe and the USA* (Oxford, Oxford University Press, 2007) and 'Conflicts of Rights as Constitutional Dilemmas' in E Brems (ed), *Conflicts between fundamental rights* (Antwerp/Oxford, Intersentia, 2008) 19. See further below.

of competing claims; and as to the hermeneutic path that the interpreter should take in order to solve instances of conflict.

Secondly, the language of the Court very much reflects this error in classification, leading to another flaw in the way in which the fundamental rights discourse is articulated in the jurisprudence. In *Schmidberger*, the Court found that the failure of the Austrian authorities to ban the demonstration which led to an interruption in the Brenner motorway was to be qualified as a measure having equivalent effect; it therefore had to be 'objectively' justified.[42] The Court then held that:

> ... since both the Community and its Member States are required to respect fundamental rights, the protection of those rights is a *legitimate interest* which, in principle, justifies a restriction of the obligations imposed by Community law, *even under* a fundamental freedom guaranteed by the Treaty such as the free movement of goods.[43]

The problem with this line of reasoning is that it suggests the demotion of fundamental rights from 'individual' rights to public policy reasons; from fundamental rights to legitimate *interests*, albeit interests which might prevail *even* over the free movement of goods. Furthermore, while at first sight it might seem that the Court either altogether rejects a hierarchy of rights; or privileges fundamental rights over Treaty rights, its analysis leads to the opposite conclusion, giving the impression of a hierarchical superiority of the Treaty rights over fundamental rights. The stress is, in fact, on the limitation of the right to move in Community law: freedom of expression is nothing but a limitation to this right which *might* (or might not) be legitimate.

The rest of the *Schmidberger* ruling confirms this reversal of priorities: thus, the Member State is called upon to justify the fact that it has *not* restricted a fundamental right. Since the right to freedom of expression can be restricted, the Member State might be under a Community law duty to do so. Whilst it is clear that there is no conflict of duties between Convention and Treaty, and that the Convention rights might sometimes be reinforced, since their breach might also constitute a breach of Community law, the *Schmidberger* ruling implies a positive duty to use the margin of appreciation recognised by the European Court of Human Rights so as to limit rights conferred by the Convention. The soundness of this interpretation might well be doubted, especially having regard to the fact that the Convention only recognises a basic floor of rights; and that the

---

[42] Case C-112/00, above n 36, para 64.
[43] *Ibid*, para 74 (emphasis added).

very idea of the margin of appreciation, and its use in relation (in particular) to the freedom of expression, has been heavily criticised.[44]

The fallacious premise which laid the foundation for the Court's reasoning—that of the homogeneity between Treaty rights and fundamental rights—then leads it to reverse the fundamental rights discourse. Fundamental rights are transformed from individual rights to a 'legitimate interest', to public policy reasons; and the Treaty rights become a vehicle to impose upon Member States a restrictive approach to fundamental rights, so that the margin of appreciation is transformed from an instrument, however debatable, which acknowledges some pluralism in our understanding of the precise content of fundamental rights, into a useful tool to enforce the primacy of Treaty rights. Furthermore, this mode of reasoning determines two important consequences: first of all, it allows the Court to claim a hermeneutic monopoly over the way in which conflicts between economic Treaty rights and fundamental rights are determined; secondly, and perhaps more importantly, it deprives the interpreter of any useful framework to assess how these conflicts should be solved, which in turn might lead to a loss of legitimacy once a decision has been taken. We shall now turn to the two cases that brought these problems into greater light.

B. The Rulings in *Viking* and *Laval*

The *Schmidberger* case was an easy one: it was unsurprising that the Court indicated that the Austrian authorities had not failed in their duties under Community law in allowing the demonstration to take place. And yet, as we have seen in the previous section, the reasoning of the Court was conceptually flawed.

Those flaws were, in the eyes of many commentators,[45] fully exposed in two subsequent cases that dealt with the conflict between Treaty rights and fundamental rights. In both cases, the issue at stake related to the extent to which the exercise of collective action could be construed as a barrier to the free movement rights. In *Viking*, the trade unions engaged in transnational collective action to prevent the flagging of convenience of a ship[46]; in *Laval*, coordinated collective action was taken in order to enforce local

---

[44] For an account, see J Sweeney, 'A "Margin of Appreciation" in the internal market: lessons from the European Court of Human Rights' (2007) 34 *Legal Issues of Economic Integration* 27.

[45] See, eg C Barnard, 'Social Dumping or Dumping Socialism?' (2008) 67 *CLJ* 262, as well as her contribution to this volume; P Sirpis and T Novitz 'Economic and social rights in conflict: political and judicial approaches to their reconciliation' (2008) 33 *EL Rev* 411; and ACL Davies 'One step forward, two steps back? The *Viking* and *Laval* cases in the ECJ' (2008) 37 *ILJ* 126.

[46] Case C-438/05, *The International Workers' Federation and the Finnish Seamen's Union v Viking Line* (judgment of 11 December 2007).

working conditions against a company which used foreign workers as posted workers.[47] The legal situation in those cases was slightly different from that at issue in *Schmidberger* in that, in the latter, the case arose as a result of a *Francovich* action taken against the state for its failure to protect the Treaty rights of the claimant, while in *Viking* and *Laval*, the Treaty was invoked directly by private parties against the trade unions.

Notwithstanding this difference, however, the starting premise of the *Viking* and *Laval* rulings is the same as that in *Schmidberger*: the protection of fundamental rights is a *legitimate interest* which must be '*reconciled* with the requirements relating to the rights protected under the Treaty and in accordance with the principle of proportionality'.[48] The stress in favour of Treaty rights is even more pronounced in *Viking* and *Laval* than it was in *Schmidberger*: it is the exercise of the fundamental right that must be proportionate. Thus, the traditional fundamental rights assessment is rebutted: rather than construing the exercise of a Treaty right as a possible interference with a fundamental right, an interference that would have to be proportionate according to the case law of the European Court of Human Rights, it is the exercise of the fundamental right that is construed as an interference with a (more) fundamental Treaty right and that must therefore be proportionate.

The consequences are far reaching and clearly visible in both cases. First of all, the assessment of the respective strengths between competing interests is centralised in the hands of the European Court of Justice.

Secondly, in both cases, the trade unions see imposed upon them a duty not to interfere with the Treaty rights of the economic operators. This fact further strengthens the Treaty right in comparison to the fundamental right, which is not horizontal unless national legislation provides for a duty upon the social partners to respect it; and, as noted by Giubboni, imposes upon the trade unions the duty to take into consideration not only the interests of the parties they represent, but also the interest of the counterparties they are acting against.[49] In this way, the very nature of collective action as a means to solve a labour *dispute* is deprived of its very *raison d'être*.

Thirdly, as a result, the conditions that determine the legitimate exercise of collective action are subsumed within the hermeneutic monopoly of the Court and are subtracted from negotiation between the different stake-holders. The social partners then lose a 'voice' in the collective process that determines the acceptable limits of the right to take collective action, on

---

[47] Case C-341/05, *Laval un Partneri* (judgment of 18 December 2007). See also C Barnard's contribution in this volume.

[48] *Viking*, para 46 (emphasis added).

[49] Paper (unpublished) presented at the Modern Law Review workshop 'Developing Solidarity in the EU: Citizenship, Governance and New Constitutional Paradigms' held at the University of Sussex (5 May 2008).

the one hand, and the duty to respect some predefined rules of the game that have been negotiated with the other social partners, on the other hand.

Fourthly, the trade unions might face financial liability for the (otherwise legitimate) exercise of a fundamental right.

The consequences of the *Viking* and *Laval* rulings are then far-reaching and deeply affect the balance of power between social parties. In this respect, those rulings exemplify the problems inherent in the premises from which the Court starts. Leaving aside the peculiarities of those cases, however, the Court's approach raises more general problems in relation to the centralisation of fundamental rights scrutiny, to which we shall now turn.

V. CENTRALISATION AND ITS PROBLEMS

The fundamental rights rhetoric endorsed by the Court in the early 1970s undoubtedly contributed to the legitimisation of the Communities/Union;[50] and such legitimising function would have been impossible without a degree of centralisation.

In relation to Union acts, and given the principle of supremacy as well as the *Foto-Frost* doctrine,[51] centralisation is not only desirable, but also essential to the Union's own functioning.[52] An act of the Union must be assessed in relation to the Union's own constitutional system. If a Union act is deemed unlawful, such an act must be void across the entire territory of the Union. In this respect, a limited degree of differentiation in fundamental rights protection is inevitable: the Union fundamental rights standard might be sometimes lower, and sometimes higher, than that which would be enforced at national level. Yet, given that, in any event, it cannot fall below the ECHR standard,[53] such oscillations are acceptable within the Union system.[54]

---

[50] See N Walker, 'Human Rights in a Postnational Order: Reconciling Political and Constitutional Pluralism' in Campbell, Ewing and Tomkins (eds), *Sceptical Essays on Human Rights* (Oxford, Oxford University Press, 2001) 119.

[51] Case 314/85, *Foto-Frost v Hauptzollamt Lübeck-Ost* [1987] ECR 4199.

[52] Although it is open to debate whether the *Foto-Frost* doctrine applies to third pillar acts where the Court's jurisdiction is reduced. Against the applicability of *Foto*-Frost to this area, see A Arnull, 'Taming the Beast? The Treaty of Amsterdam and the Court of Justice' in D O'Keeffe and P Twomey (eds), *Legal Issues of the Amsterdam Treaty* (Hart Publishing, Oxford, 1999) 109; and 'The Rule of Law in the European Union' in A Arnull and D Wincott (eds), *Accountability and Legitimacy in the European Union* (Oxford, Oxford University Press, 2002) 239. In favour, see E Spaventa, 'Remembrance of Principles Lost: on Fundamental Rights, the Third Pillar and the Scope of Union Law' (2006) 25 *Yearbook of European Law* 153.

[53] Which of course does not mean that it never falls below the ECHR standard: consider, eg the problems with the limited jurisdiction of the European Court of Justice in relation to the third pillar; or compare the ECJ's rather conservative approach in Joined Cases C-122 & 125/99, *D and Sweden v Council* [2001] ECR I-4319 with the ECtHR ruling in *Salgueiro da Silva Mouta v Portugal* (Application No 33290/96; judgment of 21 December 1999).

[54] See also the German Constitutional Law Court's ruling in the so-called *Solange 2* ruling [1987] 3 CMLR 225.

In relation to national law limiting or derogating from a Treaty right, centralisation is also not problematic from a fundamental rights perspective[55]: in those cases, fundamental rights and Treaty rights concur in affording the maximum level of protection to the individual. As mentioned above, in cases where the Member State is exercising a discretion when implementing Community law, the standard of fundamental rights protection is the highest between that set by national law and that set by Community law. In those situations in which the Member State is derogating or limiting a Treaty right, Community law fundamental rights are relevant only insofar as they afford more protection to the individual, either because the standard is higher or because of the better protection afforded by the immediate and direct applicability of Community law. Furthermore, it appears that, in such cases, the margin of appreciation left by the European Court of Justice to national authorities is narrower than that that would be accepted in the more diversified Convention system.[56] Finally, in those instances in which the Member State relies on fundamental rights in order to justify a limitation to a Treaty right, centralisation and federalisation appear balanced: subject to the supervisory role of the European Court of Justice (centralisation), the standard of fundamental rights protection is that chosen by the Member State (federalisation).[57]

However, in those cases where a Treaty right directly clashes with the exercise of a fundamental right, we see a strong push towards centralisation—and such a step is constitutionally more problematic. We have mentioned above that the starting premise in these cases is that of an ontological equation between Treaty rights and fundamental rights which leads to the qualification of those instances as clashes of rights. Here, it should be considered that true clashes of rights are always difficult to assess. Zucca has argued that 'genuine' clashes of rights are not only difficult, but *impossible* to adjudicate: the process of adjudication between two competing rights of equal force, what he identifies as a *true* clash, is the result of value judgments made by the adjudicator, be that a court or the legislature, which transcend the legal process.[58] In other words, the hermeneutic process does not help in finding a solution to true clashes of rights and, in those cases, the balancing exercise reflects the preferences of the adjudicator.

[55] While of course it still raises questions as to the boundaries of Community law and state's sovereignty.

[56] Eg it is open to debate whether the rules in *Carpenter* would have been found disproportionate by the European Court of Human Rights.

[57] Case C-36/02, above n 34.

[58] L Zucca, *Constitutional Dilemmas. Conflict of Fundamental Legal Rights in Europe and the USA* (Oxford, Oxford University Press, 2007) and 'Conflicts of Rights as Constitutional Dilemmas' in E Brems (ed), *Conflicts between fundamental rights* (Antwerp/Oxford, Intersentia, 2008) 19.

However, Zucca claims that true clashes of rights are much rarer than one might think. Rather, the majority of cases, those which he identifies as *spurious* clashes of rights, involve a clash between a right and a public interest. Here, the adjudicator might engage in a more fruitful balancing exercise, since the balancing exercise focuses on the very definition of the right at stake. Thus, hermeneutic principles and legal reasoning can perform their full function, very much in the same way as when the European Court of Justice is defining the scope of the Treaty freedoms and the extent to which Member States can invoke a public interest to limit those freedoms.

The qualification of the clash between Treaty rights and fundamental freedoms as a clash of rights then distorts the perspective, leaving us in the dark as to the way in which the respective strengths of the competing claims should be assessed. Here, it is argued that a more correct classification might be helpful in the process of adjudication. This is not only important for the sake of national courts and legal clarity; it is also crucial in order to bestow legitimacy onto the entire process. Otherwise, adjudication might be seen as transcending the hermeneutic dimension and become instead a political exercise. Here, consider the following.

The ECJ approached the *Schmidberger*-type problem in the following way:

Treaty right (including interest in European integration) → fundamental right
Fundamental right → fundamental right

As a result of this approach, the outcome of the case will include weighing up also the interest in European integration (a Community public interest) against the competing non-integrating fundamental right. This way of reasoning is unsatisfactory since, first, it does not enlighten us as to the process of adjudication and, secondly, it introduces a non-fundamental right variable in the fundamental right discourse.

A more satisfactory way to look at this question might be:

Right to exercise an economic activity → fundamental right
European integration → Community public interest
Fundamental right → fundamental right

If we were to follow this route, the outcome of the case will depend only on the mutual strengths of the two fundamental rights in competition, and the public interest of the Community would be treated exactly for what it is, ie a public interest which might in certain cases legitimately be relied upon by the Community in order to restrict a competing non-economic fundamental right.

The way of articulating the legal problem will then determine two radically different results. A theoretical example might serve to illustrate the difference. Let us consider a true clash of rights, ie a case where the conflicting claims are absolutely mutually exclusive so that the enjoyment of the right by an individual determines the loss of that same right by another. Take for instance the case of Ms Evans,[59] where the European Court of Human Rights had to determine whether Ms Evans' right to use her fertilised eggs, her only eggs that were available to her following treatment for cancer, clashed with her ex-husband's right to withdraw consent to the use of his genetic material. Now, and regardless of the merits of the case,[60] would it be intellectually defensible to say that, if the procedure for implant was to take place in another Member State, Mrs Evans' right to move and receive services should have been taken into consideration as (another) fundamental right to strengthen her claim?

If we were to accept the Court's reasoning in *Schmidberger*, then the answer would have to be positive. However, if we properly qualify the clash of rights as being a clash between Article 8 ECHR rights, the fact that Ms Evans were (or were not) to move would be irrelevant. Similarly, and as said before, in *Viking* and *Laval*, the competing claims were between the workers' rights to take collective action (either as part of their freedom of expression and association or as a free standing right)[61] and the employers' rights to pursue their trade or business (as part of their right to property). The Community dimension should have been relevant only in imposing upon the national authorities, or legislature, a duty not to discriminate between intra-Community and domestic situations, not in assessing the mutual strengths of the rights at issue.

Take for instance the case in which the political situation in another Member State attracts criticism of a human rights group elsewhere in the EU, and the latter group calls for a successful boycott of that Member State's products. Should the actions of the group, legal in the country where they took place, be called into question because they have an effect on intra-Community trade? Should the human rights group have due regard to the Treaty freedoms when organising a boycott? After all, their actions might lead to as severe consequences as those faced by the businesses in *Viking* and *Laval*. And what should we make of a strike that stops production and therefore exports? Is this the way we are going to assess the strengths of competing claims?

---

[59] *Evans v UK* (Application No 6339/05; judgment of 10 April 2007); also analysed by Zucca, n 38 above.

[60] For a reasoned critique, see R Thornton, 'European Court of Human Rights: Consent to IVF Treatment' (2008) 6 *International Journal of Constitutional Law* 317.

[61] The former would be the ECHR route, since there is no free-standing right to strike in the Convention; the latter might be the route to take following the rulings in *Viking* and *Laval*, since the Court held that the right to strike is a fundamental right recognised by the general principles of Community law (and by Art 28 of the EU Charter of Fundamental Rights). See also C Barnard, 'Social Dumping or Dumping Socialism?' (2008) 67 *CLJ* 262.

Furthermore, the different way of articulating the legal problem might also produce a different jurisdictional result. If the clash is between fundamental rights, regardless of the Community dimension, then the role of the European Court of Justice should be limited to a supervisory role, *Omega*-style, aimed at ensuring that claims containing a Community element are not treated in a different and more disadvantageous way than their purely domestic counterparts. However, if the clash is seen as a clash between a Community 'fundamental right' (ie the Treaty freedom) and another fundamental right, *Schmidberger/Viking* style, then the role of the European Court of Justice will be predominant and the latter will gain a monopoly in assessing the mutual strengths of the conflicting claims.

The way in which we choose to articulate a legal problem is of paramount importance, not only because it might determine the outcome of the case, but because it ensures the legitimacy of the adjudicating process. While it might be naive to believe that adjudication occurs in a political vacuum, the adjudicator cannot be seen as forcing his or her own societal/economic/ideological preferences as a matter of course. If the hermeneutic premises are faulty, the process of adjudication will be not only faulty, but will risk being de-legitimised. Cases involving clashes of fundamental rights are probably the most difficult to solve and surely the most controversial. However, when a court, be it national or supranational, fails to articulate its own discourse, it risks being accused of moving into a realm that it does not pertain to it, that of pure politics. Furthermore, if the legal reasoning is not articulated, it is impossible to predict.

VI. CONCLUSIONS

The development of a fundamental rights discourse in the European Union has undoubtedly strengthened the Union's constitutional foundations as well as its democratic credentials. This discourse has been embraced by all of the institutional actors at European level: if national court and European Court of Justice have provided the original impetus, the political institutions have been more than ready to provide their own contribution to the development of a fundamental rights discourse in the EU. However, the process through which the fundamental rights rhetoric is developed is far from being linear: rather, it reflects the Union's own constitutional idiosyncrasies. In this respect, the articulation of the fundamental rights discourse at the political level might appear rather schizophrenic, with different forces puling in opposite directions. These opposing forces are visible also in the case law of the European Court of Justice, albeit, naturally, the centralising force has been predominant in the Court's discourse. While this centralisation is fully justified in relation to most of the case law, to either ensure the proper functioning of the Union or the protection of individuals, in cases involving a clash of rights, such a centralising approach is more debatable. In this case, centralisation is the result of a false premise, that of an ontological homogeneity between Treaty rights and fundamental rights. This false premise determines both the artificial strengthening of some claims vis-a-vis others, solely because of the existence of a cross-border element, and also the imposition of the Court's hermeneutic monopoly. Furthermore, the fallacious starting point determines the impossibility of ascertaining the reasons behind the adjudicating process. However, once the legal discourse is articulated in a different way, so that the competing fundamental rights are properly identified, it is possible to correct these distortions and to ensure a hermeneutically consistent system. And once the competing claims are identified for what they are, and the Community interest is properly identified as no more than a public interest, the process of adjudication becomes more transparent, as well as being properly relocated in the hands of the national judiciary. After all, centralisation is not always the answer.

15

The Transformation of Union Citizenship

SAMANTHA CURRIE

I. INTRODUCTION

U NION CITIZENSHIP HAS proven to be one of the most dynamic facets of Community law in recent years. The extent of the activity surrounding the status of Union citizenship, which has more latterly been of a legislative as well as a judicial nature,[1] perhaps betrays a little the relative youth of the concept. The original Treaty of Rome may have been 'determined to lay the foundations of an ever closer union among the peoples of Europe', but it was not until Maastricht in 1992 that the status of Union citizenship was formalised by insertion into the EC Treaty.

Not only has the concept itself undergone something of a transformation, in that it has moved from a status assumed to be of mostly symbolic significance to one that can bestow meaningful rights and privileges, developments in the citizenship *acquis* have also had wider transformative effects. The influence of the Court of Justice's jurisprudence in the area has been felt by migrants (both of the non-economic and economic kind); as well as host (and home) Member States and their social welfare systems. It has also shaped the development and application of principles such as proportionality and non-discrimination on grounds of nationality.

The Court's favoured mantra, that Union citizenship is destined to be the fundamental status of nationals of the Member States, reflects the transformative nature of the concept.[2] This is clearly an aspirational statement

---

[1] Notably, much of the case law has been consolidated in Directive 2004/38 on the free movement of Union citizens and their family members to move and reside freely within the territory of the Member States [2004] OJ L158/77.

[2] This was first stated by the ECJ in its judgment in Case C-184/99, *Grzelczyk* [2001] ECR I-6193. It has been re-stated in a number of subsequent judgments and its inclusion in the preamble to Directive 2004/38 suggests that it has also been embraced by the legislature.

which suggests that the full potential of the status is yet to be unlocked. The aim of this chapter is to present some reflections on the progress (thus far) of Union citizenship and to consider potential future directions and remaining challenges for the status. Specifically, it seeks to measure the extent to which Union citizenship has truly transformed and, by corollary, how far away the current position is from constituting the fundamental status of Member State nationals.

A theme pertinent to this contribution is that of exclusion and this arises in different contexts. First, there is the question of how far the position of economically inactive migrants has been transformed by Union citizenship. Migrants exercising a non-economic right of movement have traditionally had much less extensive entitlement to residence and social rights in a host Member State. The contribution will outline the changes brought about as a consequence of Union citizenship. Secondly, there is the extent to which non-movers remain excluded from the reach of citizenship rights. Surely, if Union citizenship really is destined to be the fundamental status of Member State nationals, the effect of that status should be felt by all, regardless of whether cross-border mobility rights have been exercised. Union citizenship was linked forcibly with free movement, and the already-existing economic free movement rights, from the outset. This exclusion of those who do not exercise migratory rights from the scope of the Treaty persists to this day.[3]

More generally, the relationship that the Union citizenship provisions have with the free movement provisions applicable to economic migrants will be considered. While the Court's interpretation of Article 18 EC has been shaped by its earlier approach to Article 39 EC, the effects have also been felt in the reverse direction. Thus, the discussion will also examine how principles developed under the auspices of Article 18 EC have infiltrated reasoning under Article 39 EC.

II. STRIVING FOR LEGITIMACY: THE ORIGINS OF UNION CITIZENSHIP

It has been well rehearsed elsewhere that the creation of the Union citizenship status was part of a desire to enhance the legitimacy of the European project and to bring the European Community closer to the

---

[3] Case C-212/06, *Government of the French Community and Walloon Government v Flemish Government* (judgment of 1 April 2008). Although it is outside the scope of this contribution, the exclusionary nature of Union citizenship is also exemplified by its non-applicability to third-country national migrants. The inability of this group to derive any individual entitlement from Union citizenship remains significant.

nationals of the Member States.[4] This is a citizenship that was 'not won by the citizens but bestowed from above by a legitimacy-seeking elite'.[5]

From the outset, the development of a European citizenship was linked to the exercise of free movement rights. The 1975 Tindemans Report on the European Union, produced at the request of the Paris summit in 1974, included a chapter entitled 'Towards a Europe for Citizens'. This was the first publication to make express reference to the concept.[6] The concern of this report was to suggest ways in which the integration of Community nationals living in Member States other than their own could be enhanced. Interestingly, the idea of encouraging a greater number of trans-European student exchanges was also put forward. Throughout the remainder of the 1970s and 1980s, various other papers touched upon the idea of a European citizenship. For example, a Commission communication on a 'People's Europe' in 1988 emphasised the importance of promoting a European identity.[7] Furthermore, in a proposal for a Directive on voting rights of Community nationals in local elections, the Commission maintained that EU nationals residing in a host Member State should be entitled to vote in local elections.[8] It was not until the Intergovernmental Conference of 1990, which preceded the signing of the Maastricht Treaty, that the plans for Union citizenship took a more solid form. The Spanish delegation submitted a document entitled 'The Road to European Citizenship'. This paper, which again included proposals aimed at enhancing the status of those Community nationals residing in Member States other than that of their origin, provided the basis of the citizenship discussions in the lead-up to the adoption of the Treaty on European Union.[9] Consequently, the citizenship chapter was inserted into Part Two of the EC Treaty. Clearly, the removal of the term 'economic' from the Treaty's title and the renaming of the EEC as the EC, again a result of changes agreed at Maastricht, also linked with the broader aim of making the Union meaningful in more than an economic sense.

These formal citizenship provisions established the status of Union citizenship which is held by every person with nationality of an EU Member State.[10] As a result of the attachment of the status to Member State nationality, third-country nationals remain outside the personal scope

---

[4] For more detail on the background behind the inclusion of citizenship see S O'Leary, *The Evolving Concept of Community Citizenship* (The Hague, Kluwer, 1996).

[5] P Magnette, 'How Can One be European? Reflections on the Pillars of European Civic Identity' (2007) 13 *European Law Journal* 664.

[6] Bull EC (8) 1975 II No 12, 1.

[7] COM(88) 331 Final.

[8] COM(88) 371 Final.

[9] A Wiener, *'European' Citizenship Practice: Building Institutions of a Non-State* (Boulder, Westview, 1998).

[10] Art 17 EC. The Treaty of Amsterdam, which entered into force in 1997, added to Art 17 EC the statement that 'Citizenship of the Union shall complement and not replace national

of Union citizenship in a very absolute sense, regardless of the strength of their links to an EU Member State.[11] Thus, the drive to enhance the EU's legitimacy appears to have been concerned with courting only Member State nationals.[12] The express rights articulated include, in Article 18 EC, the 'general' right to move and reside freely within the territory of the Member States, subject to the limitations and conditions laid down by the Treaty and the measures adopted to give it effect. There is also a series of political and participatory rights: the right to vote and stand in local and European elections in a host state[13]; the right to diplomatic and consular protection from the authorities of any Member State in third countries[14]; and the right to petition the European Parliament and the right to apply to the ombudsman in any one of the official languages of the EU.[15] Like the preparatory materials and discussions prior to Maastricht, the expression of the notion of Union citizenship in the Treaty clearly resonates with the

citizenship'. The granting of nationality remains the exclusive prerogative of the individual Member States: Case C-369/90, *Micheletti* [1992] ECR I-4239; and Case C-200/02, *Zhu and Chen* [2004] ECR I-9925.

[11] Of course, third-country nationals who are family members of a migrant Union citizen derive certain rights in a host Member State (or in the Union citizen's Member State of origin when they return after a period of residence elsewhere in the EU). The relevant legislative provisions are now contained in Directive 2004/38 [2004] OJ L158/77 (previously Regulation 1612/68 [1968] OJ L257/2). On the status of third-country national family members see, inter alia, Case 267/83, *Diatta* [1985] ECR 567; Case C-413/99, *Baumbast and R* [2002] ECR I-7091; Case C-370/90, *R v Immigration Appeal Tribunal et Surinder Singh, ex p Secretary of State for Home Department* [1992] ECR I-4265; Case C-109/01, *Secretary of State for the Home Department v Akrich* [2003] ECR I-9607; Case C-1/05, *Yunying Jia v Migrationsverket* [2007] ECR I-0001; and Case C-127/08 Metock (judgment of 25 July 2008).

[12] Although Community initiatives under Title IV, Part Three of the EC Treaty have attempted to promote the integration of third-country nationals within the Member States. For example, Directive 2003/109 on the status of third-country nationals who are long-term residents [2004] OJ L16/44 and Directive 2003/86 on the right to family reunification [2003] OJ L251/12 (Ireland, the UK and Denmark are not bound by these directives). See T Kostakopoulou, 'Long-term Resident Third-Country Nationals in the European Union: Normative Expectations and Institutional Openings' (2002) 28 *Journal of Ethnic and Migration Studies* 443; T Kostakopoulou, '"Integrating" Non-EU Migrants in the European Union: Ambivalent Legacies and Mutating Paradigms' (2002) 8 *Columbia Journal of European Law* 181; G Barratt, 'Family Matters: European Community Law and Third Country Family Members' (2003) 40 *CML Rev* 369; and E Guild and C Harlow (eds), *Implementing Amsterdam: Immigration and Asylum Rights in EC Law* (Oxford, Hart, 2001).

[13] Art 19 EC. See Case C-145/04, *Spain v United Kingdom* [2006] ECR I-7917 and Case C-300/04, *Eman and Sevinger* [2006] ECR I-8055. Specifically on the aspects of political citizenship, see H Lardy, 'The Political Rights of Union Citizenship' (1997) *European Public Law* 111; J Shaw, 'Sovereignty at the Boundaries of the Polity' in N Walker (ed), *Sovereignty in Transition* (Oxford, Hart, 2003) 461; J Shaw and M Smith, 'Changing Polities and Electoral Rights: Lithuania's accession to the EU' in P Shah and W Minski (eds), *Migration, Diasporas and Legal Systems in Europe* (London, Routledge, 2006) 145; and J Shaw, *The Transformation of Citizenship in the European Union: Electoral Rights and the Restructuring of Political Space* (Cambridge, Cambridge University Press, 2007).

[14] Art 20 EC.

[15] Art 21 EC.

notion of free movement. The majority of the applicable rights, notwithstanding Article 18 EC itself, are exercisable only outside of the citizen's home state or where a cross-border element is present. Furthermore, the rights that do not depend on mobility—that is, the ability to petition the European Parliament and apply to the ombudsman—are not 'true' citizenship rights as they are available to all residents, including third-country nationals. Article 21 EC merely expresses rights set out in Part Five of the Treaty, 'Provisions Governing the Institutions'.[16]

The incorporation of the citizenship provisions at Maastricht may signify the birth of the formal concept of Union citizenship and its express entry into the Union's consciousness, but citizenship-like rights have a much longer history within the scheme of the Treaties. Specifically, the economic free movement provisions had already extended valuable social and economic rights to those exercising a right of free movement.[17] This had largely been achieved by a series of pieces of secondary legislation and by the broad interpreting case law of the European Court of Justice (ECJ).[18] In addition, the principle of non-discrimination on grounds of nationality was already enshrined in the Treaty.[19] Thus, citizenship is regarded as being present—at least in an 'embryonic' or 'incipient' sense—in the original EEC Treaty.[20] Shaw makes the point that the formalisation of Union citizenship at Maastricht:

> ... was essentially the beginning of a new stage in an on-going process of development of the status of the individual under Community law which had involved inputs from the Court of Justice, and especially its constitutionalisation of the free movement provisions and the right to non-discrimination on the grounds of nationality ...[21]

Citizenship in a European sense, therefore, stretches further than its articulation in Articles 17 to 22 EC, so as also to incorporate the

---

[16] Art 194 EC (the right to petition the European Parliament); and Art 195 EC (the right to apply to the ombudsman).

[17] Art 39 EC on the free movement of workers; Art 43 EC including the right of establishment; and Art 49 EC on the provision of cross-border services.

[18] Notably Regulation 1612/68 on freedom of movement for workers within the Community [1968] OJ L257/2. On the interpretation of 'social advantages' under Art 7(2), see, inter alia, Case 207/78, *Even* [1979] ECR 2019; Case 32/75, *Fiorini v SNCF* [1975] ECR 1085; Case 65/81, *Reina* [1982] ECR I-33; and Case C-237/94, *O'Flynn* [1996] ECR I-2617.

[19] Art 12 EC.

[20] RO Plender, 'An Incipient Form of European Citizenship' in F Jacobs (ed), *European Law and the Individual* (North-Holland, 1976); and F Jacobs, 'Citizenship of the European Union—A Legal Analysis' (2007) 13 *European Law Journal* 591.

[21] J Shaw, 'The Many Pasts and Futures of Citizenship in the European Union' (1997) 22 *EL Rev* 554.

traditional 'economic' free movement provisions, read alongside the extensive interpretation provided by the ECJ of the social rights of economic migrants. It also finds expression via the equal treatment principle in Article 12 EC and various pieces of secondary legislation.[22]

III. INCREMENTAL EVOLUTION

Given that market citizenship was already firmly established in the EEC Treaty, it is no surprise that the formal citizenship provisions, the general right of free movement in Article 18 EC in particular, have had the more transformative implications for the status of economically inactive migrants. Although the case law on the effect of the right of residence in Article 18 EC, and the attachment of the non-discrimination principle to that right, is well known, it will be considered below in order to illustrate the gradual development of the status. Attention will then turn to the impact of the citizenship provisions on the interpretation of the economic free movement rights.

A. The Court's Interpretation of the Formal Citizenship Provisions

Prior to the formalisation of Union citizenship, economically inactive migrants did not fall within the scope of the Treaty's free movement provisions. This entitlement was preserved only for those exercising economic activity. Non-economic migrants, however, had already been extended conditional rights of residence in their host Member State under a series of residence directives adopted in the early 1990s.[23] Such a right of residence was subject to the twin requirements of possessing sufficient resources so as not to become a burden on the public assistance of the host Member State, and of having taken out a policy of sickness insurance in the host state for themselves and their family.[24] The imposition of such conditions clearly represents a concern to prevent migrants from posing any sort of risk to a host Member State's social welfare system. In the aftermath of the Maastricht Treaty entering into force, it was unclear what the relationship between the Directives' requirement of self-sufficiency on the one hand, and the 'limitations and conditions' on the right of free

---

[22] Now most notably Directive 2004/38 [2004] OJ L158/77 and Regulation 1612/68 [1968] OJ L257/2.

[23] Directive 90/365 [1990] OJ L180/28 concerned retired persons; Directive 93/96 [1993] OJ L317/59 concerned students; and Directive 90/364 [1990] OJ L180/26 addressed financially independent persons. This legislation has since been repealed by Directive 2004/38 [2004] OJ L158/77.

[24] Directive 2004/38 retains these requirements (see Art 7).

movement referred to in Article 18 EC, on the other hand, would be. Although there was a feeling that the changes to the Treaty were merely of a symbolic nature, some commentators did argue from the outset that Article 18 EC at least had the potential to disentangle, to an extent, the links between the right to move freely and the need to be economically active or self-sufficient.[25] It was some time before the Court began to make significant pronouncements on the effect of the citizenship provisions.[26]

In *Martínez Sala*, the Court held for the first time that an economically inactive Union citizen who was lawfully resident in a Member State could challenge unequal treatment they experienced, in comparison to nationals of the host state, on the basis of Article 12 EC.[27] As a consequence of her lawful residence in Germany,[28] Ms Sala was within the scope *ratione personae* of the Treaty. Given that Article 17(2) EC had attached the rights in the Treaty to the status of Union citizen, she was able to rely on the principle of non-discrimination on the ground of nationality to access a child-raising allowance. This benefit fell 'indisputably' within the scope *ratione materiae* of the Treaty owing to its status as a 'social advantage' pursuant to Article 7(2) of Regulation 1612/68 and as a 'family benefit' under Article 4(1)(h) of Regulation 1408/71.[29] Even though the reasoning in this judgment was not based on Article 18 EC, and therefore it did not clarify the link between the 'limitations and conditions' and the pre-Maastricht secondary legislation on residence, it did demonstrate a willingness on behalf of the ECJ to interpret the citizenship provisions in a manner that would broaden the application of free movement entitlement under Community law and bestow more significant rights on those migrants without an economic status.[30]

---

[25] For more detail on the uncertainty surrounding the effect of the citizenship provisions, see S O'Leary, *The Evolving Concept of Community Citizenship* (The Hague, Kluwer, 1996); and S Fries and J Shaw, 'Citizenship of the Union: First Steps in the European Court of Justice' (1998) 4 *European Public Law* 533.

[26] Of course, the somewhat incremental development of the law in this area is to an extent attributable to the way in which cases make their way to the ECJ. It has been via the Art 234 EC preliminary reference procedure that the vast majority of the citizenship cases have reached the ECJ; clearly, the Court cannot influence the references made by national courts.

[27] Case C-85/96, *Martinez Sala* [1998] ECR I-2691. See C Tomuschat, Comment on *Maria Martinez Sala* (2000) 37 *CML Rev* 449; and S O'Leary, 'Putting Flesh on the Bones of European Union Citizenship' (1999) 24 *EL Rev* 68.

[28] Ms Sala's lawful residence stemmed from national law, as opposed to Art 18 EC.

[29] Last consolidated version published [1997] OJ L28/1. Note that a new regulation has been adopted which overhauls the coordination system somewhat: Regulation 883/2004 [2004] OJ L200/1.

[30] Although it was, in fact, left to the national court to decide whether or not Ms Sala did actually qualify as a worker, it was on the basis of her lawful residence read in conjunction with Arts 17(2) and 12 EC that she was entitled to the benefit.

Further details regarding both the residence right in Article 18 EC and the application of Article 12 EC emerged in the cases of *Grzelczyk*[31] and *Baumbast*.[32] In *Grzelczyk*, the Court confirmed that the requirements of having sufficient resources and medical insurance did indeed fall within the ambit of the 'limitations and conditions' relevant to the general right of residence in Article 18 EC. Therefore, it was recognised that Member States have a legitimate interest in ensuring that migrant citizens do not become an unreasonable burden on their social welfare system.[33] Nevertheless, the Court also stated that expulsion should not be an automatic consequence of a migrant's recourse to the social assistance system.[34] It was in this judgment that the Court first asserted that citizenship is destined to be the fundamental status of Member State nationals.[35] Moreover, another notable declaration was made: that the Member States had accepted a certain degree of financial solidarity between nationals and non-nationals with adoption of the residence directives.[36] The result of the reasoning in the judgment was that Mr Grzelczyk, a French national in the fourth year of his university studies in Belgium, could have a lawful right to reside in Belgium under Article 18 EC despite the fact that he clearly did not fulfil the requirement in Directive 93/96 of having sufficient resources (his application to receive the *minimex* rather gave this away). The Court placed significance on the fact that Grzelczyk was merely experiencing 'temporary difficulties' after three years of self-sufficiency.[37] As regards Mr Grzelcyk's entitlement to the *minimex* benefit, the Court applied the reasoning from *Sala* to the effect that lawfully resident migrant citizens can rely on Article 12 EC to gain access to benefits within the scope of Community law on the same basis as nationals.[38] In relation to the scope *ratione materiae*, the ECJ in *Grzelczyk* again drew a parallel with Article 7(2) of Regulation 1612/68.[39]

This is a judgment within which the transformative effects of Union citizenship are evident. The ECJ had to surmount additional obstacles to give effect to a right of equal treatment in respect of social benefits for students. Article 3 of Directive 93/96 itself made clear that migrant students had no right of access to maintenance grants; furthermore, in the earlier case of *Brown*, it had been decided that, at the stage of development

---

[31]   Case C-184/99, above n 2.
[32]   Case C-413/99, above n 11.
[33]   This has been embodies in Art 14(1) Directive 2004/38.
[34]   *Grzelczyk*, para 43. This has since been codified in Art 14(3) Directive 2004/38.
[35]   *Grzelczyk*, para 31.
[36]   *Ibid*, paras 40–44.
[37]   *Ibid*, para 44.
[38]   The principle of equal treatment for those lawfully resident has been enshrined in Art 24 Directive 2004/38.
[39]   *Grzelczyk*, para 27.

Community law was at, there was no anti-discrimination protection available in the area of maintenance or training grants.[40] The ECJ was of the opinion that the introduction into the EC Treaty of the citizenship provisions (along with a chapter on education and vocational training)[41] had altered the position of Community law. Following *Grzekczyk*, then, *Brown* is no longer regarded as a correct statement of the law[42] and the elevated status of students as Union citizens means that the equal treatment principle can apply as regards social security and assistance benefits available to students under national law.[43]

It was in the case of *Baumbast* that the Court expressly declared the right to reside in Article 18 EC to be directly effective. This was despite the argument, put forward by the German and UK governments, that the 'limitations and conditions' referred to in Article 18 EC prevented the right from being free-standing.[44] The Court confirmed that the right of residence in Article 18 EC was sufficiently clear, precise and unconditional and, thus, conferred a right upon individuals.[45] As in *Grzelczyk*, though, the ECJ also confirmed that Article 18 EC had not completely detached the right to free movement from the requirement of economic self-sufficiency. The right to free movement for citizens can be subordinated to the legitimate interests of the Member States which are perfectly entitled to prevent economically inactive migrants from becoming an unreasonable burden.[46] Importantly, the Court went on to provide that any action taken by a Member State in an attempt to limit such a right of residence must comply 'with the limits imposed by Community law and in accordance with the general principles of that law, in particular with the principle of proportionality'.[47] It was the application of the principle of proportionality that enabled Mr Baumbast's right of residence to remain intact despite the formal requirements of the

---

[40] Case 197/86, *Brown* [1988] ECR 3205. Although pre-*Brown*, in Case 293/83, *Gravier* [1985] ECR 593, the ECJ had held that there was a right to equal treatment in relation to fees for Higher Education.

[41] Title XI, Chapter 3 of Part Three of the EC Treaty.

[42] *Grzelczyk*, paras 34–5.

[43] In Case C-209/03, *Bidar* [2005] ECR I-2119, students' equal treatment rights were considered further. Mr Bidar, who was lawfully resident in the UK under Directive 90/364 (not Directive 93/96) was entitled to rely on Art 12 EC in order to gain access to a student loan on the same basis as nationals. Again, the Court held that developments in Community law precluded the exclusion of student maintenance grants and loans from Art 12 EC. See C Barnard, Comment on *Bidar* (2005) 42 *CML Rev* 1465.

[44] *Bidar*, para 78.

[45] *Ibid*, para 86.

[46] *Ibid*, para 90.

[47] *Ibid*, para 91. Essentially, the statement in *Grzelczyk* that expulsion should not be the automatic consequence of recourse to the social assistance system is an application of the principle of proportionality.

secondary legislation, specifically the health insurance condition in Directive 90/364, not being fulfilled.[48] The Baumbast family had not previously been a burden on the UK's public finances and the family was well integrated into the society after residing in the UK for a number of years; furthermore, the family had sickness insurance in Germany, where they returned when medical assistance was required. Consequently, it is no surprise that the British authorities' decision to deport Mr Baumbast was considered to be a disproportionate interference with his right to free movement.[49]

This trio of cases set the development of the notion of Union citizenship in motion. Not only did the judgments enhance the residence status of economically inactive migrants, they also provided a basis for such citizens to access rights and (a wide range of) benefits on a par with nationals.[50] Linking lawful residency, be it under national law or Article 18 EC, with the right to rely on Article 12 EC, inevitably brings to the fore tensions between the extension of rights to economically inactive migrants and the potential disruption caused to national welfare systems. The ECJ has clearly sought to strike a balance by incorporating the test of proportionality, which includes consideration of the individual's particular circumstances, and the concept of unreasonable burden, which was originally used in the residence directives and allows Member States to protect the national welfare system from excessive reliance on the right to equal treatment by non-economic migrants resident within their territory.

Both *Martínez Sala* and *Grzelczyk* involved direct discrimination in that the applications for the relevant social benefit had been refused solely on the basis of the applicant's nationality. A further judgment delivered around the same time as the latter cases, *D'Hoop*, concerned an indirectly discriminatory condition governing access to a social benefit.[51] This case is

---

[48] See further AP Van Der Mei, Comments on *Baumbast* (2003) 5 *European Journal of Migration and Law* 419; M Dougan and E Spaventa, 'Educating Rudy and the Non English Patient: A Double Bill on Residency Rights Under Art 18 EC' (2003) 28 *EL Rev* 699; and M Dougan, 'The Constitutional Dimension of the Case Law on Union Citizenship' (2006) 31 *EL Rev* 613.

[49] The situation of the Baumbast family can be contrasted with that of Mr Trojani in Case C-456/02, *Trojani* [2004] ECR I-7573. This applicant for the Bejgian *mininex* was residing in Belgium in a Salvation Army hostel and clearly did not meet the sufficient resources condition in the secondary legislation. Here, the Member State's application of limitations and conditions was held to be proportionate and Mr Trojani did not have an enforceable right of residence under Art 18 EC. Like Ms Sala, though, Mr Trojani appeared to be lawfully residing on the basis of Belgian national law as he had been issued with a residence permit. So long as national law regards such an applicant as being lawfully resident, the individual will be entitled to rely on Art 12 EC to claim equal treatment (of course, the Member State in this situation is by no means obliged to continue to grant a right of residence to such an individual who does not meet the requirements of sufficient resources and sickness insurance).

[50] The equal treatment principle has since been codified in Art 24 Directive 2004/38.

[51] Case C-224/98, *D'Hoop* [2002] ECR I-6191.

also significant in that it has provided the foundations for the Court's reasoning in future cases involving similar conditions of access.[52] In circumstances where a Member State has imposed a rule which de facto disadvantages migrants (or, indeed, nationals who have moved cross-border and are relying on their Treaty rights against their state of origin),[53] the Court signified that Member States can legitimately expect claimants of benefits to demonstrate a real link between themselves and the national territory. Requiring such a genuine connection is an additional mechanism Member States can make use of to protect their legitimate interests. Ms D'Hoop was a Belgian national who returned to Belgium after receiving her secondary education in France. She was refused access to a 'tideover allowance' due to rules which made the granting of the benefit conditional on having completed secondary education in Belgium. The rules were clearly indirectly discriminatory and, in line with its case law on indirect discrimination against economically active migrants,[54] the Court held that such treatment could be justified by reference to objective factors independent of nationality and proportionate to the legitimate aim of the national rules. Specifically, the ECJ confirmed that the Member State has a legitimate interest in seeking to ensure that the applicant for a tideover allowance could demonstrate a real and genuine link with the national employment market.[55] In this case, though, the single condition relating to the place where secondary education was completed was disproportionate to the aim of ensuring such a real and genuine link. It was too general and exclusive in nature to achieve that aim.[56]

Such notions have continued to play a significant role in the development of Union citizenship. A similar approach was taken in *Bidar*, for example, with the Court agreeing that the UK was entitled to request that the recipient of a student loan first demonstrate a certain degree of integration into the host state.[57] In this case, the UK law imposed two layers of restriction which had both an indirectly and directly discriminatory impact. Applicants for student loans were required to fulfil a test of being ordinarily resident in the UK for three years, and an additional test of being 'settled' in the UK. The 'ordinarily resident' limb was more easily satisfied by UK nationals[58]; however, the 'settled' limb amounted to a blanket ban on the ability of students from other Member States to obtain

---

[52] Notably, Case C-138/02, *Collins* [2004] ECR I-2703; Case C-209/03, above n 43; and Case C-258/04, *Ioannidis* [2005] ECR I-8275.

[53] As in Case C-224/98, above n 51.

[54] Case C-237/94, above n 18.

[55] Case C-224/98, above n 51, paras 38–9. As a Belgian national it would surely not have been difficult for Ms D'Hoop to demonstrate such a link.

[56] *Ibid*, paras 38–40.

[57] Case C-209/03, above n 43.

[58] *Ibid*, para 53.

student loans and, hence, amounted to direct discrimination on the ground of nationality.[59] The advantage was reserved exclusively for students of UK nationality. Despite this direct discrimination against students from other EU Member States, the approach of the Court was to take the two layers as a single bundle and subject it, as a whole, to the objective justification test. The Court, therefore, did suggest that the apparent direct discrimination was potentially justifiable, although it concluded in *Bidar* that the 'settled' layer of the requirement was disproportionate, since its effect was to exclude migrants, whatever the actual extent of their integration, from the ability to claim a student loan.[60]

The use of the integration, or 'genuine link', test is another method adopted by the Court to strike a fair balance between the rights of economically inactive migrants and the legitimate interests of the Member States to protect their national welfare systems. The establishment by a non-economic migrant of a genuine link with a host Member State is, essentially, equivalent to the carrying out of an economic activity by a migrant exercising a right of free movement under one of the economic freedoms. Both are a way of gaining a level of membership or belonging in a host Member State that brings with it some concomitant social rights. Thus far, the length of residence has been the main factor taken into account to assess the level of integration.[61] It is not clear if the Court will begin to consider other factors, such as the *quality* of the integration in a host society, and adopt a broader conceptualisation of what constitutes a genuine link in future.[62] Arguably, other factors in addition to residence— such as particularly strong family connections—can also demonstrate a strong link to a society.[63]

As is apparent from the brief discussion here, much of the case law has involved the non-discrimination principle being utilised in order to gain access to some form of social benefit. Clearly, this is also one of the more controversial aspects of Union citizenship as it raises issues relating to belonging and the level of solidarity non-nationals should be entitled to. It

---

[59]   *Ibid*, paras 60–63.

[60]   *Ibid*, para 61.

[61]   The case law has generally rewarded longer periods of residence: *Martinez Sala* is such an example, and this is recognised in Directive 2004/38 with the creation of a permanent resident status for those who reside in a host Member State for a period of five years (Art 16). See C Barnard, 'EU Citizenship and the Principle of Solidarity' in M Dougan and E Spaventa, (eds), *Social Welfare and EU Law* (Oxford, Hart, 2005) 157.

[62]   For further discussion of the 'genuine link' notion used in the Court's citizenship case law, see A Somek, 'Solidarity Decomposed: Being and Time in European Citizenship' (2007) 32 *EL Rev* 787.

[63]   Although this may be taken into account should expulsion be ordered in any event. Member States must take into account proportionality *and other general principles of Community law*. This includes the fundamental right of respect family life enshrined in Art 8 ECHR: see Case C-482/01, *Orfanopoulos* [2004] ECR I-5257; and Case C-109/01, above n 11.

is interesting that a status introduced with the aim of enhancing the Union's legitimacy may well have had the opposite effect in some quarters. The migration of economically inactive migrants often has connotations of 'benefit tourism' attached to it. Clearly, such negative associations can feed into anxieties at national level surrounding migration. There is also potential for these undertones to pander to anti-European Union feeling, in particular when concerns about 'foreign welfare claimants' are conflated with statements pertaining to the EU's supposed role in undermining Member States' ability to control their own borders. The expression of such sentiments, in the national press for example, does little to enhance the status of European citizenship or the EU itself.

In any event, it is important to note that the non-discrimination principle can have other positive effects outside the realm of social benefits. In *Garcia Avello*, for example, Article 12 EC was used in order to enforce a right for children of a Union citizen to take their mother's surname where the national law of the host state (Belgium) specified it had to be the father's surname.[64] One of the most interesting, and contentious, cases to arise out of the formal citizenship provisions is that of *Zhu and Chen*.[65] Although this case is somewhat different from those described directly above, it provides a further pertinent example of how Union citizenship can have profound effects on the status of individuals. The facts of the case are well known: Catherine was a baby born to Chinese parents in Northern Ireland. Belfast had deliberately been chosen as the place of birth due to the Republic of Ireland's nationality rules which extended citizenship to all persons born within the island of Ireland. Had Catherine been born in China, her parents would have been in contravention of the one-child policy. Mrs Chen later moved with Catherine to Wales and sought to rely on Article 18 EC to establish a right of residence in the UK. Despite the situation being suggestive of an abuse of rights, the ECJ accepted the argument that Catherine, a minor, could exercise a right to reside under Article 18 EC. Crucial to this was the finding that, by virtue of the financial status of the family, Catherine would satisfy the sufficient resources condition in the applicable secondary legislation.[66] Additionally, as Catherine's right to reside would be worthless without the corollary right being extended to her primary carer, Mrs Chen could also continue to reside in the UK.[67] Again, in spite of the lack of impact this outcome had for the social assistance system of the UK (the non-discrimination principle

---

[64] Case C-148/02, *Garcia Avello* [2003] ECR I-11613.

[65] Case C-200/02, above n 10.

[66] Thus, it would appear that it is not necessary for a Union citizen to demonstrate that the sufficient resources they have access to are their own.

[67] Third-country national 'primary carers' have also been granted rights of residence in a host state in the aftermath of divorce and the ceasing of economic activity by the worker when the child of a migrant worker has utilised their right to pursue their education in that

was not relevant to this case), it is easy to surmise that this case may well have had negative implications for the perception of Union citizenship. The potential connotations of this judgment not only include the suggestion that Member States lose the ability to control their own borders, but also that the citizenship provisions are open to 'abuse'.[68] Arguably, this latter concern may be particularly heightened when some of the beneficiaries of such 'misuse' are third-country national family members.[69]

B. Implications of Union Citizenship for the Market Freedoms

The market freedoms clearly impacted on the approach taken by the Court when interpreting the citizenship provisions. The connection made between Article 12 EC and the finding of lawful residence which extended access to various social rights for economically inactive migrants, for example, is clearly reminiscent of the more specific non-discrimination guarantees contained in the Treaty provisions (and secondary legislation) on the economic free movement rights. Indeed, it has already been noted above that the Court relied on the interpretation of social advantages in Article 7(2) of Regulation 1612/68 in order to determine the type of benefits non-economic migrants could gain access to. Also of significance however, has been the effect in the opposite direction—the construal of Article 18 EC has had a significant impact on the development and application of the market freedoms.

Collins provides one of the most palpable examples of principles developed under the citizenship provisions impacting on economic free movement rights.[70] Here it was held that the scope of the equal treatment principle in Article 39(2) EC must be interpreted in light of developments in the citizenship *acquis*. Specifically, the Court found that work seekers

---

territory (pursuant to Art 12 Regulation 1612/68): Case C-413/99, above n 11 (now codified in Arts 12(3) and 13(2)(b) Directive 2004/38).

[68] For discussion of such 'abuse' in the healthcare context, see L Ackers and K Coldron, '(Ab)using European Citizenship? Retirement Migrants and the Management of Healthcare Rights' (2007) 14 *Maastricht Journal of European and Comparative Law* 287.

[69] Case C-109/01, above n 11 is an example of a judgment within which the ECJ addressed abuse of national immigration law by persons seeking to rely on the free movement provisions. See AP Van Der Mei, Comments on *Akrich* (2004) 6 *European Journal of Migration and Law* 277. Note, though, that Akrich has recently been overruled by the Court, see Case C-127/08 Metock (judgment of 25 July 2008).

[70] Case C-138/02, above n 52. For discussion of *Collins*, see M Dougan, 'The Court Helps Those Who Help Themselves ... The Legal Status of Migrant Workseekers Under Community Law in the Light of the *Collins* Judgment' (2005) 7 *European Journal of Social Security* 7; O Golynker, 'Jobseekers' Rights in the European Union: Challenges of Changing the Paradigm of Social Solidarity' (2005) 30 *EL Rev* 111; and H Oosterom-Staples, Annotation of *Collins* (2005) 42 *CML Rev* 205.

are entitled to equal treatment, not only as regards access to employment, but also in respect of certain social advantages:[71]

> It is no longer possible to exclude from the scope of Article 39(2) of the Treaty—which expresses the fundamental principle of equal treatment, guaranteed by Article 12 of the Treaty—a benefit of a financial nature intended to facilitate access to employment in another Member State.[72]

In line with the reasoning employed in its earlier judgments concerning equal treatment, the Court again relied on the notion of 'genuine link' in order to try and strike a fair balance between the rights of the individual to enjoy an element of solidarity in a host territory and that of the Member State to control its social welfare system. The UK's habitual residence test, as a condition imposed to gain entitlement to jobseekers' allowance, constituted indirect discrimination against EU migrant work seekers. The UK therefore needed to demonstrate that the requirement was an appropriate (and proportionate) device for ensuring that potential claimants of the benefit had the requisite level of integration in the UK and a connection to the labour market.[73] Citizenship, therefore, fortified the status of migrant work seekers by broadening the extent of their equal treatment rights (in a manner not dissimilar to the way in which students' rights were strengthened).[74] To achieve this, the Court transferred notions developed under the auspices of Articles 18 and 12 EC to circumstances governed by Article 39 EC.

Collins provides quite an explicit example of citizenship impacting on one of the market freedoms; the ECJ expressly stated that developments in the case law on Article 18 EC necessitated a change in approach to work seekers. Work seekers are interesting because, although they fall within the scope of Article 39 EC, they are not economically active in the full sense; in essence, rights are granted to them on the basis of a future economic contribution to the host society. It is also apparent, however, that the approach taken in the citizenship cases has had implications right across the spectrum of the free movement of persons. The emphasis placed on proportionality and the claimant's individual circumstances in the cases concerning the economically inactive has also been reflected in cases involving economic migrants. *Orfanopoulos*,[75] for example, concerned an attempt by Germany to expel from its territory a Greek migrant worker on

---

[71] This judgment effectively overruled that in Case 316/85, *Lebon* [1987] ECR 2811.

[72] Case C-138/02, above n 52, para 63.

[73] *Ibid*, para 72. This logic can be seen also in the Court's reasoning in Case C-258/04, above n 52.

[74] Although Directive 2004/38 appears, on the surface, to retract slightly from the position in the case law as the equal treatment principle in Art 24 contains derogations in respect of students and work seekers. Arguably, the derogations themselves will be subject to review using the proportionality principle.

[75] Case C-482/01, above n 63.

the basis of the public policy derogation.[76] The Court made clear that Union citizenship demanded a 'particularly restrictive' interpretation of the derogations from the free movement rights of migrant workers.[77] The judgment in *Carpenter*[78] is especially interesting because, although the decision is reached on what appears to be the basis of Article 49 EC alone, the reasoning adopted by the Court is very much reminiscent of the citizenship cases.[79] Spaventa argues:

> [Carpenter] is one of those cases that most highlights the Court's concern for the protection of the individual as a citizen rather than a market actor. Whilst the case was decided on the grounds of Article 49 EC, the reasoning adopted is unconvincing and result-oriented.[80]

It is more the technique used by the Court to reach its decision, rather than the substantive pronouncements in the judgment, which betrays the influence of Union citizenship here. The Court found that the expulsion of Mrs Carpenter (a Philippine national married to a British man) from the UK would disrupt the life of the family as guaranteed by Article 8 of the European Convention on Human Rights. In turn, this disruption to family life was said to hinder Mr Carpenter's ability to provide services in other Member States. The rationale seems to have been that it was Mrs Carpenter who cared for the children from her husband's previous marriage, thus 'freeing' him to look after the business.[81] Although there is no scope here to consider the conceptual difficulties posed by the judgment,[82] the key point to note for this discussion is that the reliance on fundamental rights guaranteed by the European Convention for the Protection of Human Rights and Fundamental Freedoms (ECHR) to secure the residence status of a third-country national spouse is further evidence of a move away from an economic preoccupation, even within the context of the market freedoms. Reliance on general principles of Community law, such as proportionality and protection of fundamental rights, has been most evident in the context of Article 18 EC.[83] The convergence of the

---

[76] Art 39(3) EC; formerly Directive 64/221 [1964] OJ 850/64. Now Directive 2004/38 [2004] OJ L158/77 incorporates the relevant provisions.

[77] Case C-482/01, above n 63, para 65.

[78] Case C-60/00, *Carpenter* [2002] ECR I-6279.

[79] The Court also reasoned on the basis of Art 49 EC in the earlier ruling in Case C-274/96, *Bickel and Franz* [1998] ECR I-7637. It is clear from the judgment, though, that the decision to allow the claimants to rely on the equal treatment principle in order to have criminal proceedings they were involved in conducted in their mother tongue was clearly influenced by the existence of the citizenship provisions (Art 18 EC in particular).

[80] E Spaventa, *Free Movement of Persons in the European Union: Barriers to Movement in their Constitutional Context*, (The Hague, Kluwer, 2007) 126.

[81] Case C-60/00, above n 78, para 17.

[82] E Spaventa, above n 80, 126–33; and A Acierno, 'The Carpenter Judgment: Fundamental Rights and the Limits of the Community Legal Order' (2003) 28 *EL Rev* 398.

[83] Eg Case C-413/99, above n 11.

approaches taken towards economically active and inactive migrants is perhaps illustrative of Union citizenship beginning to fulfil the promise of constituting the fundamental status of *all* Member State nationals. Whilse the most groundbreaking (and contentious) judgments have been delivered under the sponsorship of Article 18 EC, the Court has consistently maintained that Union citizenship is a status of significance for all those bestowed with it. Surely, then, it is only right that citizenship should transform, to an extent, the traditional market freedoms.

It has been presupposed so far that any assimilation between the citizenship provisions and the economic free movement provisions will automatically result in a more expansive interpretation of the particular market freedom at issue. This assumption does not take into account the possibility of notions developed under the case law on Article 18 EC in fact having a *restrictive* impact on the status of economic migrants. In some recent judgments involving frontier workers, the Court has adopted the language of 'real and genuine link' as a measure of integration justifying entitlement to—or withholding of—a social benefit, in spite of finding Article 39 EC applicable to the situation. Traditionally, once an individual has been classified as a migrant worker, the ECJ has treated the status as absolute and applied the equal treatment principle broadly and without condition. There had been every indication in the case law that this was as true for frontier workers as for resident workers.[84] However, in *Hartmann* and *Geven*,[85] despite the Court relying on Article 39 EC and finding Article 7(2) of Regulation 1612/68 to be engaged, it also allowed for distinctions to be drawn between applicants for a German child-raising allowance on the basis of their perceived integration into the Member State of employment (based on residency and the number of hours worked). In *Hendrix*,[86] the Court took the view that a residence condition could be attached to a benefit constituting a social advantage under Article 7(2), where the applicant was a frontier worker, provided it was objectively justified and proportionate.[87] So as to ensure that the requirement of residence on the national territory did not lead to unfairness, the strength of the claimant's economic and social links to the competent Member State was to be an important part of the proportionality consideration.[88]

The Court's reliance on the real link or factor of integration test in these cases is interesting in that this language has largely been developed in cases concerning economically inactive citizens rather than economically active

---

[84] Eg Case C-337/97, *Meeusen* [1999] ECR I-3289.

[85] Case C-212/05, *Hartmann*; and Case 213/05, *Geven* (judgments of 18 July 2007).

[86] Case C-287/05, *Hendrix* (judgment of 11 September 2007).

[87] *Ibid*, para 54.

[88] *Ibid*, para 57. The following case notes consider the judgments in *Hartmann*, *Geven* and *Hendrix* in greater detail: C O'Brien (2008) 45 *CML Rev* 499; and D Martin (2007) 9 *European Journal of Migration and Law* 457.

workers. This suggests a blurring (of a more restrictive nature) of the approaches towards Articles 18 and 39 EC. When one considers the very specific situation of frontier workers, this interpretation does not appear particularly surprising: frontier workers themselves straddle the divide between economically active and inactive migrants in that they work in one Member State, yet reside in another. Thus, while they make an economic contribution to one society, they are usually more integrated in a social, political and familial sense into their country of residence. It is true that frontier workers are likely to feel a sense of belonging to the two communities they interact with and it may be that these cases represent an attempt by the Court to clarify the scope of the Member States' solidaristic responsibilities towards such individuals. However, the mere fact of being employed in a territory has historically been sufficient to demonstrate the necessary link to the Member State and activate the equal treatment principle. If it is the economic activity of migrant workers (as opposed to residence per se) that is most valued by host Member States, then, surely, this should continue to be the case whether or not the worker resides in the territory; after all, regardless of where the worker resides, they make the same economic contribution to the society of employment. At any rate, the cases of *Hartmann, Geven* and *Hendrix* do provide examples of the citizenship *acquis* influencing decisions made under Article 39 EC in a rather different manner to the way in which it did in cases such as *Collins* and *Carpenter*.

IV. THE PERSISTENCE OF THE MIGRATION MODEL

One aspect of Union citizenship that has significantly undermined claims that the status is destined to be the fundamental status of all Member State nationals is the insistence that cross-border movement must occur before any of the rights linked to citizenship become active. It was noted earlier that citizenship at European level was entwined with free movement from the very outset. Indeed, it is not only Article 18 EC, undoubtedly considered to be the principal provision added at Maastricht, but also the other (largely 'political') provisions that depend on some element of movement, thus reinforcing the correlation between the enjoyment of citizenship rights and migration. This migration fixation has persisted, meaning that the majority of those who hold the status of Union citizen remain unaffected by it, in any tangible sense, due to an absence of cross-border mobility.[89]

---

[89] See Editorial Comments, 'Two-speed European Citizenship? Can the Lisbon Treaty Help Close the Gap?' (2008) 45 *CML Rev* 1. In the same volume, Spaventa argues that Union citizenship has the potential to eradicate the need for migration as a prerequisite for the

Despite the continued importance of the cross-border link, the Court has interpreted the citizenship provisions in a way that has blurred the boundaries of the migration model somewhat. For example, in *Garcia Avello*,[90] it was the dual nationality of the children that brought the situation within the scope of the Treaty and therefore allowed them to rely on the equal treatment principle. Despite never having resided outside of Belgium, they were Spanish nationals resident in that territory and it was apparently irrelevant that they were also Belgian nationals. Consequently, any Member State nationals who bear the nationality of more than one Member State are in the rather privileged position of being exempt from the requirement to exercise cross-border movement before being entitled to invoke citizenship-based rights.[91] In other cases, notably *Chen*[92] and *Schempp*,[93] some movement had occurred, but it was not directly exercised by the Union citizen. It has already been noted that in *Chen*, Catherine was an infant who was able to rely on a right of residence as a consequence of her parents' movement (and sufficient resources). *Schempp* involved a man whose ex-wife exercised a right of free movement by migrating from Germany to Austria. As a result of her movement, the spousal support Mr Schempp paid to his former wife was subject to less favourable treatment as regards tax. Despite Mr Schempp himself being static, the ECJ found Article 12 EC applicable to the situation. These cases demonstrate a willingness on behalf of the Court to be flexible in finding the required cross-border link to bring the situation within the scope of the Treaty.[94]

Furthermore, mirroring its approach in respect of the economic free movement provisions, the ECJ has enabled migrant individuals to rely on Articles 18 and 12 EC against their Member States of origin.[95] Thus, Member States are precluded from discriminating against their own nationals who have moved to, or have previously resided in, another Member State. More recently, the Court has expanded this line of case law to incorporate action by a home Member State that, although not breaching the non-discrimination principle in Article 12 EC, constitutes a

---

enjoyment of rights under the Treaty: see E Spaventa, 'Seeing the Wood Despite the Trees? On the Scope of Union Citizenship and its Constitutional Effects' (2008) 45 *CML Rev* 13.

[90] Case C-148/02, above n 64.

[91] One of the most pertinent examples is provided by the case of Northern Ireland. As (the vast majority of) those born in Northern Ireland are entitled to both British and Irish citizenship, such individuals automatically satisfy the 'cross-border' requirement.

[92] Case C-200/02, above n 10.

[93] Case C-403/03, *Schempp* [2005] ECR I-6421.

[94] *Carpenter* is also an example of a case where the cross-border element was less than obvious.

[95] Case C-224/98, above n 51, discussed above, is such an example.

hindrance to the exercise of free movement rights by a Union citizen.[96] The reasoning here is that the relevant national rule is contrary to the right of free movement in Article 18 EC in that it may discourage the Member State's own nationals from moving abroad or residing elsewhere. Again, this reflects the approach taken in the context of the market freedoms and illustrates further convergence between Articles 18 and 39 EC.[97] One of the more blatant examples is provided by the recent case of *Morgan*.[98] Here, the ECJ held that German rules which specified that education grants for studies abroad could only be awarded if the studies in question were a continuation of education or training already carried out in Germany for at least one year constituted an 'unjustified restriction of the right to move and reside'.[99] Unquestionably, this trend further develops the notion of Union citizenship by broadening the potential applicability of the provisions. This also demonstrates how, albeit still within the migration context, Union citizenship impacts on the relationship between Member States and their own nationals.[100] In fact, as a greater number of the cases have involved claims against home Member States than host, it seems that the citizenship provisions are of particular value to those migrants disadvantaged in some way by their Member State of origin, either during or subsequent to the exercise of free movement rights.

One of the boldest steps the Court could take would be to completely disassociate the enjoyment of rights under the Treaty from the exercise of cross-border mobility. Under this analysis, Article 17 EC is capable of providing the basis for bringing individuals within the scope *ratione personae* of the Treaty, and the mere fact of being a Union citizen, as opposed to a Union citizen lawfully resident in another Member State, is sufficient to activate the equal treatment principle in Article 12 EC. After all, all Member State nationals are Union citizens (Article 17(1) EC) and Union citizens are able to enjoy the rights conferred by the Treaty (Article 17(2) EC).[101] Acceptance of this conceptualisation would pave the way for

---

[96] Case C-224/02, *Pusa* [2004] ECR I-5763; Case C-406/04, *De Cuyper* [2006] ECR I-6947; Case C-192/05, *Tas-Hagen and Tas* [2006] ECR I-10451; and Case C-76/05, *Schwarz* (judgment of 11 September 2007).

[97] In the context of the market freedoms, Case C-415/93, *Bosman* [1995] ECR I-4921 and Case C-18/95, *Terhoeve* [1999] ECR I-345 provide examples of obstacles to movement being imposed by the home Member State. As with indirect discrimination, such rules are open to justification on the basis of express derogations or imperative requirements.

[98] Case C-11/06, *Morgan* (judgment of 23 October 2007).

[99] *Ibid*, para 28.

[100] For further discussion on the exportability of benefits from home Member States, see M Dougan, 'Expanding the Frontiers of Union Citizenship by Dismantling the Territorial Boundaries of the National Welfare States?' in C Barnard and O Odudu (eds), *The Outer Limits of EU Law* (Oxford, Hart Publishing, forthcoming).

[101] See E Spaventa, above n 89.

nationals to challenge discriminatory treatment they experienced by comparison to the position of non-nationals. In addition, it would add further credence to the argument that citizenship really can constitute a fundamental status for all Member State nationals and would, arguably, serve to enhance the legitimacy of the status amongst the citizens of the Union. Although, from a normative perspective, it appears perfectly sensible and appropriate for Article 17 EC to act as the activator for enjoyment of Treaty-based rights, it is unlikely that the Court will embrace an interpretation of the citizenship provisions completely devoid of a migration element in order to challenge reverse discrimination (at least not in the short term). Citizenship has been inextricably linked with free movement from the very outset and the Court has consistently confirmed that the citizenship provisions are not applicable in wholly internal situations.[102]

Recent, and explicit, confirmation of the necessity for a cross-border element came in the *Walloon Government* judgment.[103] This case concerned a care insurance scheme set up in Belgium by the Flemish Government. The residence condition governing access to the scheme extended its scope to those persons who worked in the Dutch-speaking region and bilingual region of Brussels-Capitale (the covered regions), but resided in another Member State (in other words, frontier workers). However, two other entities of the Belgian federal state (the Government of the French Community and the Walloon Government) contended that by excluding those persons who worked in the covered regions, but *resided in another part of the national territory*, the legislation governing the care insurance scheme amounted to a restriction on the free movement of persons. In response, the ECJ distinguished between two situations of exclusion. First, there was the position of Belgian nationals who worked in the covered regions, but lived in another region of Belgium and were, therefore, denied access to the scheme. The Court was clear that such individuals, who have never exercised a right to free movement, could not gain any protection from the Treaty as 'Community law clearly cannot be applied to such purely internal situations'.[104] Furthermore, the Court rejected the argument that Article 17 EC could provide a basis for the application of citizenship rights in the absence of cross-border mobility:

> It is not possible, as the Government of the French Community suggests, to raise against that conclusion the principle of citizenship of the Union set out in Article 17 EC, which includes, in particular, according to Article 18 EC, the right of

---

[102] Joined Cases 64 & 65/96, *Uecker and Jacquet* [1997] ECR I-3171. At para 23 of the judgment, the ECJ states that 'citizenship of the Union, established by Article 8 of the EC Treaty, is not intended to extend the scope *ratione materiae* of the Treaty also to internal situations which have no link with Community law'.

[103] Case C-212/06, above n 3.

[104] *Ibid*, para 38.

every citizen of the Union to move and reside freely within the territory of the Member States. The Court has on several occasions held that citizenship of the Union is not intended to extend the material scope of the Treaty to internal situations which have no link to Community law.[105]

Secondly, there was the position of migrant workers from other Member States and Belgian nationals who had exercised a right of free movement, but since returned to Belgium. For these individuals, exclusion from the scheme could constitute a hindrance to their free movement rights. According to the Court, the possible barring from the scheme (for example, should they decide to transfer their residence in future) and the limitation that the qualifying condition could impose on the place to which individuals transfer their residence was capable of constituting a deterrence to the exercise of mobility rights.[106] Thus, the migration paradigm has been reinforced in this judgment and it remains the case that completely static individuals, without any cross-border element to rely on, gain little tangible benefit from being a Union citizen. Had the interpretation of the formal citizenship provisions not been moulded on the economic free movement provisions, particularly in the early stages of Union citizenship's development, there may have been greater potential for non-movers to enjoy more substantial benefits from the status.[107] Instead, the Court set itself on a path that it does not now seem willing to deviate from.

A possibility so far not considered here is that Union citizenship may not, in reality, be intended to be the fundamental status of *all* Member State nationals. The suggestion has been that the status should ideally offer similar, if not equal, benefits to movers and non-movers alike. It should be remembered, however, that the Court has never uncontrovertibly asserted that citizenship should comprise the fundamental status of non-migrant citizens. In those judgments in which the ECJ has made the 'fundamental status' statement, it has always been framed within the context of non-discrimination on grounds of nationality:

> Citizenship of the Union is destined to be the fundamental status of nationals of the Member States, enabling those who find themselves in the same situation to receive the same treatment in law irrespective of their nationality ...[108]

---

[105]   *Ibid*, para 39.
[106]   *Ibid*, paras 48, 51 and 53. The Court also confirmed the potential for non-discriminatory provisions of national law to constitute a hindrance to movement: para 50.
[107]   It is interesting to note, however, that an unusual example of Art 17 EC being used in an 'internal' situation, in conjunction with the general principle of equal treatment, is provided by Case C-300/04, above n 13. This case concerned Art 19 EC and the right to vote in elections to the European Parliament. Two Netherlands nationals resident in the overseas territory of Aruba successfully argued that they could rely on the right to vote in the said elections on the basis that, in being denied the right to vote, they were treated less favourably than Netherlands nationals resident in a third country.
[108]   Eg Case C-209/03, above n 43, para 31.

True, there is nothing in this statement itself to suggest that the principle of non-discrimination cannot apply in situations without a cross-border element, but it is also correct to say that the judgments in which this has been articulated have involved factual circumstances where the migration model has been held to apply.[109] The Court did not make this pronouncement, for example, in *Eman and Sevinger*, a citizenship case concerning Article 19 EC and devoid of any cross-border mobility. This is particularly interesting given that the Court relied on the general principle of equal treatment in order to reach its conclusions.[110]

The legislature's embracement of the 'fundamental status' slogan has been more explicitly exclusionary of non-migrants: Directive 2004/38 clearly addresses only migrant citizens and their family members. Recital 3 goes further than referencing the non-discrimination principle and expressly states that free movement is the key: 'Union citizenship should be the fundamental status of nationals of the Member States when they exercise their right of free movement and residence'.

Perhaps it is better to accept that Union citizenship, at least in the form of the formal citizenship provisions, is intended to be of primary benefit to those Member State nationals—all be them limited in number—who elect to exercise their right of cross-border mobility. Under this understanding, Union citizenship is not so much a tool to enhance feelings of belonging to the *Union* itself as it is a mechanism that seeks to ensure that migrants can gain access to some level of membership in an individual host society. Further, it works to prevent home Member States from punishing those who have sought to exercise a right of free movement, thus signalling an intention to shift affiliation, or at least have a form of dual membership across two societies. In other words, non-migrants actually have little to gain from a status that has as its principal aim the negotiation of migrant citizens' levels of belonging to the Member States they are affiliated with and, by corollary, individual Member States' obligations toward such migrant individuals. Even should the Court change its approach to wholly internal situations and hold that reverse discrimination, by virtue of the combined effect of Articles 17 and 12 EC, is prohibited as a consequence of the status of Union citizenship, the actual tangible impact of this on the lives of Union citizens would not be extensive. Member States do not frequently treat migrants more favourably than nationals.[111] Whereas, normatively, the claim that Union citizenship should be of value to both movers and non-movers is clearly a sound one, it is doubtful that the *current* Treaty provisions provide an adequate forum to achieve this ideal.

---

[109] Even if the finding of a cross-border element in some of the cases may be considered a little 'stretched', as in *Garcia Avello*.

[110] Case C-300/04, above n 13, para 57.

[111] Editorial Comments, above n 89, 3.

V. ASSESSING THE POTENTIAL FOR PROGRESSION UNDER THE TREATY OF LISBON

There is no doubt that Union citizenship has undergone something of a transformation since its inception. It has developed from a status largely assumed to be of limited substantive significance to one that has fundamentally altered the position and entitlement of economically inactive migrants and, furthermore, has shaped the interpretation of the economic free movement provisions. Such progress has thus far occurred largely at the Court's insistence, although the legislature has stepped in more recently with the adoption of Directive 2004/38. As the section above suggested, however, the current situation is far from constituting the fundamental status of *all* Member State nationals.

The Treaty of Lisbon[112] contains amendments, both to the Treaty on European Union and the EC Treaty (to be renamed the Treaty on the Functioning of the European Union assuming ratification progresses), that are relevant to the notion of Union citizenship.[113] Whether or not the changes will provide a basis for the status becoming more meaningful for all of those conferred with it, however, is uncertain at present. The substance of the citizenship provisions will, essentially, remain the same, but there are some innovations that deserve attention.[114] It is noteworthy that Union citizenship will be 'additional to', rather than complement, national citizenship.[115] This, albeit subtle, change in semantics may indicate recognition that Union citizenship—although clearly not a status of equal importance to national citizenship—can provide rights that are more than complementary to those provided by a nation state. The new, slightly stronger, phrasing hints at the existence of a more significant supranational status vis–a-vis the Member States. It is also significant that, as the Treaty of Lisbon effectively abolishes the pillar structure, the citizenship *acquis* (including the non-discrimination principle) will apply throughout the range of Union's competences and activities as opposed to only the first Community pillar. At present, it is unclear what practical implications (if any) this development will have. It will certainly be interesting post-Lisbon to see the extent to which the exercise of powers in the 'non-Community' areas, in particular in Police and Judicial Cooperation in Criminal Matters, will be shaped by the wider applicability of the citizenship principles.

Under the Treaty on the Functioning of the European Union, the relevant provisions will be contained in a Part Two entitled 'Non-discrimination

---

[112] The Treaty of Lisbon amending the Treaty on European Union and the Treaty establishing the European Community was signed at Lisbon on 13 December 2007 and published at [2007] OJ C306.
[113] See Editorial Comments, above n 89.
[114] Arts 17–22 EC will, on the whole, be reproduced in Arts 20–26 TFEU.
[115] Art 20 TFEU.

and Citizenship'. This appears to suggest an even greater fusing together of citizenship and the principle of equal treatment. Both the principle of non-discrimination on grounds of nationality[116] and the more general legislative power to adopt measures to combat discrimination based on sex, racial or ethnic origin, religion or belief, disability, age or sexual orientation[117] immediately precede the citizenship provisions. To return to a point considered in the preceding section, despite the ECJ's reluctance thus far, it may be possible for the enhanced connection between citizenship and non-discrimination under the new Part Two of the Treaty to provide impetus for the Court to address the reverse discrimination issue and apply the equal treatment principle to non-movers. After all, the general legislative power to combat other forms of discrimination is obviously not dependent on the existence of any cross-border movement. Given the Court's recent statements regarding wholly internal situations in the *Walloon Government* judgment, this would be a significant (and surprising) step for it to take.

One facet of Union citizenship that is genuinely strengthened under the Lisbon Treaty is the democratic dimension. There is a clear attempt to fortify the links between citizenship and democracy and a number of new provisions are geared to enhance the representative and participatory rights of citizens. The amended Treaty on European Union will include a new Title II containing Provisions on Democratic Principles.[118] The bond between democracy and citizenship is made clear from the outset as the first provision, Article 9 TEU, reiterates that every national of the Member States is also a Union citizen. Furthermore, 'in all its activities, the Union shall observe the principle of the equality of its citizens, who shall receive equal attention from its institutions, bodies, offices and agencies'. The remaining provisions of the Title include additional stipulations aimed at boosting levels of democracy and transparency within the Union. For example, Article 10(3) TEU will state that every citizen shall have the right to participate in the 'democratic life' of the Union and 'decisions shall be taken as openly and closely as possible to the citizen'.[119] In addition, Article 16 TEU will extend the scope of access to documents of the institutions whilst also strengthening the right of individuals to have their personal data protected. One of the most valuable (and publicised) rights introduced by the Treaty is the citizens' initiative which will enable citizens

---

[116] Art 12 EC; Art 18 TFEU.

[117] Art 13 EC; Art 19 TFEU.

[118] Arts 9–12 TFEU.

[119] It is not only individuals that the Treaty addresses in this respect, as Art 11 TFEU will also refer to regular and transparent dialogue with representative associations and civil society.

to invite the Commission to propose legislation in an area.[120] This resonates both with the 'new' moves to enhance participation and with the 'old' rights to petition the European Parliament and apply to the Ombudsman (not to mention the right to vote and stand in elections to the European Parliament).

The innovations relating to citizenship contained in the Treaty of Lisbon are clearly of a different ilk to those developments considered earlier in this chapter, which were predominantly court-driven, and aimed at enhancing the residence and social rights of migrants (particularly the economically inactive). It is no surprise that the transformation that has occurred within the realms of migration, particularly the cases involving the extension of solidaristic rights to non-economic migrants, have received such attention. After all, this is one of the more contentious aspects of citizenship and, moreover, this is an area that the national courts have been most inclined to seek guidance on using the preliminary reference procedure. This has (understandably) diverted attention away from the civil and political aspects of citizenship.[121] The boost given to the participatory and democratic facets of Union citizenship under the new Treaty is thus a welcome one that signifies a broader conceptualisation of what citizenship in the context of the Union means. This may prove to be the dimension of Union citizenship that is able to engage with those static individuals that have so far been outside the scope of the provisions. There is very real potential for the political voice of Union citizens to be enhanced and for identification with a European *demos* to be strengthened. The citizens' initiative may be especially effectual in increasing involvement in, and awareness of, the legislative and political process at European level. In addition to providing a counter-balance to the developments that have thus far taken place within the field of citizenship, it is also true that the Lisbon Treaty further entrenches the approach that has been fostered by the Court in the case law interpreting Articles 12, 17 and 18 EC. In particular, the changes made to the citizenship provisions, such as the strengthening of the links between the status with both the principles of democracy and non-discrimination,[122] further evidence the loosening of the connection between citizens' rights and the Single Market.

---

[120] Art 11 of the revised TEU (although the legal basis for the adoption of related legislation is found in Art 24 TFEU).

[121] However, see J Shaw, above n 13.

[122] Not to mention the further commitment to the protection of fundamental rights evidenced by the legal effect given to the Charter of Fundamental Rights under Art 6 of the revised TEU.

VI. CONCLUDING REMARKS

Despite the developments that have occurred under the auspices of Union citizenship, the full repercussions of the status have not yet been unearthed and there remains some significant expounding to be done if Union citizenship is ever to fulfil the potential of being (equally) valuable to all Member State nationals. Innovations in the Treaty of Lisbon relating to the participatory rights of citizens surely offer some hope that Union citizenship can be a status which holds significance for static individuals in the future. Nevertheless, it is clear that citizenship of the Union currently continues to offer little to those who reside in their Member State of origin without a cross-border connection.[123] Moreover, even though citizenship has been utilised most extensively within the context of migration, it has not been able to eradicate the tiered nature of free movement entitlement within the EU. It is true that the rights of economically inactive migrants have matured, but it remains the case that their residence and social rights are conditioned on the possession of a certain degree of financial wealth; indeed, the market freedoms continue to offer the greatest security of status. This suggests that economic considerations still occupy a prominent position in the Union's psyche. This view is further supported by the continued inclusion of transitional arrangements on the free movement of persons in recent Accession Treaties. The 2004 and 2007 enlargements have persisted with the policy of allowing the older Member States to restrict the mobility rights of the new citizens, despite developments in the status of Union citizenship.[124] Thus, presently, the Union does not offer a unitary status even to its migrant citizens, as distinctions are drawn between them not only on the basis of economic worth but also on grounds of nationality. This contradicts the universality of the status implied by the formal definition in Article 17 EC. That being said, the citizenship story has not yet been fully written and given the extent of the activity that has surrounded the concept in the first 50 years of the European Treaties, there is surely much scope for further transformation.

---

[123] Although it is also clear that the Court has been increasingly flexible in finding such a connection.

[124] Treaty of Accession 2003 [2003] OJ L236/17; and Treaty of Accession 2005 [2005] OJ L157/11. When Portugal, Spain and Greece acceded, although transitional arrangements were included in the Treaties, it was prior to the inclusion of the citizenship provisions in the Treaty.

16

Gender, the Acquis *and Beyond*

FIONA BEVERIDGE

I. INTRODUCTION

GENDER EQUALITY HAS occupied an important place in the EU throughout its 50-year history. and BeyondThe EU has served as an important site for the pursuit of gender equality, which has gradually been shaped into one of the key values of the Union. In the process, gender equality law has served as a spawning ground for key legal developments such as the doctrines of direct and indirect effect, the technique of prospective overruling, rules on the need for adequate remedies, and the definitions of direct and indirect discrimination, all of which have had ramifications across the whole spectrum of EU law in shaping the ways in which individual rights find recognition and protection within EU law.

The gender regime[1] created in the EU is undoubtedly *sui generis*, the result of the interplay of a range of factors. Some of these factors are structural, a manifestation of the EU's own unique polity and the influence of the evolving division of competences between the EU and Member State levels, while others are process-related—reflecting both the political compromises between the Member States and the institutional balance within the EU. The diverse gender traditions and gender regimes of the Member States feed through these structures and processes and interact in myriad ways. The EU gender regime is also complex, with traditional hard legal elements, softer policy measures and, more recently, the introduction of OMC processes in key areas, all playing an important role in shaping the overall picture. The turn to gender mainstreaming may create the impression that there is an overarching policy-making framework, but in fact this is far from true. In addition, different states are positioned differently towards the EU gender regime, influencing and being influenced by different legal and policy initiatives in a very uneven way.

---

[1] S Walby, 'The European Union and Gender Equality: Emergent Varieties of Gender Regime' (2004) 11 *Social Politics* 4.

All of these factors combine to ensure that it is extremely difficult to give an accurate account of EU gender equality law and policy which is sufficiently nuanced to capture the diversity and variation observed across different policy areas, different periods of time and from one Member State to another: a grand narrative remains distant, it seems, in this area. In its place, legal scholars bring a range of conceptual frameworks and methodologies to bear to interrogate the position of gender in EU law, resulting in a rich body of scholarship which addressees and challenges many different aspects of EU activity.

This chapter seeks to add to that body of scholarship by examining EU gender law and policy through the prism of accession. Using evidence drawn from the 2004 and 2007 enlargements, it considers how candidate countries and new entrants to the EU experience EU gender law and policy and considers what impact the turn to mainstreaming has had on pre- and post-entry expectations and requirements. Accession can be seen to have a dual character, both as a formal legal act and as a process of social and political adjustment to new political structures and realities. This chapter considers the impact of both aspects of accession on new entrant states. Accession also impacts on existing Member States and alters the make-up of the EU polity. Therefore, this chapter also looks forward to consider the future of EU gender law and policy in the enlarged EU.

The focus on accession is justified in a number of ways. First, although accession is an 'exceptional' process and each accession is different,[2] membership of the EU is assumed, at a formal legal level, to be largely homogeneous. Thus, while there may be limits to what we can learn from the experience of new entrants—the accession process was a specific response to the political and economic exigencies of the time—the 'EU' to which they acceded is assumed, up to a point, to impose similar duties and benefits on all of its members. Thus, the view from accession countries, which comprise over two-fifths of the Membership, is in itself a valid perspective on the EU.

Secondly, viewing the impacts and duties of EU Membership 'through the eyes of a newcomer' may help to illuminate the ways in which EU laws and policies shape Member State behaviour. Existing Member States have adjusted gradually over time to the current array of laws which make up the *acquis communitaire* and influenced its form to varying degrees so that in some cases very little adjustment was required. The 2004 and 2007 entrants, by contrast, had very little time to ensure that this pre-existing body of European law was transposed into national law. In addition, the policy-making processes of the EU demand particular forms of engagement

---

[2] The principle of differentiation employed in negotiations means that each applicant is treated separately on its own merits—this was the basis for the bilateral dimension of the negotiations leading up to the 2004 enlargement.

by states, which in turn may shape national institutions and policy-making processes. This 'Europeanisation' may be difficult to identify clearly in existing Member States, but, in the case of new Member States, may be more clearly traced to pre- and post-accession engagement with the EU.

Finally, the particular experiences of 12 of the existing 27 Member States in adopting and adapting to the gender laws and policies of the EU will be key in shaping their responses to further initiatives in this area in the years to come. As the European Commission has noted, the 2004 accession brought 'a wealth of experience and achievements from which the existing Member States can also learn'.[3] It has also brought the possibility of change in existing gender policy: '[t]his process of mutual amalgamation ... can be expected to refocus gender equality in Europe and to provide a fresh and promising impetus towards a gender equal society'.[4]

II. THE ACCESSION PROCESS[5]

In June 1993, a promise was made by the leaders of the EU Member States that 'the countries in Central and Eastern Europe that so desire shall become members as soon as they are able to assume the obligations of membership by satisfying the economic and political conditions'.[6] The accompanying 'Copenhagen criteria' required of prospective members:

(a) stability of institutions guaranteeing democracy, the rule of law, human rights and respect for, and protection of, minorities;
(b) the existence of a functioning market economy as well as the capacity to cope with competitive pressure and market forces within the Union; and
(c) the ability to take on the obligations of membership, including adherence to the aims of political, economic and monetary union.

As Wim Kok pointed out, the first of these, the 'political' criterion, was regarded as a precondition for the opening of negotiations, while the others had to be fulfilled by the time of accession.[7] In particular, the third

---

[3] Commission of the European Communities, Report from the Commission to the Council, the European Parliament, the European Economic and Social Committee and the Committee of the Regions, Annual Report on Equal Opportunities for Women and Men in the European Union 2002, COM(2003) 98 final of 5 March 2003, 3.

[4] *Ibid.*

[5] See generally M Cremona (ed), *The Enlargement of the European Union* (Oxford, Oxford University Press, 2003); and AE Kellerman *et al* (eds), *EU Enlargement. The Constitutional Impact at EU and National Level* (The Hague, Asser Institute, TMC, 2001).

[6] Presidency Conclusions of the Copenhagen European Council (21–2 June 1993).

[7] W Kok, 'Enlarging the European Union: Achievements and Challenges', Report of Wim Kok to the European Commission, Robert Schuman Centre for Advanced Studies (San Domenico di Fiesole, EUI, 2003) 23.

criterion on the obligations of membership 'implies that the new members should take over the policies and rules of the EU (the *acquis*) and implement and enforce them effectively'.[8]

The Luxembourg European Council in 1997 established the European Conference 'to bring together the Member States of the EU and the European States aspiring to accede to it and sharing its values and internal and external objectives'.[9] The conference was a political forum designed to foster broader and deeper cooperation on foreign and security policy, justice and home affairs, economic matters and regional cooperation and other common concerns. The Luxembourg Council also agreed to launch the accession process and established the form it would take, particularly the pre-accession elements of Accession partnerships and increases in pre-accession aid.[10] Securing the adoption and application of the *acquis* was established as a central focus both of the Accession Partnerships and of pre-accession aid programmes.[11] It was also to form a central element of the Commission's reports on the progress of the applicant countries. The Luxembourg Council also established clearly that '[i]ncorporation of the acquis into legislation is necessary, but is not in itself sufficient; it will also be necessary to ensure that it is actually applied'.[12] Hence, the European Commission had a key role to play in monitoring the progress of candidate countries, ensuring that all three criteria were met in full, including the development of a capacity and willingness to apply the *acquis*.

III. THE GENDER *ACQUIS*

Gender issues were considered in the accession process primarily, but not exclusively, in the context of the third Copenhagen criterion, concerning readiness for membership. However, a major criticism was that 'readiness' was conceived to involve gender only or primarily in respect of the equal opportunities *acquis* (a discrete area within the employment and social policy chapter), rather than as a cross-cutting issue running through all areas of preparation. Gender, it was argued, was not 'mainstreamed' throughout the accession process, but confined to the legislation and other

---

[8] *Ibid*. Maresceau gives an account of how the third Copenhagen criterion evolved into an obligation to align domestic laws and policies with the *acquis* as part of a pre-accession strategy and as a condition of membership: M Maresceau, 'Pre-accession' in Cremona (ed), above n 5, 21–3.

[9] Presidency Conclusions of the Luxembourg European Council (12–13 December 1997), paras 4–9.

[10] *Ibid*, paras 16–29.

[11] *Ibid*, paras 20 and 25 respectively.

[12] *Ibid*, para 30.

measures on equal opportunities between men and women. This argument is considered further below: first, this chapter examines the place of gender in the *acquis*.

Gender was addressed in the 2004 and 2007 accessions primarily in the context of securing the 'equal opportunities' acquis—EC law on the elimination of sex discrimination in employment, requiring legislation on equal treatment in employment and occupation, social security, occupational social security schemes, parental leave, and protection of pregnant women, women who have recently given birth and women who are breastfeeding. Sexual harassment in employment, the protection of part-time employees and the burden of proof in discrimination proceedings are also included. Directive 2000/78/EC adds inter alia a prohibition on sexual orientation discrimination in employment.[13] The *acquis* did not remain static, but was subject to regular amendment and further development through interpretation by the European Court of Justice.[14]

The position of the equal opportunities *acquis* in the accession process had not been without challenge. As Bretherton reports, in the early stage of the development of pre-accession strategies for Central and Eastern European Countries, arguments were sometimes made that some parts of the *acquis*, including within the social policy field the areas of equal opportunities between men and women and safety at work, should be ignored in the accession process to facilitate accession.[15] This argument did not succeed so that transposition and implementation of the equal opportunities *acquis* was a pre-accession requirement.

Gender issues also arose in the section of the *acquis* on employment, also in Chapter 13, under which candidate countries were required to work with the Commission on the development of employment policies, with a view to ensuring the ability of candidate countries to implement the Employment Strategy after accession. Since 1999, National Action Plans for employment have been subject to gender mainstreaming obligations[16]

---

[13] This falls within the 'anti-discrimination' part of the *acquis*, rather than the section on 'equality of treatment between men and women'.

[14] See, eg Directive 2002/73 of the European Parliament and the Council, amending Council Directive 76/207, [2002] OJ L269/15. This was not included in the negotiations for the 2004 enlargement, but was concluded during the negotiation period, so that the new Member States had to meet the same date for implementation (December 2005) as existing Member States.

[15] C Bretherton, 'Gender Mainstreaming and EU Enlargement: Swimming Against the Tide?' (2001) 8(1) *Journal of European Public Policy* 60, 69–70.

[16] Council of Ministers, The 1998 Employment Guidelines, Council Resolution of 15 December 1997. On gender and the European Employment Strategy, see J Rubery, 'Gender Mainstreaming and Gender Equality in the EU: the Impact of the EU Employment Strategy' (2002) 33 *Industrial Relations Journal* 500; J Rubery *et al*, 'Gender Equality still on the European Agenda—But for How Long?' (2003) 34 *Industrial Relations Journal* 477; J Rubery, 'Gender Mainstreaming and the OMC. Is the Open Method Too Open for Gender Equality Policy' in J Zeitlin and P Pochet, with L Magnusson (eds), *The Open Method of*

and there is evidence that the Commission carried this through into its work with the candidate countries.[17]

More generally, candidate countries were 'requested' under Chapter 13 'to effectively enforce the *acquis* through judicial and administrative systems similar to the ones of the Member States'.[18] Funding was made available in a number of instances for projects directly relating to the effective implementation of the gender *acquis*. For instance, in 1999, Slovenia received €2,000,000 to support the office for women's policy and women's networks, and the Czech Republic €700,000 for improvement of the public institutional mechanism for enforcing and monitoring equal treatment for women.[19]

Gender was, therefore, present in the *acquis*, most notably in the *acquis* relating to equal opportunities in employment: the importance of this should not be underestimated for a number of reasons. First, its inclusion was a decisive influence on law-makers in candidate countries who, sooner or later, passed legislation designed to give effect to these obligations in national law. The impetus created by the inclusion of the gender *acquis* in the pre-accession requirements existed regardless of whether, in the final analysis, the Commission was strict or lenient in reaching decisions to close negations on particular chapters of the *acquis* and allow the state in question to proceed towards membership.[20] Moreover, this impetus may be enhanced by the measures adopted by the Commission to monitor progress, such as the system of producing annual progress reports on the preparations of individual candidate countries:

> The Progress Reports concentrate mainly on what has concretely been achieved for the transposition of the *acquis* in the candidate country and what progress has been made in building up administrative and judicial capacity to implement and apply the *acquis* ... The systematic reporting ... puts enormous pressure on the candidates.[21]

Coordination in Action: The European Employment and Social Inclusion Strategies (Brussels, P.I.E-Peter Lang, 2005) 391–416; and C Fagan, D Grimshaw and J Rubery, 'The Subordination of the Gender Equality Objective: the National Reform Programmes and "Making Work Pay" Policies' (2006) 37 *Industrial Relations Journal* 57.

[17] See further K Koldinská, 'OMC in the Context of EU Gender Policy from the Point of View of New EU Member States' in F Beveridge and S Velluti, *Gender and the OMC* (Dartmouth, Ashgate, 2008).

[18] See <http://europa.eu.int/comm/enlargement/negotiations/chapters/chap13/index.htm>, accessed 28 November 2003.

[19] The picture is uneven, however: Poland is said to have received practically no funds for implementation of women's policy, although this may relate to internal factors. See also WIDE information sheet, 'Gender equality and EU accession: the situation in Poland', November 2003, available at <http:// www.wide-network.org/> accessed 23 September 2008.

[20] See further below.

[21] Maresceau, above n 8, 32.

The Commission was willing at times to highlight gaps in protection, at least at the formal level, and in some cases suggested that further attention to implementation was required. In the case of Estonia, for example, the Commission declared in its 'Comprehensive Monitoring Report'[22] that there were gaps in protection in relation to equal treatment, due to significant delays in the adoption of the draft legislation needed to give effect to gender norms and to establish the necessary institutional framework for ensuring effective implementation of those norms. Similarly, the Commission concluded that there was a need for Estonia to transpose and implement the anti-discrimination *acquis*, while in relation to the European Social Fund, including EQUAL, there was an urgent need 'to strengthen the administrative capacity for management, implementation, monitoring, audit and control at both national and regional level'.[23]

The process was broadly similar for all 2004 and 2007 entrants: during the pre-accession monitoring period, nearly all candidate countries were judged by the European Commission to have made *substantial progress* in the adoption of the equal opportunities *acquis* and, while there were undoubtedly gaps and omissions in many cases, this was never a reason for delaying accession.[24] While EC law is not the only driver here, the speed with which change has been achieved and the nature of that change seems clearly to have been fuelled by the pre-accession process.

The presence of gender in the *acquis* also served to stimulate dialogue and debate within candidate countries about gender equality policies, for instance, when legislation was required. Often, the new legislation was clearly identified in public discourse as a step required by the EU if membership negotiations were to be successful: thus, there was a clear identification of certain non-discrimination laws (such as those relating to paid labour) with the EU. This may of course have been double-edged: those who welcomed better protection from gender-based discrimination may have felt favourably disposed towards the EU as the catalyst for

---

[22] Commission of the European Communities, 'Comprehensive monitoring report on Estonia's preparations for membership', available at:
<http://ec.europa.eu/enlargement/archives/pdf/key_documents/2003/cmr_ee_final_en.pdf>
accessed 24 September 2008. Estonia is used here as an example—it is by no means the only state to have experienced criticism in this area. For a recent example, see Commission reports on the progress made by Croatia, including the repeated requirement to improve alignment of national law with the *acquis* in the area inter alia of gender equality. The most recent act does not make specific mention of gender equality as a problem, although anti-discrimination more generally remains of concern, as does judicial enforcement generally: Council Decision of 12 February 2008 on the principles, priorities and conditions contained in the Accession Partnership with Croatia, 2008/119/EC.

[23] *Ibid.*

[24] See, eg Commission of the European Communities, Report from the Commission to the Council, the European Parliament, the European Economic and Social Committee and the Committee of the Regions, Report on Equality between men and women, 2004, COM(2004) 115 final of 19 February 2004.

developments in this sphere, whereas those who opposed legislative protections in this sphere may have resented the EU's apparent interference in this area of domestic law, and these attitudes may spill over into future enforcement activity.[25]

However, while the context of accession may have stimulated debate, the conditions laid down for accession also circumscribed the terms of that debate: candidate countries were not expected to debate the *acquis*; merely to implement it as it stood.[26]

Finally, the presence of gender in the *acquis* was important because it created roles and opportunities for *civil society* groups concerned with gender equality to participate in public life by advancing debates about gender equality, by seeking to ensure that policies are based on accurate representations of the situations of women and men and the issues which concern them, by seeking to draw attention to shortfalls in national laws and policies, by raising public awareness of new legal protections and social policies and in some cases by playing a role in enforcement work. Although not the only influence on non-governmental organisation (NGO) development in transitional states,[27] clearly the orientation of a candidate country towards the EU and the specific features of EU law and policy created new or additional opportunities.

In some instances, this activity was transnational. For instance, the transnational KARAT Coalition, created around the Beijing Conference, is engaged (in its 'Gender Equality and Economic Justice' project) in training women from Central and Eastern Europe on 'economic literacy', in activism within their national states with the government and the media, in drawing attention to inadequacies in state policies, in dissemination of information about the EU and gender equality, and in lobbying the EU to persuade its representatives and institutions to pressurise candidate countries to take steps to address gender inequalities.[28] Greenberg's study of this activity points to a range of different dynamics within this process: for instance, she concludes that norms and standards that would not carry

---

[25] J Zielonka, 'How New Enlarged Borders Will Reshape the European Union' (2001) 39 *Journal of Common Market Studies* 507, 513.

[26] H Grabbe, 'How does Europeanisation Affect CEE Governance? Conditionality, Diffusion and Diversity' (2001) 8 *Journal of European Public Policy* 1013, 1015.

[27] See, eg SEELINE (South Eastern European Women's Legal Initiative) 'National Machineries Country Reports' (Zagreb, B.a.B.e, 2003), which emphasises other common influences on states, namely CEDAW, the Beijing Platform for Action and the creation of the International Criminal Court.

[28] See <http://www.karat.org> accessed 24 September 2008 for information; also <http://www.newww.pl> accessed 24 September 2008. For discussion of the role of Karat, see ME Greenberg, 'Contestation and Collaboration in EU Accession: Eastern European Women's Activism regarding Gender Equality and Economic Justice', Paper for the Cornell Mellon-Sawyer Seminar *Towards a Transnational and Trans-cultural Europe*, March 2003, available at <http://portal.is.cornell.edu/files/archives/calendar-files/1746/Mgreenberg_Paper.pdf>, accessed 21 November 2003.

much weight with national governments 'gain legitimacy when touted as EU standards', while the efforts of East European NGOs to educate Western European allies (notably the European's Women's Lobby) about the situation of Eastern European Women has been unexpectedly successful in empowering both groups to play a more prominent role in the accession process.[29]

Despite these effects, the commitment of the EU institutions to securing the equal opportunities *acquis* in the candidate countries has been questioned from time to time. One criticism is that the review process for ensuring that the *acquis* has been complied with lacks rigour. In the Commission's reports on the progress of candidate countries, for instance, it is typically concluded that national legislation largely succeeds in implementing EU anti-discrimination laws:

> [T]he entire policy area is dealt with in a few brief sentences, similar for each applicant country, and there is no reference to problem areas such as Poland's 'protective' women's policy. Rather more space is devoted to the failure of CEE governments to insist upon the EU's preferred labelling for cigarette packets.[30]

> [A] look at the Annual Progress Reports reveals that no systematic analysis of legal and *de facto* progress of candidate countries in the field of equal opportunities and treatment of women and men has taken place. Statements on the situation of women are scarce, remain very general, and do not allow for year-to-year or country-to-country comparisons of progress. Criteria and indicators for assessing progress are not explained. Moreover, information in the Annual Reports on gender equality in candidate countries is frequently incomplete or obsolete.[31]

Of course, this criticism can be made more generally of the 2004 enlargement, a particular challenge to the EU due to its sheer size and political symbolism. Accusations of a lack of rigour in scrutinising the measures adopted in candidate countries to give effect to the gender *acquis* have to be seen in this context: the political pressure to ensure the enlargement project was 'successful', together with the tight timetable pursued, probably left the Commission with little room to manoeuvre and the criticism made extends to many other areas.[32] However, the 2007

---

[29] *Ibid.*

[30] *Ibid.*

[31] S Steinhilber, 'Women's Rights and Gender Equality in the EU Enlargement. An Opportunity for Progress' (WIDE, October 2002), available at <http:// wide-network.org/> accessed 24 September 2008; see also WIDE information sheet 'Gender equality and EU accession: the situation in Poland' (November 2003), available at <http:// wide-network.org/> accessed 24 September 2008.

[32] Maresceau describes as 'astonishing' the ease with which the Commission was willing to close the environment chapters of the negotiations '[k]nowing the enormous distance between the EC environment law standards and those of the candidate countries': Maresceau, above n 8, 23. Similar observations have been made about, eg health and safety.

enlargement followed the same pattern and there is little change in this respect in the way in which ongoing enlargement processes are unfolding.

A second observation is that many of the 2004 and 2007 entrant states had a limited internal capacity to ensure effective implementation of EU laws and policies. While this was not allowed to hold up the enlargements, it remains to be seen how that capacity will develop post-accession to ensure adequate implementation in the future. Grabbe has argued that the EU's capacity in this respect is weakened by the fact that it has no 'institutional templates' to offer.[33] This shortfall in capacity has also been highlighted in the context of gender elements of OMC processes.[34]

IV. BEYOND THE *ACQUIS*

It has been argued that, beyond the *acquis*, gender did not play a significant role in the 2004 and 2007 enlargements, more precisely that the EU's *gender mainstreaming* commitment was not carried through into the accession process: 'the EU's approach to gender equality is guided by the principle of equal treatment of women and men and heavily focused on employment and labour market policies'.[35]

Evidence from other policy areas is rather thin: mainstreaming gender equality into the pre-accession strategy was an agreed 'action' in the *Social Policy Agenda* of 2000, mirroring the incorporation of gender policy inside the Community within this social policy process,[36] but it is questionable how much was achieved.[37] The Commission's Work Programme on the Framework Strategy on Gender Equality for 2001, which details the ongoing activities and new initiatives of each Commission Directorate-General and Service, shows that DG Enlargement was focusing on implementation of the *acquis* in candidate countries, and on introducing gender impact assessment and monitoring to Community-financed projects in those states. Support to women's NGOs and the development of research

---

[33] Grabbe, above n 26, 1022. Pierre Mirel, Director of DG Enlargement, confirmed to the Committee on Women's Rights and Equal Opportunities of the European Parliament that enforcement was dependent on national measures, leaving the EU to focus on institution-building measures: 'We cannot go beyond that and will not dictate how directives should be implemented' (Summary Report of the Public Hearing of 10 September 2002, 'Is enlargement also for Women?', Directorate-General for Committees and Delegations, CM\478119EN.doc, 4). Directive 2002/73 (above n 14) leaves Member States wide discretion to choose the form and functions of the equality bodies whose establishment and maintenance it requires.

[34] See, eg Koldinská, above n 17.

[35] Steinhilber, above n 31.

[36] Commission of the European Communities, Communication from the Commission to the Council, the European Parliament, the Economic and Social Committee and the Committee of the Regions, Social Policy Agenda, COM(2000) 379 final of 28 June 2000, 24.

[37] See Koldinská, above n 17.

and statistics on violence against women were also under development.[38] There is also evidence that candidate countries were exposed to Community gender policy in their shadowing of European Employment Strategy and the Social Exclusion agenda.[39] However, beyond this there is little evidence that gender mainstreaming has been carried through effectively into the accession process, and a notable lack of evidence outside the third Copenhagen criterion. Bretherton suggests that since the adoption of the *acquis* could and would be monitored in any case, dialogue on this subject was regarded within the Commission as the most effective and useful way of influencing policy and stimulating debate about gender equality in candidate countries.[40]

The European Women's Lobby (EWL) has been the EU's most vocal critic: in 2001, it stated the case for taking a much wider view of the role of gender in the accession process and laid out six recommendations for action, based on the premise that gender equality is a core value of the EU, 'a fundamental and integral part of economic, social, and democratic development'.[41] This theme was also picked up by Kinga Lohmann of the Karat Coalition, who made a clear link between gender equality issues and citizenship of the enlarged EU: 'The vision of many women of Central and Eastern Europe is for all people to be equal in Europe. They do not want to be seen as part of "another Europe", not as second-class citizens from accession countries, and third-class citizens from non-accession countries.'[42]

Women in the candidate countries were identified as facing both similar gender equality problems to women in the Member States (for example, occupational segregation, low pay and ineffective laws to combat domestic violence) and distinct problems stemming from their situation in transitional states (for example, weakening of position in the labour market, declining representation in national parliaments and reduction in childcare facilities). The conclusion of the EWL was that the situation of women in the candidate countries needed to be addressed as a horizontal issue, not merely in respect of the *acquis*.

---

[38] Commission of the European Communities, Commission Staff Working Paper, Work Programme for 2001 of each Commission service for the implementation of the Framework Strategy on Gender Equality, 2 March 2001.

[39] See text below, n 46.

[40] Above n 15.

[41] European Women's Lobby Position Paper, 'Six Areas of Action to strengthen women's rights in the accession process' (14 September 2002), available at <http://www.womenlobby.org> accessed 24 September 2008. More recently, however, there is less attention given to enlargement or the post-enlargement context, eg in the EWL's proposal in 2005 for a Roadmap, enlargement, or the situation in newly acceded countries, was ignored: EWL, 'Gender Equality Road Map for the European Community, 2006–2010' (November 2005).

[42] K Lohmann, 'Gender and Economic Justice', September 2002, available at <http://karat.org> accessed 24 September 2008.

The EWL's six recommendations for action reflect this analysis of the problem. They were:

(a) reinforcing gender equality mainstreaming in the accession process;
(b) ensuring the implementation of the gender *acquis*;
(c) combating violence against women;
(d) strengthening women's position in the economy;
(e) promoting women in decision-making; and
(f) reinforcing the role of women's NGOs in the accession process.

However, there is no evidence that these efforts by the EWL, Karat and others to widen the scope of accession-related efforts on gender equality had any impact on the approach of the Commission to the monitoring of progress in candidate countries. Moreover, both the EWL and Karat have since 'moved on' from issues stemming from enlargement to pursue other agendas, suggesting that this has not been a priority since the 2004 accession.

V. THE TRANSITION TO MEMBERSHIP

Aside from the formal accession process, there is also a sense in which preparing for EU membership requires and promotes, at a practical level, the adoption and implementation of gender equality policies and perspectives in policy-making. The premise underlying this argument is that preparation for membership requires, regardless of the formal requirements for 'admission', a substantial orientation or re-orientation of many aspects of public life in the candidate countries, for instance, the national economic policies of candidate countries, of education, employment and social policies and of the government machinery. It is this need for re-orientation which explains why accession countries face what has been described as a 'paradox': the 'need to do what is not required'.[43]

This 'need to do what is not required' can be explained by reference to two central characteristics of the accession process. First, it is expected that new Member States will, on accession, 'plug-in' to the existing political, economic and administrative activities of the institutions and the Union.[44] This is the 'big bang' element of accession. It carries the implication that to be able to operate effectively as a new Member State, and to gain the full

---

[43] P Nicolaides, 'Preparing for EU Membership: The Paradox of Doing What the EU Does Not Require You to Do' (2003) 2 *EIPA Scope* 11, available at <http://www.eipa.nl> accessed 24 September 2008.

[44] Transitional arrangements are, in theory, negotiable, but state-specific provisions were kept to a minimum in relation to the 2004 enlargement: for a review, see, eg G Avery, 'The Enlargement Negotiations' in F Cameron (ed), *The Future of Europe: Enlargement and Integration* (London, Routledge, 2004).

benefits of membership, accession countries have to anticipate these requirements and bring their state policies, machineries and capacities as closely into line as possible prior to accession.

Secondly, and following from the above, the EU expends great effort on preparations for accession, to smooth the transition from candidate state to new Member State and hence to lessen the shockwaves which the 'big bang' would otherwise release, and which would otherwise shake both existing and new Member States. While the formal requirements for membership focus on the adoption of the *acquis* and the Copenhagen criteria outlined above, in reality the preparation efforts extend into many other aspects of public life.[45] In effect, candidate countries are expected to adopt 'shadow' policies in many areas, achieving an increasing level of conformity to EU policies prior to accession.

Thus, in relation to the process of adoption of the *acquis*, it has been noted that this requires more than simply the alignment of legislation:

[C]andidate countries as well as Member States experience approximation as not just a matter of legislative formulation but also of introducing new legislation and amending existing rules. It involves permanent training and retraining at various levels, including at administrative, judicial, university etc. levels.[46]

One area in which this 'shadowing' has been encouraged is in the opening up of various 'internal' funding streams to participation by groups from the candidate countries: eight candidate countries, for example, are said to have participated in 2002 in the Commission's gender equality programme 2001–5.

Candidate countries also participated, prior to accession, in areas of Community policy operating under the Open Method of Coordination—notably the European Employment Strategy[47] and the Social Inclusion dimension of the Social Policy Agenda.[48] In both cases, candidate countries participated, with the European Commission, in developing a national plan for policy coordination in line with EU guidelines. The aim in each case was to prepare the candidate countries for full participation from the date

---

[45] See, eg D Bailey and L De Propris, 'A Bridge too Phare? EU Pre-Accession Aid and Capacity-Building in the Candidate Countries' (2004) 42 *Journal of Common Market Studies* 77.

[46] Maresceau, above n 8, 23.

[47] See above n 16.

[48] See, eg European Commission, Employment and Social Affairs DG, Outline of the Joint Inclusion Memoranda, 23 May 2002; and European Commission, 'Gender Mainstreaming in the Joint Inclusion Memoranda for future Member States: Practical Guide'. More generally, see JS Mosher and DM Trubeck, 'Alternative Approaches to Governance in the EU: EU Social Policy and the European Employment Strategy' (2003) 41 *Journal of Common Market Studies* 63; and K Koldinská, 'OMC in the context of EU Gender Policy from the point of view of new EU Member States' in Beveridge and Velluti (eds), above n 16.

of accession, and objectives included the development of fuller understanding of the socio-economic situation in the accession country, the development of suitable statistical and other information systems which would provide the necessary information on which policies would be based, the development of a national strategy in each of the fields, familiarisation of the candidate country with the broad objectives and working mechanisms of the policy area concerned and the identification of policy priorities for each candidate country. This activity was often assisted by 'twinning arrangements', discussed further below.[49]

In terms of developing capacity for future active engagement with Community gender policy, this preparation is particularly significant because of the ever-increasing importance of these areas to gender policy within the Community. Particular problems may arise in new Member States where commitment to gender equality may be low and the capacity to implement non-binding recommendations weak.

VI. POST-ACCESSION—ENGENDERING MEMBERSHIP

This penultimate substantive section of the chapter seeks to offer some reflections on what accession to the EU means in gender terms.

A. The EU as a 'Community of Law'

The first and clearest conclusion is that newly acceding Member States experience the EU as a 'community of law'. A substantial task facing candidate countries is the transposition, incorporation and implementation of the gender *acquis*. This can be clearly seen to have had a significant impact in the candidate countries, producing a flurry of legal reform and activism.

However, there is, in many new Member States, a gap between formal legal compliance (the passing of legislation) and the ability of individuals and groups to secure their legal 'rights', for example, in the workplace and through administrative and judicial processes. This should come as no surprise: leaving aside the speed with which accession negotiations took place in respect of the 2004 enlargement and the enormity of the task in some states, there is in many 'old' Member States a considerable gap between formal legal compliance and the ability of individuals and groups to secure their rights.[50] However, the speed with which accession was

---

[49] See below n 62.
[50] F Beveridge, S Nott and K Stevens, *Making Women Count: Integrating Gender into Law and Policy-Making* (Dartmouth, Ashgate, 2000).

negotiated, and the procedures adopted within candidate countries, may have exacerbated the problem in new Member States. Grabbe notes that, in relation to the 2004 enlargement, all candidate countries utilised some sort of 'fast-track' procedure for getting 'EU' legislation through parliament, resulting in many areas in a 'lack of awareness of the details of the legislation being passed on the part of parliamentarians'.[51] This was also true of Romania and Bulgaria and a similar situation exists in Croatia, although there the situation is mitigated to an extent by the passage of time since the original legislation was adopted.

Beyond this, the ability of individuals and groups to secure their rights may depend on many matters not explicitly included in the gender *acquis*, such as access to legal aid or the rules of procedure of the courts. A report prepared for the European Parliament in 2003 on the capacity of candidate countries to implement gender laws highlighted wide variation and many gaps in protection.[52]

Membership of the EU will not, in itself, address these weaknesses: indeed, compared to the pre-accession period the influence of the EU may be weakened by accession. Smith comments:

> Conditional membership is a 'consumable power resource'—once it has been used up, once the applicants have joined the EU, it could be difficult to exercise leverage over them. The carrot has been offered and consumed.[53]

However, membership exposes the new Member States to the enforcement powers of the European Commission and to the authority of the Court of Justice, both of whom may be enlisted as allies by national interest groups seeking to enhance respect for the gender *acquis*. Whether this is done merely by pursuing individual remedies through national courts, or by encouraging the Commission to pursue enforcement action and/or to 'name and shame' a state,[54] or by explicitly engaging in a litigation strategy to highlight the inadequacies of national laws and procedures,[55] the

---

[51] Grabbe, above n 26, 1017.

[52] European Public Law Centre, on behalf of the European Parliament, 'The Institutions in Candidate Countries Defending Gender Related Issues—Capacity to Implement and Control Equality 2003', available at <http://www.europarl.eu.int/comparl/femm/news_docs/ccstudy_en.pdf>, accessed 05 November 2005.

[53] KE Smith, 'The Evolution and Application of EU Membership Conditionality' in Cremona (ed), above n 5, 133.

[54] For a discussion of enforcement strategies employed by the EU institutions, see J Tallberg, 'Paths to Compliance: Enforcement, Management, and the European Union' (2002) 56 *International Organisation* 609. See also P Nicolaides, 'Preparing for Accession to the European Union: How to Establish Capacity for Effective and Credible Application of EU Rules' in M Cremona (ed), *The Enlargement of the European Union* (Oxford, Oxford University Press, 2003) 43.

[55] For a discussion of the potential of litigation strategies, see KJ Alter and J Vargas, 'Explaining Variation in the Use of European Litigation Strategies: European Community Law and British Gender Equality Policy' (2000) 33 *Comparative Political Studies* 452.

pressure on new Member States to achieve conformity with the *acquis* did not dissipate entirely when membership was achieved, although it might have assumed new forms.[56]

This points to the importance of wider features of the EU legal environment, particularly the dominant characteristic of the EU as a 'community of law', to our understanding of the gender *acquis* and the obligations it imposes. While some laggardly behaviour on the part of states may be tolerated, on the whole there is an expectation of compliance with and respect for the spirit and the letter of the law and an expectation that government bodies and courts will give effect to the gender *acquis*, even if some nudging may be required. Although there may be variations between Member States in the ease with which compliance is secured and the methods by which activists choose to operate, overall there is a shared understanding that the law will be respected and, where appropriate, that it can be relied on to redress individual wrongs. This understanding has yet to develop in the new Member States and the remaining candidate countries. Indeed, in March 2004, Eurobarometer published findings which demonstrated that citizens of the 2004 entrants placed far less trust in their country's legal system, and less significance on the European Court of Justice, than citizens of the existing Member States.[57]

B. The EU's Role in the Development of Capacities

On the ground that the preparations for accession have been influential in focusing at least some attention and resources on gender equality:

> [T]he alignment with the *acquis communitaire* has contributed decisively to the creation of institutional bodies and legal mechanisms for the support of gender equality objectives (equality legislation on issues of equal pay, parental leave, health and non-discrimination in the workplace, labour codes and creation of government offices on equal opportunities).[58]

Both the formal requirements for membership and the informal requirements referred to above raise questions about the capacity of both government bodies and civil society in the candidate countries to effectively undertake the implementation of the *acquis* and the more general mainstreaming of a gender perspective through various areas of public policy, which will be required for effective participation. Although from October 2005, Directive 2002/73 imposed a gender mainstreaming requirement on all Member States and requires the establishment of gender equality

---

[56] Smith, above n 53.
[57] European Commission, Eurobarometer 61, spring 2004, 'Public Opinion in the European Union' (2004).
[58] Bretherton, above n 15.

machinery to promote equality between women and men,[59] on a practical level EU membership already demanded this.

The EWL and Karat identified the need for gender equality awareness and training for both the EU and the candidate country *officials* involved in the accession process. It was also implied in many more of their proposals, such as the reinforcement of gender within the PHARE programme and the conducting of gender impact assessment of the economic guidelines for candidate countries.

Another area where improved capacity has been called for is in the availability of gender statistics to assist in monitoring of the gender impacts of policies, for example in relation to the labour market. The use of benchmarking, targets and indicators is central to European Employment Policy, the Social Inclusion process[60] and also required for successful participation in the Structural Funds where it is required that states demonstrate that the gender impacts of such activities are fully addressed.[61] However, Fuszara[62] argues that twinning programmes designed to boost capacity in the run-up to accession did not deliver satisfactory results and Koldinská[63] demonstrates that there remain significant problems of capacity in these areas.

WIDE has drawn attention to the need to involve *women's NGOs* in accession countries in the development of country-specific programmes, for example on labour issues, and the need to ensure that such organisations are funded. Commenting on Polish experience, they argue that the Commission assumption that NGOs will play a prominent role in ensuring that EU employment and social policy are implemented in the accession countries may be ill-founded: 'While this method of addressing gender justice may be effective in the existing member states, many of the accession countries that are characterised by relatively young democracies may have difficulty achieving this.'[64] WIDE also reports, in relation to the Czech Republic, that the lack of gender sensitivity on the part of the Czech

---

[59] Directive 2002/73 (above n 14). Art 1(1) inserts a new Art 1a into the earlier Directive 76/207. The amending Directive also requires Member States to establish and maintain a body or bodies to promote, analyse, monitor and support equality of treatment between women and men without discrimination: Art 8a, Directive 76/207/EEC, as amended by Directive 2002/73.

[60] AB Atkinson, E Marlier and B Nolan, 'Indicators and Targets for Social inclusion in the European Union' (2004) 42 *Journal of Common Market Studies* 47.

[61] Council Regulation (EC) 1260/1999 of 21 June 1999 laying down general provisions on the Structural Funds [1999] OJ L161/54, Art 41(2)(c); Communication from the Commission to the Council, the European Parliament, the European Economic and Social Committee and the Committee of the Regions, Implementation of gender mainstreaming in the Structural Funds programming documents 2000–2006, COM(2002) 0748 final of 20 December 2002.

[62] M Fuszara, 'The OMC, Gender Policy and the Experience of Poland as a New Member State' in Beveridge and Velluti (eds), above n 17.

[63] Above n 17.

[64] WIDE, 'Gender equality and EU accession: the situation in Poland', above n 31.

agencies charged with distribution of EU funds has meant that women's NGOs have experienced difficulties gaining access to these resources.[65]

These various examples point to the significance of EU membership as an influence on the development and shape of national capacities in relation to gender on a very wide range of issues. This influence extends beyond the capacities of government to include capacity within the non-governmental sector (and no doubt the private sector too). Membership also opens up a transnational dimension to this capacity-building, as witnessed by the successful deployment by KARAT of a European-wide interest group (the EWL) and, through this, a European institution (the Parliament) to draw attention to its concerns. However, despite this, it seems that there has been less focus by both these groups on enlargement issues since the 2004 accession took place, despite continuing evidence of adaptation issues.

VII. GENDER MAINSTREAMING AS A 'PUBLIC GOOD'—THE NEED FOR DEBATE

The turn in EU gender law and policy towards gender mainstreaming is well documented[66] and generally treated as non-controversial. Discussion tends to focus on whether, as a policy, it has been effectively implemented in various activities or spheres.[67] Effective participation in many EU activities, programmes and funding streams is not possible unless due concern is given to the gender dimensions of those activities. Thus, while the principle of respect for gender mainstreaming in Article 3(2) of the EC Treaty may fall short of justiciability, there is evidence that gender is 'mainstreamed' to a degree through many of the community's activities.[68]

---

[65] WIDE, 'Gender equality and EU accession: the situation in the Czech Republic', November 2003, available at <http:// www.wide-network.org/> accessed 24 September 2008.

[66] See, eg S Mazey, *Gender Mainstreaming in the EU—Principles and Practice* (London, Kogan Page, 2001); and T Rees, *Mainstreaming Equality in the European Union: Education, Training and Labour Market Policies* (London, Routledge, 1998).

[67] See, eg M Braithwaite, 'Mainstreaming Gender in European Structural Funds', paper prepared at the Mainstreaming Gender in European Public Policy Workshop, University of Wisconsin-Madison, 14–15 October 2000; S Mazey, 'Gender Mainstreaming Strategies in the EU: Delivering on an Agenda?' (2002) 10(2) *Feminist Legal Studies* 227; M Pollock and E Hafner-Burton, 'Mainstreaming Gender in the European Union' (2000) 7(3) *Journal of European Public Policy* 432; J Rubery *et al*, *Gender Mainstreaming and the European Employment Strategy and Social Inclusion Process* (EWERC, Manchester School of Management, 2004); J Shaw, 'Gender and the Court of Justice' in G de Burca and JHH Weiler (eds), *The European Court of Justice* (Oxford, Oxford University Press, 2001) 87; and F Beveridge, 'Building Against the Past: the Impact of Mainstreaming on EU Gender Law and Policy' (2007) 32 *European Law Review* 193.

[68] See the Annual Reports on Equality between Women and Men produced by the Commission, eg Commission of the European Communities, Report from the Commission to

However, the experience of European enlargement demonstrates that what many in the 'old' Member States take for granted—that attention to the gender dimension of EU activities is a 'good thing'—may not be accepted without question across the enlarged EU. Blagojevic has drawn attention to the critical importance of social, cultural and historical context in the context of gender politics in the candidate countries. Whereas the current *acquis* and the values embraced by this body of EC law were introduced gradually and through fights and negotiations in the existing Member States, that is, by the positive value of 'conquest', the situation in candidate countries is very different—an imposed gender equality is associated with communism, and hence its perceived re-imposition may be resisted. Thus, whilst feminists in the 'old' Member States may be keen to argue that the personal is political, activists in the new Member States, particularly older women, may be striving to remove state influence from what they have relatively recently reclaimed as 'private' matters. Greenberg has identified suspicion and hostility towards the very issue of gender equality as a hangover from the past which has left 'a legacy of cynicism and outright disdain for talk of gender equality'.[69] This suspicion may be heightened by the realisation that much current activity on gender in the EU takes place within the framework of the European Employment Strategy and/or the Social Policy Agenda, both increasingly directed towards the Lisbon Strategy designed to make the EU 'the most competitive and dynamic knowledge-based economy capable of sustainable economic growth with more and better jobs and greater social cohesion'.[70]

This echoes a warning issued by Anna Karamanou, then Chairperson of the Committee on Women's Rights and Equal Opportunities of the European Parliament, addressing the Women's Council in Copenhagen in 2002: enlargement, she noted, might serve to enhance mainstreaming if the opportunity was taken to focus on gender issues and the visibility of women; however, enlargement might turn sour, she suggested, if 'resistance to change and the "marketisation" of women in transitional societies gain ground in reshaping gender relations bearing the risk of a tremendous backlash against the EU'.[71]

---

the Council, the European Parliament, the European Economic and Social Committee and the Committee of the Regions, Report on equality between women and men, 2007, COM(2007) 49 final.

[69] Greenberg, above n 28, 11. See also JC Goldfarb, 'Why Is There No Feminism after Communism?' (1997) 64(2) *Social Research* 235; and J Šiklová, 'Feminism and the Roots of Apathy in the Czech Republic' (1997) 64(2) *Social Research* 258.

[70] Presidency Conclusions of the Lisbon European Council (23–4 March 2000). For a critique of the approach to employment policy embodied in the EU social model, see S Fredman, 'Women at Work: The Broken Promise of Flexicurity' (2004) 33 *Industrial Law Journal* 299. See also F Beveridge and S Velluti, above n 17.

[71] 'Gender Equality in the EU Candidate Countries', European Parliament, Statement by Anna Karamanou, MEP, Chairperson of the Committee on Women's Rights and Equal

There is also a need to accept that new Member States may have different gender regimes and hence different priorities and that not all of the gender norms developed in the 'old' Member States are appropriate in the post-accession context. For instance, questions have been raised about the Lisbon target of 60 per cent participation of women in the labour market by 2010, and how this is applied in practice in relation to part-time workers: the Netherlands can claim a female labour force participation rate of 67.5 per cent, but 74.7 per cent of these women work part-time. Bulgaria, on the other hand, falls below the target with 55 per cent of women in employment, but only 2.7 per cent of women work part-time, as this is not traditionally an employment option in 'new' Member States.[72] This gives rise to the argument that the target simply does not reflect the culture of 'new' states.

VIII. CONCLUSION

The recent enlargements provide an interesting and illuminating prism through which to examine the role of gender in the EU and consider its future. In the pre-accession period, women's groups in the accession states and candidate countries were able to use the obligation to implement the *acquis* as an opportunity to push forward debates within their own states and to develop alliances with players in the EU (the Commission, the EWL, WIDE, etc). However, the Commission itself was relatively slow to respond to calls to mainstream gender in the accession process: the political pressure to ensure a successful enlargement served to ensure that lack of commitment to the gender *acquis* did not become a barrier to accession.

Post-accession, membership of the EU provides a new set of tools for pursuing gender equality and empowers a new range of actors. However, to be an effective Member State requires the development of a wide range of capacities in relation to gender concerns in both governmental and non-governmental bodies and this may still be lacking.

More generally, the widening of the EU has also widened the political arena within which gender law and policy must be negotiated, incorporating greater political and cultural diversity. This has implications for the future development of gender equality law and policy, since new Member States bring different problems, priorities and attitudes to the table. The challenge may extend beyond the need to develop new tools, new solutions

Opportunities to the Copenhagen Women's Council, 15 September, 2002, available at <http://www.karamanou.gr/dir/sp/02–010.pdf>, accessed 21 November 03.

[72] S Jouhette and F Romans, *EU Labour Force Survey, Principal Results 2005* (EURO-STAT, Statistics in Focus, Brussels, 2006). Bulgaria has particularly low rates of part-time female employment, but this reflects the general trend across Central and Eastern Europe when compared with 'older' Member States.

and new modes of participation in policy-making: the accessions may have introduced a stronger note of dissent to the EU, contesting the very premises underlying the gender mainstreaming strategy. It seems likely that in gender equality, as in other areas of social policy, there are challenging times ahead.

17

Does the Constitutional Treaty Have a Future?

VLAD CONSTANTINESCO*

I. INTRODUCTION

WHEN I WAS invited to consider the question of whether the Constitutional Treaty has a future, for the conference on *50 Years of the European Treaties* in Liverpool, I could not have foreseen the results of the European Council meeting in Brussels on 21 to 22 June 2007, which decided to convene a new intergovernmental conference (IGC), whose negotiations resulted in the signing of the Treaty of Lisbon on 13 December 2007.[1] In a certain sense, the European Council relaunched the European dynamic by relying on a triple basis.

First, an IGC was convened to reform the Treaties: *exit* the Convention, back to intergovernmental power in Europe![2] As we can observe reading the June 2007 Presidency Conclusions, and especially the IGC mandate, little room for manoeuvre was left to the negotiations at the IGC. Some provisions were already drafted very precisely in the mandate. The incoming Portuguese Presidency was requested to draw up a draft treaty text in line with the terms of the mandate and submit this text to the IGC.[3] Moreover, the IGC was to be conducted under the overall responsibility of the heads of states or government, assisted by the members of the General Affairs and External Relations Council.[4]

---

* This chapter was initially written in June 2007 and revised in March 2008.
[1] See [2007] OJ C306 for the text of the Treaty of Lisbon and [2008] OJ C115 for consolidated texts of the amended Treaties. At the time of writing, Hungary, Malta, Slovenia, France and Romania have ratified the Treaty of Lisbon.
[2] Presidency Conclusions of the European Council meeting in Brussels on 21–2 June 2007 at p 3: the Representative of the Commission will participate in the conference. The European Parliament will be closely associated with and involved in the work of the conference with three representatives.
[3] *Ibid*, 2.
[4] *Ibid*, 3.

Secondly, the agreement reached by the IGC must be submitted to the ordinary national ratification procedures, but this time, it was hoped that ratification would take place through each national parliament: *exit* the national referenda, although one Member State (Ireland) is obliged by its constitution to organise a referendum, and others (such as Denmark and the Netherlands) had yet to decide whether to hold a popular vote.[5] [6]

Thirdly, the new Treaty of Lisbon is a text designed to amend the existing Treaty on European Union and Treaty establishing the European Community: *exit* the Constitution.[7] It is anticipated that, provided the national ratifications are completed, the Treaty of Lisbon should enter into force before the European Parliament elections in June 2009.

If 2007 was the year of the Constitutional Treaty's official death, despite the large majority of states which had already ratified it (in fact, 18 out of the 27 Member States), 2007 could also have been—in an optimistic view—the beginning of that Constitutional Treaty's second life. To answer the question about the future of the Constitutional Treaty, I therefore propose to distinguish between the short and medium terms. In the *short term*, the first impression is apparently that there is no more Constitutional Treaty at all. We shall, however, try to propose a more finely shaded judgment (Part II). In the *medium term*, the Constitutional Treaty could survive, although at the price of a metamorphosis, but perhaps more importantly, by the strength of the consensus that it has represented: a Convention and a unanimous IGC, the unanimous signatures of all the Member State governments, and a large majority of national ratifications (Part III).

---

[5] Note the *Financial Times* on 18 June 2007: a strong majority of citizens in Spain, Germany, the UK, Italy and France (75% of Spaniards, 71% of Germans, 69% of British, 68% of Italians and 64% of French) wish to have a referendum on the simplified treaty on European Union.

[6] In France, the Constitution has been amended, despite a political obstacle: the opposition asked for a referendum, arguing that only a referendum could repeal a former referendum. The *Conseil constitutionnel* admitted (in its decision of 20 December 2007) that the authorisation to ratify the Treaty amending the Treaty on European Union and the Treaty establishing the European Community would require a prior revision of the Constitution. This was done by the *Congrès* (a meeting of the *Assemblée nationale* and the *Sénat*) on 4 February 2008. See the *loi constitutionnelle* No 2008–103 of 4 February 2008. Furthermore, the Parliament has authorised the ratification of the Lisbon Treaty by Statute No 2008–125 of 13 February 2008.

[7] Presidency Conclusions of the European Council meeting in Brussels on 21–2 June 2007 at p 16: the constitutional concept, which consisted in repealing all existing treaties and replacing them by a single text called 'constitution', is abandoned.

II. THE SHORT-TERM PERSPECTIVE

In the short term, how should we appreciate what will remain of the Constitutional Treaty in the new Treaty of Lisbon?

In this regard, I would recall Walter Bagehot's famous distinction between the *dignified* and *efficient* part of the British constitution, a distinction that could be applied also to the Constitutional Treaty after the June 2007 European Council meeting. Apparently, the dignified part of the Constitutional Treaty was dropped (Section A), but the efficient one is retained (Section B).

A. The Dignified Parts of the Constitutional Treaty

The dignified parts of the Constitutional Treaty have been dropped from the new settlement in the Treaty of Lisbon. The word 'constitution' is abandoned, confirming that only states are able to have a constitution. The EU symbols should not receive the dignity of primary law: exit the flag, exit the motto and exit the anthem of the Union. However, of course, the use of the European flag, motto and anthem will not be unlawful. The same trend explains the disappearance of the designation 'Minister for Foreign Affairs of the European Union'. The same logic justifies giving up the words 'law' or 'framework law' (to replace regulations and directives, respectively). The principle of the primacy of EU/Community law is replaced by a simple IGC Declaration, recalling the existing case law of the Court of Justice.[8]

It is obvious, therefore, that those provisions which, as Bagehot once said, 'excite and preserve the reverence of the population', disappear from the new Treaty. It seems to have been the British Government (together with some others) which fought against such provisions: the EU is not a state, and Member States should avoid any ambiguity in this regard when drafting the new Reform Treaty. Maybe the same explanation applies for the British 'opt-out' from the Charter of Fundamental Rights? On that point, two short comments seem warranted. First, the Charter aims to provide better protection for citizens of the EU against the Union institutions and the Member States when they are implementing their Treaty

---

[8] *Ibid*, 16: the *TEU* and the *Treaty on the Functioning of the Union* will not have a constitutional character. The terminology used throughout the Treaties will reflect this change: the term 'Constitution' will not be used, the 'Union Minister for Foreign Affairs' will be called High Representative of the Union for Foreign Affairs and Security Policy and the denominations 'law' and 'framework law' will be abandoned, the existing denominations 'regulations', 'directives' and 'decisions' being retained. Likewise, there will be no article in the amended Treaties mentioning the symbols of the EU such as the flag, the anthem or the motto.

obligations. To refuse some such protection to UK citizens reminds me of the Social Protocol under the Maastricht Treaty, finally abandoned under the Treaty of Amsterdam. The losers here are first and foremost British citizens themselves. If they are happy with such a restriction of their rights, who should complain?[9] Secondly, one cannot complain about the lack of interest of the general population in EU matters, then deny them the incentives for identification with the EU envisaged by the Constitutional Treaty. However, the general mood these days seems not to be in favour of the same enthusiasm shown some years ago in the Laeken Declaration.[10]

B. The Efficient Parts of the Constitutional Treaty

Borrowing again from Bagehot, the efficient parts of a constitution are those provisions by which the constitution in fact works. The retention in the Treaty of Lisbon of the efficient parts of the Constitutional Treaty is thus probably more important than the withdrawal of its dignified parts.

First, the main idea of the Constitutional Treaty, to merge the Treaty on European Union (TEU) with the Treaty establishing the European Community, and to give a single legal personality to the EU, is realised. The new Treaty of Lisbon will amend the two existing Treaties. Whilst the TEU will keep its name, the EC Treaty will be called the Treaty on the Functioning of the European Union (TFEU). However, this unification of the Treaties will not eliminate all complications: the goal of simplification is not so easy to reach! Secondly, some of the obstacles raised against the new Reform Treaty were finally overcome at the IGC. For example, the Polish objections to the definition of qualified majority voting as contained in the Constitutional Treaty (55 per cent of Member States, representing 65 per cnt of the total population of the EU) were finally abandoned; the double majority system will only enter into force in 2014 and, in the event of a dispute, Member States may still invoke the definition of the qualified majority as set out in the Treaty of Nice until 2017.[11] Moreover, President Sarkozy's objection to the pursuit of 'free and undistorted' competition as one of the Union's core objectives in Article 3 of the revised TEU was accepted—not without reservations by some Member States—and again helped to pave the way for an agreement over Lisbon. Nevertheless, a protocol on the internal market and competition will be annexed to the

---

[9] According to Jean-Claude Juncker, Prime Minister of Luxemburg, '*Il reviendra au gouvernement britannique d'expliquer aux citoyens britanniques les raisons pour lesquelles ils auront moins de droits que les citoyens des autres États members*' ('It will be for the British Government to explain to British citizens the reasons why they will have less rights than citizens of other Member States').

[10] Presidency Conclusions of the European Council meeting on 14–15 December 2001.

[11] See especially the Protocol on Transitional Provisions.

revised Treaties.[12] Thirdly, the rotating six-month presidency of the European Council will be replaced, as it was proposed under the Constitutional Treaty, by a new kind of president, not being a head of state or government, chosen by the European Council for a two-and-a-half year mandate (renewable once), thus allowing for greater continuity.[13] If one expects more efficiency and continuity from this full-time President of the European Council, the main objections to the reform still remain: for example, how should this president have any influence on his or her colleagues without being supported by his or her proper national political and administrative structures? Fourthly, the Union will have its own legal personality, the word 'Community' will be replaced by the word 'Union' and, in fact, the Union replaces and succeeds to the Community.[14] Fifthly, the revised TEU is to be divided into six titles, which preserve many of the amendments agreed at the 2004 IGC, such as an enhancement of the control mechanism for the principle of subsidiarity based on an enhanced role for the national parliaments.[15] Sixthly, the former 'Minister for Foreign Affairs' is still there, but under a more sober and complicated name, as a merger of the EU representative for the Common Foreign and Security Policy and the External Affairs Commissioner: the High Representative of the Union for Foreign Affairs and Security.[16] With the creation of this new office, EU foreign policy will be given a single profile for the first time. Above all, as agreed in the 2004 IGC, an External Action Service will be created,[17] as well as a 'permanent structured cooperation' in the field of defence.[18] The visibility and efficiency of the EU in foreign policy matters will therefore be enhanced in line with the old Constitutional Treaty. Finally, it is expressly provided that the Union should accede to the European Convention on Human Rights.[19]

III. The Medium-Term Perspective

When trying to look at the medium and indeed long term, it is useful to recall the words of Winston Churchill: it is always wise to look ahead, but

---

[12] The Protocol states that the High Contracting Parties, considering that the internal market as set out in Art 3 of the revised TEU includes a system ensuring that competition is not distorted, have agreed that, to this end, the Union shall, if necessary, take action under the provisions of the treaties, including under Art 352 TFEU.

[13] See Art 15 of the revised TEU.

[14] See especially Arts 1 and 47 of the revised TEU.

[15] See Art 5(3) of the revised TEU and the Protocol on the application of the principles of subsidiarity and proportionality.

[16] See Art 18 of the revised TEU.

[17] See Art 27 of the revised TEU.

[18] See Arts 42(6) and 46 of the revised TEU.

[19] See Art 6(2) of the revised TEU.

difficult to look further that you can see. Let us remember that the Constitutional Treaty was adopted by a Convention reflecting the entire spectrum of national political cultures and ideologies, signed by *all* of the Member States, and thus seemed to represent a solid compromise and the promise of an easy success. The negative outcome of referenda in France and the Netherlands in spring 2005 opened a two-and-a-half year 'period of reflection', but, above all, a period of real uncertainty about the future of an EU which had enlarged to 27 Member States but remained confined within the provisions of the Treaty of Nice.

The coincidence of two events could explain this revival of the European dynamic: the German Presidency of the EU and the election of the new French President.

Mr Sarkozy—the new French President—launched in 2007 the idea of a 'mini-treaty', 'simplified treaty' or 'reform treaty' that would allow the EU to use some of the useful organisational reforms contained in the Constitutional Treaty: for example, a more stable Presidency of the European Council, a 'Mr X for Foreign Policy' (who would be less than a Minister, but more than a High Representative), a legal personality for the Union, the right of legislative initiative for Union citizens, etc. For her part, Mrs Merkel proposed to limit to the least degree strictly necessary modifications to the Treaties and submit before the European Council a short and limited list of questions to be discussed at their meeting in June 2007: for example, concerning a return to the classical method of amending the Treaties rather than by the Convention method; preserving the innovations contained in Part I of the Constitutional Treaty (save for the title Constitution, the new terminology of laws and framework laws, the title of Minister for Foreign Affairs, the EU symbols, the express preference to the primacy principle and incorporation of the full text of the Charter rather than its incorporation by simple cross-reference); refusing to reopen the institutional balance determined by the Constitutional Treaty (on issues such as qualified majority voting, extending co-decision with the European Parliament, etc); referring to the Union's new challenges in fields such as energy, climate change and illegal immigration; including the enlargement criteria in the Treaties; taking into account the social dimension of the EU; and opening up new possibilities for enhanced cooperation between some Member States in new areas.

As we can observe, many of these ideas were accepted by the European Council, and most of them are now contained in the Lisbon Treaty. However, in the French version, the agreement reached in Brussels, and this Lisbon Treaty, should be seen only as the first stage of a more accurate and more global answer to the different challenges threatening the Union:

The Union has to give itself a reference text—it could be named constitutional, fundamental or something else, that is not important—but this text should go further than the technical provisions in the actual treaties, and should seal the fundamentally political dimension of the European construction. This fundamental treaty should say clearly what is Europe, which implies notably to agree finally on who is called to enter in the Union, and who is not. But this text should also define what the Union wants to be, which policies for which project, and explain/suggest a process for carrying on to move forwards. This necessity calls for a great democratic debate. Why not imagine a large Convention, whose members would be chosen after a real democratic debate, notably in national Parliaments and whose mandate would be very wide. Such a Convention could meet after the 2009 elections: the electoral campaign could be for instance the opportunity for a true debate on the future of Europe.[20]

However, note that no '*clause de rendez-vous*' is foreseen in the Lisbon Treaty: the dynamic begun in Maastricht has come to a turning point, perhaps even to a stopping point.

'States are back': that is the strong message of the Lisbon Treaty, and its second strong message could be: 'the Union itself will never become a State'. The state is not dead in the European citizens' imagination: Union policies are not seen as legitimate substitutes for the states (and the new Member States in particular still need to experience fully their restoration of sovereign statehood). The Lisbon Treaty is indeed the product of the new conditions that have taken root in Europe since the fall of the Berlin Wall. It could announce the end—although maybe only temporary—of a constitutional and political perspective for the EU: European public policy objectives, such as climate change, energy, foreign relations and immigration, seem today more convincing for the citizens than purely institutional games. This does not mean that institutional reforms are useless or pointless, as many would have us think. Quite the contrary: if a clearer

---

[20] Author's translation. The French original reads: *l'Union doit se donner un texte de référence – appelons-le ou non constitutionnel, loi fondamentale ou autre, l'important n'est pas là-, qui aille au-delà des dispositions techniques contenues dans les traités actuels, et qui scelle la dimension fondamentalement politique de la construction européenne. Ce traité fondamental devra poser clairement ce qu'est l'Europe, ce qui implique notamment de se mettre enfin d'accord sur qui a vocation à rentrer dans l'Union et qui n'a pas vocation à le faire ; mais un texte qui définisse aussi ce qu'elle veut être, quelles politiques pour quel projet, et qui lui indique un processus pour continuer à avancer. Cette nécessité appelle un grand débat démocratique. Pourquoi ne pas imaginer une grande Convention, dont les membres seraient désignés après un vrai débat démocratique, notamment devant les parlements nationaux et dont le mandat serait très large? Elle pourrait se réunir après les élections européennes de 2009: ainsi la campagne européenne serait-elle l'occasion d'un véritable débat de fond sur l'avenir de l'Europe.* See N Sarkozy, speech held at the Fondation Friends of Europe/Amis de l'Europe et la Fondation Robert Schuman (Brussels, 8 September 2006), <http://www.u-m-p.org/site/index.php/ump/s_informer/discours/fondation_friends_of_ europe_amis_de_l_europe_et_la_fondation_robert_schuman_8_septembre_2006_bruxelles_ bibliotheque_solvay> accessed 25 October 2008.

public policy agenda could be established, the necessary institutional adaptations would be better understood and find their legitimacy more easily accepted by the citizens.

Finally, if we could agree that the Constitutional Treaty has 'no future' in the EU, it is for two reasons. First, the Constitutional Treaty is in fact still there, as I tried to demonstrate, in the Treaty of Lisbon. Secondly, the Constitutional Treaty was an answer, albeit a questionable one, to important and serious questions. If the answer was insufficient, perhaps even inadequate, the fundamental questions still remain: where are the limits of the EU? How should we build a 'post-national' or 'post-modern' European polity at a continental level? How are we to improve the involvement of citizens in Union affairs? In that sense, the Constitutional Treaty is very much still alive!

Index